⊙Frommer's

Alaska 2002

W9-CGL-077

Glaciers flow down from Mount McKinley, the tallest peak in North America. The dark streaks in the glacial ice are called moraine and are accumulations of rock pushed to the side as the glacier flows slowly downhill. Those in the center of the flow are called median moraine and are produced when two glaciers flow together. See chapter 8.
© Ken Graham/Accent Alaska

A Tlingit Indian wears a Button Blanket, a native ceremonial robe of intricate design and decorated with mother-of-pearl buttons. See chapter 5.
© Hollenbeck Photography

Downtown Juneau's Starr Hill neighborhood. Built up on a mountain on the side of the Gastineau Channel and surrounded by the Juneau Icefield, the city is the only state capital in the U.S. that cannot be reached by road. See chapter 5. © Mark Kelly/Alaska Stock Images

One of the most distinctive representations of Native culture in Southeast Alaska, totem poles, like this one in Juneau, are carved to depict the genealogy and history of their people. You'll see them throughout the region, particularly at Ketchikan's several totem parks and heritage centers and at the Sitka National Historic Park , which has a totem trail and a workshop where Native artists craft new poles. See chapter 5. © Randy Brandon/ Alaska Stock Images

A kayaker explores the iceberg-filled waters in Tracy Arm. The South Sawyer Glacier, located at the end of the Arm, calves off many tons of ice daily, giving the channel an otherworldly look. See chapter 5. © Jeff Foott/Alaska Stock Images

A sled dog race in Fairbanks. The city and the surrounding area host the Yukon Quest International Sled Dog Race in February and the North American Sled Dog Championships in March. See chapter 9. © Gary Schultz/Alaska Stock Images

An angler displays his trophy, a king, or chinook, salmon, considered the best-fighting salmon species in Alaska. Kings commonly grow to over 30 pounds in 5 to 7 years; the largest ever, taken by a commercial fisherman near Petersburg, weighed a whopping 126 pounds. See chapter 2. © Chip Porter/Tony Stone Images

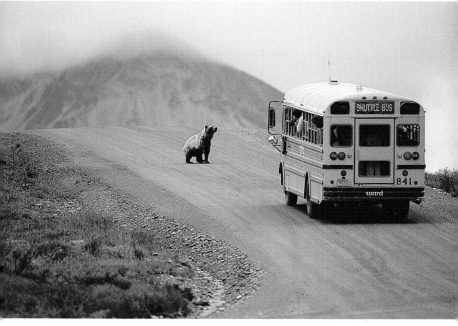

Visitors to Denali National Park encounter one of the locals. Though some complain about the buses, which are the only way to traverse the park in a vehicle, it's a system that keeps visitors from overwhelming the ecosystem, so the animals are still there to watch and their behavior remains essentially normal. It may be the only $20 safari in the world. See chapter 8. © Kim Heacox/Accent Alaska

The Yorktown Clipper cruises among the towering cliffs of Punchbowl Cove in Rudyerd Bay in the Misty Fjords National Monument. This is extreme topography: Cliffs rise vertically more than 3,000 feet from the surface of water that is 900 feet deep. See chapter 5.
© Wolfgang Kaehler Photography

A humpback whale breaching in Frederick Sound. No one knows for sure why they leap from the water like this—it may just be because they enjoy it. Humpbacks are easy to recognize by their huge, mottled tails, by the hump on their backs, and by their armlike flippers, which can grow to be 14 feet long. © David Hoffmann/Accent Alaska

A cow moose with calf in tow crosses the rolling Glenn Highway, with the Chugach Mountains rising majestically beyond. © Ken Graham/Accent Alaska

A lone canoeist glides along on Lower Summit Lake on the Kenai Peninsula, just south of Anchorage. See chapter 7. © *Jeff Schultz/Alaska Stock Images*

When should I travel to get the best airfare?
Where do I go for answers to my travel questions?
What's the best and easiest way to plan and book my trip?

frommers.travelocity.com

Frommer's, the travel guide leader, has teamed up with **Travelocity.com**, the leader in online travel, to bring you an in-depth, easy-to-use resource designed to help you plan and book your trip online.

At **frommers.travelocity.com**, you'll find free online updates about your destination from the experts at Frommer's plus the outstanding travel planning and purchasing features of Travelocity.com. Travelocity.com provides reservations capabilities for 95 percent of all airline seats sold, more than 47,000 hotels, and over 50 car rental companies. In addition, Travelocity.com offers more than 2,000 exciting vacation and cruise packages. Travelocity.com puts you in complete control of your travel planning with these and other great features:

> **Expert travel guidance from Frommer's** - over 150 writers reporting from around the world!
>
> **Best Fare Finder** - an interactive calendar tells you when to travel to get the best airfare
>
> **Fare Watcher** - we'll track airfare changes to your favorite destinations
>
> **Dream Maps** - a mapping feature that suggests travel opportunities based on your budget
>
> **Shop Safe Guarantee** - 24 hours a day / 7 days a week live customer service, and more!

Whether traveling on a tight budget, looking for a quick weekend getaway, or planning the trip of a lifetime, Frommer's guides and Travelocity.com will make your travel dreams a reality. You've bought the book, now book the trip!

A New Star-Rating System & Other Exciting News from Frommer's!

In our continuing effort to publish the savviest, most up-to-date, and most appealing travel guides available, we've added some great new features.

Frommer's guides now include a new **star-rating system.** Every hotel, restaurant, and attraction is rated from 0 to 3 stars to help you set priorities and organize your time.

We've also added **seven brand-new features** that point you to the great deals, in-the-know advice, and unique experiences that separate travelers from tourists. Throughout the guide look for:

Finds   Special finds—those places only insiders know about

Fun Fact   Fun facts—details that make travelers more informed and their trips more fun

Kids   Best bets for kids—advice for the whole family

Moments   Special moments—those experiences that memories are made of

Overrated   Places or experiences not worth your time or money

Tips   Insider tips—some great ways to save time and money

Value   Great values—where to get the best deals

We've also added a **"What's New"** section in every guide—a timely crash course in what's hot and what's not in every destination we cover.

Other Great Guides for Your Trip:

Frommer's Alaska Cruises & Ports of Call
Frommer's Canada
Frommer's British Columbia & the Canadian Rockies
Frommer's Vancouver & Victoria
Frommer's Washington State

Alaska

2002

by Charles Wohlforth

Here's what the critics say about Frommer's:

"Amazingly easy to use. Very portable, very complete."
> —*Booklist*

"The only mainstream guide to list specific prices. The Walter Cronkite of guidebooks—with all that implies."
> —*Travel & Leisure*

"Complete, concise, and filled with useful information."
> —*New York Daily News*

"Hotel information is close to encyclopedic."
> —*Des Moines Sunday Register*

"Detailed, accurate, and easy-to-read information for all price ranges."
> —*Glamour Magazine*

Wiley Publishing, Inc.

About the Author

Charles Wohlforth is a lifelong Alaskan who has been a writer and journalist since 1986. After graduating from Princeton University, he worked as a newspaper reporter in the small town of Homer, Alaska, and then for the *Anchorage Daily News,* where he covered the *Exxon Valdez* oil spill. In 1992, Wohlforth went on his own as a freelance writer for various regional and national magazines and as the author of books such as this one. His *Frommer's Family Vacations in the National Parks* covers parks all over the United States based on insights from the Wohlforth family's own camping experiences. Wohlforth lives in Anchorage with his wife, Barbara, sons Robin and Joseph, and daughters Julia and Rebecca. He welcomes reader questions through his website, www.wohlforth.net.

Published by:

Wiley Publishing, Inc.

909 Third Ave.
New York, NY 10022

ISBN 0-7645-6419-6
ISSN 1042-8283

Editor: Alexis Lipsitz Flippin
Production Editor: M. Faunette Johnston
Cartographer: John Decamillis
Photo Editor: Richard Fox
Production by Hungry Minds Indianapolis Production Services

Front cover photo: Tourists viewing icebergs in Prince William Sound
Back cover photo: Dall sheep rams on Denali's Polychrome Pass

For information on our other products and services or to obtain technical support, please contact our Customer Care Department within the U.S. at 800-762-2974, outside the U.S. at 317-572-3993 or fax 317-572-4002.

Wiley also publishes its books in a variety of electronic formats. Some content that appears in print may not be available in electronic formats.

Manufactured in the United States of America

5   4   3

Contents

List of Maps

ACKNOWLEDGMENTS

I couldn't put together a book such as this without a lot of help in covering Alaska's great distances and tracking its fast-changing visitor businesses. Friends all over Alaska show me around when I drop in for one of my visits as a "professional tourist," but a few people in particular do much more. My wife, Barbara, visits sights and hotels and keeps our family in order and happy as we travel together. My children, Robin, Julia, Joseph, and Rebecca are good sports and provide unique perspectives for "our travel book," making the discoveries of travel a joy, as only children can. My assistants in Anchorage and journalistic colleagues all over Alaska enable me to make this book as up-to-date and insider as any you'll find: Karen Datko, Kate Ripley, Kathleen Tessaro, Terry Wilson, Lynn Englishbee, Tom Morphet, Kris Capps, Peter Porco, Andrea Senn, Kerry Wilson, Tom Begich, Leslie Hines, Judy Bakeberg, Tataboline Brant, Amy Miller, Tommy Wells, and Jim Paulin. Others, who helped build previous editions, included Carol Sturgulewski, Will Swagel, Terry Williams, Carolyn Minor, Angela Baily, Kathryn Gerlek, Brian O'Donohue, Robin Mackey Hill, Joe Bridgman, Dimitra Lavrakas, Alex DeMarben, Wendy Feuer, Eric and Caroline Wohlforth, Eric Troyer, Mark Handley, Catherine Reardon, Dean Mitchell, and Laura Mathews. Many other friends offered help and advice, and I'm grateful to all of them.

—Charles P. Wohlforth

An Invitation to the Reader

In researching this book, we discovered many wonderful places—hotels, restaurants, shops, and more. We're sure you'll find others. Please tell us about them, so we can share the information with your fellow travelers in upcoming editions. If you were disappointed with a recommendation, we'd love to know that, too. Please write to:

Frommer's Alaska 2002
Wiley Publishing, Inc. • 909 Third Ave. • New York, NY 10022

An Additional Note

Please be advised that travel information is subject to change at any time—and this is especially true of prices. We therefore suggest that you write or call ahead for confirmation when making your travel plans. The authors, editors, and publisher cannot be held responsible for the experiences of readers while traveling. Your safety is important to us, however, so we encourage you to stay alert and be aware of your surroundings. Keep a close eye on cameras, purses, and wallets, all favorite targets of thieves and pickpockets.

New! Frommer's Star Ratings & Icons

Every hotel, restaurant, and attraction listing in this guide has been ranked for quality, value, service, amenities, and special features using a star-rating scale. In country, state, and regional guides, we also rate towns and regions to help you narrow down your choices and budget your time accordingly. Hotels and restaurants in the Very Expensive and Expensive categories are rated on a scale of one (highly recommended) to three stars (exceptional). Those in the Moderate and Inexpensive categories rate from zero (recommended) to two stars (very highly recommended). Attractions, towns, and regions are rated according to the following scale: zero stars (recommended), one star (highly recommended), two stars (very highly recommended), and three stars (must-see).

Finds	Fun Fact	Kids	Moments	Overrated	Tips	Value

The following abbreviations are used for credit cards:

AE	American Express	DISC	Discover	V	Visa
DC	Diners Club	MC	MasterCard		

FROMMERS.COM

Now that you have the guidebook to a great trip, visit our website at **www.frommers.com** for travel information on nearly 2,000 destinations. With features updated regularly, we give you instant access to the most current trip-planning information available. At Frommers.com, you'll also find the best prices on airfares, accommodations, and car rentals—and you can even book travel online through our travel booking partners. At Frommers.com you'll also find the following:

- Daily Newsletter highlighting the best travel deals
- Hot Spot of the Month/Vacation Sweepstakes & Travel Photo Contest
- More than 200 Travel Message Boards
- Outspoken Newsletters and Feature Articles on travel bargains, vacation ideas, tips & resources, and more!

What's New in Alaska

Here are the latest happenings in Alaska, region by region.

PLANNING YOUR TRIP Two Alaska Native–owned companies have entered the package tour business, taking on the Holland America and Princess cruise line giants. **Alaska Heritage Tours** (© 877/258-6877; www.AHTours.com) specializes in the Southcentral region, and **Goldbelt Tourism** (© 800/478-3610; www.goldbelttours.com) is primarily in the Southeast. Both have bought or built some of the best boat tours and activities in its region.

SOUTHEAST VanWinkle **and Daigler,** formerly among Sitka's best restaurants, moved across the street, changed its name to VanWinkle and Sons, and became more of a small-town family restaurant, best for pizza and simple dishes.

In Juneau, the **U.S. Forest Service Information Center** in the Centennial Hall closed, and now visitors have to travel to the Ranger District office near the airport at 8461 Old Dairy Rd., a major inconvenience. Forest contact information remains the same. The **Juneau Convention and Visitors Bureau** closed its Log Cabin Visitor Center and moved into the space vacated by the Forest Service (no indication yet on what will happen to the historic log cabin). I've also rewritten the **Juneau Walking Tour** to make it easier and have excluded the closed center and the less impressive sites near the dock.

The newly expanded **Mt. Juneau Inn** (© 907/463-5855; www.mtjuneauinn.com) is a beautifully restored Craftsman-style house originally built by a ship's captain and now transformed into attractive rooms. Also in Juneau, the wonderful hosts at **Cashen's Quarters B&B** sold out and now the B&B will be operated more as a no-host guest house.

Puffin B&B in Gustavus closed, as did **Frontier Air.** Try Gustavus-based **Air Excursions** (© 907/697-2375) for Glacier Bay flightseeing instead.

In Haines, the historic **Chilkat Dancers** stopped regular performances in 2001 due to a reduction in cruise ship dockings. Locals hope the group will revive. An interesting new attraction in Haines is **Tsirku Canning Co.,** at Fourth Avenue and Main Street, a cannery museum with antique fish packing equipment that really works.

In Skagway, the **Alaskan Wildlife Adventure and Collection Showcase** appears to have closed permanently. A new attraction is **Klondike Gold Dredge Tours** (© 877/983-3175; http://klondikegolddredge.com). Although overpriced and a bit out of place historically, it does show off how industrial placer mining really worked and offers gold panning.

We discovered a great new restaurant in Skagway called **Sabrosa's,** a tiny sidewalk cafe at Sixth and Broadway.

For more on the Southeast, see chapter 5.

ANCHORAGE VICINITY In downtown Anchorage, the **Snowshoe Inn** changed hands and raised rates, putting it well above the moderate category; I no longer recommend it at these prices. However, the **Caribou Inn,** at Fifth Avenue and L Street (© **800/272-5878** or **907/272-0444**), charges very reasonable rates.

Downtown Anchorage has a large new restaurant at Fifth Avenue and G Street, its ornate and theatrical dining rooms constructed at what must have been great cost. The Italian food at **Orso** (© **907/222-3232**) is good, and a meal there is an experience. For an inexpensive meal downtown, it's hard to beat the new **Cilantro's Mexican Restaurant,** at 611 W. Ninth Ave. (© **907/279-8226**).

The Whale's Tail at the Hotel Captain Cook no longer has nightly dance music.

At Portage, the **Begich-Boggs Visitor Center** has been remodeled to update the interpretive displays. Instead of concentrating on glaciology (the Portage Glacier melted so that it can no longer be seen from the center), the museum covers Chugach National Forest in general.

The stabilization and renovation of **Independence Mine Historic Park** should be complete for visits in 2002, reopening the Mat-Su area's most interesting site.

For more on Anchorage and environs, see chapter 6.

KENAI PENINSULA & PRINCE WILLIAM SOUND In Hope, the **Discovery Café,** the town's center of activity, reopened in 2001, having been rebuilt by community volunteers after a fire destroyed it in 1999.

The **Russian Lakes Trail** and **Resurrection River Trail** no longer connect, and the Forest Service has no plans to rebuild the washed-out sections.

After a year of operation, it is evident that users of the **tunnel to Whittier** must check the schedule of open times and arrive well in advance. At busy times, lines of cars can't always get through during the openings and must wait an hour or more for the next chance.

The **Alaskon Express** bus line no longer serves Seward, but the Seward Bus Line and Park Connection still offer van and bus service.

Rainbow Tours in Homer has stopped its tours to Gull Island and the **Alaska Center for Coastal Studies.** The center has gone to a more flexible schedule using a water taxi, giving visitors more opportunities to join low-tide walks at its Peterson Bay facility. Also in Homer, **Kachemak Air Service** no longer offers bear viewing or marine landings (Bill de Creeft still does air tours in his antique plane); instead, book bear viewing from Homer with Emerald Air Service (© **907/235-6993;** www.emeraldair service.com).

The **World Extreme Skiing Championships** and the **Snow Man Festival** in Valdez will no longer be held. The **Westmark Valdez Hotel** has closed indefinitely pending demolition and reconstruction. I no longer recommend the **Rodeway Inn** in Valdez. However, I've added a strong recommendation for the **Alaska Woollybugger B&B** (© **907/835-8505**), which has a fly-fishing theme. Also in Valdez, **Oscar's** closed and a much better restaurant took its place, **Harbor's Edge.**

For more on the Kenai Peninsula and Prince William Sound, see chapter 7.

DENALI NATIONAL PARK The old **Park Hotel,** the only accommodation within Denali National Park, closes for the last time at the end of the 2001 season. The site will eventually become a learning center.

South of the park, **Denali Mountain Morning Hostel and Lodge**

(© **907/683-7503**) is a good addition, with inexpensive accommodations and the area's only backpacking gear rental.

For more on Denali National Park, see chapter 8.

THE INTERIOR In Fairbanks, **Grandma Shirley's Hostel** has closed.

Due to construction, tours of the **Geophysical Institute** at the University of Alaska Fairbanks have been canceled; tours should begin again when the work is complete, but exactly what they will comprise is undetermined.

Chena Hot Springs Resort opened an outdoor rock-lined pond for swimming in the hot mineral springs, addressing the biggest shortcoming of the resort, its small indoor pool. A fountain and waterfall provide evaporative cooling of otherwise scalding water. Sadly, **Tack's,** everyone's favorite stop on Chena Hot Springs Road, burned to the ground on Memorial Day 2001.

A new inn/hotel and a new restaurant have opened in downtown Dawson City, raising the standards in that remote community. **Bombay Peggy's Inn and Lounge** (© **867/993-6969;** www.klondikeweb.com/bombay) occupies a restored gold rush building with high ceilings and elaborate service. **Ruby's Hideaway,** at Second and Queen streets (© **867/993-5721**), brings handcrafted fine dining to the downtown area for the first time.

Princess Cruises and Tours is building a grand new lodge in Copper Center, the first luxury or even standard accommodation near **Wrangell–St. Elias National Park.** They expect to open for the 2002 season. (Contact information for Princess is in chapter 2.) Also in Copper Center, don't miss the elaborate model train and diorama of the historic copper mining operation in the **Copper Rail Depot** bar (© **907/822-3522**).

For more on the Alaskan Interior, see chapter 9.

THE BUSH A $1-million visitor center has opened at the Dutch Harbor airport for the **Aleutian WWII National Historic Area** (© **907/ 581-1276;** www.nps.gov/aleu), with interpretive information on the island's war ruins. Volunteer archaeological digs continue in connection with the **Museum of the Aleutians,** but not at the site right next to the museum.

The Frozen Family exhibit at the **Inupiat Heritage Center** will be taken down and an exhibit of dolls and figurines from ancient times to the present will be installed.

For more on the Alaskan Bush, see chapter 10.

1

The Best of Alaska

As a child, when my family traveled outside Alaska for vacations, I often met other children who asked, "Wow, you live in Alaska? What's it like?" I never did well with that question. To me, the place I was visiting was far simpler and easier to describe than the one I was from. The Lower 48 seemed a fairly homogeneous land of freeways and fast food, a well-mapped network of established places. Alaska, on the other hand, wasn't—and isn't—even completely explored. Natural forces of vast scale and subtlety were still shaping the land in their own way, inscribing a different story on each of an infinite number of unexpected places. Each region, whether populated or not, was unique far beyond my ability to explain. Alaska was so large and new, so unconquered and exquisitely real, as to defy summation.

In contrast to many places you might choose to visit, it's Alaska's unformed newness that makes it so interesting and fun. Despite the best efforts of tour planners, the most memorable parts of a visit are unpredictable and often unexpected: a humpback whale leaping clear of the water, the face of a glacier releasing huge ice chunks, a bear feasting on salmon in a river, a huge salmon chomping onto your line. You can look at totem poles and see Alaska Native cultural demonstrations, and you can also get to know living indigenous people who still live by many of the traditional ways. And sometimes grand, quiet moments come, and those are the ones that endure most deeply.

As the writer of this guidebook, I aim to help you get to places where you may encounter what's new, real, and unexpected. Opening yourself to those experiences is your job, but it's an effort that's likely to pay off. Although I have lived here all my life, I often envy the stories visitors tell me about the Alaska places they have gone to and what happened there. No one owns Alaska, and most of us are newcomers here. In all this immensity, a visitor fresh off the boat is just as likely as a lifelong resident to see or do something amazing.

1 The Best Views

- **A First Sight of Alaska:** Flying north from Seattle, you're in clouds, so you concentrate on a book. When you look up, the light from the window has changed. Down below, the clouds are gone, and under the wing, where you're used to seeing roads, cities, and farms on most flights, you see instead only high, snowy mountain peaks, without the slightest mark of human presence, stretching as far as the horizon. Welcome to Alaska.

- **Punchbowl Cove** (Misty Fjords National Monument): A sheer granite cliff rises smooth and implacable 3,150 feet straight up from the water. A pair of bald eagles wheels and soars across its face, providing the only sense of scale. They look the size of gnats. See chapter 5.

- **From the Chugach Mountains Over Anchorage, at Sunset:** The city sparkles below, on the edge of an orange-reflecting Cook Inlet, far below the mountainside where you stand. Beyond the pink and purple silhouettes of mountains on the other side of the inlet, the sun is spraying warm, dying light into puffs of clouds. And yet it's midnight. See chapter 6.
- **Mount McKinley From the Air** (Denali National Park): Your bush pilot guides his plane up from the flatlands of Talkeetna into a realm of eternal white, where a profusion of insanely rugged peaks rises in higher relief than any other spot on earth. After circling a 3-mile-high wall and slipping through a mile-deep canyon, you land on a glacier, get out of the plane, and for the first time realize the overwhelming scale of it all. See chapter 8.
- **The Northern Lights** (Alaska's Interior): Blue, purple, green, and red lines spin from the center of the sky, draping long tendrils of slow-moving light. Bright, flashing, sky-covering waves wash across the dome of stars like ripples driven by a gust of wind on a pond. Looking around, your companions' faces are rosy in a silver, snowy night, all gazing straight up with their mouths open. See chapter 9.

2 The Best Alaska Cruises

Cruises provide comfortable, leisurely access to the Inside Passage and the Gulf of Alaska. Here are some of the best bets. See chapter 4 for details.

- **Best Up-Close Alaska Experience:** Glacier Bay Cruiseline *Wilderness Adventurer* and *Wilderness Explorer* sail itineraries that shun overcrowded port towns in favor of wilderness areas and small fishing villages. Both carry sea kayaks for off-ship exploration, and both feature naturalist-led hikes as central features of the experience. The line is owned by an Alaska Native corporation and the ships are small (carrying 74 and 36 passengers, respectively) and very casual. They're not fancy, but that's the point—it's where they take you that counts.
- **Best Itinerary:** World Explorer Cruises' *Universe Explorer* is unmatched, offering a 14-day round-trip itinerary from Vancouver that includes all the major ports of call and a few others, too. They also offer a 9-night round-trip out of Vancouver, featuring the best of the Inside Passage. The ship is large, though not huge, and stresses education rather than the typical big-ship cruise diversions.
- **Most Comfortable Small Ships:** Cruise West's *Spirit of Endeavor* and *Spirit of '98* (a 19th-century coastal steamer re-creation) and Clipper's *Yorktown Clipper* offer a higher level of comfort than the other small ships in Alaska while still giving you an intimate, casual, up-close small-ship experience.
- **Most Luxurious Big Ships:** *Crystal Harmony* is the top-of-the-line ship in the Alaska market, with superb cuisine, elegant service, lovely surroundings, great cabins, and sparkling entertainment. If you want a more casual kind of luxury, Radisson Seven Seas' *Seven Seas Navigator* (which is slightly smaller than the *Harmony*) offers just that. Among the mainstream cruise ships, Celebrity's *Mercury* and *Galaxy* are the big winners, offering cutting-edge modern ships with great service, dining, and design.

Alaska

MILEAGE CHART Approximate driving distances in miles between cities.	Anchorage	Circle	Dawson City	Eagle	Fairbanks	Haines	Homer	Prudhoe Bay	Seattle	Seward	Skagway	Tok	Valdez
Anchorage		520	494	501	358	775	226	847	2234	126	832	328	304
Circle	520		530	541	162	815	746	1972	2271	646	872	368	526
Dawson City	494	530		131	379	548	713	868	1843	619	430	189	428
Eagle	501	541	131		379	620	727	868	1974	627	579	173	427
Fairbanks	358	162	379	379		653	584	489	2121	484	710	206	364
Haines	775	815	548	620	653		1001	1142	1774	901	359	447	701
Homer	226	746	713	727	584	1001		1073	2455	173	1058	554	530
Prudhoe Bay	847	1972	868	868	489	1142	1073		2610	973	1199	695	853
Seattle	2243	2271	1843	1974	2121	1774	2455	2610		1361	1577	1931	2169
Seward	126	646	619	627	484	901	173	973	1361		958	454	430
Skagway	832	872	430	579	710	359	1058	1199	1577	958		504	758
Tok	328	368	189	173	206	447	554	695	1931	454	504		254
Valdez	304	526	428	427	364	701	530	853	2169	430	758	254	

Chukchi Sea

Little Diomede Island

Nome

Norton Sound

Yukon Delta National Wildlife Refuge

Bethel

Yukon Delta National Wildlife Refuge

Bering Sea

Nunivak Island

Pribilof Islands

Bristol Bay

Attu Island

Cape St. Stephen

Rat Islands

Alaska Peninsula

Unimak Island

Cold Bay

Dutch Harbor

Adak

Adak Island

Atka Island

Atka

Unalaska

Aleutian Islands

PACIFIC

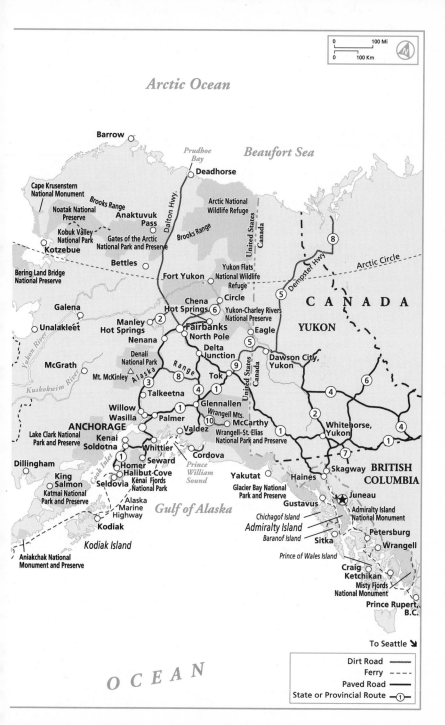

Arctic Ocean

Barrow

Prudhoe Bay

Beaufort Sea

Deadhorse

Cape Krusenstern National Monument

Brooks Range

Noatak National Preserve

Anaktuvuk Pass

Arctic National Wildlife Refuge

Kobuk Valley National Park

Gates of the Arctic National Park and Preserve

Dalton Hwy.

Brooks Range

United States Canada

Kotzebue

Bettles

Arctic Circle

Bering Land Bridge National Preserve

Fort Yukon

Yukon Flats National Wildlife Refuge

Dempster Hwy.

⑧

Galena

Chena Hot Springs ⑥

Circle

⑤

CANADA

Unalakleet

Manley Hot Springs

②

Fairbanks

North Pole

Yukon-Charley Rivers National Preserve

Eagle

YUKON

Yukon River

Nenana

Delta Junction

⑤

McGrath

Denali National Park

Alaska Range

⑨

Dawson City, Yukon

Mt. McKinley △

③

⑧

Tok

United States Canada

⑥

Kuskokwim River

Talkeetna

④

①

④

Willow

Glennallen

②

Whitehorse, Yukon

④

Wasilla

Palmer

①

Wrangell Mts.

ANCHORAGE

⑩

McCarthy

①

Lake Clark National Park and Preserve

Kenai

Valdez

Wrangell–St. Elias National Park and Preserve

⑦

Soldotna

Whittier

Cordova

Dillingham

Homer

Seward

Prince William Sound

Yakutat

Haines

Skagway

BRITISH COLUMBIA

King Salmon

Halibut Cove

Kenai Fjords National Park

Seldovia

Glacier Bay National Park and Preserve

Katmai National Park and Preserve

Alaska Marine Highway

Gustavus

Juneau

Kodiak

Gulf of Alaska

Chichagof Island

Admiralty Island

Admiralty Island National Monument

Kodiak Island

Baranof Island

Sitka

Petersburg

Aniakchak National Monument and Preserve

Prince of Wales Island

Wrangell

Craig

Ketchikan

Misty Fjords National Monument

Prince Rupert, B.C.

Cook Inlet

OCEAN

To Seattle ↘

Dirt Road	————
Ferry	– – – –
Paved Road	————
State or Provincial Route	—①—

0   100 Mi
0   100 Km

- **Best Cruisetours:** Holland America Line and Princess are the leaders in linking cruises with land tours into the Interior, either before or after your cruise. They own their own hotels, deluxe motor coaches, and railcars, and after many years in the business, they both really know what they're doing. Princess concentrates more on the Anchorage/Denali/Fairbanks routes, while Holland America has many itineraries that get you to the Yukon Territory's Dawson City and Whitehorse.

3 The Best Glaciers

More of Alaska—more than 100 times more—is covered by glacier ice than is settled by human beings.

- **Grand Pacific Glacier** (Glacier Bay National Park): Two vast glaciers of deep blue meet at the top of an utterly barren fjord. They rubbed and creased the gray rock for thousands of years before just recently releasing it to the air again. Boats that pull close to the glaciers appear surrounded by the intimidating walls of ice on three sides. See chapter 5.

- **Childs Glacier** (Cordova): Out the Copper River Highway from Cordova, this is a participatory glacier-viewing experience. The glacier is cut by the Copper River, a quarter-mile broad; standing on the opposite shore (unless you're up in the viewing tower), you have to be ready to run like hell when the creaking, popping ice gives way and a huge berg falls into the river, potentially swamping the picnic area. Even when the glacier isn't calving, you can feel the ice groaning in your gut. See chapter 7.

- **Exit Glacier** (Seward): You can drive near the glacier and walk the rest of the way on a gravel path. It towers above like a huge blue sculpture, the spires of broken ice close enough to breathe a freezer-door chill down on watchers. See chapter 7.

- **Western Prince William Sound:** In this area of western Prince William Sound, you can see a couple of dozen glaciers in a day. Some of these are the amazing tidewater glaciers that dump huge, office-building-size spires of ice into the ocean, each setting off a terrific splash and outward-radiating sea wave. See chapter 7.

4 The Most Beautiful Drives & Train Rides

You'll find a description of each road in chapter 9 under "Alaska's Highways a la Carte." Here are some highlights:

- **White Pass and Yukon Route Railway** (Skagway to Summit): The narrow-gauge excursion train, sometimes pulled by vintage steam engines, climbs the steep grade that was chiseled into the granite mountains by stampeders to the Klondike gold rush. The train is a sort of mechanical mountain goat, balancing on trestles and steep rock walls far above deep gorges. See chapter 5.

- **Seward Highway** (Turnagain Arm): Just south of Anchorage, the highway has been chipped into the side of the Chugach Mountains over the surging gray water of Turnagain Arm. Above, Dall sheep and mountain goats pick their way along the cliffs, within easy sight. Below, white beluga whales chase salmon through the turbid water. See chapter 7.

- **Alaska Railroad** (Anchorage to Seward): The line follows the same stretch of Turnagain Arm as the Seward Highway, then splits off as it rises into the mountains of the Kenai Peninsula, rumbling close along the face of a glacier and clinging to the edge of a vertically walled gorge with a roaring river at the bottom. See chapter 7.
- **Denali Highway:** Leading eastwest through the Alaska Range, the Denali Highway crosses terrain that could be another Denali National Park, full of wildlife and with views so huge and grand, they seem impossible. See chapter 8.
- **Richardson Highway:** Just out of Valdez heading north, the Richardson Highway rises quickly from sea level to more than 2,600 feet, switching back and forth on the side of a mountain. With each turn, the drop down the impassable slope becomes more amazing.

North of Glennallen, the highway rises again, bursting through the tree line between a series of mountains and tracing the edge of long alpine lakes, before descending, parallel with the silver skein of the Alaska Pipeline, to Delta Junction. See chapter 9.
- **Top of the World and Taylor Highways:** Leading over the top of rounded, tundra-clothed mountains from Dawson City, Yukon Territory, to the Alaska Highway near Tok, this gravel route floats on a waving sea of terrain, with mountains receding to the infinite horizon in every direction. See chapter 9.
- **The Roads Around Nome:** You can't drive to Nome, but 250 miles of gravel roads radiate from the Arctic community into tundra that's populated only by musk oxen, bear, reindeer, birds, and other wildlife. See chapter 10.

5 The Best Fishing

The quality of salmon fishing in Alaska isn't so much a function of place as of time. See chapter 2 for how to find the fish when you arrive.

- **Bristol Bay:** This is the world's richest salmon fishery; lodges on the remote rivers of the region are an angler's paradise. See chapter 2.
- **Prince of Wales Island:** Fly-in trips or roadside streams yield some of the most prolific salmon fishing and peaceful fly-fishing anywhere. See chapter 5.
- **Copper River Delta, Cordova:** The Copper itself is silty with glacial runoff, but feeder streams and rivers are rich with trout, Dolly Varden, and salmon. See chapter 7.
- **The Kenai River:** The biggest king salmon—up to 98 pounds—come from the swift Kenai River.

Big fish are so common in the second run of kings that there's a special, higher standard for what makes a trophy. Silvers and reds add to a mad, summer-long fishing frenzy. See chapter 7.
- **Homer:** Alaska's largest charter-fishing fleet goes for halibut ranging into the hundreds of pounds. Beyond the road system, Unalaska has the biggest halibut. See chapters 7 and 10.
- **Kodiak Island:** The bears are so big because they live on an island that's crammed with spawning salmon in the summer. Kodiak has the best roadside salmon fishing in Alaska, and the remote fishing, at lodges or fly-in stream banks, is legendary. See chapter 10.

6 The Best Tips for Cooking Salmon

Now that you've caught a Pacific salmon, you need to know how to cook it—or order it in a restaurant—to avoid spoiling the rich flavor. Tips for getting your fish home are in chapter 7, section 10.

- **Freeze As Little As Possible:** It's a sad fact that salmon loses some of its richness and gets more "fishy" as soon as it's frozen. Eat as much as you can fresh, because it'll never be better. Ask if the salmon is fresh when you order it in a restaurant. Don't overlook smoking, the traditional Native way of preserving fish for the winter.

- **Choose the Best Fish:** The finest restaurants advertise where their salmon comes from on the menu. In early summer, Copper River kings and reds are the richest in flavor; later in the summer, Yukon River salmon are best. King, red, and silver are the only species you should find in a restaurant. The oil in the salmon gives it the rich, meaty flavor; the fish from the Copper and Yukon are high in oil content. Avoid farm-reared salmon, which is mushy and flavorless compared with wild Alaska salmon.

- **Keep It Simple:** When ordering salmon or halibut in a restaurant, avoid anything with cheese or heavy sauces. When salmon is fresh, it's best with light seasoning, perhaps just a little lemon, dill weed, and pepper and salt, or basted with soy sauce; or without anything on it at all, grilled over alder coals.

- **Don't Overcook It:** Salmon should be cooked just until the moment the meat changes color and becomes flaky through to the bone, or slightly before. A minute more, and some of the texture and flavor are lost. That's why those huge barbecue salmon bakes often are not as good as they should be—it's too hard to cook hundreds of pieces of fish just right and serve them all hot.

- **Filets, Not Steaks:** Salmon is cut two ways in Alaska: lengthwise filets or crosswise steaks. The filet is cut with the grain of the flesh, keeping the oil and moisture in the fish. Do not remove the skin before cooking—it holds in the oils, and will fall off easily when the fish is done. If you have a large group, cook the salmon bone-in (sometimes called a roast), stuffing seasonings in the body cavity. When it's done, the skin easily peels off and, after eating the first side, you can effortlessly lift out the skeleton.

7 The Best Bear Viewing

There are many places to see bears in Alaska, but if your goal is to make *sure* you see a bear—and potentially lots of bears—these are the best places:

- **Anan Wildlife Observatory:** When the fish are running, you can see many dozens of black bear feeding in a salmon stream from close at hand. Access is easiest from Wrangell. See chapter 5.

- **Pack Creek** (Admiralty Island): The brown bears of the island, which is more thickly populated with them than anywhere else on earth, have learned to ignore the daily visitors who stand on the platforms at Pack Creek. Access is by air from Juneau. See chapter 5.

- **Katmai National Park:** During the July and September salmon runs, dozens of giant brown bears congregate around Brooks Camp, where, from wooden platforms a few yards away, you can watch the full range of their behaviors. Flight services from Homer and Kodiak also bring guests at any time of the summer to see bears dig clams on the park's eastern seashore. See chapters 7 and 10.

- **Denali National Park:** The park offers the best and least expensive wildlife-viewing safari in the state. Passengers on the buses that drive the park road as far as the Eielson Visitor Center usually see at least some grizzlies. See chapter 8.

8 The Best Marine Mammal Viewing

You've got a good chance of seeing marine mammals almost anywhere you go boating in Alaska, but in some places it's almost guaranteed.

- **Frederick Sound** (Petersburg): A humpback jumped right into the boat with whale-watchers here in 1995. Petersburg boats also see otters and baby seals sitting on icebergs floating in front of LeConte Glacier. See chapter 5.
- **Point Adolphus** (Gustavus): Humpback whales show up off the point in Icy Strait, just a few miles from little Gustavus, a town of luxurious country inns, and in Bartlett Cove within Glacier Bay National Park. See chapter 5.
- **Sitka Sound:** Lots of otters and humpback whales show up in the waters near Sitka. In fall, when the town holds its Whale Fest, you can spot them from a city park built for the purpose. See chapter 5.
- **Kenai Fjords National Park** (near Seward): You don't have to go all the way into the park—you're pretty well assured of sea otters and sea lions in Resurrection Bay, near Seward, and humpbacks and killer whales often show up, too. See chapter 7.
- **Prince William Sound:** Otters, seals, and sea lions are easy—you'll see them on most trips out of Valdez, Whittier, or Cordova—but you also have a good chance of spotting both humpback and killer whales in the Sound. See chapter 7.

9 The Best Encounters with Native Culture

- **Ketchikan Totem Poles:** The town has two totem pole parks. At the park in Saxman, you can meet carvers in a workshop. At a museum, the real historic poles are on display. At Totem Bight, the poles stand in a natural setting. See chapter 5.
- **Alaska Native Heritage Center** (Anchorage): All of Alaska's Native groups joined together to build this grand living museum and gathering place, where dance and music performances, storytelling, art and craft demonstrations, and simple meetings of people happen every day. See chapter 6.
- **Alutiiq Museum** (Kodiak): The Koniag people are recovering their culture from the ground and from artifacts repatriated from the world's museums. Visitors can even join in archaeological fieldwork. See chapter 10.
- **Museum of the Aleutians** (Unalaska): Built by Aleuts to preserve and exhibit their own heritage, the museum stands right beside a major dig still in progress. See chapter 10.
- **Inupiat Heritage Center** (Barrow): Another brand-new living museum, this is a place to meet and enjoy performances by the Native people who built it, and to

see extraordinary artifacts they have made and recovered from frozen digs. See chapter 10.

- **NANA Museum of the Arctic** (Kotzebue): Eskimos of this still-traditional city/village proudly show off their Inupiat way of life with a combination of high-tech and age-old entertainment. See chapter 10.

10 The Best Community Museums & Historic Sites

- **Sitka National Historical Park:** The site of the 1804 battle between the Tlingits and Russians, in a totem pole park and seaside stand of old-growth forest, allows you to really appreciate what the Native people were fighting for. Inside the visitor center, Native craftspeople carry on their traditional work and talk with visitors. See chapter 5.
- **The Alaska State Museum** (Juneau): This richly endowed museum doesn't just show off its wealth of objects—it also uses them to teach about the state. A visit will put Alaska's Native cultures and pioneer history entirely in context. See chapter 5.
- **Anchorage Museum of History and Art:** Alaska's largest museum has the room and expertise to tell the story of Native and white history in Alaska, and to showcase contemporary Alaskan art and culture. See chapter 6.
- **The Pratt Museum** (Homer): The Pratt explains the life of the ocean in an intimate and clear way you'll find nowhere else in Alaska. See chapter 7.
- **University of Alaska Museum** (Fairbanks): The wealth of the university's study of Alaska, in all its forms, is put on display in galleries and daily shows, from equipment used to study the aurora borealis to a petrified bison. See chapter 9.

11 The Best Gold Rush Sites

The Klondike Gold Rush of 1898 transformed Alaska from a blank map at the periphery of America's consciousness to a fast-growing frontier and magnet for thousands of dreamers with visions of wealth. A century later, Alaska's best historic sites preserve that extraordinary time.

- **Skagway:** The little town at the top of Lynn Canal was where most of the gold rush stampeders got off the boat to head to the Klondike. Spared from fire, flood, or even much significant economic development other than tourism, Skagway contains a large collection of gold rush era buildings protected by the National Park Service. See chapter 5.
- **Fairbanks:** The gold rush in Fairbanks, just after the turn of the century, is not entirely done yet—there's a big new mine north of town. The city is large enough to provide lots of fun activities that exploit gold rush history. See chapter 9.
- **Dawson City:** A group of prospectors made the Klondike gold strike in 1896 and returned to tell of it in 1897, and in 1898 tens of thousands of greedy gold seekers arrived after an arduous stampede. Dawson City is ground zero, and the town is dedicated to preserving and sharing the history of the gold rush phenomenon. See chapter 9.
- **Eagle:** Unlike the other tourist-thronged gold rush towns, Eagle is a forgotten backwater where the gold rush was the last significant

thing to happen. The town is real and unspoiled, with lots to see but few other people to see it with. See chapter 9.

12 The Best Winter Destinations

- **Sitka:** Much of historic Sitka is just as good in winter as at any other time of year, but with fewer crowds and lower prices. The humpback whale-watching is exceptional in the late fall and early winter, as the whales stop off here on their migration. See chapter 5.
- **Juneau:** Although many tourist attractions close down, the steep and stunning Eaglecrest Ski Area opens up, and the best the town has to offer remains available—and you'll have it all pretty much to yourself. See chapter 5.
- **Anchorage:** The Fur Rendezvous and Iditarod sled dog races keep a winter-carnival atmosphere going through much of February and March, but those who enjoy participatory winter sports will enjoy Anchorage most, with some of the best Nordic and telemark skiing anywhere, close access to three downhill skiing areas, dog mushing, and lake skating. See chapter 6.
- **Alyeska Resort** (Girdwood): Alaska's premier downhill skiing area has lots of snow over a long season, fantastic views, new lifts, and a luxurious hotel. See "The Best Hotels," below, and chapter 6.
- **Chena Hot Springs Resort:** A 90-minute ride from Fairbanks and you're out in the country, where the northern lights are clear on a starry winter afternoon and night. The resort has lots of activities to get you out into the snowy countryside, or you can just relax in the hot mineral springs. See chapter 9.

13 The Strangest Community Events

- **Cordova Ice Worm Festival:** The truth is, ice worms do exist. Really. This winter carnival celebrates them in February. The highlight is the traditional annual march of the ice worm (a costume with dozens of feet sticking out) down the main street. See chapter 7.
- **Midnight Sun Baseball Game** (Fairbanks): The semipro baseball game, played without lights, doesn't begin until 10:30pm on the longest day of the year. See chapter 9.
- **Bering Sea Ice Golf Classic** (Nome): The greens are Astroturf, as the sea ice won't support a decent lawn in mid-March. Hook a drive and you could end up spending hours wandering among the pressure ridges, but you must play the ball as it lies. See chapter 10.
- **Nome Polar Bear Swim/Bathtub Race:** Nome has so *many* strange community events. Memorial Day is marked by the polar bear swim, sea ice permitting. Labor Day is celebrated by a bathtub race down Front Street, with water and a bather in each tub. See chapter 10.
- **Pillar Mountain Golf Classic** (Kodiak): The course is one hole, par is 70, and elevation gain is 1,400 feet. Having a spotter in the deep snow of late March is helpful, but use of two-way radios, dogs, and chain saws is prohibited. Also, there's no cutting down power poles, and cursing tournament officials carries a $25 fine. See chapter 10.

• **Community Softball** (Barrow): Play in the Arctic requires some special considerations. Spectators watch from their cars, and if a ball disappears in a puddle so that no part of it is showing, runners can advance no more than two bases. See chapter 10.

14 The Best Hotels

• **Westcoast Cape Fox Lodge** (Ketchikan; ☎ **866/225-8001** toll-free or 907/225-8001): Standing in its own little forest atop a rocky promontory that dominates downtown Ketchikan, this cleanly luxurious hotel has the feel of a mountain lodge or resort. A funicular tram carries visitors to the Creek Street boardwalks, or you can take the wooded cliff-side path. The rooms and common areas, accented with masterpieces of Tlingit art, have exceptional views of the city and Tongass Narrows through the trees. See chapter 5.

• **Hotel Captain Cook** (Anchorage; ☎ **800/843-1950**): This is the grand old hotel of downtown Anchorage, with a heavy nautical theme, teak paneling, and every possible amenity. It also remains the state's standard of service and luxury. See chapter 6.

• **Alyeska Prince Hotel** (Girdwood; ☎ **800/880-3880**): The first sight of this ski resort hotel—designed in a château style and standing in an undeveloped mountain valley—will make you catch your breath. Wait till you get inside and see the starscape and polar bear diorama in the lobby atrium, or the swimming pool, with its high-beamed ceiling and windows looking out on the mountain. A tram carries skiers and diners to the mountaintop. See chapter 6.

• **Kenai Princess Lodge** (Cooper Landing; ☎ **800/426-0500**): Princess Cruises and Tours has several superb hotels in Alaska; I especially like this one because it really is like a lodge, with working fireplaces and balconies in the romantic rooms. They're like luxury backwoods cabins. See chapter 7.

• **River's Edge Resort Cottages** (Fairbanks; ☎ **800/770-3343** or 907/474-0286): A village of trim little cottages with nicely appointed rooms watches the Chena River flow by from patios with sliding-glass doors. The owners thought of building the place when they saw how guests in their RV park enjoyed socializing. You feel like you've moved into a friendly neighborhood. Guests can canoe right from their front yards. See chapter 9.

• **The Grand Aleutian Hotel** (Unalaska/Dutch Harbor; ☎ **800/ 891-1194**): This large, lodge-style luxury hotel, which is competitive with the best in the state, gets extra points for the sheer audacity of building it on this remote, volcanic island. The hotel's existence creates a unique opportunity for those who want to stay in a fine hotel and see the Bush, with the best unexploited fishing and wildlife- and bird-watching. See chapter 10.

15 The Best Bed & Breakfasts

• **Alaska Ocean View Bed & Breakfast** (Sitka; ☎ **907/747-8310**): Here a family has set out to turn its home into perfect accommodations, with every detail attended to and warm, overflowing hospitality. See chapter 5.

- **Pearson's Pond Luxury Suites and Adventure Spa** (Juneau; © 888/658-6328): Diane Pearson takes the prize for the most obsessive attention to detail at any B&B in Alaska. Not only are the bathrooms stocked with condoms and computers, but the private pond, with a spraying fountain, is stocked with fish. See chapter 5.
- **Glacier Trail Bed & Breakfast** (Juneau; © 907/789-5646): The hosts built their house to be the perfect B&B, with Jacuzzi tubs, stunning glacier views from the bedrooms, and many amenities. Others could have done that, but only this fascinating and very Alaska couple could make their guests feel so welcome. See chapter 5.
- **Meadow's Glacier Bay Guest House** (Gustavus; 877/766-2348): This house full of art is itself a work of art in how it uses a movingly beautiful setting, in a grassy estuary with views of surrounding mountains. See chapter 5.
- **Aurora Winds Inn B&B Resort** (Anchorage; © 907/346-2533): This enormous house on the hillside above Anchorage has rooms so completely and theatrically decorated you'll feel as if you're sleeping in a movie set. See chapter 6.
- **The Oscar Gill House Bed & Breakfast** (Anchorage; © 907/279-1344): A beautifully restored historic B&B right in downtown Anchorage with low rates. See chapter 6.
- **Forget-Me-Not Lodge and the Aurora Express Bed and Breakfast** (Fairbanks; © 800/221-0073): The owners bought an old-fashioned railroad train, hauled it up the side of a mountain above Fairbanks, and remodeled the cars in luxurious theme decor as a bed-and-breakfast. See chapter 9.

16 Best Websites

Many useful websites are listed throughout the book; some of the best are under "Visitor Information," near the beginning of each town section.

- **www.trollart.com.** Ketchikan artist Ray Troll has created a website that carries you deep into his mind, which is full of odd and resonant humor about the evolution of fish, man, and our common relations. His vibrantly colored art makes it an aesthetic journey.
- **www.state.ak.us/adfg.** The Alaska Department of Fish and Game posts valuable information for anyone interested in fishing, hunting, wildlife watching, or just learning about creatures. Everyone from children to wildlife biologists will find something at his or her level.
- **www.adn.com.** The site for Alaska's largest newspaper, the *Anchorage Daily News*, contains an exhaustive state visitor guide, event and cultural information, and an informative fishing report, with south-central streams rated weekly.
- **www.awrta.org.** The Alaska Wilderness Recreation and Tourism Association unites hundreds of small eco-tourism operators. Authentic local guides and lodges can be hard to find, but they're all listed here on a comprehensive and well-organized site.
- **www.alcanseek.com.** This is a sort of Yahoo! of the north, with links and reports on the Alaska Highway and related regions organized by topic channels. (Alcan is the nickname for the

highway, which runs from British Columbia to Alaska.)

- **www.gi.alaska.edu**. They haven't put together a pretty site at the Geophysical Institute at the University of Alaska Fairbanks, but it's loaded with fascinating and cool science information about Alaska, such as aurora predictions, volcano watches, real-time earthquake and tsunami information, rocketry and space science, and more.
- **akweathercams.faa.gov**. It seems that every B&B has a webcam now; this site, posted for pilots by the FAA, is neat because it lets you see tiny, remote communities all over the state from a clickable map.
- **Favorite small-town sites:** Alaska communities too small to have a newspaper are communicating through the Internet; visitors to these sites can vicariously experience the pleasures and pitfalls of remote living. The best I've found are **www.seldovia.com** and **www.mccarthy-kennicott.com/ WSEN.htm**.

Planning Your Trip to Alaska

Planning a trip to Alaska can be a bit more complicated than traveling in the rest of the United States. Aside from the vast distances and range of climatic conditions, the best places book up for the high summer season. This chapter provides the general information to get oriented, then covers when and how to plan a trip to Alaska, including where to find guides, outfitters, and Internet resources. I've also included advice on fishing and shopping for Alaska Native art.

1 The Regions in Brief

SOUTHEAST ALASKA The Southeast Panhandle is the relatively narrow strip of mountains and islands that lies between Canada and the Gulf of Alaska. To Alaskans, it's Southeast, but to the rest of the country, it's more like the northernmost extension of the lush Pacific Northwest. It's a land of huge rain forest trees, glacier-garbed mountains, and countless islands ranging in size from the nation's third largest to tiny, one-tree islets strewn like confetti along the channels and fjords. The water is the highway of Southeast Alaska, as the land is generally too steep and rugged to build roads, but there are lots of towns and villages reachable by the ferry system or cruise ships. Southeast contains **Juneau,** Alaska's capital and third-largest city, and **Ketchikan,** next in size to Juneau. Southeast's towns are as quaint and historic as any in Alaska, especially **Sitka,** which preserves the story of Russian America and its conflict with the indigenous Native people. Alaska Native culture—Tlingit and Haida—is rich and close at hand. No other region offers more opportunities for boating or seeing marine wildlife. Likewise, no other region is as crowded with tourists, with well over half a million cruise-ship passengers jamming the little towns all summer. The weather is wet and temperate.

SOUTHCENTRAL ALASKA As a region, Southcentral is something of a catchall. The area is roughly defined by the arc of the Gulf of Alaska from the Canadian border on the east to Cook Inlet and the end of the road network to the west. It's a microcosm of the state, containing **Prince William Sound,** which is similar to the wooded island habitat of Southeast; the **Kenai Peninsula,** a roaded fishing, boating, and outdoor mecca; **Anchorage,** the state's modern, major city; and the **Matanuska and Susitna valleys,** an agricultural and suburban region of broad flatlands between steep mountains. Southcentral dominates Alaska, with most of the state's population and a more highly developed transportation system than elsewhere, including a network of highways and the Alaska Railroad. Southcentral's weather is influenced by the ocean, keeping it from being very hot or very cold. The coastal areas are wet, while just behind the coastal mountains the weather is drier.

THE INTERIOR The vast central part of the state is crossed by highways and by rivers that act as highways. Big river valleys lie between great mountain

Alaska by the Numbers

This chart shows some comparative indicators for 17 of Alaska's most popular destinations. The third column is the best season to visit, when there's enough going on and weather is suitable (that includes weather that's good for winter sports). The "Transportation" column shows ways of getting to each destination (see more on this in "Getting There," later in this chapter).

Place	Pop.	Season	Transportation	Precip. (in.)	Snow (in.)
Anchorage	260,283	May–Sept Jan–Mar	Road, air, rail	15.7	71
Barrow	4,581	June–Aug	Air	4.5	30
Cordova	2,454	May–Sept	Air, ferry	93.1	119
Denali National Park	169	June–Sept	Road, rail	15.3	83
Fairbanks	82,840	May–Sept Jan–Mar	Road, air, rail	10.5	68
Glacier Bay National Park	429	May–Sept	Air, boat	70	117
Haines	1,811	May–Sept/Nov	Road, ferry, air	48	123
Homer	3,946	May–Sept	Road, air, ferry	24.6	55
Juneau	30,711	May–Sept	Air, ferry	56.3	99
Kenai	6,942	May–Oct	Road, air	19.3	61
Ketchikan	14,070	May–Sept	Air, ferry	150.7	37
Kodiak Island	13,913	May–Sept	Air, ferry	76.3	73
Kotzebue	3,082	June–Aug	Air	9.5	50
Nome	3,505	June–Aug/Mar	Air	16.1	61
Petersburg	3,224	May–Sept	Air, ferry	110.4	67
Seward	2,830	May–Sept	Road, rail, ferry, air	66.4	81
Sitka	8,835	May–Sept/ Nov	Air, ferry	86.4	39
Skagway	862	May–Sept	Road, ferry, air	26.4	50
Unalaska/ Dutch Harbor	4,283	June–Sept	Air, ferry	59.9	88
Valdez	4,036	May–Sept	Road, air, ferry	61.5	304

ranges, the largest of which are the Alaska Range, which contains **Mount McKinley,** North America's tallest peak, and the Brooks Range, the northern end of the cordillera that includes the Rockies. McKinley is the centerpiece of **Denali National Park,** Alaska's premier road-accessible wildlife-viewing destination. The region's dominant city is **Fairbanks,** Alaska's second largest, which lies on the lazy Chena River roughly in the middle of the state. The natural

environment is drier and less abundant than that in Southeast or Southcentral. The Athabascans, the Interior's first people, still subsist on this sparse land in tiny villages and river fish camps. Summer days can be hot and winters very cold in the Interior, because of the distance from the ocean.

THE BUSH Bush Alaska is linked by lifestyle rather than by geography. One good definition would be that the Bush is the part of the state that's closer to the wilderness than to civilization. It's also the only part of the state where Native people outnumber whites and other relative newcomers. In many Bush villages, readily accessible to the outside world only by small plane, people still live according to age-old subsistence hunting-and-gathering traditions. The Bush region includes the majority of Alaska outside the road network, ranging from the north end of the Canadian border all the way around the coast, out the Aleutians, and the Alaska Peninsula and Kodiak Island, south of Anchorage. But some towns in each of the other regions also could be called "Bush villages." The Bush contains many regions, including the Arctic, Northwest, and Southwest Alaska.

2 Visitor Information

The **Alaska Tourism Industry Association,** P.O. Box 143361, Anchorage, AK 99514-3361 (© **800/862-5275** or 907/929-2200; www.travelalaska.com) is the state's main visitor information agency. Real live people answer prospective visitors' questions, and they'll be happy to send out a free vacation planner.

For outdoor recreation, the **Alaska Public Lands Information Centers** are centralized sources of information on all government lands, which include more than 85% of the state. The centers, in Anchorage, Fairbanks, Ketchikan, and Tok, are operated cooperatively by many land agencies, including the National Park Service and U.S. Forest Service. The Anchorage center is at 605 W. Fourth Ave., Suite 105, Anchorage, AK 99501 (© **907/271-2737,** TTY 907/271-2738; www.nps.gov/aplic).

3 Money

Alaska is an expensive destination any way you slice it. With the exception of a few out-of-the-way spots, good standard motel rooms are rarely less than $100 in the high season, and usually over $120. Airfare from Seattle to Anchorage fluctuates wildly with competition among the airlines, but a $300 round-trip, with 14-day advance purchase, is a fair deal. (Flying is cheaper than the alternatives, driving or taking the ferry and bus.) You can easily pay twice that to fly to an Alaska Bush community. Even the train is expensive, with a one-way fare from Anchorage to Fairbanks (a 350-mile trip) costing $175 on the least luxurious of three choices of cars.

A couple ordering a good salmon dinner, appetizers, and wine will likely pay $100 in a fine restaurant, including tip. One reason cruise ships have become such a popular way to visit Alaska is that, for the same quality level, they're less expensive on a daily basis than independent travel, and offer the chance to see remote coastal areas that can be quite costly to get to for land-based visitors. (See chapter 4 for details on cruising.)

To travel at a standard American comfort level, a couple should allow $120 per person, per day, for room and board. The cost of an activity such as flightseeing, wildlife cruises, or guided fishing typically is $75 to $250 per person. Add ground transportation—a car is the best way to see much of the state, and you won't do much better than $50 a day for an economy model from the major national firms, although you can save with an unknown brand. Weekly rentals generally cost the same as renting for 5 individual days. You also may need train and ferry tickets.

You can trim your costs, however, by cutting your demands. You'll learn more about the real Alaska staying in

---

Questions, Anyone?

If you can't find the answers you are looking for in the book, check out my personal website, at www.wohlforth.net, where I post and answer reader questions and offer some of my other writings about Alaska, without charge. In addition, online updates of this book are posted at frommers.travelocity.com.

B&B accommodations than in a standard hotel room. Expect to pay $85 to $100 for a nice room with a shared bath, $100 to $120 for a private bath. The complimentary breakfast cuts down on food costs, too. And there are plenty of family restaurants where you can eat a modest dinner for two for $30, with a tip and a glass of beer. Traveling in that style will bring the cost of room and board down to about $85 per person, per day, for a couple.

Another way to save money is to travel in the shoulder season, before and after the peak summer season. Hotel and guided activity prices drop significantly, typically 25% or more. May and September are solidly in the shoulder season, and sometimes you get bargains as late as June 15 or as early as August 15. Traveling in the winter is a whole different experience, but certainly saves a lot of money—where hotels are open, you'll find their rates typically running half of their high-season levels. For other considerations on off-season and shoulder-season travel, see "When to Go," later in this chapter.

You can save the most money by giving up a private room every night

and cooking some of your own meals. Camping is a fun way to really see Alaska and costs only $10 to $15 a night in state and federal government campgrounds. Hostels are available in most towns for under $20 a night. Even small Bush communities now have ATMs; the main exceptions these days are remote outdoor destinations such as lodges or parks. In the "Fast Facts" section for each town in this book, I'll tell you if there's an ATM and where to find it. There's even a website where you can locate the nearest PLUS Network ATM wherever you are in the world: **www.visa.com/pd/atm/**. Alaska ATMs generally are on the Cirrus, PLUS, or MAC networks, and other major ATM networks.

In larger towns, you'll find that every business you'd expect to take credit, charge, or debit cards at home will accept them. Even most bed-and-breakfasts and inexpensive restaurants usually take cards now. Few businesses of any kind will take an out-of-state personal check. Traveler's checks are good just about anywhere, but there's no longer any reason to go through the hassle and expense.

4 When to Go

CLIMATE & SEASONS

The weather in Alaska can be extreme and unpredictable. The state is the first to get whatever Arctic Siberia or the void of the North Pacific have to throw at North America. The extremes of recorded temperatures are a high of 100°F and low of –80°F. At

any time of year your vacation could be enlivened by weeks of unbroken sunny weather or weighed down by weeks of unbroken rain. All you can do is play the averages, hope for the best, and, if you do get bad weather, get out and have fun anyway—that's what Alaskans do. A statistical summary of weather probabilities in various Alaska places is found below in "Alaska's Climate, by Months & Regions." I've summarized the best visitor season in each destination in "Alaska By the Numbers," above.

JUNE, JULY & AUGUST Summer in Alaska is a miraculous time, when the sun refuses to set, the salmon run upriver, and people are energized by limitless daylight. The sun dips below the horizon in Anchorage for only about 4 hours on June 21, the longest day of the year, and the sky is light all night. The state fills with people coming to visit and to work in the seasonal fishing, timber, and construction industries. Weather gets warmer, although how warm depends on where you go (see the chart below). June is the driest of the summer months, July the warmest, and August generally the rainiest month of the brief summer, but warmer than June. In most respects, June is the best summer month to make a visit, but it does have some drawbacks to consider: In the Arctic, snow doesn't all melt until mid-June; in Southcentral Alaska, trails at high elevation or in the shade may be too muddy or snowy; and not all activities or facilities at Denali National Park open until late June. It's also the worst time for mosquitoes.

Summer also is the season of high prices. Most operators in the visitor industry have only these 90 days to make their year's income, and they charge whatever the market will bear. July is the absolute peak of the tourist season, when you must book well ahead and when crowds are most prevalent. (Of course, crowding depends on where you are. With a population density of roughly one person per square mile, Alaska is never *really* crowded.) Before June 15 and after August 15, the season begins to decline, providing occasional bargains and more elbow room, with real

off-season conditions most places before Memorial Day and after Labor Day. But the length and intensity of the visitor season vary widely in different areas: In cruise-ship ports, it's busy from chilly early May into stormy October.

MAY & SEPTEMBER More and more visitors are coming to Alaska during these shoulder months to take advantage of the lower prices, reduced crowds, and special beauty.

May is the drier of the two months and can be as warm as summer, if you're lucky, but as you travel farther north and earlier in the month, your chances increase of finding cold, mud, and even snow. In Alaska, there is no spring—the melt of snow and resultant seas of mud are called **breakup.** Flowers show up with the start of summer. Many outdoor activities aren't possible during breakup, which can extend well into May. Except for in cruise-ship towns, most tourist-oriented activities and facilities are still closed before May 15, and a few don't open until Memorial Day or June 1. Where visitor facilities are open, they often have significantly lower prices. Also, the first visitors of the year usually receive an especially warm welcome. The very earliest salmon runs start in May, but for a fishing-oriented trip it's better to come later. Cruise ships begin calling May 1, and the towns they visit swing into action when they arrive.

Sometime between late August to mid-September, weather patterns change, bringing clouds, frequent rainstorms, and cooling weather, and signaling the trees and tundra to turn bright, vivid colors. For a week or two (what week it is depends on your latitude), the bright-yellow birches of the boreal forest and rich red of the heathery tundra make September the most lovely time of year. But the rain and the nip in the air, similar to late

October or November in New England, mean you'll likely have to bundle up; and September is among the wettest months of the year. Most tourist-oriented businesses stay open, with lower prices, till September 15, except in the Arctic.

Alaska's Climate, by Months & Regions

	Jan	Feb	Mar	Apr	May	June	July	Aug	Sept	Oct	Nov	Dec

Anchorage: Southcentral Alaska

	Jan	Feb	Mar	Apr	May	June	July	Aug	Sept	Oct	Nov	Dec
Avg. high/low**	21/8	26/11	33/17	44/29	55/39	62/47	65/51	63/49	55/41	40/28	28/16	22/10
Hours of light*	6:53	9:41	12:22	15:20	18:00	19:22	18:00	15:15	12:19	9:29	6:46	5:27
Sunny days†	12	10	13	12	11	10	9	9	9	10	10	10
Rain/snow days	8	8	8	6	7	8	11	13	14	12	10	11
Precipitation‡	0.8	0.8	0.6	0.6	0.7	1.0	1.9	2.7	2.6	1.9	1.1	1.1

Barrow: Arctic Alaska

	Jan	Feb	Mar	Apr	May	June	July	Aug	Sept	Oct	Nov	Dec
Avg. high/low**	-8/-20	-12/-24	-8/-21	6/-8	25/15	39/30	46/34	43/34	34/27	20/10	5/-6	-6/-17
Hours of light*	0:00	8:05	12:33	17:43	24:00	24:00	24:00	17:34	12:30	7:46	0:00	0:00
Sunny days†	7	18	21	18	8	9	11	5	4	6	8	4
Rain/snow days	4	4	4	4	4	5	9	11	11	11	6	5
Precipitation‡	0.2	0.2	0.1	0.2	0.2	0.3	0.9	1.0	0.6	0.5	0.2	0.2

Cold Bay: Aleutian Archipelago

	Jan	Feb	Mar	Apr	May	June	July	Aug	Sept	Oct	Nov	Dec
Avg. high/low**	33/24	32/23	35/25	38/29	45/35	50/41	55/46	56/47	52/43	44/35	39/30	35/27
Hours of light*	8:05	10:10	12:17	14:36	16:32	17:25	16:33	14:34	12:17	10:04	8:01	7:08
Sunny days†	8	6	8	4	3	3	3	2	4	6	6	7
Rain/snow days	19	17	18	16	17	16	17	20	21	23	22	21
Precipitation‡	2.8	2.5	2.3	2.0	2.5	2.3	2.4	3.7	4.3	4.2	4.2	3.3

Fairbanks: Interior Alaska

	Jan	Feb	Mar	Apr	May	June	July	Aug	Sept	Oct	Nov	Dec
Avg. high/low**	-2/-19	8/-15	24/-2	42/20	60/38	71/52	73/52	66/47	55/36	32/17	11/-5	1/-16
Hours of light*	5:46	9:14	12:22	15:54	19:22	21:48	19:26	15:52	12:24	9:04	5:39	3:43
Sunny days†	15	14	17	14	16	13	12	10	10	9	12	12
Rain/snow days	8	7	6	5	7	11	12	12	10	11	11	9
Precipitation‡	0.6	0.4	0.4	0.2	0.6	1.4	1.8	1.8	1.1	0.8	0.7	0.8

Juneau: Southeast Alaska

	Jan	Feb	Mar	Apr	May	June	July	Aug	Sept	Oct	Nov	Dec
Avg. high/low**	29/18	34/23	39/27	48/32	55/39	62/45	64/48	63/48	56/43	47/37	37/28	32/23
Hours of light*	7:31	9:55	12:18	14:55	17:11	18:17	17:13	14:54	12:20	9:49	7:27	6:22
Sunny days†	8	7	7	8	8	8	8	9	6	4	6	5
Rain/snow days	18	17	18	17	17	15	17	17	20	24	20	21
Precipitation‡	4.3	3.9	3.5	2.9	3.5	3.1	4.2	5.3	7.2	7.8	5.4	5.1

Valdez: Prince William Sound

	Jan	Feb	Mar	Apr	May	June	July	Aug	Sept	Oct	Nov	Dec
Avg. high/low**	27/18	30/19	37/24	45/31	53/39	60/45	63/48	61/46	54/41	43/33	33/23	29/19
Hours of light*	6:54	9:41	12:22	15:19	17:58	19:20	17:57	15:14	12:20	9:30	6:48	5:29
Sunny days†	9	9	11	11	9	8	8	10	8	8	10	7
Rain/snow days	17	14	16	14	17	15	17	17	20	20	16	18
Precipitation‡	5.7	5.5	4.7	3.2	3.2	2.8	3.6	6.5	9.3	7.9	5.7	7.6

*Hours of light is sunrise to sunset on the 21st day of each month.
**All temperatures are given in degrees Fahrenheit.
†Sunny days include the average observed clear and partly cloudy days per month.
‡Precipitation is the average water equivalent of rain or snow.

After September 15, it's potluck. Some areas close up tight, but the silver salmon fishing hits prime time on the Kenai Peninsula, and the season stays active until the end of the month. A lucky visitor can come in September and hit a month of crisp, sunny, perfect weather, and have the state relatively to him- or herself. Or, it can be cold and rainy all month. Cruise ships continue to ply the Inside Passage well into October, while the sky dumps torrential rains: Ketchikan averages 22 inches and 24 rainy days in the month.

WINTER   One of the most spectacular trips I ever took was a train ride from Fairbanks to Anchorage in January. Outside the windows, Mount McKinley stood clear and so vivid in a vast, smooth landscape of pale blue and rich orange that I felt as if I could reach out and touch it. A young woman from South Africa was on the train. When I asked her why she came to Alaska in January, she only had to point out the window.

She was right, but visitors and the people who serve them generally haven't figured that out yet. Some towns (such as Skagway and Dawson City) close down almost completely. In others—most places on the ocean, for example—nearly all activities and attractions are closed for the season, but services remain open for business travelers. Where facilities are open, hotel prices are often less than half of what you'd pay in the high season. Quite luxurious rooms sometimes go for the cost of a budget motel. Visitors who seek out places of interest can have an exceptional and memorable time, enjoying some of the best alpine, Nordic, and backcountry skiing, outdoor ice-skating, dog mushing, snowmobiling, and aurora and wildlife watching available anywhere, at any time. The best time to come is late winter, from February through mid-March, when the sun is up longer and winter carnivals and competitive dog mushing hit their peak.

WHAT TO WEAR

SUMMER   You're not going to the North Pole, and you don't need a down parka or winter boots weighing down your luggage. But you do need to be ready for a variety of weather, from sunny, 80° days to windy, rainy 50° outings on the water. The way Alaskans prepare for such a range is with layers. The content of the layers depends on what you'll be doing, but everyone should bring at least this: warm-weather clothes, heavy long-sleeved shirts and pants, a wool sweater, a warm jacket, and a raincoat. Gloves and wool hats are a good idea, too, especially for boating trips. If you'll be camping, add synthetic thermal long underwear and wool socks and make your jacket thick synthetic fleece. Combining these items, you'll be ready for any summer conditions. For hiking, bring sturdy shoes or cross trainers.

WINTER   Most visitors can get by in town with a normal greatcoat, sweater, hat, gloves, and wool socks. If you're like most Alaskans, you'll just make a quick dash from car to heated building when really cold weather hits. The key to warmth and safety during vigorous outdoor activities is to wear layers of breathable clothing that will stay warm when wet, such as wool or synthetics. With the following layers, you can be ready for temperatures well below zero (at which point you won't want to ski or skate anyway): synthetic thermal long underwear, synthetic fleece pants and coat, wool sweater, wind-resistant pants and jacket, wool socks and hat, and lined mittens. Reduce the layers for warmer temperatures. Snowmobiling and dog mushing are less active, so you need warmer clothing. On guided trips, they'll tell you what to bring or provide it for you. A full outfit for backcountry survival in extreme cold includes synthetic thermal long underwear, the stoutest Sorel-style or Air Force bunny boots, insulated snow pants, a heavy down parka with a hood, thick, insulated mittens (not gloves), a wool hat, and a face-insulating mask; all that costs at least $500. You can buy it in Anchorage or Fairbanks when you arrive, but no one should go for an outing in such conditions without experience or skilled guidance.

ALASKA CALENDAR OF EVENTS

Here are some of the biggest community events of the year in Alaska's cities and towns. Many of the dates are estimates, simply because of the timing of our deadlines. Don't plan a vacation around them without checking for up-to-date details. I haven't listed fishing derbies, which go on in almost every town in the summer.

February

The Yukon Quest International Sled Dog Race (℃ 907/452-7954; www.yukonquest.org) runs between Fairbanks and Whitehorse, Yukon Territory, trading the direction each year. Mushers say this rugged 1,000-mile race is even tougher than the Iditarod. Starts February 9, 2002, in Fairbanks.

The Anchorage Fur Rendezvous Winter Carnival (℃ 907/274-1177; www.furrondy.net) is a huge, citywide winter celebration, with many community events, fireworks, craft fairs, snowshoe softball, dogsled rides, and other fun. The main event is the **World Champion Sled Dog Race,** a 3-day sprint event of about 25 miles per heat. February 8–17, 2002.

March

The Nenana Ice Classic (℃ 907/832-5446; www.ptialaska.net/~tripod), in Nenana, starts with Tripod Days, when a "four-legged tripod" that will mark the breakup of ice on the Tanana River is erected,

ushering in a weekend celebration of dance performances, dog mushing, and other activities. The ticket buyer who guesses the minute the tripod moves, usually in May, wins the jackpot. Tripod Days is the first weekend in March.

The Iditarod Trail Sled Dog Race (℃ 907/376-5155; www.iditarod.com) starts with fanfare from **Anchorage.** Then the teams are loaded in trucks for the **Iditarod Restart,** in **Wasilla,** which is the real beginning of the race. Here the historic gold rush trail becomes continuous for the dogs' 1,000-mile run to Nome. The event enlivens Wasilla at the end of a long winter. The finish in Nome is the biggest event of the year in the Arctic, drawing world media attention and turning Nome into a huge party for a few days (they even play golf out on the sea ice). The race solicits volunteers to help, which is a much better way to experience it than just watching. Starts first Saturday in March.

The World Ice Art Championships (℃ 907/451-8250; www.icealaska.com) brings carvers from all over the world to sculpt immense chunks of clear ice cut from a Fairbanks pond. Among ice carvers, Fairbanks' ice is famous for its clarity and the great size of the chunks. Some spectacular ice sculptures stand as tall as a two-story building. March 6–17, 2002.

April

The Alaska Folk Festival (℃ 907/463-3316; www.juneau.com/aff) is Juneau's community-wide celebration, drawing musicians, whether on the bill or not, from all over the state. April 8–14, 2002.

May

Copper River Delta Shorebird Festival (℃ 907/424-7260; www.ptialaska.net/~midtown) revolves around the coming of dizzying swarms of millions of shorebirds that use the delta and beaches near the town as a migratory stopover in early May. The whole community gets involved to host birdwatchers and put on a 5-day schedule of educational and outdoor activities.

The Kachemak Bay Shorebird Festival, Homer (℡ **907/235-7740;** homeralaska.org/shorebird. htm), held in early May, includes guided bird-watching hikes and boat excursions, natural-history workshops, art shows and performances, a wooden boat festival, and other events.

Little Norway Festival, Petersburg (℡ **907/772-4636;** www. petersburg.org), celebrates the May 17, 1814, declaration of the independence of Norway from Sweden. The town has 4 days of community events the third full weekend of the month.

Kodiak Crab Festival (℡ **907/ 486-5557;** www.kodiak.org/crab fest.html), lasting 5 days over Memorial Day weekend, is the town's biggest event of the year and includes many fun events and the solemn blessing of the fleet and memorial service for lost fishermen.

June

Celebration, in Juneau (℡ **907/ 463-4844**), is a huge Alaska Native dance and cultural gathering that happens only every other year. June 6–8, 2002.

The Sitka Summer Music Festival (℡ **907/747-6774;** www.sitkamusic festival.org), a chamber-music series that began in 1972, draws musicians from all over the world for 3 weeks in June. Performances take place Tuesdays and Fridays, and other events all week.

Midnight Sun Baseball Game, Fairbanks. A summer-solstice event:

the local semipro baseball team, the Fairbanks Goldpanners, plays a game without artificial lights beginning at 10:30pm. Call ℡ **907/ 451-0095** for information. Around June 21.

Midnight Sun Festival, Nome. Celebrates the summer solstice, when Nome gets more than 22 hours of direct sunlight, with a parade, softball tournament, bank "holdup," raft race, and similar events. Call ℡ **907/443-5535** for information. June 21.

The Last Frontier Theater Conference (℡ **907/834-1612;** www.uaa. alaska.edu/pwscc/) brings famous playwrights and directors to the community for seminars and performances in June. Arthur Miller, Edward Albee, and other famous writers have met the public here in fairly intimate settings.

July

The Yukon Gold Panning Championships and Canada Day Celebrations, Dawson City. The Canadian equivalent of the Fourth of July. July 1.

Independence Day. Most of the small towns in Alaska make a big deal of the Fourth of July. Seward always has a huge celebration, exploding with visitors, primarily from Anchorage. Besides the parade and many small-town festivities, the main attraction is the **Mount Marathon Race,** from the middle of town straight up rocky Mount Marathon to its 3,022-foot peak and down again. **Seldovia, Ketchikan, Skagway,** and **Juneau** also have exceptional Fourth of July events. See the individual town sections for more information.

August

The Southeast Alaska State Fair and **Bald Eagle Music Festival** (℡ **907/766-2476**), Haines. Held for 5 days in early August; it's a regional small-town get-together, with livestock, cooking, a logging show, a parade, music, and other entertainment.

The Alaska State Fair (© 907/ 745-4827; www.akstatefair.org), Palmer. The biggest event of the year for the Matanuska Valley, and one of the biggest for Anchorage. It's a typical state fair, except for the huge vegetables. The good soil and long Valley days produce cabbages the size of beanbag chairs. A mere beach ball–size cabbage wouldn't even make it into competition. The 11 days before Labor Day.

October

Alaska Day Festival, Sitka. Alaska Day, commemorating the Alaska purchase on October 18, 1867, is a big deal in this former Russian and U.S. territorial capital city.

November

Sitka WhaleFest (© 907/747-5940; www.sitka.org/whale.htm). Over a weekend in early November, during the fall and early winter period when humpback whales congregate in Sitka Sound, there are workshops, whale-watching tours, a concert, and other community events. The event coordinates with the Alaska Bald Eagle Festival.

The Alaska Bald Eagle Festival (© 907/766-2202; www.bald eaglefest.org), Haines. Seminars and special events mark an annual congregation of 3,000 eagles near Haines. It's timed to allow visitors to also attend the WhaleFest in Sitka.

Carrs/Safeway Great Alaska Shootout (© 907/786-1230; www.goseawolves.com or www. shootout.com), Anchorage. The University of Alaska Seawolves host a roster of the nation's top-ranked NCAA Division I men's and women's basketball teams at the Sullivan Arena. Thanksgiving weekend.

5 Escorted Tour or Do-It-Yourself?

Hundreds of thousands of visitors come to Alaska each year on escorted package tours, leaving virtually all their travel arrangements in the hands of a single company that takes responsibility for ushering them through the state for a single, lump-sum fee. But more and more visitors are cutting the apron strings and exploring Alaska on their own, and in the process discovering a more relaxed, spontaneous experience. Each approach has advantages and disadvantages, of course, and which way you choose to visit depends on how you value those pros and cons. Unfortunately, some people make the choice based on expectations that aren't valid, so it's important to know what you're getting into.

An escorted package tour provides security. You'll know in advance how much everything will cost, you don't have to worry about making hotel and ground-transportation reservations, you're guaranteed to see the highlights of each town you visit, and you'll have someone telling you what you're looking at. Often, a package price saves money over traveling at the same level of comfort independently. If there are weather delays or other travel problems, it's the tour company's problem, not yours. Everything happens on schedule, and you never have to touch your baggage other than to unpack when it magically shows up in your room. If you sometimes feel like you're a member of a herd on an escorted tour, you'll also meet new people, a big advantage if you're traveling on your own. Many passengers on these trips are retired, over age 65.

If you're short on time, escorted package tours make the most of it, as they often travel at an exhausting pace. Passengers get up early and cover a lot of ground, with sights and activities scheduled solidly through the day. Stops last only long enough to get a taste of what the sight is about, not to dig in and learn about a place you're especially interested in. On an escorted trip, you'll meet few if any Alaska residents, since most tour companies hire college students from "Outside" (a term coined by Alaskans to refer to anyplace that's not in Alaska) to fill summer jobs. You'll stay in only the largest hotels and eat in the largest, tourist-oriented restaurants—no small, quaint places loaded with local character. For visiting wilderness, such as Denali National Park, the quick and superficial approach can, in my opinion, spoil the whole point of going to a destination that's about an experience, not just seeing a particular object or place.

Studies by Alaska tourism experts have found that many people choose escorted packages to avoid risks that don't really exist. Alaska may still be untamed, but that doesn't mean it's a dangerous or uncomfortable place to travel. Visitors who sign up for a tour to avoid having to spend the night in an igloo or use an outhouse may wish they'd been a bit more adventurous when they arrive and find that Alaska has the same facilities found in any other state. Except for tiny Bush villages that you're unlikely to visit anyway, you'll come across the standard American hotel room almost anywhere you go. The tourism infrastructure is well developed even in small towns—you're never far from help unless you want to be.

It's also possible for an independent traveler to obtain some of the predictability a package tour provides. You can reserve accommodations and activities and control your expenses by using a good travel agent experienced in Alaska travel. Some even offer fixed-price itineraries that allow you to travel on your own (see "Independent Travel Planning," at the end of this section). But independent travelers never have the complete security of those on group tours. Once you're on the road, you'll be on your own to take care of the details, and weather delays and other cancellations can confound the best-laid plans. If you can't relax and enjoy a trip knowing unforeseen difficulties could happen, then an escorted package tour is the way to go.

LARGE TOUR COMPANIES

A few major tour and cruise-ship companies dominate the Alaska package-tour market with "vertically integrated" operations that allow them to take care of everything you do while in Alaska with tight quality control. Each also offers tours as short as a couple of hours to independent travelers who want to combine their own exploring with a more structured experience. Two Native-owned upstarts also offer land and boat tours. All can be booked through any travel agent.

Holland America Tours   The Holland America cruise line became the giant of Alaska tourism by buying local tour companies such as Gray Line and Westours to carry visitors in buses, trains, and boats, and the Westmark hotel chain to put them up for the night. Today the Alaska/Yukon operation employs 2,000 workers operating 184 buses, 13 railcars, and 2 day boats. Most clients arrive in the state on one of the company's ships (see chapter 4), but even within Alaska, chances are good that a tour you sign up for will put you on a Gray Line coach and exclusively in Westmark hotels. The quality of the Westmark chain is inconsistent; most are described in the town sections of this book. Other than the classy Baranof in Juneau, they tend to have standard to small rooms with typical amenities.

Native Art: Finding the Real Thing

In a gift shop in Southeast Alaska, I watched as a woman who said she was an artist's assistant sanded a Tlingit-style carving. When I asked who made the carving, the artist said, "It's my work." At the time, that seemed like an odd way of putting it. Only later did I learn from one of the artist's former assistants that his "work" involved ordering the carvings from Southeast Asia and shipping them to Alaska, where he hired locals to pretend to be working on them in the shop. A journalist friend of mine met a boy in the alley behind a gift store in Ketchikan removing "MADE IN TAIWAN" stickers from merchandise with a razor blade. Several years ago, the Federal Trade Commission fined an art dealer for peddling fake Native art. He was able to go on selling carvings signed by a person with a made-up, Native-sounding name along with the name of an Alaska village. The artist was Cambodian and had spent only a few months in the village.

You may not care if the gifts and souvenirs you buy in Alaska really come from Alaska. But if you do, especially if you plan to spend a lot of money on authentic Alaska Native art, you must pay attention.

The most serious kind of counterfeit is fake Alaska Native fine art. Pieces sell for $500 or more, and the scam both defrauds the buyer and takes food off the tables of Alaska's village artists, who can't compete in price with Indonesian carvers. Repeated newspaper exposés seem to have little effect. In 1995, an Anchorage reporter visited villages in Bali where hundreds of workers were turning out Eskimo masks and moose, otter, and sheep carvings from fossilized walrus ivory, whalebone, and other Alaskan materials, using designs taken from books sent from Alaska. In 2001, a Juneau paper documented that half the shops in

On a group tour, you don't spend much time in the room, as schedules generally are tightly planned and daily departures are early. You'll find a description of the company's railcars on the Anchorage-Denali-Fairbanks run in chapter 8. Gray Line coaches are first-rate, especially several super-luxurious, extra-long vehicles that bend in the middle and have a lounge in the back. And the company goes more places than any other, with a catalog that covers just about anything in the state that could possibly be done with a group. They also have self-drive tours. Some of the tour excursions—on the Yukon River between Dawson City and Eagle, for example—are entirely unique. Prices depend on a

variety of factors, but in general a tour of a week is about $1,600 per person. 300 Elliot Ave. W, Seattle, WA 98119. ✆ 800/544-2206. www.graylineofalaska.com or www.hollandamerica.com.

Princess Cruises and Tours The Princess cruise line has built its land-tour operation from the ground up instead of buying it (as Holland America did), and the result is a smaller but consistently top-quality collection of properties. The five Princess hotels are all among Alaska's best. Two are near Denali National Park, and one each are in Fairbanks and Cooper Landing, on the Kenai Peninsula; the fifth, near Wrangell-St. Elias National Park, is expected to be completed in 2002. Princess operates its own coaches and town were selling counterfeits, with some removing foreign labels and attaching "MADE IN ALASKA" stickers.

How can you avoid being scammed? Ask questions before you buy. Any reputable art dealer will provide you with a biography of the artist who created an expensive work. Ask specifically if that artist actually carved the piece: Some Native artists have sold their names and designs to wholesalers who produce knockoffs. Price is another tip-off. An elaborate mask is more likely to cost $3,000 than $300. Another indicator is the choice of materials; most soapstone carvings are not made in Alaska.

The **Alaska State Council on the Arts** (© 907/269-6610) authenticates Native arts and crafts with a **silver hand** label, which assures you it was made by the hands of an Alaska Native with Alaskan materials. But the program isn't universally used, so the absence of the label doesn't mean the work definitely isn't authentic. Other labels aren't worth much: An item could say **Alaska Made** even if only insignificant assembly work happened here. Of course, in Bush Alaska, and in some urban shops, you can buy authentic work direct from craftspeople. Buying in Native-owned co-ops is also safe.

For gifts that don't claim to be made by Natives but do at least purport to originate in the state, a symbol of two bears that says **Made in Alaska** (www.madeinalaska.org/mia) indicates that a state contractor has determined that it was at least substantially made here. Non-Natives produce Alaskan crafts of ceramics, wood, or fabric, but not plastic—if it's plastic, it probably wasn't made here. Again, price is an indicator: As with anywhere else in the United States, the cheapest products come from Asia.

has superb railcars on the Alaska Railroad route to Denali. Descriptions of each hostelry can be found in the appropriate chapter. Most people on the tours come to Alaska on a cruise ship, but tours are for sale separately, too, and they have recently begun offering fly-drive packages that put you in your own car rather than a bus. The company's network of tours is less extensive than Holland America's but visit the places most people want to go. 2815 Second Ave., Ste. 400, Seattle, WA 98121-1299. © 800/426-0442. www.princess.com.

Alaska Heritage Tours Chugach Natives recently created this tour company to show off the Southcentral region, Denali, and Fairbanks. They own attractive lodges in Talkeetna and Seward (listed in those sections) and top boat-tour operations in Kenai Fjords National Park and Prince William Sound (from Whittier or Valdez). Where they don't own hotels, they stay at some of the best. Prices are quite competitive. Several self-drive packages are also offered. 2525 C St., Anchorage, AK 99503. © 877/258-6877. Fax 907/263-5559. www.AHTours.com.

Goldbelt Tourism The Juneau Native corporation bought or built some of the best tours and cruises Southeast Alaska has to offer, including the Glacier Bay National Park concession, an excellent small-ship cruise line, the Misty Fjords National Monument tour, and some of the most popular Juneau activities.

Besides selling these to independent travelers and helping them plan trips, they offer packages that take guests to the very best of the region, as well as provide a few departures to other parts of the state.

9109 Mendenhall Mall, Ste. 5C, Juneau, AK 99801. ℂ 800/478-3610 or 907/789-4183. www. goldbelttours.com.

INDEPENDENT TRAVEL PLANNING

With this guidebook, you can book everything yourself, but for a long trip it can get quite complicated to keep track of all the dates and deposits. If you're using a trusted travel agency to make trip arrangements, our reviews can help you make smart, informed decisions. Read through the book, make your selections, and bring the agent as detailed a plan as possible, derived from your own research, for the agent to do the bookings for you. Most agents who don't specialize in Alaska are aware of only the biggest attractions and best-marketed companies. Another option is to use a travel agency or trip-planner based in Alaska. They'll know much more about the place and can help you more in picking out what you want to do. I've listed a few below.

Unfortunately, there are cautions to be offered in using the agencies. They work on commission, which means they're being paid by the establishments you're buying from. A good agent will disregard the size of the commission and really look out for you, but I've encountered too many visitors on poorly planned itineraries not to advise caution. Some travel agents book visitors on trips to far-flung corners of the state in quick succession, so they wind up staying only briefly in expensive places and then zooming off somewhere else, all with little concern for the visitors' true interests. Your best defense is to do enough research so you can actively participate in the planning.

Here I've gathered the names of some agencies that book Alaska trips. Expect to pay booking fees and to have the agent collect commissions from the businesses you use. My knowledge of these agencies is limited to contacting them as a journalist. I have removed any about whom I received justified complaints.

Alaska Bound This Michigan-based agency is the only one in the Lower 48 that specializes in Alaska. It started as a cruise planner, working primarily with Holland America, but now plans many independent trips, too, charging $100 per person. Although they don't take credit cards, they will use yours to book your stays, so you get the security and frequent-flier mileage.

321 East Lake St., Petoskey, MI 49770. ℂ 888/ ALASKA-7 or 231/439-3000. www.alaskabound.com.

All Ways Travel This is a solid old travel agency in downtown Anchorage, with many years of experience in arranging Alaska trips. Fees depend on the effort expended and type of bookings you need.

302 G St., Anchorage, AK 99501. ℂ 800/676-2946 or 907/276-3644. allways@alaska.net.

Fantasia Travel This agency, under the same ownership as Camp Alaska Tours, gladly puts clients in B&Bs and cabins, not just the high-priced places most agents prefer to use. Sign up for notification of airfare sales by e-mail on their website.

290 N. Yenlo, L-2, Wasilla, AK 99654. ℂ 800/478-2622 or 907/376-2622. www.alaskaflights.com.

Sport Fishing Alaska Choose this company for a fishing vacation. The owners, former guides and float, charter, and air-taxi operators Larry and Sheary Suiter, know where the fish will be week to week. They also can book the balance of your trip at fun and interesting places. They charge a $95 upfront fee. (See "Fishing," below.)

9310 Shorecrest Dr., Anchorage, AK 99515. ℂ 907/ 344-8674. www.alaskatripplanners.com.

Tips **Cost-Cutting Ideas for your Alaska Trip**

A coupon book called **The Great Alaskan Tour Saver** (© 907/278-7600; www.toursaver.com), which costs $100, is well worth the price if you plan on traveling as a couple, especially in the Southcentral region. Among more than 100 coupons, there are some freebies and many two-for-one deals on some of the best activities and tours, valuable enough to pay for the book with just a couple of uses. For example, the 2000 book contained a free ticket anywhere on the Alaskon Express Bus Line, worth over $200 all by itself. It's harder to get a savings payoff from the **Alaska-Pass** (© 800/248-7598 or 206/463-6550; www.alaskapass.com), an unlimited travel pass on Alaska's two unconnected railroads, Alaskon Express and Alaska Marine Highway ferry system. You can save if you are traveling in Alaska purely by ground transportation without renting a car, and you don't plan to stay long; but then you would spend an inordinate proportion of your time on buses and ferries. For the same money, you could buy a round-trip plane ticket and rent a car.

Viking Travel   An entrepreneur in the small Southeast Alaska town of Petersburg built this travel agency, initially specializing in independent trips emphasizing the outdoors but now planning trips for the whole state. Instead of a fee or percentage, they charge a package price. The firm also books Alaska and B.C. ferries without surcharge; get on their list and they will book your cabins and vehicle reservations on the first day the system makes them available.

P.O. Box 787, Petersburg, AK 99833 © 800/327-2571 or 907/772-3818. http://alaska-ala-carte.com or www.alaskaferry.com.

6 Planning an Outdoor Vacation

Most people visit Alaska to experience wilderness. It's ironic, then, that so many visitors spend their time in crowded ships, buses, trains, and airplanes, all of which are the antithesis of a wilderness experience. You do need technology to get to the wilderness of Alaska, but unless you at least partly let loose of that umbilical cord, you'll never really arrive at your destination.

Every town in Alaska is a threshold to the wild. There's always a way to go hiking, biking, or sea kayaking, or to get on the bank of a stream or the deck of a boat to hook into a furiously fighting wild salmon—and end up in the evening back in a comfortable hotel room. Or take it a step further: Plan to go out overnight, perhaps with a friendly local guide at first, and then go out on your own. I've included lots of details on how to do this throughout the book. Scary? If it weren't a little scary, it would be Disneyland, and that it definitely is not. It's real, and that's why it's worth doing.

Wilderness lodges are listed in the following sections: Gustavus, Prince of Wales Island and Admiralty Island in chapter 5; across Kachemak Bay from Homer in chapter 7; and in Denali National Park and near Talkeetna in chapter 8. Remote Forest Service cabins in Tongass and Chugach national forests are covered in chapters 5 and 7, respectively.

Here are the outdoor activities we've covered in our pages. Checks mark places where the activity is good and developed for visitors (not everywhere it's possible). Stars are our

Outdoor Choices

	Backpacking	Bear Viewing	Bird-Watching	Canoeing	Day Hiking	Diving	Fishing: Halibut	Fishing: Salmon	Mountain Biking	River Floating	Skiing: Alpine	Skiing: Nordic	Sea Kayaking	Whale-Watching
Southeast														
Ketchikan				✓			✓	✓					✓	
Prince of Wales				★	✓	★	✓	★						
Wrangell		★	✓		✓		✓	✓	✓	★			✓	
Petersburg	✓				★		✓	✓	✓			✓	✓	★
Sitka		✓	★		★	✓	✓	✓	✓				★	✓
Juneau	✓	★	✓	✓	★	✓	✓	✓	✓		✓	✓	★	✓
Glacier Bay/Gustavus					✓		★	✓	✓				★	★
Haines			★		✓		✓	✓	✓	✓			✓	
Skagway	✓				✓				✓					
Anchorage (includes day trips from Anchorage)	★		✓	✓	★			✓	★	★	★	★	✓	
Kenai Peninsula/PWS														
Whittier			✓				✓	✓					✓	✓
Seward/Kenai Fjords NP	✓		★		✓		✓	★	✓				✓	★
Cooper Landing	★				✓			★	✓	★				
Kenai/Soldotna/ Kenai NWR			✓	★				★	✓					
Homer/Halibut Cove/Seldovia		✓	✓		★		★	✓	★				✓	★
Valdez			✓		✓		✓	★	✓	✓			✓	✓
Cordova	✓		★	★	✓		✓	✓	★	★	✓		✓	✓
Denali NP	★	★	✓		★				✓	✓				
Interior														
Fairbanks				✓				✓	✓		✓	✓		
Chena Hot Springs Rd.	★			✓	★			✓	★			✓		
Steese Hwy.	✓				✓			✓	✓					
Dalton Hwy.	✓		✓		✓									
Dawson City/Eagle									★					
Wrangell–St. Elias NP	★				✓				✓	★				
Bush														
Kodiak		✓			✓		✓	★	✓				✓	
Katmai NP	✓	★			✓			★						
Dutch Harbor/Unalaska			★		✓		★	✓						
Pribilof Island			★		✓									
Nome*			★		✓				★					
Kotzebue			✓							✓				
Barrow			✓						✓					

* Must bring bike.

favorites. Note, this chart is not exhaustive, and is certainly subjective.

ACTIVITIES

BACKPACKING Alaska's best backpacking country for trail hikes is in **Chugach State Park** near Anchorage (chapter 6), on Chena Hot Springs Road and on the Steese Highway near Fairbanks (chapter 9), and in the **Chugach National Forest** on the Kenai Peninsula (chapter 7). For hiking beyond trails, go to **Denali** or **Wrangell–St. Elias national parks** (chapters 8 and 9). Alaska trail hikes require the same skills as backpacking anywhere else, plus preparation for cold and damp (see "What to Wear," earlier). Hiking beyond the trails is a glorious experience, but you need to know how to cross rivers and find your way—it's best if you have some outdoor experience. Or go with a guide; they're listed below. See section 10, later in this chapter, for some backcountry safety tips.

BIKING Most every town in Alaska has a bike-rental agency. There are excellent bike routes all over the state and few restrictions on where you can ride. A bike is a great way into Denali National Park (chapter 8); Anchorage has an extensive network of paved trails and many mountain biking routes (chapter 6); and guided mountain biking is available in Haines, Skagway, and Wrangell (chapter 5). **Alaska Bicycle Adventures,** below, leads longer tours.

CANOEING Paddling a canoe on a remote Alaska lake or river is the best way to get into the wilderness without a backpack, a guide, or a great deal of expense. For beginners, it's easy to rent a canoe in Fairbanks (chapter 9) for a day trip. If you're ready to go overnight, the choices of routes are extraordinary, including the rivers of the Interior (chapter 9), canoe routes with rental cabins in Southeast Alaska's Tongass National Forest (chapter 5), the bird-watching country of the Copper River Delta near Cordova, or the supreme lake canoe routes of the Kenai National Wildlife Refuge (both in chapter 7).

CAR OR RV CAMPING Campgrounds are almost everywhere in Alaska, many in extraordinarily beautiful natural places. Public campgrounds far outnumber commercial ones. They're usually located where they are because there's something special about the place: a great view or beach, an exceptional fishing stream or trailhead. Rarely will you find running water or flush toilets; most are seasonal, with hand pumps for water. (When it's time to wash up, stay at a commercial campground, which I've noted in each town section in the destination chapters throughout this book.) I've mentioned some great campgrounds throughout the book, but there are many more than I had space to cover. A map that lists all the public campgrounds is available from the Alaska Public Lands Information Centers (see "Visitor Information," earlier) for 25¢. If you are planning to camp the whole way, get a copy of *Traveler's Guide to Alaskan Camping,* by Mike and Terri Church (Rolling Homes Press; $20), which contains detailed reviews of virtually every

---

Tips **Guide Gratuities**

As a general rule, tip fishing guides and outfitters $10 to $20 per person per day. For outings of less than a day, adjust the tip accordingly. At wilderness lodges, which normally have all-inclusive rates, it's often best to add the tip to your final payment when you leave and let the proprietor distribute it to the staff rather than try to do it at each meal. A blanket tip of $15 per person per day is acceptable.

public and commercial campground in the state.

FISHING   Fishing in Alaska may spoil you for fishing anywhere else. The world's largest salmon and halibut were caught here in recent years, and Pacific salmon are so plentiful that catching and processing them still provides the state's largest source of employment. Fly fishermen also come for thriving wild stocks of steelhead, cutthroat, and rainbow trout and Dolly Varden char.

There's no room here to tell you how to fish in Alaska—the best way is to pick it up from other anglers, most conveniently by going with a guide on your first outing. If you can afford it, a day of guided fly-in fishing to a remote stream is the ultimate (you can do it from virtually any town listed in chapter 5, 6, or 7). You can also study up by getting the encyclopedic and endlessly useful *Alaska Fishing,* by Rene Limeres and Gunnar Pederson (Foghorn Press; $21). The best all-around source of information is the **Alaska Department of Fish and Game Sport Fish Division** (© 800/ 874-8202;   www.state.ak.us/adfg). The agency not only produces printed guides and a handy website (including fishing licenses for sale online), but it will also field questions from the public. They update sportfishing hotlines for each part of the state (listed in each town section).

If fishing is the primary goal of your trip, think about booking time at a fishing lodge. The remote rivers of the Bristol Bay region have Alaska's most prolific salmon fishing, and the only way out there is to take a floatplane to a remote site. You'll be on streams jammed with salmon and with few other anglers around to compete with. But you'll waste your money if you book a date that's not near the peak of the local salmon run (that does happen). Consequently, I've listed few river-fishing lodges in this book. (The

exceptions: on the Kenai River in Cooper Landing and Kenai-Soldotna, in chapter 7; and ocean fishing lodges in Ketchikan and on Prince of Wales Island in chapter 5.) Instead, I recommend booking through **Sport Fishing Alaska,** 9310 Shorecrest Dr., Anchorage, AK 99515 (© **907/344-8674;** www.alaskatripplanners.com).   The business is run by a couple, Larry and Sheary Suiter, with years of experience on the Kenai River and in Southwest Alaska. After receiving a $95 advance fee, they plan a fishing vacation tailored to your budget that puts you right where fishing is hot at the time when you can travel.

FLIGHTSEEING   No one should come to Alaska without seeing the scenery at least once from a small plane. The most spectacular rides of all are the Mount McKinley flights from Talkeetna (chapter 8) and the Glacier Bay National Park flights from Haines or other surrounding communities (chapter 5). But just about anywhere you go is worth seeing from the air; only then can you grasp how huge and complex the land is and how little changed it is by mankind. Fixed-wing flights give you the most time aloft for your money, with seats going for around $100 for an hour-long flight. If you can't afford that, consider taking scheduled prop service between small communities, which can cost less than $50 and allow you to see almost as much.

RAFTING   Letting an Alaskan river pull you through untouched wild country in a raft provides a unique perspective without the sweat and toil of backpacking. Alaska has many great rivers, virtually all undeveloped and, with perhaps a single exception, never crowded. White-water guides operate on rivers all over the state offering day trips in many towns. Outfitters also lead trips deep into Alaska, using the rivers to visit extraordinary places that can be reached no other way. Many companies offer floats; some are listed below and still others are in the destination chapters throughout this book.

SEA KAYAKING   Just about every coastal town from Kodiak east through Kachemak Bay, Prince William Sound, and the Southeast Panhandle has a kayak outfitter taking visitors on day trips or expeditions. I think it would be a shame for any fit person to come to Alaska and not take a sea-kayaking day trip. It is your best chance to get close enough to really know the wilderness and see whales, sea otters, seabirds, and marine life in an intimate way. Local guides are listed in each town section. Outfitters offering longer trips to a variety of places are listed below.

OUTFITTERS & OUTDOOR PACKAGE TRIPS

Besides the outfitters and tour guides listed below, I've noted other operators in the destination chapters covering the towns where they are based. Browse through those chapters before deciding on a trip, as a trip with a small-town guide service can be wonderful. There are many other larger operators, too; increasingly, international adventure travel companies bring groups to Alaska, renting equipment or even hiring guides here. Although those trips may be excellent, I've listed only homegrown operators who know their territory intimately.

Alaska Bicycle Adventures   The well-run operation provides all the arrangements for bicycle expeditions over Alaska's rural highways, including a support van that follows the group and ferries bicyclists over the dangerous or boring patches of road, or picks them up just because they're tired— allowing strong and weaker riders to tour together. Sea-kayaking and fishing excursions break up some trips. Choose from many itineraries; one appealing program lasts a week, looping from Anchorage, over the Denali Highway, down the Richardson Highway, a little bit into Wrangell–St. Elias National Park, then to Valdez and across Prince William Sound (by boat) and back to Anchorage. It costs $2,595.

907 E. Dowling Rd. no. 29, Anchorage, AK 99518. ✆ **800/770-7242** or 907/243-2329. www.alaskabike.com.

Alaska Discovery   A homegrown ecotourism pioneer that's developed a national reputation, Alaska Discovery still offers some of the best sea-kayaking trips in Southeast Alaska, including Glacier Bay and Admiralty Island outings that cater to both beginners and the truly rugged. Their inn-to-inn trips are essentially outdoor-oriented package tours, taking groups to the best spots for day activities like kayaking, rafting, or watching wildlife. Extended river trips float through the Arctic and on the Tatshenshini and Alsek rivers. They also offer outdoor packages for complete vacations. A 3-day kayak expedition near Juneau is $495 or $595, while 10 days in the Arctic is around $3,000.

5130 Glacier Hwy., Juneau, AK 99801. ✆ **800/586-1911** or 907/780-6226. www.akdiscovery.com.

Alaska Wildland Adventures   This company specializes in trips for regular folks who may not have done a lot of arduous outdoor activities before. Concentrating in the area from Denali National Park to the Kenai Peninsula, where they operate four wilderness lodges, most of the company's trips link together a series of outdoor day activities, such as rafting, hiking, or wildlife watching, with beds and indoor plumbing in the evening. A 10-day safari is around $4,000; trips for families with kids or with tent camping included are available, too.

P.O. Box 389, Girdwood, AK 99587. ✆ **800/334-8730** or 907/783-2928. www.alaskawildland.com.

A Salmon Primer

In Alaska, it's not so much where you wet your line, but when. The primary catch, Pacific salmon, lives in salt water but spawns in fresh water, with each fish returning to the stream of its birth during a certain, narrow window of time called a "run." When the salmon are running, fishing is hot; when they're not running, it's dead. And the runs change from day to day, typically lasting only a few weeks. (Halibut, on the other hand, are bottom-dwelling ocean fish; you can fish them from a boat every day when the tide is right.) You can fish salmon all over the state in fresh and salt water, but the closer you are to the ocean, the better the fish are. Salmon flesh softens in fresh water and the skin turns dull and red. Salmon right from salt water that haven't started their spawning cycle are called silver bright—when you see one, you'll understand why. No Pacific salmon feeds in fresh water, but kings and silvers, meat eaters at sea, strike out of habit when they reach the river.

There are five species of Pacific salmon, each preferring its own habitat, and, even when the habitat overlaps, each timing its run differently. Each species has two names.

King (or **chinook**) is the most coveted, best fighting fish, commonly growing to 30 pounds in 5 to 7 years at sea (the sport record, from the Kenai River, was 97 pounds, and the largest ever, taken by commercial fishermen near Petersburg, was 126 pounds). It takes a lot of effort to hook and land a big king, but it's the ultimate in Alaska fishing. You also need a special king stamp from the Alaska Department of Fish and Game, in addition to your fishing license. King runs come mostly from late May to early July.

The **silver** (or **coho**) is smaller than the king, typically 6 to 9 pounds, but it fights and jumps ferociously, making it nearly as big a prize.

Alaskan Wilderness Sailing & Kayaking Safaris Crusaders for protecting the Sound long before the *Exxon Valdez* oil spill, Jim and Nancy Lethcoe have written a shelf of books about its history, nature, and best spots. In these trips, based on an island near Prince William Sound's Columbia Glacier, they share the waters they love with warmth and a great depth of knowledge. Offerings include day sailing and short paddles in inflatables and longer expeditions on a yacht or in a rigid kayak. P.O. Box 1313, Valdez, AK 99686. ℂ 907/835-5175. www.alaskanwilderness.com.

Camp Alaska Tours Readers have told me about the wonderful time they had with these folks, traveling in a van with only 12 adults and camping each night along the way. Trips last 6 days to 3 weeks, with hiking, rafting, kayaking, and an opportunity to see the outdoors with a new group of outdoors-oriented friends. Their philosophy is to keep things loose and allow people to pursue their own interests. Prices are around $125 per day, and one itinerary is available for families with children as young as age 10. P.O. Box 872247, Wasilla, AK 99687. ℂ 800/376-9438 or 907/376-9438. www.campalaska.com.

Colors of Nature Rich Reid, an accomplished professional nature photographer, leads tours for photographers and those who just want to

Silvers run mostly in the fall, beginning in August and lasting into October in some streams.

Red (or **sockeye**) salmon, so named for their tasty red flesh, are the trickiest to catch. They usually weigh 4 to 8 pounds and can run in any of the summer months, depending on the region and stream. Reds feed primarily on plankton at sea, and when they strike a fly, it's out of an instinct that no one really understands; you need perfect river conditions to catch reds legally.

Pinks (or **humpies**) grow to only a few pounds and aren't as tasty as the other three species; their flesh lacks the fat that makes salmon so meaty in flavor and deteriorates quickly in fresh water. Pinks are so plentiful that Alaska anglers usually view them as a nuisance to get off the line, but visitors often enjoy catching them: There's nothing wrong with a hard-fighting 4-pound fish, especially if you use light tackle.

Chum (or **dog**) salmon return plentifully to streams over much of the state but are rarely targeted by anglers. Yet a typical 5- to 10-pound chum hits and fights hard. Like pinks, chums aren't prized for the table and are mostly used for subsistence by Alaska Natives, who smoke or dry the fish for winter use or freeze it to feed dog teams.

The gear you use depends on the species you are after and the regulations for the area you're fishing. You have to catch the fish in the mouth; snagging is allowed only in special circumstances. On salt water, boats troll for kings and silvers with herring bait and gear to hold it down. Lures, salmon eggs, or flies will work on silvers and kings in the rivers, but regulations vary. Flies work best with reds. Most Alaska fishermen use spinning gear on the larger salmon species—landing such a large fish is iffy with a fly rod.

observe closely. Rather than workshops, these are trips oriented to seeing: Reid takes his groups, limited to six, where they can expect good lighting and spectacular sights, such as migrations, foliage, or the aurora. You stay in comfortable lodgings and ride in a 15-passenger van. A 10-day tour is $3,205.

P.O. Box 1086, Ojai, CA 93024. ✆ 888/385-5595. www.colorsofnature.com.

Equinox Wilderness Expeditions Karen Jettmar, author of *The Alaska River Guide,* the standard guidebook on floating Alaska's rivers, leads challenging rafting, sea-kayaking, and hiking trips and base-camp wildlife viewing each summer in some of the wildest and most exotic places around the state. Her groups are tiny, with five to eight members, and she specializes in trips for women; family and coed trips are available, too. A 10-day Arctic float trip costs around $3,000.

618 W. 14th Ave., Anchorage, AK 99501. ✆ 907/2 74-9087. www.equinoxexpeditions.com.

Nova These guys started commercial rafting on Alaska's rivers in 1975, but as the industry developed, they kept the company small, keeping their base in a tiny village on the Matanuska River, northeast of Anchorage, and primarily employing Alaskan guides. Their catalog covers longer expeditions on some of the state's wildest rivers, but also includes

---

> ### *Tips* Make Yourself Useful
>
> You don't have to see Alaska only as an observer—you can be a partici-
> pant. The **Iditarod Trail Sled Dog Race** (© **907/376-5155**; www.iditarod.
> com) uses hundreds of volunteers as it passes through remote villages on
> the 1,000-mile trek from Anchorage to Nome in March. Visitors can be
> part of it, and see the real Alaska along the way, contributing only their
> own time and travel to Alaska. Other races and events also use volunteers
> but don't have a formal program like the Iditarod's. Two archaeological
> programs use visitors to help dig Alaska Native sites and process the
> artifacts they find: the **Museum of the Aleutians,** in Unalaska, and **Dig
> Afognak,** in Kodiak (both in chapter 10). These programs will cost you a
> bit in travel and accommodations, but it's a great opportunity to learn
> and do something real.

---

itineraries of 2 or 3 days that more of us can afford. Two days on the Matanuska costs $275; 3 days on the Talkeetna, including the 14-mile long, Class IV rapids of the Talkeetna Canyon, costs $950.

P.O. Box 1129, Chickaloon, AK 99674. © **800/ 746-5753** or 907/745-5753. novalaska.com.

St. Elias Alpine Guides When you're ready for a real expedition, these are the real professionals to contact. Having given up on McKinley years ago as too crowded, they special-ize in trekking, climbing, and floating the deep and rugged wilderness of Wrangell–St. Elias National Park. Theirs is the only trip catalog I know of that offers first ascents as part of the product line; so far, they've taken clients to the top of previously unclimbed mountains more than 45 times. For details, go to chapter 9.

P.O. Box 111241, Anchorage, AK 99511. © **888/ 933-5427** or 907/345-9048; summer 907/554-4445. www.steliasguides.com.

7 Getting There & Getting Around

BY PLANE

Anchorage is the main entry hub, served by several major carriers to the rest of the United States. Most passen-gers come through Seattle, but for a bit more you can fly nonstop to Anchor-age from many major cities. **Alaska Airlines** (© **800/252-7522;** www.alaskaair.com) has more flights than all other airlines combined, nonstop to five cities. Three other airlines have five flights a day to Anchorage, mostly from their hubs: **United** (Chicago; © **800/241-6522;** www.ual.com), **Delta** (Salt Lake City; © **800/ 221-1212;** www.delta.com), and **Northwest** (Minneapolis; © **800/ 225-2525;** www.nwa.com). Four other airlines have a flight or two daily in summer.

The Seattle-Anchorage route is competitive and prices are volatile, sometimes as low as $200 if you're lucky, so shop around before booking. You can usually count on paying around $300 with advance purchase and flexibility on when you fly. Sum-mer sales sometimes hit in April. If you can make a last-minute decision, sign up for web specials on the Alaska Airlines site and other airline sites, as there often are bargains to be had you can't get any other way. Most airlines also continue to Fairbanks, but **Alaska Airlines** is the only jet carrier to any-where else in Alaska. It also has arrangements with commuter lines that fan out from its network to smaller communities.

To fly to a roadless village, or to fly between most towns without returning to a hub, you will take a small, prop-driven plane with an Alaska Bush pilot at the controls. Small air taxis also charter to fishing sites, lodges, remote cabins, or anywhere else you want to go. An authentic Alaskan adventure can be had by taking a Bush mail plane round-trip to a village and back. The ticket price is generally much less than a flightseeing trip, and you'll have at least a brief chance to look around a Native village. Kodiak, Nome, Kotzebue, Barrow, and Fairbanks are places from which you can do this.

BY SHIP

The most popular way to get to Alaska is on a **cruise ship** (chapter 4, "Cruising Alaska's Coast," provides an in-depth look at your options).

For a more affordable trip, with a chance to stop as long as you like along the way, take the **Alaska Marine Highway System** (© 800/642-0066; TDD 800/764-3779; www.dot.state. ak.us/external/amhs/home.html). It's my favorite way to travel. The big blue, white, and gold ferries ply the Inside Passage from Bellingham, Washington, and Prince Rupert, B.C., to the towns of Southeast Alaska, with road links to the rest of the state at Haines and Skagway. In summer, one ferry a month connects from that system across the Gulf of Alaska to the central part of the state. From there, smaller ferries connect towns in Prince William Sound and the Kenai Peninsula to Kodiak Island and the Aleutian Archipelago. For a complete discussion of the system and its intricacies, see "Getting Around by Ferry: The Alaska Marine Highway" in chapter 5.

BY RAIL

You can't get to Alaska by train, but you can get close. **Amtrak** (© 800/ USA-RAIL; www.amtrak.com) serves Bellingham, Washington, a couple of times a day; from there, you can catch the Alaska ferry north. From the east, it makes more sense to catch the ferry in Prince Rupert, B.C., getting there on Canada's **Via Rail** (© 888/ VIA-RAIL; www.viarail.ca); you change from the transcontinental route in Jasper.

BY CAR OR RV

Driving to Alaska is a great adventure, but it requires thousands of miles on the road, and you have to have plenty of time. By car, Anchorage is 2,250 miles from Seattle and 3,400 miles from Los Angeles. By comparison, New York to L.A. is 2,800 miles.

Some of the 1,400-mile **Alaska Highway** is dull, but there are spectacular sections of the route, too, and few experiences give you a better feel for the size and personality of Alaska. Putting your car on the ferry cuts the length of the trip considerably, but raises the cost; you could rent a car for

---

Tips **The Cheapest Way to Alaska**

Flying is the cheapest and by far the simplest way to get to Alaska. Take other means only for the adventure, not for the cost. Round-trip train, ferry, and bus fare between Seattle and Anchorage costs four times as much as a good plane fare between the same cities. Driving is expensive, too, when you count rooms, food, and wear and tear on your vehicle. Fuel for the 4,500-mile drive from Seattle to Anchorage and back would cost about $400 in a car that gets 20 miles to the gallon—more than a plane ticket. (Okay, maybe a foursome in a car, camping every night and eating rice and beans, can do it cheaper.)

2 weeks for the same price as carrying an economy car on the ferry one-way from Bellingham to Haines. I love riding the ferry up the Inside Passage, but I usually rent a car or bike to get around in the towns on the way. Details on the Alaska section of the Alaska Highway, and other highways, are contained in chapter 9. *The Milepost* (Morris Communications; $25), contains mile-by-mile logs of all Alaska highways and approaches, and is sold widely (the commercial listings are advertisements, and are not objective).

Renting a car is the easiest way to see the Interior and Southcentral part of the state. All the major national car-rental companies are represented in Anchorage as well as many local operators, who may have lower prices for older cars and possibly will allow you to drive on gravel roads (see chapter 6). In smaller cities and towns, there are usually a couple of agencies; our town descriptions provide details on firms in each town. Base rates for major rental companies are in the range of $50 a day for an economy car.

One-way rentals between Alaska towns are an attractive way to travel, but you generally pay steep drop-off charges, so a more popular plan is to fly into and out of Anchorage and pick up and return the car there. There are two popular circular routes from Anchorage: to Denali and Fairbanks on the Parks Highway and back on the Richardson and Glenn highways, or to Valdez by ferry from Whittier and back on another part of the Richardson Highway and the Glenn Highway.

Many retirees come to Alaska in their motor homes, park the RV by a salmon stream, and spend the summer. Sounds nice, but for most of the rest of us, with limited time, it makes more sense to rent an RV after flying to Alaska. An RV rental saves nothing over traveling with a rental car, staying in hotels, and eating in restaurants (RVs rent for around $1,400 a week, plus gas and possibly mileage charges), but you gain freedom and spontaneity. You save and have even more freedom with a tent, but an RV is more fun in cold, rainy weather. I've listed two major rental agencies in Anchorage (see chapter 6).

8 Tips for Travelers with Special Needs

FOR TRAVELERS WITH DISABILITIES

The Americans with Disabilities Act and economic competition have sped the process of retrofitting hotels and even B&Bs to be accessible for people with disabilities. The result is often the best rooms in the house. Hotels without such facilities now are the exception; however, check when making reservations.

There are several Alaska agencies for people with disabilities. **Challenge Alaska,** P.O. Box 110065, Anchorage, AK 99511 (✆ **907/344-7399;** www. challenge.ak.org), is a nonprofit organization dedicated to providing accessible outdoor activities. They have a skiing center on Mount Alyeska (✆ **907/783-2925**), in Girdwood, and

also offer summer camping, sea kayaking, fishing, and other trips; get on their mailing list for current listings. Prices are low: a 2-day sea-kayaking outing was only $115, and volunteer helpers can go free. Challenge Alaska also keeps track of tourism operators who are authentically accessible and welcomes inquiries.

Alaska Welcomes You! Inc., P.O. Box 91333, Anchorage, AK 99509-1333 (✆ or TTY **800/ 349-6301,** or 907/349-6301; www. accessiblealaska.com), books accessible cruises, tours in Southcentral Alaska, and extended travel packages to Denali National Park and the Kenai Peninsula, and does trip planning for independent travelers with special needs. The operator is a respected community worker for the disabled who field-checks the places he books to make sure they really are accessible.

FOR SENIORS

People over age 65 get reduced-admission prices to most Alaska attractions, and some accommodations have special senior rates. National parks offer free admission and special camping rates for people over 62 with a Golden Age Passport, which you can obtain at any of the parks for $10 and which never expires. Also mention your age when booking your airfare; most domestic airlines offer senior discounts.

Most towns have a senior citizens center where you'll find activities and help with any special needs. The **Anchorage Seniors Center** (© 907/258-7823) offers guidance for visitors, as well as use of the restaurant, showers, gift shop, and fitness room; a big band plays Friday nights for dancing. **Elderhostel,** 11 Avenue de Lafayette, Boston, MA 02111-1746 (© 877/426-8056; TTY 877/426-2167; from overseas, © 978/323-4141; www.elderhostel.org), operates many weeklong Alaska learning vacations for groups of people 55 and older. The catalog of choices is on the website.

FOR GAY & LESBIAN TRAVELERS

Anchorage, Juneau, and Fairbanks have active gay and lesbian communities. In Anchorage, **Identity Inc.** (© 907/258-4777; www.alaska.net/~identity) offers referrals, publishes a newsletter called *Northview,* and sponsors activities throughout the year, including the June Pridefest, with many events, including a parade and picnic. They are planning a community center. The **S.E. Alaska Gay/Lesbian Alliance** (© 907/586-4297; www.ptialaska.net/~seagla) is a similar organization in Juneau. **QnetAK** is a website with statewide information

(www.mosquitonet.com/~qnetak). In Alaska, Bob DeLoach at **Whitsett Travel** (© 907/892-1888; apollo@ alaska.net) specializes in gay and lesbian travel.

FOR STUDENTS

Many museums offer free or reduced admission for students and anyone under 18, although sometimes you have to ask. Make sure to bring a student ID card.

There are hostels in most towns in Alaska. Except for those in Anchorage, Fairbanks, and Juneau, they tend to be open in the summer only. I have described hostels in the text for each town. Some, but far from all, are members of **Hostelling International/American Youth Hostels,** 733 15th St. NW, Suite 840, Washington, DC 20005 (© 202/783-6161; www.hiayh.org), listed on their website or in a directory, *Hostelling North America,* which you can order there or by phone (free to members, $3 for nonmembers). Membership gives you discounts at member hostels, and is free for youths 17 and under. For ages 18 to 54, membership is $25, 55 and over $15.

Many students travel to Alaska for summer work. It's usually possible to get a job in a fish cannery in most coastal towns. Work on the slime line is hard and unpleasant and the pay is low, but if the season is good and you work long hours, camping to keep your expenses low (most canneries have tent cities of summer workers nearby), you can take home more money for your summer's work than you would normally earn elsewhere. Hillary Rodham Clinton worked an Alaska slime line when she was in school, and you can, too. Stay onshore, however, as offshore fish-processing ships are truly miserable and dangerous places to work, and if the ship doesn't get any fish, you don't make any money. Also, don't come north expecting to make fabulous wages. The stories of college students making huge crew shares on fishing boats are legends—there are plenty of experienced deckhands to take those jobs before boats hire raw hands they have to train. Jobs are always available in the tourism industry, too, although you'll have to plan ahead more for that. The **Alaska Department of Labor Job Service** posts job openings and advice on its website, **www.labor.state.ak.us/esjobs/jobs**. A search function allows you to narrow it down by area and field—just point your web browser to seafood processing.

FOR FAMILIES

When we researched our first edition of this book, my son, Robin, was 3, and my daughter, Julia, was 6 months. As I write this, Robin is 9, Julia is 6, Joseph is 2, and Becky is 4 months. You might run into us in a campground or on a boat dock anywhere in the state as we travel to research the next edition of "our Alaska book." Robin loves to surprise people he sees carrying the book. We also write *Frommer's Family Vacations in the National Parks* together. Yes, it's a great job, and bringing the family along is the best part.

Alaska's magnificent scenery is something even young children can understand and appreciate. Also, an Alaska vacation is largely spent outdoors, which is where kids like to be. Robin and Julia never get enough ferry riding, and all three older children enjoy camping immensely. I'm sure Becky will, too; our extensive experience camping with babies, even as young as 3 months, has been entirely positive. Having everyone sleep in a tent, at baby level, is an infant's idea of vacation paradise.

There are drawbacks to Alaska as a family destination. The primary one is the expense. The airlines' half-off companion fares are inconsistently applied, and we haven't yet gotten one on the Alaska route. Activities like flightseeing and tour-boat cruises tend to have less-than-generous children's discounts and cost too much for most families. Often, bed-and-breakfast rooms are too small for a family. Hotel rooms and restaurant meals are expensive in Alaska. Car camping solves many of those problems, with stops in a hotel every few days to get everyone cleaned up. I wouldn't take kids over the Alaska Highway, however; instead, I'd fly to Anchorage and rent a car and any bulky camping gear there (see "Getting Outside; Equipment," in chapter 6).

You have to be careful in choosing your itinerary and activities with children. The highways in Alaska are long, and children will require a gradual approach to covering a lot of ground. They also need time to play, explore, and rest. Frankly, children often don't enjoy activities like wildlife watching. It takes a long time to find the animals, and when you do, they're usually off in the distance—kids younger than 8 often don't have the visual skills or patience to pick out the animals from the landscape. Don't overtax children with walks and hiking trips; we keep track of the longest hike we've managed without excessive whining, then try to extend that record just a little bit each time out. Short sea-kayaking excursions, on the other hand, are great for children who are old enough, riding in the front of a double-seat boat with a parent in back; we began with Robin at age 7, and I have friends who have done it with a 3-year-old. In practice, the age limit depends on the outfitter and your child's level of responsibility.

If you're flawed mortals like us, after the end of a few weeks on the road, you'll be getting on each other's nerves. We found success by leaving time for low-key kid activities, like beachcombing and playing in the park, while one grown-up splits off for

> **Tips Using the Internet on the Road**
>
> Don't take your laptop on vacation. For one thing, it's pathetic. For another, it's unnecessary. Even tiny Alaska towns have some kind of web access these days; most have a trendy Internet cafe of some kind, while in others you can log on at the public library. Internet access for each Alaska community is listed in the appropriate section of the book. Relying on this kind of access is easier than lugging a computer around, worrying about it being stolen, and trying to connect through spotty phone lines on weird hotel phone systems. Typically, you can find the information you want for less than $5.
>
> There are three ways to get your e-mail on the web, where you can check it from any computer. One: Your Internet Service Provider may have a web-based interface. Just find out how it works before you leave home. Two: You can open an account on a free, web-based e-mail provider before you leave home, such as Microsoft's **Hotmail** (hotmail.com) or **Yahoo! Mail** (mail.yahoo.com). Your home ISP may be able to forward your home e-mail to the web-based account auto-matically. Or, three: Use **www.mail2web.com**. This amazing free service allows you to type in your regular e-mail address and password and retrieve your e-mail from any web browser, anywhere, so long as your home ISP hasn't blocked it with a firewall.

a museum visit, shopping, or a special, more expensive activity. Of course, if you want to preserve your marriage, you'll have to be scrupulously fair about who gets to go flightseeing and who has to stay behind and change diapers, as you won't have my all-purpose excuse (research).

If you're interested in a package tour with your family, most of the companies listed in this chapter will take children, but research carefully to make sure you will have enough down time. A better choice would be an out-door-oriented trip designed for chil-dren by an outfitter. **Alaska Wildland**

Adventures (© **800/334-8730**) has various trips for kids as young as 12, and even offers a "Family Safari" for families with children ages 6 through 11 that strings together day trips in various places with stays at wilderness lodges, including a float trip on the Kenai River and several days in Denali National Park. The 9-day trip costs $3,795 for adults and $3,495 for kids, exclusive of air travel. **Alaska Discovery** (© **800/586-1911**) takes children as young as 10 on some of its extended Southeast Alaska sea-kayaking trips, which start at $495 to $595 for 3 days and 2 nights.

9 Health, Safety & Traveler's Insurance

CRIME & EMERGENCY SERVICES

CRIME Sadly, crime rates are not low in Alaska's larger cities, although muggings are rare. Take the normal precautions you'd take at home. You're safe in daylight hours anywhere

tourists commonly go, less so late at night leaving a bar or on a wooded bike trail. Women need to be espe-cially careful on their own, as Alaska has a disproportionately high rate of rape. Most women I know avoid walking by themselves at night, especially in wooded or out-of-the-way areas. The late-night sunlight can be deceiving—just because it's light out doesn't mean it's safe. Sexual assaults occur in towns big and small. Women should never hitchhike alone. If you are a victim of a crime, you can reach police almost anywhere by calling 911, or, if it is not an emergency, using the numbers listed under "Fast Facts" in each community section.

MEDICAL EMERGENCIES You'll find modern, full-service hospitals in each of Alaska's larger cities, and even in some small towns that act as regional centers. There's some kind of clinic even in the smallest towns, although they often are staffed by physicians' assistants rather than medical doctors. I've listed the address and phone numbers for medical facilities in each destination under "Fast Facts." Call those numbers, too, for referrals to a dentist or other health professional. In an emergency, call 911.

If you suffer from a chronic condition such as epilepsy, diabetes, or heart problems, wear a **Medic Alert Identification Tag** (© **888/633-4298;** www.medicalert.org), which will inform doctors of your condition and give them access to your records through a 24-hour hotline.

OUTDOORS HEALTH & SAFETY
BEARS & OTHER WILDLIFE
Being eaten by a bear is probably the least likely way for your vacation to end. Deaths from dog bites are much more common, for example. But it's still wise to be prepared for bears, and to know how to avoid being trampled by moose.

The first rule of defense is simple: *Don't attract bears.* All food and trash must be kept in airtight containers when you're camping. When car camping, the trunk of the vehicle will do. When backpacking, you can protect your food by hanging it from a long tree branch or, above treeline, storing it in a bear-resistant canister (for rent at Denali or in Anchorage, chapters 6 and 8). Be careful not to spread food odors when you're cooking and cleaning up. Never keep food, pungent items, or clothing that smells like fish in your tent. Clean fish away from your campsite.

When walking through brush or thick trees, make lots of noise to avoid surprising a bear or moose. Bells you can hang on your belt are for sale at sporting-goods shops, or you can sing or carry on loud conversation. You might not scare a bear away this way, but you could keep from startling it.

At all costs, avoid coming between a bear and its cubs or a bear and food. Moose are strongly defensive of their young, too, and can attack if they feel you're getting too close.

If you see a bear, stop, wave your arms, make noise, and, if you're with others, group together so you look larger to the bear. Don't tempt the bear to chase; depart by slowly backing away, at an angle if possible. If the bear follows, stop. Once in a great while, the bear may bluff a charge; even less often, it may attack. If you're attacked, fall and play dead, rolling into a ball facedown with your hands behind your neck. The bear should lose interest. In extremely rare instances, a bear may not lose interest, because it's planning to make a meal of you. If this happens, fight back for all you're worth. Many Alaskans carry a gun for protection in bear country, but that's not very practical for visitors. We carry bear mace, a spray that can deter a bear with a burning fog of capsaicin pepper (except in wind or rain). A can costs about $50 at sporting-goods stores, or order direct from **Counter Assault** (© **800/695-3394** or 406/257-GRIZ; www.counterassault.com). Unlike a gun, it is legal in the national parks. If you take a gun, it had better be a big one. A .300-Magnum rifle or 12-gauge shotgun loaded with rifled slugs is the weapon of choice.

BOATING SAFETY Because of the cool temperatures, unpredictable weather, and cold water, going out on the ocean or floating a fast river is more hazardous in Alaska than in most other places, and you should go only with an experienced, licensed operator unless you know what you're doing. There's little margin for error if you fall into the water or capsize—you have only minutes to get out and get warm before hypothermia and death. A life jacket will keep you afloat, but it won't keep you alive in 40°F water. If you're sea kayaking or canoeing, stay close to shore and take plastic dry bags with everything you need to quickly warm a person who gets wet (see "Hypothermia," below).

HYPOTHERMIA A potentially fatal lowering of core body temperature can sneak up on you. It's most dangerous when you don't realize how cold you are, perhaps in 50-degree weather on a damp mountain hike or rainy boating trip. Dress in material (whether wool or synthetic) that keeps its warmth when wet, choosing layers to avoid chilling perspiration. (See "What to Wear," earlier in this chapter.) Eating well and avoiding exhaustion also help. Among the symptoms of hypothermia are cold extremities, being uncommunicative, displaying poor judgment or coordination, and sleepiness. A shivering victim still has the ability to warm up if better dressed; a lack of shivering means the body has gone beyond that point and warmth must be added from the outside or from warm drinks. Get indoors, force hot liquids (except in cases of shock), and, if shelter is unavailable, apply body heat from another person, skin on skin, in a sleeping bag.

INSECT BITES The good news is that Alaska has no snakes or poisonous spiders. The bad news is that Alaska makes up for it with mosquitoes and other biting insects. They're not dangerous, but they can ruin a trip. Effective insect repellent is a necessity, as is having a place where you can get away from them. Hikers in the Interior, where mosquitoes are worst, sometimes use head nets. Mosquitoes can bite through light fabric, which is why people in the Bush wear heavy Carhart pants and jackets even on the hottest days. You might want to pack Benadryl or some other antihistamine cream to relieve itching if you do get bitten.

DANGEROUS PLANTS Two shrubs common in Alaska can cause skin irritation, but there is nothing as bad as poison ivy or poison oak. **Pushki,** also called cow parsnip, is a large-leafed plant growing primarily in open areas, up to shoulder height by late summer, with white flowers. The celerylike stalks break easily, and the sap has the quality of intensifying the burning power of the sun on skin. Wash it off quickly to avoid a rash. **Devil's Club,** a more obviously dangerous plant, grows on steep slopes and has ferocious spines that can pierce through clothing. Also, don't eat anything you can't positively identify, as there are deadly poisonous mushrooms and plants.

RIVER CROSSINGS Hiking in Alaska's backcountry often requires crossing rivers without bridges. Use great caution: It's easy to get in trouble. Often, the water is glacial melt, barely above freezing and heavy with silt that makes it opaque. The silt can fill your pockets and drag you down. If in doubt, don't do it. If you do decide to cross, unbuckle your pack, keep your shoes on, face upstream, use a heavy walking stick if possible, and rig a safety line. Children should go in the eddy behind a larger person, or be carried.

SHELLFISH Don't eat mussels, clams, or scallops you pick or dig from the seashore unless you know they're safe. To find out, call the **Alaska Department of Environmental Conservation** (✆ **907/269-7501**), which tests the beaches. Most of Alaska's remote beaches are not tested and so are not safe. The risk is paralytic shellfish poisoning, a potentially fatal malady caused by a naturally occurring toxin. It causes total paralysis, including your breathing. A victim may be kept alive with mouth-to-mouth resuscitation until medical help is obtained.

SWIMMING Ask about lake water before swimming in it. In recent years, some lakes have been infested with a bug that causes an itchy rash.

WATER Unpurified river or lake water may not be safe to drink. Hand-held filters available from sporting-goods stores for around $75 are the most practical way of dealing with the problem. Iodine kits and boiling also work. The danger is a protozoan cyst called *giardia lamblia,* which causes diarrhea and has been spread to thousands of water bodies all over the United States by dog feces. It may not show up until a couple of weeks after exposure and could become chronic. If symptoms show up after you get home, tell your doctor you may have been exposed so that you can get tested and cured.

DRIVING SAFETY

SUMMER Keep your headlights on all the time for safety on the highway. Drivers are required to pull over at the next pull-out whenever five or more cars are trailing on a two-lane highway, regardless of how fast they're going. This saves the lives of people who otherwise will try to pass. When passing a truck going the other way on a gravel highway, slow down or stop and pull as far as possible to the side of the road to avoid losing your windshield to a flying rock. Always think about the path of rocks you're kicking up toward others' vehicles. Make sure you've got a good, full-size spare tire and jack if you're driving a gravel highway. For remote driving, bring along a first-aid kit, emergency food, a tow rope, and jumper cables.

WINTER Drivers on Alaska's highways in winter should be prepared for cold-weather emergencies far from help. Take all the items listed for rural summer driving, plus a flashlight, matches and materials to light a fire, chains, a shovel, and an ice scraper. A camp stove to make hot beverages is also a good idea. If you're driving a remote highway (such as the Alaska Highway) between December and March, take along gear adequate to keep you safe from the cold even if you have to wait overnight with a dead car at –40°F (see "What to Wear," earlier in this chapter, and add blankets and sleeping bags). Never drive a road marked "Closed" or "Unmaintained in Winter." Even on maintained rural roads, other vehicles come by rarely. All Alaska roads are icy all winter. Studded tires are a necessity—nonstudded snow tires or so-called "all-weather" tires aren't adequate. Also, never leave your car's engine stopped for more than 4 hours in temperatures of –10°F or colder. Alaskans generally have electrical head-bolt heaters installed to keep the engine warm overnight; you'll find electrical outlets everywhere in cold, Interior Alaska areas.

TRAVEL INSURANCE

There are three kinds of travel insurance: **trip-cancellation, medical,** and **lost-luggage** coverage. Trip-cancellation insurance is a must if you have paid the large cash deposits demanded by many Alaska outfitters, fishing guides, wilderness lodges, package tour operators, and cruise companies. A premium of 8% of the cost of the trip is well worth the protection against the uncertainty of Alaska weather (most deposits are lost in case of weather delays or cancellations) or unexpected crises that might prevent you from being able to depart as planned.

Medical insurance for travelers from outside the United States is a worthwhile investment, too, but probably doesn't make sense for most travelers from the U.S., who likely are already covered under their regular health insurance. Likewise, your baggage is probably covered under your homeowners' policy or credit card benefits. Besides, if the airline loses your bags, they are usually responsible for up to $2,500 per piece on domestic flights, $640 on international flights; don't check baggage worth more than that. Some credit- and charge-card companies may also insure you against airplane crashes and other travel accidents if you buy tickets with their cards.

Various companies sell travel insurance; you can conveniently buy online. Reputable firms include **Access America** (✆ **800/284-8300;** www.accessamerica.com) and **Travel Guard International** (✆ **877/216-4885;** www.travel-guard.com).

 ## FAST FACTS: Alaska

Area Code All of Alaska is in area code **907.** In the Yukon Territory, the area code is **867.** When placing a toll call within the state, you must dial 1, the area code, and the number. See "Telephone," below, for important tips.

Banks & ATMs There are banks and automated teller machines in all but the tiniest towns.

Business Hours In the larger cities, major grocery stores are open 24 hours a day and carry a wide range of products (even fishing gear) in addition to food. At a minimum, **stores** are open Monday through Friday from 10am to 6pm, are open on Saturday afternoon, and are closed on Sunday, but many are open much longer hours, especially in summer. **Banks** may close an hour earlier and, if open on Saturday, only in the morning. Under state law, **bars** don't have to close until 5am, but many communities have an earlier closing, generally around 2am.

Cellular Phone Coverage Most of the populated portion of the state has cellular coverage. Your cell-phone provider should be able to give you a brochure detailing roaming charges, which can be steep.

Emergencies Generally, you can call ✆ **911** for medical, police, or fire emergencies. On remote highways there sometimes are gaps in 911 coverage, but dialing 0 will generally get an operator, who can connect you to emergency services. Citizens Band channels 9 and 11 are monitored for emergencies on most highways, as are channels 14 and 19 in some areas.

Holidays Besides the normal national holidays, banks and state and local government offices close on two state holidays: Seward's Day (the last Mon in Mar) and Alaska Day (Oct 18, or the nearest Fri or Mon if it falls on a weekend). See chapter 3 for a listing of national holidays.

Internet/E-mail Access See "Using the Internet on the Road," earlier.

Liquor Laws The minimum drinking age in Alaska is 21. Most restaurants sell beer and wine, while a minority have full bars that serve hard liquor as well. Packaged alcohol, beer, and wine are sold only in licensed stores, not in grocery stores, but these are common and are open long hours every day. More than 100 rural communities have laws prohibiting the importation and possession of alcohol (this is known as being "dry") or only the sale but not possession of alcohol (known as being "damp"). With a few exceptions, these are tiny Bush communities off the road network; urban areas are all "wet." Of the communities featured in this book, Kotzebue and Barrow are damp, and the rest are wet. Before flying into a Native village with alcohol, ask about the law—bootlegging is a serious crime (and serious bad manners), or check a list on the Alcoholic Beverage Control Board website, at www.abc.revenue.state.ak.us/localopt.htm.

Maps I've noted the best trail maps in each applicable section throughout this book. For the most popular areas, I recommend the excellent trail maps published by **Trails Illustrated** (© **800/962-1643;** www.trails illustrated.com). They're sold in park visitor centers, too. The maps are printed on plastic, so they don't get spoiled by rain; however, they don't cover the whole state. Buy **official topographic maps** from the U.S. Geological Survey in person or by order at USGS–ESIC, 4230 University Dr., Anchorage, AK 99508 (© **907/786-7011**), open Monday to Friday, 8:30am to 4:30pm.

Newspapers The state's dominant newspaper is the *Anchorage Daily News* (www.adn.com); it's available everywhere but is not always easy to find in Southeast Alaska. Seattle newspapers and *USA Today* are often available, and in Anchorage you can get virtually any newspaper.

Taxes There is no state sales tax, but most local governments have a sales tax and a bed tax on accommodations. The tax rates are listed in each town section throughout the book under its "Fast Facts."

Telephone I am assured that all major calling cards will work in Alaska, but this certainly hasn't been the case in the past. To make sure, contact your long-distance company, or buy a by-the-minute card.

Time Zone Although the state naturally spans five time zones, in the 1980s Alaska's middle time zone was stretched so almost the entire state would lie all in one zone, known as Alaska time. It's 1 hour earlier than the U.S. West Coast's Pacific time. Crossing over the border from Alaska to Canada adds an hour and puts you at the same time as the West Coast. As with almost everywhere else in the United States, daylight saving time is in effect from 1am on the first Sunday in April (turn your clocks ahead 1 hour) until 2am on the last Sunday in October (turn clocks back again).

3

For International Visitors

Visitors from the rest of the United States sometimes say Alaska is like a foreign country full of Americans. If you are coming from overseas, it may be doubly unfamiliar. This chapter aims to help you through the details so you can better enjoy the differences.

Information on border crossings between the United States and Canada on the Alaska Highway is contained in chapter 9.

1 Preparing for Your Trip

ENTRY REQUIREMENTS
Check at any U.S. embassy or consulate for current information and requirements. You can also obtain a visa application and other information online at the **U.S. State Department's** website at **http://travel.state.gov**.

DO YOU NEED A VISA? Most tourists coming to the United States do not need a visa. Canadian citizens only need proof of residence (not even a passport), and citizens of 29 other countries need hardly more under the U.S. State Department's **Visa Waiver Program.** At press time, the list included: Andorra, Argentina, Austria, Australia, Belgium, Brunei, Denmark, Finland, France, Germany, Iceland, Ireland, Italy, Japan, Liechtenstein, Luxembourg, Monaco, The Netherlands, New Zealand, Norway, Portugal, San Marino, Singapore, Slovenia, Spain, Sweden, Switzerland, the United Kingdom, and Uruguay. Citizens can enter for up to 90 days of pleasure travel with only a valid passport and a round-trip air or cruise ticket in their possession upon arrival. Further information is available from any U.S. embassy or consulate.

Citizens of all other countries must obtain visas.

OBTAINING A VISA To obtain a visa, a traveler must submit a completed application form (either in person or by mail) along with a $45 fee and two photos (1½ inches or 37mm square), and may need evidence of plans to return home at the end of the visit. If you cannot go in person, contact the nearest U.S. embassy or consulate or check the State Department website (http://travel.state.gov) for directions on applying by mail. Your travel agent or airline office may also be able to provide you with visa applications and instructions.

MEDICAL REQUIREMENTS Unless you're arriving from an area known to be suffering from an epidemic (particularly cholera or yellow fever), inoculations or vaccinations are not required for entry into the U.S.. If you have a disease that requires treatment with narcotics or syringe-administered medications, carry a valid signed prescription or letter from your physician to allay any suspicions that you may be smuggling narcotics.

Upon entering the United States, foreign nationals are required to declare any dangerous contagious diseases they carry, which includes infection with HIV, the AIDS virus. Anyone who has such a disease is excluded from entry as a tourist. However, you may be able to apply for a waiver if you are attending a conference or have another compelling non-tourism reason for your visit. If you will be entering the country in Alaska, contact the **Immigration and Naturalization Service** in Anchorage (© **907/271-6855;** www.ins.usdoj. gov) to inquire about a waiver or related issues. If you're entering the United States at another point, contact the **INS** at © **800/375-5283** (TTY 800/767-1833). Doubtless many HIV-positive visitors come in without declaring their condition, their way of dealing with an archaic law that was originally intended to halt the spread of tuberculosis and the like.

DRIVER'S LICENSES Foreign driver's licenses are mostly recognized in the United States, although you may want to get an international driver's license if your home license is not written in English.

CUSTOMS
WHAT YOU CAN BRING IN
Personal effects, such as cameras and fishing rods, are exempt from duties. In addition, every visitor over 21 years of age may bring in the following without paying duties: (1) 1 liter of wine or hard liquor; (2) 200 cigarettes, or 50 cigars (but not from Cuba), or 2 kilograms (4.4 pounds) of smoking tobacco; and (3) $100 worth of gifts. To claim the gift exemption, you must spend at least 72 hours in the United States and cannot have claimed it within the preceding 6 months.

The duty on goods exceeding these exemptions is 10% of the value on the first $1,000; above that amount, it depends on the item. Importation of most raw food and plant material is prohibited or requires a special license. Foreign tourists may bring in or take out up to $10,000 in U.S. or foreign currency, traveler's checks, or securities with no formalities; larger sums must be declared to U.S. Customs on entering or leaving and paperwork must be filed.

Declare any medicines you are carrying and be prepared to present a letter or prescription from your doctor demonstrating you need the drugs; you may bring in no more than you would normally use for the duration of your visit.

For more details on what you can and cannot bring, go to the **U.S. Customs** website at **www.customs. ustreas.gov** and click on "Traveler Information," or call © **202/927-1770.**

WHAT YOU CAN BRING HOME
WILDLIFE PRODUCTS Alaska Native art and crafts made from protected marine mammals are perfectly legal (even though possessing the raw animal pelts is not legal for non-Natives), but you do need to get permits to take these items out of the country. Permits also are required to export products made from brown or black bear, bobcat, wolf, lynx, or river otter. The best solution is to have the shop where you buy the item mail it to you insured, and have them take care of the paperwork. If you carry it with you, or buy from a shop that can't handle the paperwork, you'll need to get your own permits. To go into or through Canada, get a Personal Effects Exemption Certificate for the item by calling the **U.S. Fish and Wildlife Service** in Anchorage (© **907/271-6198**). They can handle it in a few days. Call them also for permits for products made of nonmarine mammals. To take **marine mammal products** to a country other than Canada, you need a permit from the **Fish and Wildlife Service** in Washington, D.C. (© **800/358-2104;**

international.fws.gov). It can take a month to get these permits. There may be other regulations for bringing walrus ivory into your home country because of the international ban on elephant ivory. It's important to note that Alaska Natives have used these materials for thousands of years, and their harvest poses no threat to the species.

OTHER GOODS Rules governing what you can bring back duty-free vary from country to country, and generally are posted on the web. **Canadians** should check the booklet *I Declare*, which you can download or order from Revenue Canada (𝄞 **506/636-5064;** www.ccra-adrc.gc.ca). **British** citizens should contact HM Customs & Excise (𝄞 **020/7202-4227;** www.hmce. gov.uk). **Australians** can contact the Australian Customs Service (𝄞 **1-300/ 363-263** within Australia, 61-2/ 6275-6666 from outside Australia; www.customs.gov.au). **New Zealand** citizens should contact New Zealand Customs (𝄞 **09/359-6655;** www. customs.govt.nz).

INSURANCE

Although it's not required of travelers, health insurance is a very good idea. Unlike many European countries, the United States does not generally offer free or low-cost medical care to its citizens or visitors. Doctors and hospitals are expensive, and except in emergencies they require that patients work out how to pay before rendering services. Buy a travel insurance policy that covers the costs of an accident, repatriation, or death. Packages such as **Europ Assistance** in Europe are sold by automobile clubs and travel agencies at attractive rates. **Worldwide Assistance Services, Inc.** (𝄞 **800/ 777-8710,** ext. 417, or 202/ 331-1609; www.worldwideassistance. com) is the United States branch of the company.

I also strongly recommend trip-cancellation and interruption insurance

if you place deposits on Alaska services or accommodations. Insurance providers are covered under "Health, Safety & Traveler's Insurance," in chapter 2.

MONEY

The most common **bills** are the $1 (colloquially, a "buck"), $5, $10, and $20 denominations; $50 and $100 bills usually are not welcome as payment for small purchases. Four denominations of **coins** are commonly used: 1¢ (1 cent, or a penny); 5¢ (5 cents, or a nickel); 10¢ (10 cents, or a dime); 25¢ (25 cents, or a quarter). Occasionally you will also encounter coins for 50¢ (50 cents, or a half dollar) and any of three designs of the $1 piece. New designs for U.S. currency have been introduced, but the old-style bills and coins are still legal tender. See chapter 2 for a discussion of **credit cards, ATMs, traveler's checks,** and other payment methods in Alaska. Though traveler's checks are widely accepted, make sure that they're denominated in U.S. dollars, as foreign-currency checks are often difficult to exchange. You'll need identification, such as a driver's license or passport, to change a traveler's check.

The "foreign-exchange bureaus" so common in Europe are rare even at airports in the United States, and non-existent outside major cities. The only foreign-exchange service in Alaska is at the **Wells Fargo Bank** branch in the Fifth Avenue Mall in Anchorage (𝄞 **907/267-5700;** www.wellsfargo. com). You can change money elsewhere, but it generally is not a good idea. Obtain U.S. dollars before you leave home. You can pay for almost anything with a credit or charge card, with the exchange automatically made by your bank.

SAFETY

Robberies (like muggings) are quite rare in Alaska, even in Anchorage, but the incidence of rape is high. Precautions are covered in chapter 2. Thefts can happen even in tiny towns. Keep an eye on your belongings and lock your car and hotel doors. Don't leave valuables in sight in the car. Guns are ubiquitous in Alaska. I'm not aware of a tourist ever being shot, but you could be if you get in a fight or transport illegal drugs.

2 Getting to the United States

Most flights to Alaska come from domestic airports, requiring trips from overseas to pass through Seattle or another major city, but service is available direct to Anchorage from Seoul, South Korea, on **Korean Air Lines** (© **800/436-5000** or 907/243-3329; www.koreanair.com), and occasionally other cities by charter airlines. Canadians can drive to Alaska over the Alaska or Top of the World highways, covered in chapter 9, or on an Alaska Marine Highway System ferry from Prince Rupert, B.C., covered in chapter 5.

Getting through immigration control and Customs can take 2 or 3 hours, especially if you enter the country at a big-city airport on a busy summer day. Leave at least that much time to connect to a domestic flight. Passing between Alaska and Canada takes no time at all unless you have special complications. See chapter 9 for Canadian border requirements.

 FAST FACTS: **For the International Traveler**

See Fast Facts, in chapter 2, for information not listed here.

Currency & Exchange See section 1 of this chapter.

Electricity Like Canada, the United States uses 110 to 120 volts AC (60 cycles), compared to 220 to 240 volts AC (50 cycles) in most of Europe, Australia, and New Zealand. If your small appliances use 220 to 240 volts, you'll need a 110-volt transformer and a plug adapter with two flat parallel pins to operate them here. Downward converters that change 220 to 240 volts to 110 to 120 volts are difficult to find in the United States, so bring one with you.

Embassies & Consulates All embassies are located in Washington, D.C. If your country isn't listed, call for directory information in Washington, D.C. (© **202/555-1212**) for the number of your national embassy. **Australia:** Embassy, 1601 Massachusetts Ave. NW, Washington, DC 20036 (© **202/ 797-3000;** www.austemb.org). **Canada:** Embassy, 501 Pennsylvania Ave. NW, Washington, DC 20001 (© **202/682-1740;** www.canadianembassy. org). **Ireland:** Embassy, 2234 Massachusetts Ave. NW, Washington, DC 20008 (© **202/462-3939;** www.irelandemb.org). **Japan:** Embassy, 2520 Massachusetts Ave. NW, Washington, DC 20008 (© **202/238-6700;** www.embjapan.org). **New Zealand:** Embassy, 37 Observatory Circle, Washington, DC 20008 (© **202/328-4800;** www.nzemb.org). **United Kingdom:** Embassy, 3100 Massachusetts Ave. NW, Washington, DC 20008 (© **202/ 588-6500;** www.britainusa.com). **Japan** has a consulate-general in Anchorage, the only nation that does, at 3601 C St., Ste. 1300, Anchorage, AK 99503 (© **907/562-8428**).

Emergencies Call ✆ **911** to report a fire, call the police, or get an ambulance almost anywhere in the United States. This is a toll-free call (no coins are required at public telephones).

Gasoline (Petrol) Petrol/gasoline stations are known as both gas stations and service stations. Gasoline costs less here than in Europe (about $1.75 per gallon at press time). Taxes are already included in the pump price. One U.S. gallon equals 3.8 liters or .85 Imperial gallons.

Holidays Banks, government offices, post offices, and many stores, restaurants, and museums are closed on the following legal national holidays: January 1 (New Year's Day), the third Monday in January (Martin Luther King Jr. Day), the third Monday in February (Presidents' Day, Washington's Birthday), the last Monday in May (Memorial Day), July 4 (Independence Day), the first Monday in September (Labor Day), the second Monday in October (Columbus Day), November 11 (Veterans' Day/Armistice Day), the fourth Thursday in November (Thanksgiving Day), and December 25 (Christmas). Additionally, banks and state government offices in Alaska close on two state holidays: the last Monday in March (Seward's Day) and October 18 (Alaska Day, which is celebrated on the nearest Friday or Monday if the 18th falls on a weekend).

Legal Aid If you are stopped for a minor traffic infraction (such as speeding), never attempt to pay the fine directly to a police officer; this could be construed as attempted bribery, a much more serious crime. Pay fines by mail, or directly into the hands of the clerk of the court. Alaska law carries harsh penalties, including mandatory jail time, for drunk driving. Even some traffic tickets, such as speeding more than 15 miles per hour over the limit, can involve a mandatory court appearance, a major inconvenience. If accused of a serious crime, say and do nothing before consulting a lawyer. Here the burden is on the state to prove a person's guilt beyond a reasonable doubt, and everyone has the right to remain silent, whether he or she is suspected of a crime or is actually arrested. Once arrested, a person can make one telephone call to a party of his or her choice. Call your embassy or consulate.

Mail The locations of the post offices in each town in this book are listed in the appropriate Fast Facts sections. You can send mail from your hotel or the post office. Mail in the United States must have a five-digit postal code (or ZIP code), after the two-letter abbreviation of the state to which the mail is addressed. At press time, domestic postage rates were 20¢ for a postcard and 34¢ for a letter. For international mail, mailing a first-class letter of up to one ounce costs 80¢ (60¢ to Canada and to Mexico), a first-class postcard 70¢ (50¢ to Canada and Mexico).

Taxes Neither the U.S. nor the state of Alaska impose a value-added tax (VAT) or sales tax, but most Alaska communities, with the exception of Anchorage, levy their own sales taxes, and all communities impose taxes on hotel rooms and rental cars. See the individual town sections' "Fast Facts" for local tax rates.

Telephone & Fax Before using a telephone in a hotel, check for surcharges on long-distance and local calls, which can be astronomical. If so, you're better off using a **public pay telephone,** which you'll find clearly marked in most public buildings and private establishments as well as in hotel lobbies and on the street. Many convenience stores sell **prepaid calling cards** in denominations up to $50; these can be the least expensive way to call home. **Local calls** made from public pay phones usually cost 25¢. In smaller Alaska communities, you may have to wait for the person you are calling to answer before quickly putting the money in the phone. Pay phones do not accept pennies or anything larger than a quarter.

Most long-distance and international calls can be dialed directly from any phone. For **long-distance calls within Alaska and the United States and to Canada,** dial 1 followed by the three-digit area code and the seven-digit number. For **international calls to places other than Canada,** dial 011 followed by the country code, city code, and telephone number of the person you are calling. U.S. area codes and international country codes are listed in the front of the White Pages telephone directory, or dial 0 to get a country code from the operator. If you're calling the **United States** from another country, the country code is 01.

For **collect, operator-assisted, and person-to-person calls,** dial 0 (the number zero) followed by the area code and number you want; an operator will then come on the line, and you should specify that you are calling collect, or person-to-person, or both. If your operator-assisted call is international, ask for the overseas operator.

For **local and national directory assistance** ("information"), dial ✆ **411;** for a number in a particular area code, dial the area code followed by ✆ 555-1212. Typically, you'll be charged around 50¢ for this service.

There are two kinds of telephone directories in the United States. The so-called **White Pages** list private households and business subscribers in alphabetical order; the **Yellow Pages** list businesses and organizations categorized by the services they provide. In Alaska, the two directories are contained in the same book in all towns except Anchorage. Look in the front of the White Pages for emergency numbers and instructions on making long-distance calls. Blue pages near the front of the White Pages directory list numbers for government agencies.

Time Most of the U.S. is divided into six time zones. From east to west, they are: eastern, central, mountain, Pacific, Alaska, and Hawaii/Aleutian. For example, noon in New York City is 11am in Chicago, 10am in Denver, 9am in Los Angeles, 8am in mainland Alaska, and 7am in Honolulu and the outer Aleutians. Daylight saving time is in effect from 1am on the first Sunday in April through 1am the last Sunday in October, except in Arizona, Hawaii, part of Indiana, and Puerto Rico. Daylight saving time moves the clock 1 hour ahead of standard time.

Tipping Tips make up a major part of the compensation for many service workers. To leave no tip in a restaurant is socially unacceptable.

In restaurants, bars, and nightclubs, tip your server 15% to 20% of the check, depending on the quality of service. Tip **bartenders** 10% to 15%, tip **checkroom attendants** $1 per garment, and tip **valet-parking attendants** $1 per vehicle. Tipping is not expected in cafeterias or fast-food restaurants where you order at a counter. In hotels, tip **bellhops** $1 per bag ($2 to $3 if you have a lot of luggage) and tip the **housekeeper** at least $1 per day. Tip **cab drivers** 15% of the fare, tip **skycaps** at airports $1 per bag ($2 to $3 if you have a lot of luggage), and tip **hairdressers** and **barbers** 15% to 20%. Do not tip gas-station attendants and ushers at movies and theaters.

See "Guide Gratuities" under "Planning an Outdoor Vacation," in chapter 2, for tipping of guides and outfitters.

Toilets You won't find public toilets (or "restrooms") on the streets in most U.S. cities, but they can be found in hotel lobbies, bars, restaurants, museums, department stores, railway and bus stations, or service stations.

4

Cruising Alaska's Coast

Alaska is one of the top cruise destinations in the world, with almost three quarters of a million people sailing the state's coast annually, visiting the towns and wilderness areas of the Southeast and the Gulf of Alaska by day and burrowing into their ships for effortless travel by night. This element of cruise travel—the fact that it's *easy*—is one of its main drawing cards for visitors to the Southeast, where the lack of roads between towns makes the waters of the Inside Passage the region's de facto highway. You could do the same routes on the Alaska State Ferry, but you'd have to be willing to invest more time, both for the actual traveling and for the planning.

Now for the bad news: All those cruise ships aren't necessarily good for Alaska and its residents. Alaskans are known for their hospitality, but we all have our limits. Imagine living in a coastal settlement and having an entire town full of new people arriving all at once—as many or more as live there—mobbing your streets and hiking trails, spewing pollution into the air and water, and creating a tremendous racket of helicopters. Imagine it happening every day, without respite, all summer. Suppose all the old, community businesses on the waterfront area were driven out by seasonal gift shops? You might not mind if you were one of the few local visitor-industry entrepreneurs who snags fleeting cruise-ship spending, but most people would find their sense of hospitality wearing thin.

For years, the cruise-ship industry exploited the hospitality of Southeast Alaska as if it were an inexhaustible resource, but a dam of resentment burst when two of the lines, Royal Caribbean and Holland America, were caught and convicted of felonies for dumping pollution such as dry-cleaning fluid, photo chemicals, and used oil in the pristine waters of the Inside Passage, and then lying about it. Marine pilots—the local experts who guide the ships through tricky passages—disclosed that some of the lines routinely asked to be brought to small "doughnut holes" of water just outside the state's 3-mile limit of control to dump sewage. Those sites also happened to be Alaska's prime whale-watching grounds. Huge plumes of black smoke some ships belched into the air of Southeast towns also turned out to be illegal. So determined was Alaska Governor Tony Knowles to give the state real power to deal with polluters that he called the legislature back into session in 2001 during its summer recess to thrash out a new set of laws giving the job of enforcement to the state itself, not the lines. The changes make Alaska the first state with its own environmental laws for the cruise industry.

Whether the legislature manages to pass new pollution regulations in the face of a powerful cruise lobby remains to be seen. But the tide of public sentiment about the industry has turned. Some communities feel the environmental damage and cultural bulldozing brought by these floating cities is not worth the economic benefit. Haines, for one, has put a limit on the amount of cruise-tour traffic it will tolerate, and Juneau residents voted in a $5 per passenger head tax on cruise-ship visitors (it is included in your fare) in 2000. And, after years of fast growth, the industry, too, has begun talk of a "carrying capacity." Perhaps a bit late, they are recognizing that quaint little towns aren't such fun to visit if overrun by other visitors. To this end, Princess began in September 2000 to shut down its ships' engines while in dock in Juneau, drawing electrical power from the city grid and thus reducing the pollution coming from its ships' smokestacks. This is a new practice in cruising, and signifies a willingness in the industry to help preserve its most valuable asset: the pristine destinations that people are paying good money to see. Still, any substantial change that occurs will depend on what the lines hear from their customers. Your enjoyment of a trip is the cruise lines' stock in trade, and few would enjoy these beautiful places so much with the knowledge they were contributing to their demise.

But don't let all this legislative wrangling frighten you off. You'll find the residents of Southeast Alaska remain warm to visitors, whether they come from cruise ships or travel independently. In this chapter we'll go through the cruise options available in the state, focusing primarily on those that give a real in-depth experience. For even more information, pick up a copy of *Frommer's Alaska Cruises & Ports of Call.*

1 Weighing Your Cruise Options

Your two main questions in choosing a cruise in Alaska are, "Where do I want to go?" and "How big a ship?"

INSIDE PASSAGE OR THE GULF OF ALASKA?

Typically, the cruise lines offer two basic weeklong itineraries. **Inside Passage cruises** generally sail round-trip from Vancouver, British Columbia, visiting three or four port towns (typically Juneau, Skagway, Ketchikan, and either Sitka, Haines, or Victoria, B.C.) along the Inside Passage, spending a day in Glacier Bay or one of the other glacier areas, and spending 2 days "at sea," meaning they just cruise along, allowing you to relax and enjoy the scenery.

Gulf of Alaska cruises generally sail north- and southbound between Vancouver and Seward (the port for Anchorage) in alternating weeks, visiting many of the same towns and attractions as the Inside Passage cruises but—since they don't have to turn around and sail back to Vancouver—also tacking on a visit to Valdez, Hubbard Glacier, College Fjord, or one or more of the other Gulf towns or natural attractions.

Though most of the major operators stick pretty closely to these two basic routes, the small-ship cruise lines tend to offer more **small-port and wilderness-oriented itineraries,** some sailing round-trip from Juneau or Sitka, some sailing between Juneau and Ketchikan, and one even sailing between Juneau and Glacier Bay. Many of these ships visit the major ports of call, but may also include visits to small ports that aren't accessible to the bigger ships, towns like Petersburg, Wrangell, Gustavus, Elfin Cove, and possibly the Native village of Metlakatla. Some ships sail itineraries where passengers can explore by kayak or take hiking treks.

Cruisetours combines a cruise with a land tour, either before or after the cruise. Typical packages link the cruise with a 3- to 5-day Anchorage/Denali/Fairbanks tour, a 7-day Yukon tour (which visits Anchorage, Denali, and Fairbanks on the way), or a 5- to 7-day tour of the Canadian Rockies. Holland

America, Princess, and Cruise West (a distant third) are the three leaders in the cruisetour market. Even if you book with another cruise line, chances are your land tour will be through one of these operators.

BIG SHIP OR SMALL?

Imagine an elephant. Now imagine your pet pug dog, Sparky. That's about the size difference between your options in the Alaska market: behemoth modern megaships and small, more exploratory coastal vessels.

The **big ships** offer you heated pools, theatrical productions, organized activities, spas, jogging tracks, discos, generally spacious accommodations, fine dining, and more, but their size comes with three major drawbacks for passengers: (1) they can't sail into narrow passages or shallow-water ports, (2) their size and inflexible schedules limit their ability to stop or even slow down when wildlife is spotted, and (3) when their passengers disembark in a town, they tend to overwhelm that town, limiting your ability to see the real Alaska.

The **small ships** offer little in terms of amenities: they usually have small cabins, only one lounge/bar and dining room, and no exercise facilities, entertainment, or organized activities. Despite all of this, they're universally more expensive than the big ships, and offer fewer discounts. That's the minus side. On the plus side, (1) they can sail almost anywhere (including far into Misty Fjords, where no large ship can penetrate), (2) since they tend to have more flexibility in their schedules than the large ships, they can usually take time to linger if whales or other wildlife are sighted nearby, (3) their small size doesn't scare off wildlife as easily as the big ships, and the fact that you're at or near the waterline (rather than 10 stories up, as on the large ships) means you get a more close-up view, and (4) they're almost all completely casual—no dressing up required.

Visitors aboard large ships may physically be in Alaska, but unless they're reminded of it they might never know, such is the disjunction between the glitzy modern ships and the real world outside. Visitors aboard small ships, however, get an experience that's many times more intimate, allowing them to really get in touch with the place they've come to see. For all these reasons, my advice to anyone wanting to experience Alaska rather than just get a postcard impression of it is to spend the extra money for a small-ship cruise. As with any product, you get what you pay for, and by paying extra in the short term for a more intimate cruise, you're almost guaranteed of having an Alaska experience that you'll remember your whole life.

2 The Best Cruise Lines in Alaska

Cruise lines are in the business of giving their guests a good time, so they've all got something going for them. Here's my pick of Alaska's best, though, in a few different categories.

- **Best Line for an Up-Close Alaska Experience:** There's almost no contest here. **Glacier Bay Cruiseline** is the only line offering itineraries that take you into the heart of natural Alaska, avoiding the usual tourist towns entirely on their adventure-oriented cruises and concentrating instead on hiking, kayaking, and wildlife watching. The overall experience is 100% casual and the spartan ships act more like base camps than resorts.
- **Best Lines for an Educational Experience:** With its single old ocean liner, **World Explorer Cruises** focuses on wildlife education and on helping passengers really learn about Alaska and Alaska Native culture. The ship is budget and casual all the way, but its staff of naturalists and guest lecturers

is among the best in the business. Among small ships, **Clipper Cruise Line, Lindblad Expeditions,** and **Glacier Bay Cruiseline** all focus on education, with naturalists giving lectures onboard and leading groups ashore.

- **Best Lines for a Stress-Free Cruise:** For years, **Holland America**'s stock-in-trade has been providing a comfortable, low-key vacation experience for seniors, and though the line has been making some changes to attract a younger clientele as well, it's still the best bet for someone wanting to visit Alaska in reassuring comfort. On the small-ship side, **Cruise West** caters to many seniors, though those who want to add some excitement to their trip can opt for boating, kayaking, and biking excursions.

- **Best Lines for Pampering:** If you want to cruise in style, sailing through Alaska like a pasha in a sedan chair, you've got a few choices. **Crystal Cruises** and **Radisson Seven Seas Cruises** are the two real luxury lines in the market, offering a white-glove experience. Among mainstream ships, **Celebrity Cruises** is the best by far, with exceptional service, dining, and decor. In the small-ship category, **American Safari Cruises** offers an experience that's as close as you can get to sailing aboard a private yacht. Its two ships carry only 12 and 22 passengers each, with all expenses covered, including excursions and alcoholic beverages.

3 Booking Your Cruise

Almost every cruise line publishes brochure prices that are the travel equivalent of a new car's sticker price: wildly inflated in the hope that someone, somewhere, might take them at face value. In reality, especially as sailings gets close and it looks as if the line will get stuck with unsold space, cruise lines are almost universally willing to sell their cruises for much, much less. (The small-ship lines tend to be the exception to this rule. Since they have less space to sell and appeal to a more specific market niche, they can often get their initial asking price.)

More than ever, there are numerous ways to book a cruise and find the best discounts. In the United States, 90% to 95% of all cruise bookings are arranged through **travel agents,** but instead of using the services of a traditional travel agent, these days you can also head for your computer and check out what the **online cruise agencies and discounters** are offering; a handful even allow you to actually submit your credit card online and make a reservation without ever having to talk to a soul. And some cruise lines, like Carnival, NCL, Royal Caribbean, and Celebrity, even have their own booking sites (although at press time, they aren't particularly user-friendly).

BOOKING A SMALL-SHIP CRUISE

The small-ship companies in Alaska—Glacier Bay Cruiseline, American Safari Cruises, Clipper, Cruise West, and Lindblad Expeditions—all offer real niche-oriented cruise experiences, attracting passengers who have a very good idea of the kind of experience they want (usually educational and/or adventurous, and always casual and small-scale). In many cases, a large percentage of passengers on any given cruise will have sailed with the line before. Because of all this, and because the passenger capacity of these small ships is so low (from 12 to 138), in general you're not going to find the kind of deep discounts you do with the large ships. Still, for the most part these lines rely on agents to handle their bookings, taking very few reservations directly. (Clipper is the exception to this rule, taking most of their Alaska bookings directly, rather than through agents.)

Tips **Shopping for Shore Tours**

Most cruise-ship passengers sign up for onshore activities and excursions that leave from the dock when they arrive on board. It's easy and convenient, and you can be sure the outing will be timed to your port of call. On the down side, these tend to be the most superficial and highest-priced choices in town and almost always involve large groups. For outdoor activities, trooping down a trail or paddling a sea kayak in a big mob can spoil the experience. There is an alternative, however. A large part of the high shipboard price for shore tours is the cut taken by the cruise line. You can get a much better deal (as much as half off) by arranging your own activities in advance. Most guides will be happy to tailor an outing to your limited time, and you'll probably have a far more intimate experience in the bargain. It only takes a little advance prepwork: Study your ports of call, the activities and operators there (for which this book will be an invaluable guide), and the time you will be ashore, and then make your reservations before you leave, putting down the appropriate deposits and getting directions for making transfers.

All of the lines have a list of agents with whom they do considerable business and can hook you up with one or another of them if you call (or e-mail) and ask for an agent near you.

AGENCIES SPECIALIZING IN MAINSTREAM CRUISES

The following cruise-only and full-service agencies have solid reputations in selling mainstream cruises such as Princess, Carnival, Royal Caribbean, Celebrity, Holland America, and Norwegian Cruise Line, and operate from a combination of walk-in business and 800-number telephone-based business.

- **Admiral of the Fleet Cruise Center,** 12920 Bluemound Rd., Elm Grove, WI 53122 (© **800/462-3371** or 262/784-2628).
- **Admiral of the Fleet Cruise Center,** 3430 Pacific Ave. SE, Ste. A–5, Olympia, WA 98501 (© **800/877-7447** or 360/866-7447).
- **The Cruise Company,** 10760 Q St., Omaha, NE 68127 (© **800/289-5505** or 402/339-6800; www.thecruisecompany.com).
- **Cruises By Brennco,** 508 E. 112th St., Kansas City, MO 64131 (© **800/955-1909** or 816/942-1000).
- **Cruise Value Centers,** 6 Edgeboro Rd., East Brunswick, NJ 08816 (© **800/231-7447;** www.cruisevalue.com).
- **Hartford Holidays,** 129 Hillside Ave., Williston Park, NY 11596 (© **800/828-4813** or 516/746-6670).
- **Just Cruisin' Plus,** 5640 Nolensville Rd., Nashville, TN 37211 (© **800/888-0922** or 615/833-0922; justcruisinplus.vacation.com).
- **Kelly Cruises,** 1315 W. 22nd St., Ste. 105, Oak Brook, IL 60523 (© **800/837-7447** or 630/990-1111; www.kellycruises.com).

- **Mann Travel & Cruises American Express,** 4400 Park Rd., Charlotte, NC 28209 (✆ **800/835-9828** or 866/591-8129; www.manntravels.com).
- **National Leisure Group,** 100 Sylvan Rd., Ste. 600, Wobrun, MA 01801 (✆ **800/435-7683** or 617/424-7990; www.nlg.com).
- **The Travel Company,** 220 Congress Park Dr., Delray Beach, FL 33445 (✆ **800/242-9000;** www.mytravelco.com).

THE COST: WHAT'S INCLUDED & WHAT'S NOT

However you arrange to buy your cruise, what you basically have in hand at the end is a contract for transportation, lodging, dining, entertainment, housekeeping, and assorted other miscellaneous services that will be provided to you over the course of your vacation. It's important, though, to remember what extras are *not* included in your cruise fare. Aside from **airfare,** which is usually not included in your cruise fare (see more on air arrangements below), the most pricey addition to your cruise fare, particularly in Alaska, will likely be **shore excursions.** Ranging from about $29 for a bus tour to $250 or more for a helicopter or fixed-wing flightseeing excursion, these sightseeing tours are designed to help cruise passengers make the most of their time at the ports the ship visits, but they can add a hefty sum to your vacation costs.

You'll also want to add to your calculations **tips for the ship's crew.** Tips are given at the end of the cruise, and passengers should reserve at least $9 per person, per day ($63 per passenger for the week) for tips for the room steward, waiter, and busperson. (In practice, I find that most people tend to give a little more.) Additional tips to other personnel, such as the head waiter or maitre d', are at your discretion. On the small ships, all tips often go into one pot, which the crew divides up after the cruise.

All but a very few ships charge extra for **alcoholic beverages** (including wine at dinner) and for soda. Nonbubbly soft drinks such as lemonade and iced tea are included in your cruise fare.

Port charges, taxes, and other fees are usually included in your cruise fare but not always, and these charges can add as much as $175 per person onto the price of a 7-day Alaska cruise. Make sure you know whether these are included in the cruise fare when you are comparing rates.

Of course, just as at a hotel, you also pay extra for items like ship-to-shore phone calls or faxes, e-mails, spa treatments, and so on.

MONEY-SAVING STRATEGIES

Cruise pricing is a fluid medium, and there are a number of strategies you can use to save money off the booking price.

LATE VERSUS EARLY BOOKING

More than ever before, there are no steadfast rules about pricing—policies differ from line to line, and from week to week, depending on supply and demand. If there's empty space on a ship as the sailing date nears, lines would rather sell a cabin for a lower fare than not sell it at all. While booking early will still get you as much as a 50% discount off the brochure rates and give you a better pick of cabins, booking late (just a few weeks or month or two before sailing) will often get you an even better rate. Of course, you have to consider when booking at the last minute that if you have to fly to the port of embarkation, you may have to pay an airfare so high that it cancels out your savings on the cruise. You'll find last-minute deals advertised online and in the travel section of your Sunday newspaper. You should also check with a travel agent or an agency or discounter that specializes in cruises.

SHOULDER SEASON DISCOUNTS

You can think of the Alaska cruise season as three distinct periods: (1) peak season, late June, July, and early to mid-August; (2) value/standard season, early June and late August; and (3) budget season, May and September. You can save by booking a cruise during this last period, in the shoulder months of May or September, when cruise pricing is lower. The weather might be a little chillier, and September is known for rain, but a lot fewer people visit during those months, allowing you a bit more pristine experience of the place, especially if you're sailing on a small ship. Frommer's cruise editor recently took an early May sailing with Glacier Bay Cruiseline and reported that he felt like he had the state all to himself.

DISCOUNTS FOR THIRD & FOURTH PASSENGERS & GROUPS

Most ships offer highly discounted rates for third and fourth passengers sharing a cabin with two "full-fare" passengers (even if those two have booked at a discounted rate). It may mean a tight squeeze, but it'll save you a bundle. Some lines offer **special rates for kids,** usually on a seasonal or select-sailings basis, that may include free or discounted airfare. Those under age 2 generally cruise free.

One of the best ways to get a cruise deal is to book as a **group** of at least 16 people in at least eight cabins. The savings include a discounted rate, and at least the cruise portion of the 16th ticket will be free. A "group" in this instance can be a real group (friends, relatives, and so on) or simply a block of passengers booked by a travel agency on the same cruise. You don't have to even pretend you know these people, but the savings are the same. Ask your travel agent about any group deals they may offer.

SENIOR-CITIZEN DISCOUNTS

Senior citizens may be able to get extra savings on their cruise. Some lines will take 5% off the top for those 55 and up, and the senior rate applies even if the second person in the cabin is younger. Membership in groups such as AARP is not required, but such membership may bring additional savings.

BOOKING AIR TRAVEL THROUGH THE CRUISE LINE

Except during special promotions, airfare to the port of embarkation is rarely included in the cruise rates, so you'll have to purchase airfare on your own or buy it as a package with your cruise through your travel agent or online cruise site. You can usually find information on these "air/sea" programs in the back of cruise line brochures, along with prices. The benefit of booking through the cruise line is that round-trip transfers between the airport and the ship are usually included. Also, the cruise line will know your airline schedule, and in the event of delayed flights and other unavoidable snafus, will be able to do more to make sure you and the other people on your flight get on the ship; if you've booked your air transportation separately, you're on your own. On the downside, air add-ons may not be the best deal and it might be cheaper to book your own airfare. Also, you probably won't be able to use any frequent-flier miles you may have accumulated.

CHOOSING YOUR CABIN

Cruise-ship cabins run from tiny boxes with accordion doors and bunk beds to palatial multiroom suites with hot tubs on the balcony. Which is right for you? Price will likely be a big factor here, but so should the vacation style you prefer. If, for instance, you plan to spend a lot of quiet time in your cabin, you should probably consider booking the biggest room you can afford. If, conversely, you plan to be out on deck all the time checking out the glaciers and wildlife, you might be just as happy with a smaller (and cheaper) cabin to crash in at the end of the day. Cabins are either **inside** (without a window or porthole) or **outside** (with), with the latter being more expensive. On the big ships, the more deluxe outside cabins may also come with **private verandas.**

SPECIAL MENU REQUESTS

The cruise line should be informed at the time you make your reservations about any special dietary requests you have. Some lines offer kosher menus, and all will have vegetarian, low-fat, low-salt, and sugar-free options available.

4 The Small-Ship Cruise Lines

Small ships allow you to see Alaska from sea level, without the kind of distractions you get aboard the big ships—no glitzy interiors, no big shows or loud music, no casinos, no spas, and no crowds, as the largest of these ships carries only 138 passengers. You're immersed in the 49th state from the minute you wake up to the minute you fall asleep, and for the most part left alone to form your own opinions. Personally, I feel that, despite these ships' higher cost, they provide by far the better cruise experience for those who really want to get the feel of Alaska.

Small-ship itineraries can be categorized as **port-to-port,** meaning they mimic the larger ships in simply sailing between port towns; **soft-adventure,** meaning they provide some outdoors experiences like hiking and kayaking, while not requiring participants to be trained athletes; and **active-adventure,** meaning the hiking and kayaking will be the real focus of the trip, and may be strenuous.

On all of these types of cruises, the small-ship experience tends toward an education rather than glitzy entertainment. You'll likely get **informal lectures** and sometimes video presentations on Alaska wildlife, history, and Native culture. Meals are served in open seatings, so you can sit where and with whom you like, and time spent huddled on the outside decks scanning for whales fosters great camaraderie among passengers.

Cabins on these ships don't generally offer TVs or telephones and tend to be very small and sometimes spartan (see the individual reviews for exceptions). Alaska Sightseeing's *Spirit of '98* and *Spirit of Oceanus* and Clipper Cruise Line's *Clipper Odyssey* have elevators, but in general the small ships are not good choices for travelers who require the use of wheelchairs or have other mobility problems.

AMERICAN SAFARI CRUISES

19101 36th Ave. W, Ste. 201, Lynnwood, WA 98036. (C) **888/862-8881.** Fax 425/776-8889. www. americansafaricruises.com.

Directed to the demanding high-end traveler, American Safari Cruises promises an intimate, all-inclusive yacht cruise to some of the more out-of-the-way stretches of the Inside Passage. The company books only 12 to 22 people per cruise, guaranteeing unparalleled flexibility and privacy. Black-bear aficionados can chug off in a Zodiac boat for a better look; active adventurers can explore the shoreline in one of the yacht's four kayaks; and lazier travelers can relax aboard ship. Another big plus: All off-ship excursions—including flightseeing and trips to boardwalked cannery villages and Tlingit villages—are included in the cruise fare, as are drinks. The price is considerable, as is the pampering.

TYPICAL PASSENGERS   Passengers, almost always couples, tend to be more than comfortably wealthy and range from 45 to 65 years of age. Most hope to get close to nature without sacrificing luxury.

SHIPS   More private yachts than cruise ships, the 22-passenger *Safari Quest* and 12-passenger *Safari Spirit* look like Ferraris, all sleek, contoured lines and dark glass. Cabins are comfortable, and sitting rooms are intimate and luxurious, almost as if they had been transported whole from a spacious suburban home. A big-screen TV in the main lounge forms a natural center for impromptu lectures during the day and movie-watching at night. **Sample rates per person:** Lowest-price outside cabins $3,695 for 7-night cruise; no inside cabins or suites.

CLIPPER CRUISE LINE

7711 Bonhomme Ave., St. Louis, MO 63105. ℭ 800/325-0010 or 314/727-2929. Fax 314/727-6576. www.clippercruise.com.

Honored by *Condé Nast Traveler* as one of the top-10 cruise lines in the world, Clipper's operation is more sophisticated and service-oriented than most other lines with ships this size. Its ships sail port-to-port itineraries, and as aboard Alaska's other small-ship lines, the onboard atmosphere is casual; what lies out there beyond the ship's rail is most passengers' real focus. Lectures and videos on Alaska make up the bulk of the entertainment program, and a nightly social hour encourages passengers to mix and mingle. Motorized landing craft, carried aboard the ship, ferry passengers to remote beaches, pristine forests, small villages, and wildlife refuges, where naturalists and/or historians and other experts may conduct walking tours.

TYPICAL PASSENGERS   Passengers are generally over 55, educated, and financially sound, with relatively high expectations when it comes to food, comfort, and overall experience. While they want to experience Alaska's natural wonders—whales, glaciers, woodlands—they're not necessarily run-the-rapids types.

SHIPS   Along with Alaska Sightseeing's *Spirit of Endeavor* and *Spirit of Oceanus* and Glacier Bay's *Executive Explorer*, the 128-passenger *Clipper Odyssey* and 138-passenger *Yorktown Clipper* are two of the best choices in Alaska for someone who wants small-ship intimacy and flexibility but doesn't want to skimp on comfort. Their public rooms are larger and more appealing than those aboard competing ships, and all cabins are outside. Except for those at the lowest level, all have picture windows, and the top suite on the *Odyssey* offers a private veranda. **Sample rates per person:** Lowest-price outside cabins on *Yorktown Clipper*: $2,310 for 7-night cruise; on *Odyssey:* $4,520; no inside cabins on either ship.

CRUISE WEST

2401 4th Ave., Ste. 700, Seattle, WA 98121. ℭ 800/426-7702 or 206/441-8687. Fax 206/441-4757. www.cruisewest.com.

Cruise West is the largest operator of small ships in Alaska, offering port-to-port itineraries, friendly service, and a casual onboard atmosphere. As with Clipper Cruise Line, Cruise West's ships are for people who want to visit Alaska's port towns and see its wilderness areas up close and in a relaxed, small-scale environment without big-ship distractions; they're not for people who want to spend their days hiking and kayaking.

The line's friendly, enthusiastic staffs are a big, big plus, making guests feel right at home. A cheerful and knowledgeable cruise coordinator accompanies each trip to answer passengers' questions about Alaska's flora, fauna, geology, and history, and Forest Service rangers, local fishermen, and Native Alaskans sometimes come aboard to give informal talks about the culture and industry of the state.

TYPICAL PASSENGERS   Cruise West passengers tend to be older (typically around 60 to 75), financially stable, well educated, and independent-minded.

SHIPS   The 70-passenger *Sheltered Seas* is a cabinless excursion ship that cruises Alaska's waterways by day and deposits passengers at a hotel ashore at night, generally after the crowds from larger cruise ships have left and in time to enjoy some nightlife. If you can't decide between cruising Alaska and seeing it by land, this is an option worth exploring. The 96-passenger *Spirit of '98,* a replica of a 19th-century steamship, carries its Victorian flavor so well that fully two-thirds of the people I met on board thought the ship had been a private yacht at the turn of the 20th century. (*Note:* The *'98* is the only small ship in Alaska that has an elevator and a cabin that's wheelchair friendly.) The 78-passenger *Spirit of Alaska* and *Spirit of Columbia,* and 84-passenger *Spirit of Discovery* are all spartan ships designed to get passengers into small ports and allow them to see the state up close. The 102-passenger *Spirit of Endeavor,* on the other hand, offers among the highest levels of small-ship comfort of any small ship in Alaska, comparable to Clipper's *Yorktown Clipper* and Glacier Bay's *Executive Explorer.* At press time, Cruise West had just announced the acquisition of a new vessel, the 114-passenger *Spirit of Oceanus* (the former *Renaissance V* of Renaissance Cruises). It will be the largest and, from the sound of it, poshest vessel in the fleet, with 12 high-end cabins boasting private teak balconies. **Sample rates per person:** Lowest-price inside cabins $919, lowest outside $1,319.

GLACIER BAY CRUISELINE

226 2nd Ave. W, Seattle, WA 98119. ℂ **800/451-5952** or 206/623-2417. Fax (206) 623-7809. www. glacierbaycruiseline.com.

Glacier Bay Cruiseline—the only **Native-owned** cruise line in Alaska—offers three types of cruises: soft-adventure (aboard the *Wilderness Explorer*), active-adventure (aboard the *Wilderness Adventurer*), and port-to-port (aboard the slightly more luxurious *Executive Explorer*). The *Wilderness Discoverer* is a hybrid, sailing itineraries that mix 3 days of adventure activities with 3 days spent visiting popular ports of call.

The adventure sailings are for a particular type of traveler, one interested in exploring Alaska's wilds rather than its towns. On the *Wilderness Explorer's* soft-adventure cruises, for example, the biggest town you're likely to encounter after departing Juneau is tiny little Elfin Cove, population around 30 to 35 (at least in the summer). Other than this, days are spent hiking in remote regions, exploring the glaciers, cruising the waterways looking for whales and other wildlife, and **kayaking**—the *Wilderness Adventurer, Wilderness Explorer,* and *Wilderness Discoverer* carry fleets of stable two-person sea kayaks, which are launched from dry platforms at the ships' sterns. A weeklong sailing typically includes three kayak treks. **Naturalists** sail with every cruise to point out natural features and lead off-ship expeditions, all of which are included in the cruise price. On board, the atmosphere is casual and friendly, with the staff establishing a friendly, casual rapport with passengers, providing just enough attention while leaving you the space to enjoy your vacation however you want. Entertainment facilities on all ships are minimal: board games, books, and a TV/VCR in the lounge, on which passengers can view tapes on wildlife, Alaska history, Native culture, and a few feature films.

TYPICAL PASSENGERS   On the *Wilderness Explorer, Adventurer,* and *Discoverer,* passengers tend to be on the youngish side, with as many couples in their 40s and 50s as in their 60s and 70s, and a scattering of 30-somethings (and a few 80- or 90-somethings) filling out the list. Whatever their age, passengers tend to be active and interested in nature and wildlife. On the *Executive Explorer,* passengers tend to be older (60 and up) and less active and adventurous, though they still enjoy the same informality as aboard the line's other vessels.

SHIPS   The 49-passenger catamaran-style *Executive Explorer* is Glacier Bay's most luxurious ship, sailing port-to-port itineraries. The spartan, 74-passenger *Wilderness Adventurer* and almost identical 86-passenger *Wilderness Discoverer* are the line's soft-adventure ships, outfitted with sea kayaks and kayak dry-launch platforms in their sterns. The 36-passenger *Wilderness Explorer* is the line's most basic ship, with tiny cabins and bunk-style beds. It visits no ports, instead offering the most active cruise experience available in Alaska, with cruises structured so passengers are out kayaking and hiking most of each day and only use the vessel to eat, sleep, and get from place to place. **Sample rates per person:** Lowest-price inside cabins $2,415, lowest outside $2,735 for 7-night cruise; no suites.

LINDBLAD EXPEDITIONS
720 Fifth Ave., New York, NY 10019. **(℃** 800/397-3348 or 212/765-7740. Fax 212/265-3770. www.expeditions.com.

Lindblad Expeditions specializes in environmentally sensitive, soft-adventure vacations that are explorative and informal in nature, designed to appeal to the intellectually curious traveler seeking a cruise that's educational as well as relaxing. Days aboard are spent learning about the Alaskan outdoors from high-caliber expedition leaders trained in botany, anthropology, biology, and geology, and observing the world around you either from the ship or on shore excursions, which are included in the cruise package. Educational films and slide presentations aboard ship precede nature hikes and quick jaunts aboard Zodiac boats.

TYPICAL PASSENGERS   Passengers tend to be over 55, educated, relatively well off, and physically active (even so, the ships become very quiet not long after dinner; everyone crashes early to store up energy for the next day).

SHIPS   The shallow-draft, 70-passenger *Sea Lion* and *Sea Bird* are identical twins. With just two public rooms and utilitarian cabins, they're very similar to other "expedition style" small ships, such as Glacier Bay's *Wilderness Adventurer* and ASCW's *Spirit of Alaska* (as a matter of fact, the *Spirit of Alaska* and the two Special Expedition ships all sailed at one time for the now-defunct Exploration Cruise Lines). Cabins are small and functional, and public space is limited to the open sun deck and bow areas, the dining room, and an observation lounge that serves as the nerve center for activities. **Sample rates per person:** Lowest-price outside cabins $3,690 for 7-night cruise; no inside cabins or suites.

5 Mid-size Educational Cruising

WORLD EXPLORER CRUISES
555 Montgomery St., San Francisco, CA 94111-2544. **(℃** 800/854-3835 or 415/393-1565. Fax 415/391-1145. www.wecruise.com.

This is a real one-of-a-kind Alaska cruise experience that combines a relatively large ship (the dowdy, 731-passenger *Universe Explorer*) with an education-oriented approach more typical of a small-ship line. The ship offers an incredible itinerary—a 14-night round-trip cruise out of Vancouver that visits all the popular ports of call along with Haines, Wrangell, Valdez, and Seward—an educational lecture series, an atmosphere of friendly informality, and some truly high-caliber shore excursions. There's also a library stocked with 16,000 volumes (many on Alaska nature, history, and culture), a 150-seat cinema for movie watching, and a 16-terminal computer learning center operated by a company called SeniorNet. Entertainment-wise, one night it might be a string quartet, the next a cello soloist, a classical pianist, or an operatic soprano, cabaret singer, or ballad singer. The ship's **lecture circuit** features talks on ecology and the cultures of Alaska, presented by experts in their subject.

TYPICAL PASSENGERS The *Universe Explorer* tends to attract an older clientele, though the average age of its passengers is declining, mostly due to bike/hike-and-cruise options that allow passengers to bike or hike their way through the ports of call. These more active shore excursions appeal to a family market. It's not unusual for the ship to sail with between, say, 15 and 30 teens and preteens on board. There is a youth program and a team of counselors.

SHIPS The 731-passenger *Universe Explorer* has nice but not spectacular public spaces and adequate if not palatial cabins. The bulk of the ship is taken up with double-occupancy rooms with twin beds (convertible to queen-size). Some also are capable of accommodating third passengers in foldaway sofa beds. Public areas are fairly spartan. The ship has a functional reception area, lounge/bar facilities, a comfortable but not glamorous show room, and a huge library, with many selections on nature and wildlife. **Sample rates per person:** Lowest-price inside cabins $1,988, lowest outside $2,885, lowest suite $3,990 for 14-night cruise.

6 The Big-Ship Cruise Lines

The ships featured in this section vary in size, age, and offerings, but share the common thread of having more activities and entertainment options than any one person can possibly take in over the course of a cruise. You'll find swimming pools, health clubs, spas, nightclubs, movie theaters, shops, casinos, multiple restaurants, bars, and special kids' playrooms, and in some cases sports decks, virtual golf, computer rooms, and cigar clubs, as well as quiet spaces where you can get away from it all. In most cases you'll find lots and lots of onboard activities including games, contests, classes, and lectures, plus a variety of entertainment options and show productions, some very sophisticated.

CARNIVAL CRUISE LINES

3655 NW 87th Ave., Miami, FL 33178-2428. ✆ 800/CARNIVAL. Fax 305/471-4740. www.carnival.com.

Carnival is the big kahuna of the cruise industry, but translating the line's warm-weather "24-hour orgy of good times" philosophy to Alaska's "look at the bears and whales!" temperament isn't an easy trick. In one of its Alaska brochures, the line says that, like the prospectors, you might find yourself shouting "Eureka"— but in the ship's casino, not at a gold rush site. Kinda makes you wonder why you aren't just going to Vegas.

On the plus side, entertainment is among the industry's best, with each ship boasting a dozen dancers, a 12-piece orchestra, comedians, jugglers, and numerous live bands, as well as a big casino. Activity is nonstop. Cocktails begin to flow before lunch, and through the course of the day you can learn to country line-dance or ballroom dance, take cooking lessons, learn to play bridge, watch first-run movies, practice your golf swing by smashing balls into a net, join in a knobby-knee contest, or just eat, drink, shop, and then eat again. Alaska-specific naturalist lectures are delivered daily. In port, Carnival offers more than 60 **shore excursions,** divided into categories of easy, moderate, and adventure. For kids, the line offers Camp Carnival, an expertly run children's program with activities that include Native arts and crafts sessions, lectures conducted by wildlife experts, and special shore excursions for teens.

TYPICAL PASSENGERS   Overall, Carnival has some of the youngest demographics in the industry: mostly under 50, including couples, lots of singles, and a good share of families. It's the same Middle America crowd that can be found in Las Vegas and Atlantic City and at Florida's megaresorts.

SHIPS   The 2,112-passenger, 84,000-ton *Carnival Spirit* is big, new, and impressive, with four swimming pools, a wedding chapel, conference center, and, in addition to the formal dining room and casual buffet restaurant, an alternative restaurant sitting high up by the ship's smokestack. The ship also has more of what makes Carnival tick, including a two-level gym, balconies on over half the cabins, a large children's center, and two consecutive decks of bars, lounges, and nightspots, one with an outdoor wraparound promenade. **Sample rates per person:** Lowest-price inside cabins $1,579, lowest outside $1,879, lowest suite $2,929 for 7-night cruise.

CELEBRITY CRUISES

1050 Caribbean Way, Miami, FL 33132. © **800/437-3111** or 305/539-6000. Fax 800/437-5111. www.celebritycruises.com.

Celebrity Cruises offers a great combination: a classy, tasteful, and luxurious cruise experience at a moderate price—it's definitely the best in the midpriced category. The line's ships are real works of art; its cuisine—guided by Michel Roux, one of the top French chefs in Britain—is outstanding; its service first-class, friendly, and unobtrusive; and its spa facilities among the best in the business.

A typical day might offer bridge, darts, a culinary art demonstration, a trapshooting competition, a fitness fashion show, an art auction, a volleyball tournament, and a none-too-shabby stage show. Lectures on the various ports of call, the Alaskan environment, glaciers, and Alaskan culture are given by resident experts. For children, Celebrity ships employ a group of counselors who direct and supervise a camp-style children's program. Activities are geared toward different age groups. There's an impressive kids' play area and a separate lounge area for teens.

TYPICAL PASSENGERS   The typical guest is less party-oriented, more sophisticated, and more independent-minded than aboard a lot of other megaships. You'll find everyone from kids to retirees.

SHIPS   Sleek, modern, and stunningly designed, both the 1,870-passenger *Mercury* and the larger, 1,950-passenger *Infinity* have a lot of open deck space and lots of large windows that provide access to the wide skies and the grand Alaskan vistas. Overall, there are no really bad cabins on these ships—inside cabins are about par for the industry standard, outside cabins are larger than usual, and suites (which come with butler service) are particularly spacious. Startlingly modern art—by the likes of Robert Rauschenberg, Jasper Johns, David Hockney, Pablo Picasso, Andy Warhol, and Richard Serra—is scattered throughout both vessels. Both ships (but especially *Infinity*) feature incredible spas with hydrotherapy pools, steam rooms, and saunas, plus health and beauty services and exceptionally large fitness areas. **Sample rates per person:** Lowest-price inside cabins $1,729, lowest outside $2,399, lowest suite $4,949.

CRYSTAL CRUISES

2049 Century Park E, Ste. 1400, Los Angeles, CA 90067. ℂ **800/446-6620** or 310/785-9300. Fax 310/785-3891. www.crystalcruises.com.

Luxury all the way. Crystal offers all the amenities of much bigger ships, but in a more luxurious and intimate atmosphere, with only 940 passengers. Everything on the **Crystal Harmony** is first class, with fine attention paid to detail and to making guests feel comfortable. Service on the ship is nothing short of superb. The ship carries a battery of Alaska naturalists, environmentalists, and National Park Service rangers to educate and entertain passengers in the wilderness areas of the 49th state. The line's food-and-wine series presents well-known chefs and wine experts who put on food preparation demonstrations, lecture on the art of cookery, and prepare dinner one night during the cruise. A PGA-approved golf pro accompanies practically every *Harmony* cruise, conducting clinics along the way. The *Harmony* also has a flourishing computer room on board, with training for the uninitiated. There's dazzling show-lounge entertainment, first-run movies, and a casino operated by Caesar's World.

TYPICAL PASSENGERS   Passengers aboard Crystal tend to be successful businesspeople who can afford to pay for the best. Many are under 50, with the average age probably closer to 60 than 70. Whatever their age, they tend to be people who like to dress up rather than down. "Casual night" doesn't mean the same thing to Crystal guests as it means to other people.

SHIPS   A handsome ship by any standard, the *Harmony* has one of the highest passenger-space ratios of any cruise ship. Its cabins are large, well appointed, and tastefully decorated with quality fittings and in agreeable color tones. Almost half of them have private verandas. Public rooms are classy throughout. Two alternative restaurants, Prego (Italian, mostly northern) and Kyoto (Asian/Japanese), introduce variety to the dining experience. **Sample rates per person:** Lowest-price inside cabins $4,050, lowest outside $4,515, lowest suite $9,435 for 12-night cruise.

HOLLAND AMERICA LINE

300 Elliott Ave. W, Seattle, WA 98119. ℂ **800/426-0327** or 206/281-3535. Fax 206/286-7110. www.hollandamerica.com.

Holland America can be summed up in one word: *tradition.* The company was formed way back in 1873 as the Netherlands-America Steamship Company, and its ships today strive to present an aura of history and dignity, like a European hotel where they never let rock stars register. Service is provided primarily by Filipino and Indonesian staff members who are uniformly fantastic—gracious and friendly without being cloying.

Though most of the line's Alaskan fleet is relatively young, the ships are designed with a decidedly "classic" feel—no flashing neon lights here. Similarly, Holland America's ships are heavy on more mature, less frenetic kinds of activities. You'll find good bridge programs and music to dance (or just listen) to in the bars and lounges, plus health spas and the other amenities found on most large ships. The line has improved its nightly show-lounge entertainment, which was once, frankly, not so hot. Each week includes a crew talent show in which the Indonesian and Filipino staff members perform their countries' songs and dances. Club HAL is one of the industry's more creative children's programs, though the children's playrooms (often no more than a meeting room stocked with a few toys) are no match for what you find on the latest Princess or Celebrity megaships.

TYPICAL PASSENGERS   Though it still caters mostly to the older crowd that's long been its bread and butter, the average age is dropping, partly thanks to an increased emphasis on its children's program.

SHIPS   The 1,266-passenger *Ryndam, Statendam,* and *Veendam* are more or less identical. All cabins have a sitting area and lots of closet and drawer space, and even the least expensive inside cabins run almost 190 square feet, quite large by industry standards. Outside doubles have either picture windows or verandas. The striking dining rooms, two-tiered showrooms, and Crow's Nest forward bar/lounges are among these ships' best features. The newer, 1,440-passenger *Volendam* and *Zaandam* are larger and fancier, with triple-decked oval atriums, 197 suites and deluxe staterooms with private verandas, five showrooms and lounges, and an alternative restaurant designed as an artist's bistro, featuring drawings and etchings. The smallest cabin is a comfortable 190 square feet. The very long, stately, 1,494-passenger *Westerdam* is reminiscent of an old-time ocean liner, with portholes on some decks, a wide wraparound promenade, a truly lovely showroom, and spacious cabins and lounges. Cabins are large, though none have verandas. **Sample rates per person:** Lowest-price inside cabins $1,532, lowest outside $1,892, lowest suite $2,625.

NORWEGIAN CRUISE LINE

7665 Corporate Center Dr., Miami, FL 33126. (800/327-7030. Fax 305/448-7936. www.ncl.com.

Norwegian Cruise Line (NCL) offers an informal and upbeat onboard atmosphere on both the medium-sized *Norwegian Wind* and the megaship *Norwegian Sky,* sailing from Seattle. The line excels at activities, and its recreational and fitness programs are among the best in the industry. Last year NCL inaugurated a casual-dining policy that allows passengers to dine when they want (within a certain time frame), with whomever they want, dressed however they want.

In Alaska, NCL offers an Alaskan lecturer, wine tastings, art auctions, trap shooting, cooking demonstrations, craft and dance classes, incentive fitness program, and bingo, among other activities. Passengers can choose from a good selection of soft-adventure shore excursions, including hiking, biking, and kayaking. Entertainment is generally strong, and includes Broadway-style musical productions. For kids, there's an activity room, video games, an ice-cream bar, and guaranteed babysitting aboard, plus sessions with park rangers and escorted shore excursions.

TYPICAL PASSENGERS   In Alaska, the demographic tends more toward retirees than on the line's warmer-climate sailings, but you'll find families as well, including grandparents bringing along the grandkids.

SHIPS   The 2,002-passenger *Norwegian Sky* is the newest and biggest ship in the NCL fleet, with an Internet cafe, a huge sun deck (complete with a driver in a golf cart delivering drinks), a basketball court and batting cage, and a wedding chapel (for in-port ceremonies only). In contrast to its large public spaces, standard cabins are small at 154 square feet and have little storage space. The smaller, less fancy, 1,700-passenger *Norwegian Wind* has three main dining rooms, an alternative restaurant, and the typical range of lounges, bars, and entertainment facilities. Closet and drawer space in cabins is quite limited, so pack lightly.

Sample rates per person: Lowest-price inside cabins $1,400, lowest outside $1,899, lowest suite $4,452 for 7-night cruise.

PRINCESS CRUISES

10100 Santa Monica Blvd., Los Angeles, CA 90067. 🕻 **800/LOVE-BOAT** (568-3262) or 310/553-1770. Fax 310/277-6175. www.princess.com.

Consistency is Princess's strength. With new ships joining its fleet like so many cars off a Detroit assembly line, you'd think that maintaining acceptable service standards could be a problem. All things considered, though, Princess accomplishes this rather well. Throughout the fleet, the service in all areas—dining room, lounge, cabin maintenance, and so on—tends to be of consistently high quality.

Princess passengers can expect enough onboard activities to keep them going morning to night, if they've a mind to, and enough nooks and crannies to allow them to do absolutely nothing, if that's their thing. Kids are well taken care of, with especially large children's playrooms. On shore, the line's shore-excursion staffs get big points for efficiency.

TYPICAL PASSENGERS Typical Princess passengers are likely to be between, say, 50 and 65. Recent additional emphasis on its youth and children's facilities has begun to attract a bigger share of the **family market,** resulting in the passenger list becoming more active overall.

SHIPS The 1,950-passenger *Dawn, Sea, Sun,* and *Ocean Princess* are virtually indistinguishable from one another except for cosmetics. Despite their size, you'll probably never feel crowded; there always seems to be lots of space on deck, in the buffet dining areas, and in the lounges. There are beautiful libraries, patisseries for pastries and cappuccino, and pizzerias for good made-to-order Italian fast food. The ships have extensive children's playrooms with ball drop, castles, computer games, puppet theaters, and more. As for cabins, even the smallest is a spacious 175 square feet, and more than 400 have private verandas. The 1,590-passenger *Regal Princess* is warm and inviting inside, and on the outside looks like—what? A spaceship? A *Star Wars* storm trooper's helmet? Spacious, well-furnished cabins are one of the ship's better features (standard dimensions are about 190 sq. ft.), and there are some interesting public rooms, like the huge observation lounge/casino/bar. **Sample rates per person:** Lowest-price inside cabins $1,848, lowest outside $2,030, lowest suite $4,102 for 7-night cruise.

RADISSON SEVEN SEAS CRUISES

600 Corporate Dr., Ste. 410, Fort Lauderdale, FL 33334. 🕻 **800/285-1835.** www.rssc.com.

Radisson offers the best in food, service, and accommodations in an environment that's a little more casual and small-shiplike than Crystal's more determined luxury.

The line assumes for the most part passengers want to entertain themselves on board, so organized activities are limited, but they do include lectures by local experts, well-known authors, and the like, plus facilities for card and board games and the occasional dance lesson. There are three computers in the library to allow guests to send e-mail and use CD-ROMs. Entertainment includes production shows, cabaret acts, and local acts that come on board at ports. The library stocks books and also movies guests can play on their in-cabin VCRs. The line has a no-tipping policy, and offers creative shore excursions.

TYPICAL PASSENGERS Radisson tends to attract high-income, low-key passengers ages 50 and up. The typical passenger is well educated, well traveled, and inquisitive.

SHIPS Cabins on the 490-passenger *Seven Seas Mariner* are all oceanview suites, most with private verandas. The standard suite is a large 301 square feet; some suites can interconnect if you want to book two for additional space. In the public areas, the show lounge is designed to resemble a 1930s nightclub. There are two additional lounges plus a casino and the Connoisseur Club, a cushy venue for predinner drink and after-dinner fine brandy and cigars. The ship's spa offers Judith Jackson European spa treatments using a variety of herbal and water-based therapies. **Sample rates per person:** Lowest-price suite $2,595 for 7-night cruise; no inside or standard outside cabins.

ROYAL CARIBBEAN INTERNATIONAL

1050 Caribbean Way, Miami, FL 33132. ℂ **800/327-6700** or 305/539-6000. www.rccl.com.

Royal Caribbean sells a mass-market style of cruising that's reasonably priced and offered aboard casual, well-run ships with plenty of the standard cruise line fare—craft classes, horse racing, bingo, shuffleboard, deck games, line-dancing lessons, wine-and-cheese tastings, cooking demonstrations, art auctions, and the like—plus elaborate health clubs and spas, covered swimming pools, large open sun deck areas, and innumerable bars, lounges, and other entertainment centers. The Viking Crown Lounge and other glassed-in areas make excellent observation rooms to see the Alaska sights. Royal Caribbean spends big bucks on entertainment, which includes high-tech show productions. Headliners are often featured. Port lectures are offered on topics such as Alaska wildlife, and the line offers some 65 shore excursions. The line's children's activities are some of the most extensive afloat.

TYPICAL PASSENGERS The crowd on Royal Caribbean ships, like the decor, rates pretty high on the whoopee scale, though not quite at the Carnival level. Passengers represent an age mix from 30 to 60, and a good number of families are attracted by the line's well-established and fine-tuned kids' programs.

SHIPS The 2,000-passenger *Rhapsody* and *Vision of the Seas* are almost identical, and offer plenty of nice touches that give them the feel of top-flight shore resorts. You'll find sumptuous, big-windowed health club/spas and loads of fine shopping, dining, and entertainment options. Cabins are not large but do have small sitting areas. All outside cabins on both ships' Bridge and Commodore decks have balconies and can sleep up to four quite comfortably. The 2,100-passenger *Radiance of the Seas* will also be sailing in Alaska in 2001 but had not been launched at press time, so details are not available. **Sample rates per person:** Lowest-price inside cabins $1,579, lowest outside $2,179, lowest suite $3,229 for 7-night cruise.

5

Southeast Alaska

Rich, proud people have lived in Southeast Alaska for thousands of years, fishing its salmon and hunting all through its primeval forests, where the tree trunks grow up to 10 feet thick. In canoes, they explored the hundreds of misty, mossy, enchanted islands where the animals, trees, and even the ice had living spirits. The salmon lived under the sea in human form, becoming fish in the summer to swim in seething masses up the rivers and streams as a gift of food to feed their kin, the people. In return, the people treated the salmon with respect and ceremony, allowing their spirits to return to human form under the sea to live another year. So blessed, the Tlingit and Haida built great, carved houses and poles, fought wars, owned slaves, traded with faraway tribes, and held rich contests of giving called potlatches, where they passed on the stories that still help explain their mysterious world. Even for a modern non-Native walking in the grand quiet of the old-growth rain forest, it's easy to find yourself listening for the spirits of the trees speaking their mysteries.

Discovery subsists on mystery, and Southeast Alaska is still being discovered. A honeycomb of limestone caves under Prince of Wales Island wasn't found until 1987. Explorers continue to map its endless miles of caverns, finding the bones of extinct animals, the artifacts of some of North America's earliest prehistoric people, bear dens, strange eyeless shrimp that live nowhere else, and even underground streams that host spawning salmon. The caves network at every step into

passages that lead straight up or down or off to either side, some only large enough to carry a cool wind. The unfathomable intricacy is exhilarating but also a bit disquieting, like a breath of the supernatural, for it is proof of the unknowable.

Southeast Alaska unfolds like the intricate, hidden world below the tree roots. This land of ice and forest may not look as large on the map as other parts of Alaska, but the better you know it, the bigger it becomes, until you have to surrender to its immensity. You don't need to go underground to experience the sensation—you can feel it by gazing from a boat at the fractal geometry of the endlessly folded, rocky shoreline. The discoveries you make depend only on how closely you look. On a cruise through the Inside Passage, you'll marvel at all the little beaches and rocky outcroppings you pass, hundreds of inviting spots each day you steam through. If you were to stop at random on any one of those uninhabited beaches in a skiff or kayak, you'd find you could spend a day surveying just a few acres of rocks, the overhanging forest, and the tiny pools of water left behind by the tide. And if you gazed down into any one of those pools, you'd find a complex world all its own, where tiny predators and prey live out their own drama of life in the space of a few square feet.

The area stands apart from Alaska, and not only because most of it can't be reached by road. No other part of the state shares the mysterious, spirit-ridden quality of the coastal rain forest. No other area has such mild weather, more akin to the Pacific Northwest than to the heart of Alaska. Certainly no other area in Alaska gets so much rain, nor do many other places on earth. The traditional Native people here differed from other Alaska Natives, too: They were far richer and left behind more physical artifacts. The Tlingit, Haida, and Tsimshian exploited the wealth nature gave them and amplified it by being successful traders with tribes to the south and over the mountains in today's British Columbia and Yukon Territory. In their early contact, the Tlingits even briefly defeated the Russian invaders in the Battle of Sitka, and after white dominance was established, managed to save many of their cultural artifacts and stories.

Along with its other riches and complexities, Southeast Alaska also has many charming small towns and villages that seem to have grown organically from the mountainsides bordering the fjords and channels of the islands. With economies that predate Alaska's oil boom, they developed slowly, their fishermen building houses to hand down to their children. The smaller towns remain completely exempt from the American blight of corporate sameness. Real, old-fashioned main streets are prosperous with family businesses where the proprietors know their customers by first name.

1 Exploring Southeast Alaska

A unique and inviting aspect of traveling in Southeast Alaska is that no roads connect most of the communities. People are forced to get out of their speeding cars and ride on boats, where they can meet their fellow travelers and see what's passing by—slowly. The islands of the region form a protected waterway called the **Inside Passage,** along which almost all of the region's towns are arrayed. Thanks to the **Alaska Marine Highway** ferry system, it's inexpensive to travel the entire passage, hopping from town to town and spending as much time in each place as you like. And if you're short on time, air service is frequent, with jets to the major towns and commuter planes to the villages.

GETTING AROUND BY FERRY: THE ALASKA MARINE HIGHWAY

The state-run **Alaska Marine Highway System,** 6858 Glacier Hwy., Juneau, AK 99801-7909 (© **800/642-0066** or 907/465-3941, TDD 800/764-3779; www.state.ak.us/ferry), is a subsidized fleet of blue-hulled, ocean-going ferries whose mission is to connect the roadless coastal towns of Alaska for roughly the same kind of cost you'd pay if there were roads and you were driving. Call for a free schedule or download it from the website.

PROS & CONS The ferry system's strengths are its low cost, frequent summer sailings, free stopovers, exceptional safety, and the fact that kids love it. In the summer, Forest Service guides offer interpretive talks on board. Its weaknesses are crowding during the July peak season, sometimes many-hour delays, generally lackluster food, and a shortage of cabins, which means that most people camp on deck or in chairs during overnight passages.

ROUTES The system mostly serves Southeast, though it does cover most of coastal Alaska, with one sailing a month connecting Southeast Alaska with the Southcentral region nearer Anchorage, and two smaller ferries there that link communities all the way out the Aleutian Chain (see chapters 7 and 10).

To the south, five large, main-line ferries call on Prince Rupert, British Columbia, and run about 30 hours north to Haines and Skagway. Each of these towns is connected to the rest of the world by roads, but none of the towns in

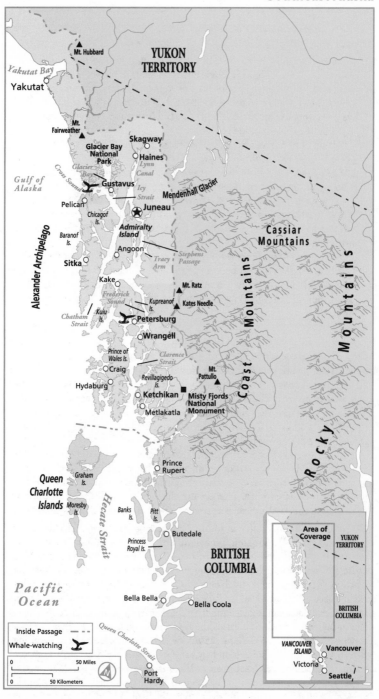

Mt. Hubbard

YUKON TERRITORY

Yakutat Bay

Yakutat

Mt. Fairweather

Gulf of Alaska

Skagway

Glacier Bay National Park

Haines

Glacier Bay

Lynn Canal

Cross Sound

Gustavus

Icy Strait

Mendenhall Glacier

Pelican

Chicagof Is.

Juneau

Baranof Is.

Admiralty Island

Cassiar Mountains

Alexander Archipelago

Angoon

Stephens Passage

Sitka

Tracy Arm

Kake

Frederick Sound

Mt. Ratz

Kupreanof Is.

Kates Needle

Kuiu Is.

Petersburg

Chatham Strait

Wrangell

Prince of Wales Is.

Clarence Strait

Coast Mountains

Craig

Revillagigedo Is.

Mt. Pattullo

Hydaburg

Ketchikan

Misty Fjords National Monument

Metlakatla

Rocky Mountains

Prince Rupert

Queen Charlotte Islands

Graham Is.

Hecate Strait

Moresby Is.

Banks Is.

Pitt Is.

Butedale

Princess Royal Is.

BRITISH COLUMBIA

Pacific Ocean

Bella Bella

Bella Coola

Inside Passage

Whale-watching

Queen Charlotte Strait

0   50 Miles

0   50 Kilometers

Port Hardy

Area of Coverage

YUKON TERRITORY

BRITISH COLUMBIA

VANCOUVER ISLAND

Vancouver

Victoria

Seattle

Tips **Ferry System Booking**

The **Alaska Marine Highway's** statewide toll-free number (© **800/ 642-0066**) can be understaffed, but there are ways around that problem. You can reserve online at **www.dot.state.ak.us/external/amhs/**. Or, if you need to talk to someone, call the staff at the office in Anchorage, where they have less to do, at © **907/272-7116**. That office is staffed for walk-ins, too, in the Alaska Public Lands Information Center, at Fourth and F streets in Anchorage.

In addition, the contractors who operate ferry terminals in Kodiak (© **800-526-6731**; www.akferry.com) and Homer (© **800/382-9229**, or 907/235-8449; www.akmhs.com) maintain toll-free numbers and websites where you can reach an agent quickly, get detailed advice, and reserve for anywhere in the system. **Viking Travel,** in Petersburg (**800/327-2571** or 907/772-3818; www.alaskaferry.com), will hold your early booking until the first day it becomes available on the system, making sure you are the first in line.

You can avoid some crowds on the boats by scheduling around them. Ferries are crowded northbound in June and southbound in August and both ways in July. If you're planning to fly one way and take the ferry the other, go against the flow (southbound in June and northbound in August).

---

between are. In the summer, the large ships stop at least daily (although sometimes in the middle of the night) in Ketchikan, Wrangell, Petersburg, Juneau, Haines, and Skagway. Some make a side trip to Sitka on the way. Juneau is the hub, with many extra sailings north on the Lynn Canal to Haines and Skagway. One ship, the *Columbia,* goes all the way south to Bellingham, Washington; from there, it makes a 37-hour nonstop run to Ketchikan before continuing up through the other towns to Haines.

The two smaller, feeder ferries, the *LeConte* and *Aurora,* connect the larger towns to tiny villages up and down the coast. They mostly take local residents back and forth to their villages, so they're rarely crowded. Those routes are definitely off the beaten track, offering the cheapest and easiest way to the real wilderness of the Alaska Bush. The feeder ferries have restaurants but no cabins.

CONNECTIONS **From the south:** The appeal of taking the ferry to Alaska from Bellingham, Washington, is obvious, but it does not save money over flying and it takes 2 days just to get to Ketchikan. The popular alternative is to board in Prince Rupert, B.C. Getting there by rail is covered under "Getting There & Getting Around" in chapter 2. Or you can drive and leave your vehicle at a secured lot operated by Park Avenue Corner Store, © **888/437-1373,** for $5 a day Canadian for cars, up to $9 for RVs, with monthly discounts; they have a shuttle to the dock. Or ride the **B.C. Ferries** system, 1112 Fort St., Victoria, B.C., Canada V8V 4V2 (© **250/386-3431;** www.bcferries.bc.ca), touring British Columbia's Victoria Island by car. Get to the island by ferry from the south at Nanaimo from Vancouver or Victoria from Port Angeles, Washington (that route is operated by **Black Ball Transport;** © **360/457-4491;** www.northolympic.com/coho), then drive north to Port Hardy and take the B.C. ferry to Prince Rupert, where it docks right next to the Alaska ferry.

From the north: The choices for continuing into Alaska at the end of a ferry ride are limited: rent a car or ride a bus. Bus service connects Skagway to the rest of the state, and rental cars are available in Skagway or Haines. See those sections, below, for details.

By air: By flying to your starting point, you can save time and reduce the chance of having to spend the night sleeping in a chair on board. Long hauls on the ferry can be uncomfortable and don't save much money over flying, but the ferry is much less expensive and more appealing for connecting towns within the Southeast region. Fly into Juneau, Sitka, or another sizable town and plan a ferry trip from there, stopping at various places before returning to catch your plane home.

STOPPING OVER   Buying ahead or booking round-trip tickets saves you nothing on the ferry, and stopovers of any length add little to the cost of your passage. Use the ferry system to explore the towns along the way, grabbing the next ferry through to continue your journey. If you travel without a vehicle, you generally don't need reservations (major exceptions include the Bellingham sailings and passages across the Gulf of Alaska). Bring along a bike, or even a sea kayak, to have total freedom in exploring Southeast. Don't count on port calls to be long enough to see the towns; if the boat is running late, they may not let you off at all.

WALK-ON FARES   The adult walk-on fare from Prince Rupert to Skagway is $143. Bellingham to Ketchikan is $180, Bellingham to Skagway $277. Juneau to Sitka is $29. Fares for children 11 and under are roughly half price, and children 2 and under ride free.

BRINGING VEHICLES   You must reserve a place to take a vehicle on the ferry in the summer, often several months ahead. Fares vary according to the size of the car as well as your destination; a passage from Prince Rupert to Haines for a typical 15-foot car is $298, or $607 from Bellingham. You also have to buy a ticket for each person, including the driver. Renting a car at your destination may save money and the inconvenience and wear-and-tear of bringing your own. You can carry a kayak, canoe, or bike on the ferry (without a car) quite inexpensively.

CABIN RESERVATIONS   Sometimes you can snag a cabin from the standby list (approach the purser quickly upon boarding), but generally you must reserve ahead for the summer season. Cabins on the Bellingham book up many months ahead. An overnight, two-berth outside cabin (one with a window) with a bathroom is around $60 on most sailings, or $134 from Prince Rupert to Haines, $299 from Bellingham to Haines, plus the cost of your ticket. The great majority of the cabins are small and spartan, coming in two- and four-bunk configurations, but for a premium you can reserve a more comfortable sitting-room unit on some vessels. Most cabins have tiny private bathrooms with showers. Try to get an outside cabin so that you can watch the world go by. Cabins can be stuffy, and the windowless units can be claustrophobic as well.

DO YOU NEED A CABIN?   If you do a lot of layovers in Southeast's towns, you can arrange to do most of your ferry travel during the day, but you'll probably have to sleep on board at least once. You can't sleep in your vehicle. One of the adventures of ferry travel is finding a chair to sleep in or setting up a tent on deck with everyone else. The covered outdoor solarium, on the top deck, is the best sleeping spot on board, in part because the noise of the ship covers other sounds. The recliner lounges are comfortable, too, but can be stuffy. If the ship looks crowded, grab your spot fast to get a choice location. **Showers** are available, although there may be lines. Lock the valuables and luggage you don't need in the **coin-operated lockers.** If you're tenting, the best place is behind the solarium, where it's not too windy. On the *Columbia,* that space is small, so grab it early. Bring duct tape to secure your tent to the deck in case you can't find a sheltered spot, as the wind over the deck of a ship in motion blows like an endless gale. If all that sounds too rugged, or if you have small children and no tent, reserve a cabin. It offers a safe and private home base and a good night's rest, and there's a certain romance to having your own compartment on a public conveyance.

FERRY FOOD   If you can, bring your own food on the ferry. Ferry food isn't positively bad, but it's quite inconsistent from one ship to the next. It's often greasy, and you can get awfully tired of it after several meals in a row. Also, during peak season, the food lines are sometimes unreasonably long. We usually bring a cooler or picnic basket. Even if you're traveling light, you can pick up some bagels and deli sandwiches on a stopover or long port call.

THE BEST RUNS   Going to Sitka through **Peril Straits,** the ferry fits through extraordinarily narrow passages where no other vessel of its size ventures; the smooth, reflective water is lovely, and you may see deer along the shore. The **Wrangell Narrows,** between Petersburg and Wrangell, also is an incredible ride, day or night, as the ship accomplishes a slalom between shores that seem so close you could touch them, in water so shallow the schedules must be timed for high tide. **Frederick Sound,** between the Narrows and Wrangell, is prime for whale sightings. Approaching Skagway through the towering mountains of the **Lynn Canal** fjord also is impressive.

GETTING AROUND BY AIR & ROAD

BY AIR   Air travel is the primary link between Southeast's towns and the rest of the world. Major towns without road access have jet service, provided by **Alaska Airlines** (© **800/252-7522;** www.alaskaair.com), the region's only major airline. Juneau is Southeast Alaska's travel hub. Ketchikan and Sitka each have a few flights a day, while Wrangell, Petersburg, and Yakutat each have one flight going each direction daily. Gustavus is served from Juneau once daily during the summer. Some of these "milk runs" never get very far off the ground on hops between small towns: On the 31-mile Wrangell-to-Petersburg flight, the cabin attendants never have time to unbuckle. Haines and Skagway, which have highway connections, don't receive visits from jets, but all the towns and even the tiny villages have scheduled prop service.

Like the ferries, the planes can be quite late. Each of the airports in Southeast has its own challenges caused by the steep, mountainous terrain and the water. In bad weather, even jet flights are delayed or they "overhead"—they can't land at all at the intended destination and leave their passengers somewhere else. Your only protection against these contingencies are travel insurance, a schedule that allows plenty of slack in case you're significantly delayed, and low blood pressure.

BY ROAD   Three Southeast Alaska communities are accessible by road: Haines, Skagway, and the village of Hyder, which lies on the British Columbia border east of Ketchikan and is accessible from the gravel Cassiar Highway through Canada. If you're driving the Alaska Highway, passing through Haines and Skagway adds 250 miles of very scenic driving to the trip. Take the ferry the 15 miles between the two towns (they're separated by 362 road miles). This ferry route is not as heavily booked as the routes heading between either town and Juneau, but it's a good idea to reserve ahead anyway. You also can rent a car from

---

Tips **Southeast From Above**

If you can possibly afford it, you'll want to take a **flightseeing** trip at some point during your trip. The poor man's way of doing this is to fly a small prop plane on a scheduled run between two of your destinations instead of taking the ferry. If you ask, the pilot may even go out of his or her way to show you the sights; even if not, you'll gain an appreciation for the richness and extreme topography of the region. Each operator also offers flightseeing tours, which cost as little as $90 for a brief spin. Flight services are listed in each town section.

Haines or Skagway for travel to the rest of the state at the end of a ferry journey (Haines will save you only 60 miles over Skagway); buses serve Skagway; details are listed in the sections on each of those towns. If you're driving the highway in winter, you should be prepared for weather as cold as 40°F below zero. Alaska winter driving information is under "Health, Safety & Traveler's Insurance," in chapter 2.

Bikes make a lot of sense for getting around Southeast's small towns, which tend to be compact. You can rent one almost anywhere you go, or bring your own on the ferry. The networks of abandoned or little-used logging roads on some islands offer limitless routes for mountain biking. Elsewhere, Forest Service hiking trails are often open for riding.

GETTING OUTSIDE IN THE TONGASS NATIONAL FOREST

Nearly all of Southeast Alaska, stretching 500 miles from Ketchikan to Yakutat, is in Tongass National Forest. The towns sit in small pockets of private land surrounded by 17 million acres of land controlled by the U.S. Forest Service—an area nearly as large as the state of Maine, and considerably larger than any other national forest or any national park in the United States. The majority of this land has never been logged, and the rate of logging has dropped dramatically in recent years, preserving one of the world's great temperate rain forests in its virgin state. It's an intact ecosystem full of wildlife, and mostly free of human development. Indeed, you quickly forget it *is* the Tongass National Forest. Since it always surrounds you when you're in this region, it's simply the land.

FOREST SERVICE CABINS

One of the best ways to get into Southeast's wilderness is by staying at one of the scores of remote Forest Service Public Recreation Cabins. These are simple cabins without electricity or running water where you can lay your sleeping bag on a bunk and sit by a warm woodstove out of the rain. You need to bring everything with you, as if camping, but it's a good deal more comfortable than a tent. And you will probably find yourself in a stunningly beautiful spot, perhaps with your own lake and a boat for fishing. Cabins are along canoe trails, on beaches best reached by sea kayak, on high mountain lakes accessible only by floatplane, and along hiking trails. We do this with our family several times a summer by boat or canoe or on foot. I've learned three important things to pass on: Do your research, pack carefully to keep your load as light as you can, and spend at least 3 nights, preferably a week, to make all the effort pay off with real relaxation.

GETTING CABIN INFORMATION   I've listed a few of the cabins in the text with the towns they're nearest, but for complete information check the

---

Why There Are No Highways

A tectonic plate that underlies the Pacific Ocean brought the islands of the Southeast Alaska Panhandle from across the globe and squished them up against the plate that carries the land mass of Canada. Along the line of this glancing collision, large glacial mountains thrust up, and the islands were stretched and torn into the fractured geography that makes the area so interesting. In short, it's just too expensive to build roads through those icy mountains and across the steep, jumbled terrain of the islands. In 2000, Gov. Tony Knowles shelved a plan to build a road to Juneau, the capital city, because of the cost, electing to add more ferries instead.

Tongass website (**www.fs.fed.us/r10/tongass**) or get copies of the free publications for each of the three major areas in the national forest: the southern area, which includes Ketchikan, Prince of Wales Island, and Misty Fjords National Monument; the Stikine Area, around Petersburg and Wrangell; and the Chatham Area, around Juneau, Sitka, and Admiralty Island. Each cabin is briefly described. You can get the booklets from the visitor centers and ranger offices listed with each town, or write ahead to the **Tongass National Forest,** 648 Mission St., Ketchikan, AK 99901-6591 (✆ **907/228-6202** or TTY 907/228-6222; fax 907/228-6215).

You'll need a good map to figure out where the cabins are, and an idea of how to get there and how much travel will cost—generally, this will be many times the cabin rental of $25 to $45 a night. Few cabins can be reached without a boat or aircraft. A flight service can help you choose according to your interests and how far you can afford to fly. You may be able to rent the gear you need, but you'll have to reserve that ahead, too. The solution to these puzzles is different for each town; I've listed where to find help in the town sections later in this chapter.

RESERVING A CABIN   The cabins are reserved through a national system. Don't rely on the reservations operators or website for advice or cabin information—they're in upstate New York—but pose your questions instead to the ranger station nearest where you plan to go. The rangers are friendly and have probably stayed in the cabin you're interested in. Use the reservations system when you're ready to book; you can check cabin availability dates and reserve on the Internet (**www.reserveusa.com**). Contact the **National Recreation Reservations Service (NRRS),** operated by **Reserve America,** at ✆ **877/444-6777,** 877/833-6777 TDD, or 518/885-3639 with toll from overseas. The phone lines are open summer daily 8am to midnight EST, winter daily 10am to 7pm. They take American Express, Discover, MasterCard, and Visa, or you can reserve on the phone and then pay by certified check. Cabins are available for reservation on a first-come, first-served basis, starting 180 days ahead.

2 Ketchikan: On the Waterfront

Had they known about it, the film noir directors of the 1950s would have chosen the Ketchikan (*ketch*-e-kan) waterfront for Humphrey Bogart to sleuth. One can picture the black-and-white montage: A pelting rain drains from the brim of his hat, suspicious figures dart through saloon doors and into the lobbies of concrete-faced hotels, a forest of workboat masts fades into the midsummer twilight along a shore where the sea and land seem to merge in miles of floating docks. Along Creek Street, salmon on their way to spawn swim under houses

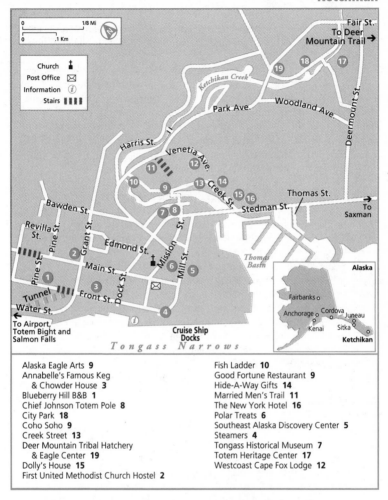

Alaska Eagle Arts **9**
Annabelle's Famous Keg
   & Chowder House **3**
Blueberry Hill B&B **1**
Chief Johnson Totem Pole **8**
City Park **18**
Coho Soho **9**
Creek Street **13**
Deer Mountain Tribal Hatchery
   & Eagle Center **19**
Dolly's House **15**
First United Methodist Church Hostel **2**

Fish Ladder **10**
Good Fortune Restaurant **9**
Hide-A-Way Gifts **14**
Married Men's Trail **11**
The New York Hotel **16**
Polar Treats **6**
Southeast Alaska Discovery Center **5**
Steamers **4**
Tongass Historical Museum **7**
Totem Heritage Center **17**
Westcoast Cape Fox Lodge **12**

chaotically perched on pilings beside a narrow boardwalk; inside, men are spawning, too, in the arms of legal prostitutes. Meanwhile, the faces of totem poles gaze down on the scene disapprovingly, mute holders of their own ancient secrets.

Today, the director hoping to re-create that scene would have his work cut out for him removing the T-shirt shops and bright street-front signs that seek to draw throngs of cruise passengers in to buy plastic gewgaws. Not so long ago, Ketchikan was a rugged and exotic intersection of cultures built on the profits of logging Southeast's rain forest, but in a decade it has transformed itself into a tourist center, softening its rough edges while selling their charm to visitors. And the changes can only accelerate. More and bigger ships are coming, and Southeast Alaska's last major timber mill—the Louisiana Pacific–owned pulp plant in Ward Cove, north of town—closed in 1997 due, in part, to environmental concerns. A major portion of the mill was blown up in 1999; they sold tickets to see who would get to press the button on the explosives, but the occasion was less than festive, as former employees saw the scene of their work lives disappear into dust. A smaller, more labor-intensive operation, intended to replace the jobs by sawing lumber and making veneer, closed down in 2001. In the meantime, the economy has moved on.

On summer days, the white cruise ships tower above the town like huge new buildings on the dock facing Front Street, the downtown's main drag. Each morning their gangways disgorge thousands of visitors, clogging the streets and, for a few hours, transforming the town into a teeming carnival. With only a few hours to spend, the passengers explore the closest of the twisting streets, see the museum at the Southeast Alaska Discovery Center, or take a tour to one of the totem pole parks. Then evening comes, the streets empty, and the cruise ships slide off quietly on the way to their next port.

That is when a sense of the old, misty, mysterious Ketchikan starts to return. Visitors with a little more time to spend, and the willingness to explore beyond the core tourist areas, can drink fully of the history and atmosphere of the place. Stay in a quaint old hotel, hike a boardwalk path through the primeval rain forest, and visit the museums, clan house replicas, and totem pole parks that make Ketchikan a center of Tlingit and Haida culture.

Ketchikan also makes a great jumping-off point for some spectacular outdoor experiences, including a trip to **Misty Fjords National Monument** (see section 3, later in this chapter). As the state's fourth-largest city, Ketchikan is the transportation hub for the southern portion of Southeast Alaska. (The nickname "Gateway City" refers to its geographical location and transportation function.) Seaplanes based on docks along the waterfront are the taxis of the region, and a big inter-agency visitor center can get you started. Ketchikan also is one of the wettest spots on earth, with rain measured in the hundreds of inches; quality rain gear is requisite for any activity, in the wilds or in the streets of town.

ESSENTIALS
GETTING THERE
BY AIR   **Alaska Airlines** (© **800/252-7522** or 907/225-2145; www.alaskaair. com) provides Ketchikan with nonstop jet service from Seattle and with flights to the north stopping in Petersburg, Wrangell, Sitka, Juneau, and Anchorage. Commuter lines run wheeled planes and floatplanes from Ketchikan to the neighboring communities, as well as offer fishing packages and flightseeing.

The airport is on Gravina Island and can be reached only by a ferry that runs each way every half-hour (more frequently at peak times). Believe the airline when it tells you when to catch the ferry for your plane. The fare is $2.50 for adults, $1.50 ages 6 to 11, and free under 6. Returning the same day is free. The fare for cars is $5 each way, no matter how soon you come back. See "Getting Around," below, for how to get from the airport ferry dock to town.

BY FERRY   The dock is 2½ miles north of downtown. **Alaska Marine Highway** ferries (© **800/642-0066;** www.state.ak.us/ferry) run 6 hours north to Wrangell and 6 hours south to Prince Rupert, B.C. The walk-on fare from Prince Rupert is $42, from Wrangell it's $26; children under 12 go half price. Call the local terminal at © **907/225-6182** or 907/225-6181 for a recording of updated arrival and departure times.

ORIENTATION
Ketchikan is on huge **Revillagigedo Island,** popularly known as **Revilla Island.** The downtown area, pretty much taken over by tourism, is quite compact and walkable, but the whole of Ketchikan, including a second commercial area used

by locals, is long, strung out between the Tongass Narrows and the mountains. A waterfront road goes under various names through town (it's Water Street on our map), becoming North Tongass Highway as it stretches about 16 miles to the north. Saxman is 2½ miles to the south of downtown on the 14-mile South Tongass Highway.

GETTING AROUND

You can spend a day seeing the downtown sights on foot, but you will need transportation to get to the totem pole parks or airport.

BY SHUTTLE OR BUS   The **Airporter Shuttle** (© **907/225-5429**) meets each flight and picks up at the major hotels according to a schedule you can get at the front desk. They'll pick up anywhere else by arrangement. The $15 fare downtown is comparable to what you'd pay for a taxi, and includes the airport ferry fare. Since it drives right to the terminal, it's the best way to go if you have a lot of luggage. **The least costly way to the airport or ferry dock is the Ketchikan Gateway Borough bus** (© 907/247-7442), which runs a single route through town every half-hour from 5:15am to 9:45pm Monday to Saturday and once an hour Sunday 8:45am to 3:45pm. The fare is $1.50, and luggage must fit under the seat.

BY TAXI   The local taxis, mostly minivans, are convenient and usually easy to flag down on the single main road through town. Try **Sourdough Cab** (© 907/225-5544) or **Yellow Taxi** (© **907/225-5555**). Taking a cab to the airport terminal is costly because of the ferry to the airport and the time it will run up on the meter. Take the cab just to the airport ferry dock and walk on. If you have a lot of luggage, take the shuttle, which goes to the terminal.

BY RENTAL CAR   **Alaska Car Rental** (© **800/662-0007** or 907/225-5000) has offices at the airport and at Third Avenue and Tongass, or will pick up or deliver the car for free. **Avis** (© **800/230-4898** or 907/225-4515; www. avis.com) has a desk at the airport, too. Rental rates begin at about $50 for an economy car.

BY BIKE   A bike is a good way to get around Ketchikan. A 2½-mile bike trail runs along the water to Saxman, stopping a few blocks short of the totem pole park there, and another goes north 6.4 miles to the Ward Lake Recreation Area. **Southeast Exposure,** 515 Water St. (© **907/225-8829;** www.southeastexposure. com), rents bikes for $12 half day and $22 full day, and offers guided bike outings.

VISITOR INFORMATION

The **Southeast Alaska Discovery Center,** 50 Main St., Ketchikan, AK 99901 (© **907/228-6220** or 907/288-6237 TDD; fax 907/228-6234; www.fs.fed/ r10/tongass, click on "Office Directory"), is much more than a visitor center. Housed in a large, attractive building of log and concrete a block from the cruise-ship dock, the center contains Alaska's best museum on the interaction of the state's natural ecology and human society, including both traditional Native and contemporary uses. Although a bit defensive in spots about logging, exhibits make you feel deep down what's special about these lands. There's also an auditorium showing a high-tech slide show. Admission to those facilities in summer costs $5, free ages six and under, with a $15 family maximum; in winter it's free. Without paying, you can get guidance about planning your time and activities in the outdoors. An information kiosk and bookstore are located near the entrance, and downstairs you'll find a trip-planning room like an explorer's private den, for information about outdoor pursuits all around the state. The center is open May to September daily from 8am to 5pm, October to April Tuesday to Saturday from 10:30am to 4:30pm.

The **Ketchikan Visitors Bureau,** 131 Front St., Ketchikan, AK 99901 (© **800/770-2200** or 907/225-6166; fax 907/225-4250; www.visit-ketchikan. com), stands right on the cruise-ship dock, offering town information and desks where tourism businesses sell their wares, including tickets for tours. The center is open daily in the summer 8am to 5pm and when cruise ships are in town; weekdays only in winter.

SPECIAL EVENTS

There's a detailed **events calendar** at **www.visit-ketchikan.com**.

Celebration of the Sea, a 10-day event beginning around the first of May, includes a variety of art, music, and community events; you can get a schedule from the Ketchikan Visitors Bureau. **King Salmon Derby,** a 50-year-old tradition, takes place at the end of May and the beginning of June.

The Fourth of July celebration is huge, with a long parade on Front Street attended by mobs of locals and cruise-ship passengers. After the parade, there's a **Timber Carnival** with an all-afternoon loggers' competition at the baseball field near City Park on Park Avenue; admission is free.

The crowd-pleasing **Great Alaskan Lumberjack Show** goes on all summer long behind the Alaska Discovery Center (© **888/320-9049;** www.lumberjack sports.com). Canadian and U.S. professional teams compete three or more times daily, mostly to an audience of cruise-ship passengers. Tickets are $29 adults, half price ages 5 to 12.

The Blueberry Arts Festival, held the second Saturday of August, has booths, music, and food, and is put on by the very active Ketchikan Area Arts and Humanities Council, 338 Main St. (© **907/225-2211;** www.ketchikanarts. org). Check with the council for winter performing-arts events, too, including the **Monthly Grind** music and poetry show in the Saxman Tribal House the third Saturday from September to April, and a wearable art show in February.

 ***FAST FACTS:* Ketchikan**

Banks Several banks have ATMs, including the one at 306 Main St., as do grocery stores and the visitor center.

Hospital **General Hospital** is at 3100 Tongass Ave. (© **907/225-5171**).

Internet Access **Cyber-by-the-Sea** (© **907/247-6904;** www.cyberbythesea. com) is at 5 Salmon Landing on the second floor.

Police Call © **907/225-6631** for nonemergencies.

Post Office 3609 Tongass Ave.; a more convenient downtown substation is at the Great Alaska Clothing Company, 422 Mission St.

Taxes **Sales tax** is 5.5%. **Room taxes** for accommodations total 11.5%.

EXPLORING KETCHIKAN

Schoolteacher Lois Munch, of **Classic Tours** (© **907/225-3091;** www.classic tours.com), makes her tours fun: She wears a poodle skirt to drive visitors around in her '55 Chevy. A 2-hour tour to the Saxman totem poles is $50; a

3-hour tour adds a natural history stop and costs $65. Rates are per person and include the admission to Saxman and tax. The maximum group size is five. Check at the town visitor center for many more choices.

TLINGIT, HAIDA & TSIMSHIAN CULTURAL HERITAGE

The Ketchikan area has two totem pole parks and a totem pole museum, as well as a wealth of contemporary Native art displayed all over town. Notable pieces stand at Whale Park at Mission and Bawden streets and at the Westcoast Cape Fox Lodge. Most of what you see in Southeast Alaska is Tlingit—the Haida and Tsimshian generally live to the south and east in British Columbia—but Ketchikan is near the boundary between the three peoples, so their similar cultures mix here.

Totem Heritage Center ★★Located near City Park, the center contains the largest collection of original 19th-century totem poles in existence. The poles, up to 160 years old, are displayed indoors, mostly unpainted, many with the grass and moss still attached from when the poles were rescued from the elements in villages. Totem poles were never meant to be maintained or repainted—they generally disintegrate after about 70 years, and were constantly replaced—but these were preserved to help keep the culture alive. A high ceiling and muted lighting highlight the spirituality of the art. Well-trained guides are on hand to explain what you're looking at, and there are good interpretive signs. The gift shop carries authentic Native crafts in the summer.

601 Deermount St. ✆ **907/225-5900**. Admission $4 in summer, free in winter. Summer daily 8am–5pm; winter Mon–Fri 1–5pm.

Totem Bight State Historical Park ★★★   The park presents poles and a clan house carved beginning in 1938 by elders working with traditional tools to copy fragments of historic poles that had mostly rotted away. The project, funded by the New Deal's Civilian Conservation Corps, helped save a Tlingit and Haida culture that had been essentially outlawed until that time. The setting, the site of a traditional fish camp, is a peaceful spot on the edge of Tongass Narrows, at the end of a short walk through the woods, so the experience is both aesthetic and educational. The park also stands out for its excellent interpretive signs, a printed guide, and interpretive website. There's a small park bookstore.

10 miles out of town on N. Tongass Hwy. Ketchikan Area State Park Office, 9883 N. Tongass Hwy. ✆ **907/247-8574**. www.dnr.state.ak.us/parks/units/totembgh.htm.

Saxman Native Village Totem Pole Park ★   Saxman's park has artifacts similar to those at Totem Bight park, but with an added resource: You can see carvers work in the building to the right of the park. You can visit the studio and the poles without joining a tour, but there are no interpretive materials. To get inside the clan house and find out what it's all about, you need to join a tour. Cape Fox Corp., the owner of the park, caters mainly to cruise-ship passengers with its 2-hour tour, which includes a short performance of a Tlingit legend and a demonstration of traditional dance and song by the Cape Fox Dancers. The tour schedule is different each day, depending on the ships. The site is more like a city park than the lovely setting at Totem Bight.

In Saxman, 2½ miles south of Ketchikan on the S. Tongass Hwy. ✆ **907/225-4421** for tour times and tickets. Tour $30 adults, $15 children 12 and under; unguided visits free.

DOWNTOWN ATTRACTIONS

Ketchikan's best downtown attractions are all within walking distance of one another. See Creek Steet, then walk up Park Avenue past the Ketchikan Creek

---

Tips   **Avoiding the Crowds**

Ketchikan is overrun with as many as 8,000 cruise-ship passengers every day from May through September, far more than the small visitor attractions or even the streets can comfortably handle. Independent travelers can avoid the crush by planning to visit popular spots in the afternoon. Spend the morning instead on an outdoors activity. At the Deer Mountain Tribal Hatchery and Eagle Center, the buses all come through before noon. At Totem Bight State Park, the trails quiet down by midafternoon. Ships usually leave entirely in early evening.

---

fish ladder and up to lovely **City Park,** site of the Totem Heritage Center, described above. The park is among my favorite places in Ketchikan. The creek splits into a maze of ornamental pools and streams once used as a hatchery, with footbridges, a fountain, and large trees with creeping roots.

Creek Street ✪   The boardwalk starts at the Stedman Street bridge, running over the tidal creek. It was Ketchikan's red-light district until fairly recently; now it's a quaint tourist mall. Prostitution was semi-legal in Alaska until 1952, recently enough to survive in local memories but distant enough to have made Creek Street historic and to transform the women who worked there from outcasts to icons. Dolly Arthur, who started in business for herself on the creek in 1919 and died in 1975, lived through both eras, and her home became a commercial museum not long after her death. **Dolly's House** (✆ **907/225-6329**) is amusing, mildly racy, and a little sad. Admission is $4; it's open 8am to 4pm during the summer and when cruise ships are in town. Creek Street has some interesting shops, described below, but it's also fun just to walk on the creekside boardwalk, into the forest above, and over the "Married Men's Trail"—a discreet way for married men to reach the red-light district. **The Cape Fox Hill–Creek Street Funicular** (known as "the tram"), a sort of diagonal elevator, also runs 211 feet from the boardwalk up to the Westcoast Cape Fox Lodge on top of the hill. Take it up and then enjoy the walk down through the woods. The summertime fare is $1, but if no one is around, just press the "up" button and go.

Tongass Historical Museum   This one-room museum is where Ketchikan talks back to itself, with well-executed revolving exhibits that have always held my interest. A small permanent area shows Native artifacts. In the same building the attractive Ketchikan Public Library is a great place to recharge, especially the children's section downstairs, where big windows look out on Ketchikan Creek's falls.

629 Dock St. ✆ **907/225-5600.** Summer daily 8am–5pm; winter Wed–Sat afternoons. Admission is $2 summer, free winter.

Deer Mountain Tribal Hatchery and Eagle Center ✪✪✪   This remarkable nonprofit center combines one of Alaska's best hatchery tours with its very best place to see a bald eagle close up. The wooden buildings stand right over Ketchikan Creek. The eagles hunt salmon swimming naturally right through their enclosure. You can see other fish climbing the current up into pools where they are sorted before being cut open to complete their biological purpose (salmon die when they spawn anyway). The hatchery tours are special for letting you get so close, right in the action, where you can feed the fry yourself. They produce king and silver salmon and steelhead trout. Visitors walk right through the eagle enclosure. Remarkably, the resident pair of injured, flightless bald eagles have mated for life and built a nest, and lay eggs each year. There's no glass between you and this activity.

1158 Salmon Rd. ℂ **800/252-5158** or 907/225-6760. Summer daily 8:30am–4:30pm, winter by arrangement. Admission $6.95.

SHOPPING

The Ketchikan art scene is one of Alaska's liveliest, thanks in part to the Ketchikan Arts and Humanities Council, whose helpful staff operates the **Main Street Gallery,** at 338 Main St. (www.ketchikanarts.org). Shows change monthly.

Note: Ketchikan is a shopping and art destination, but if you want something authentically Alaskan you have to be careful. For some important tips, see "Native Art: Finding the Real Thing," in chapter 2.

Ray Troll is Alaska's leading fish-obsessed artist. His gallery, **Soho Coho,** at 5 Creek St., is worth a visit even if you aren't a shopper. It shows Troll's own work and that of other Ketchikan artists from the same school of surreal rain-forest humor. In Troll's art, subtle ironies and silly puns coexist in a solidly decorated interior world. T-shirts are his most popular canvas; "Spawn Till You Die" is a classic. Troll's incredible art website trips far into his strange mind (and sells shirts), at www.trollart.com. The gallery is open summer daily from 9am to 6pm; winter, Wednesday to Saturday noon to 5:30pm; or order at ℂ **800/ 888-4070.**

Adjacent to Soho Coho, **Alaska Eagle Arts** is a serious gallery featuring the bold yet traditional work of Native artist Marvin Oliver. Upstairs, don't miss **Parnassus Books,** a wonderfully cluttered browsing nirvana with broad, sophisticated collections of Alaskana, art, and women's art, among other strong subject areas. Down the boardwalk at 18 Creek St., craftspeople carve and interact with visitors at **Hide-A-Way Gifts.**

At 123 Stedman St., across the creek, **Blue Heron Gallery and Gifts** carries Alaska arts and crafts that appeal to locals as well as visitors: jewelry, stained glass, clothing, jam, prints, and so on. Just to the south, at 229 Stedman, **Herring Cove Originals** is Sharon Huffman's studio and gallery of sharp, vivid prints made with fish, plants, and other things from nature; pieces cover a broad price range. Also nearby, at 633 Mission St., **Exploration Gallery** uniquely specializes in antique maps and prints, and also carries contemporary prints, pottery, and Native art, with more thoughtful selections than the sameness found in most other shops. Farther down the same street, **Scanlon Gallery,** at 318 Mission St., carries a huge selection of contemporary art, Alaska Native art, and affordable prints and other items in various media.

You'll also find local beer and chocolate on Mission: **Ketchikan Brewing Company,** at 607 Mission, and **KetchiCandies,** at 315 Mission.

GETTING OUTSIDE

There's lots to do outdoors around Ketchikan, but most of it will require a boat or plane; drive-by attractions are limited. See the sections on Misty Fjords National Monument and Prince of Wales Island (both later in this chapter) for more options. In any event, your first stop should be the trip-planning room at the Southeast Alaska Discovery Center (see "Visitor Information," near the beginning of the Ketchikan section), for details on trails, fishing, and dozens of U.S. Forest Service cabins.

SPECIAL PLACES

REMOTE CABINS The U.S. Forest Service maintains more than 50 **cabins** around Ketchikan; all are remote and primitive, but at $25 to $45 a night, you can't beat the price or the settings. This is a chance to be utterly alone in the wilderness; many of the lake cabins come with a boat for fishing and exploring. For details and descriptions of all the cabins, contact the **Southeast Alaska Discovery Center** (© **907/228-6220;** www.fs.fed.us/r10/tongass). The reservations system to use when you're actually ready to book a cabin is described in "Getting Outside in the Tongass National Forest," in section 1 of this chapter.

You'll need all your camping gear except a tent, including sleeping bags, a camp stove, your own cooking outfit, a lantern, and so on. **Alaska Wilderness Outfitting and Camping Rentals,** 3857 Fairview St. (© **907/225-7335;** www.latitude56.com/camping/index.html), rents most of the gear you need, including small outboards for the skiffs, and will even take care of your grocery shopping. They don't rent sleeping bags, however. (The same folks have a water taxi, kayak delivery, and charter service called **Experience One Charters,** listed later in the Misty Fjords section of this chapter.)

The cabins are remote. You can hike or take a boat to some of them, but most are accessible only by floatplane (unless you have loads of stuff, flying is probably the cheapest way to go). Expect to pay $225 to $400 per person round-trip. For a recommended carrier, see "The Coolest Flights," later, in the section on Misty Fjords National Monument.

SCENIC TRAILS The wide, gravel **Ward Lake Nature Trail** circles 1.3 miles around a smooth lake among old-growth Sitka spruce large enough to put you in your place. Ward Creek has steelhead and cutthroat trout, Dolly Varden char, and silver salmon; check current regulations before fishing. To reach the trail, campgrounds, and picnic area, travel about 8 miles out North Tongass Highway and turn right on Revilla Road. For a slightly more challenging hike, **Perseverance Lake Trail** climbs up boardwalks with steps from the Three Cs Campground, across the road from Ward Lake, to a lake 2.3 miles away, with good berry picking on the way.

Deer Mountain Trail, right behind downtown, is a steep but rewarding climb through big, mossy trees up to great views. You can walk from City Park to the trailhead, half a mile and 500 feet higher on steep Fair Street and Ketchikan Lakes Road, but if you take a cab you will save energy for the trail. The first mile rises 1,000 feet to a great ocean view south of Tongass Narrows, and the next mile and 1,000 feet to another great view, this time of Ketchikan. The alpine summit, at 3,001 feet, comes near the 3-mile mark. The Deer Mountain Forest Service cabin is a bit farther, and the trail continues to another trailhead 10 miles away. Pick up a trail guide sheet from the Forest Service at the Southeast Alaska Discovery Center.

OUTDOOR ACTIVITIES

FISHING The **Alaska Department of Fish and Game,** 1255 W. Eighth St. (P.O. Box 25526), Juneau, AK 99802-5526 (© **907/465-4180;** www.state.ak. us/adfg), produces a 24-page fishing guide to Ketchikan, with details on where to find fish in both fresh and salt water, listing 17 spots accessible from the roads. You can also pick up a copy at the Southeast Alaska Discovery Center. For licenses and other help, the local **Fish and Game office** is at 2030 Sea Level Dr., Suite 205, Ketchikan, AK 99901 (© **907/225-2859**).

Guided fishing charters can get out on the water for salmon and halibut, and bareboat rental also is available. The Ketchikan Visitors Bureau can put you in contact with an operator. A day-long guided charter costs around $200 per person, half-day about $130. If you want to devote your time in Ketchikan to fishing, check out the fishing lodges listed below.

SEA KAYAKING   The islands, coves, and channels around Ketchikan create protected waters rich with life and welcoming for exploration by kayak. Any reasonably fit adult can enjoy a kayak outing. **Southeast Exposure,** 515 Water St. (✆ **907/225-8829;** www.southeastexposure.com), rents kayaks and guides day trips and overnights. Day trips are $50 to $110; a 4-day Misty Fjords National Monument paddle is $708 per person.

ACCOMMODATIONS

In addition to the hotels and B&Bs listed below, the **Ketchikan Reservation Service,** 412 D–1 Loop Rd., Ketchikan, AK 99901 (✆ **800/987-5337** or phone/fax 907/247-5337; www.ketchikan-lodging.com), books many bed-and-breakfasts and outfitted apartments online.

EXPENSIVE

Best Western Landing ✪   This is a regularly remodeled establishment with a variety of good, unremarkable rooms on long hallways. The newer rooms are large, with two queen beds, good-size bathrooms, tables, and microwave ovens; the older wing has slightly smaller rooms with one queen and are $30 less. All are well kept, but none are a bargain, by my reckoning. The location, right across from the ferry dock, is distant from the downtown sights, so you'll need to rent a car or use the courtesy van.

The **Landing Restaurant,** a fountain and grill with lots of chrome, is a local favorite. Lunch is $5.75 to $10; a burger is $7.25. Dinner is $11 to $26, with a steak and seafood menu that's a bit pretentious for the setting. I prefer to eat dinner upstairs, at **Jeremiah's** bar, which serves sandwiches, pizza, and quite good pasta in a sumptuous room; the nonsmoking area is glassed off and not smoky.

3434 Tongass Ave., Ketchikan, AK 99901. ✆ **800/428-8304** or 907/225-5166. Fax 907/225-6900. www. landinghotel.com. 75 units. High season $140–$170 double; $175–$230 suite. Low season $100–$120 double; $130 suite. AE, DC, DISC, MC, V. **Amenities:** 2 restaurants (grill, Italian); 1 bar; exercise room; room service (6am–10pm); same-day laundry and dry cleaning. *In room:* TV, dataport, unstocked refrigerator, coffeemaker, hair dryer, iron.

Edgewater Bed and Breakfast ✪   Situated on the coastal bike trail about 1½ miles south of town over the water, this place is a great choice for long stays or if you want to cook for yourself. The rooms are large and light, if sparsely decorated, with big bathrooms and access to a large kitchen stocked with food. All but one has a private entry from the wraparound deck. An upstairs suite is enormous, perfect for a family or group—the host doesn't charge extra for more people. Best of all, the ocean is at your doorstep. You can fish right from the property, and on my brief inspection I saw a sea otter and a nesting bald eagle. You can bike here, but you'll probably want a car.

2070 S. Tongass Hwy. (P.O. Box 9302), Ketchikan, AK 99901. ✆ **907/247-3343.** Fax 907/247-3343. www.edgewaterbb.com. 4 units. Summer $125–$150, winter $100; rates for rm without regard to number of guests. Rates include continental breakfast. MC, V. **Amenities:** Free laundry machines. *In room:* TV, phone.

The Narrows Inn ✪   The motel buildings sit above the water, where fishing charters and floatplanes collect guests for outings. The rooms, done up in an outdoors theme, are fresh and nicely decorated, with wallpaper borders, but they're small for the price—the TV is mounted on the wall. Bathrooms are large. Rooms with balconies rent for $10 more. The location, 4 miles from town, requires that you have a car.

4871 N. Tongass Hwy. (P.O. Box 8296), Ketchikan, AK 99901. ✆ **888/686-2600** or 907/247-2600. Fax 907/247-2602. www.narrowsinn.com. 46 units. High season $135–$155 double. Low season $84–$90 double. Extra person $10. AE, DC, DISC, MC, V. **Amenities:** Restaurant (steak and seafood); bar; marina. *In room:* TV, dataport, coffeemaker, hair dryer.

Salmon Falls Resort ★★   If fishing is your goal, a stay at this huge on-island lodge has several advantages. First, there's the incredible setting, on island-dotted Clover Pass next to a waterfall where 10,000 pink salmon spawn. Next is the cost savings of a road-accessible lodge, since you don't have to fly out. Finally, you're not trapped in the middle of nowhere if one of you doesn't want to fish—the attractions of Ketchikan are a 17-mile drive down the road. The facilities are quite good: large, up-to-date white-walled motel rooms, but without TVs or phones and with small bathrooms. Those in the upper building are slightly preferable and cost the same. The restaurant and bar are in a massive log octagon held up in the center by a section of the Alaska pipeline, with great views and a well-prepared menu of steak and seafood ranging from $18 to $29. It's worth a drive out the road for dinner, even if you aren't staying here. Some 40 lodge-operated boats tie at the dock. Inclusive fishing packages start at $900 per person, double occupancy, for a 3-day stay with 2 days on the water, self-guided. With a guide, the price is $1,300 per person. Without fishing, room and board is $600.

16707 N. Tongass Hwy. (P.O. Box 5700), Ketchikan, AK 99901. ✆ **800/247-9059** (reservations) or 907/225-2752. Fax 907/225-2710. www.salmonfallsresort.net. 52 units. MC, V. Closed Sept 15–May 15. **Amenities:** Restaurant; bar; inclusive guided fishing.

Westcoast Cape Fox Lodge ★★★   This is Alaska's most beautiful hotel. It stands on a wooded pinnacle above downtown, reached from Creek Street by a funicular; the sheer drop-off and tall rain-forest trees give the rooms and restaurant a treehouse feel. The perfectly proportioned buildings are done in extraordinary taste, complementing the stunning views from double-hung windows framed in warm wood. The hotel was built by the Cape Fox Native corporation, and the lobby and parking area are a museum of Tlingit art masterpieces, adding to the sense of the peace and rain-forest spirit. All but a dozen rooms share the view (rooms on the opposite side are $10 less). They're large and airy, appointed in rich-toned wood, with attractively tiled bathrooms.

The **Heen Kahidi** restaurant ★★ is the best in town. The dining room, a tall, narrow rectangle of windows with a fireplace, is a beautiful, calming place to eat. The service is highly professional, and the cuisine, emphasizing local seafood with rich sauces, is plentiful and skillfully turned out. Lunch ranges from $7 to $20, dinner main courses from $17 to $37, with most around $25. It is open 7am to 9pm daily.

800 Venetia Way, Ketchikan, AK 99901. ✆ **866/225-8001** or 907/225-8001. Fax 907/225-8286. www.westcoasthotels.com. 72 units. High season $159–$169 double. Low season $129–$139 double. Year-round $200 suite. AE, DC, DISC, MC, V. **Amenities:** Restaurant; bar; room service (7am–9pm); coin-op laundry; dry cleaning. *In room:* TV, dataport, coffeemaker, hair dryer, iron.

MODERATE

Blueberry Hill B&B ★★ *Finds*   This gracious 1917 house, once a residence for nuns, stands atop the rocky cliff that bounds the north side of the downtown waterfront, above the tunnel. The center of the action is a short drive or 117 steps away on a public stairway, but up here all is peaceful in common rooms with high ceilings and stately dimensions and trim. Talented, solicitous Vicki Zahler presides, bringing her background in Oregon as an interior decorator and caterer to her role as innkeeper. Her experience shows in the antiques, art, and comfortable, just right country decor, and the candles and soft New Age music in the living room. Each of the guest rooms is large and light, with its own bathroom and phone. Smoking is not allowed in the house.

500 Upper Front St. (P.O. Box 9508), Ketchikan, AK 99901. ✆ **877/449-2583** or 907/247-2583. Fax 907/ 247-2584. www.blueberryhillbb.com. 4 units. High season $90–$105 double; $135 suite. Low season $60–$95. Extra person $25. Rates include breakfast. DC, DISC, MC, V. *In room :* Queen-size beds with down comforters.

INEXPENSIVE

Captain's Quarters Bed & Breakfast ★★ *Value*   These rooms, large, quiet, and immaculate, with sweeping views of the city and ocean, and a self-contained, self-service breakfast room, rival the best hotel rooms in Ketchikan, but cost half as much. A nautical theme carries through with oak woodwork. One room has a full kitchen. The setup allows as much privacy as you want—socialize with hostess Toni Bass, a gregarious school secretary, or come and go without seeing anyone. The house is perched in a mountainside neighborhood just north of the tunnel where half the streets are stairs. It's a reasonable walk from downtown. There's no smoking in the house.

325 Lund St., Ketchikan, AK 99901. ✆ **907/225-4912.** www.ptialaska.net/~captbnb. 3 units. High season $85 double. Low season $69 double. Extra person $20. Rates include continental breakfast. MC, V. *In room:* TV, telephones with private lines, hair dryer.

New York Hotel ★★ *Value*   This funny little 1924 building, in a perfect central location just off Creek Street, contains charming, antique-furnished rooms that look out on a small boat harbor. They are an almost unreal value, far more attractive than those of other hotels in town that cost much more, and come with a continental breakfast and a courtesy van to the airport and hiking trails. Energetic new owners are keeping it sparkling clean, adding new carpets and quality linens and making improvements to the building, which is on the National Register of Historic Places, consistent with its quirks and charms. The lobby is tiny and rooms are not large. Steep, narrow stairs may be a barrier to some.

The same new owners have made the attached **New York Café** into an evening scene, with music, poetry, and even yoga and quilting meetings. They serve healthy and hearty breakfasts and lunches as well as espresso, quiche, salads, sandwiches, and pastries baked in-house. Everything is under $10. They're open at least 6am to 10pm, sometimes earlier or later. The dining room restores an old-fashioned lunch counter and has tables as well. Light floods in from high windows on a black, white, and red tiled floor. It's smoke free.

207 Stedman St., Ketchikan, AK 99901. ✆ **866/225-0246** or 907/225-0246. Fax 907/225-1803. wwwthe newyorkhotel.com. 8 units. High season $79–$89 double. Low season $49–$59 double. Rates include continental breakfast. AE, DISC, MC, V. **Amenities:** Restaurant (coffeehouse); courtesy van. *In room:* TV, dataport.

A Hostel

First United Methodist Church   This church hostel is right in the downtown area. Dorms are male and female, and guests have use of the church kitchen. Bring a sleeping bag. It is open only June through August, office hours 7 to 9am and 6 to 11pm.

400 Main St. (P.O. Box 8515), Ketchikan, AK 99901. ✆ **907/225-3319.** www.hosteltravelers.com. 23 beds. $10 per person AYH/HI member, $13 nonmembers. Closed Sept–May.

CAMPING

Three Forest Service campgrounds with a total of 47 sites are located at **Ward Lake** (see "Special Places," above). A salmon stream runs through the middle of the lakeside Signal Creek Campground, which, along with the Last Chance Campground, can be reserved through the national system described in "Getting Outside in the Tongass National Forest," in section 1 of this chapter.

Eighteen miles out North Tongass Highway, the **Settler's Cove State Park** includes a sandy beach (a good place to watch whales, beachcomb, or even swim); the 1-mile Lunch Falls Loop Trail, a handicapped-accessible path to a spectacular waterfall; and a short coastal trail. There are 14 campsites, half of which will take rigs of up to 30 feet, without hookups. Camping costs $10 a night. For information, contact the **Alaska Division of Parks** (© **907/ 247-8574**), 9883 N. Tongass Hwy.

If you need hookups for an RV, try **Clover Pass Resort,** about 13 miles north of the ferry terminal on North Point Higgins Road (© **800/410-2234** or 907/247-2234). They charge $26 a night.

DINING

The best restaurant in town is in the Westcoast Cape Fox Lodge. See the Salmon Falls Resort, Best Western Landing, and New York Hotel listings for other good choices. A popular espresso place is **The Edge,** at 5 Salmon Landing Market, in an airy water-view corner space (© **907/225-1465**).

Annabelle's Famous Keg and Chowder House ✩ STEAK AND SEAFOOD The dining room is formal, with high-backed armchairs at well-spaced tables, dark wood, and floral patterns, all done in a heavy late-19th-century theme. The straightforward dinner menu includes steak and seafood, plus a few more-ambitious selections, one of which I ordered on my last visit: a stuffed halibut special that was nicely seasoned but overdone, with excellent vegetables and rice pilaf. A more limited selection, including the tasty chowder, is served in the spacious bar.

326 Front St. © **907/225-9423.** Lunch $7.25–$14; dinner $19–$37. AE, DC, DISC, MC, V. Sun–Thurs 7am–9:30pm, Fri–Sat 7am–10:30pm.

Good Fortune Chinese Restaurant CHINESE   The restaurant stands on pilings in Creek Street, with small upstairs and downstairs dining rooms. The food is consistently good year after year, with a long and varied menu that allows you to choose by style of cuisine—Cantonese, Szechuan, and so on.

4 Creek St. © **907/225-1818.** Lunch $6.50; dinner $7–$20. MC, V. Mon–Sat 11am–9pm, Sun noon–9pm.

Ocean View Restaurante ✩✩ (Finds) MEXICAN/ITALIAN   When you find food as good as this at an apparently typical family restaurant, you want to stop people in the street to tell them about it. But everyone in Ketchikan already knows, one reason the place is so lively and festive even on an off-season week-night. Few tourists know about it or make the drive a mile from downtown. The menu is long and all reasonably priced, with separate columns of Mexican and Italian cuisine (and an occasional Greek item slipped in the Italian column), a page of seafood and sautéed entrees, plus chicken, veal, steak, pasta, and pizza. Variety is a common technique used by small-town restaurants to make it through the winter; the difference here is remarkably good cooking. Service is friendly and efficient, and a meal need not take long. Alcohol is not served, and smoking is not allowed. The pizza, delivered free, is the best in town.

1831 Tongass Ave. © **907/225-7566.** Reservations recommended. Lunch $6.50–$9; dinner $6–$16. MC, V. Daily 11am–11pm.

Polar Treats DELI/WRAPS   The chairs are plastic and the tableware dispos-able, but if you're looking for a quick, inexpensive, and delicious lunch break while sightseeing, you'll do no better. The wraps are huge, messy, and flavorful, and the panini and other sandwiches are good, too. Stop in for the hand-packed ice cream. Seating is minimal, so much of the business is take-out or delivered.

410 Mission St. © **907/247-6527.** Lunch $5.75–$6.75. MC, V. High season daily 9am–7pm. Low season Mon–Sat 11am–4pm.

Steamers ⚐ STEAK/SEAFOOD   On the third floor right on the dock (take the corner elevator to the top), this bar and grill has a high ceiling and lots of light wood, good service, and widely separated tables, giving it a clean, relaxed feel. Some 20 beers are on tap, and there is live jazz Wednesday through Saturday nights. Each meal we've had here has been done just right—fish grilled not a moment too long, lightly seasoned seafood stir-fry, and very spicy blackened prime rib. Dinner prices make this a place for a special meal, as a fish-and-chips dinner is $17 and you can easily spend more than $50 per person; lunches are around $10.

76 Front St. © **907/225-1600.** Complete lunch $10; complete dinner $17–$50. AE, DC, DISC, MC, V. Daily 11am–11pm.

3 Misty Fjords National Monument

Among the vast, uninhabited islands, bottomless bays and fjords, massive trees, and inconceivably towering cliffs of the southern Alaska Panhandle are 2.3 million acres of inviolate wilderness, which Jimmy Carter set aside as a national monument with a stroke of his presidential pen in 1978. There are sheer cliffs as high as Yosemite Valley's that rise straight from remote Punchbowl Cove, where only passengers of boats, kayaks, or floatplanes can see them. There's no question that this land, larger than Yellowstone National Park, qualifies scenically as among America's greatest wild places, but without roads or trails, it's more like a great national park a century ago than the busy places we know now. Here, a seemingly endless untouched wilderness forces you to admit that your own imagination is sadly puny by comparison.

There's no cheap way to see the bulk of the monument; the only practical way to get there is by boat or floatplane. The only places to stay are 14 primitive U.S. Forest Service cabins. The most popular way to see the monument is on a tour boat from Ketchikan. The monument is also a good place for sea kayaking—that's how the backcountry Forest Service rangers get around.

There are several noteworthy things to see. **New Eddystone Rock,** standing in the middle of Behm Canal, is a 237-foot-tall exclamation point of weathered rock, the remaining lava plug from an eroded volcano. **Rudyerd Bay** is like a place where the earth shattered open: The cliffs in its Punchbowl Cove rise vertically 3,150 feet from the surface of water that's 900 feet deep—topography in a league with the Grand Canyon. Waterfalls pound down out of the bay's granite. These are the places boat tours go. A floatplane can also show you the high lakes and high country ice. But the vast majority of the monument receives no visitors at all. Don't go to Misty Fjords to see animals. You may see harbor seals, but here the attraction is the land itself and its outrageous geology. Also, the name is accurate: It's misty. Or it could be pouring rain. This is among the rainiest spots on earth, and if the weather is very bad, what you see will be limited.

ESSENTIALS
GETTING THERE
BY BOAT   The most affordable way to see the fjords is to go on one of the tour-boat excursions offered by Ketchikan operators. The largest and most

experienced of these is **Alaska Cruises,** owned by Juneau's Goldbelt Native corporation, 220 Front St., Ketchikan (© **800/228-1905** or 907/225-6044; www.goldbelttours.com). They run a high-speed, 92-passenger catamaran on daily day-long trips out to Rudyerd Bay and back. The tour travels up the Behm Canal, passes New Eddystone Rock, then drifts through Punchbowl Cove before finally coming to a floating dock at the head of Rudyerd Bay, where passengers from cruise ships board floatplanes. The fare is $145. They serve a continental breakfast on the outbound trip, snacks and chowder on the way back. If you're susceptible to seasickness, consider seeing the fjords by air, instead; the water is smooth in the fjords but can be rough on the way there. (Take Dramamine *before* you set out; once you're underway, it's generally too late.)

If you have a larger group, consider a private charter, of which many are available in Ketchikan. **Experience One Charters,** 3857 Fairview, Ketchikan (© **907/225-7335;** www.latitude56.com), takes groups of up to 16 to Misty Fjords on an itinerary and at a pace you control; they'll supply the kayaks, too, for a paddle once you get there. It's expensive without a large group, however, because you must pay for a minimum of eight passengers at $225 each for an all-day trip. They also specialize in outfitting visits to Forest Service cabins.

BY PLANE Flying over Misty Fjords and landing in a floatplane is mind-blowing. The landing is crucial. As you're flying, you see this breathtaking terrain unfold below; when you stand on the ground, you get your first sense of scale, and everything you've seen is suddenly magnified (at the same time you have shrunk). Go in the late afternoon when the light is pretty and the swarms of planes carrying cruise-ship passengers are gone. Several air-taxi operators in Ketchikan take flightseeing day trips or drop clients at remote cabins. The largest is **Promech Air** (© **800/860-3845** or 907/225-3845), which charges $180 for a 50-minute flight, with 10 minutes on the ground. My favorite is under "The Coolest Flights," below.

BY KAYAK There are few more spectacular places for overnight kayak expeditions. If you have only a few days, concentrate on Rudyerd Bay. Don't miss Punchbowl Cove or the waterfall trail to Punchbowl Lake, where there is a shelter and good camping, or a trail and shelter at Nooya Lake. Both lakes have public rowing skiffs.

Southeast Exposure, 507 Stedman St., Ketchikan (© **907/225-8829;** www.southeastexposure.com), offers guided trips to the monument, starting at 4 days for $708 per person. They also rent kayaks for $30 to $50 a day; a 90-minute training class is mandatory.

I don't recommend an unguided trip deep into the fjords for first-time kayakers, but I can't imagine a more appealing destination for experienced paddlers. **Alaska Cruises** (see "By Boat," above) drops off or picks up kayakers at Rudyerd Bay for $200 per person. Larger groups can charter a boat, gaining the advantage of a choice of drop-off points. **Experience One Charters** (see "By Boat," above) offers that service and rents camping equipment.

VISITOR INFORMATION

The **Southeast Alaska Discovery Center,** 50 Main St., Ketchikan, AK 99901 (© **907/228-6220;** www.fs.fed.us/r10/tongass), can give you a trip-planning packet about Misty Fjords. Get the names of charter operators from the **Ketchikan Visitors Bureau,** 131 Front St., Ketchikan, AK 99901 (© **800/ 770-2200** or 907/225-6166; fax 907/225-4250; www.visit-ketchikan.com).

Moments The Coolest Flights

You can fly to Misty Fjords for an hour, listening to tape-recorded commentary on headphones with a pilot hired for the summer by the flight service, or you can go for twice as long and have more fun with Michelle Madsen and Jeff Carlin, a cool flying couple who, when they go out together, have to argue about whose plane to take. Michelle flies her Cessna 185 with her long blond hair flowing and her little white dog Perro at her side (although she'll gladly leave him behind), letting passengers pick out a CD for the stereo as background to her impromptu commentary about the fjords. We soared with Van Morrison while she told us about her favorite places down below, then landed for as long as anyone wanted to soak in the awesome surroundings. It felt like an outing with old friends. The business is called **Island Wings Air Service,** 1935 Tongass Ave., Ketchikan (© **888/ 854-2444** or 907/225-2444; www.islandwings.com). They charge $159 to $179 per person for a 2-hour flight that includes 45 minutes on the ground at the fjords. Michelle and Jeff also help plan cabin trips; they know these places intimately, and will take the time to help you choose a Forest Service cabin that suits your interests and budget. They've devised flat round-trip fares ($225 to $400 per person) to each of the cabins; check the list on their informative website, which makes planning far easier than trying to figure hourly charter times.

ACCOMMODATIONS

The only lodgings are 14 **U.S. Forest Service cabins** and several three-sided shelters. Many are little used and extremely remote, and all those on lakes come with their own rowboats. The cabins cost $25 to $45 per night, but that's only a small part of the cost of using them. You also have to pay for a floatplane (about $300 to $450 an hour) to take you there and back. See "By Air," and "The Coolest Flights," above. Ella Lake is relatively near Ketchikan—so it's a shorter, cheaper trip to get there—but it's still very secluded. For a complete listing of cabins, contact the Forest Service; their website, with an interactive map, is the best source of information (keep digging at **www.fs.fed.us/r10/ tongass** and you'll find it). For reservation information, see "Getting Outside in the Tongass National Forest," in section 1 of this chapter.

4 Prince of Wales Island

If you have plenty of time, the Alaska Bush is just a short ferry or small-plane ride from Ketchikan, ready to be explored by car. Prince of Wales Island, known locally as "POW," is 135 miles long and 45 miles wide, making it the third-largest island in the United States (after Alaska's Kodiak Island and Hawaii's Big Island), yet it is populated by only a few tiny towns and Native villages. What makes the island unique in Alaska is that it's traversed by a network of more than 1,000 miles of gravel roads, built and maintained by the U.S. Forest Service to facilitate logging. That means you can drive to beautiful places rich with fish, exploring without the expense of an airplane or boat, but rarely seeing another person. It can be a strange feeling to drive for hours without seeing a building or another car. The flip side of such accessibility is that large clear-cuts now mar many once-beautiful parts of the island.

Fishing, in both salt and fresh water, is by far the biggest reason to visit the island. The Forest Service lists 32 good fishing streams and maintains some 20 public cabins, built mainly for their access to remote fishing lakes and streams. Many fishing lodges operate on the island, taking guests out on boats to fish salmon in the ocean; most visitors to the island have booked inclusive packages at one of the lodges well in advance.

But some people discover more of the island. Divers find clear waters and a rich profusion of marine life; two canoe routes cross wilderness areas of the island; and few other places offer families such opportunities for solitude and discovery along the road and trails. Plus, POW contains hundreds of barely explored caves, two of which casual visitors can safely enter, albeit with some effort.

ESSENTIALS

GETTING THERE & GETTING AROUND   The simplest way to Prince of Wales is to fly with an air service such as **Promech Air** (© 800/860-3845 or 907/225-3845), which has scheduled service to four POW communities, with fares ranging from around $90 to $380 round-trip; call ahead to try to get a better deal.

If you fly, and you're not at a lodge or on a package, you'll need to rent a car. **Wilderness Rent-a-Car,** in Klawock (© 907/755-2691), charges $99 a day plus 30¢ a mile after 100 miles, which can add up fast if you explore the whole island. If you plan to drive a lot on the island, you'll do better by renting a car in Ketchikan and taking it over on the ferry, making sure it's okay to take the rental on unpaved roads. The **Alaska Marine Highway** serves Hollis roughly once a day (see section 1 of this chapter, "Exploring Southeast Alaska"; the number on Prince of Wales is © 907/826-3432). The fare for a small car from Ketchikan to Hollis is $44, and each passenger is $22 more. It's safest to reserve a ferry spot a week or two in advance in high season, but it's entirely possible to just show up and luck into a space, too. The new **Inter-Island Ferry Authority** (© 907/826-4848) planned to start serving the area in 2002; call for details. For $25, **Sea Otter Taxi** (© 907/755-2362) will drive you from the dock in Hollis to Craig; call to reserve ahead.

VISITOR INFORMATION   Before going to Prince of Wales, stop at the **Southeast Alaska Discovery Center** at 50 Main St. in Ketchikan (© 907/228-6220; www.fs.fed.us/r10/tongass), and pick up the Forest Service recreation guides and the $4 road guide, which is a large map showing the roads and topography and listing the cabins and facilities available around the island. Fishermen will also want to get a copy of the Alaska Department of Fish and Game's *Sport Fishing Guide* for the island, as well as other guidance from the **Ketchikan Division of Sport Fish** office, at 2030 Sealevel Dr., Suite 207, Ketchikan, AK 99901 (© 907/225-2859). You also can order the map and get tourist information from the **Prince of Wales Chamber of Commerce,** P.O. Box 497, Craig, AK 99921 (© 907/826-3870; fax 907/826-5467; prince ofwalescoc.org).

ORIENTATION   The largest town is **Craig,** on the west side of the island. Here you'll find good hotels, restaurants, a bank with an ATM, various stores, and a floatplane dock. Seven miles east is **Klawock,** a large Native village with the island's only paved landing strip, a shopping center, more restaurants and accommodations, and a rotting totem pole park built under the New Deal in the 1930s. The other towns and villages on the island are quite small and have limited services. **Hollis,** where the ferry lands on the east side of the island, has few visitor services.

GETTING OUTSIDE

CANOEING & SEA KAYAKING   A couple of lovely backwoods canoe routes cross parts of the island, on Sarkar Lake and through the Honker Divide, each with Forest Service cabins along the way. Here's an inexpensive way into deep wilderness, with the relative comfort of a roof over your head at night. You can bring your own canoe or rent one from **Log Cabin Sporting Goods** in Craig (© **888/265-0375** or 907/826-2205; www.seaatours.com). They charge $40 a day for a canoe or $50 a day for a double sea kayak; they also rent camping packages, do water taxi drop-offs, and carry anything you might need to buy. Their guided sea kayaking costs $50 for a 2-hour paddle, $100 all day. Most intriguing is their 4-day sea kayaking expedition based from a 42-foot motor yacht. When you arrive at each day's destination, a seafood dinner and warm bed are waiting for you on board. If some of your party don't want to paddle, they can ride. It costs $1,400 per person.

CAVING   The limestone of Prince of Wales Island contains a honeycomb of miles of caves. Though the caves are wet, cold, and challenging, advanced cavers consider these to be among the world's most exciting, for their complexity and for the wonder of exploring areas that have never been seen by human eyes. The caves weren't discovered until 1987, and there's still plenty left to be mapped by explorers.

Two caves have been developed for the public. Forest Service guides lead visitors on highly recommended 2-hour treks into **El Capitan** cave three times a day Thursday to Saturday during the summer (reservations required). Although the tour goes only about 600 feet into the 12,000-foot cave, it feels like you've been to the center of the earth in these incredibly complex, twisting chambers. The hike is only for the fit and starts with a climb up 370 steps to the mountainside cave opening. Ten miles away, visitors can walk into the grottolike **Cavern Lake Cave** on their own—you never lose daylight in this broad crack in the earth. Tall rubber boots or other preparations for the flowing cavern stream will help. The caves are a 3-hour drive from Craig, and you'll need the Forest Service's **road guide** (see above) to find them. Reserve with the **Thorne Bay Ranger District,** 1312 USFS Dr. (P.O. Box 19001), Thorne Bay, AK 99919 (© **907/828-3304;** www.fs.fed.us/r10/tongass).

DIVING   Craig Sempert's **Craig's Dive Center,** 107 Main St., Craig (© **907/ 826-3481** or 800/380-DIVE in Alaska only; craigdiv@aptalaska.net), offers rentals and fully guided diving packages. The water here is clearer and the invertebrate and marine mammal life even richer than in the Inside Passage part of Southeast Alaska. Plankton blooms can cloud things up in the summer, but winter is always clear. Sempert dives in wet and dry suits, and tailors packages to visitors' interests, diving in unexplored areas, and even in caves. He also rents out a pair of attractive kitchenette apartment units by the night, for $95 double—a great place for families to stay, whether divers or not.

FISHING   The fishing opportunities on Prince of Wales are legendary. Fly-fishermen talk of rain forest surrounding streams and lakes that yield steelhead, cutthroat, and other trout by the dozen in a day's fishing. Many lodges on the island offer river or ocean trips, and guides are booked up many months in advance. Some are described below. You can also go on your own, using the Forest Service cabins or camping. Some cabins come with boats that allow access away from the road, or you can rent a canoe (see below). Even without a boat, there are enough roads and enough good fishing that anyone with a car and a copy of the *Sport Fishing Guide* (see above) can find a good fishing spot.

ACCOMMODATIONS & DINING

In Craig, I've mentioned the rooms at **Craig's Dive Center** above. **Haida Way Lodge** (© 800/347-4625 or 907/826-3268; www.haidawaylodge.com) rents good standard rooms for reasonable prices, and helps independent travelers make their other arrangements. It and a sister Native-owned property, **Sunnahae Lodge** (© 907/826-4000), offer popular fishing packages. Three days of charter fishing and four of meals and lodging cost $2,195 per person, based on double occupancy. **Papa's Pizza** in Craig (© 907/826-2244) has good food and delivery, and there are several other restaurants in town.

In Thorne Bay, on the northern end of POW, **McFarland's Floatel** (© 888/828-3335 or 907/828-3335; www.mcfarlandsfloatel.com) is a neat concept, a do-it-yourself lodge with four two-bedroom cabins with full kitchens (you cook for yourself); the cost is for $240 per night for up to four people, and includes a dock where a lodge building and rental boats float on placid water. The boats and a Chevy Suburban rent for reasonable rates, and they offer fishing charters.

The island's most famous fishing lodge is on the west side, reached only by floatplane. **The Waterfall Resort** (© 800/544-5125 outside Alaska only, or 907/225-9461; www.waterfallresort.com) is a luxury property built in a 1912 cannery. A 3-night stay is $3,060 per person, including guided boat fishing.

CABINS & CAMPING

If you enjoy roughing it, nothing can be more appealing than a stay on POW in a primitive **Forest Service cabin** on a remote lake all your own. Several of the cabins on Prince of Wales are reached by skiffs that the Forest Service leaves tied up at the bank by the road—you load your gear and row to your lodgings. This accessibility makes them far more affordable than cabins elsewhere in the forest that can be reached only with a floatplane or charter boat. See section 2 of this chapter, on Ketchikan, for information on renting camping gear, and "Outside in the Tongass National Forest," in section 1, for more on how to rent a cabin.

If you don't need a solid roof, you can camp almost anywhere on the island. The **Eagles Nest Campground,** two miles east of the Control Lake Junction on the road to Thorne Bay, has 11 well-separated sites among huge trees by the edge of Balls Lake. A 2-mile trail circles the lake. A ½-mile boardwalk ends at Control Creek, where you can see red salmon spawning amid a grove of Sitka spruce of staggering girth and height. Sites can be reserved through the same system as cabins.

5 Wrangell

Wrangell, valued for its position near the mouth of the Stikine River, began as a Tlingit stronghold and trading post and became the site of a Russian fort built in 1834. The British leased the area from the Russians in 1840, and their flag flew until the U.S. purchase of Alaska in 1867. Over the balance of the 19th century, Wrangell experienced three gold rushes and the construction of a cannery and sawmill.

Then, time pretty much stopped.

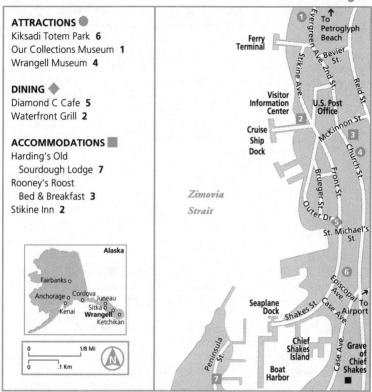

ATTRACTIONS ●
Kiksadi Totem Park **6**
Our Collections Museum **1**
Wrangell Museum **4**

DINING ◆
Diamond C Cafe **5**
Waterfront Grill **2**

ACCOMMODATIONS ■
Harding's Old
 Sourdough Lodge **7**
Rooney's Roost
 Bed & Breakfast **3**
Stikine Inn **2**

While the world outside changed, Wrangell stayed the same from the mid–20th century on. It even moved backward. Elsewhere, Wal-Mart and shopping malls were invented and small-town main streets deflated. Then people noticed what they had lost and tried to bring back their communities. Not out here, beyond the road system. With little incentive for anyone to visit, Wrangell stayed as it was after a 1952 fire burned the downtown: a burly, blue-collar American logging town, simple and conservative. Wrangell cut trees, processed them, and shipped them. The bars stayed busy, and no one thought of opening a health food restaurant. As long as there were trees to saw into lumber, the future was safe in the past.

Or so it seemed until environmental and economic concerns closed the mill. Some feared the town would die, too. Sawing lumber had sustained the local economy for more than 100 years, and a third of the paychecks in town came from that one plant. But, as it turned out, change hasn't destroyed Wrangell. The town is quieter, and some trailer houses have disappeared and stores closed, but the year-round population is down only modestly, at about 2,300. In its new incarnation, Wrangell is working to improve on its positive qualities, and the residents show an endearing eagerness to please. A big new museum is planned, and two ecotourism operators are offering kayaking, hiking, and the like. Tour boats take guests up the wild Stikine River, out on the water for Southeast's great salmon fishing, and over to the mainland to see hordes of bears at the Anan

Wildlife Observatory. The U.S. Forest Service maintains gravel roads that lead to some spectacular places. The town even built a golf course called Muskeg Meadows. Named for the area's hummocky swamps, it was built up on wood waste from the old mill.

Wrangell can't change its stripes—it's still a muscular town with narrow horizons—but that's part of the attraction. The town has a nonthreatening, small-scale feel that allows a family to wander comfortably and make friends. My family and I were even invited home to dinner by another family we had just met. There is no crime, so there is no fear of strangers. We picnicked in one of the totem pole parks, hiked in the rain forest, and looked at ancient art strewn across Petroglyph Beach. We were sorry to have to leave.

On the ferry back to Juneau, a class of Wrangell sixth-graders sat next to us. They talked with excited innocence of all the new things they hoped to experience in the state capital, the most electrifying of which seemed to be the prospect of eating for the first time at McDonald's. Wrangell, I thought, still has a long way to go to catch up with the rest of the world, and that is a condition much to be envied.

ESSENTIALS

GETTING THERE   **Alaska Airlines** (© 800/252-7522; www.alaskaair.com) serves Wrangell once daily with a jet flying 28 minutes north from Ketchikan and another 19 minutes south from Petersburg, a flight that skims low over the treetops the entire way.

Wrangell is on the main line of the **Alaska Marine Highway System** (© 800/642-0066; www.state.ak.us/ferry), with landings six times a week in the summer. The voyage through the narrow, winding **Wrangell Narrows** north to Petersburg is one of the most beautiful and fascinating in Southeast Alaska. It's quite a navigational feat to watch as the 400-foot ships squeeze through a passage so slender and shallow the vessel's own displacement changes the water level onshore as it passes. The route, not taken by cruise ships (which approach through larger waterways), is also a source of delays, as the water in the narrows is deep enough for passage only at high tide. The walk-on fare is $26 from Ketchikan, $20 from Petersburg. The terminal is downtown (© 907/874-2021), a block from the Stikine Inn.

VISITOR INFORMATION   The small office of the **Wrangell Chamber of Commerce Visitor Center** is located in the Stikine Inn (P.O. Box 49), Wrangell, AK 99929 (© 800/367-9745 or 907/874-3901; www.wrangell.com/Chamber), facing the city dock, where cruise ships tie up. The center is open Monday to Friday 10am to 4pm in summer, and additional hours when a cruise ship is in town.

The U.S. Forest Service also has an information desk at the **Wrangell Ranger District Office,** 525 Bennett St. (P.O. Box 51), Wrangell, AK 99929 (© 907/874-2323; www.fs.fed.us/r10/tongass), located on the hill behind town. Here you can draw on local knowledge of the logging roads and fishing holes, obtain guides to each Forest Service cabin and path, and, for $4, buy a detailed Wrangell Island Road Guide topographic map that shows and describes the island's outdoor attractions. The office is open Monday to Friday only, 8am to 5pm in summer and 7:30am to 4:30pm in winter.

ORIENTATION   The main part of town is laid out north to south along the waterfront at the northern point of Wrangell Island. **Front Street** is the main business street, leading from the small-boat harbor and **Chief Shakes Island** at the south to the city dock and the ferry dock at the north. Most of the rest of the town is along **Church Street,** which runs parallel a block higher up the hill. **Evergreen Avenue** and **Bennett Street** form a loop to the north which goes to the airport. The only road to the rest of the island, the **Zimovia Highway,** heads out of town to the south, paved for about 12 miles, then connects to over 100 miles of gravel logging roads built and maintained by the Forest Service, most of which are usable for two-wheel-drive vehicles in the summer.

GETTING AROUND   You can do the town on foot, but you will need wheels for the airport or Zimovia Highway.

The guys at **Practical Rent A Car** are friendly; they're at the airport (© 907/ 874-3975), or you can have them deliver the car to you.

For a taxi, try **Northern Lights Taxi** (© 907/874-4646).

Rent **bikes** from **Solo Cat Sports** (© 907/874-2923), described in more detail below.

FAST FACTS: Wrangell

Bank **Wells Fargo** is at 115 Front St., with an ATM.

Hospital **Wrangell General** is at 310 Bennett St. (© 907/874-7000).

Internet Access Go to **Amethyst Rose Florist,** Front Street, © 907/ 874-4554.

Police For nonemergency calls, dial © 907/874-3304.

Post Office At 105 Federal Way, near the ferry dock.

Taxes **Sales tax** is 7%. Rooms carry a **$4 bed tax** on top of that.

SPECIAL EVENTS   **The Garnet Festival,** the third week of April, marks the arrival of the sea lions, hooligan, shorebirds, and bald eagles on the Stikine River Delta, a spring tornado of wildlife in the region's largest coastal marshes. Community activities take place in town while jet boat tours traverse the delta. **The Wrangell King Salmon Derby,** the last 2 weeks of May and first part of June, started in 1953. Contact the Wrangell Chamber of Commerce (listed above under "Visitor Information"), or check their website for details. Wrangell also puts on a classic small-town **Independence Day** celebration.

EXPLORING WRANGELL & ENVIRONS

Before white settlers arrived, the Tlingits already had warred for centuries over this strategic trading location near the mouth of the Stikine River. The first Chief Shakes was a successful conqueror who enslaved his enemies, then handed down power through the female line, in the Tlingit tradition, for 7 generations. Charlie Jones was recognized as the last of the line, Chief Shakes VII, at a pot-latch in 1940, but the position had long since lost most of its status. The decline began after the Alaska purchase, in 1867. Word came of the Emancipation Proclamation, which theoretically freed a third of the residents of the coast's Tlingit villages. Chief Shakes VI sent his slaves in canoes to dry halibut; they kept paddling home to Puget Sound, never looking back. (An excellent pamphlet, "Authentic History of Shakes Island and Clan," by E. L. Keithhahn, sells for $4 at the Wrangell Museum, described below.)

Chief Shakes Island, a tiny islet in the middle of the small-boat harbor, is the site of a Tlingit clan house and collection of totem poles constructed by Native workers, using traditional tools, in the Civilian Conservation Corps during the 1930s. Unlike some CCC clan house replicas in the region, which mix Tlingit styles, this house is an exact, scaled-down copy of the 1834 house in which Chief Shakes VI lay in state in 1916. The inside of the clan house is fascinating, both in the sense it gives of the people's ways, and for some extraordinary artifacts. Unfortunately, it takes some effort to get inside. Call Nora Rinehart at © **907/ 874-2023,** or, if you can't reach Nora, Margret Sturdevant at © **907/874-3747.** For a $20 minimum fee, they'll come down and open the house and give you the talk. Even if you can't manage that, visit the island to see the rotting totem poles and the charming setting (and, with extra time, visit the overgrown grave of Chief Shakes V, on Case Avenue just across the harbor). There's a resident otter that you can often see near the island's footbridge, sometimes feeding its young.

The carved house posts in the clan house are replicas of the mid-18th-century originals that now stand in the **Wrangell Museum,** 318 Church St. (© **907/ 874-3770**). These are probably the oldest and certainly the best-preserved Tlingit house posts in existence, still bearing the original fish egg and mineral paints, and a gash where, during a potlatch, a chief hacked off an image that a visitor admired and gave it to him—a gesture that, as intended, demonstrated the extent of his wealth. The museum has many other important Alaska Native pieces, and a lot of other just plain old stuff that tells the story of Wrangell, one of Alaska's most historic towns. As director Theresa Thibault told me, "We were the economic center of Alaska at one time—for a short time—believe it or not." This is a special museum, connecting visitors and locals in many ways other than just showing off artifacts. Admission is $3 for adults, free ages 16 and under. Summer hours are Monday to Friday 10am to 5pm, Saturday 1 to 5pm, and when the ships are in. In winter, they're open Tuesday to Friday 10am to 4pm.

One of the museum's projects has been the preservation of an impressive set of petroglyphs that lie on the beach a mile north of town. The 50 carvings of **Wrangell Petroglyph Beach State Historic Park** probably represent the work of forgotten indigenous people pre-dating the Tlingit, and were made over a long period of time. The images, chipped into rocks, are of animals and geometric forms. Their purpose is lost to time. Walk north on Evergreen Avenue and follow the signs down to the beach (don't go within an hour of high tide). Replicas of the petroglyphs were recently carved so that visitors who want to take rubbings will not destroy the originals; also try not to step on them. The great pleasure here is simply to search for the carvings—they're just lying out there, and it takes some looking—and to wonder at their meaning and age.

Wrangell has one more museum, a good place to stop on the way back from the Petroglyph Beach, meet a delightful old lady, and see her favorite things. Elva Bigelow maintains her **Our Collections Museum** in a big old boat shed on Evergreen Avenue (© **907/874-3646**). It's an all-inclusive gathering of her family's 60 years in Wrangell: old tools, nautical equipment, sewing machines, a collection of 60 dolls, a large diorama of the town assembled for the 1967 centennial celebration, and anything else you can imagine. Mrs. Bigelow's museum is open when cruise ships are in town, or you can reach her by phone and she'll gladly show it to you—she loves visitors. Donations are appreciated, and Mrs. Bigelow sells her own crochet work and other crafts.

On Front Street near the center of town, the **Kiksadi Totem Park** was built by the Sealaska regional Native corporation in the mid-1980s on the former site of a clan house. The grass is a comfortable place to sit, and the totem poles are truly beautiful.

GETTING OUTSIDE: ON WRANGELL ISLAND

Wrangell Island's network of gravel roads, maintained by the Forest Service, leads to places of awesome beauty rarely visited by non-Alaskans. There are a few day-hike trails, some lovely campsites, and paths to remote cabins and fishing lakes you can have to yourself. There are a couple of calm and scenic places to start a kayak paddle.

There's only one way out of town: south on the Zimovia Highway along narrow Zimovia Strait. The Forest Service map (see "Visitor Information," above) is helpful for anything you might want to do along this route.

The first stop is **City Park,** just south of town. Besides having a picnic area on the shore among big trees, it's a fine **tide pooling** spot. Go a couple of hours before a good, low tide.

Five miles out Zimovia Highway you reach the **Shoemaker Bay Recreation Area,** with a small boat harbor, campground, and picnic sites (see "Camping," below).

Continuing south, **Eight Mile Beach** is a good stop for a ramble, and don't miss **Nemo Point,** a high, oceanside overlook from which you can see more than 13 miles along Zimovia Strait all the way back to town. The campsites here are gorgeous.

All the way across the island, about 45 minutes from town, **Earl West Cove** gives access to the protected wilderness waters on the Eastern Passage. There's a good campground there, too.

HIKING   Across the road from the Shoemaker Bay Recreation Area, the **Rainbow Falls Trail** climbs steeply for just under a mile (and 500 feet in elevation gain) on a boardwalk with steps, up a ridge between two creeks, forested with big, mossy Sitka spruce and western hemlock. The falls seem to tumble down between the branches. From that point, you can continue another 2.7 miles and another 1,100 feet higher into open alpine terrain on the **Institute Creek Trail** to the Shoemaker Overlook, where there are great views, a picnic area, and a shelter. Marie Oboczky, who owns **Rainwalker Expeditions** (© **907/874-2549;** www.rainwalkerexpeditions.com), leads nature walks on the lower part of the trail, and longer hikes all over the island. The advantage of going with Oboczky is that she is a skilled naturalist and teacher and knows all the best places to go.

The Rainbow Falls Trail is the island's busiest, especially when cruise ships are in town. If you want to be sure you won't see anyone, take one of the less developed walks you can reach along the logging roads—the Forest Service can point the way. One good choice is the **Salamander Ridge Trail,** which leads a mile to subalpine terrain, where you can go off-trail hiking. The trail begins 27 miles from Wrangell on Salamander Road, also known as Forest Road 50050. The **Long Lake Trail** leads over a half-mile boardwalk to a public shelter and rowboat on the lake, on Forest Road 6271 (you'll need a map).

BIKING   A paved bike trail leads all the way from town, between the Zimovia Highway and the water, 6 miles to the Shoemaker Bay Loop Road. There are many more miles of appealing mountain-bike routes on Forest Service roads all over the island. **Solo Cat Sports** (© **877/874-2923** or 907/874-2923;

www.thetongass.com), owned by the warm and enthusiastic Steve Prysunka, leads backcountry tours and rents quality mountain bikes and other gear from a shop behind the car wash near the Forest Service office on Bennett Street. Prices range from $32 a day for a standard bike to $69 for a full suspension model. They also have child trailers.

SEA KAYAKING **Solo Cat Sports** (see "Biking," above) and **Alaska Vistas** (© 866/874-3006 or 907/874-3006; www.alaskavistas.com) both offer guided sea kayaking and rentals from Wrangell. Solo Cat aims to make independent sea kayakers of beginners; Alaska Vistas offers a wide variety of ecotourism services and has been around longer. Either will do day trips starting from the boat harbor, or guided trips of many days.

An interesting longer day trip starts from Earl West Cove, on the east side of the island. Solo Cat uses it as a launch point. Among the destinations is Berg Bay, where there's a Forest Service cabin for rent, excellent bird-watching, and an old mining trail for hiking. They also offer water taxi service.

One of Alaska Vistas' most popular trips starts with a jet-boat trip on the Stikine River to Shakes Lake, and then paddles back to Wrangell with stops at the natural hot springs and other sites along the way.

You can rent all the equipment you need in Wrangell, including boats and camping gear, or bring it on the ferry.

FISHING Wrangell Island allows anglers access to rarely visited streams and lakes, some with public cabins, that you can reach by car or a drive and short hike. The Forest Service provides a list, and the Alaska Department of Fish and Game publishes a 20-page *Petersburg/Wrangell Sport Fishing Guide* (for a copy, call © 907/465-4180; www.state.ak.us/adfg). May and June are the prime months for king salmon fishing, silvers start in July, and halibut are available all summer.

The well-run **Alaska Waters,** listed below, offers a long day of saltwater fishing for $225 per person. Many other charter boats are available at the harbor; ask at the visitor center. You can often arrange to take part of the day on the boat for sightseeing and wildlife watching, too.

GETTING OUTSIDE: OFF THE ISLAND

Wrangell lies in an extraordinary place, surrounded by vast, rich wild lands for fishing, rafting, sea kayaking, or simply enjoying. I've described two of the main off-island destinations below—the Stikine River and the Anan Wildlife Observatory—but there are many more, too many to mention. The guides I've listed can give ideas, or contact the Forest Service to get a list of the cabins they rent to the public, many of which provide exclusive access to exceptional fishing.

To get anywhere, you need a boat or floatplane. You can go independently, hiring a water taxi for $90 to $120 an hour; it costs about $450, one-way, to get to a remote Forest Service cabin. That service is offered by various operators, including the impressive, Native-owned **Alaska Waters,** 241 Berger St. (© 800/347-4462 or 907/874-2378; www.alaskawaters.com). They also rent all the outdoor stuff you'll need, including camping equipment and canoes, and offer guided fishing, Stikine River jet boat tours and expeditions, and trips to the Anan Wildlife Observatory. Commentary includes natural history and Tlingit cultural traditions and legends.

If you're going by air, **Sunrise Aviation** (© 800/874-2311 or 907/874-2319; www.pnw.com/sunrise) is a Wrangell-based operator.

> **Fun Fact** **Why the Garnet Stands?**
>
> In the streets of Wrangell, you sometimes encounter kids selling garnets the way children at other places sell lemonade. The gems come from the Garnet Ledge, near the mouth of the Stikine River, a mine that is still productive recreationally 130 years after its discovery. A visit isn't worth the effort for most travelers, but the story is interesting. The ledge was exploited from 1907 to 1936 by the first all-woman corporation in the nation, a group of investors from Minneapolis. Its current ownership is unusual, too: a 1962 deed gave the mine to the Boy Scouts and the children of Wrangell, which is interpreted to mean only children have the right to remove the stones. You can get a water taxi out there, but take a kid along if you intend to remove garnets. Of course, it's easier simply to buy garnets from a child at a card table in the street.

THE STIKINE RIVER

The Stikine's gray, glacial water rushes all the way from the dry Interior of British Columbia to a broad, shallow delta in the rain forest a few miles from Wrangell. It's among the fastest navigable rivers in North America, and in early gold rush years was a route through the Coastal Range. Tours that sometimes go as far as Telegraph Creek, B.C., use high-powered jet boats to manage the swift current (see above).

The shallow delta is an exceptionally rich wildlife-viewing area, with sea lions, eagles, and many other species of birds. When the salmon are running, you can see them thrashing in their spawning pools. Farther upriver, tours see Sitka black-tailed deer, moose, brown and black bears, mountain goats, river otters, and beavers.

Traveling upriver, tours usually stop at the **Shakes Glacier** and **Shakes Lake,** where there are 3,000-foot cliffs and some 50 waterfalls. Bring a swimsuit for a dip in the Forest Service–owned **Chief Shakes Hot Springs,** where there's an indoor and an outdoor tub for public bathing. The temperature is adjustable up to 120°F. Some tours go all the way to Telegraph, B.C., 160 miles upriver, where Alaska Waters (see above) brings travelers to a remote homestead lodge. A 3-day, 2-night package is $575. The going rate for a 6-hour jet boat tour from Wrangell is around $145.

Rafting the Stikine offers fast water, expansive scenery, and the potential for a remote, many-day journey. The two firms listed above under "Sea Kayaking," Alaska Vista and Solo Cat Sports, offer these guided trips, lasting about 10 days to 2 weeks, for an inclusive price of around $2,500 per person. Solo Cat also takes kayakers down the river. Alaska Vista and Alaska Waters rent rafts and other gear for floating the Stikine. A raft rents for about $100 a day.

ANAN WILDLIFE OBSERVATORY

When the pink salmon are running in July and August (peak is mid-July to Aug 20), more than 40 individual **black bears** and a few brown bears gather at a waterfall on Anan Creek, on the mainland southeast of Wrangell Island, often walking close to a platform where visitors stand watching. Don't go outside this season, however, unless you have it on good authority that bears are actively using the creek. Forest Service guides are on duty during the bear months; visitors must also follow safe bear behavior (they'll brief you when you arrive;

also, see "Outdoors Health & Safety," in chapter 2). Most visitors will enjoy a guided day trip from Wrangell more than going on their own. **Alaska Waters** goes by boat, charging about $145 per person for the hour-long run from Wrangell and a few hours with the bears. Sunrise Air flies to Anan. It's also possible to go without a guide, and no permit is needed; there's even a Forest Service cabin for rent, although it's in high demand during the bear season. The walk to the observatory is half a mile from the shore where you land, on a good trail.

ACCOMMODATIONS

Grand View Bed and Breakfast ⋆
This house overlooking Zimovia Straits, near the bike path, has an apartment with full cooking facilities and three other comfortable rooms. It is warm and well kept and the rooms have all the attributes of a good hotel, with private entrances and all but one with VCRs and telephones. The hosts, 50-year residents, do breakfast to your specifications.

Mile 2 Zimovia Hwy. (P.O. Box 927), Wrangell, AK 99929. ☎ or fax 907/874-3225. www.grandviewbnb.com. 4 units. $85 double, $105 apt; $15 each additional person over age 12. Rates include breakfast. No credit cards. **Amenities:** 8-person Jacuzzi; free mountain bike loan; courtesy car; free laundry machines. *In room:* Hair dryer, bathrobes, fan.

Harding's Old Sourdough Lodge ⋆
The energetic Bruce Harding, a large dog, and a cat run the hotel in the style of a fishing lodge. Harding rents the rooms alone or as packages for fishing, kayaking, rafting or other outdoor activities. The attractive building with a wraparound porch is about a mile from the center of town in a waterfront area, but Harding will drive you where you want to go. Some rooms are small, without TVs, and most have only shower stalls, not tubs. Decoration is on an outdoors theme. The suites are huge. Fresh seafood dinners are served nightly, family style (you eat what they cook). Dinner prices are $16 to $24 per person; nonguests by reservation only.

1104 Peninsula (P.O. Box 1062), Wrangell, AK 99929. ☎ **800/874-3613** or 907/874-3613. Fax 907/ 874-3455. www.akgetaway.com. 16 units. $85 double; $135 triple or quad; $150–$195 suite. Rates include continental breakfast. AE, DC, DISC, MC, V. **Amenities:** Sauna; bike rental; activities booking; car rental; courtesy car; coin-op laundry; fish freezing. *In room:* Dataport.

Rooney's Roost Bed & Breakfast ⋆⋆
Located downtown, this attractive old house with dormer windows was recently restored by a new generation of the family that has operated it for years. They didn't miss a detail, adding antiques on the hardwood floors for an elegance otherwise unknown in Wrangell. The rooms, decorated according to themes, all have four-poster beds with thick mattresses, comforters, and oversize pillows. The bathrooms attached to three of the rooms also are brand new; two have showers only, one a claw-foot tub. Elaborate breakfasts with local ingredients, such as seafood or berries, are served in a sunny dining room at the guests' own time.

206 McKinnon (P.O. Box 552), Wrangell, AK 99929. ☎ **907/874-2026.** Fax 907/874-4404. www. rooneysroost.com. 6 units, 3 with private bathroom. $95 double private bathroom, $75 double shared bathroom, $10 each additional person. Rates include full breakfast. MC, V. **Amenities:** Free bike loan; courtesy car; laundry service. *In room:* TV w/VCR, iron, fan.

Stikine Inn
The town's main hotel is close to the ferry dock and stands right on the water's edge. A center of community activity, it has the town visitor center on-site. The rooms tend to be worn and outdated, with unmatched fabrics. The more modern units have only one bed. But they're all perfectly comfortable, and you can hear the water lapping the shore outside as you fall asleep or watch the sunset on the ocean.

The restaurant is described under "Dining," below. The art gallery and gift shop on the ground floor, **River's Edge Fine Arts & Gifts,** is the largest in town, with fine art, pottery, and inexpensive gifts.

107 Front St. (P.O. Box 990), Wrangell, AK 99929. © **888/874-3388** or 907/874-3388. Fax 907/874-3923. www.stikine.com. 34 units. $89 double; $114 suite. Extra person over age 12 $5. AE, DISC, MC, V. **Amenities:** Restaurant (diner); activity desk. *In room:* TV.

HOSTELING & CAMPING

Wrangell Hostel is at the First Presbyterian Church, 220 Church St., Wrangell, AK 99929 (© **907/874-3534**). They're open mid-June to Labor Day, and the rate is $10 a night.

There are several attractive campgrounds in Wrangell. I've never seen a campground in a spot like the mountaintop **Nemo Point Forest Service Campground** (see "Getting Outside: On Wrangell Island," earlier in this section), but it's more than a dozen miles out of town. Five miles south of town, the **Shoemaker Bay Recreation Area** has sites by the road overlooking the boat harbor, right across from the Rainbow Falls Trail. There are water and electric hookups for RVs. Contact the **Wrangell Recreation and Parks Department** at © **907/874-2444** for information. They also manage **City Park,** right at the edge of town on Zimovia Highway, where camping is permitted. For a full hookup RV site, try **Alaska Waters'** small park, at 241 Berger St. (© **907/ 874-2378**). They charge $15 a night, and $3 for access to the shower room. Showers also are available for $3 at the town swimming pool, at the school.

DINING

Dining in Wrangell is not great, but you can get an adequate meal. The **Waterfront Grill** at the Stikine Inn (see "Accommodations," above) is a typical family restaurant serving three meals a day. When you sit down for dinner, they bring two menus, one for fine dining and another for the less expensive fare favored by the locals. Nothing is terribly expensive or terribly exciting among the steak, seafood, sandwiches, or pizza. The dining room is trim and bright, with superb ocean views.

Harding's Old Sourdough Lodge (see "Accommodations," above) serves meals to guests, and to others by reservation. It's a family-style dinner without a menu.

The **Diamond C Cafe,** at 215 Front St. (© **907/874-3677**), is a comfortable small-town coffee shop open 6am to 3pm daily in summer, closing at 1pm Sundays in the winter. It's lighter, cleaner, and better decorated than these places usually are, and the service is fast and friendly. Besides the hearty breakfasts, they serve burgers and sandwiches in the $4 to $8 range.

6 Petersburg: Unvarnished Threshold to the Outdoors

Petersburg is the perfect small town, the sort of prosperous, picturesque, quirky place that used to be mythologized in Disney films. Except that Petersburg would never let Disney in the door. People here are too smart for that, and too protective of a place they know would be spoiled by too much attention. For the same reason, Petersburg is just as glad the big cruise ships can't enter their narrow harbor. They've got something too good going here to spoil it with throngs of tourists and seasonal gift shops. Instead, locals spend the money that keeps Nordic Drive, the main street, thriving with family-owned grocery and hardware stores, restaurants, a fish market, a cybercafe, and other businesses. Wooden streets over Hammer Slough still serve utilitarian purposes, making them far more appealing than if they were prettied up as tourist areas. When you walk along Sing Lee Alley and check out the stylish little bookstore, you rarely see others like yourselves—instead, you see Norwegian fishermen in pickup trucks and blond-haired kids on bikes.

Keeping Petersburg insular and authentic also means that the outdoor opportunities to which it provides an entryway are sublime but little used. There are wonderful trails, mountain-biking routes, and secret places. On the water, the humpback whale–watching is as reliable as anywhere in Alaska, and still undiscovered. There's a glacier to visit, terrific fishing, and limitless sea-kayaking waters. The in-town attractions are few—a day is plenty for simple sightseeing—and little attempt has been made to accommodate lazy gawkers. But Alaska's best is waiting for those willing to spend the effort to look.

Petersburg is named for its founder, Peter Buschmann, who killed himself after living here for only 4 years. But that shouldn't be a reflection on the town, which is in an ideal location and has flourished since that inauspicious beginning. In 1898, or thereabouts (historians differ), Buschmann founded a cannery on Mitkof Island facing the slender, peaceful Wrangell Narrows in what was to become Petersburg. The stunning abundance of salmon and halibut and a nearby source of ice—the LeConte Glacier—made the site a natural. Buschmann had emigrated from Norway in 1891 and, as a proud old Son of Norway told me, he always hired Norwegians. Any Norwegian who came to him, he hired. In a few years, the cannery failed. Perhaps an excessive payroll? My suggestion was met with an icy glance and a change of subject. Teasing aside, Buschmann's mistake was merging his cannery with a firm trying to challenge a monopolistic canning operation, and they went down together.

Buschmann's suicide followed his financial reverses, but the promise of Petersburg remained. The Norwegians stayed and slowly built a charming town of white clapboard houses with steeply pitched roofs, hugging the water. Their living came from the sea, as it still does. Appropriately, the downtown area doesn't stop at water's edge. Roads, boardwalks, and buildings continue over the smooth waters of Wrangell Narrows, out to the cannery buildings that survive on long wooden piers, and into the boat harbors, which branch out in a network that far surpasses the city streets.

Today the town's economy, based on fishing and government work—the Stikine Ranger District of the Tongass National Forest is headquartered here—makes for a wealthy, sophisticated, and stable population.

ESSENTIALS

GETTING THERE   Petersburg has the most welcoming **ferry terminal** in the system (✆ **907/772-3855**), with a grassy lawn and a pier from which to watch the boats and marine animals. It's about a mile to the town center. To the north, the **Alaska Marine Highway** (✆ **800/642-0066**; www.state.ak.us/ferry) can take you from Juneau directly (an 8-hour run), or by way of Sitka (10 hours to Sitka from Juneau, then 9 more from Sitka to Petersburg). The fare is $20 from Wrangell (3 hours), $29 from Sitka, and $48 from Juneau.

Petersburg is served by **Alaska Airlines** jets (✆ **800/252-7522;** www.alaskaair.com) once north and once south each day, with the nearest stops on the puddle jumper being Juneau and Wrangell. **L.A.B. Flying Service** (✆ **800/427-5966** or 907/772-4300; www.labflying.com) connects Petersburg to Juneau with prop service, stopping in Kake on the way. From the airport, call **Maine Cab** (✆ **907/772-6969**) for a taxi into town.

Petersburg

ACCOMMODATIONS ■
Bear Necessities Guest House **9**
Bumbershoot Bed & Breakfast **1**
Petersburg
  Bunk and Breakfast Hostel **7**
Scandia House **6**
Tides Inn Motel **4**

Waterfront Bed & Breakfast **12**
Water's Edge Bed & Breakfast **1**

DINING ◆
AlasKafe **5**
Joan Mei Restaurant **12**
Northern Lights Restaurant **10**

ATTRACTIONS ●
Clausen Memorial Museum **3**
Eagle's Roost Park **2**
Hammer Slough **8**
Sing Lee Alley/
  Sons of Norway Hall **11**

VISITOR INFORMATION   The Petersburg Chamber of Commerce and the U.S. Forest Service jointly operate the informative **Visitor Information Center,** corner of First and Fram streets (P.O. Box 649), Petersburg, AK 99833 (© 907/772-4636; www.petersburg.org). A ranger offers detailed guidance on the outdoor opportunities that really make Petersburg fun as well as trail guides and natural history publications. A chamber representative helps with hiring a boat, finding lodgings, and other arrangements. This also is the place for details on Forest Service cabins in the ranger district, which you can reserve through the national system described in "Getting Outside in the Tongass National Forest," in section 1 of this chapter. The center is open in summer daily from 9am to 5pm, winter Monday to Friday 10am to 2pm.

The full-service **Viking Travel** agency, corner of Nordic Drive and Sing Lee Alley (© **800/327-2571** or 907/772-3818; http://alaska-ala-carte.com or www.alaskaferry.com), also specializes in booking local guides for tours, kayaks, whale-watching, flights, fishing charters, and other activities. Owners Dave and Nancy Berg are knowledgeable and helpful. They also sell custom Alaska tour packages and ferry tickets.

ORIENTATION   Petersburg is on Mitkof Island, divided from the much larger Kupreanof Island by the long, slender channel of the Wrangell Narrows.

There are three small-boat harbors, and so many docks, boardwalks, and wooden streets that the town seems to sit on the ocean. **Nordic Drive** is the main street, running from the ferry dock through town, then becoming **Sandy Beach Road** as it rounds Hungry Point to the north. At Sandy Beach, you can circle back, past the cannery workers' tent city and the airport, which stands above the town, to **Haugen Drive,** which meets Nordic again near **Hammer Slough,** right in town. To the south, Nordic becomes the **Mitkof Highway,** which runs to the undeveloped balance of the island.

GETTING AROUND   You can walk downtown Petersburg, but you'll need wheels or a boat to get to most outdoor activities.

The **Tides Inn Motel** and **Scandia House** (see "Accommodations," later) both rent cars, but not many are available in town, so book well in advance for summer.

Biking is a great way to see Petersburg. You can rent a bike for $4 to $5 an hour or $20 a day from **Northern Bikes,** located in the Scandia House Hotel (© **907/772-3978**). They're open summer Tuesday to Saturday 11am to 5pm.

The Scandia House also rents small boats, a wonderful way to explore Wrangell Narrows and get to trails across on the other side, or go fishing inexpensively. An 18-footer with a 40-horse outboard rents for $160 a day, gas included, $25 less for guests of the hotel. They don't provide fishing gear.

 FAST FACTS: Petersburg

Banks There are two banks, with ATMs, at the corner of Nordic Drive and Fram Street.

Hospital **Petersburg Medical Center** is at Second and Fram streets (© **907/ 772-4291**).

Internet Access At **AlasKafe,** upstairs at 306 N. Nordic (© **907/772-5282**), you can also get lunch and a haircut (see "Dining," later).

Police Find them on Nordic Drive near Haugen; nonemergencies © **907/ 772-3838**.

Post Office Near the airport.

Taxes **Sales tax** is 6%. The tax on **accommodations** totals 10%.

SPECIAL EVENTS   The Little Norway Festival, which celebrates the May 17, 1814, declaration of independence of Norway from Sweden, is an occasion for Petersburg to go wild. The 4-day schedule of events is the third full weekend of the month, with a street fair, parade, beauty pageant, seafood feast, and so on. **The King Salmon Derby** offers $30,000 in prizes over Memorial Day weekend. **July 4th** is a very big deal in Petersburg. **The Canned Salmon Classic** lasts June 1 to August 15, with a first prize of up to $4,000 going to the person who guesses how many cans of salmon will be packed in Petersburg during the season. **Julebukking,** a Norwegian tradition, happens on Christmas Eve, when merchants offer food and drink to their customers and the streets fill with people.

For information on any of the above events, contact the **Petersburg Chamber of Commerce** (© **907/772-3646;** www.petersburg.org).

EXPLORING PETERSBURG

A walk around Petersburg should include the boardwalk streets of **Hammer Slough,** the tidal mouth of a creek that feeds into the waterfront. **Sing Lee Alley** leads from North Nordic Drive at the charming center of town, passing by several interesting little shops, including **Sing Lee Alley Books,** at no. 11 (© 907/772-4440), where there's a good collection on natural history and local culture. Petersburg has so many thriving little shops because of its isolation and healthy economy—so far, it's been too small to attract the predation of Wal-Mart and other chains.

Sing Lee Alley turns from solid ground to wooden dock before you reach the **Sons of Norway Hall,** a town center where a large model Viking ship used in the Little Norway Festival is often parked. Next door, also on pilings, is the **Fishermen's Memorial Park.** Plaques memorialize Petersburg mariners lost at sea under a bronze statue of Bojer Wikan, a fisherman and lifelong resident.

Across the street, on the outboard side, **Tonka Seafoods** (© 907/772-3662; www.tonkaseafoods.com) is a specialty fish processor with a shop and mail-order operation; they will process your sport-caught fish, too. They offer tours ($5) during the summer, 1 to 3pm Monday to Saturday. Call ahead if you're really interested, as times can change.

Continue on to Nordic Drive, then turn left, crossing back over the slough to **Birch Street,** which follows the slough's bank on pilings upstream past old, weathered houses that hang over the placid channel. Many have one door for the road and another for the water. It's a charming, authentic place. Step out of the way of cars on the one-lane dock/street.

Back down at the waterfront, stroll the harbor floats to see the frenetic activity of the huge commercial fishing fleet in the summer, then continue north on Nordic Drive to **Eagle's Roost Park,** where there is a grassy area to sit and a stairway that leads down to the water. At low tide, an interesting if rugged beach walk starts here. You're almost guaranteed to see eagles, which congregate for the fish waste from the nearby cannery. Look in the tops of the trees. (In fact, you can see eagles almost anytime and anywhere along the water in Petersburg.) Another nice walk leads on a boardwalk a third of a mile over muskeg swamp from the uphill side of the elementary school, at Fourth Street.

The **Clausen Memorial Museum,** at Second and Fram streets (© 907/772-3598; www.clausenmuseum.alaska.net), interprets Petersburg and its history for the people who live here. It has a living, community feel. When I last visited, a portfolio of old photographs was on display with notes for visitors who want to write down the names of anyone they can identify and other memories. The office of a leading fish packer is displayed just as he left it in the 1970s, a time capsule of the ordinary that says much about the town. No doubt the local fishermen are fascinated by the obsolete fishing gear, rugged old nautical equipment, and a model fish trap, outlawed in 1959 when Alaska became a state. It's like being invited into the town's collective memory. The museum is open in summer Monday through Saturday from 10am to 4:30pm; call for hours in the winter. Admission is $2 for adults, free for children 12 and under.

GETTING OUTSIDE

I have listed only a few highlights from Petersburg's wealth of outdoor opportunities. For other choices, many of them just as good as those I've written about here, or for the detailed trail and backcountry information you'll need, contact the U.S. Forest Service at either of two locations in Petersburg—the visitor center, listed above, or the **Petersburg Ranger District** offices at 12 North Nordic Dr. (P.O. Box 1328), Petersburg, AK 99833 (© **907/772-3871; www.fs.fed.us/r10/tongass**).

Some of the best places to go around Petersburg require a boat. **Viking Travel** (see "Visitor Information," above) books most of the dozen or so small charter boats that are operating from the harbor at any one time, allowing them to consolidate small groups into six-person boatloads for whale-watching, sightseeing, or fishing.

Some operators have made a specialty of natural history and environmentally responsible tours. Barry Bracken, a retired marine fish biologist, offers these kinds of trips on his 28-foot vessel. Contact **Kaleidoscope Cruises** (© **800/ TO-THE-SEA** or 907/772-3736; www.alaska.net/~bbsea). Ron Compton's **Alaska Scenic Waterways** (© **800/ASW-1176** or 907/772-3777; akscenic. com) also specializes in natural history cruises using his aluminum jet boat, the *Motivator*, which has a landing craft bow that makes it easy to stop for picnics or beach walks.

SPECIAL PLACES

SANDY BEACH It's an easy bike ride or a longish walk 1.6 miles up Nordic Drive, around Hungry Point at the northern tip of the island, then along Sandy Beach Road to the beach and picnic area. Return by way of the airport, coming back into town on Haugen Drive. The beach itself is coarse sand and fine gravel, and you won't swim in the frigid water, but it's a lovely spot, facing Frederick Sound on the east side of Mitkof Island.

If you go at high tide, you can beachcomb and bird-watch—a great blue heron was hanging out last time I visited—but a better plan is to time your visit at a low tide (free tide books are widely available, or ask at the visitor center). At tides of 1 foot or lower, you can see the outlines of ancient fish traps built on the beach beginning 2,000 years ago. They look like V-shaped rows of rocks, and at times you can see stakes. The indigenous people who built them knew how to create channels that would corral salmon at high tide, leaving them stranded to be gathered up when the water receded. These ancient people presumably also created the petroglyphs on rocks near the traps, which may depict the traps or could have something to do with the sun. Finding the traps and petroglyphs isn't easy—it's best if you can get someone to lead you, perhaps by joining the occasional Forest Service walks that you can ask about at the visitor center. But, if you have the time and inclination to explore, walk out to the left from the picnic area, to the edge of the lagoon near the house with the greenhouse. A major petroglyph is on a black bedrock face, visible when you are looking back toward the picnic area, and the traps are just offshore from there.

RAVEN TRAIL & RAVEN'S ROOST CABIN About 4 miles up the steep but spectacular Raven Trail, which begins behind the airport off Haugen Drive near the water tower (roughly a mile from town), the Raven's Roost Forest Service cabin sits atop a mountain with a sweeping view of the town and surrounding waters and islands. It's the sort of place that inspires artists and poets. Allow 3 to 4 hours for the climb along a boardwalk, then up a steep muddy slope, then along a ridge, with an elevation gain of over 1,000 feet. It's possible to continue hiking over the steep, subalpine terrain of the Twin Ridge Ski Trail another 4.9 miles to the Twin Creek Road, and then get a ride 11 miles back to town. Check with the visitor center for trail conditions. You'll need sleeping bags, cooking gear, lights, and food. Reserve the cabin through the national system described in section 1 of this chapter, "Getting Outside in the Tongass National Forest," and check there for information sources on the other 19 cabins in the area, most of which are reached by plane or boat.

MITKOF ISLAND The Mitkof Highway, leading south from Petersburg, opens most of Mitkof Island, with its king salmon fishing; views of swans, fish, and glaciers; salmon hatchery; hiking trails; lakes; and many miles of remote roads for mountain biking. The town's swimming hole and ice-skating pond are out the road, too. Anyone can enjoy a day's sightseeing drive over the island, and if you like hiking and the outdoors, you'll find days of fun. Pick up the $4 *Forest Service Mitkof Island Road Guide* map at the visitor center or ranger office; it shows what you'll find along the way.

The **Three Lakes Loop Road** intersects with the highway twice, once 10 miles from Petersburg, and again 20 miles from town. From the north intersection, the one closest to town, it's 15 more miles to the level, 4.5-mile boardwalk **Three Lakes Trail,** which circles four small lakes, each of which contains trout, and three of which have Forest Service rowboats for public use. Besides the fish, it's a place of abundant wildflowers and berries, where you may see deer, beavers, bear, and many birds, including seasonal sandhill cranes.

Fourteen miles down Mitkof Highway from Petersburg, a quarter-mile boardwalk leads across the damp, hummocky ground of the rain-forest muskeg to **Blind River Rapids,** a peaceful spot with a three-sided shelter where you can watch and fish for king salmon in June and silvers in September, and sometimes see eagles and bears feeding on the fish. A mile-long loop leads farther into the forest and muskeg.

At 17 miles, somewhat hidden in the trees on the right, a bird-watching blind looks out on **Blind Slough,** where trumpeter swans winter. Swans normally will be gone by mid-March.

At 18 miles, at the end of the pavement, you'll reach the **Blind Slough Recreation Area,** where locals go to swim in amber water in the summer. Water warms in the narrow slough, more than 5 miles from Wrangell Narrows. These are appealing canoeing or sea-kayaking waters as well. In the winter much of the town congregates here for ice-skating and bonfires.

A branch road at the recreation area leads over the slough to the **Crystal Lake Hatchery** (© 907/772-4772), which raises king and silver salmon. I've toured a lot of hatcheries, but enjoyed this one especially because it's so informal—they get so few visitors that you can just wander through on your own and ask questions of the friendly technicians. A guy who was using a machine to count millions of fish let my son help.

At 22 miles from Petersburg, you reach the **Ohmer Creek campground,** with a 1-mile trail, a floating bridge over a beaver pond, and access to king salmon in June and July and trout and some salmon in late summer. The road continues from here along the south shore of Mitkof Island, with great ocean views, to its end at mile 32.

PETERSBURG CREEK The lovely, grassy Petersburg Creek area can be an afternoon's family frolic among the meadows of wildflowers that meet the water, or the start to a challenging 21-mile, multiday hike into the **Petersburg Creek–Duncan Salt Chuck Wilderness.** The fishing is exceptional. You'll need a skiff or sea kayak, or get a charter to drop you off, as the creek is on Kupreanof Island, across Wrangell Narrows from town; the state maintains a dock there. **Guided sea-kayak day trips** go up the creek (see "Sea Kayaking," below), which contains four species of salmon and two of trout. The trail is maintained by the

---

For a Takeout Lunch

Stop in at **Coastal Cold Storage,** at Excel Street and Nordic Drive (© **907/772-4177**), where they sell seafood from freezers and live from tanks. Order burgers, sandwiches, fish specials, and ice-cream cones at the counter.

Forest Service and has miles of boardwalks and two cabins, one at Petersburg Lake and one at East Salt Chuck, each with a boat for public use (reservations are required). Petersburg Lake has trout, and odds are good you'll see ducks, geese, loons, trumpeter swans, bald eagles, and black bears. The Kupreanof dock also provides access to the 3-mile, 3,000-foot trail that climbs Petersburg Mountain, a challenging hike that has spectacular views from the top.

LECONTE GLACIER/STIKINE RIVER DELTA   Ice calving from the glacier has choked the waters in front, making approach difficult, but in June you can see seal pups on the floating ice and possibly mountain goats on shore. A bit farther on is the Stikine River Delta, a wildlife habitat of grasslands, braided channels, and marshes with excellent bird-watching. In late April and early May, when the hooligan run, more than 1,500 bald eagles congregate, and some two million other birds rest on their West Coast migration. The charter operators listed above can take you, or Viking Travel can book one of the others who offer these trips. Boat tours based in Wrangell specialize in going to the Delta, too, and they're closer to the river. The going rate for a 4- to 5-hour tour to LeConte Glacier from Petersburg is about $125 per person. Going on to the delta would be more like $175 per person and take all day.

ACTIVITIES

FISHING   There are many fishing streams and lakes you can reach on the roads—several are mentioned above, under "Mitkof Island." For more choices, check at the visitor center, or send away before you come for a *Petersburg/ Wrangell Sport Fishing Guide* from the **Alaska Department of Fish and Game,** 1255 W. Eighth St. (P.O. Box 25526), Juneau, AK 99802-5526 (© **907/ 465-4180;** www.state.ak.us/adfg).

For expert advice and regulation information, you also can contact the Petersburg office (© **907/772-3801**). The boat harbor has a couple dozen licensed charter fishing boats, mostly six-passenger vessels. As elsewhere, halibut and salmon are usually the target. You can get a list of operators at the visitor center, or book through **Viking Travel** (see "Visitor Information," earlier). Salmon charters usually last half a day and cost around $100 per person, while halibut charters go all day and average $165.

MOUNTAIN BIKING   The largely abandoned logging roads on the island and on surrounding islands that can be reached by boat provide long bike rides without cars or other people. **Northern Bikes,** in the Scandia House Hotel (© 907/772-3978), rents gear and can give ideas on where to go.

SEA KAYAKING   The waters of Wrangell Narrows are protected and interesting, with plenty to see. On longer trips of 3 days to a week, you can get out among the glaciers, Stikine River Delta, and even the whales—there's as much variety here, among these rain-forest islands, as anywhere in the region. It's possible to set up a trip linking some of the Forest Service cabins, too, or to use one as a base camp for a few days of exploration. **Tongass Kayak Adventures**

(© **907/772-4600;** www.tongasskayak.com) offers guided and unguided versions of each of these adventures (they rent equipment, too). Their 4-hour paddle crosses Wrangell Narrows from the harbor and penetrates Petersburg Creek, where they stop for a snack and often see bear and deer. No experience is required; they charge $55. A 3-night base camp tour costs $675 per person; an 8-night version begins at $1,320.

WHALE-WATCHING   Most summers, **Frederick Sound** is one of the best places in the state to see humpbacks feeding. Whale-watching charters can go any day from May 15 to September 15, but the height is July and August. You'll likely see stunning bubble-net feeding, when the whales confine a school of fish in a circle of bubbles, then lunge upward to scoop them up, bursting through the surface in a great swoosh. Whales have even been known to spy hop, poking their heads as high above the surface as possible in order to look down into the boats that are watching them. In summer 1995, a humpback jumped right into one of these boats, presumably accidentally. (No one was injured, but a few people fell into the water.) Several charter operators offer trips in small, six-passenger boats. Some, including Kaleidoscope Cruises (under "Getting Outside," above), have hydrophones on board, so you may be able to hear the whales' vocalizations while waiting for them to surface, if their feeding behavior and the water conditions are right. Book through Viking Travel or directly with one of the operators. Trips usually leave around 8am and stay out 6 to 10 hours, with several hours with the whales. Prices are $120 to $180 per person. A non-profit **Petersburg Marine Mammal Center** is hoping to open an information center downtown by 2002.

ACCOMMODATIONS

Bear Necessities Guest House ⚓ *Value*   This is a large one-bedroom apartment unit on pilings right on Sing Lee Alley. Although it lacks a view, the decor is cute and the facilities are perfect for a family or a long stay, with a full, outfitted kitchen, lots of beds, and the amenities of home. The bathroom has a shower, no tub.

18 Sing Lee Alley (P.O. Box 923), Petersburg, AK 99833. © **907/772-2279.** www.alaska.net/~bearbnb. 1 unit. $90 double. Extra person $10. Rates include continental breakfast. MC, V. *In room:* TV, fax/copier, full kitchen, iron.

Bumbershoot Bed & Breakfast ⚓ *Finds*   The industrious Gloria Ohmer, who also owns the Tides Inn Motel (see below), has opened her extraordinary waterfront home on Frederick Sound to guests as well. The rooms are large, decorated with quilts she made. Gloria and her husband, Don Koenigs, also will share their beadwork, woodwork, sewing, stained glass, lapidary, music room, fish-cleaning room, and deck barbecue with you. It's hard to come away without gaining a little of their enthusiasm for life. Rooms with water views—and the water is only barely beyond your reach—rent for $10 more. For $150 a night, you can rent the entire downstairs apartment, with two rooms, a kitchen, and a large living room with a fireplace. They also lend bicycles, offer free use of the laundry machines, and arrange transportation from the ferry dock or airport.

901 Sandy Beach Rd. (P.O. Box 372), Petersburg, AK 99833. © **907/772-4683.** Fax 907/772-4627. ohknigs@pobox.alaska.net. 4 units, 2 with shared bathroom. $80–$90 double. Extra person $10. Rates include continental breakfast. DISC, MC, V. **Amenities:** Free bicycle loan; courtesy car; free laundry machines. *In room:* TV/VCR, hair dryer, iron.

Scandia House ⚓⚓   Rebuilt in the town's distinctive Norwegian style after a fire in 1995, this building's solid simplicity puts it in a class by itself. White rooms with blonde-wood trim are blessed with natural light. You have a choice: front rooms with king-size beds, rooms with kitchenettes, twin-bedded rooms, or a magnificent fourth-floor suite with towering ceilings. Most rooms have only one bed and a few have shower stalls, not tubs. When I inspected it, the house-keeping was immaculate. Book well in advance for the busy summer season.

110 Nordic Dr. (P.O. Box 689), Petersburg, AK 99833. ℂ **800/722-5006** or 907/772-4281. Fax 907/772-4301. scandia@alaska.net. 33 units. $90–$110 double, $130 double with kitchenette; $185 suite. Extra person over age 12 $10. Rates include continental breakfast. AE, DC, DISC, MC, V. **Amenities:** Skiff rental; courtesy van; car rental. *In room:* TV.

Tides Inn Motel ★ *Value*   Few hotels in Alaska have such good rooms at such affordable prices. The kitchenette rooms, which rent for the same rate, are an incredible bargain. The biggest difference among the rooms is the views. Those in the older part face an air shaft, while nonsmoking units in the front of the new section get a sweeping view. I watched bald eagles doing aerobatics less than 50 feet from my front window. The management is efficient and committed to quality, slowly remodeling rooms while keeping those that remain outdated in clean, attractive condition. The hotel has the Avis car-rental franchise and serves a continental breakfast in the lobby.

307 N. First St. (P.O. Box 1048), Petersburg, AK 99833. ℂ **800/665-8433** or 907/772-4288. Fax 907/772-4286. tidesinn@alaska.net. $85 double. Extra person $10. Rates include continental breakfast. AE, DC, DISC, MC, V. **Amenities:** Car rental; courtesy van. *In room:* TV.

Waterfront Bed & Breakfast ★   The building, designed as a bed-and-breakfast as well as a family home, sits on pilings over the Wrangell Narrows near the ferry dock. It combines supreme ocean views and the essential, watery feel of Petersburg. The kids' yard is on the wooden pier, and the canoe down below is free for guests to borrow. Rooms are decorated with Mission-style oak furniture and comforters; they have shower stalls, not tubs. Two rooms each have a single queen-size bed while the third, with two doubles, costs $10 more; the rate is the same no matter how many people stay in the room.

Nordic Dr. near the ferry dock (P.O. Box 1613), Petersburg, AK 99833. ℂ **907/772-9300**. Fax 907/772-9308. www.alaska.net/~h20frbnb. 3 units. $95–$105 per rm. Rates include continental breakfast. No smoking. MC, V. **Amenities:** Covered outdoor Jacuzzi; courtesy car; free laundry machines. *In room:* Hair dryer.

Water's Edge Bed & Breakfast ★ *Finds*   Barry and Kathy Bracken's house sits right on the beach on Frederick Sound, about a mile from town, with a creek running next to one room. You can sit in the large common room and bird-watch from there, or borrow the canoe for a paddle along the shore. Probably the best thing to do here is to book a package combining a stay at the B&B and an excursion on Barry's 28-foot boat. A retired state marine fish biologist, he leads natural history and whale-watching excursions. His knowledge of the area is deep and his enthusiasm infectious. Book well ahead, as it's a rare and popular opportunity.

705 Sandy Beach Rd. (P.O. Box 1201), Petersburg, AK 99833. ℂ **800/TO-THE-SEA** (800/868-4373) or phone/fax 907/772-3736. www.alaska.net/~bbsea. 2 units. High season $95 double. Low season $70 double. Extra person $10. 2-night minimum stay. Rates include continental breakfast. No credit cards. No smoking. No children under 12. **Amenities:** Free canoe and bike loan; courtesy car; laundry facilities. *In room:* Hair dryer.

HOSTEL & CAMPING

Friendly little **Petersburg Bunk and Breakfast Hostel,** at 805 Gjoa St. (ℂ **907/772-3632;** www.bunkandbreakfast.com), has male and female dorm rooms with four beds in each. The $25 nightly rate includes a continental breakfast and room tax. They're open May 15 to September 15; there is a 9:30am to 5pm lockout and 11pm curfew.

Petersburg's most famous campground is the **Tent City** at 1800 Haugen Dr. (© **907/772-4224;** ci.petersburg.ak.us/~park&rec/). The summer's young cannery workers set up tents and plastic sheeting on 50 wooden platforms for $5 a night. It's a bit rowdy for most tourists, but young people looking to make friends should enjoy it. A central pavilion has coin-op showers, sinks, phones, cooking areas, and firewood.

The closest natural camping is found 22 miles out the Mitkof Highway at **Ohmer Creek** (see "Special Places: Mitkof Island," above). **Twin Creek RV Park** is 6.5 miles out the highway (© **907/772-3244**), charging $18.85 for full hookups.

DINING

Petersburg mostly has typical small-town family restaurants, and not much else that rises above that level. For take-out pizza, try **Pelleritos** (© **907/772-3727**), across from the ferry terminal, open daily 7am to 9pm and a little later on weekends.

AlaaKafe ★ *Finds* COFFEEHOUSE/BISTRO   It looks like a coffee shop, but they also serve delicious panini sandwiches, pasta, soup, vegetarian food, and salad, and they offer a kid's menu. In fact, it's the best lunch we've had in Petersburg. You can log on to the Internet, talk or read on the couch, or even get your hair cut—Glenn and Valerie Miller started the place as a hair salon, and their customers wouldn't let them shut down the salon in the back rooms when they decided to shift to selling food and coffee. On summer nights, they sometimes add live music, poetry readings, or even gourmet food.

Upstairs at 306B N. Nordic, at the corner of Excel St. © 907/772-JAVA. www.clik.to/alaskafe. All items $6–$10. No credit cards. Summer, Mon–Fri 7:30am–5pm, Sat 7:30am–midnight, Sun 9am–1pm. Winter, Tues–Sat 7:30am–5pm.

Joan Mei Restaurant ★ CHINESE   The whole family works together in this large, bright dining room, serving flaky egg rolls and entrees with vegetables that remain crisp and flavorful rather than being smothered or overcooked. Locals come here for a nice dinner out, and we saw many happy faces.

1103 S. Nordic, across from the ferry dock. © 907/772-4222. Lunch $6.25–$14.50, Dinner $6.25–$20. MC, V. Mon–Tues and Thurs–Fri 11am–8:30pm, Sat–Sun 7am–8pm. Closed mid-Jan to mid-Feb.

Northern Lights Restaurant ★ *Kids* SEAFOOD/DINER   You couldn't find a much better site for a restaurant than here, sitting on pilings in Hammer Slough, overlooking two boat harbors. The service is friendly and the food is good and plentiful, including the burgers, salads, pasta, and specials they do all year for the locals and the fine dining seafood entrees added in the summer for visitors. The ice cream parlor furniture, video games, and ice cream counter remain from a previous incarnation; kids can entertain themselves while you linger.

203 Sing Lee Alley. © 907/772-2900. Lunch $7–$8.50, dinner $12–$15; summer dinner to $28. MC, V. Summer Mon–Fri 6am–11pm, Sat 7am–11pm, Sun 7am–10pm; winter Mon–Fri 6am–8pm, Sat 7am–8pm, Sun 7am–3pm.

7 Sitka: Rich Prize of Russian Conquest

If I could visit only one Alaska town, it would probably be Sitka.

Sitka preserves the Russian buildings of Alaska's earliest white settlement and, more deeply, the story of the cultural conflict between Alaska Natives and the invaders, and their resistance and ultimate accommodation to the new ways.

Here, 18th-century Russian conquerors who had successfully enslaved Aleuts to the west met their match in battle against the rich, powerful, and sophisticated Tlingit. A visit to Sitka reveals the story of that war, and also the cultural blending that occurred in the uneasy peace that followed under the influence of the Russian Orthodox church—an influence that remained even after the Russians sold Alaska to the U.S. in 1867 (that also happened here), and that continues today.

Sitka's history is Alaska's richest, and there's more of real interest in this town than anywhere else you might visit. The fact is, most Alaska towns haven't been on the map long enough to have accumulated much history. Those that have been around for a while often have been wiped out a time or two, leaving little to remind you of the distant past. There's usually a small museum and a few gold rush sites that can be seen in half a day. Not so in Sitka. Historic photographs bear a surprising resemblance to today's city. The National Park Service protects buildings and grounds of major historic significance—places where the pioneers spoke Russian, with ways so much more European than those of the rest of the American West. Even a superficial exploration of the attractions takes a day, and that's without time for the out-of-the-way points of interest or the outdoors.

In 1799, the Russians chose these protected waters on Sitka Sound, on the ocean side of Baranof Island, for a new fort as part of a strategy of pushing their sea otter hunting operations and territorial claims east and south along the west coast of North America. The Tlingit understandably considered this to be an invasion, and in 1802 they attacked the Russian's redoubt and killed almost everyone inside. The Russians counterattacked in 1804 with the cannons of the ship *Neva* and a swarm of Aleut warriors, eventually forcing the Tlingit battle leader, Katlian, to withdraw. But the Russians never rested easy in their new capital, named New Archangel, and the hostility of the proud and dangerous Tlingit long remained.

Some Russian laborers intermarried and essentially adopted Tlingit culture, but the bureaucrats and naval officers sent to run the colony for the czar tended to view Alaska as purgatory and left as soon as they could. Under their ineffective and uninterested control, the Russians made surprisingly little impression on the great mass of Alaska. They failed to explore the Interior and held only tenuous control of the vast coastline.

The departing Russians rushed home, leaving only three significant towns—Unalaska, Kodiak, and Sitka—of which only Sitka retains more than a single Russian building. During their century of rule the Russians had nearly wiped out the sea otter and the culture of the Aleuts, but both would eventually bounce back. The Russian Orthodox church stood as their only lasting cultural gift. Thanks to the efforts of one extraordinary cleric, Father Ivan Veniaminov, Alaska Natives were able to worship in their own languages, winning for the Russian Orthodox church many villages' continuing loyalty over less tolerant Protestant churches that came under American rule.

Besides its historic significance, Sitka also is fun to visit. Somehow it has retained a friendly, authentic feel, despite the crush of thousands of visitors. Perhaps because cruise-ship travelers must ride shuttle boats to shore, or because Sitka is a slightly inconvenient, out-of-the-way stop on the Alaska Marine Highway's main-line ferry routes, the city's streets haven't been choked by solid rows of seasonal gift shops, as has occurred in Ketchikan, Skagway, and a large part of Juneau. It remains picturesque, facing Sitka Sound, which is dotted with islands

Jugglers, dancers and an assortment of acrobats fill the street.

She shoots you a wide-eyed look as a seven-foot cartoon character approaches.

What brought you here was wanting the kids

to see something magical while they still believed in magic.

America Online Keyword: Travel

With 700 airlines, 50,000 hotels and over 5,000 cruise and vacation getaways, you can now go places you've always dreamed of.

Travelocity.com
A Sabre Company
Go Virtually Anywhere.

"WORLD'S LEADING TRAVEL WEB SITE, 5 YEARS IN A ROW." WORLD TRAVEL AWARDS

I HAVE TO CALL THE TRAVEL AGENCY AGAIN. DARN, OUT TO LUNCH. NOW I HAVE TO CALL THE AIRLINE. I HATE CALLING THE AIRLINES. I GOT PUT ON HOLD AGAIN. "INSTRUMENTAL TOP-40" ... LOVELY. I HATE GETTING PUT ON HOLD. TICKET PRICES ARE ALL OVER THE MAP. HOW DO I DIAL INTERNATIONALLY? OH SHOOT, FORGOT THE RENTAL CAR. I'M STILL ON HOLD. THIS MUSIC IS GIVING ME A HEADACHE. I WONDER IF SOMEONE ELSE HAS CHEAPER FLIGHTS. FORGET IT, CAN'T TAKE IT ANYMORE ... I'M HANGING UP.

YAHOO! TRAVEL
100% MUZAK-FREE

Booking your trip online at Yahoo! Travel is simple. You compare the best prices. You click. You go have fun. Tickets, hotels, rental cars, cruises & more. Sorry, no muzak.

YAHOO!®
Travel
travel.yahoo.com

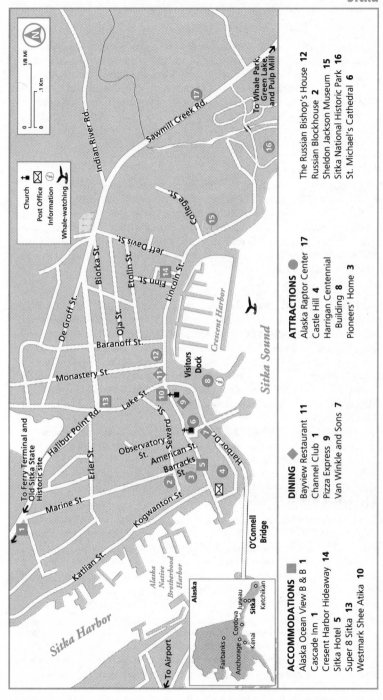

Sitka

Church †
Post Office ⊠
Information ⓘ
Whale-watching ✈

ACCOMMODATIONS ■
Alaska Ocean View B & B **1**
Cascade Inn **1**
Cresent Harbor Hideaway **14**
Sitka Hotel **5**
Super 8 Sitka **13**
Westmark Shee Atika **10**

DINING ◆
Bayview Restaurant **11**
Channel Club **1**
Pizza Express **9**
Van Winkle and Sons **7**

ATTRACTIONS ●
Alaska Raptor Center **17**
Castle Hill **4**
Harrigan Centennial
Building **8**
Pioneers' Home **3**

The Russian Bishop's House **12**
Russian Blockhouse **2**
Sheldon Jackson Museum **15**
Sitka National Historic Park **16**
St. Michael's Cathedral **6**

(*Fun Fact* **Thank You. No, Thank *You.***

In 1867, Russia's Czar Alexander feared that he couldn't hold the unprofitable colony of Alaska and saw a political advantage in doing his American allies the favor of selling it to them. Ironically, the Americans thought they were doing Russia a favor by buying it. Congress balked at paying the $7 million price Secretary of State William Seward had negotiated for this worthless waste, relenting more than a year later partly out of fear of offending the Czar. Americans didn't change their dim view of "Seward's Folly" until gold discoveries decades later.

---

and populated by feeding eagles. Tourism is important here, but Sitka's community remains its center. The process of being "spoiled" hasn't even begun.

Even beyond the town and its history, Sitka is a gateway to a large, remote portion of Southeast Alaska, in the western coastal islands. This area contains some of Tongass National Forest's least-used outdoor opportunities. The ocean halibut and salmon fishing are excellent and not overexploited, the bird- and wildlife-watching exceptional.

ESSENTIALS

GETTING THERE Sitka sits on the west side of Baranof Island, a detour from the Inside Passage. The big, main-line ferries on the **Alaska Marine Highway System** (© 800/642-0066; www.state.ak.us/ferry) don't always stop here, but the small *LeConte* adds more connecting trips each week, often stopping at villages in the region. The ride through narrow Peril Straits into Sitka is definitely worth the trip. The shore seems close enough to touch, and if you look closely you can sometimes see deer. The fare from either Juneau (9 hrs. away) or Petersburg (10 hrs.) is $29. The ferry dock (© 907/747-3300) is 7 miles out of town.

Alaska Airlines (© 800/252-7522, or 907/966-2422 locally; www.alaskaair.com) links Sitka daily to Juneau and Ketchikan, flights that then continue nonstop to Seattle and Anchorage.

Sitka Tours charges $5 to get to town from the airport or ferry dock. **Sitka Cab** is at © 907/747-5001; the ride from the ferry dock is around $15.

VISITOR INFORMATION Although only a desk, the city-operated **Harrigan Centennial Hall visitor center,** 330 Harbor Dr., next to the Crescent Boat Harbor (© 907/747-3225), provides refreshingly straightforward printed information. They're open in summer Monday through Wednesday 8am to 10pm, Thursday and Friday and most weekend days 8am to 5pm; in winter, Monday through Friday 8am to 5pm. If you are writing ahead for information, instead contact the **Sitka Convention and Visitors Bureau,** at P.O. Box 1226, Sitka, AK 99835 (© 907/747-5940; fax 907/747-3739). They maintain a very useful website at **www.sitka.org**.

The **Sitka National Historic Park Visitor Center,** 106 Metlakatla St., Sitka, AK 99835 (© 907/747-6281; www.nps.gov/sitk), run by the National Park Service, maintains the most important historic sites in Sitka, and is an essential stop where you can gather information and learn about what happened here. The Historic Sites of Sitka map produced by the Park Service and Sitka Historical Society is an indispensable guide to the buildings and parks around town. You can easily see Sitka's history on foot with one of these maps. The center is open daily 8am to 5pm in summer, Monday to Friday 8am to 5pm in winter. Also see "Exploring Sitka," below, for more on the park.

ORIENTATION   Sitka, on the west side of Baranof Island, has only a few miles of road. The **ferry terminal** is located at its north end, 7 miles out, on **Halibut Point Road;** the site of the abandoned pulp mill is at the south end, 5 miles out **Sawmill Creek Boulevard.** The town faces Sitka Sound. Across Sitka Channel is **Japonski Island** and the **airport** (don't worry, it only looks as if your plane is going to land in the water). **Lincoln Street** contains most of the tourist attractions.

GETTING AROUND   The airport has locations of **Avis** (© **800/331-1212** or 907/966-2404; www.avis.com) and **Allstar** (© **800/722-6927** or 907/ 966-2552; www.ptialaska.net/~rfahey).

The Visitor Transit Bus operated by **Sitka Tribal Tours** (see "Exploring Sitka," below) makes a continuous circuit of the sites May to September, Monday to Friday, 12:30 to 4:30pm, with added hours when cruise ships are in. The fare is $7 all day, $3 one-way, and kids ride free.

S.E. Diving, at 105 Monastery, just uphill from the Russian Bishops House (© **907/747-8279**), rents bikes for $5 an hour or $20 a day. **Sitka Bike and Hike** (© **877/292-5325** or 907/747-4821) rents bicycles and leads road and mountain biking tours.

 FAST FACTS: **Sitka**

Banks **ATMs** are at grocery stores and banks at 300 and 318 Lincoln St.

Hospital **Sitka Community** (© **907/747-3241**) is at 209 Moller Dr.

Internet Access Try **Highliner Coffee,** on Lake St. near Seward St. (© **907/ 747-4924**), or at the downtown post office.

Police Call © **907/747-3245** for nonemergency business.

Post Office At 338 Lincoln St.; it is open Saturday.

Taxes **Sales tax** is 5%. The tax on **rooms** totals 11%.

SPECIAL EVENTS   The **Starring Ceremony,** in early January (the exact date depends on the church calendar), marks Russian Orthodox Christmas with a procession through the streets and song and prayer at the doors of the faithful. Call St. Michael's Cathedral for information (© **907/747-8120**).

The **Sitka Salmon Derby** occurs at the end of May and beginning of June, when the kings are running; contact the Sitka Sportsman's Association (© **907/ 747-8886**). The **Sitka Summer Music Festival,** a chamber-music series that began in 1972, is one of Alaska's most important cultural events, drawing musicians from all over the world for 3 weeks in June. Performances take place Tuesdays and Fridays, and other events all week. Contact the festival office for information (© **907/747-6774;** www.sitkamusicfestival.org).

Alaska Day, October 18, commemorating the Alaska Purchase, is a big deal in this former Russian capital city; the **Alaska Day Festival** lasts 4 days leading up to the big event. The Convention and Visitors Bureau has information. The **Sitka Grind,** a music and arts celebration at varying sites around town, takes place the third Saturday of each month from October to March. The **Sitka**

WhaleFest (© 907/747-5940; www.sitka.org/whale.htm) takes place over a weekend in early November, during the fall and early winter period when humpback whales congregate in Sitka Sound. There are workshops, whale-watching tours, and other community events. Consider combining it with the Haines Bald Eagle Festival, coordinated to follow (see section 11 of this chapter, on Haines).

EXPLORING SITKA

The **Sitka Tribal Tours** Community House is a good starting point, where you can join walking or bus tours, dance performances (see below), kayaking, and other outdoor activities. It is at 456 Katlian St. (© **888/270-8687** or 907/747-7290; www.sitkatribal.com). **Sitka Tours** (© **907/747-8443**) also offers tours, taking more of the Russian perspective. Prices for each range from about $12 for a brief downtown tour to $33 for a longer town tour that includes most of the attractions and either Native or Russian dancing, depending on which firm you go with.

SITKA'S TLINGIT & RUSSIAN HERITAGE

Sitka National Historic Park ★★★ In 1799, the Russian America Company, led by Alexander Baranof, landed from their base in Kodiak, established Redoubt St. Michael (today the **Old Sitka State Historic Site,** 7½ miles north of town—just a grassy picnic area with interpretive signs), and claimed the Pacific Northwest of America for Russia. The Tlingit, who were sophisticated traders and already had acquired flintlocks, attacked with knives, spears, and guns, and destroyed the redoubt in mid-June 1802, killing almost all of the Russians. The Natives immediately began building fortifications on the site now within the national historical park, anticipating a Russian counterattack, which came in 1804. Baranof returned with an attacking force of a Russian gunship and a swarm of Aleut kayaks, which towed the becalmed vessel into position to begin the bombardment. The Tlingits withstood the siege for 6 days, then vacated their fort at night, after taking heavy losses from the shelling and from a bomb-laden canoe. The Russians founded and heavily fortified the town of New Archangel, and in 1808 it became their administrative capital. But the Tlingit name is the one that stuck: Shee Atika, since contracted to Sitka.

The historic significance of the battle site was recognized early, and Pres. Benjamin Harrison, a friend of Alaska missionary Sheldon Jackson, set the land aside in 1890. In 1905, a collection of totem poles from around Southeast was brought here (the originals are in storage; replicas are on display), and in 1910 the site was designated a national historic park. The park emphasizes the Native perspective. In the newly remodeled visitor center, a display explains the history, and Alaska Native artisans from the Southeast Alaska Indian Cultural Center work in a series of windowed workshops in wood, silver, and cloth, making traditional carvings, jewelry, drums, and regalia. An auditorium shows films and other programs.

I found the totem park and battle site most impressive. The totems stand tall and forbidding along a pathway through massive spruce and hemlock, where misty rain often wanders down from an unseen sky somewhere above the trees. The battle site is along the trail—only a grassy area now—but among the trees and totems, with the sound of the lapping sea and raven's call, you can feel deep down what the Tlingits were fighting for.

And, in fact, the park and center are full of evidence of the Tlingit's living heritage. In 1996, a gathering of clans erected a major new pole in front of the center to explain their story back to mankind's arrival in North America. It took quite a bit of debate to settle the story the pole would tell. For example, the crests of the eagle and raven tribal moieties are traditionally never shown on the same pole, but they had to be to tell the whole history of the Tlingits. At the bottom of the pole, the last step in the story, is the raven helmet worn by Katlian, the Tlingit's leader in the battle of Sitka. You can see the helmet itself in the Sheldon Jackson museum (see below).

106 Metlakatla St. ℂ **907/747-6281.** Free admission. Visitor center open summer daily 8am–5pm; winter, Mon–Fri 8am–5pm. Park open summer daily 6am–10pm, winter daily 7am–8pm.

The Russian Bishop's House ★★★   Father Ivan Veniaminov (a.k.a. Bishop Innocent), born in 1797, translated the Bible into Tlingit and trained deacons to carry Russian Orthodoxy back to their Native villages. Unlike most of the later missionaries of other faiths (who were led by Sitka's other historic religious figure, Sheldon Jackson), Veniaminov allowed parishioners to use their own language, a key element to saving Native cultures. When the United States bought Alaska in 1867, few Russians remained, but thanks to Veniaminov's work, the Russian Orthodox faith remains strong in Native Alaska; today there are 89 parishes, primarily in tiny Native villages. In 1977, Veniaminov was canonized as St. Innocent in the Orthodox faith.

In 1842, the Russian America Company retained Finnish shipbuilders to construct this extraordinary house for him as a residence, school, and chapel. It survived many years of neglect in part because its huge beams fit together like a ship's. In 1972, the National Park Service bought and began restoring the building, which is the best of only four surviving from all of Russian America (one is in Kodiak, one in California, and one at 206 Lincoln Street, occupied by the Log Cache Gifts). The Bishop's House is Alaska's most interesting historic site. Downstairs is a self-guided museum; upstairs, the bishop's quarters are furnished with original and period pieces. It's an extraordinary window into an alternate stream of American history, from a time before the founding of Seattle or San Francisco when Sitka was the most important city on North America's Pacific Coast. The tour concludes with a visit to a beautiful little chapel with many of the original icons Innocent brought from Russia.

Lincoln and Monastery sts. No phone; call Sitka National Historical Park Visitor Center (ℂ **907/747-6281**). Admission $3 per person or $10 per family. Summer daily 9am–5pm; by appointment in winter.

Sheldon Jackson Museum ★★   Sheldon Jackson, a Presbyterian missionary with powerful friends in Washington, was Alaska's first General Agent for Education, a paternal guardian of the welfare, schooling, and spiritual lives of Alaska's Natives. Although his assimilationist views today appear misguided, he tried to defend Natives from exploitation and abuse while, on the side, gathering an omnivorous collection of some 5,000 of their art, cultural, and everyday objects during his travels from 1888 to 1898. That collection, the best in Alaska, has been displayed for a century in a concrete building on the college campus that bears Jackson's name. It's a jewel box; the overwhelming wealth is displayed by the state museum curators in such ingenious ways that it avoids feeling cluttered. Many drawers open to reveal more displays. Despite the age of many of the pieces, they appear as new as if just made. Don't miss Katlian's helmet, worn by the Kiksadi clan's war leader in the Battle of Sitka in 1804; raven-shaped, it is that rare piece of great history that's also great art. Native artists demonstrate their skill on summer days, and the gift shop contains almost exclusively authentic Native arts and crafts, with few items under $100.

104 College Dr. © 907/747-8981. www.museums.state.ak.us. Admission $4 adults, free for ages 18 and under. Mid-May to mid-Sept, daily 9am–5pm; mid-Sept to mid-May, Tues–Sat 10am–4pm.

St. Michael's Cathedral ⋇   The first Orthodox cathedral in the New World stands grandly in the middle of Sitka's principal street, where it was completed in 1848. Father Veniaminov (see above) designed it and oversaw construction. The cathedral contains several miraculous icons, some dating from the 17th century. The St. Michael, the farthest right of six on the front screen, was bound for Sitka aboard the *Neva* in 1814 when the ship went down in the Pacific. Thirty days later the icon, in its crate, washed ashore undamaged and was recovered by Sitka's townspeople. The original building burned down in a fire that took much of Sitka's downtown in 1966, but almost all the contents were saved by a human chain in the 30 minutes before the building was destroyed. One man lifted down the huge central chandelier, which later took six men to carry. Orthodox Christians all over the United States raised the money to rebuild the cathedral exactly as it had been, using a Russian architect who could interpret Veniaminov's original plans. It was completed in 1976. A knowledgeable guide is on hand to answer questions or give talks when large groups congregate. Sunday services are sung in English, Slavonic, Tlingit, Aleut, and Yupik.

Lincoln and Cathedral sts. © 907/747-8120. $2 donation requested. Summer Mon–Fri 9am–4pm, Sat–Sun varies. Call for winter hours.

Sitka Tribe Dance Performances ⋇   The Sheet'ka Kwaan Naa Kahidi Community House, standing on the north side of the downtown parade ground, is a modern version of a Tlingit Clan House, with an air handling system that pulls smoke from the central fire pit straight up to the chimney. The magnificent house screen at the front of the hall, installed in 2000, is the largest in the Pacific Northwest. Performances last 30 minutes, including three dances and a story. It's entirely traditional and put on by members of the tribe. You can also sign up for tours and activities in the lobby.

The **New Archangel Dancers** (© **907/747-5516**) perform Russian dance frequently in summer at the Harrigan Centennial Hall; of course, they're not Russians.

429 Katlian St. © **888/270-8687** or 907/747-7290. www.sitkatribal.com. $6 adults, $3 children. Call for times.

OTHER ATTRACTIONS IN TOWN

Isabel Miller Museum   The highlight of this one-room Sitka Historical Society museum is a diorama of the town as it looked in 1867, the time of the Alaska purchase. The hall is in the park near the Crescent Harbor downtown.

Harrigan Centennial Hall. © 907/747-6455. www.sitka.org/historicalmuseum. Free admission. Summer daily 8am–5pm, winter Tues–Sat 10am–4pm.

Alaska Raptor Center ⋇   The nonprofit center takes in injured birds of prey (mainly bald eagles, but also owls, hawks, and other species) for veterinary treatment and release or, if too badly injured, for placement in a zoo or to join the collection of 25 that live on-site. Visitors get to see the impressive birds up close in a lecture setting, through the glass wall of the veterinary clinic, or in cages and pens outside. A pleasant, disabled-accessible nature trail leads down to a river where eagles sometimes feed.

1101 Sawmill Creek Blvd. (*(C)* **907/747-8662;** www.alaskaraptor.org. $10 adults, $5 ages 12 and under. Summer Sun–Fri 8am–4pm. Winter by appointment.

WALKING DOWNTOWN   The grassy park at Lincoln and Katlian was the site of the Russians' barracks and parade ground. Just north on Marine Street is a replica of a **Russian Blockhouse;** across Lincoln Street to the south and up the stairs is **Castle Hill,** a site of historic significance for the ancient Tlingits, for the Russians, and for Native Alaskans. The first American flag raised in Alaska was hoisted here in 1867. There are historic markers and cannons. Walking east past the cathedral and Crescent Harbor, several quaint historic buildings are on the left. My favorite is **St. Peter's by-the-Sea Episcopal Church,** a lovely stone-and-timber chapel with a pipe organ, consecrated in 1899. At the east end of the harbor is a **public playground;** turn left, uphill on Jeff Davis Street (named for the first commander of the Alaska garrison, not the Confederate president) past **Sheldon Jackson College** to the Sitka National Cemetery, which has some old and interesting graves.

SHOPPING

There are some good shops and galleries in Sitka, mostly on Lincoln and Harbor streets. Several are across the street from St. Michael's Cathedral, on the uphill side. **Impressions,** at 239 Lincoln St., carries prints by many of Alaska's best contemporary artists. **Fairweather Prints,** at 209 Lincoln St., has a fun, youthful feel; it is large and has a diverse selection, including wearable art (including T-shirts), watercolors, prints, ceramics, and cute, inexpensive crafts. Continue west on Lincoln to **Baranov's Russian and American Store** on the right, and **Log Cache Gifts,** a typical gift store except that it occupies an 1835 Russian cabin. **Old Harbor Books,** at 201 Lincoln St., is a good browsing store with an excellent selection of Alaska books (**The Backdoor** espresso shop inside is covered under "Dining," later). Back in the other direction, near the boat harbor, the **Sitka Rose Gallery** occupies a Victorian house at 419 Lincoln St., featuring higher-end work, mostly local: sculpture, original paintings, engraving, and jewelry. It's quite grand. The **Sheldon Jackson Museum Gift Shop,** 104 College Dr., is an excellent place to buy Alaska Native arts and crafts with assurance of their authenticity.

GETTING OUTSIDE: ON THE WATER

The little islands and rocks that dot Sitka Sound are an invitation to the sea otter in all of us; you must get out on the water. Humpback whales tend to show up in large groups in the fall but are also sometimes seen in the summer. There are so many bald eagles that you're pretty well guaranteed to see them from shore. But the lowly sea otter is the most common and, in my experience, most amusing and endearing of marine mammals, and you'll certainly see them from a tour boat.

SIGHTSEEING & WILDLIFE TOURS

Tour boats visit **St. Lazaria Island,** a bird rookery where you can expect to see puffins, murres, rhinoceros auklets, and storm petrels by the hundred thousand, as well as other pelagic birds. The volcanic rock drops straight down into deep water, so even big boats can come close. Trips also commonly encounter otters and sometimes whales. The public tubs at **Goddard Hot Springs,** 17 miles south of town, are another possible stop for charters.

The **Sitka Wildlife Quest,** operated by Allen Marine Tours (*(C)* **888/ 747-8101** or 907/747-8100; www.allenmarinetours.com), does a terrific job, with well-trained naturalists to explain the wildlife. You have a good chance of encountering humpback whales and sea otters. The 2-hour cruise costs $49 adults, $30 children, and leaves from the Crescent Harbor Visitors Dock Wednesday at 6pm and Saturday and Sunday at 9am late May to August. The Sunday excursion includes a visit to St. Lazaria Island. Buy tickets on board. These are different excursions from the ones offered cruise-ship passengers.

For $90 per person, you can charter a six-passenger boat for a 4-hour tour to St. Lazaria Island with a married couple who are both retired wildlife biologists, Kent Hall and Beverly Minn, at **Sitka's Secrets** (© 907/747-5089; www. sitkasecret.com). For a multi-day exploration with an experienced naturalist, try Barbara Bingham's **Raven's Fire** (© 888/747-4789 or 907/747-5777; www. ravensfire.com).

Sea Life Discovery Tours (© 907-966-2301), brand new in 2001, plans to offer tours to see underwater life in a boat with huge windows in the hull. They charge $65 for a 90-minute tour; call for times.

SALTWATER FISHING
Many charter boats are available for salmon or halibut. The Sitka Convention and Visitors Bureau (see "Visitor Information," earlier) keeps a detailed charter boat list, including rates, that goes on for pages. **Alaska Adventures Unlimited** (© 907/747-5576; akafish@ptialaska.net.) is a booking agent handling more than half the charter boats in the harbor. If you can handle your own boat, skiffs rent for $85 half-day from **Sitka Ocean Adventures** (© 907/747-6375; www.ptialaska.net/~delongb).

SEA KAYAKING
Sitka's protected waters and intricate shorelines are perfect for sea kayaking. Your almost sure to see sea otters, seals, sea lions, and eagles, and could see whales. Various companies offer guided paddles; links to five are found at **www. sitka.org/tours.htm**, or call the visitor center.

Beginners will do well with **Sitka Sound Ocean Adventures** (© 907/ 747-6375; www.ptialaska.net/~delongb), run by the same friendly couple as the Camp Coogan Bay Hideaway (see "Accommodations," below). Their small-group, 2-hour paddles cost $50 per person.

Baidarka Boats is the place to go if you want to do more than briefly dip a paddle in the water, or if you seek to rent boats. Their well-stocked shop for sales or rental is at 320 Lincoln St. (© 907/747-8996; www.kayaksite.com). They take raw beginners, too, but their shortest paddle is 4 hours, with time for beachcombing, tide pooling, and snacks. The competitive rates depend on the size of your group.

DIVING
These waters tend to be clear and biologically rich, making them appealing to divers. Winter is best, when plankton isn't blooming, but good periods come in summer, too. **Clay's Dive Shop,** 246 Katlian St. (© 907/747-7871), is one of two dive shops in town.

GETTING OUTSIDE: ONSHORE
FRESHWATER FISHING
Anglers should pick up the *Sitka Area Sport Fishing Guide,* which has lots of tips on streams, lakes, and methods in the area. You can write ahead for it from the **Alaska Department of Fish and Game,** 1255 W. Eighth St. (P.O. Box 25526), Juneau, AK 99802-5526 (© 907/465-4180; www.state.ak.us/adfg). The local Fish and Game office is at 304 Lake St., Room 103, Sitka, AK 99835 (© 907/747-5355).

FOREST SERVICE CABINS

The **Sitka Ranger District,** 201 Katlian St., Suite 109, Sitka, AK 99835 (✆ **907/747-4420;** www.fs.fed.us/r10/tongass), maintains two dozen wilderness cabins on Baranof, Chichagof, and Kruzof islands, in sea kayaking coves and on remote fishing lakes, where rowing skiffs generally are provided. The cabins and their facilities are described in a Forest Service booklet or on their website. You will need camping gear and a boat or floatplane to get there, a much greater cost than the nightly rental of $35 to $45. Perhaps the most affordable way is via **Sitka Sound Water Taxi** (✆ 907/747-5970; home. gci.net/~snewell/). **Harris Aircraft Services,** 400 Airport Rd. (✆ **907/ 966-3050;** www.harrisaircraft.com) offers floatplane charters. Check "Getting Outside in the Tongass National Forest," in section 1, for information on researching and reserving a cabin. Another remote cabin option is listed below, under "Accommodations."

HIKING

Already a great hiking area, Sitka is busily building more trails to thread all over the mountains behind the town. There are a dozen U.S. Forest Service hiking trails accessible from the roads around Sitka and another 20 you can get to by plane or boat. A handy map, the *Outdoor Recreation Guide,* shows all the road-accessible trails, including easy walks from downtown. Get it and advice from the visitor center or ranger district.

From downtown, the 4.1-mile (one-way) **Indian River Trail** is a relaxing rain-forest walk rising gradually up the river valley to a small waterfall. Take Indian River Road off Sawmill Creek Road just east of the downtown. For a steeper mountain-climbing trail to alpine terrain and great views, the **Gavan Hill–Harbor Mountain Trail** is near the end of Baranof Street, which starts near the Russian Bishop's House. It gains 2,500 feet over 3 miles to the peak of Gavan Hill, then continues another 3 miles along a ridge to meet Harbor Mountain Road. The **Sitka Cross Trail** connects these trails and neighborhood streets, allowing you to start almost anywhere.

At the north end of Halibut Point Road, 7½ miles from downtown, several wonderful trails loop through the **Starrigavan Recreation Area.** On the right the **Estuary Life Trail** and **Forest Muskeg Trail,** totaling about a mile, are exquisitely developed and accessible to anyone, circling a grassy estuary rich with birds and fish. The well-built **Mosquito Cove Trail,** starting from the far end of the campground loop on the left, loops 1¼ miles along the shore to the secluded gravel beach of the cove, returning over boardwalk steps through the old-growth forest.

TIDE POOLING & SHORE WALKS

Halibut Point State Recreation Area, 4.4 miles north of town on Halibut Point Road, is a great place for a picnic, shore ramble, and tide pooling. The Mosquito Cove Trail (above) is also promising. To find the best low tides, check a tide book, available all over town. It's best to go on the lowest tide possible, arriving on the shore an hour before the low. To identify the little creatures you'll see, buy a plastic-covered field guide at the National Park Service visitor center at the historical park.

WHALE-WATCHING

Humpback whales stop to feed in Sitka Sound on their way south in the winter migration. During October, November, December, and March, you can watch from shore—the local government has even built a special park for the purpose.

At **Whale Park,** 3½ miles south of town on Sawmill Creek Boulevard, spotting scopes are mounted on platforms along a boardwalk and at the end of staircases that descend the dramatic, wooded cliffs. Excellent interpretive signs, located near surfacing concrete whales in the parking lot, explain the whales. The Sitka WhaleFest, in November (see "Special Events," earlier), is the best time for whale enthusiasts; you can watch whales in the company of cetacean scientists from all over the west coast.

ACCOMMODATIONS

In addition to the places below, you'll find excellent standard rooms in a quiet building downtown at the **Super 8 Sitka,** 404 Sawmill Creek Blvd. (© **800/ 800-8000** for reservations, or 907/747-8804). Also, the **Sitka Convention and Visitors Bureau** (© **907/747-5940;** www.sitka.org) has links to many B&Bs on its website, and can send you a printed list as well.

Alaska Ocean View Bed & Breakfast ★★   Ebullient Carol Denkinger and her husband, Bill, have a passion for making their bed-and-breakfast one you'll remember. They've thought of everything—the covered outdoor Jacuzzi where you can watch the eagles, toys and games for the kids, thick robes and slippers, an open snack counter, and big, delicious full breakfast, even wildflower seeds to take home. Rooms are plush, and guests are pampered. It's on a residential street with a view of the water about a mile from the historic district.

1101 Edgecumbe Dr., Sitka, AK 99835. © **907/747-8310.** Fax 907/747-3440. www.sitka-alaska-lodging.com. 3 units. High season $119–$179 double; extra person $15–$30. Low season $79–$129 double; extra person $5–$20. Rates include breakfast. AE, MC, V. No smoking. **Amenities:** Outdoor Jacuzzi; business center. *In room:* TV/VCR and free video library, CD player, dataport, microwave, unstocked refrigerator, coffeemaker, hair dryer, iron.

Cascade Inn ★   Although the gas station and convenience store out front suggest something else, once you get into the rooms of this waterside building, you find a clean oasis of ocean light. Each has a balcony right over the water's edge; the views over Sitka Sound are remarkable and you can sleep to the sound of the sea. The rooms themselves are small but crisp, with one or two queen-size beds. Kitchenette units cost $15 more. The sauna has a glass front to take advantage of the view. It's 2.5 miles to town. *Note:* Stay elsewhere if you have trouble with stairs.

2035 Halibut Point Rd. © **800/532-0908** outside Alaska, or 907/747-6804. www.travelsitka.com/cascade. 10 units. High season $110–$125 double, low season $85–$95 double; $10 each additional person. AE, DC, MC, V. **Amenities:** Sauna; fishing charters; coin-op laundry. *In room:* TV/VCR, voice mail, coffeemaker, hair dryer, iron.

Crescent Harbor Hideaway ★ *(Finds)*   This stately 1897 house, one of Sitka's oldest, stands across a quiet street from Crescent Harbor and the lovely park at the harbor's edge, with a glassed-in porch to watch the world go by. One unit is a large, one-bedroom apartment with a full kitchen and a private patio and phone line; it's the best unit I've seen in Sitka. The other nestles adorably under the eaves. The style is simple elegance, with antiques and colonial reproductions, Berber carpet and attractive bathrooms. Everything is clean and fresh. Hostess Susan Stanford is an artist and enjoys her guests. The common areas are shared with an Australian shepherd named Lacy. Susan's neighbors, Ron and Barbara Lessard, have a very nice single unit, **Finn Alley Inn** (© **907/747-3655;** www.ptialaska.net/~seakdist/finn.htm).

709 Lincoln St., Sitka, AK 99835. ©/fax **907/747-4900.** www.ptialaska.net/~bareis/B&B.htm. 2 units. High season $110–$145 double. Low season $85–$115 double. Extra person $25. Rates include continental breakfast. No credit cards. No smoking, even outside. *In room:* TV, VCR, clock, radio, hair dryer.

Finds **Rent a Floathouse**

Southeast Alaska has a unique kind of dwelling called a floathouse, a house on a barge, permanently anchored in some quiet, forgotten cove. There have even been float-towns, with houses, schools, and other buildings tied together, usually at remote logging sites. **Camp Coogan Bay Hideaway** (© 907/747-6375; www.ptialaska.net/ ~delongb) is a floathouse you can rent. It floats in a narrow, placid bay out of a wilderness fantasy, 20 minutes from Sitka by boat (it's the best place in the area to see bears). A charming, peeling old bunkhouse from town was stuck on a 1940s barge and anchored here, with a rainwater system, a woodstove for heat, propane appliances, and a diesel generator if you want light. A wood-fired sauna and a gas barbecue are out on deck. Don't expect the Hilton: It's primitive and a little grubby. You'll want to rent a boat or sea kayaks for mobility; owners John and Barbara DeLong offer those services too, and have two other floathouses for rent.

Sitka Hotel *Value*   This is a good, family-owned budget hotel. Each year the proprietors take on another improvement project in the 1939 building. The small rooms will never be luxurious, but the owners have put together many comfortable, quirky units and keep them clean and well maintained. The location is prime, right across from the Russian parade grounds. The rooms without private bath are about four to a bathroom, and the facilities are in good shape. **Victoria's Restaurant,** with about a dozen tables in the storefront downstairs, tries, like the hotel, for a high Victorian feel, but it's more a friendly small-town diner, with hearty breakfasts and lunches in winter and an inexpensive fine-dining dinner menu added in the summer.

118 Lincoln St., Sitka, AK 99835. © 907/747-3288. Fax 907/747-8499. www.sitkahotel.com. 60 units, 45 with private bathroom. $60 double with shared bathroom, $75 double with private bathroom. Extra person $7. AE, MC, V. **Amenities:** Restaurant and bar; coin-op laundry. *In room:* TV.

Westmark Shee Atika ✹   The community's main upscale hotel, overlooking Crescent Harbor in the heart of the historic district, falls short of being the first-class place Sitka deserves, mostly because of the structure itself, a brown, five-story wooden building with plywood siding, hanging ceilings in the halls, and small rooms. The furniture, carpets, TVs, and other amenities were new on my inspection and the rooms well kept, but blah browns and cramped spaces took away from the effect. The restaurant, lounge, and most rooms have very good waterfront views; harborside rooms are $10 more.

The **Raven Dining Room** is everything you'd expect from an upscale hotel cafe with a long menu of seafood and beef in the evening.

330 Seward St., Sitka, AK 99835-7523. © 800/544-0970 for reservations, or 907/747-6241. Fax 907/ 747-5486. www.westmarkhotels.com. 101 units. High season $139–$149 double. Low season $139–$149 double. Extra person over age 13 $15. AE, DC, DISC, MC, V. **Amenities:** Restaurant and bar; summer tour desk. *In room:* TV, dataport, coffeemaker, hair dryer, iron.

HOSTELLING & CAMPING

Hostelling International—Sitka is located at 303 Kimsham St. (© 907/ 747-8661), more than a mile from downtown. The 18 beds are $10 per night, but they don't provide linens. It's open June to August; office hours and dorm access are 8 to 10am and 6pm to 10pm. Reservations are required, and they start taking them April 1.

The Forest Service's **Starrigavan Campground,** at the north end of Halibut Point Road, 7½ miles from town and ½ mile from the ferry dock, is one of the loveliest in Alaska. One loop of sites branches from the Estuary Life Trail, widely separated under huge trees. The other loop is at the water's edge, with some sites situated next to the ocean to make you feel like you're way out in the wilderness. The 28 sites, with pit toilets, are first-come, first-served, with an $8 fee, open May 1 to Labor Day. Gates are locked 10pm to 7am.

There are two RV parks, each with water and electric hookups only and charging under $22: city-run **Sealing Cove RV Park** (© 907/747-3439) is near the airport, and **Sitka Sportsman's Association RV Park** (© 907/747-6033) is near the ferry dock.

DINING

See other restaurant choices at the Westmark Shee Atika and Sitka Hotel above, under "Accommodations." A Subway sandwich shop is at Seward and Lake streets, behind the Westmark.

Bayview Restaurant BURGERS/PASTA/SEAFOOD   The view of the boat harbor and good food make this small second-story restaurant popular year-round, although it's sometimes noisy and a bit cramped. Everything I've tried from the extensive menu has been well prepared and quickly served. The clam chowder sings, and people come back for the halibut and burgers. Some lunch items are priced a little high, however; my lunch of halibut fish and chips was tasty and done just right, but the portion and plate were quite small for $10. A BLT is $8. Dinner prices are more competitive. The wine list has a nice selection and reasonable prices. It's a great spot for breakfast.

407 Lincoln St. © 907/747-5440. Main courses $5.50–$27. AE, DISC, MC, V. Spring–fall, Mon–Sat 5am–9pm, Sun 5am–8pm. Winter, Mon–Thurs 7am–8pm, Fri–Sat 7am–9pm, Sun 8am–8pm.

Channel Club STEAK/SEAFOOD   The steaks have always been great here, and the salad bar, which comes with every meal, is legendary. It's really an appetizer bar, and the crab alone is worth the trip. The restaurant is in one big room, with a swordfish on one wall and the menu on another, and the dress code seems to be T-shirts and baseball caps. The service is as casual as in the greasiest greasy-spoon diner. That's all part of the manly club thing, and it works. But in this setting there's no escape from the copious cigarette smoke, and if you ask for refuge you're shunted off by the bathroom, where it's still smoky and worse. The restaurant is several miles out Halibut Point Road, but a courtesy van will come get you and take you home at the end of the evening. They have a full bar.

2906 Halibut Point Rd. © 907/747-9916. Reservations recommended. Main courses $12–$41.50. AE, DC, MC, V. Sun–Thurs 5–10pm, Fri–Sat 5–11pm.

Pizza Express *Value* MEXICAN/PIZZA   Come here when you want a filling, inexpensive meal in a light, pleasant dining room. The owners and most of the menu are Mexican, but they also serve and deliver good pizza.

236 Lincoln St., Ste. 106. © 907/966-2428. Main courses $6–$13. MC, V. Mon–Sat 11am–10pm, Sun noon–10pm; closes at 9pm in winter.

Van Winkle and Sons SEAFOOD/PASTA/PIZZA   Formerly a funky and stylish little place across the street, this has become more of a typical small-town family restaurant since its name and venue changed. The simple seafood, beef,

Hip Eats & Coffee in Sitka

The same cool couple owns two of the coolest places in town: **Mojo Café**, at 256 Katlian St. (© **907/747-0667**), and **The Backdoor Café**, in the back half of Harborside Books at 104 Barracks St. (© **907/747-8856**). These are the kinds of places that develop a following among the local poets, musicians, and the like. Mojo, in a tiny cinderblock room, is open Monday through Friday 6:30am to 2pm, serving cold breakfasts and soup, sandwiches, and specials for lunch. The Backdoor is more of a coffee place, with the owner's own bagels and the day's lunch special from the Mojo. It's a great hangout, open Monday through Saturday 7am to 5pm, Sunday 9am to 3pm. Neither place takes credit cards. **Highliner Coffee**, on Lake Street just above Seward Street (© **907/747-4970**), is a fancier place, with Internet access ($5.25 for the first half-hour). A "highliner" is a top commercial fisherman; the name here is a bit of a boast for its fisherpeople owners, who hope to educate customers about their way of life. It's open Monday through Saturday 5:30am to 5pm, Sunday 8am to 4pm.

and pizza receive good reviews, but the more sophisticated fare I sampled fell flat and the service was poor. The dining room is on the second floor with two tiers of booths and a good view to the water.

205 Harbor Dr. © **907/747-7652**. Reservations recommended. Lunch items $6–$10.25; dinner main courses $11–$24. AE, MC, V. High season, Mon–Sat 11:30am–1:45pm; daily 5–9:45pm. Low season, Mon–Sat 11:30am–1:45pm and 5–8:45pm, Sun 5–9pm.

8 Juneau: Forest Capital

Juneau (*June*-oh) hustles and bustles like no other city in Alaska. The steep downtown streets echo with the mad shopping sprees of cruise-ship passengers in the summer tourist season and the whispered intrigues of politicians during the winter legislative session. Miners, loggers, and ecotourism operators come to lobby for their share of Southeast's forest. Lunch hour arrives, and well-to-do state and federal bureaucrats burst from the office buildings to try the latest trendy restaurant or brown-bag on one of the waterfront wharves, the sparkling water before them and gift store malls behind. The center of town becomes an ad hoc pedestrian mall as the crush of people forces cars to creep.

My Juneau is close at hand, but very different. As a child, at a magical age, I lived here with my family in a house on the side of the mountains above downtown. My Juneau is up the 99 steps that lead from the cemetery to the bottom of Pine Street—the way I walked home from school—and then to the top of residential Evergreen Avenue, where the pavement gives way to a forest trail among fiddlehead ferns and massive rain-forest spruces. That trail leads to the flume (a wooden aqueduct that used to bring water down from the mountains), upon which we would walk into the land of bears and salmon, the rumbling water at our feet. It's still a short walk from the rackety downtown streets to a misty forest quiet, where one can listen for the voices of trees.

Juneau is Alaska's third-largest city (Anchorage and Fairbanks are larger), with a population of 30,000, but it feels like a small town that's just been stuffed with people. Splattered on the sides of Mount Juneau and Mount Roberts along Gastineau Channel, where there isn't room for much of a town, its setting is picturesque but impractical. Further development up the mountains is hemmed in by avalanche danger; beyond is the 1,500-square-mile **Juneau Icefield,** an impenetrable barrier. Gold-mine tailings dumped into the Gastineau created the flat land near the water where much of the downtown area now stands. The Native village that originally stood on the waterfront is today a little pocket of mobile homes several blocks from the shore. There's no road to the outside world, and the terrain forbids building one. Jets are the main way in and out, threading down through the mountains to the airport.

Gold was responsible for the location; it was found here in 1880 by Joe Juneau and Richard Harris, assisted by the Tlingit chief Kowee, who told them where to look. All three men are buried in the Evergreen Cemetery. Their find started Alaska's development. The territory's first significant roads and bridges and its first electrical plant were built in the mountains here, which were carved with miles of hard rock tunnels well before the Klondike Gold Rush began. In a few years these mines removed more gold than the United States paid for all of Alaska, as attested to by a photograph in the State Museum showing comparative piles. There's plenty of gold left, but mining died out with World War II and environmental controls and low gold prices have stymied recent efforts to start again. There are several interesting gold mining sites.

In 1900, Congress moved the territorial capital here from Sitka, which had fallen behind in the rush of gold rush development. Alaskans have been fighting over whether or not to keep it here for many decades since, but Juneau's economy is heavily dependent on government jobs, and it has successfully fought off a series of challenges to its capital status, most recently in 1994. The closest the issue came was in the 1970s, when the voters approved moving the capital, but then balked at the cost of building a whole new city to house it—a necessity since neither Anchorage nor Fairbanks, which have their own rivalry, would support the move if it meant the other city got to have the capital nearby.

There's plenty to see in Juneau, and it's a good town to visit because the relatively sophisticated population of government workers supports excellent restaurants and amenities not found elsewhere in Southeast. Alaska's most accessible glacier, the Mendenhall, is in Juneau, and businesses ranging from the fish hatchery to the brewery to an abandoned mine have set up tours for visitors. There are three good museums, too. Juneau is also a starting point for outdoor travel all over the northern Panhandle. Because the city is a travel hub, you'll likely pass through on your way to Glacier Bay or virtually anywhere else you want to go in the region. But you don't have to go that far to get into the outdoors from Juneau: You can start from the capitol building for a hike to the top of Mount Juneau or Mount Roberts, or up the Perseverance Trail that leads in between. Sea-kayaking and whale-watching excursions are nearby, as well as some of Alaska's most scenic tide pooling and beach walking.

Downtown, the crush of visitors can be overwhelming when many cruise ships are in port at once, and the streets around the docks have been entirely taken over by shops and other touristy businesses. Many of these are owned by people from outside who come to the state for the summer to sell gifts made outside. But only a few blocks away are quiet mountainside neighborhoods of houses with mossy roofs, and only a few blocks farther are the woods and the mountains, populated by bear, eagles, and salmon.

ESSENTIALS
GETTING THERE
BY AIR   Jet service is available only from **Alaska Airlines** (✆ **800/252-7522;** www.alaskaair.com), with several daily nonstop flights from Seattle and

---

Tips **Flying to Juneau**

Don't schedule anything tightly around a flight to Juneau: The mist-shrouded airport, wedged between ocean and mountain, is tough to get into and can be a hair-raising place to land. It even has its own verb: *to overhead*. That means that when you fly to Juneau, you could end up somewhere else instead. The airline will put you on the next flight back to Juneau when the weather clears, but they won't pay for hotel rooms or give you a refund. Your only protection is travel insurance and a loose itinerary. This situation is such an ingrained part of Juneau's way of life that a channel on the cable TV system broadcasts the view from the airport 24 hours a day, showing the weather over the Gastineau Channel (it's called the Channel Channel, 23 on the dial). Residents know the view so well they can tell from the silent image if they'll get out that day.

Anchorage and from the smaller Southeast Alaska towns. Many of the region's commuter and air-taxi operators also maintain desks at the airport and have flights out of Juneau, including **L.A.B. Flying Service** (② 800/427-5966 or 907/789-9160; www.labflying.com) and **Wings of Alaska** (② 907/789-0790; www.wingsofalaska.com).

BY FERRY All the ferries of Southeast's main-line **Alaska Marine Highway System** (② 800/642-0066; www.state.ak.us/ferry) stop at the terminal in Auke Bay (② 907/465-3940), 14 miles from downtown. The *Malaspina* runs daily up the Lynn Canal to Haines and Skagway and back in the summer. The passenger fare is $26 to Haines, $35 to Skagway. Cabins with outside windows have been made into inexpensive private day rooms, a relaxing, private way to travel.

GETTING INTO TOWN FROM THE AIRPORT & FERRY TERMINAL
The **Hotel Express** van (② 907/463-6916) meets flights and takes passengers downtown for $8; it picks up at major hotels or smaller ones by prior arrangement. At this writing, there is no public transportation from the ferry dock, so you have to take a cab. **Capital Cab** (② 907/586-2772 or 907/789-2772) offers **taxi service** (as well as tours by the hour). A cab in from the airport will cost you $20, the ferry dock $25. An express **Capital Transit** city **bus** (② 907/789-6901) comes to the airport at 11 minutes past the hour on weekdays from 8:11am to 5:11pm and costs $1.25; your luggage has to fit under your seat or at your feet.

ORIENTATION

Juneau has three main parts: downtown, the Mendenhall Valley, and Douglas. Downtown Juneau is a numbered grid of streets overlying the uneven topography like a patterned quilt over a pile of pillows. As you look at Juneau from the water, Mount Juneau is on the left and Mount Roberts on the right; Mount Roberts is a few hundred feet taller, at 3,819 feet. **Franklin Street** extends south of town 5½ miles to good hiking trails and the hamlet of Thane. When the city outgrew its original site downtown, housing spread to the suburban **Mendenhall Valley,** about a dozen miles north out the Egan Expressway or the parallel, two-lane Glacier Highway. The glacial valley also contains the Juneau International Airport, University of Alaska Southeast, and **Auke Bay** area, where the ferry terminal is located. The road continues 40 miles, to a place known as **"The End of the Road."** Across a bridge over the Gastineau Channel from downtown Juneau is Douglas Island. Turn left for the town of **Douglas,** mostly a bedroom community for Juneau, and turn right for the North Douglas Highway, which leads to the ski area and some beautiful rocky beaches.

GETTING AROUND

BY RENTAL CAR A car is a hindrance in compact downtown Juneau, but if you're going to the Mendenhall Glacier or to any of the attractions out the road or on Douglas Island, renting a car for a day or two is a good idea. Hertz, Avis, Budget, and National are based at the airport.

BY BIKE If you can handle hills, bikes make good sense in Juneau, where separated paths parallel many of the main roads and downtown traffic is slow. The 24-mile round-trip to Mendenhall Glacier keeps you on a bike path almost all the way. **Mountain Gears,** at 126 Front St. (☎ **907/586-4327**), rents 21-speed mountain bikes for $6 an hour or $25 a day, full suspension for $35. This full-service bike shop can give you ideas for mountain biking rides and provide maps and directions.

 FAST FACTS: **Juneau**

Banks Among many banks and stores, **Wells Fargo,** at 123 Seward St. (☎ 907/586-3324), has an ATM.

Hospital **Bartlett Regional,** at 3260 Hospital Dr. (☎ **907/586-2611**), is 3 miles out on the Glacier Highway.

Internet Access **Uncle Arty's,** 493 S. Franklin St., second floor (☎ **907/463-2543**), is open summer daily 8am to 11pm.

Police At 210 Admiral Way, ☎ **907/586-2780** for nonemergencies.

Post Office Downtown in the federal building, 709 W. Ninth St.; and in the Mendenhall Valley at 9491 Vintage Blvd., by the airport.

Taxes **Sales tax** is 5%. You pay 12% tax on **rooms.**

VISITOR INFORMATION

The **Visitor Information Center** is in the Centennial Hall at 101 Egan Dr., near the State Museum (☎ **888/581-2201** or 907/586-2201; fax 907/586-6304; www.traveljuneau.com). Operated by the Juneau Convention and Visitors Bureau, the center distributes a *Juneau Travel Planner,* online or on paper, that contains exhaustive listings of hotels and B&Bs, charter boats, tours, and other services, including information such as rates that booster organizations usually don't publish. The center is open Monday to Friday 8:30am to 5pm, Saturday and Sunday 9am to 5pm in summer; Monday to Friday 9am to 5pm in winter. Volunteers also staff a **visitor information desk** at the airport, near the door in the baggage-claim area, during the summer.

The **Tongass National Forest Juneau Ranger District** is near the airport at 8465 Old Dairy Rd., Juneau, AK 99801 (☎ 907/586-8800, TTY 907/790-7444, fax 907/586-8808; www.fs.fed.us/r10/tongass).

SPECIAL EVENTS

An exhaustive event calendar is posted on the visitors' bureau website: www.traveljuneau.com/discover.

Tips   Where Do You Get Off?

Cruise-ship passengers disembark in Juneau's attractive **Marine Park** waterfront area, where a kiosk dispenses information and tour operators sell their services. Downtown shops and attractions are close by. Among the most popular sights is right at the dock, the statue of a small dog facing the ships as they come in. This is *Patsy Ann,* a bull terrier that in the 1930s always seemed to know when a steamer was arriving and faithfully stationed herself on the dock to meet the disembarking passengers.

The **Alaska Folk Festival** (© 907/463-3316; www.juneau.com/aff) is the state's biggest annual drawing together of musicians, at Centennial Hall, April 8 to 14, 2002. **The Juneau Jazz and Classics Festival** (© 907/463-3378; www.juneau.com/music), May 17 to 26, 2002, includes concerts at various venues, even on a boat. **Celebration** (© 907/463-4844) is a huge Alaska Native dance and cultural gathering that happens only every other year, June 6 to 8, 2002. **Gold Rush Days** (© 907/586-2497) includes logging and mining events and competitions anyone can join, June 30 to July 1, 2002. **The Golden North Salmon Derby** (© 907/789-2399; www.salmonderby.org), held annually since 1947, targets kings and silvers over a weekend in mid-August. Unlike some other such derbies around the state, this isn't just a tourist thing—it empties the town, and is even covered live on the radio.

DOWNTOWN ATTRACTIONS & ACTIVITIES

Alaska-Gastineau Mill and Gold Mine Tour ★   A half-day tour visits the overgrown ruins of a hard rock gold operation that operated from 1915 to 1921, then goes 360 feet into one tunnel for a demonstration of how it was done. Although Princess Tours provides the buses and sells the tickets, the tour is the work of people who came to Juneau to reopen the A.J. mine (of which this was a part), and stayed to turn it into a tourist attraction when that project failed; their fascination is infectious. The mine site is south of town, but buses pick up visitors at the state museum downtown. The tour is quite in-depth; those without interest in mining history or mechanical matters may get bored. Dress warmly.

Book though Princess Tours, 151 Mill St. © 907/463-3900. $59 adults, $39 children. Daily departures during summer; call ahead to reserve.

Alaska State Museum ★★★   The museum contains a large collection of art and historical artifacts, but it doesn't seem like a storehouse at all because the objects' presentation is based on their meaning, not their value. Come here to put the rest of your visit in context. A clan house in the Alaska Native Gallery contains authentic art you'd really find in its functional place. The Lincoln Pole is here, carved by an artist who used a picture of the president as his model to represent his clan's first encounter with whites. Native cultures from around the state contributed superb artifacts, presented to explain the lifestyle of those who made them. The ramp to the second floor wraps around the natural history display, with an eagle in a tree, and at the top a state history gallery uses significant pieces to tell Alaska's story. The children's area is among the best we've seen, with a ship they can play in—I just about needed a crowbar to get my son out. The gift store carries authentic Native arts and crafts, plus books, maps, and so on.

395 Whittier St. ✆ **907/465-2901.** www.museums.state.ak.us. Admission $5 adults, free for ages 18 and under. Winter discount $3. High season, Mon–Fri 9am–6pm, Sat–Sun 10am–6pm; winter, Tues–Sat 10am–4pm.

The Juneau-Douglas City Museum ★ This fun little museum displays artifacts and photographs from the city's pioneer and mining history. There are gorgeous stained-glass windows. The tiny bookshop is stocked with handy information for your visit, including the historic hike guide booklet, historic walking-tour map, and maps of the Evergreen Cemetery and the old Treadwell Mine. The plaza in front is where the 49-star U.S. flag was first raised in 1959—they didn't make many of those, as Hawaii was admitted as the 50th within a year, but you'll still find one flying here.

At the corner of Fourth and Main sts. ✆ **907/586-3572.** www.juneau.lib.ak.us/parksrec/museum. Admission $3 adults ($2 in winter), free for ages 18 and under. High season, Mon–Fri 9am–5pm, Sat–Sun 10am–5pm. Low season, Fri–Sat noon–4pm and by appointment.

The Last Chance Mining Museum ★ *Finds* The museum preserves old mining buildings on forested Gold Creek with some of their original equipment, including an immense 1912 air compressor and layered glass map of the tunnels. This was once a nerve center for one of the world's biggest hard-rock mines. The highlight is its energetic and learned guide, Renee Hughes, who lives above the compressor with her husband and fellow leader of the Gastineau Channel Historical Society, Gary Gillette. Ask her about the cave-in of the Treadwell Mine to hear her riveting storytelling.

1001 Basin Rd. (From downtown, take Gold St. to the top, then turn left onto Basin Rd., continuing 1½ miles up the valley to the end of the road.) ✆ **907/586-5338.** Admission $3. Daily 9:30am–12:30pm and 3:30–6:30pm. Closed Oct to mid-May.

Mount Roberts Tramway ★ The tram takes only 6 minutes to whisk passengers from tourist-clogged Franklin Street to the clear air and overwhelming views at the tree line (1,760 ft.), a destination that used to require a day of huffing and puffing to witness. The tram can be crowded; it's once you're up there that the beauty hits you. The Alaska Native owners seem to understand that, and they have done a good job of building a network of paths that take advantage of the views as you pass through a fascinating alpine ecosystem; the owners have even carved artwork into the living trunks of some of the trees. If you're energetic, you can start a 6-mile round-trip to Mount Roberts's summit (at 3,819 ft.), or you can hike the 2.5 miles back to downtown. There's an auditorium at the top tram station showing a film on Tlingit culture and a multimedia performance on wildlife. A bar and grill serves three meals a day. Don't bother with the tram on a day of fog or low overcast—it's not worth the money without the view.

490 South Franklin St., at the waterfront near the cruise-ship dock. ✆ **888/461-8726** or 907/463-3412. www.goldbelttours.com. All-day pass $19.75 adults, $10.50 children 12 and under, tax included. Daily 9am–9pm. Closed Oct–Apr.

WALKING TOUR | **JUNEAU**

Start & Finish:	Alaska State Capitol, Fourth and Seward streets.
Time:	1 to 1½ hours for standard tour; 2½ hours for the extended tour, with minimal stops.

❶ **The Alaska State Capitol**
This structure fills the block between Fourth and Fifth and Main and Seward streets. Except for the marble portico on the Fourth Street side, it is a nondescript brick box, probably the least

Alaska

- Fairbanks
- Anchorage
- Cordova
- Juneau
- Kenai
- Sitka
- Ketchikan

1 Alaska State Capitol
2 Courthouse
3 Juneau-Douglas City Museum
4 The State Office Building
5 Governor's Mansion
6 Gold Creek
7 Wickersham House State Historic Site
8 St. Nicholas Orthodox Church
9 Holy Trinity Episcopal Church
10 The Evergreen Cemetery
11 Abandoned wooden flume
12 The Last Chance Mining Museum

Church ⛪
Information ⓘ
Post Office ✉

impressive state capitol in the most beautiful setting in the nation. The federal government built the structure in 1931, when Alaska was still a territory. Inside, some of the old-fashioned woodwork and decorative details are interesting, and the building is mostly without security to block your wanderings. During the summer, free tours start every half hour Monday through Friday 9am to 4:30pm; other times, pick up a self-guided tour brochure in the lobby. Call ℂ **907/465-3800** for information. The legislature is in session January to early May.

Across Fourth is the:
❷ State Courthouse
The statue of a bear in front defines Alaskan taste in art: It replaced a hated abstract steel sculpture called *Nimbus* that was removed by an act of the legislature and that finally came to rest in front of the state museum a few blocks away.

On the opposite, northwest corner is the:
❸ Juneau–Douglas City Museum
Stop in here now to buy the Evergreen Cemetery map if you plan to include that in your walk, or get the *Historic*

Downtown Juneau Guide to learn more on the whole walk.

④ The State Office Building

This building stands on the fourth corner. It's built into the edge of a cliff that forms a major barrier through the downtown area; if you're headed for the lower land where the State Museum and Centennial Hall are located, you can avoid eight flights of steps in between by taking the building's elevator down. In any event, visit the towering atrium, with its great views and a 1928 movie theater pipe organ that's played on Fridays at noon. The state library historical collections off the lobby contain historic photographs and artifacts, some of which are often on exhibit. On sunny days, the patio off the atrium is a warm place for a picnic, with a fabulous view.

Returning out the door you entered, turn left and follow Calhoun Street around the curve. An outdoor staircase here leads down to the flat area of town below (but you know about taking the elevator). Those lowlands originally were mostly underwater and this embankment stood just above the shoreline, which continued along Front and South Franklin streets. The land you see below you is mine tailings that were dumped in the Channel. The pedestrian overpass across Calhoun is used by the governor and his black labs, Shadow and Cody, to get to the Capitol from the white, neoclassical:

⑤ Governor's Mansion

Located on the left, it was built by the federal government in 1912. Call ⓒ **907/465-3500** to arrange a tour. If you see a tall, slender man with dark hair running a dog in the yard, that's Gov. Tony Knowles. He's a Democrat from Anchorage; his 8 years will end late in 2002.

Shortcut: To save yourself some hill-climbing, continue on Calhoun and turn right on Goldbelt Street, climbing past some beautiful houses to Seventh, then pick up the tour at the Wickersham House.

Continuing down Calhoun, you'll come to:

⑥ Gold Creek

Juneau's founders made their gold strike in this stream in 1880. Trace it upstream in peaceful **Cope Park,** past the playground and tennis courts to the unique ballfield, which is bounded by the stream's forested canyon walls. (To continue this walk to Evergreen Cemetery and up to the top of the town and through the woods on the flume—a long, strenuous walk—return to Calhoun Street and continue in the direction you were going. That's covered below under "The Extended Walk.") At the end of the baseball diamond's left field line is a lovely path and public stairway through the woods up to Seventh Street. Seventh runs along a narrow ridge between downtown Juneau and the creek. Across the street from the top of the stairway is:

⑦ The Wickersham House State Historic Site

It's at 213 Seventh St. (ⓒ **907/586-9001**). This white, 1899 frame house was the retirement home of Judge James Wickersham, revered by Alaskans for bringing law to the gold rush in Eagle, Nome, and Fairbanks, for exploring the Denali area and helping make it a national park, for convincing the federal government to build the Alaska railroad, and for winning Alaska's right to make its own laws when he represented the territory in Congress. The house was in the family from 1928 until the state bought it in 1984, so it still contains Wickersham's belongings, including an Edison cylinder gramophone he took to Fairbanks, and his assignment to go to Alaska signed by Theodore Roosevelt. The house badly needs work, but the short tour is charming. A live-in guide requests a $2 donation. It is open mid-May through September, 10am to noon and 1 to 5pm, winter by appointment.

Continue on Seventh to Gold Street, turn right and follow it downhill to Fifth, site of the tiny:

⑧ St. Nicholas Orthodox Church

This structure is a significant architectural landmark. The octagonal chapel was built in 1893–94 by Slavic miners and Tlingits. Many Tlingits chose the Russian Orthodox faith in the 19th century when government-sponsored missionaries sought to convert Alaska Natives to Christianity, for it was the only faith that allowed them to worship in their own language. Father Ivan Veniaminov (see p. 123) had translated the Bible into Tlingit 50 years earlier when the Russians were still in Sitka. Today, Alaska Natives make up the bulk of the Russian Orthodox church congregation in Alaska, and St. Nicholas still has an active Tlingit parish. Lengthy services are sung in English, Tlingit, and Slavic for Saturday vespers at 6pm and on Sunday morning at 10am; the congregation stands throughout the service. Otherwise, a guide is on hand 9am to 6pm, May 15 to September, to answer questions, and excellent written guides are available, too. A $2 donation is requested.

⑨ Holy Trinity Episcopal Church

A block down Gold at Fourth, this is also worth a stop for its peaceful turn-of-the-century sanctuary of dark wood under a steeply pitched roof; it's unlocked all day. The church was built in 1896 by Alaska's first Episcopal bishop, when he established their first mission in Juneau. A little-known piece of church history: As an undersize acolyte at age 8, I almost smashed the stained glass in the back of the church when I lost control of the heavy crucifix and had to run down the aisle to keep up with it.

Turn right and walk 2 blocks to the start/finish point.

THE EXTENDED WALK

This walk of roughly 3 miles includes some steep stairways and streets. Follow the walking tour until you reach Gold Creek (see number 6, above), then cross the creek and stay on the same road, bearing right as it becomes Martin Street.

⑩ The Evergreen Cemetery

The cemetery slopes toward the ocean, opening a wonderful vista over the clear green lawn. One reason it's so broad and open is that the markers are flush with the ground. The old Alaska Native graves are in the wooded portion on the far side. Joe Juneau and Richard Harris, the city's founders, are buried near the cross at this top end of the cemetery.

Across the road from the cross, Hermit Street reaches a little way into the mountainside. Follow the steep public stairs next to house no. 430 up to the bottom of Pine Street. This is the walk I described in the introduction. The views get better and better as you rise to the top of Pine Street then go right on Evergreen Street, following to where it gives out among shadowy spruce and western hemlock. Continue on the peaceful forest trail among the ferns and evergreens up the valley from here, coming to the:

⑪ Abandoned wooden flume

Once the town's aqueduct, it now is maintained as a boardwalk into the forest. Since it carried water, it's nearly level, but watch your step in wet weather, as it crosses some high trestles over gullies.

At the end of the flume, cross over the valley to Basin Road. Stop here to see:

⑫ The Last Chance Mining Museum

The museum is described above under "Downtown Attractions & Activities."

To the left is the Perseverance Trail, described below, which continues up between the mountains, and the trailhead for a challenging hike up Mount

Juneau. To get back to town, follow Basin Road 1½ miles back down the valley. Taking the first right will put you at the top of Gold Street. Descend a block to Seventh and pick up the walking tour at paragraph 7 (the Wickersham House is a block down Seventh) or continue down Gold to St. Nicholas Orthodox Church, paragraph 8.

SHOPPING

The shops near the dock cater primarily to the cruise-ship passengers. After the last of more than 500 summer port calls, many close their doors. The year-round community and more local shops tend to be farther up the hill. If you're looking for authentic Alaska Native arts and crafts, be warned that counterfeiting is widespread. For buying tips, read "Native Art: Finding the Real Thing" in chapter 2.

The Raven's Journey, 175 S. Franklin (✆ **907/463-4686**), a brightly lit, museumlike gallery, shows Tlingit and other Northwest Indian carvings and masks, and whalebone, ivory, and fossil ivory carvings and jewelry from the Yup'ik and Inupiat of western and northern Alaska. Works are displayed with biographical placards of the artists. **Juneau Artists Gallery,** upstairs in the same buildings (✆ **907/586-9891**), is a co-op of local artists who take turns staffing the gallery. Only their work shows, and much of it is good and inexpensive.

Rie Muñoz is one of Juneau's best known artists, producing simple, graphic, generally cheerful watercolors of coastal Alaska communities and Native people. Her prints and tapestries are shown downtown at the **Decker Gallery,** 233 S. Franklin (✆ **907/463-5536**), and in the Mendenhall Valley at the **Rie Muñoz Gallery,** at 2101 Jordan Ave. (✆ **800/247-3151** or 907/789-7449; www. riemunoz.com).

For gifts, try **Annie Kaill**'s fine arts and crafts gallery, 244 Front St. It's a little out of the cruise-ship shopping area and gets business from locals. The shop has a rich, full, homey feeling, with local work at various price levels. The long-established **Ad Lib,** at 231 S. Franklin St., also is reliable and oriented to items made in Alaska. **Galligaskins,** 219 S. Franklin St. (www.galligaskins.net), features clothing with Alaska-theme designs. **Hearthside Books** is a cubbyhole of a bookstore at the corner of Franklin and Front streets, but has a good selection for its size. (Their larger branch is in the Mendenhall Valley's Nugget Mall, at 8745 Glacier Hwy.) **The Observatory,** at 200 N. Franklin St. (✆ **907/586-9676;** www.observatorybooks.com), specializes in rare maps and books, and is owned by a real expert.

Bill Spear sells his own brightly colored enamel pins from his studio upstairs at 174 S. Franklin (✆ **907/586-2209;** www.wmspear.com). Alaskans collect the vividly executed fish, birds, airplanes, dinosaurs, vegetables, and many other witty, provocative, or beautiful pins.

Taku Smokeries, at 550 S. Franklin, across the parking lot from the tram station (✆ **800/582-5122** or 907/463-3474; www.takusmokeries.com), is worth a stop even if you're not in the market for the pricey delicacies in the case: It's interesting to watch workers fillet, smoke, and pack salmon through large windows, and to read the explanatory signs about what they're doing. They'll ship the smoked fish anywhere.

ATTRACTIONS BEYOND WALKING DISTANCE

Mendenhall Glacier Transport (✆ **907/789-5460**) does a 2½-hour town and Mendenhall Glacier tour for $20. Otherwise, take a rented car or, for vigorous people, bike 24 miles out to the Mendenhall Glacier and back. I've listed these sites by distance from downtown.

Alaskan Brewing Company

Beer lovers and aspiring capitalists will enjoy the tour of Alaska's most popular craft brewery. Now too big to be called "micro," the brewery started in 1986 when 40 friends bet $5,000 each on Geoff and Marcy Larson's idea of bringing a local gold rush–era brew back to life. It worked, and now Alaskan Amber is everywhere in Alaska and in much of the Northwest, and the brewery has won a long list of national and international awards for its brews. The short free tour includes tasting of the Amber, Pale Ale, and ESB beers, and starts every half-hour.

5429 Shaune Dr. ℂ 907/780-5866. www.alaskanbeer.com. May–Sept, Mon–Sat 11am–4:30pm. Oct–Apr, Thurs–Sat 11am–4:30pm. Turn right from Egan Dr. on Vanderbilt Hill Rd., which becomes Glacier Hwy., then right on Anka St. and right again on Shaune Dr.

Macaulay Salmon Hatchery ⋆

The hatchery, known by locals as DIPAC (Douglas Island Pink and Chums), was ingeniously designed to allow visitors to watch from outdoor decks the whole process of harvesting and fertilizing eggs. From mid-June to October, salmon swim up a 450-foot fish ladder, visible through a window, into a sorting mechanism, then are "unzipped" by workers who remove the eggs. Guides and exhibits explain what's happening. You can often see seals and other wildlife feeding on the returning salmon just offshore from the hatchery at these times. Inside, large saltwater aquariums show off the area's marine life as it looks in the natural environment. It's less impressive in May and June, before the fish are running, when the tour includes the incubation area, where the fish eggs develop in racks of trays. The tours don't take long; allow 45 minutes for your entire visit.

2697 Channel Dr. (3 miles from downtown, turn left at the first group of buildings on Egan Dr.). ℂ 877/463-2486 or 907/463-4810. www.dipac.net. Admission $3 adults, $1 children ages 12 and under. Summer, Mon–Fri 10am–6pm, Sat–Sun 10am–5pm. Sept 15–May 15, call ahead.

Glacier Gardens

This is the place to see the rain forest if you have mobility problems. The heart of the hour-long tour is a ride in vehicles similar to golf carts up a steep mountainside, past a stream and pools, to a platform with a great view of the Gastineau Channel. If you're planning a hike in the area, that will have less interest. Gardeners will especially enjoy the extraordinary hanging baskets and other bright and ingenious plantings in the lower area.

7600 Glacier Hwy. (near the Fred Meyer store about 1 mile from the airport). ℂ 907/790-3377. www. glaciergardens.com. Admission $14.95 adults, $8.95 ages 6–12. Summer daily 9am–6pm. Closed Oct–Apr.

Mendenhall Glacier ⋆⋆

At the head of Mendenhall Valley, the Mendenhall Glacier glows bluish white, looming above the suburbs like an Ice Age monster that missed the general extinction. Besides being a truly impressive sight, Mendenhall is the most easily accessible glacier in Alaska and one of the state's most visited attractions. The parking lot has a great view across the lake to the glacier's face, with several short paths and a covered viewing area. A wheelchair-accessible trail leads down to the lake. The land right near the parking lot shows the signs of the glacier's recent passage, with little topsoil, stunted vegetation, and in many places bare rock that shows the scratch marks of the glacier's movement. Atop a bedrock hill, reached by stairs, a ramp, or an elevator, the recently remodeled Forest Service visitor center contains a glacier museum with excellent explanatory models, computerized displays, and ranger talks. Admission is $3 for adults, free for children under 12. In late summer, you can watch red and silver salmon spawning in **Steep Creek,** just short of the visitor center on the road.

There are several trails at the glacier, ranging from a half-mile nature trail loop to two fairly steep, 3½-mile hikes approaching each side of the glacier. At the visitor center and a booth near the parking lot, the Forest Service distributes a brochure, "Mendenhall Glacier: Carver of a Landscape," which includes a trail map. The **East Glacier Loop Trail** is a beautiful day hike leading through the forest to a waterfall near the glacier's face and parts of an abandoned rail tram and an abandoned dam on Nugget Creek; the trail has steep parts but is doable for school-age children. The **West Glacier Trail** is more challenging, leaving from 300 yards beyond the Skater's Cabin and following the edge of the lake and glacier, providing access to the ice itself for experienced climbers with the right equipment. Take the Mendenhall Loop Road to Montana Creek Road, turn right, then turn right again on Skater's Cabin Road.

The Skater's Cabin is also the starting point for a groomed cross-country-ski loop on Mendenhall Lake in front of the glacier. Don't go beyond the orange safety markers near the glacier's face. Other trails weave through the pothole lakes across from the glacier.

At the head of Glacier Spur Rd. (right from Egan Dr. on Mendenhall Loop to Glacier Spur). Visitor center (𝄐 907/789-0097) open daily in summer 8am–6pm; call for winter hours.

ATTRACTIONS & ACTIVITIES OUT ON THE ROAD

On sunny summer weekends, Juneau families get in the car and drive out on the road (northwest along the Glacier Highway, as it's officially known). The views of island-stippled water from the paved two-lane highway are worth the trip, but there also are several good places to stop. To use this road guide, set your trip odometer to zero at the ferry dock (which is 14 miles from downtown Juneau).

The **Auke Village Recreation Area** is a mile beyond the ferry dock and is a good place for picnics and beach walks. Less than a mile farther is a Forest Service campground.

The **Shrine of St. Therese** 𝄐 (𝄐 907/780-6112; www.juneau-diocese. addr.com), 9 miles beyond the ferry dock, stands on a tiny island reached by a foot-trail causeway. The wonderfully simple chapel of rounded beach stones, circled by markers of the 15 stations of the cross, stands peaceful and mysterious amid trees, rock, water, and the cries of the raven. It is the most spiritual place I know. The vaguely Gothic structure was built in the 1930s of stone picked up from these shores and dedicated by Alaska's first Catholic bishop to St. Therese of Lisieux, who died in 1897 at the age of 24. Liturgy services are held June to August at 1:30pm. The Juneau Catholic Diocese maintains a log retreat hall on the shore facing the island; be quiet when descending the gravel driveway from the highway. The shrine's island is a good vantage from which to look at **Lynn Canal** for marine mammals or, at low tide, to go tide pooling among the rocks.

Eagle Beach, 14 miles beyond the ferry dock, makes a good picnic area in nice weather, when you can walk among the tall beach grass or out on the sandy tidal flats and look for eagles, or go north along the beach to look for fossils in the rock outcroppings.

The road turns to gravel, then comes to **Point Bridget State Park,** 24 miles beyond the ferry dock (𝄐 907/465-4563; www.dnr.state.ak.us/parks/units/ ptbridg1.htm). A flat 3½-mile path leads through forest, meadow, and marsh to

ACCOMMODATIONS ■
Blueberry Lodge **6**
Glacier Trail B&B **4**
Mt. Juneau Inn **12**
Pearson's Pond Luxury
Inn & Spa **3**
DINING ◆
Chan's Thai Kitchen **1**
Douglas Cafe **11**
Hot Bite **2**

ATTRACTIONS ●
Alaskan Brewing Company **9**
Glacier Gardens **7**
Macauley Salmon Hatchery **10**
Mendenhall Glacier
Visitor Center **5**
Mendenhall Wetlands Refuge **8**

the shore, where you may see sea lions and possibly humpback whales. Two public-use cabins rent for $35 a night. See "State Parks Cabin Reservation Tricks," in chapter 7. The road ends 26 miles from the ferry dock at pretty **Echo Cove.**

GETTING OUTSIDE: ONSHORE

BIRD-WATCHING   Bald eagles are more common than pigeons in Juneau. A few years ago, one of them made off with a tourist's Chihuahua, starting a statewide debate about whether it was funny or horrible. Eagles are most common on the shoreline, especially where fish are plentiful, such as at the hatchery. For more variety, visit the **Mendenhall Wetlands State Game Refuge** (© 907/ 465-4290), which encompasses 4,000 acres of tidal estuaries in the Gastineau Channel near the airport. Some 140 species of birds use the refuge, mainly during the April and May migrations. Access points are on either side of the channel, including a viewing platform on the downtown-bound side of Egan Drive, at mile 6.

FRESHWATER FISHING Juneau isn't known particularly for its stream fishing, but there are a few places on the roads where you can put in a line. The advice you need is in the printed sport-fishing guide or on the website published by the Alaska Department of Fish and Game, 1255 W. Eighth Ave. (P.O. Box 3-2000), Juneau, AK 99801 (© **907/465-4180;** www.state.ak.us/adfg).

For a remote fly-in experience with fly or spinning gear, contact **Alaska Fly 'N' Fish Charters,** 9604 Kelly Ct. (© **907/790-2120;** www.alaskabyair.com). A guided 4 ½-hour trip is $350 per person, with a two-person minimum.

HIKING I've mentioned several good hikes at Mendenhall Glacier and out the road, above. *In the Miner's Footsteps,* a guide to the history behind 14 Juneau trails, is available for $3 from the Juneau–Douglas City Museum. The Juneau city **Department of Parks and Recreation** (© **907/586-5226;** www.juneau.lib.ak.us/parksrec/) leads hikes (and other activities) through the year; call or check the website.

The **Perseverance Trail** climbs up the valley behind Juneau and into the mining history of the area it accesses. It can be busy in summer. The trailhead is about 1½ miles from town on Basin Road. The trail is 3 miles of easy walking on the mountainside above Gold Creek to the Perseverance Mine, at the Silverbow Basin, a mining community from 1885 to 1921. Use caution on icy patches, as there are steep drop-offs. A well-documented $1 historic guide is for sale at the Juneau–Douglas City Museum.

Two trails start from points along the Perseverance. The challenging **Mount Juneau Trail** rises more than 3,500 feet in about 2 miles from a point 1 mile from the Perseverance trailhead. Go only in dry weather to avoid disastrous falls. The **Granite Creek Trail,** starting 2 miles in, climbs 1,200 feet over 1.5 miles to an alpine basin. Both are quieter than the Perseverance Trail.

Another hike right from downtown climbs **Mount Roberts**—just follow the stairway from the top of Sixth Street, a neighborhood called Star Hill. The summit is 4½ miles and 3,819 vertical feet away, but you don't have to go all the way to the top for incredible views and alpine terrain. At the 1,760-foot level, you come to the restaurant at the top of the Mount Roberts tram, mentioned earlier. Of course, it's easier to take the tram up and hike down, or start from the tram stop to hike to the summit.

The **Treadwell Mine Historic Trail,** on Douglas Island, is a fascinating hour's stroll through the ruins of a massive hard-rock mine complex that once employed and housed 2,000 men. Since its abandonment in 1922, big trees have grown up through the foundations, intertwining their roots with rails and

---

Gearing Up for Juneau's Outdoors

You can rent the gear you need for outings or Forest Service cabin visits. **Mountain Gears,** listed earlier under "Getting Around," has mountain bikes and offers guidance on where to ride. **Juneau Outdoor Center,** in the Douglas boat harbor at 101 Dock St. (© **907/586-8220;** www.juneaukayak. com), rents sea kayaks, camping gear, and skiffs with outboard motors you can use for fishing or exploring, and offers guidance in planning where and how to go. Any of these can recommend one of the several water taxis doing remote drop-offs.

machinery and adding to the site's exceptional power over the imagination. A well-written guide to numbered posts on the trail is available from the Juneau–Douglas City Museum. This is a great hike for kids. To find the trailhead, take Third Street in Douglas, bearing left at the Y onto Savikko Street, which leads to Savikko Park, also known as Sandy Beach Park. The trail starts at the far end.

Another great family outing is to the **Outer Point Trail,** 1.3 miles on a forest boardwalk to a beach with good tide pooling, lots of eagles, and possible whale sightings. Nowhere else I know are there so many kinds of lovely spots in such a short walk: the mossy rain forest, the stunted muskeg swamp, a glassy little creek, and the pebbled beach and bedrock ocean pools. From there, on the western point of Douglas Island—the opposite side from Juneau—you can see Auke Bay and the airport back to the east, Admiralty Island to the west, and the tiny islands of Stephens Passage before you. The only drawback is crowding, especially when tour groups tromp through; avoid them by going early or late. To get there, drive over the bridge to Douglas, then right on North Douglas Highway 11½ miles to the trailhead.

RAFTING   The Mendenhall River isn't a wild or scary ride, so the guides on the Native-owned **Auk Ta Shaa Discovery,** 76 Egan Dr. (© **800/820-2628;** www.goldbelttours.com), offer commentary on Native legends and natural history. The 4-hour rides cost $89 for adults, $44.50 age 16 and under (no kids under 50 lb. allowed). Transportation from downtown is included in the price.

SKIING   For **downhill skiing,** the city-owned **Eaglecrest Ski Area** (© **907/ 790-2000;** www.juneau.lib.ak.us/eaglecrest) is the large, steep home hill of Olympic silver medalist Hillary Lindh, Juneau's favorite daughter (her father helped choose the site in the 1970s). A chair goes right to the top of Douglas Island, opening 360° views and 640 acres of skiing terrain. There are 31 runs with a total vertical drop of 1,400 feet, rated 40% expert, 40% intermediate, and 20% novice. It's only 12 miles from downtown on North Douglas Highway. An all-day lift ticket is $26 for adults. In Alaska, Eaglecrest is second only to Alyeska Resort near Anchorage, yet no one knows about it outside Juneau.

There are 8 kilometers of **cross-country-skiing** trail at Eaglecrest. Juneau's warm, damp winters don't always provide enough snow for good cross-country skiing at the lower elevations, but many of the hiking trails into the mountains become winter backcountry routes, and snow does stick up there. Before going out, always check with the Forest Service (see "Visitor Information," earlier) for advice on your route and on avalanche conditions. Several of the Forest Service cabins also serve as winter warm-up houses during the day, and make good skiing destinations. If conditions permit, a network of trails is set around the Mendenhall Glacier (see above).

GETTING OUTSIDE: ON THE WATER
SEA KAYAKING   The protected waters around Juneau welcome sea kayaking, and the city is a popular hub for trips on the water farther afield. Besides the sublime scenery, you'll almost certainly see eagles, sea birds, and seals, and possibly humpback whales.

There are at least five operators offering sea-kayaking excursions, but the area's most established ecotourism operator is **Alaska Discovery,** 5310 Glacier Hwy. (© **800/586-1911** or 907/780-6226; www.akdiscovery.com), with trips all over

---

Finds Remote Cabins on Foot

Five U.S. Forest Service cabins and two Alaska State Parks cabins are accessible by hikes of less than a day on trails connected to Juneau's road system. That means that you can get there without an expensive plane or
boat charter, and that's a rarity. Two cabins are at Bridget Point State Park
(see "Attractions & Activities Out the Road," above). The Forest Service
cabins include: **Peterson Lake,** with lake and stream fishing for Dolly Varden char, cutthroat and steelhead trout, and silver and pink salmon; **John
Muir,** on a 1,500-foot ridge top above Auke Bay, up the Auk Nu Trail; **Dan
Moller,** on Douglas Island right across from town; **Eagle Glacier,** overlooking the glacier upriver from Eagle Beach and reached by the Amalga Trail;
and beautiful **Windfall Lake,** with fishing. Each rents for $35 a night, and
generally there's a 2-night maximum stay. All are popular and must be
reserved well in advance. If you can afford a charter, or if you are an
expert sea kayaker, there are many more choices farther afield, especially
on Admiralty Island (see below). You'll need camping gear to stay at the
primitive cabins (see "Gearing Up for Juneau's Outdoors," above). Get
information on cabins from the Ranger District (see "Visitor Information,"
earlier), then reserve through the national system described in "Getting
Outside in the Tongass National Forest," in section 1 of this chapter.

Southeast and beyond. Part of the company's ethic and reason for being is to
build support for protecting Southeast's wild places. A multiday kayak trip is
your chance to really know the Alaska wilderness. Alaska Discovery will even
custom-design a trip for your group. If you haven't spent much time in the outdoors but would like to see real Alaska wilderness, I couldn't recommend a better
introductory trip than the Coastal Escape, a 3-day, 2-night camping trip to
Berner's Bay, on Lynn Canal north of the end of the road. Besides paddling,
groups spend plenty of time exploring the beaches and rain-forest shorelines. Fit
beginners will do fine, with teens as young as 14 normally invited; some trips
may include kids as young as 10. No whiners, however: There's a good chance
of rain, you'll sleep in a two-person tent, and paddling is work. The cost is $495
to $595 per person. Alaska Discovery's other trips range up to 12 days and go to
some truly incredible places, including Glacier Bay National Park (see section 9
of this chapter); they're best for those with some sea-kayaking experience.

If you don't have that kind of time, Alaska Discovery is a partner in **Auk Ta
Shaa Discovery** (© **800/820-2628** or 907/586-8687; www.goldbelttours.com),
with a sea-kayak day trip that starts from an unspoiled spot way out the road for
$95 per person, $47.50 ages 12 to 16. The 7-hour trip includes 5 hours of
kayaking and a beach picnic.

Several businesses that rent kayaks are listed under "Gearing Up for Juneau's
Outdoors" (p. 144). Typically, you'll pay about $40 a day for a single, $50 for a
double. Delivery is easy to arrange on the road system.

SALTWATER FISHING & WHALE-WATCHING   The closest I ever came
to a humpback whale—I almost touched it—was on the way back from king
salmon fishing out of Juneau on a friend's boat. More than two dozen charter
companies offer fishing from Juneau and Auke Bay; you can go to **watch whales**
or fish, or both. Juneau is well protected behind layers of islands, so the water
generally is calm.

A lot of companies offer trips. The Juneau Convention and Visitors Bureau maintains a list of businesses with details on their services and prices; their website has links to many. **Juneau Sportfishing and Sightseeing,** 2 Marine Way, Suite 230 (© **907/586-1887;** www.juneausportfishing.com), is one of the largest operators, and their rates are typical: $195 per person for a full day of fishing, $120 for 4 hours, or $85 for a 2½-hour whale-watching trip.

CRUISING   A motor yacht can put you in the Inside Passage wilderness in perfect comfort, but with the freedom usually reserved only for hardy outdoors people. Imagine motoring up to a glacier or landing on a remote beach on an uninhabited island for a picnic, or catching your own salmon dinner and watching humpback whales from your own deck. Of course, it's also quite expensive to go this way.

Various Juneau operators offer multiday cruising charters on motor yachts. **Adventures Afloat** (© **800/323-5628** or 907/789-0111; www.ptialaska.net/~valkyrie/) offers crewed boats of various sizes for around $430 per person, per day. **Alaska Yacht Charters** (© **800/725-3913** or 907/789-1978; www.alaska yachtcharters.com) is owned and operated by a couple with much fishing experience. **ABC Alaska Yacht Charters** (© **800/780-1239** or 907/789-1239; www.abcalaska.com) represents a fleet of 27- to 140-foot vessels. You may enjoy daydreaming with their website even if you can't afford it. The all-inclusive prices for a cruise with a crew start around $2,000 a day. They also charter bareboat motor yachts, without skippers, starting around $2,200 a week for the smallest vessels.

DIVING   The **Channel Dive Center,** 8365 Old Dairy Rd. (© **907/790-4665,** www.channeldive.com), offers instruction, rentals, and guiding for drysuit diving. Guided dives include historic shipwrecks near town. From fall through spring, you can dive among sea lions. Diving is not as good in the summer, when plankton blooms tend to cloud the water.

GETTING OUTSIDE: ON THE ICE

More than 36 major glaciers around Juneau flow from a single ocean of ice behind the mountains, the 1,500-square-mile **Juneau Icefield.** You can land on it in a helicopter just to touch the ice, or for a nature hike or dogsled ride. It's expensive, but there are few other places to see, let alone explore, the kind of ice sheet that carved North America in the last ice age. From the air, glaciers look unreal, like creations by a graphic artist, their sinuous lines of blue and white ice striped with darker gray gravel debris. Only standing on the ice, which on closer inspection resembles the crusty compressed snow of springtime snow berms, do you get a clear sense of this entirely unfamiliar kind of terrain.

It's worth noting that these tours have had some major mishaps in recent years. While the accidents represent a tiny fraction of all the safe flights, they're a reminder that flying a helicopter to a glacier is not like flying an airliner.

Era Helicopters (© **800/843-1947** or 907/586-2030; www.eraaviation.com) is among Alaska's oldest and most respected operators. Their 1-hour glacier landing flight costs $195. They also offer a program of **dogsled rides** on the ice. This is a neat idea: A lot of visitors to Alaska want to ride a dogsled, but it's a winter sport that really can't be re-created with sleds on wheels, as most dogsled tours try to do in the summer. Here, you do it on snow, as it's meant to be done. That excursion costs $329 per person. One caveat: Poor or even overcast weather makes it difficult to see the ice clearly, but if you wait for a sunny morning all

A Day Trip to Tracy Arm

Readers gush to me about the **boat tours to Tracy Arm**, south of Juneau. One reason, I suspect, is that the fjords of the Tracy Arm–Fords Terror Wilderness (part of Tongass National Forest) are relatively unknown outside the area, but the scenery and wildlife viewing easily rivals that of Glacier Bay National Park, which was rated the best national park to visit by the readers of *Consumer Reports.* For those not riding a cruise ship, Tracy Arm has a significant advantage over Glacier Bay: It's much easier and less expensive to get to. Day trips to Tracy Arm from Juneau cost about $110 and take 8 hours; a trip to Glacier Bay costs at least three times as much and is exhausting as a day trip—it's wiser to overnight there, though that adds still more to the cost.

The Tracy Arm fjord is a long, narrow, twisting passageway into the coastal mountains, with peaks up to a mile high that jut straight out of the water, waterfalls tumbling thousands of feet down their sides. At its head, Sawyer Glacier and South Sawyer Glacier calve ice into the water with a rumble and a splash. Whales and other wildlife usually show up along the way. And, as at Glacier Bay, John Muir paid a visit. No second-best here!

The largest operator is the Native-owned **Auk Nu Tours** (part of Goldbelt, which owns most of the big tourism businesses in town), 76 Egan Dr., Juneau (© 800/820-2628 or 907/586-8687; www.goldbelttours.com). They offer a day-long trip daily at 9am in the summer. A naturalist provides commentary on the high-speed catamaran. Light meals and the use of binoculars are included in the price.

Other large boats compete, and you can shop around. The family-operated **Adventure Bound Alaska**, at 215 Ferry Way, Juneau (© 800/228-3875 or 907/463-2509; www.adventureboundalaska.com), prides itself on slower tours that allow more time to soak up the sights. The total time on the water is 90 minutes more than Auk Nu and is priced $10 less. The 56-foot single-hull boat has deck space all the way around.

Another way to go is to charter a six-passenger boat. Although it may cost twice as much or more per person, you'll decide when to linger with the animals or ice. Check with the visitor center for a referral, or **Juneau Sportfishing and Sightseeing** (© 907/586-1887), listed in this section under "Saltwater Fishing & Whale-Watching."

seats will likely be booked. They have a 48-hour cancellation policy, so you have to gamble to some extent on good viewing conditions. Of course, they don't fly in unsafe conditions.

Another company with its own helicopters specializes in hiking and teaching about glaciers: **NorthStar Trekking** (© 907/790-4530; www.glaciertrekking.com). Their small groups (a maximum of 11, with two guides) go on hiking excursions of up to a few miles, with the speed determined by the group. The 4-hour trip, which includes half an hour of flight time, costs $315 per person.

GETTING OUTSIDE: ON ADMIRALTY ISLAND

Beyond Douglas Island from Juneau, near the entrance to Gastineau Channel, is 900,000-acre Admiralty Island, one of the largest virgin blocks of old-growth forest in the country. The vast majority of the island is the protected **Kootznoowoo Wilderness.** Kootznoowoo, Tlingit for "fortress of bears," is said to have the highest concentration of brown bears on earth. Despite the town of Angoon on the western side of the island, there are more bears than people on Admiralty. The island's **Pack Creek Bear Viewing Area** is the most famous and surefire place to see bears in Southeast. The area has been managed for bear viewing since the 1930s, when hunting was outlawed. There's a platform for watching the bears up close as they feed on salmon spawning in the creek in July and August. Peak viewing occurs in the middle of that period. The bears generally pay no attention to the people watching them.

Only 25 miles from Juneau, Pack Creek is so popular that the Forest Service uses a permit system to keep it from being overrun during the day (from 9pm to 9am, no humans are allowed). There are no facilities in this wilderness area, but a platform allows safe bear viewing. Book early.

The easiest way to go is with a tour operator who has permits. The Forest Service District Ranger Office can give you a list of guides. **Alaska Discovery,** 5310 Glacier Hwy. (© **800/586-1911** or 907/780-6226; www.akdiscovery.com), has many permits for sea kayak trips. Their 1-day excursion flies out, then paddles to the creek; no experience is necessary, but you must be physically capable of hiking and paddling. It costs $450 per person. A 2-night campout and sea kayak near the creek offers more time to see the bears and appreciate the scenery. It costs $895 per person. **Alaska Fly 'N' Fish Charters,** 9604 Kelly Ct. (© **907/ 790-2120;** www.alaskabyair.com), also has permits for its naturalist-guided 5½-hour fly-in visits, which cost $400 per person, with everything you need included. Twelve permits per day go to the commercial operators and 12 to people who go without any guide (and you aren't allowed to hire a guide after getting the permit); 8 of those 12 can be booked in advance with the Forest Service, and the other four are held out to be distributed 3 days before they're good, or the previous Friday for Tuesday and Wednesday, at 9am at the Juneau Ranger District Office. In the peak season, permits cost $50 for adults, $25 for those ages 16 or under or 62 and over. After you have the permit, you'll still need a way to get there and your own gear (including rubber boots and binoculars). **Alaska Fly 'N' Fish Charters** charges $200 per person round-trip to drop off customers with their own permits; the price drops to $140 for groups of three to five.

Protected **Seymour Canal,** on the east side of the island, is good for canoeing and kayaking, and has two other sites besides Pack Creek where bears often show up: Swan Cove and Windfall Harbor. Outfitters are listed above. There are 15 Forest Service cabins on Admiralty, and the well-regarded **Thayer Lake Lodge,** Auke Bay (© **907/247-8897;** www.AlaskaOne.com/thayerlake), is located on a wilderness inholding near Angoon. For information on the island and cabins and an excellent $4 map, contact the **Admiralty Island National Monument,** 8461 Old Dairy Rd., Juneau (© **907/586-8790;** www.fs.fed.us/r10/chatham/anm).

ACCOMMODATIONS

Hotel rooms are tight in the summer, so book ahead. Bed-and-breakfasts are the way to go in Juneau. You can get a better room and have more fun for less money. The Juneau Convention and Visitors Bureau *Juneau Travel Planner* and website contain listings of the hotels and B&Bs, with their features and price ranges (© **888/581-2201;** www.traveljuneau.com). **Bed & Breakfast Association of Alaska, INNside Passage Chapter,** communicates through its website (**www.accommodations-alaska.com**), where you will find more than a dozen Juneau B&Bs listed with links to their own pages.

EXPENSIVE

Baranof Hotel ★★   The Baranof is the only lodging in Alaska with the pedigree and style to pull off the role of the old-fashioned grand hotel. Built of concrete in 1939, it served for decades as an informal branch of the state capitol. Legislators and lobbyists still confer in the dark, opulent lobby and restaurants. The structure itself constrains modernization—the bathrooms and many rooms tend to be small—but features such as glass doorknobs and pressed-tin ceilings remain to show that it comes by its faults honestly. Recent remodeling has lightened many rooms while keeping the style. The upper-floor rooms have great views on the water side, while lower rooms were redone most recently. There are many appealing suites.

The Art Deco **Gold Room** ★ restaurant is Juneau's most traditional fine-dining establishment. The dining room combines intimacy and grandeur, a real showplace of shining brass, frosted glass, and rich wood. The food varies greatly in quality year to year. Most entrees are $20 to $25.

127 N. Franklin St., Juneau, AK 99801. © **800/544-0970** or 907/586-2660. Fax 907/586-8315. www.west markhotels.com. 193 units. High season $149–$169 double, low season $129–$139 double. $15 each additional person over age 12. AE, DC, DISC, MC, V. **Amenities:** 2 restaurants (continental and cafe); bar; tour desk; salon; room service (7am–2pm, 5–10pm); dry cleaning. *In room:* TV, telephone with dual-line dataport, iron, kitchenettes available.

Goldbelt Hotel Juneau ★★   The Goldbelt Native corporation bought this somewhat heartless upscale hotel near the water and brought its public spaces to life with masterpieces of Tlingit art, including a new totem pole out front, a huge yellow cedar bas-relief by Nathan Jackson in the lobby-restaurant area, and a museum-quality Chilkat blanket in a display case. The large bedrooms, with either two full-size or one king bed, were upgraded with bold colors and new furniture in a dark cherry finish. They're noticeably quiet and immaculate. Those on the front, $10 more, have good views of the Gastineau Channel.

51 W. Egan Dr., Juneau, AK 99801. © **888/478-6909** or 907/586-6900. Fax 907/463-3567. www.goldbelt tours.com. 105 units. High season $169–$179 double. Low season $139–$149 double. Extra person $15. AE, DC, DISC, MC, V. **Amenities:** Restaurant (beef and seafood); tour desk; room service (7am–10pm). *In room:* TV w/pay movies, dataport, coffeemaker, hair dryer, iron.

Pearson's Pond Luxury Suites and Adventure Spa ★★★   Imagine you're a slightly obsessed bed-and-breakfast host and you decide to give your guests every amenity you can possibly think of. Now go to Diane Pearson's house and count how many you missed. A refrigerator and coffee machine? Child's play: Pearson provides a kitchenette stocked with food, wine, and her own home-baked bread. Maybe you thought of a private duck pond with a dock, a rowboat, and a fountain? But did you stock the pond with fish? And did you remember massage, yoga, two separate hot tubs in the garden, and a laptop in your room? There's much more, as Pearson is constantly adding: When I last visited, carpenters were finishing two Jacuzzi suites and an atrium entrance. But I also have to add two caveats. First, it is still a house, not a luxury hotel, and not all rooms

ACCOMMODATIONS ■

Baranof Hotel **12**
Cashen's Quarters **9**
Driftwood Lodge **3**
Goldbelt Hotel Juneau **14**
Juneau International
 Hostel **8**
Prospector Hotel **5**
Silverbow Guest Inn **10**

DINING ◆

Armadillo Tex-Mex Cafe **18**
The Back Room **13**
Di Sopra / The Fiddlehead
 Restaurant & Bakery **2**
Douglas Cafe **1**
The Hangar **15**
Heritage Coffee Co. & Café **13**
Rainbow Food **13**
Red Dog Saloon **16**
The Summit Restaurant **19**
Valentine's Coffee House
 & Bakery **11**

ATTRACTIONS ●

Alaska State Museum **4**
Centennial Hall **6**
 Juneau-Douglas City
 Museum **7**
The Last Chance Mining
 Museum **11**
Mount Roberts Tramway **20**
Patsy Ann statue **17**
*See Juneau Walking Tour
map for other attractions*

are suites, or even large; some have showers, not tubs. Second, all the extras may be a bit much unless you're planning a honeymoon-like stay. Pearson's is in the Mendenhall Valley, 15 minutes from downtown.

4541 Sawa Circle, Juneau, AK 99801. ℂ **888/658-6328** or 907/789-3772. Fax 907/789-6722. www. pearsonspond.com. 5 units. High season $169–$269 double. Low season $70–$159 double. Extra person $30. AE, DISC, DC, MC, V. **Amenities:** Exercise room; 2 Jacuzzis; rowboat and paddleboat loan; bike loan; concierge; car rental; business center; massage in room or studio; free laundry; fishing gear loan. *In room:* TV w/VCR, high-speed Internet port, CD player, computer , kitchenette, stocked refrigerator, coffeemaker, hair dryer, iron.

MODERATE

Glacier Trail Bed & Breakfast ★★ *Finds* You wake up to an expansive view of the Mendenhall Glacier filling a picture window in a big, quiet, tastefully decorated room. Luke and Connie Nelson built the house with this moment in mind. Before beginning construction, they researched B&Bs all over the

---

Tips **Lodging at the Airport**

The new **Guest House Inn & Suites** (📞 **888/559-9846** or 907/790-6435; www.guesthousealaska.com) is nearer your gate than the check-in desk at most airports, and it's also among Juneau's best hotels, with large, elegantly decorated rooms with high ceilings and every amenity. They have a small pool; and a continental breakfast comes with the room. A room for two people is $139 summer, $79 winter.

---

country, finding ideas for the amenities in the rooms and gaining inspiration for how to put the rooms together—not just as a bedroom with a lot of stuff in it, but as a cohesive, calming whole. A family apartment downstairs is perfect for large groups. The Nelsons are fascinating, literate people with varied interests and a lifetime of experience with Alaska's outdoors. Luke's family owns a lodge on Admiralty Island, and with them he does Pack Creek tours (see "Getting Outside: On Admiralty Island," above). You'll need to rent a car if you stay here. The Nelsons also rent kayaks for outings on nearby Mendenhall Lake.

1081 Arctic Circle, Juneau, AK 99801. 📞 **907/789-5646.** Fax 907/789-5697. www.juneaulodging.com. 3 units. High season $120–$145 double. Low season $85–$100 double. Extra person $20. Rates include full breakfast. AE, MC, V. **Amenities:** Bike loan; laundry machines. *In room:* TV w/VCR, stocked refrigerator, microwave oven, coffeemaker, hair dryer, iron, Jacuzzi bathtubs.

Mt. Juneau Inn 🌠 A pair of big old Craftsman-style houses—one was built by a ship's captain—overlook the channel among overhanging evergreens a short drive or reasonable bike ride from downtown. Newly remodeled rooms with private baths are large and light, with Berber carpets and fresh country and floral decor. Some have claw-foot tubs but no shower, while others have shower only. In the other building, connected by a breezeway, older rooms share baths. They're cozy and cute, with stenciled borders, quilts, and antiques. There's some road noise from the Egan Drive freeway that runs between the inn and the water. The common areas are large and attractive; weddings are held here. The full breakfast comes buffet style. The inn also includes two two-bedroom apartments and a cottage.

1801 Old Glacier Hwy., Juneau, AK 99801. 📞 **907/463-5855.** Fax 907/463-5423. www.mtjuneauinn. com. 15 units, 9 with private bathroom; 2 apts; 1 cottage. Summer $89 double shared bathroom, $119 double private bathroom, $15 each additional person. Suites, cottage $149 double, apts $195 for 4. Winter $89 double. AE, DC, DISC, MC, V. **Amenities:** Coin-op laundry. *In room:* Speaker telephones, high-speed Internet, robes.

Prospector Hotel 🌠 I've always found this a comfortable waterfront hotel, with large, standard rooms. Then, when I made my inspection in 2001, every room had been stripped completely for remodeling—even the lighting fixtures and two dozen kitchenette units. The new look is washed pine, wrought iron, and marble with fabrics of rich brown and red. Rooms facing the channel have good views but suffer from highway noise. The lower level, called the first floor, is a half-basement and lacks an elevator. A parking garage takes care of the chronic shortage of downtown parking.

375 Whittier St., Juneau, AK 99801-1781. 📞 **800/331-2711** or 907/586-3737. Fax 907/586-1204. www.prospectorhotel.com. 58 units. High season $110 double; $135–$145 double with kitchenette. Low season $80 double; $95–$120 double with kitchenette. AE, DC, DISC, MC, V. **Amenities:** Restaurant (beef and

seafood); bar; exercise room; business center; limited room service; In room massage; laundry; dry cleaning. *In room:* TV, coffeemaker.

Silverbow Guest Inn ★ The young proprietors have found an original and oddly pleasing style in their little downtown hotel. The 1914 building with wood floors, bare brick, and stained glass is decorated with family pictures and weird postcards. In the rooms, the overlay of new on old is a charming Pottery Barn style. Considerate touches show up repeatedly, such as the shelf of supplies you may have forgotten, answering machines on the direct-line phones, hard candies, and breakfast in a sack if you have to leave very early. Otherwise, breakfast comes from the family bakery, famed for its authentic bagels. Rooms and bathrooms are small, reminiscent of a European pension (for which the summer rate is a bit high). The restaurant and on-site art cinema are described below.

120 Second St., Juneau, AK 99801. ℃ **800/586-4146** or 907/586-4146. Fax 907/586-4242. www. silverbowinn.com. 6 units. High season $138 double. Low season $88 double. Extra person $15. $10 surcharge for 1-night stays. Rates include continental breakfast. DISC, MC, V. **Amenities:** Restaurant; bar. *In room:* TV, hair dryer.

INEXPENSIVE

Blueberry Lodge ★ *Finds* Staying here is like visiting a first-class wilderness lodge, except you're only 6 miles from downtown Juneau. Jay and Judy Urquhart built the spectacular log building themselves in the woods of Douglas Island, looking out on an eagle's nest and the Gastineau Channel's Mendenhall Wetlands State Game Refuge. They keep a spotting scope in the living room and will lend you binoculars and rubber boots for an exploration by the water. Rooms are large, contemporary, and very clean, with rich colors that contrast with the huge logs of the walls, but they lack phones or TVs. It's possible to be alone and to enter without passing through the family's quarters, but the general atmosphere is social, with two teenagers, two dogs, and a cat in residence. Judy serves a big, fancy breakfast. You'll need to rent a car for the 10-minute drive to town.

9436 N. Douglas Hwy., Juneau, AK 99801. ℃ and fax **907/463-5886.** www.blueberrylodge.com. 5 units, all with shared bathroom. High season $85–$95 double. Low season, $75 double. Extra person over age 4 $15. Rates include full breakfast. AE, DISC, MC, V. **Amenities:** Babysitting; free laundry machines.

The Driftwood Lodge *Value* This downtown motel, next door to the State Museum, is popular with families, and houses legislators and aides in the winter in its apartmentlike kitchenette suites. Although the building can't hide its cinderblock construction and old-fashioned motel exterior, small bathrooms, or lack of elevators, the rooms are remarkably comfortable and well kept. The management has held prices low while slowly improving the place, so adjoining rooms could have old shag carpeting or a brand new interior. For the price of an ordinary room elsewhere, you can get a huge suite with a full kitchen here. The round-the-clock courtesy van saves big money to the airport or ferry, and offers inexpensive town tours.

435 Willoughby Ave., Juneau, AK 99801. ℃ **800/544-2239** or 907/586-2280. Fax 907/586-1034. www. driftwoodalaska.com. 63 units. High season $85 double; $93–$104 suite. Low season $62 double; $89 suite. Extra person $7. AE, DC, DISC, MC, V. **Amenities:** Bike rental; coin-op laundry. *In room:* TV, coffeemaker.

Tips **Ask Before You Light Up**

Generally, **smoking** is not permitted at bed-and-breakfasts and inns; smokers should ask when they book if smoking is allowed even outside.

A HOSTEL

Juneau International Hostel *Finds*   This place seems too good to be a hostel. The historic yellow house among the downtown sights is a showplace of custom cabinetry and big, light common rooms. The shared kitchen was squeaky-clean when I visited. Office hours are 7 to 10am and 5 to midnight in the summer, 8 to 9am and 5 to 10:30pm in the winter, with lockout during the day. There's a coin-op laundry. Prepaid reservations by mail are required and there is a 3-night maximum stay.

614 Harris St., Juneau, AK 99801. ✆ 907/586-9559. www.home.gci.net/~juneauhostel. 47 beds. $10 per person nonmembers, $7 members. No credit cards.

CAMPING

Juneau has two exceptional Forest Service campgrounds open mid-May through mid-September. For information, call the Juneau Ranger District at ✆ 907/586-8800 or contact them at www.fs.fed.us/r10/tongass; neither takes reservations. **The Mendenhall Glacier Campground,** overlooking the lake and glacier and next to the Mendenhall River, is the most-improved public campground in the state, with granite block construction. The new bathrooms have showers and flush toilets and there is a ½-mile disabled-accessible nature trail. The 68 sites are huge and broadly separated; nine have full RV hookups and another nine electricity and water. Tents and RVs are segregated. To get there, turn right on Montana Creek Road from Mendenhall Loop Road. Tent sites are $10, RV sites $24 and $26. The 12-site **Auke Village Campground,** 1.7 miles north of the ferry dock, lies along an ocean beach, with pit toilets and running water. Sites are $8 per night.

Spruce Meadow RV Park, at 10200 Mendenhall Loop Rd. (✆ 907/789-1990; www.juneaurv.com), has full hookups in a natural setting with many amenities. Full hookups are $26, cable TV $2.50 extra.

DINING
EXPENSIVE

DiSopra/The Fiddlehead Restaurant and Bakery ★★ VEGETARIAN/SEAFOOD/ITALIAN   Upstairs, DiSopra serves finely crafted northern Italian cuisine in a dining room with big windows, a mural, and solicitous service. The menu changes quarterly, and Juneau friends have complained of inconsistency, but it's still the most sophisticated food available in town. Meanwhile, downstairs, the Fiddlehead has butcher-block tables, knotty pine paneling, and ferny stained glass. It serves from a long menu of flavorful food, with a great variety of ethnic influences, delicacies made into sandwiches, and many rice and vegetarian dishes. You can have lunch or dinner here for around $10, or more expensive dinner entrees of seafood or beef, or pasta similar to that upstairs.

429 W. Willoughby Ave. ✆ 907/586-3150. Reservations recommended for DiSopra. Dinner main courses $9–$25; lunch $8–$12. 15% gratuity added for parties of 6 or more. AE, DISC, MC, V. Summer, DiSopra daily 5–10pm; Fiddlehead daily 7am–10pm. Winter, DiSopra Tues–Sat 5–9pm; Fiddlehead daily 7am–9pm.

The Summit Restaurant ★★★ STEAK/SEAFOOD   A great place for a romantic meal. The dining room, with only 10 tables, looks out over the cruise-ship dock from big windows. The formal service manifests an easy, world-weary elegance not easily faked, and the Summit is the only restaurant in Alaska that really has it. If you're lucky enough to get a reservation during the summer season, you'll find the seafood and vegetables from the constantly changing, sometimes creative menu perfectly prepared and occasionally truly inspired,

Quick Bites in Juneau

You can pick up a tasty picnic at the deli at the **Rainbow Food** health-food grocery at the corner of Seward and Second streets ((C) **907/ 586-6476**). **Hot Bite,** a stand at the Auke Bay boat harbor, is a local secret, serving charcoal-broiled burgers and mind-blowing milk shakes. Downtown Juneau's young, professional population supports several good coffeehouses. **Valentine's Coffee House and Bakery,** 111 Seward St. ((C) **907/463-5144**), serves light hot meals and microbrews in an authentic old-fashioned storefront. **Heritage Coffee Co. and Café,** 174 S. Franklin St. ((C) **907/586-1087**), also serves light meals and is a good people-watching place.

such as the halibut with spinach and Grand Marnier sauce on mashed potatoes. A little European-style hotel, the Inn at the Waterfront, is upstairs.

455 S. Franklin St. (C) **907/586-2050**. Reservations recommended. Main courses $15–$28. AE, DC, DISC, MC, V. Daily 5–11pm. Closed Oct.

MODERATE

The Back Room/Silverbow Bakery ⭐ SANDWICHES/ECLECTIC   This place has several faces. In the small, sunny bakery, you can get great bagels for breakfast or a hearty sandwich for lunch. In the rough brick Back Room you can get a microbrew, kielbasa and pirogies, an Indonesian peanut pasta, a teriyaki salmon grill, or many other items from an eccentric menu (the food generally is quite good and entree prices inexpensive). In the same room, on Tuesday, Thursday, and Saturday night they show classic films (they still serve beer and food during the movies). Call or check the website for listings. The masterminds for this melange are a cosmopolitan young couple who landed here from graduate school in Seattle. The ingredients seem to have gelled, creating a scene for Juneau.

120 Second St. (C) **907/586-4146**. www.silverbowinn.com. All main courses $5–$18. DISC, MC, V. Mon 7am–5:30pm, Tues–Fri 7am–9pm; Sat 7:30am–4:30pm, 5:30pm–9pm; Sun 8am–3:30pm. (These hours combine the bakery and restaurant; the restaurant is closed Mon; slightly shorter hours in winter.)

Douglas Cafe ⭐ *Finds* ECLECTIC   It's a great pleasure to find a place like this hiding in the guise of an ordinary small-town burger joint. The key, I'm convinced, is the two owners working in the kitchen, indistinguishable from the other young guys in baseball caps back there. They turn out wonderful seafood, meat, and vegetarian dinners, drawing on many world cuisines, and lunches that translate such food into sandwiches and a great array of burgers. The small dining room is lively, bright, and casual but somewhat cramped, with stacking chairs and wooden benches that can get hard by the end of a meal. Weekend breakfasts are an event, filling the place with townspeople. Service is quick and casual. Craft brews are on tap.

916 Third St., Douglas (turn left after crossing the bridge from Juneau, then continue until you see the cafe on the left). (C) **907/364-3307**. Lunch items $6.50–$9; dinner main courses $8.25–$17. MC, V. Summer, Tues–Fri 11am–8:30pm, Sat 9am–8:30pm, Sun 9am–1:30pm. Closed Tues in winter.

The Hangar ⭐⭐ STEAK/SEAFOOD/PASTA   Situated in a converted airplane hangar on a wooden pier with large windows, this bar and grill has great views and a fun atmosphere; even off-season, it's packed. It's a fine place to drink beer (with 24 brews on tap), listen to live music, or play at one of the three pool tables. What's surprising is that the food is quite good, too. The seared ahi sashimi appetizer, a kind of tartar, had a pleasant texture and taste, and the jambalaya, a huge portion for $12, was spicy but balanced—the shrimp didn't get smothered, as they often do. It's a great place to finish a day.

2 Marine Way. © 907/586-5018. Reservations recommended. Main courses $12–$21. AE, DISC, MC, V. Daily 11am–11pm.

INEXPENSIVE

Armadillo Tex-Mex Cafe 😊 *Value* TEX-MEX   You order lunch at a counter and choose drinks from a cooler, but this casual, infectiously cheerful place is where some of Alaska's best Southwestern food comes from. Locals, who swear by it, know the restaurant merely as "Tex-Mex." Chicken is a specialty, and the homemade salsa is famous, served free with a basket of chips for each diner. The tiny dining room is located near the docks. They serve wine and beer, brewing their own brand periodically. With an output of only 32 barrels a year, they've kept supply well below demand.

431 S. Franklin St. © 907/586-1880. Main courses $6–$16. MC, V. Summer daily 11am–10pm. Winter Mon–Sat 11am–9pm.

Chan's Thai Kitchen ★★ *Finds* THAI   The small, overlit dining room in the half-basement level of a steak house sees few tourists, but locals brag to each other about how long they were willing to stand in the small entrance area to get a table. For a year after it opened, everyone I met would ask me, "Have you been to the Thai place yet?" When I did finally go, I became a believer, too—the authentic Thai food is that good, the service quick and professional, and the atmosphere, if lacking in polish, conducive to a good time. Reservations are not accepted and they do not have a liquor license (it's BYO).

11820 Glacier Hwy. (in Auke Bay, across the boat harbor). © 907/789-9777. Main courses $9–$13. MC, V. Tues–Thurs 11am–2pm and 5–8pm, Fri 11am–2pm and 5–8:30pm, Sat 4:30–8:30pm.

NIGHTLIFE

Two **salmon bakes** take place nightly during the summer, each offering entertainment with the fish. Alaska Travel Adventures has offered its **Gold Creek Salmon Bake** for more than 30 years. It's touristy, yes, but fun, with marshmallow roasting, music, and other entertainment—great for families. (I'd avoid it in the rain, though.) The cost is $26.50 for adults, $17.75 for children. Call © 907/789-0052 to arrange pickup by van.

The Gold Nugget Revue plays summer nights at 7pm at the Thane Ore House, 4 miles out Thane Road, south of Juneau (© 907/586-3442). The show includes can-can dancing and a gold rush melodrama—corny, but people leave smiling. The meal of salmon, halibut, or beef ribs costs $27, or skip the meal and pay $8.50 for the show alone. There is indoor or outdoor seating.

For more substantial performances, try to catch a show by Juneau's **Perseverance Theatre,** Alaska's largest professional theater. Their stage is usually dark midsummer, but the winter season often starts in September and sometimes lasts until early June. To find out what's playing, contact the theater's office at 914 Third St., Douglas (© 907/364-2421), or check the website at www.perseverancetheatre.org.

A political scandal or two have put a damper on some of the infamous legislative partying that once occurred in Juneau, far away from home districts, but there still are good places to go out drinking and dancing. The **Red Dog Saloon,** at 278 S. Franklin St., is the town's most famous bar, with a sawdust-strewn floor and slightly contrived but nonetheless infectious frontier atmosphere. It's a fun place, with walls covered with lots of Alaska memorabilia. The nightly live music is free of cover charge. Across the street, **The Alaskan Bar,** 167 S. Franklin, is in an authentic gold rush hotel, with a two-story Victorian bar room that's the scene of boisterous parties and music all year. **The Hangar,** listed above under "Dining," is the place for beer drinkers. They have a big-screen TV and live music Friday and Saturday nights, as well as pool and darts.

9 Glacier Bay National Park

Glacier Bay is a work in progress; the boat ride to its head is a chance to see creation unfolding. The bay John Muir discovered in a canoe in 1879 didn't exist a century earlier. Eighteenth-century explorers had found instead a wall of ice a mile thick where the entrance to the branching, 65-mile-long fjord now opens to the sea. Receding faster than any other glacier on earth, the ice melted into the ocean and opened a spectacular and still-unfinished land. The land itself is rising 1½ inches a year as it rebounds from the weight of now-melted glaciers. As your vessel retraces Muir's path—and then probes northward in deep water where ice stood in his day—the story of this new world unravels in reverse. The trees on the shore get smaller, then disappear, then all vegetation disappears, and finally, at the head of the bay, the ice stands at the water's edge surrounded by barren rock, rounded and scored by the passage of the ice but not yet marked by the waterfalls cascading from the clouds above.

Glacier Bay, first set aside by Calvin Coolidge in 1925, is managed by the National Park Service, which has the difficult job of protecting the wilderness, the whales, and the other wildlife while showing them to the public. This rugged land the size of Connecticut can be seen only by boat or plane, and the presence of too many boats threatens the park. The whales appear to be sensitive to the noise of vessels and, since the 1970s, when only a single whale returned all year, the park service has used a permit system to limit the number of ships that can enter the bay. Any tour boat sees several other ships on a day's journey up the bay, but how much it bothers the whales really can't be proved. After a bitter controversy, the park service increased the number of cruise ships entering the bay recently, and whale sightings have continued to be quite frequent. In 2001, however, environmentalists won a court ruling that cruise ships must be reduced pending further study. Some cruise visits to Glacier Bay were canceled in 2001, and cruise ships will visit even less often in 2002, depending on the courts and what the study shows.

On my longest trip, I saw humpback whales breaching (leaping all the way out of the water) every day. I saw orcas, too. One day, while fishing for halibut from a small boat in foggy Icy Strait, just outside the park, I heard a sound like thunder not far off. Like thunder, the sound repeated, growing closer, but its source remained hidden behind the white circle of fog that surrounded us. Then the smooth water suddenly bulged and a huge, barnacled creature shot upward and crashed down with a sharp clap and a splash that rocked the boat. And then it happened again. The whale went on performing for most of an hour. A day later, I encountered the same spectacle while sea kayaking in the park's Bartlett Cove.

Leaping whales and falling glaciers are hard to beat. But the park also has major drawbacks to consider. Sightings aren't guaranteed, so there's a risk that you'll spend a lot of money and not see any whales. And even though this is a huge wilderness, the opportunities to see it are limited and therefore crowded. The lone concessionaire-operated tour boat into the bay costs $157 per person and is usually full of people. The large cruise ships that bring most visitors to the park view the scenery without getting up close to the shore or wildlife and miss the shore-based attractions. Smaller ships see more, with smaller groups and more chances to get outdoors. Independent travelers can spend a few days in some of Alaska's most attractive wilderness accommodations, in Gustavus, with great fishing, hiking, sea kayaking, and tour boat rides into the park. But the only way to see the heart of the park in true solitude is on a boat you charter for yourself (out of range of most budgets) or on a rugged overnight sea-kayaking adventure.

As an alternative, consider the other places to see Alaska's glaciers and whales that are easier and less expensive to visit. If you're in Juneau, consider a day trip to Tracy Arm instead. In Southcentral Alaska, plan a day trip from Whittier to see the glaciers of western Prince William Sound or from Seward to see Kenai Fjords National Park. There are other places in Southeast rich with marine wildlife, as well. Still, Glacier Bay beats them all—and just about anyplace on earth—for the combination of lots of whales and lots of big glaciers.

ESSENTIALS
GETTING THERE

Gustavus, covered in the next section of this chapter, is the gateway to Glacier Bay. Unless you're on a cruise ship, you'll fly or take a passenger ferry to Gustavus. Those arrangements are covered in that section. Vans to the park headquarters at Bartlett Cove meet planes and boats and cost $10 to make the 10-mile trip to the park, plus $2 for baggage. It's free if you are traveling with a package; also, most of the inns and lodges in Gustavus offer free transfers to the park.

BY TOUR BOAT   The *Spirit of Adventure* tour boat is the main way for independent travelers to see the park. It is operated by park concessionaire **Glacier Bay Cruiseline,** based at 226 Second Ave. W, Seattle, WA 98119 (© **800/ 451-5952** or 206/623-2417; fax 206/623-7809; www.glacierbaytours.com), or, locally, in the summer only, at P.O. Box 199, Gustavus, AK 99826 (© **907/ 697-2226;** fax 907/697-2408). The boat is fast and quiet, carrying up to 250 passengers in upper and lower lounges. Its shortcomings are inadequate outdoor deck space and a tendency for the windows to fog up inside. The 9-hour voyage is too long for most children. There's a snack bar and a simple lunch is provided. Bring good rain gear and layers of warm clothing. Binoculars, a necessity, are provided. A park service ranger does the commentary, so you can count on accuracy and a didactic approach missing from most commercial tours. The fare is $156.50 for adults, half price for children.

The company offers a same-day trip from Juneau, Haines, or Skagway, but it makes for too long a day, and the schedule leaves no shore time in Glacier Bay or Gustavus. The package fare from Juneau is $346.50, more from Haines or Skagway. A better choice is to take their 2-day package, riding from Juneau to Gustavus on the *Auk Nu* passenger ferry, including a whale-watching trip in Icy Strait (see the Gustavus section, below), then spend the night at Bartlett Cove and do the *Spirit of Adventure* tour the second day, and fly back to Juneau, Haines, or Skagway. That package costs $481 from Juneau. See the Gustavus section for more choices.

BY SMALL CRUISE SHIP   If your budget allows, there may be no better way to see Glacier Bay than on a small cruise ship on an excursion of a couple of days or more. **Glacier Bay Cruiseline** has developed a whole small-ship cruise fleet around this idea, and visitors come back overjoyed. Two vessels, the *Wilderness Explorer* and the larger *Wilderness Adventurer,* carry racks of sea kayaks. **Cruise West** also offers small-ship itineraries including Glacier Bay. See chapter 4 for complete reviews of each.

Local family operators based in Gustavus also do these trips. If you have a large group, you can have a boat and guide to yourself. Mike Nigro, a former backcountry ranger and long-time resident, takes groups of four to six for $1,400 to $1,650 per day on a 42-foot yacht. His **Gustavus Marine Charters** is reached at © **907/697-2233** or www.gustavusmarinecharters.com.

VISITOR INFORMATION

Contact the **Glacier Bay National Park and Preserve** at P.O. Box 140, Gustavus, AK 99826 (© **907/697-2230**; www.nps.gov/glba). The park service interprets the park mainly by placing well-prepared rangers on board all cruise and tour vessels entering the bay. The park also maintains a modest visitor center with displays on the park on the second floor of the lodge at wooded Bartlett Cove. Nearby are the park's offices, a free campground, a backcountry office, a few short hiking trails, a dock, sea-kayak rental, and other park facilities. Rangers lead daily nature walks and present an evening slide show.

ACTIVITIES AT THE PARK

AT BARTLETT COVE   There are three short hiking trails through the rain forest of Sitka spruce and western hemlock at Bartlett Cove. Each weaves through the cool, damp quiet that these huge trees and the moss create on the forest floor. Wet spots are often crossed by boardwalks with railings. A free trail guide is available at the visitor center.

The **Forest Loop** is an easy trail about 1 mile long, beginning at the lodge and passing through the woods and past some park buildings to the cove's pebble beach. The **Bartlett River Trail** is a 4-mile round-trip leading to the Bartlett River Estuary, a good bird-watching spot, especially during migrations. The **Bartlett Lake Trail** branches off the Bartlett River Trail after about 0.25 mile, a 3-mile one-way forest hike to the lake.

KAYAKING IN THE PARK   You won't forget seeing a breaching humpback whale from a sea kayak, sitting just inches off the water, and feeling the waves from its stupendous splash passing under your hull. Here, it's a common experience. When we breathlessly told our innkeepers about this life-expanding revelation, they smiled politely. They hear the same descriptions all the time.

Inexperienced paddlers should choose a guided trip. **Alaska Discovery,** 5310 Glacier Hwy., Juneau (© **800/586-1911** or 907/780-6226; www.akdiscovery.com), is Alaska's best large sea-kayak guide organization. They offer paddles ranging from 6 hours to 8 days in Glacier Bay. A 6-hour guided paddle from Bartlett Cove is the best choice for beginners. Although the trip goes nowhere near the glaciers, the paddlers stand a good chance of seeing whales, sometimes quite close up. The guides are well trained and know how to teach and make the trip an adventure. Any fit person can enjoy the trip. It costs $125, including a tasty lunch and a ride from your lodgings or the airport. The longer tours also are well guided and outfitted, but I wouldn't recommend a week of sea kayaking to anyone who hasn't tried it before. You should have spent enough time in a kayak and camping to know you'll enjoy such a remote, physically demanding trip even if it rains the whole time. If you're up to it, however, this is the most intimate and authentic way to experience this wilderness, with almost unlimited time to see the glaciers and wildlife. The 5-day trip to the bay's more visited west arm is $1,695; 8 days in the spectacular but forgotten east arm is $1,995. The company also has a simple bed-and-breakfast in Gustavus, for 1- or 2-night stays at the beginning or end of a sea-kayaking excursion.

It's also possible to paddle around Bartlett Cove or near Gustavus without a guide. Raw beginners can try it, but a safer course is to take a guided outing first. **Glacier Bay Sea Kayaks,** based in Gustavus (© **907/697-2257;** www.glacierbayseakayaks.com), is the park service concessionaire, operating May 1 to September 30. They offer day rentals, which begin with an instructional briefing, for $60 a day. Drop-offs up the bay are $167.50 round-trip. You will need a backcountry permit from the park service to make such a self-guided trip, and you'll have to attend their briefing. Permits are readily available at the park headquarters, but research what to bring before you leave for the park.

FLIGHTSEEING   The other way to get into the park is by flightseeing. Gustavus-based **Air Excursions** (✆ **907/697-2375**) offers air tours, as do other operators from various towns, Haines being the closest (see section 11, later). You'll see the incredible rivers of ice that flow down into the bay, and you may even see wildlife. What you give up is a sense of scale.

ACCOMMODATIONS, CAMPING & DINING

Glacier Bay Lodge ✮   Operated by the park concessionaire, Glacier Bay Cruiseline, this is the only place to stay in the park (although Gustavus, 10 miles down the road, has some of the most attractive accommodations in Alaska). The lodge rooms are comfortable but, for the price, nothing special. Although well maintained, they're in need of updating. The buildings' setting, accessed from the main lodge by boardwalks and steps, is amid the soothing quiet of large rain-forest trees.

The **restaurant** has huge windows looking onto Bartlett Cove, where you can sometimes see whales. There are inexpensive main courses on the dinner menu, but mainly it's a beef and sea establishment with white tablecloths and dishes in the $20 range. For a pleasant, less expensive meal, order from the menu on the deck. Breakfast is available as early as 5:30am and dinner as late as 10pm. Drinks are served in the restaurant or on a deck over the cove; on rainy days, visitors congregate around the fire in the comfortable lobby. Laundry facilities and bike rentals are available.

The area's least expensive beds are the bunks in men's and women's dorms with six beds each. The lodge also provides public showers for the free Park Service **campground.** About a quarter-mile from the dock, the campground lacks running water but has a warming hut, firewood, and bear-resistant food caches. You have to cook in a fire ring in the intertidal zone and observe other bear avoidance rules the rangers will explain. Get a camping permit at the ranger station when you arrive; the campground is almost never full.

Bartlett Cove (P.O. Box 199), Gustavus, AK 99826. ✆ **800/451-5952** or 907/697-2226. Fax 206/623-7809 or 907/697-2408. www.glacierbaytours.com. 56 units. $165 double. Extra person $9. Hostel bunks $28 per person. AE, DC, DISC, MC, V. Closed mid-Sept to mid-May.

10 Gustavus: Country Inns & Quiet

The unincorporated town of Gustavus (gus-*tave*-us) remains an undiscovered treasure—or at least it succeeds in making itself feel that way. It's wonderfully remote, accessible only by air or a small passenger ferry, but has a selection of comfortable and even luxurious inns and lodges, plus several days' worth of outdoor activities, excellent salmon and halibut fishing, nearly surefire whale-watching, close access to the sea kayaking and other activities at Glacier Bay National Park, and places for casual hiking and bicycle outings. Neither large cruise ships nor the Alaska State Ferry land here, leaving the roads free of their throngs of shoppers. Miraculously, the 400 townspeople have been smart enough to value what they've got and build on it. Even the gas station is a work of art. Walking, biking, or driving down the quiet roads, everyone you pass—every single person—waves to you.

The buildings, mostly clapboard houses and log cabins, are scattered widely across an oceanfront alluvial plain. Several of the founding homesteads were farms, and the broad clearings of sandy soil wave with hay and wildflowers. The setting is unique in Alaska, and when I had a choice to go anywhere in the state for a 4-day trip with extended family, this is the place I chose. Each of us took something lasting from the trip. My older son, then 8, learned what it was like to be able to bike anywhere at will, making discoveries in the woods and friends on the quiet lanes without his parents reining him in. My parents, in their 60s, glowed when they returned from kayaking among the breaching humpback whales in the park's Bartlett Cove. I often reminisce about a day at the beach when I built dams and sand castles with the children, looking up to see a family of orcas romping just off shore. My cousin won't forget the huge platters of Dungeness crab that came for dinner one night at the inn.

The problem with Gustavus is the expense (and the dampness, but you get used to that). The best outdoor activities involve charters or rentals, which can add more than $200 a day per person to the cost of your trip. Most accommodations have all-inclusive plans, which include great meals but come with price tags typically around $150 per person per night. Less expensive B&Bs exist, but the choice of restaurants for dinner is limited.

ESSENTIALS

GETTING THERE The **Auk Nu** passenger ferry, a high-speed catamaran (© **800/820-2628** or 907/586-8687; www.auknutours.com), leaves Juneau's Auke Bay harbor from 11789 Glacier Hwy., near the ferry terminal, at 11am daily mid-May through mid-September. The adult fare is $30 one-way, $60 round-trip. The *Auk Nu* lands at the Gustavus dock at 1:15pm, goes on an afternoon whale-watching cruise in Icy Strait (sightings guaranteed or your money back), then leaves for Juneau at 5:45pm, arriving at 8pm. Adding the whale watch, which I recommend unless you are planning to see the whales of Icy Strait some other way, brings the adult round-trip fare to $104 (more on that below). On the ferry run, they also carry kayaks, bikes, and other cargo, for an added fee, and serve light meals. Transfers from downtown Juneau to the dock are $10, from the airport area $5.

During the summer, **Alaska Airlines** (© **800/252-7522;** www.alaskaair. com) flies a jet once a day from Juneau to Gustavus and back in the late afternoon. The fare is around $100, round-trip. Various commuter carriers serve Gustavus from Juneau and other nearby towns, generally charging more. One is **L.A.B. Flying Service** (© **800/427-5966** or 907/766-2222; www.labflying. com).

VISITOR INFORMATION There are no public buildings in Gustavus because there is no government. Only the informal community association holds sway. Generally, you contact a lodge, and once you're comfortable with them, allow them to advise you and book your activities. Be certain to reserve a place to stay before showing up in Gustavus.

GETTING AROUND There are just a few roads. The main one starts at the airport and runs about 10 miles to **Bartlett Cove,** the Glacier Bay National Park base of operations. **Dock Road** branches off to the left, at the gas station, and

---

Tips **Be Prepared**

Gustavus isn't formally a town; it has no bank or ATM and few other businesses. Bring cash, as credit cards aren't always accepted, and don't count on being able to buy incidentals.

leads to the ocean dock. Most businesses will give you a good free map, which shows everything in town, for exploring by bicycle. Many inns and B&Bs have courtesy vans and free bicycles. **TLC Taxi** (✆ **907/697-2239**) will carry you and your kayak; the fare depends on the number of travelers (reserve ahead if you need the taxi).

EXPLORING GUSTAVUS

Everything to do in Gustavus involves the outdoors.

WHALE-WATCHING & FISHING   Whales keep their own schedule, but you're almost certain to see them on a whale-watching excursion from Gustavus, where the swirling current of Icy Strait creates such a rich feeding ground that humpbacks come back every summer without fail. Whale-watching trips aboard the *Auk Nu,* a large, comfortable catamaran, leave the town dock for Point Adolphus every day at 2pm. The commentary is first rate, and a good, light meal is included in the price. The fare for the 3-hour cruise is $59, and you get your money back if you don't see whales—which virtually never happens. (A combination fare with the ride from Juneau is $104.)

Other, smaller operators will provide a more intimate experience on smaller boats, usually getting you closer to the whales. They'll also combine the trip with superb halibut and salmon fishing if salmon are running. The advantage of halibut fishing here are the spectacular protected waters; seasickness generally is not a concern. Your inn host in Gustavus can make the arrangements. A boat typically charters for $200 or more per person for a full day, plus the cost of having your fish professionally packed and shipped home to you.

SEA KAYAKING   **Alaska Discovery,** 5310 Glacier Hwy., Juneau (✆ **800/586-1911** or 907/780-6226; www.akdiscovery.com), offers an easy 2½-day, 2-night kayaking expedition among the whales for $795 per person. They take a boat to a base camp, then kayak among the whales from there. The outing is suitable for fit beginners and older children. Gustavus-based **Spirit Walker Expeditions** (✆ **800/KAYAKER** or 907/697-2266; www.seakayakalaska.com) has a good reputation locally. They lead guided 1- to 7-day trips to the whale-watching grounds and beyond. **Sea Otter Kayak** (✆ **907/697-3007;** www.he.net/~seaotter) rents kayaks on Dock Road.

HIKING & BICYCLING   There are few cars in Gustavus—they have to be hauled here on a barge or plane—but most inns provide bikes. The roads are fun to explore, and the sandy beaches, accessed from the town dock, are great for a walk and a picnic, to watch eagles and other birds and wildlife. You can go many miles, if you are of a mind for a run or long walk, but we saw little reason to go far before stopping to play and picnic on a broad sand beach undisturbed by any other human footprint.

ACCOMMODATIONS & DINING

Gustavus contains many of Alaska's best remote accommodations. There are many more good places to stay than I have room to describe here, some of them so good they'd be the best on the list in most other Alaska towns. I can wholeheartedly recommend these: **Growley Bear Inn,** Dock Road (✆ **907/697-2730;** www.growleybear.com); and the **Glacier Bay Country Inn,** Tong Road (✆ **800/628-0912** or 907/697-2288; www.glacierbayalaska.com).

Most accommodations are "Gustavus style," which means charging a daily per-person price for rooms, breakfast and dinner served family style, brown-bag lunches, bicycles and some other outdoor equipment, transportation around the area, and booking fishing, sea kayaking, hiking, and Glacier Bay tours (which cost extra). It's expensive, but it's a great way to visit. Another set of accommodations charges less, but leaves you on your own for lunch and dinner.

If you choose the less costly, a la carte approach, you'll likely take your evening meals at the inns anyway, as Gustavus is short on restaurants. You'll have to make prior arrangements; you can't just show up and eat. The Glacier Bay Lodge serves three meals a day—but it's 10 miles away at the park's Bartlett Cove head-quarters. Several free-standing restaurants have gone out of business periodically around town; your innkeeper can direct you to one that's currently operating. One that's been going strong for several years is **A Bear's Nest Cafe,** on Rink Creek Road (© **907/697-2440**), where the often braided Lynne Morrow serves organic dishes, homemade bread, seafood specials, soup, and sandwiches in a dining room that's also the ground floor of her house, 11am to 8pm daily in the summer. She accepts Discover, MasterCard, and Visa. Also, a country store on Dock Road sells basics for picnics or to cook yourself.

Except as noted, rooms don't have phones. Some of the inns do not have licenses to serve alcohol; if that's a consideration, be sure to ask before you book your stay.

Blue Heron Bed and Breakfast at Glacier Bay ★

Stay here if your budget doesn't allow a pricey all-inclusive package, and you'll still get many of the same comforts in fresh, attractive rooms with features such as VCRs, comforters, and superior linens. The hosts, long-time residents, are enthusiastic about their guests and serve large breakfasts. If you rent one of the cabins, you can cook your own evening meal; even the rooms have limited cooking facilities. The location is among the wildflowers and marshland near the Gustavus waterfront.

Off Dock Rd. (P.O. Box 77), Gustavus, AK 99826. © and fax **907/697-2293**. www.blueheronbnb.net. 2 units, 2 cabins. $125 double, $150 double cabin; $40 each additional adult, discounts for children. No credit cards. **Amenities:** Free bike loan; courtesy van; In room massage; laundry machines. *In room:* TV/VCR.

Glacier Bay's Bear Track Inn ★★★

Six miles from Gustavus, this extraor-dinary log building faces its own field of wildflowers, which, if you walk half a mile across it, leads to the sea. You look out on this scene from a lobby with a huge fireplace, a ceiling 28 feet high, and a wall of windows. The immense logs of the walls and the isolation give the place the feeling of a wilderness lodge, but the rooms are as good as those of any upscale hotel, and have the advantage of large dormer windows with sweeping views. Objectively, it's the best place in Gustavus, and one of the best remote lodges in Alaska; however, I found it too perfect to hold much charm. Unlike other lodges and inns in Gustavus, meals are cooked to order from a varied menu; the inn serves beer and wine. Those not staying here can buy dinner, too.

255 Rink Rd., Gustavus, AK 99826. © **888/697-2284** or 907/697-3017. Fax 907/697-2284. www. beartrackinn.com. 14 units. $393 per person, double occupancy; discounts for additional nights. Rates include round-trip air from Juneau and all meals. AE, DISC, MC, V. Closed Nov–Jan. **Amenities:** Restaurant; bike loan; children's programs; concierge; tour desk; car rental; business center; room service (5am–8pm); In room mas-sage; babysitting; laundry service. *In room:* Hair dryers.

Gustavus Inn at Glacier Bay ★★★

This is the original and still my favorite of the Gustavus full-service inns. By objective standards of modern luxury, imi-tators have surpassed the old homestead farmhouse, but no one could duplicate the extraordinary hospitality of the Lesh family, honed over 35 years of running the inn. They know how to make guests feel immediately a part of the place. The site is unsurpassed, too, standing at the center of the community amid blowing grass and with a huge vegetable garden that provides much of the dining room's wonderful food. Dave, the chef, has published a cookbook. The seasonings he uses on seafood are a real revelation, served on big, inexhaustible platters in the dining room, where there's also a beer and wine bar and sushi appetizers. Before going, talk over what you want to do with Dave or his father, Jack, and let them book everything.

Gustavus Rd. (P.O. Box 60), Gustavus, AK 99826. © **800/649-5220** or 907/697-2254. Fax 907/697-2255. www.gustavusinn.com. 11 units. $150 per person per night. Children under 12 half price. Rates include all meals. AE, MC, V. Closed Sept 16–May 15. **Amenities:** Restaurant; bike loan; laundry service; fishing rods (bring your own tackle). They drive guests around and offer free bikes.

Meadow's Glacier Bay Guest House ★★   At high tide the sea comes to the base of the lawn by the grassy meadow and estuary where this house stands, a rich foreground for stunning views in every direction. If any house could live up to such a setting, this is it. Designed by owner Chris Smith's father, its cool, airy spaces interpret those outside with big geometric shapes, shining wood floors, and great white walls hung with some of the best of Alaska's contemporary art. Each guest room is its own small work of the decorator's art: fashionable, immaculate, and perhaps a little too good for mere mortals. Smith's wife, Meadow Brook, presides, serving elaborate breakfasts and providing advice and equipment for the area's outdoors.

Off Dock Rd. (P.O. 93), Gustavus, AK 99826. © **877/766-2348** or 907/697-2348 (phone or fax). www. glacier-bay-alaska.com. 4 units. $139–$199 double. Extra person $69. Rates include full breakfast. AE, MC, V. **Amenities:** Bike loan; babysitting; laundry service. *In room:* Telephone with dataport, coffeemaker, hair dryer.

11 Haines: Eagles & the Unexpected

For years we always just passed through Haines on the way from the ferry up the highway. I didn't know what I was missing until I stopped and took a couple of days to really investigate. Now Haines is one of my favorite Alaska towns.

Haines is casual, happy, and slightly odd. It waits for you to find it, but once found, it unveils wonderful charms. If you're looking for the mythical town of Cicely from television's *Northern Exposure,* you'll get closer in Haines than any-place else I know (in fact, the producers scouted here before choosing to shoot in Roslyn, Washington). As I walked down a sidewalk, I saw a sign in a storefront that said to look in the big tree across the street. I looked, and there was an eagle peering back at me. At the Alaska Indian Arts Native cultural center, seeking an office or a ticket window or someone in charge, I wandered into a totem pole studio where a carver was completing a major commission. He gladly stopped to talk. It turned out there wasn't anyone in charge. Issues that are a big deal in some other towns just aren't in Haines.

Haines's dominant feature, the 1904 **Fort William H. Seward,** gives the town a pastoral atmosphere. The fort is a collection of grand white-clapboard buildings arranged around a 9-acre parade ground, in the middle of which stands a Tlingit clan house—out of place, yes, but wonderfully symbolic of Haines. The town is a friendly, accessible center of Tlingit culture as well as a retired outpost of seemingly pointless military activity.

And Haines has **bald eagles**—always plenty of bald eagles, and in the fall, a ridiculous number of bald eagles. More, in fact, than anywhere else on earth. The chance to see the birds draws people into the outdoors here. There are well-established guides for any activity you might want to pursue, all cooperating and located together. There are some excellent hiking trails right from town, as well as protected sea kayaking waters. Also, it's worth noting that because of its location in relation to the flow of weather, Haines is not quite as rainy as towns father south.

ESSENTIALS

GETTING THERE The **Alaska Marine Highway System,** 1591 Glacier Ave., Juneau, AK 99801-1427 (© **800/642-0066,** or 907/766-2111 locally; www.state.ak.us/ferry), is how most people get to Haines, and the cruise on the Lynn Canal fjord from Juneau or Skagway is among the most beautiful in the Inside Passage. The fare is $26 from Juneau and $19 from Skagway. The dock is 5 miles north of town. Unfortunately, since this is the northern highway connection where nearly all vehicles get off or on, there are often delays.

If you're just going to or from Skagway without a car, a good alternative is one of the summer-only private passenger ferries. The Haines-Skagway Fast Ferry, operated by **Chilkat Cruises and Tours** (© **888/766-2103** or 907/766-2100; www.chilkatcruises.com), runs a 150-passenger catamaran, the *Fairweather Express,* at least three 35-minute round-trips a day. It leaves from the Port Chilkoot dock, below Fort William Seward, where they have a local booking service and serve halibut and chips. Adult round-trips are $36, one-way $24; children 12 and under pay half price. Weekend cruises to Juneau are $99 roundtrip. **The Haines-Skagway Water Taxi and Scenic Cruise** (© **888/766-3395** or 907/766-3395; www.lynncanal.com) makes the run to Skagway and back a sightseeing cruise, following the shoreline and stopping for wildlife sightings. The 80-passenger vessel leaves from the small boat harbor, charging adults $35 round-trip, $24 one-way; children under 12 go half price. Their daily sightseeing cruise to Juneau, including a bus tour of the capital city, is $109 ($119 from Skagway).

If you're driving, the **Haines Highway** leads 155 miles to Haines Junction, Yukon Territory, an intersection with the Alaska Highway (you must pass through Canadian Customs—see the "Alaska Highway" section in chapter 9 for rules). The road runs along the Chilkat River and the bald eagle preserve, then climbs into spectacular alpine terrain. Anchorage is 760 driving miles from Haines, Fairbanks is 644. One-way car rentals to Anchorage, Fairbanks, and Skagway are available from **Avis,** at the Hotel Hälsingland (© **907/766-2733**), with a $300 drop-off charge plus the rental cost. You can also rent an RV one-way to Anchorage. **ABC Motorhome Rentals,** 3875 W. International Airport Rd., in Anchorage (© **800/421-7456** or 907/279-2000; www.abcmotorhome. com), charges $500 plus a 1-week rental, starting around $1,400 in the high season.

Three air services offer scheduled prop service, air taxi, and flightseeing tours to surrounding communities. One is **L.A.B. Flying Service,** based at Main Street and 4th Avenue (© **800/427-5966** or 907/766-2222; www.labflying.com), with frequent flights, charging $70 one-way for the 30-minute trip from Juneau.

VISITOR INFORMATION The small but well-staffed and -stocked **Haines Convention and Visitors Bureau Visitor Information Center,** Second Street near Willard (P.O. Box 530), Haines, AK 99827 (© **800/458-3579** or 907/ 766-2234; www.haines.ak.us), is operated by the city government, which also sends out a vacation-planning packet. It's open summer Monday to Friday 8am to 6pm, Saturday 9am to 5pm, Sunday 11am to 5pm; in winter, hours are

ACCOMMODATIONS ■
Captain's Choice Motel **4**
Eagle's Nest Motel **1**
Fort Seward Bed & Breakfast **14**
Hotel Hälsingland **11**
Mountain View Motel **8**
A Sheltered Harbor B&B **12**
The Summer Inn
  Bed & Breakfast **3**

DINING ◆
The Bamboo Room **5**
The Commander's Room **11**
Fireweed Bakery **10**
Fort Seward Lodge, Restaurant & Saloon **9**
Port Chilkoot Potlatch Salmon Bake **15**

ATTRACTIONS ●
Alaska Indian Arts cultural center **13**
American Bald Eagle Foundation
  Natural History Museum **7**
Sheldon Museum & Cultural Center **6**
Tsirku Canning Co. **2**

Monday to Friday 8am to 5pm.

ORIENTATION   Haines sits on the narrow Chilkat Peninsula near the north end of the Southeast Alaska Panhandle. Highways run north and east on either side of the peninsula; the one on the east side goes to the ferry dock, 5 miles out, and ends after 11 miles at **Chilkoot Lake.** The other is the **Haines Highway,** which leads to the Canadian border, the Alaska Highway, and the rest of the world.

The town has two parts: the sparsely built downtown grid and, a short walk to the west down Front Street or Second Avenue, the Fort William Seward area. Vans and buses that meet the ferry offer free or inexpensive transfers, seeking to take you on a town tour. Hotel Hälsingland books tours, too, but your feet or a bicycle will get you around handily.

GETTING AROUND Bikes are available from **Sockeye Cycle,** just uphill from the Port Chilkoot Dock on Portage Street in the Fort William Seward area (© 907/766-2869; www.cyclealaska.com), for $6 an hour or $30 a day.

Haines Taxi and Tours can be reached at © 907/766-3138.

Avis car rental has an outlet at the Hotel Hälsingland. **Affordable Cars** is at the Captain's Choice Motel (see "Accommodations," below).

SPECIAL EVENTS The **Great Alaska Craftbeer and Homebrew Festival** (© 800/542-6363) takes place over 3 days in mid-May. The **Kluane to Chilkat International Bike Relay** (© 907/766-2202) is held around the summer solstice, June 21, heading down the Haines Highway, with more than 1,000 entrants; it's quite a downhill.

The **Southeast Alaska State Fair and Bald Eagle Music Festival** (© 907/766-2476) is the biggest event of the summer, held for 5 days in early August; it's a regional small-town get-together, with livestock, cooking, a logging show, a parade, music, and other entertainment. Buildings constructed for the filming of the movie *White Fang* in 1990 were donated to the fair, and now form the nucleus of a retail area here. (One stop of interest here, at any time, is the local microbrewery, Haines Brewing Co., which offers samples and informal tours.)

The **Alaska Bald Eagle Festival** (© 907/766-2202; www.baldeaglefest.org) offers seminars and special events to mark the annual eagle congregation. It's held in mid-November, timed to allow visitors to also attend the WhaleFest in Sitka.

 FAST FACTS: **Haines**

Bank **First National Bank of Anchorage** is at Main Street and Second Avenue.

Hospital The **Haines Medical Clinic** (© 907/766-2521) is on First Avenue, near the visitor center.

Internet Access **Mountain Market,** at Third Avenue and the Haines Highway (© 907/766-3340), charges $8 an hour. Next door, at the **Haines Borough Library,** Third Avenue and Willard Street (© 907/766-2545), you can log on for free.

Police Reach city police in nonemergencies at © 907/766-2121. Outside city limits, call the **Alaska State Troopers** at © 907/766-2552.

Post Office At 55 Haines Hwy.

Taxes The local **sales tax** is 5.5%.

EXPLORING HAINES

The main feature of Haines is **Fort William H. Seward National Historic Site,** a collection of large, white, wood-frame buildings around sloping parade grounds overlooking the magnificent Lynn Canal fjord. (Get the informative walking-tour map of the National Historic Site from the Haines Convention and Visitors Bureau.) The fort led a peaceful life, for a military installation. By the time the U.S. Army built it, in 1904, the Klondike gold rush was over, and there's no evidence it ever deterred any attack on this little peninsula at the north end of the Inside Passage. It was deactivated at the end of World War II, when it was used for training.

In 1947 a group of five veterans from the Lower 48 bought the fort as surplus with the idea of forming a planned community. That idea didn't really work out, but one of the new white families helped spark a Chilkat Tlingit cultural renaissance in the 1950s. The Heinmillers, who still own a majority of the shares in the fort, were looking for something to do with all that property when someone suggested a Tlingit tribal house on the parade grounds. The project, led by a pair of elders, took on a life of its own, and the **Chilkat Dancers** and **Alaska Indian Arts** cultural center followed. Lee Heinmiller, a member of the second generation, still manages the arts center, where you can see totem carving and silversmithing practiced. The dance troupe stopped performing except for special occasions in 2001 after more than 40 years on stage here and around the world, but may yet revive. The cultural center is open from 9am to 5pm Monday to Friday and evenings when cruise ships are in town. It occupies the old fort hospital on the south side of the parade grounds.

In the downtown area, the **Sheldon Museum and Cultural Center,** 11 Main St. (℃ **907/766-2366;** www.sheldonmuseum.org), contains an upstairs gallery of well-presented Tlingit art and cultural artifacts; downstairs is a collection on the white history of the town. There's a uniquely personal feel to the Tlingit objects, some of which are displayed with pictures of the artisans who made them and the history of their relationship with the Sheldons, for whom the museum is named. It's open in summer, daily from 1 to 5pm, plus mornings and evenings that are posted weekly; call for winter hours. Admission is $3 for adults, free for children under 12.

Also downtown, the **Tsirku Canning Co.,** at Fourth Avenue and Main Street (℃ **907/766-3474**), is a museum of Alaska salmon canneries, full of 80-year-old machinery salvaged from abandoned canneries around the state, including a 120-foot line you can see doing its work on imaginary fish. The fishing industry remains the state's largest employer, and was long its largest industry by any measure; in 1929, 157 canneries stood all along the coast, teeming with summer workers and served by frequent steamer service in places where nothing remains today but broken dock pilings. Haines had nine. The 90-minute tour, including a 20-minute video, costs $10. Independent travelers can join the tour May to mid-September Monday through Saturday at 1pm.

The entirely unique **American Bald Eagle Foundation Natural History Museum,** at Second Avenue and Haines Highway (℃ **907/766-3094;** www. baldeagles.org), is essentially a huge, hair-raising diorama of more than 180 eagles and other animal mounts. Dave Olerud sits in a wheelchair behind the desk and will talk your ear off about the museum if you want him to—he worked on it for 18 years and was paralyzed in a fall during construction. Admission is $3 adults, $1 ages 8 to 12. It's open summer daily 9am to 6pm, winter Monday, Wednesday, and Friday 1 to 4pm.

GETTING OUTSIDE

EAGLE VIEWING   Haines is probably the best place on earth to see bald eagles. The **Chilkat Bald Eagle Preserve** protects 48,000 acres of river bottom along the Chilkat River. From October to January, up to 3,000 eagles gather in the cottonwood trees (also known as western poplar) on a small section of the river, a phenomenon known as the Fall Congregation. (A healthy 200 to 400 are resident the rest of the year.) The eagles come for easy winter food: A very late salmon run spawns here into December in a 5-mile stretch of open water known as the Council Grounds.

During the Congregation, dozens of eagles stand in each of the gnarled, leafless cottonwoods on the riverbanks, occasionally diving for a fish. The best places to see them are pull-outs, paths, and viewing areas along the Haines Highway from mile 18 to 21. Don't walk on the flats, as that disturbs the eagles. The preserve is managed by Alaska State Parks, 400 Willoughby, 3rd Floor, Juneau, AK 99801 (www.dnr.state.ak.us/parks/units/eagleprv.htm), but the Haines Convention and Visitors Bureau may be a better source of information for planning a visit.

Local guides offer trips to see the eagles by raft, bicycle, or bus—mostly in the summer, when the eagles are fewer but visitors more numerous. **Chilkat Guides,** based at 1 Mile Haines Hwy. along Sawmill Road (© 907/766-2491; www.raftalaska.com), does a rafting trip twice a day during the summer down the Chilkat to watch the eagles. The water is gentle—if it's too low, there's a chance you'll be asked to get out and push—and you'll see lots of eagles, mostly at a distance. The company is run by young people who create a sense of fellowship with their clients. The 4-hour trip, with a snack, costs $80 for adults, $40 for children.

Sockeye Cycle (see "Biking," below) has guided bike tours to see eagles and Fort Seward on a 90-minute trip that costs $42; and **Alaska Nature Tours** (© 907/766-2876; http://kcd.com/aknature) takes 3-hour bus and walking tours to the preserve for $50 per person in summer.

BIKING   **Sockeye Cycle,** at 24 Portage St., near the dock (© 907/766-2869; www.cyclealaska.com), leads a variety of guided trips—a couple of hours, half or full day, or even a 9-day trek. A 3-hour ride along Chilkoot Lake costs $90. Or you can go on your own for $30 a day. The area is quite conducive to biking.

FISHING   There are several charter operators in Haines for halibut or salmon, or guided freshwater fishing for king and silver salmon, halibut, Dolly Varden, or cutthroat trout. The Haines Convention and Visitors Bureau can help you find a guide through the links on their website or the list of operators they keep at the office. For self-guided fishing advice, contact the local office of that Alaska Department of Fish and Game at © 907/766-2625; www.state.ak.us/adfg.

FLIGHTSEEING   This is one of Alaska's best flightseeing trips. The Inside Passage is beautiful, and one mountain away is Glacier Bay National Park; the ice field and the glaciers spilling through to the sea are a sight you can't forget. It's possible to land on an immense glacial ice field and see the sun slicing between the craggy peaks. **Alaska Mountain Flying and Travel,** 132 2nd Ave. (© 800/954-8747 or 907/766-3007; www.flyglacierbay.com), offers these flights; the owner and pilot is known for his glacier and beach landings. Prices range from $115 to $259 per person, and reservations are recommended. **L.A.B. Flying Service** (© 800/427-5966; www.labflying.com) is a larger operator, offering flights from Haines starting at $105 per person.

HIKING   There are several good trails near Haines, ranging from an easy beach walk to a 10-mile, 4,000-foot climb of **Mount Ripinsky,** north of town (it starts at the top of Young Street). Get the *Haines Is for Hikers* trail guide from the visitor center. The easiest for families is the **Battery Point Trail,** which goes 2.4 miles along the beach, decorated with wild iris, from the end of the shore road that leads southeast from the Port Chilkoot cruise-ship dock. **Mount Riley**

is south of town, with three trail routes to a 1,760-foot summit that features great views and feels much higher than it is; get the trail guide or ask directions to one of the trailheads. **Seduction Point Trail** is 7 miles long, starting at Chilkat State Park at the end of Mud Bay Road south of town and leading to the end of the Chilkat Peninsula. It's a beach walk, so check the tides; they'll give you a tide table at the visitors bureau.

SEA KAYAKING   Deishu Expeditions, 425 Beach Rd. (© **800/552-9257** or 907/766-2427; www.seakayaks.com), offers instruction, short guided trips, longer expeditions, and rentals ($45 a day for a single, plus $25 for drop-off and pickup anywhere on the Haines Road system). A half-day guided paddle is $85, including a snack; a full day, including lunch, is $125.

ACCOMMODATIONS

Many towns have a lot of chainlike hotels and only one or two unique places with character. In Haines, the situation is reversed.

Besides the hotels I've listed, you'll find good economy rooms at these other places: **A Sheltered Harbor B&B,** 57 Beach Rd. (©/fax **907/766-2741;** www.geocities.com/asheltered); **Mountain View Motel,** at Mud Bay Road and Second Avenue (© **907/766-2900**); **Fort Seward Lodge, Restaurant & Saloon,** in the old fort exchange (© **800/478-7772** or 907/766-2009; www.ftsewardlodge.com); and **Eagle's Nest Motel,** Mile 1, Haines Hwy. (© **800/354-6009**).

Captain's Choice Motel ✦   These trim, red-roofed buildings house the one standard chainlike motel in town, with all the anticipated amenities. Yet it still has a certain amount of charm, making it—objectively, anyway—probably the best hotel in town. The room decor is on the dark side, with paneling, and is somewhat out-of-date, but it's quite clean, and many of the rooms have good views on a large sun deck.

108 N. Second St. at Dalton St. (P.O. Box 392), Haines, AK 99827. © 800/478-2345 or 907/766-3111. Fax 907/766-3332. www.capchoice.com. 39 units. High season $104 double; $145 suite. Low season $76 double; $120 suite. Extra person $5. AE, DC, DISC, MC, V. **Amenities:** Tour desk; car rental; courtesy van; limited room service. *In room:* TV, dataport, fridge, coffeemaker.

Fort Seward Bed and Breakfast ✦ *(Finds)*   The fort surgeon's quarters overlook the parade grounds and the Lynn Canal with a big wraparound porch and an unspoiled historic feel. Norm Smith has lived in this house most of his life and in 1981 started the B&B with his wife, Suzanne, a gifted hostess who instantly makes you feel like an old friend. The rooms have high ceilings, fireplaces, wonderful cabinetry—all kinds of authentic charm. It's a social place, with a barbecue on the porch, and guests are welcome to use the kitchen, where Norm produces a fine full breakfast.

1 Fort Seward Dr. (P.O. Box 5), Haines, AK 99827. © 800/615-NORM or phone/fax 907/766-2856. www.haines.ak.us/norm. 7 units, 2 with private bathroom. High season $84–$125 double. Low season $78 double. Extra person $25. Rates include full breakfast. DISC, MC, V. Closed Oct 15–Apr 7. No smoking. **Amenities:** Bike loan; courtesy car. *In room:* TV/VCR.

Hotel Hälsingland ✦   This National Historic Landmark has been operating continuously as a hotel in the same family since 1947, a year after it stopped functioning as the commanding officer's quarters at Fort William Seward. Owner Arne Olsson has worked hard to renew the rooms, however, and his work has paid off in upgrading the huge, white clapboard structure, although some of the furniture still looks not antique but just plain old. Every room is different, so it's wise to choose when you check in. Some are priced for backpackers, with fewer amenities. Most rooms with private bathrooms have only showers, not tubs. When I stayed in a big, oddly shaped room with a nonworking fireplace and windows on the parade grounds, I felt like I could almost hear the commander walking across the floor in his spurs. The hotel serves as a center for tours, buses, and other activity.

The **Commander's Room** restaurant has a wide selection of fresh seafood with views of the ocean and parade grounds, and prompt service. It's open for dinner and a continental breakfast that comes with the room. The small bar has craft brews on tap. It's a friendly, low-key place in the evening.

Fort William Seward parade grounds (P.O. Box 1589), Haines, AK 99827. ℂ **800/542-6363** or 907/766-2000. Fax 907/766-2445. www.haines.ak.us/halsingland. 50 units, 45 with private bathroom. $59 double without bathroom, $93 double with private bathroom; $119 suite. Rates include continental breakfast. AE, DISC, MC, V. Closed mid-Nov to mid-Mar. **Amenities:** Restaurant; bar; tour desk; Avis car rental; courtesy van; coin-op laundry. *In room:* TV.

The Summer Inn Bed & Breakfast *(Value)* This lovely old clapboard house downtown has a big porch and living room, decorated in whites and pale, lacy fabrics, like Grandma's house. The five rooms are cozy but small, and share three bathrooms among them (bathrooms were immaculate when we last visited). The house was built by a reputed former member of Soapy Smith's gang in 1912 (see Skagway section for more on Soapy). No smoking or drinking allowed.

117 Second Ave. (P.O. Box 1198), Haines, AK 99827. ℂ and fax **907/766-2970.** www.summerinn. wytbear.com. 5 units, none with private bathroom. High season $80 double; $100 suite. Low season $70 double; $90 suite. Extra person $15. Rates include full breakfast. MC, V.

DINING

Haines doesn't have a great restaurant, but you can eat well at the Hotel Hälsingland (see "Accommodations," above) during the summer, and there are lots of places for a burger or a slice of pizza. Among the best lunch places is the **Mountain Market & Café** *(star)*, a health-food store at Third Avenue and the Haines Highway (ℂ **907/766-3340**). A youthful hangout, it serves hearty and reasonably priced sandwiches, wraps, and soups. It's great for picnics, or stop by for coffee or breakfast.

The Bamboo Room *(star)* DINER/SEAFOOD This small restaurant, in the same family for nearly 50 years, was recently rescued from being a smoky adjunct to the bar. It has been divided off by attractive etched glass and made into a first-class diner serving burgers, salads, pasta, and lots of seafood. Many light and healthful items are on the menu along with the solid fried foods. The new incarnation fits a building that started as a French restaurant during the gold rush era and then became a brothel and speakeasy before the Tengs family got it in 1953. The history is on the back of the menu. Get the halibut and chips.

Second Ave. near Main St. ℂ **907/766-2800.** Lunch $6–$12.50; dinner $6–$23. AE, DISC, DC, MC, V. Summer daily 6am–midnight. Winter daily 6am–8pm.

Fireweed Bakery *(star)* *(Value)* ORGANIC/MEDITERRANEAN In this dining room just 2 blocks from the Port Chilkoot dock, in the Quartermaster's Building at old Fort Seward, thoughtful restoration has come closer than anywhere else in the fort to re-creating the elegance enjoyed by early-20th-century officers. Captains' chairs and eight tables made by a Haines craftsperson sit amid ample hardwood, wainscoting, and local art—a clean, stylish look. The menu, posted on a blackboard, changes daily, but it is consistently wholesome and expertly seasoned, with items such as gyro sandwiches or mushroom ravioli. The bagels are top-notch, as are all the fine baked goods. At this writing, they're still hoping for a beer and wine license.

Fort Seward Bldg. 37, Blacksmith Rd. © **907/766-3838.** Lunch $6–$11; dinner $7–$11. MC, V. Mon–Sat 7am–9pm. Closed winter.

Fort Seward Lodge, Restaurant & Saloon ✯ STEAK/SEAFOOD   A favorite of the locals, the restaurant resides in a tall room in the old Post Exchange of the historic fort, where patrons have long speared dollar bills to the ceiling. It's now papered with money. This is a fun place, with a friendly and gregarious staff and partying tradition (although the bar is in a separate room). The food—simple, fresh fish, meat, and vegetables—may be the best in town. The prime rib is especially famous. The full bar has Alaska microbrews on tap.

Mile 0 Haines Hwy., in Fort William Seward. © **907/766-2009.** www.ftsewardlodge.com. Dinner $8–$25. DISC, MC, V. Summer daily 5–10pm. Winter daily 5:30–9pm.

Port Chilkoot Potlatch Salmon Bake SALMON BAKE   Salmon bakes are touristy by nature, but this long-established event is a *good* salmon bake. The sockeye is grilled on alder and not overcooked or ruined with overseasoning. Dining is at picnic tables, either in tents or in the clan house on the parade grounds. After you go through the line, waiters replenish your plate. One glass of beer or wine is included in the price as well as dessert and other trimmings.

Fort William Seward parade grounds. © **907/766-2000.** Reservations recommended. $23.75 per person. AE, DC, DISC, MC, V. Mon–Thurs 5–8:30pm. Closed Oct–Apr.

12 Skagway: After the Gold Rush

It's only been 100 years since white civilization came to Alaska. There were a few scattered towns in Southeast before that—Juneau, Sitka, and Wrangell, for example—but until the Klondike Gold Rush, the great mass of Alaska was populated only by Natives who had never seen a white face, for only a few explorers and prospectors had ever ventured there. Then, in a single year, 1898, the population exploded. (See "The Gold Rush in Context," in chapter 9.) It still stands as the greatest event in Alaska's short but eventful history, for the flow of people in a few short years set the patterns of development ever since.

For Skagway, the rush created a long-term living based on showing off to visitors the wildest boomtown of the era, a true Wild West outpost that in its biggest years was completely without law other than the survival of the meanest. And a good living it's been, for in today's Skagway, more money and more than 20 times as many visitors come through in a year as made the trip to the Klondike during the gold rush.

In 1896 there was a single log cabin in Skagway, in 1897 the word of the Klondike strike made it to the outside world, and in 1898 Skagway was a huge gold rush boomtown. In 1899 the gold rush was ending, and in 1903, 300 tourists arrived in a single day to see where the gold rush happened. By 1908, local businessmen had started developing their tourist attractions, moving picturesque gold rush buildings to Broadway, the main street, to create a more unified image when visitors arrived on the steamers. By 1920, tourism had become an important part of the economy. By 1933, historic preservation efforts had started. Today, you can see history in Skagway, and you can see the history of history.

With 862 residents and nearly half a million visitors annually, the "real" town has all but disappeared, and most of the people you'll meet are either fellow visitors or summer workers brought north to serve them. Most of the tourists are from cruise ships—it's not unusual for several ships to hit town in a single morning, unleashing waves of people up the wharf and into the one historic street. There are plenty of highway and ferry travelers, too, and outdoor enthusiasts come to do the Chilkoot Trail, just as the stampeders did.

Is it worth all those visits? Skagway, spared from fire and recognized so long ago for its history, is probably the best-preserved gold rush town in the United States. What happened here in a 2-year period was certainly extraordinary, even if the phenomenon the town celebrates is one of mass insanity based on greed, inhumanity, thuggery, prostitution, waste, and, for most, abject failure. In the rush years of 1897 and 1898, Skagway or its ghost-town twin city of Dyea were the logical places to get off the boat to head off on the trek to the gold fields near the new city of Dawson. (That fascinating town is covered in chapter 9.) Skagway instantly grew from a single homestead to a population of between 15,000 and 25,000—no one knows exactly how many, in part because the people were flowing through so fast but also because there was no civil authority to count the people. Dawson City ended up with 30,000.

While Canada was well policed by the Mounties, Skagway was truly lawless—a hell on earth, as one Mountie described it. Soapy Smith ruled, a con artist turned organized crime boss; the governor offered to put him officially in charge as a territorial marshal and rode with him in the 1898 Independence Day parade. Four days later, Smith was shot dead in a gunfight with Frank Reid, who led a vigilante committee upset over one of Smith's thefts. Reid died of his wounds in the shoot-out, too, but Smith's gang was broken. Of course, the gold rush was about to end anyway.

In 1976 the National Park Service began buying many of Skagway's best old buildings for the **Klondike Gold Rush National Historic District,** and now it owns about 15, having completed restoration in 1999. Broadway is a prosperous, freshly painted 6-block strip of gold rush era buildings. A few that look like real businesses turn out to be displays showing how it was back then. Other buildings restored by the Park Service are under lease to gift shops and such. Visitors also can ride the gold rush era narrow-gauge **White Pass and Yukon Route railroad** into the White Pass, hike the **Chilkoot Trail,** or join in some other, limited outdoor activities.

ESSENTIALS

GETTING THERE   The **Alaska Marine Highway System** (© **800/ 642-0066,** or 907/983-2941 locally; www.state.ak.us/ferry) connects Skagway daily with Haines and Juneau. The fare is $19 to Haines, $35 to Juneau. If you're headed to Haines without a vehicle, consider the two private passenger ferries listed under "Getting There" in the Haines section. Haines is 15 miles away by boat but more than 350 miles by road.

Since 1978, **Klondike Highway 2** has traced the route of the stampeders through the White Pass into Canada, a parallel route to the Chilkoot Trail. The road runs 99 miles, then meets the Alaska Highway a dozen miles southeast of the Yukon capital of Whitehorse. The border is at the top of the pass, 14 miles from Skagway. (Information on Customs is in chapter 9 in the Alaska Highway section.) This is one of the most spectacular drives anywhere in Alaska, and the

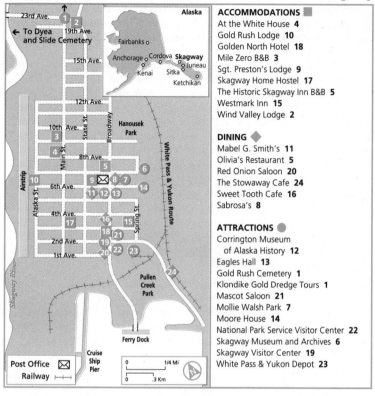

ACCOMMODATIONS ■
At the White House **4**
Gold Rush Lodge **10**
Golden North Hotel **18**
Mile Zero B&B **3**
Sgt. Preston's Lodge **9**
Skagway Home Hostel **17**
The Historic Skagway Inn B&B **5**
Westmark Inn **15**
Wind Valley Lodge **2**

DINING ◆
Mabel G. Smith's **11**
Olivia's Restaurant **5**
Red Onion Saloon **20**
The Stowaway Cafe **24**
Sweet Tooth Cafe **16**
Sabrosa's **8**

ATTRACTIONS ●
Corrington Museum
  of Alaska History **12**
Eagles Hall **13**
Gold Rush Cemetery **1**
Klondike Gold Dredge Tours **1**
Mascot Saloon **21**
Mollie Walsh Park **7**
Moore House **14**
National Park Service Visitor Center **22**
Skagway Museum and Archives **6**
Skagway Visitor Center **19**
White Pass & Yukon Depot **23**

road is a well-maintained two-lane highway with wide shoulders. The views are basically equivalent to those from the White Pass and Yukon Route railway, but a lot cheaper. Do it in clear weather, if possible, as in cloudy weather all you'll see is whiteout. Car rentals are available from **Avis** (© **800/331-1212** or 907/983-2247), with an office at the Westmark Inn Skagway, at Third and Spring streets.

It takes 2 days to travel by bus between Skagway and Anchorage. Gray Line's summer-only **Alaskon Express** (© **800/544-2206** or 907/983-2241;www.gray linealaska.com/alaskon.cfm) leaves from the Westmark Inn Skagway, at Third and Spring streets. **Alaska Direct Busline** (© **800/780-6652**) operates year-round from the ferry terminal. Either service charges about $220 one-way to Anchorage.

Several air taxi operators serve Skagway. **L.A.B. Flying Service** (© **800/427-5966** or 907/983-2471; www.labflying.com) has scheduled flights from Juneau for $140 round-trip.

VISITOR INFORMATION In the restored railroad depot, the **National Park Service Visitor Center,** Second Avenue and Broadway (P.O. Box 517), Skagway, AK 99840 (© **907/983-2921;** www.nps.gov/klgo), is the focal point for activities in Skagway. Rangers answer questions, give lectures and show films, and five times a day lead an excellent guided walking tour. The building houses a small museum that lays the groundwork for the rest of what you'll see. Most of the Park Service's programs are free. It's open daily 8am to 8pm from June to August, daily 8am to 6pm in May and September, and Monday to Friday 8am to 5pm from October to April.

The **Skagway Convention and Visitors Bureau Center,** 245 Broadway (P.O. Box 1025), Skagway, AK 99840 (© **907/983-2854;** fax 907/983-3854; www.skagway.org), occupies the historic Arctic Brotherhood Hall, the building with the driftwood facade. The website contains links to hotels, restaurants, and activities, or they'll send you the information on paper (order at © 888/762-1898). Stop in especially for the handy and informative **Skagway Walking Tour Map** of historic sites. It's open daily 8am to 6pm in the summer, Monday to Friday 8am to 5pm in the winter.

GETTING AROUND Skagway is laid out on a simple grid, with streets branching off from Broadway. All the main sights can be reached on foot.

If you want to go to Dyea (2 miles along Klondike Hwy. 2, then 8 miles on a gravel road) or the gold rush graveyard, a bike is a fun way to do it. **Sockeye Cycle,** on Fifth Avenue off Broadway (© **907/983-2851;** http://cyclealaska.com), rents good mountain bikes for $6 an hour and leads guided day trips (see "Getting Outside," below).

SPECIAL EVENTS Skagway's **July 4th Parade and Celebration,** organized by the city, has been a big deal since Soapy Smith led the parade in 1898, with lots of small-town events. **The Klondike Road Relay,** a 110-mile overnight footrace over the pass, brings hundreds of runners in teams of 10 from all over the state. It's held in early September. Call the visitor center for information.

 FAST FACTS: Skagway

Bank **Wells Fargo,** at Broadway at 6th Avenue, has an ATM.

Hospital The **Skagway Medical Clinic,** staffed by a physician's assistant, can be reached at © **907/983-2255** during business hours, or © 907/983-2418 after hours.

Internet Access There are three choices, including **Alaska Cruiseship Services,** at Third Avenue and Broadway (© 907/983-3398).

Police For nonemergency business, call © **907/983-2232.**

Post Office On Broadway between Sixth and Seventh avenues.

Taxes **Sales tax** is 4%. The **bed tax** totals 8%.

EXPLORING SKAGWAY

You can see most of Skagway on foot, and everything by bike. Many companies also offer car, van, or bus tours, too. None goes to greater lengths for a unique experience than Steve Hites, whose **Skagway Streetcar Company,** 270 Second Ave. (© **907/983-2908**), uses antique touring vehicles with costumed guides who consider their work "theater without walls." The very personal and amusing 2-hour streetcar tour, based on a tour originally given to President Harding in 1923, is $36 for adults. Hites also offers a 90-minute van ride up the highway to the White Pass Summit for $31 and a 5-hour tour into the Yukon Territory for $69; children are charged half fare. Hites operates out of his big gift shop with an espresso counter and a theater, where he completes his tour. Book the tour at least 2 weeks in advance, as they're always sold out.

TOURING THE HISTORIC PARK

The main thing to do in Skagway is to see the old buildings and historic gold rush places. Do it with the *Skagway Walking Tour Map* or join a fascinating National Park Service guided walking tour (see "Visitor Information," above).

Start with a visit to the **museum** at the National Park Service Visitor Center and next door. It helps put everything else in context. Of greatest interest is a collection of food and gear similar to the ton of supplies each prospector was required to carry over the pass in order to gain entry into Canada, a requirement that prevented famine among the stampeders, but made the job of getting to Dawson City an epic struggle.

While they prepared to go over the pass, gold rush greenhorns spent their time in Skagway drinking and getting fleeced in the many gambling dens and brothels. Nothing was against the law in the town's heyday because there was no civil authority. It's hard to picture at times, because everything looks so orderly now, but the Park Service has tried. For example, the **Mascot Saloon,** at Broadway and Third Avenue, has statues bellying up to the bar. It's open daily from 8am to 5pm and admission is free.

The Park Service offers free tours of the 1897 **Moore House,** near Fifth Avenue and Spring Street, 1pm to 5pm during the summer. Ten years before the gold rush happened, Capt. William Moore brilliantly predicted it and home-steaded the land that would become Skagway, knowing that this would be a key staging area. He built a cabin in 1887, which stands nearby. But when the rush hit, the stampeders simply ignored his property claims and built the city on his land without offering compensation. Years later, he won in court.

A block east, on Sixth Avenue, is **Mollie Walsh Park,** with a good children's play area, public restrooms, and phones. A sign tells the sad story of Skagway's first respectable woman, who chose to marry the wrong man among two suitors and was killed by him in a drunken rage. The other suitor—who'd previously killed another rival for her affections—commissioned the bust of Walsh that stands at the park.

The **Gold Rush Cemetery** is 1½ miles from town, up State Street. Used until 1908, it's small and overgrown with spruce trees, but some of the charm and mystery of the place is lost because of the number of visitors and the shiny new paint and maintenance of the wooden markers. The graves of Soapy Smith and Frank Reid are the big attractions, but don't miss the short walk up to Reid Falls. A map is available at the visitor center. The closely spaced dates on many of the markers attest to the epidemics that swept through stampeders living in squalid conditions. Remember, there was no sanitation for the tens of thousands who passed this way in 1898.

About 9 miles north of Skagway is the ghost town of **Dyea,** where stampeders started climbing the Chilkoot Trail. It's a lovely coastal drive or bike ride: From Skagway, go 2 miles up Klondike Highway 2 and then turn left, continuing 8 miles on gravel road. Dyea is a lot more ghost than town. All that remains are a few boards, broken dock pilings, and miscellaneous iron trash. On a sunny day, however, the protected historical site is a perfect place for a picnic, among beach grasses, fields of wild iris, and the occasional reminder that a city once stood here. The National Park Service leads an interesting guided history and nature walk once a week; check at the visitor center. (See "Getting Outside," below, for other ideas on going to Dyea.)

The little-visited **Slide Cemetery,** in the woods near Dyea, is the last resting place of many of the 60 to 70 men who died in an avalanche on the Chilkoot Trail on Palm Sunday, April 3, 1898. No one knows how many are here, or exactly who died, or how accurate the wooden markers are. In 1960, when the state reopened the Chilkoot Trail, the cemetery had been completely overgrown, and the markers were replaced. But somehow the mystery and forgetting make it an even more ghostly place, and the sense of anonymous, hopeless hardship and death it conveys is as authentic a gold rush souvenir as anything in Skagway.

MUSEUMS & ATTRACTIONS

The White Pass and Yukon Route ★★   A narrow-gauge railroad line that originally ran to Whitehorse, the White Pass was completed after only 2 years in 1900. It's an engineering marvel and a fun way to see spectacular, historic scenery. The excursion ride begins at a depot with the spine-tingling sound of a working steam engine's whistle. The steamer pulls the train a couple of miles, then diesels take the cars—some of them originals more than 100 years old— up steep tracks that were chipped out of the side of the mountains. They "recommend" you don't get out of your seat, but it's a long ride on a slow train, and most people get up and socialize; however, you cannot move from car to car while the train is moving. The trick is to go in clear weather. When the pass is socked in all you see is white clouds. Tickets are expensive, however, and you have to reserve ahead. Take the gamble: Cancellation carries only a 10% penalty and you can change dates for no charge. Also, try to go on a weekend, when fewer cruise ships are in town taking up all the seats; weekend trains can be booked as little as a week ahead, while midweek excursions can book up months ahead. The summit excursion—which travels 20 miles with an elevation gain of 2,865 feet, then turns back—takes about 3 hours and costs $82 for adults. All fares except the Chilkoot Pass hiker's fares are half price for ages 3 to 12.

The biggest treat for train lovers are the steam-powered trips. An all-day round-trip to Lake Bennett, where the stampeders launched their boats for the trip to Dawson City, leaves each Saturday morning June to August. The fare is $156 including lunch and a walking tour at Lake Bennett. The same tour pulled by a diesel engine happens 3 days a week for $128. These days, the line operates only as a tourist attraction, closing down mid-September to mid-May.

Second Ave. depot (P.O. Box 435, Dept. B), Skagway, AK 99840. ℂ **800/343-7373** or 907/983-2217. www.whitepassrailroad.com.

Skagway Museum and Archives ★   The museum contains a fine collection of gold rush artifacts and other items reflecting Skagway's colorful history. The building is the town's most impressive, and one of the state's most dignified architectural landmarks, its crisp granite walls and high pitched roof standing among tall shade trees on the edge of town. It began life as a short-lived gold rush era college and later was a federal courthouse, city hall, and jail. Extensive renovations were completed in 2000.

Seventh and Spring sts. ℂ **907/983-2420.** Admission $2 adults, $1 students, free for children 12 and under. Summer daily 9am–5pm. Call for winter hours.

Corrington Museum of Alaska History   The eclectic exhibit that leads into the gift shop is well worth a brief stop. Alaska's history is told in 32 pieces of walrus ivory scrimshaw. Besides owning some interesting items, they've done a good job of putting it all together in an understandable way.

Fifth Ave. and Broadway, in Corrington's gift shop. © 907/983-2580. Free admission. Mid-May to mid-Sept 9am–7pm. Closed winter.

Klondike Gold Dredge Tours   Gold mining never happened in Skagway; it was only a transit point, but more gold rush tourists come here than anywhere else, so promoters brought a dredge to where the people are. The 1937 rig dug up and digested gravel to remove gold first in Idaho and then near the border on the Top of the World Highway. A 2-hour tour includes a 20-minute video and gold panning. If you will visit Dawson City or Fairbanks, you can see larger dredges in authentic historic settings for less money, but if not, this stop can satisfy your mechanical curiosity.

Mile 1.7 Klondike Hwy. © 877/983-3175 or 907/983-3175. http://klondikegolddredge.com. $28 adults, $20 under age 12. Add $5 for transfer from Skagway. Summer daily 8:30am–4:30pm.

GETTING OUTSIDE
BACKPACKING   The National Park Service and Parks Canada jointly manage the famous **Chilkoot Pass Trail,** publishing a trail guide and offering information at their offices in Skagway and Whitehorse. Some 20,000 stampeders used the trail to get from Dyea—9 miles from Skagway—to Lake Bennett, 33 miles away, where they could build and launch boats bound for Dawson City. Today about 3,000 people a year make the challenging hike, taking 3 to 5 days. The Chilkoot is not so much a wilderness trail as an outdoor museum, but don't underestimate it, as so many did during the gold rush.

To control the numbers, **Parks Canada,** 205–300 Main St., Whitehorse, Yukon Y1A 2B5 Canada (© 800/661-0486; fax 867/393-6701; http://parkscan.harbour.com/ct), allows only 50 hikers with permits per day to cross the summit. To buy the permits, call with a Visa, American Express, or MasterCard and the date you plan to start. If you mail the money, your reservation isn't guaranteed till it arrives. Permits are $35 for adults, $17.50 ages 6 to 15, plus a $10 per person reservation fee. Eight of the 50 daily permits are held for walk-ins, distributed along with any no-shows at the Park Service's visitor center in Skagway. Once over the pass, you're on Lake Bennett, on the rail line 8 miles short of the road. You can walk to the road, or get back to Skagway on the White Pass and Yukon Route railway (see "Museums & Activities," above), which runs at 1pm daily, June through August. The one-way fare to Frasier, B.C., is $30 (no children's discount) and the scenic 3-hour ride to Skagway is $65 adults, half price children. Be certain to make your reservations well in advance. Although you can stock up on groceries in Skagway, you'll need to rent any equipment in Juneau or Whitehorse.

There are two **U.S. Forest Service cabins** near Skagway, and official access to both is by the White Pass and Yukon Route railway. Both are on trails described in the *Skagway Trail Map,* mentioned below. One cabin is an old, red White Pass caboose parked next to the tracks 6 miles up the line at the trailhead for the 4.5-mile **Denver Glacier Trail.** Another cabin is 1½ miles off the track, 14 miles up on the spectacular **Laughton Glacier Trail.** For either, you need a $35 cabin permit (see "Getting Outside in the Tongass National Forest," in section 1 of this chapter, for reservations information) and a train ticket from the railroad. For details, contact the National Park Service visitor center (see above), or the **Juneau Ranger District,** 8465 Old Dairy Rd., Juneau, AK 99801 (© 907/586-8800; www.fs.fed.us/r10/tongass).

BIKING **Sockeye Cycle,** on Fifth Avenue off Broadway (ⓒ **907/983-2851;** http://cyclealaska.com), leads bike tours, including one that takes clients to the top of the White Pass in a van and coasts down on bikes; the 2-hour trip is $69. They also lead a tour of the quiet ghost town site of Dyea for $69, going over in a van. I rode to Dyea from Skagway on my own over the hilly, 10-mile coastal road, one of the most pleasant, scenic rides I can remember.

HIKING A *Skagway Trail Map* is available from the visitor center, listing 11 hikes around Skagway. An easy evening walk starts at the suspension footbridge at the north end of First Avenue, crossing the Skagway River to **Yakutania Point Park,** where pine trees grow from cracks in the rounded granite of the shoreline. Across the park is a shortcut taking a couple of miles off the trip to Dyea and to the **Skyline Trail and A.B. Mountain,** a strenuous climb to a 3,500-foot summit with great views. On the southern side of town, across the railroad tracks, a network of trails heads up from Spring Street between Third and Fourth avenues to a series of mountain lakes, the closest of which is **Lower Dewey Lake,** less than a mile up the trail.

FLIGHTSEEING Skagway, like Haines, is a good place to choose for a flight-seeing trip, as Glacier Bay National Park is just to the west. **L.A.B. Flying Service** (ⓒ **800/427-5966** or 907/983-2471; www.labflying.com) is one of several companies offering fixed-wing service. Expect to pay $120 with a two-person minimum. **Temsco Helicopters** (ⓒ **907/983-2900;** www. temscoair.com) takes 55-minute tours over the Chilkoot Trail, including a 25-minute landing on a glacier (not in Glacier Bay); those flights cost $169. A helicopter and dogsled tour on Denver Glacier is $303.

ACCOMMODATIONS

All the accommodations in Skagway are within close walking distance of the historic district, except as noted. In addition to the accommodations listed, you'll find good standard rooms, reasonably priced and about a mile from the sights, at **Wind Valley Lodge,** 22nd Avenue and State Street (ⓒ **907/983-2236;** www.alaskan.com/windvalleylodge). You'll also find inexpensive rooms at **Sgt. Preston's Lodge,** Sixth Avenue and State Street (ⓒ **907/983-2521**).

At The White House ⭑ The Tronrud family essentially rebuilt a burned 1902 gable-roofed inn, which has dormer and bow windows and two porticos with small Doric columns. They made the rooms comfortable and modern while retaining the style of the original owner, Lee Guthrie, a successful gambler and saloon owner of the gold rush years. The inn has hardwood floors and fine woodwork. Bedrooms vary in size, but all have handmade quilts and other nice touches.

Corner of Eighth and Main sts. (P.O. Box 41), Skagway, AK 99840-0041. ⓒ **907/983-9000.** Fax 907/983-9010. www.skagway.com/whitehouse. 10 units. High season $104–$120 double. Low season $60 double. Extra person $10. Summer rates include full breakfast, winter continental breakfast. AE, DISC, MC, V. **Amenities:** Courtesy van. *In room:* TV, ceiling fan.

Gold Rush Lodge ⭑ *Value* This is a clean, comfortable motel by the airstrip, 3 blocks from the historic district, with a grassy picnic area out back. The rooms are on the small side but modern and attractively decorated in light colors and have many amenities. Bathrooms have shower stalls, no tubs. The hosts provide fruit, coffee, and a cookie jar in the lobby, and write the guests' names and hometowns on an erasable board so they can get to know each other.

Sixth Ave. and Alaska St. (P.O. Box 514), Skagway, AK 99840. ℭ 877/983-3509 or 907/983-2831. Fax 907/983-2742. www.goldrushlodge.com. 12 units. High season $80–$105 double. Low season $60–$75 double. Extra person $10. AE, DC, DISC, MC, V. No smoking. **Amenities:** Courtesy car. *In room:* TV/VCR, dataport, microwave, fridge, coffeemaker, hair dryer, fan.

Golden North Hotel 🏆🏆 This big yellow landmark on Broadway was built in 1898 and is Alaska's oldest operating hotel. It's a fun place to stay. New owners spent $1.6 million to restore the creaking wooden building while keeping its campy character intact, including the placards in each room about a different gold rush family and the big claw-foot tubs. They strive to make it like sleeping in your own museum. Eight rooms have showers only, two have shower-tub combinations, and the remainder have only tubs. Four rooms share bathrooms. Room 24 has a lovelorn gold rush ghost.

Third Ave. and Broadway (P.O. Box 343), Skagway, AK 99840. ℭ 888/222-1898 or 907/983-2294. Fax 907/983-2755. www.goldennorthhotel.com. 31 units, 27 with private bathroom. $75 double with shared bathroom; $105–$120 double with private bathroom. Extra person $10. Rates include continental breakfast. AE, DC, DISC, MC, V. **Amenities:** Restaurant; brewpub; courtesy car.

The Historic Skagway Inn Bed and Breakfast Built in 1897, this cute and authentic little Victorian inn has frilly rooms ranging from small single bedrooms to a large front room, above the street, with a porch. They don't have phones, and 12 guest rooms share 6 bathrooms. The lobby is a welcoming parlor full of books where guests visit over tea. The courtesy van will take hikers to the Chilkoot Trail trailhead, and free Coleman fuel is provided for hikers.

A full breakfast is served in the windowed dining room, which at night becomes **Olivia's,** an intimate fine-dining establishment. It has only seven tables, so guests can't help feeling special. The menu emphasizes fresh local seafood and garden produce. Reservations are usually necessary.

Seventh Ave. and Broadway (P.O. Box 500), Skagway, AK 99840. ℭ 888/752-4929 or 907/983-2289. Fax 907/983-2713. www.skagwayinn.com. 12 units, none with private bathroom. High season $99–$119 double. Low season $69–$89 double. AE, DISC, MC, V. **Amenities:** Restaurant; courtesy van.

Mile Zero Bed & Breakfast 🏆 In 1995, Howard and Judy Mallory specially built this place a few blocks from the historic area to be a B&B, creating large, crisp, soundproofed rooms all with two entrances: from an internal hall and through French doors that lead to a porch. The idea is to give guests the privacy and convenience of a motel and the warmth and character of a B&B, and it works.

Ninth Ave. and Main St. (P.O. Box 165), Skagway, AK 99840. ℭ 907/983-3045. Fax 907/983-3046. www.mile-zero.com. 7 units. High season $105 double; extra person $25. Low season $70 double; extra person $20. Rates include continental breakfast. DISC, MC, V. No smoking. **Amenities:** Courtesy car.

HOSTELS & CAMPSITES

A primitive **National Park Service Dyea Campground** has 22 well-separated sites near the water; camping is free. There are several RV parks. You'll find full hookups for $22 at **Garden City RV Park,** between 15th and 17th streets on State Street (ℭ **907/983-2378**). The city also maintains the **Pullen Creek/Skagway RV Park** (ℭ **800/936-3731** or 907/983-2768) near the small-boat harbor, with coin-operated showers open to the public. RV sites with power and water are $22, dry sites $16 or $12 if you have a tent and no vehicle.

Skagway Home Hostel Frank Wasmer and Nancy Schave have really opened up their historic home to hostelers, sharing their meals, refrigerator, bathrooms, laundry machines, bicycles, and hospitality side by side with guests. The atmosphere is like off-campus shared housing at college, except the house is nicer and better kept. Bunks are in separate male and female dorm rooms. To reserve, you have to send the money ahead—they don't return long-distance calls. In winter, reservations are required, as Frank and Nancy might otherwise not be there. Summer registration hours are 5:30 to 10:30pm. No pets, alcohol, or smoking.

Third Ave. near Main St. (P.O. Box 231), Skagway, AK 99840. ℂ **907/983-2131**. skagwayhomehostel@ yahoo.com. 1 private rm, 3 dorms. $15 per bunk, $40 double private rm. No credit cards. **Amenities:** Bike loan; free laundry machines.

DINING

Restaurants go out of business and open up faster in Skagway's fully seasonal economy than anywhere else I know, so you may need to ask around for a current recommendation. Besides those listed here, also see **Olivia's,** in the Historic Skagway Inn, above. Stop off for espresso and baked goods at **Mabel G. Smith's** (ℂ **907/983-2609**), a bakery, card, and coffee shop on Fifth Avenue off Broadway.

Sabrosa's ★ *Finds* DELI/VEGETARIAN   This tiny sidewalk cafe down an alley across from the post office feeds locals. The tables are in a pleasant fenced area, a sort of patio arrangement (although not great in the rain). It's an island of intimacy out of the stream of the tourist rush. Our halibut, pasta salad, and vegetarian sandwich were tasty, wholesome, filling, and inexpensive, a rare combination in Skagway. They also serve Mexican specials and fresh baked goods. Service is quick and friendly.

Sixth and Broadway. ℂ **907/983-2469**. All items $3.50–$9. No credit cards. Mon–Fri 6am–4pm, Sat–Sun 8am–2pm. Closed off-season.

The Stowaway Cafe ★★ SEAFOOD/CAJUN   In a small, gray clapboard house overlooking the boat harbor, a 5-minute walk from the historic sites, Jim and Kim Long's little restaurant is a labor of love—they met here when she hired him to fix it up, then married and bought the place. Jim cooks the grilled and blackened salmon and halibut that anchor the menu; there's also beef, pasta, and all the usual waterfront restaurant items. Service is fast. The tiny dining room is decorated with a miscellaneous collection of knickknacks that will keep your attention almost as well as the harbor view. Avoid the alcove on the street side, however, where you're out of the flow and lose the view. Inexpensive lunches are available 11am to 4pm only from a take-out window. They have a beer and wine license.

End of Congress Way near the small boat harbor. ℂ **907/983-3463**. Reservations recommended. Dinner $12.50–$28.50. V. Summer daily 4–10pm. Closed winter.

Sweet Tooth Café DINER   One of Skagway's few year-round restaurants, the Sweet Tooth makes it through the winter with good, simple food, quick service, reasonable prices, and hearty portions. The dining room is light and keeps with the town's quaint theme. Alcoholic beverages are not available.

315 Broadway. ℂ **907/983-2405**. Lunch $5.75–$7.25. MC, V. Daily 6am–3pm.

NIGHTLIFE

Incredibly, the **Days of '98 Show** has been playing since 1927 in the Fraternal Order of Eagles Hall No. 25, at Sixth Avenue and Broadway (ℂ **907/ 983-2545**). Jim Richards carries on the tradition each summer with actors imported from all over the United States, doing three shows a day. The evening shows begin with mock gambling at a casino run by the actors. The performance includes singing, cancan dancing, a Robert Service reading, and the story of the shooting of Soapy Smith. Matinees are $12, and evening shows are $14; senior citizens pay $2 less, and children are charged half price.

The **Red Onion Saloon,** at Second Avenue and Broadway, is an authentic-feeling old bar that often has terrific live jazz and other styles of music, but the players sometimes jump up suddenly and leave—they're cruise-ship musicians who enjoy coming here to stretch out and jam, and they can't afford to miss the boat. It was a brothel originally—what wasn't in this town?—and a mock madam is on hand offering tours. **Moe's Frontier Bar,** at Fifth Avenue and Broadway, is more of a gritty local hangout.

6

Anchorage & Environs

As teenagers living in Anchorage, my cousin and I got a job from a family friend painting his lake cabin. He flew us out on his floatplane and left us there, with paint, food, and a little beer. A creek that ran past the lake was so full of salmon that we caught one on every cast until we got bored and started thinking of ways to make it more difficult. We cooked the salmon over a fire, then floated in a boat on the lake under the endless sunshine of a summer night, talking and diving naked into the clear, green water. We met some guys building another cabin one day, but otherwise we saw no other human beings. When the week was over, the cabin was painted—it didn't take long—and the floatplane came back to get us. As we lifted off and cleared the trees, Anchorage opened in front of us, barely 10 minutes away.

The state's largest city, Anchorage—where 40% of Alaska's population resides—is accused crushingly of being just like a city "Outside," not really part of Alaska at all. It's true that the closer you get to Anchorage, the more the human development reminds you of the outskirts of Anytown, USA, with fast-food franchises, occasional traffic jams, and the ugly big-box retail development inflicted everywhere by relentless corporate logic. You often hear the joke, "Anchorage isn't Alaska, but you can see it from there," and

writers piously warn visitors to land in Anchorage but move on as soon as possible, as if it's catching.

When I hear that advice, I think of the many great experiences I've had here—like painting that cabin, years ago. Anyone in Anchorage with a few hundred dollars for a floatplane can be on a lake or river with the bears and salmon in a matter of minutes, in wilderness deeper than any you could find in the Lower 48. **Chugach State Park** is largely within the city limits, but it's the size of Rocky Mountain National Park, and has similar alpine terrain, with the critical difference that most of it is virtually never visited. Yet you can be climbing those mountains in half an hour's journey from your downtown hotel. **Chugach National Forest,** the nation's second largest, is less than an hour down the road. In downtown's **Ship Creek,** people catch 40-pound salmon from under a freeway bridge. Even within the city, you can bike dozens of miles along the coast or through wooded greenbelts, or ski in one of the nation's best Nordic skiing parks.

Anchorage is indeed a big American city, with big-city problems of crime and pollution, but it's also entirely unique for being surrounded by pristine and spectacular wild lands. Anywhere else, Anchorage would be known not for its shortcomings, but as one of America's greatest cities for outdoor enthusiasts.

ANCHORAGE YESTERDAY & TODAY

Anchorage isn't old enough to have a sharp identity as a city—its first generation is just now passing away. The city started as a tent camp for workers mobi-
lized to build the Alaska Railroad in 1915. A few houses and businesses went up
to serve the federal employees who were building and later running the railroad,
as Steve McCutcheon's father did. McCutcheon, who died in 1998, remembered
a remote, sleepy railroad town enlivened by a couple of large World War II military bases, but never more than strictly functional. As one visitor who came in
the early 1940s wrote, the entire town looked like it was built on the wrong side
of the tracks.

A couple of years ago, McCutcheon looked out the picture window from his
living room on a placid lake surrounded by huge, half-million-dollar houses,
each with a floatplane pulled up on the green front lawn, and he recalled the year
people started to take Anchorage seriously. It was the year, he said, when they
started thinking it would be a permanent city, not just an encampment where
you went for a few years to make money before moving on—the year they
started building Anchorage to last. That year was 1957. Oil was discovered on
the Kenai Peninsula's Swanson River, south of here. It was around that time that
McCutcheon built his own house all by itself on a lake, far out in the country.
At that time, you could homestead in the Anchorage bowl. Those who had the
opportunity but chose not to—my wife's family, for example—gave it a pass
only because it seemed too improbable that the flat, wet acreage way out of town
would ever be worth anything.

Oil fueled Anchorage's growth like nitrogen fertilizer poured on a shooting
weed. Those homesteads that went begging in the 1950s and early 1960s now
have shopping malls and high-rise office buildings on them. Fortunes came fast,
development was haphazard, and a lot was built that we'd all soon regret. I had
the bizarre experience of coming home from college to the town I'd grown up
in and getting completely lost in a large area of the city that had been nothing
but moose browse the last time I'd seen it. Visitors found a city full of life but
empty of charm.

In the last 15 years, that has started to change. Anchorage is slowly outgrow-
ing its gawky adolescence. It's still young, prosperous, and vibrant—and
exhausting when the summer sun refuses to set—but now it also has some excellent restaurants, a good museum, a new Native cultural center and a nice little
zoo, and things to do in the evening besides the tourist melodramas you'll find
in every Alaska town. People still complain that Anchorage isn't really Alaska—
in Fairbanks, they call it "Los Anchorage" (and in Anchorage, Fairbanks is
known as "Squarebanks")—yet the great wilderness around the city remains
intertwined with its streets. Along with a quarter million people, Anchorage is
full of moose—so many, they're becoming pests and wintertime hazards, inspiring debate about hunting them within the city limits. Bears and bald eagles also
show up in town, though less frequently, on the system of greenbelts and bike
trails that brings the woods into almost every neighborhood.

Anchorage stands on broad, flat sediment between the Chugach Mountains
and the silt-laden waters of upper Cook Inlet. At water's edge, mud flats not yet
made into land stretch far offshore when the tide is at its low point, up to 38
vertical feet below high water. There's a **downtown area** of about 8 by 20 blocks,
near Ship Creek where it all started, but most of the city lies on long commercial strips. Like many urban centers built since the arrival of the automobile, the

Anchorage

ACCOMMODATIONS ■
Anchorage RV Park **35**
Aurora Winds Inn B&B Resort **28**
Centennial Camper Park **33**
Courtyard by Marriott **4**
Hillside on Gambell Motel
  & RV Park **17**
A Homestead Bed and Breakfast **2**
Lakeshore Motor Inn **6**
Microtel Inn and Suites **3**
Millenium Hotel Anchorage **5**
Raven House Bed & Breakfast **10**
Spenard Hostel International **8**

DINING ◆
Arctic Roadrunner **18, 24**
Atlasta Deli **21**
The Bear Tooth Theatrepub **12**
Campobello Bistro **20**
Jens' Restaurant **19**
The Lucky Wishbone **14**

The Moose's Tooth
  Pub and Pizzeria **23**
New Sagaya's City Market **13**
Roscoe's Skyline Restaurant **22**

ATTRACTIONS ●
Alaska Aviation Heritage Museum **7**
Alaska Botanical Garden **31**
Alaska Native Heritage Center **34**
The Alaska Zoo **26**
Anchorage Golf Course **25**
Campbell Creek Science Center **30**
Earthquake Park **9**
Glen Alps Trailhead **27**
Goose Lake **32**
Hilltop Ski Area **29**
Kincaid Park **1**
Mulcahy Stadium **16**
Sullivan Arena **15**
Westchester Lagoon **11**

layout is not particularly conducive to any other form of transportation. But the roads go only so far. Just beyond, wilds beckon in the Chugach, along the trails of Turnagain Arm, at Alyeska Ski Resort in Girdwood, in Prince William Sound and the Matanuska and Susitna valleys. You'll find ways to that wilderness, and the urban pleasures by its side, throughout this chapter.

1 Essentials

GETTING THERE

BY PLANE　You'll probably get to Anchorage at the start of your trip by air, as it has by far the most flights linking Alaska to the rest of the world on many airlines. The **Ted Stevens Anchorage International Airport** is a major hub. Seattle has the most frequent flights, with numerous domestic carriers flying nonstop all day. Within Alaska, most flights route through Anchorage, even for communities that are much closer to each other than either is to Anchorage. **Alaska Airlines** (✆ 800/252-7522; www.alaskaair.com) is the dominant carrier for Alaska destinations, and the only jet operator to most Alaska cities. Various commuter carriers link Anchorage to rural destinations not served by jet. **Era Aviation** (✆ 800/866-8394 or 907/266-8394; www.eraaviation.com) is one of the largest for Southcentral Alaska destinations and can be booked directly or through Alaska Airlines.

　A **taxi ride** downtown from the airport runs about $14. Try **Alaska Cab** (✆ 907/563-5353). Taxis generally are expensive to use in Anchorage because of the spread-out urban design. The **Borealis Shuttle** (✆ 888/436-3600 or 907/276-3600; www.borealisshuttle.com) covers the whole city, charging by zones; to get downtown from the airport they charge $12 for the first person plus $2 for each additional person. **Alaska Tourquest** (✆ 907/344-6667; www.alaskatourquest.com) charges $5 per person and $2 for baggage between the airport, downtown, and points in between.

BY CAR　There's only one road to the rest of the world: the Glenn Highway. It leads through the Mat-Su Valley area and Glennallen to Tok, and the Alaska Highway, 330 miles from Anchorage. Thirty miles out of town the Glenn meets the Parks Highway, which leads to Denali National Park and Fairbanks. The other road out of town, the Seward Highway, leads south to the Kenai Peninsula. See "Alaska's Highways a la Carte," in chapter 9.

BY BUS　Gray Line's **Alaskon Express,** 745 West Fourth Ave. (✆ 800/478-6388 or 907/277-5581; www.graylinealaska.com/alaskon.cfm), links Anchorage to Girdwood, Whittier, Valdez, Denali National Park, and down the Alaska Highway to Whitehorse and Skagway, and to points along the way. The

---

Tips　Construction Delays

If a delay happens every time you go somewhere, is it really a delay or is it the normal state of affairs? You can ponder that while waiting for construction on Alaska's roads and for the perpetual construction at the airport in Anchorage. On some highways, you should plan around periodic road closures. Get the details on major projects at (✆ 800/478-7674 or www.dot.state.ak.us/external/state_wide/dnc/advise_c.html). At the airport plan extra time for departures or for changes between another airline and Delta, which is in a satellite terminal during the work.

fare to Denali National Park is $78, to Skagway $219. The **Parks Highway Express** (℃ **888/600-6001;** www.AlaskaShuttle.com), a van and bus service, offers service from Anchorage to Fairbanks, Talkeetna, Valdez, and even Dawson City, and anywhere on the way. In Anchorage they stop at the downtown Youth Hostel. A ticket to Denali National Park is $49. Various other van and bus services offer service to and from Seward, Homer, Fairbanks, and Denali National Park; see the sections on each of those places for details.

BY RV A recreational vehicle is a popular way to explore the region. High-season rates are around $1,400 a week, plus the large amount of fuel you use. **ABC Motorhome Rentals,** 3875 W. International Airport Rd. (℃ **800/ 421-7456** or 907/279-2000; www.alaskan.com/abcmotorhomes), charges no mileage fee and, if you want to drive to Alaska, you might be able to get a special rate by bringing up one of their new units. **Cruise America,** 8850 Runamuck Place (℃ **800/327-7799** or 907/349-0499; www.cruiseamerica.com), charges comparable prices, but you pay a mileage fee over a certain limit. They charge $750 for a one-way rental to or from Anchorage and one of their other centers around the country.

BY RAIL The **Alaska Railroad** (℃ **800/544-0552,** 907/265-2494, or 907/265-2620 TDD; www.akrr.com) connects Anchorage with Seward and Whittier to the south and Fairbanks and Denali National Park to the north. It's a fun way to travel, with expert commentary in the summer, good food, and clean, comfortable cars, but the train is priced as a tourism excursion and costs much more than ordinary transportation. For example, the spectacular Seward run, only about 120 miles, costs $55 one-way. Most trains run only in the summer, but a snowy 12-hour odyssey to Fairbanks runs once a week all winter (the summer fare is $175 one-way, winter $105). See chapter 8 on Denali National Park, and sections on other destinations, for fares and service details to other points.

ORIENTATION

Many visitors never make it beyond the **downtown** area, the old-fashioned grid of streets at the northwest corner of town where the large hotels and gift shops are located. Street numbers and letters work on a simple pattern, and navigation is easy. Beyond downtown, most of Anchorage is oriented to commercial strips, and you'll need a map to find your way. The map on p. 186 will suffice for major thoroughfares, but to find anything on smaller streets, pick up a detailed map at the visitor centers or in any grocery store. Some parts of greater Anchorage are in distinct communities outside the bowl formed by the Chugach Mountains, including **Eagle River** and **Eklutna,** out the Glenn Highway to the northeast, and **Girdwood** and **Portage,** on the Seward Highway, to the south. The suburban **Matanuska and Susitna valleys** lie north of the city on the Glenn and Parks highways.

GETTING AROUND

BY RENTAL CAR A car helps a lot in Anchorage and the Southcentral region. Most major car-rental companies operate in Anchorage, largely from desks at the airport in a tunnel off the domestic baggage-claim area. An economy car for $50 a day, with unlimited mileage, is a fair deal. Cars can sell out in summer, so reserve ahead.

BY BUS It takes a long time to go far using the **People Mover** bus system (℃ **907/343-6543;** www.peoplemover.org), but if you have the time, it's inexpensive and covers most of the whole city (but not the airport). Bus fares all over town are $1 for adults, 50¢ for ages 5 to 18, and transfers are 10¢. There is a free zone in the downtown core called DASH. The transit center bus depot is at Sixth Avenue and G Street. Buses generally come every half hour but are less frequent on weekends.

BY BIKE   The network of bike trails is a great way to see the best side of Anchorage, but not a practical means of transportation for most people. The **Tony Knowles Coastal Trail** comes right downtown (see "Getting Outside," later). Bikes are usually for rent in Elderberry Park downtown, at the start of the Coastal Trail. Exact arrangements seem to change annually, but at the moment the provider is **CycleSights** (© 907/344-1771 or 907/227-6109). **The Bicycle Shop,** in midtown at 1035 W. Northern Lights Blvd. (© **907/272-5219**), rents and services a wide selection of bikes, charging $20 the first day, $15 for additional days, or $85 a week.

VISITOR INFORMATION

The **Anchorage Convention and Visitor Bureau,** 524 W. Fourth Ave., Anchorage, AK 99501-2212 (© **907/276-4118;** fax 907/278-5559; www.anchorage.net), offers information for the whole state at its centers and extensive website. The main location is the **Log Cabin Visitor Information Center,** downtown at Fourth Avenue and F Street (© **907/274-3531;** open daily June–Aug 7:30am–7pm, May and Sept 8am–6pm, Oct–April 9am–4pm). If it's crowded, go to the storefront office right behind it. You'll also find visitor information desks at the airport: one in the baggage-claim area in the domestic terminal and two in the international terminal (in the lobby and the transit area).

The **Alaska Public Lands Information Center,** located at 605 W. Fourth Ave. (across the intersection from the log cabin at Fourth and F), Suite 105, Anchorage, AK 99501 (© **907/271-2737,** or 907/271-2738 TTY; www.nps.gov/aplic; open daily 9am–6pm in summer; Mon–Fri 10am–5:30pm in winter), has guidance for anyone planning to spend time outdoors anywhere in Alaska, as well as exhibits of interest even for those who aren't. The center occupies a grand room with high ceilings in the 1930s post office and federal courthouse. All the land agencies are represented, you can buy ferry tickets from the Alaska Marine Highway System, there's an excellent selection of trail and field guides, and rangers are on hand with advice based on personal experience.

SPECIAL EVENTS

For an exhaustive event listing, with something almost every day of the year, check www.anchorage.net. See the "Out from Anchorage" sections later for events in communities farther afield.

The **Fur Rendezvous Winter Carnival** (© **907/274-1177;** www.furrondy. net; Feb 8–17, 2002) is a huge, citywide winter celebration, with many community events, fireworks, craft fairs, snowshoe softball, dogsled rides, and other fun. The main event is the **World Champion Sled Dog Race,** a 3-day sprint event of about 25 miles per heat. The **Iditarod Trail Sled Dog Race** (© **907/ 376-5155;** www.iditarod.com) starts from Anchorage the first Saturday in March at 10am, then the teams are loaded into trucks a few miles out of town and restarted the next day in Wasilla for the 1,000-mile run to Nome (see the section on the Matanuska and Susitna valleys, later in this chapter, and the Nome section in chapter 10). **The Native Youth Olympics** (© **907/265-5986**), in late April at the University of Alaska Sports Center, is a tough competition in traditional Native sports. The **Saturday Market** is a big street fair and farmer's market held during the summer at Third Avenue and E Street (© 907/ 277-5634). **Music in the Park** presents free band performances in the park at Fourth Avenue and E streets Wednesdays and Fridays at noon all summer (© 907/276-5015). The **Mayor's Midnight Sun Marathon** (© 907/ 343-4474), Alaska's largest, brings more than 3,000 runners for a race on the weekend nearest the summer solstice. The **Ship Creek Salmon Derby,** for 10 days in early June and again in August, offers a chance to win $5,000 and bene- fit charity by catching big salmon in downtown Anchorage (© 907/ 276-6472).

The annual convention of the **Alaska Federation of Natives** (© 907/ 274-3611), held in late October, brings villagers from all over the state, and with them dance celebrations and an exceptional opportunity to buy Native crafts at a fair. The **Carrs/Safeway Great Alaska Shootout men's basketball tournament** (© 907/786-1230; www.shootout.net), hosted by the University of Alaska-Anchorage, brings top-ranked college teams to the Sullivan Arena over Thanksgiving weekend.

 FAST FACTS: **Anchorage**

Banks A bank is rarely far away, and grocery stores also have **ATMs.** Downtown, **Wells Fargo** (© 907/267-5700) has a branch in the Fifth Avenue Mall (5th Ave. and D St.), which offers full foreign currency exchange and wire transfer services. It is open Monday through Saturday 10am to 6pm.

Business Services **Kinko's Copies** is at 2210 E. Northern Lights Blvd. (© 907/276-4228; fax 907/276-8357).

Hospitals **Alaska Regional Hospital** is at 2801 DeBarr Rd. (© 907/ 276-1131), and **Providence Alaska Medical Center** is at 3200 Providence Dr. (© 907/562-2211).

Internet Access Downtown, **Oscar's Roast N Smoke** (508 W. Sixth Ave., © 907/868-3028; www.oscarscigars.com), a cigar and coffee shop, has four computers with fast access for $2 for 15 minutes. The **Z. J. Loussac Library,** midtown at 3600 Denali St. (© 907/343-2975; www.muni.org/library), offers free access.

Police The **Anchorage Police Department** has main offices at 4501 S. Bra- gaw Rd., south of Tudor Road; for a nonemergency call © 907/786-8500. For nonemergency police business outside the city, call the **Alaska State Troopers,** 5700 E. Tudor Rd. (© 907/269-5511).

Post Office Downtown, it's downstairs in the brown building at Fourth Avenue and D Street.

Taxes There's no **sales tax** in Anchorage. The **bed tax** is 8%.

2 Accommodations

Hotel rooms are overpriced in Anchorage, so it's a good place to choose a B&B or small inn. I've searched for such places, choosing those with character and reasonable prices. There are hundreds more, many of them just as good.

One cool way to shop for a room is on the cooperative web directory maintained by the **Anchorage Alaska Bed and Breakfast Association** at **www.Anchorage-BnB.com**. The many links go straight to the B&Bs' own sites. Members police each other's quality. Their **B&B Hotline** (© 888/584-5147 or **907/272-5909**), answered by members in turn, offers referrals to places that meet callers' requirements.

Alaska Private Lodgings, P.O. Box 200047, Anchorage, AK 99520-0047 (© **800/401-7444** or 907/746-1439; fax 907/746-7470; www.alaskabandb. com), represents B&Bs in Anchorage and over much of the state and can help with itinerary planning. Their directory of B&Bs is on the website, with pictures.

DOWNTOWN
VERY EXPENSIVE
Besides the Hotel Captain Cook, described in full below, three other high-rise hotels downtown offer a similar level of service without as much character or quite as many amenities. The large **Hilton Anchorage,** 500 W. Third Ave. (© **800/245-2527** or 907/272-7411; www.hilton.com), is right at the center of downtown activities. The **Sheraton Anchorage,** 401 E. Sixth Ave. (© **800/325-3535** or 907/276-8700; www.sheraton.com), is comparable to the Hilton, but is located in a less attractive area a few blocks off the downtown tourist area. The new **Anchorage Marriott Downtown,** 820 W. Seventh Ave. (© **800/228-9290** or 907/279-8000; www.marriotthotels.com), has a nice pool and fabulous views from rooms with wall-size picture windows.

Hotel Captain Cook ★★★   This is Alaska's great, grand hotel, where royalty and rock stars stay. Former governor Wally Hickel built the first of the three towers after the 1964 earthquake, and now the hotel fills a city block. Inside, the brown decor has a fully realized (maybe a little excessive) nautical theme, with art memorializing Cook's voyages and enough teak to build a square-rigger. The standard rooms are large, with great views from all sides—you don't pay more to be higher. The place has real character and style; but it's a dark, sumptuous style that's not currently fashionable. Some bathrooms are smaller than they should be. The pool in the basement is one of the best in town.

Sophisticated continental food and elaborately formal service justifies the high prices at **The Crows Nest** ★★★, the city's most traditional fine-dining restaurant, on the hotel's top floor. Pheasant, quail, bison, and venison were on recent menus, as well as the usual seafood, beef, and lamb. All tables have stupendous views, and high-backed booths lend a sense of intimacy. The deliberate service requires that you set aside a full evening for a special meal—dinner unfolds gradually, with almost theatrical formality. Main courses range from $26 to $50. **Fletcher's,** off the lobby, is an English pub serving good Italian-style pizza and sandwiches. **The Pantry** is more than a typical hotel cafe, with excellent service and interesting entrees mixed in with more predictable choices.

Fourth Ave. and K St. (P.O. Box 102280), Anchorage, AK 99510-2280. © 800/843-1950 or 907/276-6000. Fax 907/343-2298. www.captaincook.com. 547 units. High season $240–$250 double; $260–$1,500 suite. Low season $130–$140 double; $150–$1,500 suite. Extra person $20. AE, DISC, MC, V. **Amenities:** 3 restaurants; 2 bars; large indoor pool; large health club with racketball, Jacuzzi, and sauna; concierge; car-rental desk; business center; lobby arcade of 16 shops; salon; 24-hour room service; massage; same-day dry cleaning; concierge-level rooms. *In room:* TV w/pay movies, dataport, hair dryer, iron.

ACCOMMODATIONS
Copper Whale Inn **2**
Caribou Inn **4**
Duke's 8th Avenue Hotel **20**
G Street House **22**
Hostelling International,
Anchorage **23**
Hotel Captain Cook **8**
Leopold David House B&B **13**
The Oscar Gill House Bed and
Breakfast **25**
Susitna Place **24**
The Voyager Hotel **7**

DINING
Cafe del Mundo **5**
Cilantro's Mexican Restaurant **21**
Club Paris **17**
The Crows Nest **8**
Dianne's Restaurant **19**
Downtown Deli and Cafe **15**
Glacier Brewhouse **9**
Kumagoro **16**
The Marx Brothers Cafe **14**
Orso **9**
Sacks Cafe **12**
Side Street Espresso **11**

Simon and Seafort's
Saloon and Grill **3**
Snow City Cafe **6**

ATTRACTIONS
Anchorage Museum of
History and Art **18**
The Imaginarium **10**
The Oscar Anderson
House Museum **1**

EXPENSIVE

Here are a few more chain-hotel options downtown: the **Days Inn** (© **800/325-2525** or 907/276-7226; www.alaskalife.net/daysinn), which has a courtesy van to the airport and many amenities; the **Holiday Inn-Anchorage** (© **800/465-4329** or 907/279-8671; www.holiday-inn.com), which has a pool; the **Clarion Suites** (© **800/517-4000** or 907/274-1000; www.hotel-choice.com), across from the Federal Building, with a small pool and suites as standard rooms; and the **Hawthorn Suites** (© **888-777-7511** or 907/222-5005; www.hawthorn.com), with similar facilities, plus a Benihana Restaurant on site.

Copper Whale Inn ★★   A pair of clapboard houses overlook the water and Elderberry Park right on the Coastal Trail downtown, with charming rooms of every shape and size. There's a wonderfully casual feeling to the place, with a host who serves a full breakfast and befriends guests. The rooms in the newer building, lower on the hill, are newer, with cherry-wood furniture and high ceilings on the upper level. Two rooms that share a bathroom have great views. Rooms lack TVs, but in some you can get one hooked up by request.

440 L St., Anchorage, AK 99501. © **907/258-7999.** Fax 888/WHALE-IN or 907/258-6213. www.copper-whale.com. 18 units, 16 with private bathroom. High season $110 double with shared bathroom, $135–$160 double with private bathroom. Low season $69 double with shared bathroom, $79 double with private bathroom. Extra person $10. Rates include full breakfast. AE, DISC, MC, V. **Amenities:** Access to health club; bicycles; concierge (host). *In room:* Dataport, iron.

Duke's 8th Avenue Hotel _(Value_ This cinderblock apartment house downtown was converted into surprisingly light and comfortable one- and two-bedroom suites with full kitchens. Each unit has two telephones and an extra line for your computer. A family or business party on a long stay can save a lot of money here: The basic rate on two-bedroom units accommodates four adults, and children 12 and under stay free (the one-bedroom-unit rates are for two people). Moreover, the cooking and dining setup is adequate for real meals. On the downside, the four-story building has no elevator and is not accessible for the disabled, and the 100-level is a half basement.

630 W. Eighth Ave., Anchorage, AK 99501. © 800/478-4837 or 907/274-6213. Fax 907/272-6308. www.hotel.alaska.com. 28 units. High season $140–$165 suite. Low season $80–$105 suite. Children 12 and under stay free in parents' rm. AE, DC, DISC, MC, V. **Amenities:** Inexpensive self-serve laundry. _In room:_ TV, dataport, kitchen, coffeemaker.

The Voyager Hotel 👁👁 Thanks to its exacting proprietor, Stan Williams, The Voyager is just right, right down to the quality of the linen. The size is small, the location central, the rooms large and light, all with well-designed kitchenettes, and the housekeeping exceptional. The desks have speaker phones, high-speed dataports, and extra electrical outlets; and the hospitality is warm yet highly professional. There's nothing ostentatious or outwardly remarkable about the hotel, yet the most experienced travelers rave about it the loudest.

501 K St., Anchorage, AK 99501. © 800/247-9070 or 907/277-9501. Fax 907/274-0333. www.voyager hotel.com. 38 units. High season $169 double. Low season $89 double. Extra person $10. AE, DC, DISC, MC, V. No smoking. **Amenities:** Restaurant (continental); bar; nearby health club with $7.50 day pass; same-day dry cleaning; no smoking on property. _In room:_ A/C, TV, dataport, kitchenette, coffeemaker, hair dryer.

MODERATE

The Oscar Gill House Bed & Breakfast 👁👁 On the Delaney Park strip, just a few blocks from downtown, this is truly the oldest house in Anchorage—it was built in 1913, in Knik, before Anchorage was founded, and moved here on a barge a few years later. Oscar Gill was an early civic leader. The house was to be torn down in 1982 but was moved to storage by a historic preservation group; Mark and Susan Lutz saved it in 1994, transferring it to its present location and, with their own labor, restoring it authentically as a cozy, friendly

---

More Exceptional B&Bs in Anchorage

Birch Trails Bed & Breakfast (© 907/688-5713), in the Chugiak area a half hour out of town, belongs to a dog-mushing family that offers rides (see "Getting Outside," later). The 24 dogs bed down in the yard right outside the windows of comfortable, country-style rooms renting for $95 double. A reasonably priced choice downtown, **Leopold David House B&B,** in one of the most historic and interesting houses in Anchorage, is at 605 W. Second Ave. (© 888/279-1225 or 907/279-1917; www.alaskaholiday.com). Hosts speak French, German, Polish, Russian, and Spanish. I also especially like the following downtown places: **G Street House** (© 800/401-7444 or 907/746-1439), an elegant home hosted by a wonderful family (he's on the city assembly and she's an expert on local history); and **Susitna Place** (© 907/274-3344; www.susitnaplace.com), with lovely rooms overlooking Cook Inlet from atop a bluff on a quiet side street.

bed-and-breakfast. Now it's on the National Historic Register. The house is full of appropriate antiques, and manages to be both homey and immaculate. The Lutzes are good people and like to get to know their guests, and the breakfast is great. Free bikes are available. Book early, as they fill. There's a 5% discount for paying cash and a 2-week cancellation policy.

1344 W. 10th Ave. (P.O. Box 200047), Anchorage, AK 99520-0047. *C* and fax **907/279-1344.** www.oscargill.com. 3 units, 1 with private bathroom. High season $95 double with shared bathroom, $110 double with private bathroom. Low season $65 double with shared bathroom, $75 double with private bathroom. Extra person $15. Rates include full breakfast. AE, MC, V. **Amenities:** Bike loan; babysitting. *In room:* TV, dataport, hair dryer, iron.

INEXPENSIVE

Caribou Inn   Some of the rooms are quite large and the location is prime, right downtown. The carpet and fabrics were in good shape when I visited and the rooms very clean, but this is an old wooden building in need of some work, and much of the furniture is garage-sale style. A cigarette odor hung in some rooms. Full kitchens are available, and many rooms have VCRs or refrigerators. You will do no better on price for respectable hotel lodgings downtown, especially when you count the money saved on the included breakfast, airport transfer, and parking pass. Here you'll run into other budget-conscious summer visitors, not the flophouse clientele at downtown hotels charging comparable rates.

501 L St., Anchorage, AK 99501. *C* **800/272-5878** or 907/272-0444. Fax 907/274-4828. www. alaska.net/~caribou. 14 units, 9 with private bathroom. Summer $89 shared bathroom, $99 private bathroom; winter $49 shared bathroom, $59 private bathroom. Rates include full breakfast. AE, DC, DISC, MC, V. **Amenities:** Courtesy van; self-service laundry. *In room:* TV.

HOSTEL

Hostelling International, Anchorage, 700 H St. (*C* **907/276-3635,** fax 907/276-7772; www.alaska.net/~hianch), is a 95-bed hostel right downtown, with an impersonal, urban feel. A coin-op laundry, kitchen, and baggage storage are available, and they have Internet access in the lobby. Dorm rooms are small, with just a few bunks each. Members pay $16, nonmembers $19; private rooms are $40 to $50 for two. The hostel closes between noon and 5pm daily and the curfew is 1am. A homier hostel outside the downtown area is detailed below.

BEYOND DOWNTOWN
VERY EXPENSIVE

Millennium Hotel Anchorage ★★   With a good view of the floatplanes on Lake Spenard, near the airport, the large lobby, with its warm colors and fly rods and animal mounts on display, suggests a huge fishing and hunting lodge. There's a big patio to catch the sun and watch the planes, but it's the rooms that are really special—decorated in a style of tasteful opulence and packed with thoughtful details, they're a delight to the eye and an invitation to relaxation. A courtesy van runs a regular schedule downtown, but this is an airport hotel, and for convenience you really need to rent a car if you stay in this area. The hotel was formerly the Regal Alaskan.

4800 Spenard Rd., Anchorage, AK 99517-3236. *C* **800/544-0553** or 907/243-2300. Fax 907/243-8815. www.millenium-hotels.com. 248 units. High season $270–$285 double; $325–$600 suite. Low season $165–$185 double; $250–$400 suite. AE, DC, DISC, MC, V. **Amenities:** 2 restaurants (steak and seafood, cafe); health club (no pool); Jacuzzi; sauna; concierge; tour desk; 24-hour room service; laundry; dry cleaning; concierge-level rooms. *In room:* TV w/pay movies and Nintendo, dataport, fridge, coffeemaker, hair dryer, iron.

EXPENSIVE

Aurora Winds Inn B&B Resort ★★★   This massive house far up the hillside in South Anchorage (near the zoo and Glen Alps trailhead) has rooms so grand and theatrically decorated you'll feel as if you're in a James Bond movie. Each bedroom has a sitting area and decorative details that make it unique, elegant, or even campy. The bathrooms are also showplaces: Three have Jacuzzis, and one is larger than a lot of hotel rooms, with an "environmental habitat chamber." One lovely room has windows on the deck and forest on three sides. Besides the outdoor hot tub set in luxuriant gardens, there is a gym with a tiny, jetted lap pool—a sort of water treadmill—and a theater with a large video screen.

7501 Upper O'Malley Rd., Anchorage, AK 99516. ℂ 907/346-2533. Fax 907/346-3192. www. aurorawinds.com. 5 units. High season $125–$175 double. Low season $55–$125 double. Extra person $15 in high season, $10 in low season. Rates include full breakfast. AE, DC, DISC, MC, V. **Amenities:** Lap pool; exercise room; Jacuzzi; sauna; concierge; limited room service; laundry machines; fish freezing. *In room:* TV w/VCR, dataport, coffeemaker, hair dryer, iron.

MODERATE

Raven House Bed and Breakfast ★   On a huge, sloping lot on the Coastal Trail in the Turnagain residential area, the house has a sleek, opulently modern style. Maxine Quist's extraordinary housekeeping helps maintain the clean lines—it's as if the place were brand-new. Two simple but nicely decorated bedrooms share a bathroom. A huge and luxuriously appointed suite downstairs has a bar, fridge, entertainment center, and two-person Jacuzzi; it's often used as a honeymoon suite. Maxine lends bicycles, which can quickly and safely get you downtown on the trail.

3315 Iliamna Ave., Anchorage, AK 99517. ℂ **907/248-9587.** Fax 907/248-6600. ravenbnb@alaska.net. 3 units, 1 with private bathroom. $85 shared bathroom, $125 private bathroom. Rates include full breakfast. No credit cards.

INEXPENSIVE

Hillside on Gambell Motel and RV Park *Value*   On a busy highway with a car dealership and self-storage business, this funny little hotel is a friendly oasis. Rooms are clean and well maintained and have features such as microwave ovens that make them quite practical, if not beautiful or luxurious. Six have kitchenettes and there's a new cabin for four. The wooded Lanie Fleischer Chester Creek Trail, for biking, walking, or Nordic skiing, is just beyond a gate in the RV park (full hookups are $24.)

2150 Gambell St., Anchorage, AK 99503. ℂ **800/478-6008** or 907/258-6006. Fax 907/279-8972. www. hillside-alaska.com. 26 units. High season $89–$129 double. Low season $60–$86 double. Extra person $10. AE, DISC, MC, V. **Amenities:** Coin-op laundry. *In room:* TV, dataport, fridge, coffeemaker, hair dryer.

A Homestead Bed and Breakfast *Finds*   This is a real 1930s homestead house built of logs, once remote but now a few minutes from the airport and Kincaid Park. Frank and Patricia Jasper have lived here more than 30 years, and they've kept it as an authentic slice of Alaska. One of the rooms is a charming log cabin with plank floors, the other is a many-room upstairs suite with four beds, an outside entrance, and many odd corners and pieces of furniture. Both rooms have cooking facilities. It's a great deal. (Beware, an entirely different place on Spenard Road has an almost identical name.)

6141 Jewel Lake Rd., Anchorage, AK 99502. ℂ **907/243-5678.** Fax 907/248-6184. jasper@chugach.net. 2 units. Summer $95 double. Winter $65 double. Extra person $20. Rates include full breakfast in summer, continental in winter. MC, V (5% surcharge for credit cards). No smoking. *In room:* TV/VCR, kitchenette, coffeemaker.

Affordable Rooms Near the Airport

Good, inexpensive standard motel rooms near the airport are rare to the vanishing point, although luxurious rooms (like those at the Millennium Hotel Anchorage) and B&Bs are readily available. The lowest priced, consistently acceptable standard hotel rooms I could find, after extensive searching, were $129 a night, at peak season, at two places: the **Lakeshore Motor Inn** (© 800/770-3000 or 907/248-3485; www.lakeshoremotorinn. com), and the mass-produced **Microtel Inn and Suites** (© 888/771-7171 or 907/245-5002; www.microtelinn.com). Various other hotels charge less, but none met my standards to recommend here (I do recommend the Homestead Bed and Breakfast, below). Two good chain hotels stand near the airport, with higher rates: **Courtyard by Marriott** (© 800/321-2211 or 907/245-0322; http://courtyard.com/ANCCY), with many amenities and a pool; and the **Holiday Inn Express** (© 800/HOLIDAY or 907/248-8848; www.holiday-inn.com).

HOSTEL

Spenard Hostel International, 2845 W. 42nd Ave. (© **907/248-5036;** www.alaskalife.net/spnrdhstl/hostel.html), is a friendly place near the airport, with free phones, inexpensive bike and storage rental, Internet access, a laundry, and a black Lab, Magnet. There are three lounges for different activities and three kitchens. You can come and go 24 hours a day. It feels more like communal housing than a hostel. The office is open daily 9am to 1pm and 7 to 11pm in summer, 7 to 11pm winter. Beds are $15.

CAMPING

Anchorage is a big city, but you can find natural camping fairly near town. The municipally owned **Centennial Park** is on Boundary Road at the Muldoon Road exit from the Glenn Highway (© **907/333-9711,** or 907/343-4474 off-season; www.muni.org/parks/camp.cfm), just as you enter town from the north. Although it is near a Muldoon's run-down commercial strip, many of the 83 sites are nicely wooded. The campground has a dump station and free showers and charges $13 a night. There are several RV parks within the Anchorage bowl, of which the best is the wooded and landscaped **Anchorage RV Park,** 7300 Oil-well Rd. (© **800/400-7275** or 907/338-7275; www.anchrvpark.com), near Centennial Park and the Alaska Native Heritage Center. It has full services and excellent facilities, and charges $30 to $35 per night on the 195 sites. They don't take tenters. Near downtown, the **Hillside on Gambell Motel and RV Park** is listed above under "Inexpensive."

For a real camping experience, you need to head out of town to Chugach State Park (see "Getting Outside," later) or Chugach National Forest (see chapter 7). Here are the two closest state park campgrounds. One of my favorites is the 28-site, $10-per-night **Bird Creek Campground,** 25 miles south on the Seward Highway (mile 101), next to Turnagain Arm and the salmon-filled creek. The 56-site **Eagle River Campground** sits in a thickly wooded riverside spot, and it's well developed with paved roads and large sites with lots of privacy. It costs $15 a night with a 4-night maximum; some sites can be reserved up to a year ahead at © **907/694-7982.** From the Glenn Highway, 12 miles from Anchorage, take the Hiland Road exit.

3 Dining

DOWNTOWN
EXPENSIVE

Club Paris ★★ STEAK/SEAFOOD   Coming in from a bright spring afternoon into midnight darkness, under a neon Eiffel Tower and past a smoke-enshrouded bar, I sat down at a secretive booth for two, and felt as if I should lean across the table and plot a shady 1950s oil deal with my companion. And I would probably not have been the first. In contrast to Sullivan's Steakhouse, across the street, which contrives a masculine, retro feel, Club Paris is the real thing, decorated with mounted swordfish and other cocktail-era decor. The smoky club is too authentic for some, but it's the essence of old Anchorage boomtown years, when the streets were dusty and an oil man needed a class joint in which to do business. Steak, of course, is what to order, and rare really means rare. Ask for the blue cheese stuffing; the stuffed filet is worth the years it probably takes off your coronary arteries. Full liquor license.

417 W. Fifth Ave. ✆ 907/277-6332. Reservations recommended. Lunch $5.75–$15; dinner main courses $14–$44. AE, DC, DISC, MC, V. Mon–Sat 11:30am–2:30pm, 5–11pm; Sun 5–10pm.

The Marx Brothers Cafe ★★★ ECLECTIC/REGIONAL   A restaurant started by three friends back when gourmet food was an exotic hobby in Anchorage is now a standard of excellence in the state. Treatments of Alaska seafood that started as cutting-edge creative cuisine here now turn up in many of the best restaurants. Chef Jack Amon still presides in the kitchen of the cottage downtown, one of the city's first houses. Maître d' Van Hale still presides out front, preparing his famous Caesar salad at tableside, a ritual that allows him to schmooze with anyone he chooses in the tiny dining rooms. His attitude mirrors the casual elegance of the entire evening, which feels like dinner at the home of friends with perfect taste; some have told me, however, that they felt excluded from the beam of warmth, as if they weren't insiders. The cuisine is varied and creative, ranging from Asian to Italian. A meal is an experience that takes much of the evening. Waiting in the small entryway can be uncomfortable if your table isn't ready. The wine cellar is famous.

627 W. Third Ave. ✆ 907/278-2133. www.marxcafe.com. Reservations required. Main courses $17.50–$28.50. AE, DC, MC, V. Summer daily 5:30–10pm. Winter, Mon–Thurs 6–9:30pm, Fri–Sat 5:30–10pm.

Orso ★★ ITALIAN   Anchorage is growing up. Although the city has long had little boutique restaurants to show off the talents of particular chefs, only with this large, theatrically decorated place has a big investment been made in sophisticated dining. It's fun to eat in the ornate rooms, and the food, a combination of northern and southern Italian cuisine with some local seafood inventions, is generally good and occasionally exceptional. Perhaps concerned about over-shooting our provincial tastes, however, I had the sense they'd toned down some dishes. In that vein, our waitress was at pains to explain the menu and translate all her Italian flourishes—at the end, she said *"Ciao,"* and then added, "That means goodbye." The menu is set up in the multi-course Italian style, but the huge portions are designed to make a meal of just one course. Save by skipping the *piatti secondi* (that means second course).

737 W. Fifth Ave. ✆ 907/222-3232. Reservation recommended. Lunch $8–$14, dinner pasta or main course $12–$26. AE, DC, DISC, MC, V. Summer Mon–Fri 11am–2:30pm, 4:30–11pm, Sat–Sun 4:30–11pm; winter Sun–Mon 4:30–9:30pm, Tues–Thurs 4:30–10pm, Fri–Sat 4:30–11pm.

The Best Take-out in Town

Anchorage has great take-out food (as my family's continued survival attests). The best, most original burgers are at **Arctic Roadrunner,** with locations on Arctic Boulevard at Fireweed Lane and on Old Seward Highway at International Airport Road. Try the Kodiak Islander, which has peppers, ham, onion rings, and God knows what else on top.

The best gourmet deli, with legendary sandwiches, is **Atlasta Deli** (℃ **907/563-3354**), in the shopping mall at Arctic Boulevard and Tudor Road. I had a sub that cost $11.50, and I didn't regret it. They deliver.

We get carry-out Chinese from **New Sagaya's City Market** (℃ **907/ 274-6173;** www.newsagaya.com) at the corner of 13th and I streets. It's also a wonderful gourmet grocery and community meeting place, and has a good deli and Italian-style brick-oven pizza. Pack a picnic here, or eat in the enclosed or sidewalk dining areas.

Sacks Cafe ★★★ CREATIVE/ECLECTIC   This is the most fashionable restaurant in town, and also one of the best. The storefront dining room, in warm Southwest colors and sharp angles, resembles a showcase for the food and diners, who can sit at tables or a tapas bar. It was remodeled by one of the city's most exciting architects, Mike Mense. The cuisine defies categorization, but is consistently interesting and creative, frequently with Thai influences. The menu changes, but one recent offering was chicken with scallops, shiitake mushrooms, snow peas, udon noodles, ginger cream sauce, and black bean salsa. Vegetarians do as well as meat eaters. For lunch, the sandwiches are unforgettable, with choices such as shrimp and avocado with herb cream cheese on sourdough. The beer and wine list is extensive and reasonably priced.

328 G St. ℃ **907/274-4022.** www.sackscafe.com. Reservations recommended for dinner (reserve a few days ahead for weekend nights). Lunch $5.25–$12.95; dinner main courses $15–$28. AE, MC, V. Mon–Wed 11am–3pm, Thurs–Sun 11am–3pm; Thurs and Sun 5–9:30pm; Fri–Sat 5–11pm.

Simon and Seafort's Saloon and Grill ★★ STEAK/SEAFOOD   Simon's, as it's known, is the most fun fine-dining place in town, a jolly beef and seafood grill where voices boom off the high ceilings. On sunny summer evenings, the rooms, fitted with brass turn-of-the-century saloon decor, fill with light off Cook Inlet, down below the bluff; the views are magnificent. The food is consistently very good. A long list of nightly specials includes items as exotic as a tasty crab- and macadamia-stuffed halibut, but most of the cuisine is simpler. The service, too, stands out: warm and professional, and quick enough to allow time for other evening activities. Children are treated well. To enjoy the place on a budget, order a sandwich and soup for lunch in the well-stocked bar.

420 L St. ℃ **907/274-3502.** Reservations recommended (make dinner reservations a couple of days in advance in summer). Lunch $7–$15; dinner main courses $16–$40. AE, MC, V. Mon–Fri 11:15am–3:30pm and 4:30–11pm, Sat 4:30–11pm, Sun 4:30–10pm.

MODERATE

Glacier Brewhouse ★ GRILL/SEAFOOD/PIZZA   An eclectic and ever-changing menu is served in a large dining room with lodge decor, where the pleasant scent of the wood-fired grill hangs in the air. They brew eight or more hearty beers behind a glass wall. It's noisy and active, with lots of agreeable if trendy touches, such as the bread, made from spent brewery grain, that's set out on the tables with olive oil. An advantage for travelers is the wide price range—a feta cheese, spinach, and artichoke pizza is $10; crab legs are $34. The food is usually quite good. This is not a good choice for groups, however, as it's too loud to carry on a conversation across a large table; service can be rushed; and a table can take time to acquire, even if you have a reservation.

737 W. Fifth Ave. ℂ 907/274-BREW. www.glacierbrewhouse.com. Reservations recommended for dinner. Lunch $8–$15; dinner main courses $9–$34. AE, MC, V. High season daily 11am–11pm. Low season Mon–Sat 11am–10pm, Sun 4–9pm.

Kumagoro ✶ JAPANESE Anchorage has several good, authentic Japanese restaurants, but this one, right on the main tourist street downtown, has the most convenient location. Among my favorite lunches anywhere is their lunch box ($14.30), a large sampler of many dishes, including sushi, sashimi, and other tasty things I couldn't identify. The dining room is pleasantly low-key, with tables in rows, so you may have the opportunity to meet those seated next to you. Beer and wine license.

533 W. Fourth Ave. ℂ 907/272-9905. Lunch $6.50–$14.30; dinner main courses $13.20–$39. AE, DISC, DC, MC, V. Summer daily 11am–10:45pm. Winter daily 11am–9:45pm.

INEXPENSIVE

Cilantros Mexican Restaurant ✶ *Finds* MEXICAN Authentic, inexpensive Mexican food is served in this charming little house on the park strip. Each cheerful but sparsely decorated dining room is large enough for only a few tables, the Spanish-speaking staff whizzing past over scuffed wood floors. Our meals were just right, from the warm, thick chips with salsa that hit the table when we did, to the ample and flavorful main courses that came not much later, to the bill, which, including everything for two, amounted to $14. They serve from the entire, very long menu all day, including breakfast: The huevos rancheros are great. They serve no alcohol.

611 W. Ninth Ave. ℂ 907/279-8226. Breakfast $4.25–$6, lunch and dinner $5–$11. MC, V. Mon–Fri 11am–9:30pm, Sat–Sun noon–9:30pm.

Dianne's Restaurant *Value* SOUP/SANDWICH This is my first choice for a quick, healthful, inexpensive lunch downtown. Located in the base of a tall, glass office building, Dianne's cafeteria line fills with well-dressed folk seeking the hearty, freshly baked bread, soups, sandwiches, and specials turned out for the lunch hour. The atmosphere is bright and casual and you don't waste your day eating. No liquor license.

550 W. Seventh Ave., Ste. 110. ℂ 907/279-7243. All items $4–$7.75. AE, DISC, MC, V. Mon–Fri 7am–4pm.

Downtown Deli and Cafe DELI Governor Tony Knowles started this Fourth Avenue sandwich restaurant before his success in politics. In 1994, President Clinton came for dinner. Knowing his appetite, I hope he ordered some side dishes, for much of the food here is served strictly a la carte; it can be a shock to receive a plate containing only the exact item you ordered and nothing else. Best choices are the quiche of the day, breakfasts, and the salmon dinner. Prices are reasonable for dinner, when downtown is short on inexpensive sit-down places, and kids are treated well. Service can suffer on summer mornings when the place is overrun with tourists. They serve beer and wine.

525 W. Fourth Ave. ℂ 907/276-7116. All items $6.25–$12. AE, DC, DISC, MC, V. Summer daily 6am–10pm. Winter Sun 9am–4pm, Mon 7am–4pm, Tues–Sat 7am–9pm.

Snow City Cafe ✶ VEGETARIAN/HOME STYLE This is a meeting place for a young, environmentally conscious crowd, and also a good restaurant. The

Coffeehouses

There are coffeehouses all over the city where people go for a cup of java and a pastry, and to meet people and engage in conversation. My favorite is **Side Street Espresso,** on G Street between Fourth and Fifth, a gathering place for artists, radicals, musicians, and other people who want to trade ideas. **Cafe del Mundo,** at Fourth and K downtown and at Northern Lights and Denali midtown, gathers an older crowd of businesspeople, yuppies, stay-at-home parents, and anyone else looking for a comfortable meeting spot.

food, served by a friendly, committed staff in a light storefront dining room, is laced with interesting flavors and styles of preparation, including many vegetarian dishes. For lunch, the sandwiches are filling and various. The Reindeer Reuben, made with reindeer sausage instead of corned beef, is better than an ordinary Reuben on several counts. It's a good stop for breakfast, too, and it's sometimes open for dinner, but not consistently enough to list hours; on weekends they have live acoustic music.

1034 W. Fourth Ave. ℂ 907/272-CITY. Lunch $5–$10; dinner main courses $9–$15. AE, DISC, MC, V. Mon–Fri 7am–4pm, Sat–Sun 8am–4pm.

BEYOND DOWNTOWN
EXPENSIVE

Jens' Restaurant ✸✸✸ INTERNATIONAL   Chef Jens Hansen is truly gifted. His restaurant is for the kind of diner who loves exciting food, surprises, beautiful plates of new tastes and textures, and meals that are about the food, sharing bites, saying "Wow," and "How did he do that?" I won't call it experimental, because I've never had a meal here that wasn't perfect, but the cuisine is highly eclectic and there's often only one item on the changing menu that isn't unusual or challenging: the superb pepper steak. Like everything, even that dish has a sauce, and it is complex and memorable. The wine list is exceptional and reasonably priced, and you can sip it while dining inexpensively on appetizers in a pleasant bar area; try the incredible spinach ravioli with Gorgonzola, for example. Desserts also are sublime, such as the chocolate pâté with chocolate sauce, laced with black raspberry sauce. The dining room is light and clean, decorated with modern art. Service is highly professional, with each formally attired waiter assigned to just a few tables.

701 W. 36th Ave. ℂ 907/561-5367. www.jensrestaurant.com. Reservations recommended. Lunch $9–$16.50; dinner main courses $18–$28. AE, DC, DISC, MC, V. Mon–Fri 11:30am–2pm; Tues–Sat 6–10pm. Closed Jan.

MODERATE

Campobello Bistro ✸✸ NORTHERN ITALIAN/BISTRO   This quiet little midtown restaurant is amazingly like stepping into northern Italy, except for the Alaska seafood. Even the service has the quality of jocular professionalism I remember from Italy. Unlike most of Anchorage's best restaurants, they don't try to reinvent the cookbook here. Most of the menu consists of recognizable dishes, such as veal Marsala or Italian sausage and polenta, but, with a single exception on our many visits, meals have been bold, highly flavored, and entirely satisfying. Those seeking the bland tomatoes and cheese of a typical Italian family restaurant should go elsewhere (Sorrento's and Romano's, both on Fireweed

Lane, each do that tried-and-true formula well). The wine list and food are reasonably priced.

661 W. 36th, Ste. 10. © **907/563-2040.** Lunch $8–$13; dinner main courses $13–$19.50. DC, MC, V. Mon–Fri 11am–2:30pm; Tues–Sat 5–9pm.

INEXPENSIVE

The Lucky Wishbone *Finds* DINER   This Anchorage institution (in high school we called it "The Bone") is where the real pioneer Alaska meets families out for a delicious, not-too-greasy fried chicken dinner and famous milk shakes (try the hot fudge) and other delights from the fountain. One section of the counter is reserved for discussion of aviation and golf. When the beloved owners outlawed smoking years ago, it made the front page of the newspaper. You'll see few other tourists, as the location, among the car dealerships at the extreme east end of downtown, is too far to walk to from the hotels, but I recently ran into Alaska's powerful senior U.S. senator, Ted Stevens. They have a drive-in.

1033 E. Fifth Ave. © **907/272-3454.** All items $3–$9.25. Summer daily 10am–11pm. Winter daily 10am–10pm. MC, V.

The Moose's Tooth Pub and Pizzeria *Kids* PIZZA   The best pizza and beer in Anchorage undoubtedly come from this fun and friendly place. The microbrewery came first, but the pizza really is the greater accomplishment. It has a soft, light crust like Italian pizza but the oomph of American pizza. They offer many ingenious toppings, but not just to dump on—the combinations really work. Dine inside (perhaps in the "hippie pad"), or at picnic tables outside in a tent that's open year-round. That's the best place in town to take kids for dinner. See "Nightlife," later, for details on their cinema/pub.

3300 Old Seward Hwy. © **907/258-2537.** www.moosestooth.net. Large pizza $12.50–$25. DISC, MC, V. Summer, Sun–Thurs 11am–midnight, Fri–Sat 11am–1am. Winter, Sun–Mon 11am–11pm, Tues–Thurs 11am–midnight, Fri–Sat 11am–1am.

Roscoe's Skyline Restaurant *Finds* SOUL FOOD/SOUTHERN   Roscoe built up this large mall restaurant from a shack where he used to barbecue out back in a cut-off steel barrel. The place hasn't lost any of the authenticity or friendly, homey service in the transition, but now the dining room is comfortable and well appointed. Roscoe still table-hops to make friends talking about food and his impressive collection of black entertainment memorabilia. The barbecue and fried chicken are justly famous.

600 E. Northern Lights Blvd. (in the Sears Mall). © **907/276-5879.** Lunch $4.50–$8; dinner main courses $11–$16. AE, MC, V. Mon–Thurs 11am–9pm, Fri–Sat 11am–10pm, Sun noon–6pm.

4 Attractions & Activities

I've arranged this section starting with a walking tour through downtown Anchorage, followed by details on the downtown museums and then attractions that are farther afield.

The best **guided tour** of the historic downtown area is by **Anchorage Historic Properties,** 645 W. Third Ave. (© **907/274-3600;** www.customcpu.com/np/ahpi), a city-endowed historic preservation group, offering 2-hour, 2-mile walks June to August, Monday to Friday at 1pm. The volunteer guides are fun and knowledgeable. Meet at the lobby of Old City Hall, 524 W. Fourth Ave., next door to the Log Cabin Visitor Information Center. Tickets cost $5 for adults, $4 for seniors over age 65, and $1 for children.

> ### *Tips* Helper Bees
>
> The people you see downtown on bikes and on foot in bright yellow-and-black outfits are the Anchorage Downtown Partnership Security Ambassadors, sometimes known as the "bumblebees" for their color scheme. They are funded by several downtown businesses in part to help visitors. Stop one to ask a question or report a problem.

Motorized city tours are available from many operators; check with the visitor center to make your choice. Frankly, there's not that much to see. On the less expensive tours, you can get a feel for the city, while the costlier ones go inside key sites but don't allow much time there. **Anchorage City Trolley Tours,** at Fourth and F Street (© **907/276-5603**), offers hourly tours—in buses that have been made to look like San Francisco streetcars—just to give a taste of Anchorage. They leave every hour from 9am to 6pm May to September and cost $10 per person. The major tour companies described in section 5 of chapter 2 under "Escorted Tour or Do-It-Yourself?" also sell city tours to independent travelers.

WALKING TOUR	DOWNTOWN ANCHORAGE

Start & Finish: Fourth Avenue and F Street.

Time: 2 hours (use the shortcuts noted for a briefer tour).

Start at the **Log Cabin Visitor Information Center** at Fourth Avenue and F Street. Outside is a sign that shows the distance to various cities and a 5,114-pound jade boulder put on display by Stewart's Photo Shop, an Anchorage institution that is just across the street. Walk east, toward the mountains, to:

---

❶ Old City Hall (1936)

It's on the right, at Fourth Avenue and E Street. Recently renovated, its lobby contains a fun display on city history, including dioramas of the early streetscape, old photographs, and the fire bell and fire pole that once were used in this building.

Crossing E Street, notice on the left side of Fourth Avenue that all the buildings are modern—everything on that side from E Street east for several blocks collapsed in the 1964 earthquake. The street split in half, lengthwise, with the left side ending up a dozen feet lower than the right. That land was later reinforced with a gravel buttress by the U.S. Army Corps of Engineers and the slope below forever set aside from new construction because of the earthquake risk. This stretch of Fourth Avenue is where the **Iditarod Trail Sled Dog Race** and the **Anchorage Fur Rendezvous World Championship Sled Dog Race** start each year in March and February, respectively.

At Fourth Avenue and D Street is the:

❷ Wendler Building (1915)

The old Club 25 is among the oldest buildings in Anchorage. The bronze statue of the dog commemorates the sled-dog races that start here. Across D Street is a mural that depicts a map of coastal Alaska and B.C., with the Iditarod Trail dimly marked.

Turn right, walking a block south on:

❸ D Street

Several interesting little businesses and restaurants inhabit this block, sometimes joining together for a street fair. First on the left is **Cyrano's Off-Center Playhouse** (© **907/274-2599**), with its Eccentric Theater Company, Bistro Bergerac, and book store. Stop in for a snack or cultural offering. On the right, **The Rondy Shop** (© **907/274-1196;** www.furrondy.net/rondyshop.htm) carries memorabilia from the annual Fur Rendezvous winter carnival and sled dog races, and has a campy little history display.

❹ The 5th Avenue Mall

This grand, four-story shopping center faces D from the south side of Fifth.

Turn left on Fifth.

❺ A series of interesting shops

are on the north side of Fifth, including **Laura Wright Alaskan Parkys,** where seamstresses sew custom Eskimo coats, and **Russian Gift Shop "Aleksandr Baranov"** (www.russiangiftshop.com), which carries an amazing array of nested Russian dolls, lacquered boxes, and the like.

From Fifth Avenue turn right on C Street and follow it to the corner of Sixth Avenue, where you'll find:

❻ Wolf Song of Alaska

The nonprofit museum and gift shop (© **907/274-9653;** www.wolfsongalaska.org) aims to educate and elevate the public about Alaska's most controversial mammal. Inside you'll find dioramas, exhibits, artwork, videos, and eager volunteers. Admission is $3 for adults, $1.50 ages 6 to 18. Unless your interest in wolves is strong, you'll spend only 10 or 15 minutes here. Summer hours are at least 10am to 6pm Monday through Saturday, noon to 5pm Sunday; winter Monday through Saturday 11am to 5pm.

A door or two west (away from the mountains) is the free:

❼ Alaska State Troopers Museum

I don't know why I so enjoy this trove of law enforcement insignia, equipment, a 1952 Hudson Hornet, photographs, and other memorabilia—maybe it's the way these things convey the positive spirit of pioneer Alaska combined with the troopers' obvious pride. It's open year-round Monday to Friday, 10am to 5pm, Saturday noon to 4pm (© **907/279-5050;** www.alaska.net/~foast).

Continue west, past the mall, to Sixth Avenue and E Street, which is one corner of the beautifully planted:

❽ Town square

The community raised money for the improvements by collecting donations of $40 each for the granite bricks, with an inscription of the contributor's choosing. There are 13,344 (bet you can't find mine). On the east side of the square, behind you, the huge whale mural was painted freehand by Wyland in 1994. He painted similar whale murals in cities all along the West Coast. On the west side of the square is the massive, highly decorated, dominating:

❾ Alaska Center for the Performing Arts

Anchorage's most controversial building, the center was completed in 1988 at a cost of over $70 million. The lobby is usually open, and whatever your opinion of the decor, a look inside will spark a discussion. Tours are Wednesday at 1pm; a $1 donation is requested (reach the center's administrative offices at © **907/263-2900**). Thespians believe the building is haunted by the ghost of painter Sydney Lawrence, who makes lights mysteriously vary and elevators go up and down with no one in them. An auditorium demolished to make room for the center was named for Lawrence.

**Map legend:**

1 Old City Hall
2 Wendler Building
3 D Street
4 The 5th Avenue Mall
5 Series of interesting shops
6 Wolf Song of Alaska
7 Alaska State Troopers Museum
8 Town square
9 Alaska Center for the Performing Arts
10 City Hall
11 Decker/Morris Gallery
12 Offbeat businesses
13 Holy Family Cathedral
14 Elderberry Park
15 Resolution Park
16 The Last Blue Whale
17 Totem poles
18 Ship Creek overlook
19 Saturday Market
20 Old federal building
21 4th Avenue Theater

Check the box office for current performances in the three theaters, Alaska's premier performance venues (and see "The Performing Arts," later).

Take a Break
From the Alaska Center, cross Sixth Avenue at the F Street light and turn right (west) to **Humpy's,** a popular tavern on the south side of Sixth with a huge selection of microbrews, live music, and good casual meals.

The square green office building next door to Humpy's is:

⑩ City Hall

Turn left through the pedestrian walkway between Humpy's and City Hall. A large mural showing a timeline of the history of Anchorage faces the parking lot. A much better mural, by Duke Russell, is on the wall in Humpy's outdoor seating area on the near side of the parking lot.

Walk west through the city hall parking lot to G Street, turn right, and proceed to Sixth Avenue and G. On the northeast corner of Sixth Avenue and G Street, in the corner of the Performing Arts Center, is the:

⑪ Decker/Morris Gallery

It's one of Alaska's best and most uncompromising.

Walk a block north to Fifth Avenue. The west side of G Street between Fourth and Fifth avenues contains some of the downtown's best:

⑫ Offbeat businesses

First comes **Aurora Fine Arts,** which is hardly offbeat, but is an attractive arts and craft shop; next, **Uncle Joe's**

Pizzeria, with good pie by the slice; next, **Darwin's Theory,** a friendly, old-fashioned bar with character that shows up in an Indigo Girls song; next, **Suzi's Woolies** (www.suzis woollies.com), a Celtic shop carrying imported sweaters, jewelry, and CDs, and with live Irish music Saturday afternoons; next, **Denali Wear,** which is Tracy Anna Bader's studio and shop of bright, graphic wearable art; next, **Side Street Espresso,** where you can get into a lively discussion on art or politics and make contact with thinking people; next, **Charlie's Alaska Trains** (www.ptialaska.net/~aktrains), a retired couple's labor of love, which sells little other than Alaska Railroad models and memorabilia.

Shortcut: You can cut an hour off the tour here by continuing north on G Street to Fourth, then turning right and walking 1 block to F Street.

Backtrack to Fifth and G, then proceed west (away from the mountains) on Fifth. The Imaginarium, described under "Downtown Museums," below, is on the right. Continuing west on Fifth Avenue and crossing H Street, you'll see the:

⑬ Holy Family Cathedral
This concrete Art Deco church is the seat of the Roman Catholic archbishop. The interior is unremarkable.

Keep going toward the water, crossing L Street and going down the hill to:

⑭ Elderberry Park
The yellow-and-brown house is the **Oscar Anderson House,** described under "Downtown Museums," below. Besides the good playground equipment, the park offers the easiest access point to the **Coastal Trail** (see "Walking & Biking," later). The trail tunnels under the Alaska Railroad tracks from the bottom of the park.

Now hike back up the hill to L Street and turn left. At Third Avenue is:

⑮ Resolution Park
The bronze **Captain Cook Monument** stands on a large wooden deck,

but he's gazing out to sea—the opposite of the way he was facing when he explored Cook Inlet in 1778 aboard HMS *Resolution.* Cook didn't personally come as far as Anchorage, instead sending a boat with his ship's master, William Bligh (later the inspiration of mutiny on the HMS *Bounty*). Failing to find the Northwest Passage here, Cook considered his 2 weeks in Cook Inlet a waste of time, grousing in his journal, "Nothing but a trifling point in geography has been determined." The park's informative signs, powerful mounted binoculars, and commanding vantage point make this a rewarding stop for gazing out at the water and the mountains beyond. The waters you see are ferocious and wild, with whirlpool currents and a tidal range of almost 40 vertical feet. The shore across the Inlet, about 2 miles away, is virtually uninhabited.

Follow Third Avenue east (back toward the mountains) 1 block and turn right on K Street. On the right is:

⑯ The Last Blue Whale
Joseph Princiotti's huge 1973 bronze of combat between a whale and whalers in small boats shows the whale's point of view.

Cross K Street to walk through the plaza toward the opposite Nesbett State Courthouse. The sinuous shapes of the concrete are supposed to suggest both the flow of people through the court system and the shape of a braided glacial river. At the courthouse, at 4th Avenue and I Street, take a look at the two:

⑰ Totem poles
Carved of red cedar by Lee Wallace, of Ketchikan, and erected in 1997, they represent the eagle and raven moieties of the Tlingit people, intended to symbolize the balance of justice. A Tlingit creation story tells of how raven stole the moon and stars and brought them to mankind; here, the moon and stars are the stars of the Alaska flag.

Walk around past the courthouse on Fourth Avenue and turn left onto H Street. Follow H as it crosses Third Avenue and becomes Christensen Drive. Descend the hill on Christensen and turn right on Second Avenue, toward the mountains. Many of the **old houses** that line Second are marked, and a kiosk at Second and F tells some town history. If you imagine houses like this over much of downtown, you'll know what Anchorage looked like before oil.

Continue east on Second Avenue to E Street, where you will find:

⑱ A Ship Creek overlook with a monument to President Eisenhower

The bust commemorates Alaska's 1959 admission to the Union (in fact, Eisenhower was a major barrier to statehood). More interesting is the overlook. You can see the Alaska Railroad yards from here, and part of the port of Anchorage and the neighborhood of Government Hill across the Ship Creek river bottom. This is where the tent city of Knik Anchorage, later shortened to Anchorage, was set up in 1914. An informative set of historic signs on the overlook explains. The Alaska Railroad, which helped build Anchorage, still has its headquarters in a modern brick building that stands by the creek. The nearer concrete building is the railroad's stately depot. The beautifully restored steam engine on the pedestal in front was used on construction of the Panama Canal, then worked in the yard here as a switch engine. The creek itself is full of salmon in June and August (see "Fishing," later), and a

walkway that crosses a dam just upstream from here is a good place to watch the fish and to feed ducks. But the walk down the stairs to the river bottom and back is strenuous.

Walk up the hill on E Street to Third Avenue. Every weekend in the summer, the extensively landscaped parking lot on the left becomes the:

⑲ Saturday Market

The street fair draws hundreds of vendors and thousands of shoppers. You can buy everything from local vegetables to handmade crafts to somebody's old record collection. There are food booths and music, too.

Turn right on Third Avenue, then left on F Street. F Street Station, on the left, is a fun bar with an after-work crowd. Proceed to Fourth Avenue, and you're back at the Log Cabin Visitor Information Center, but don't stop. Turn right on Fourth Avenue. On the right side is the:

⑳ Old federal building

This grand, white, Depression-era structure now contains the Alaska Public Lands Information Center, with interesting displays and lots of information about the outdoors. Across the street is Anchorage's most attractive historic building, the restored:

㉑ 4th Avenue Theater

It was built by Cap Lathrop, Alaska's first business magnate, who created it as a monument to the territory and the permanence of its new society. Today it's a gift store. Don't miss going in and looking at the bas-relief murals and the blinking big dipper on the ceiling, which during many a movie over the years was more entertaining than whatever was on the screen.

DOWNTOWN MUSEUMS

Anchorage Museum of History and Art ★★★   The state's largest museum doesn't have its largest collection, but unlike the Alaska State Museum in Juneau or the University of Alaska Museum in Fairbanks, the Anchorage museum has the room and staff both to teach and to serve as a center of contemporary culture of a regional caliber. Most visitors tour the large Alaska Gallery, an informative and enjoyable walk through the history and some of the anthropology of large enclosures with natural flora for bears, seals and otters, musk oxen, mountain goats, moose, caribou, waterfowl—all the animals you were supposed to see in Alaska but may have missed. (Don't get the elephant or Siberian tigers in your snapshots—they'll blow your story.) A snack bar serves basic meals, and there is a large gift shop.

4731 O'Malley Rd. © 907/346-3242. Admission $8 adults, $7 seniors, $5 children 12–17, $4 children 3–12. AE, MC, V. Opens daily at 10am; closing time varies by season. Drive out the New Seward Hwy. to O'Malley Rd., then turn left and go 2 miles; it's 25 min. from downtown, without traffic.

Earthquake Park   The 1964 Good Friday earthquake was the biggest ever in North America, registering at 9.2 on the Richter Scale, killing 131 people, and flattening much of the region. Downtown Anchorage and the Turnagain residential area, near the park, suffered enormous slides that turned neighborhoods into chaotic ruins. A sculpture and excellent interpretive signs commemorate and explain the event and point out its few remaining marks on the land. This also is a good access point to the Coastal Trail.

West end of Northern Lights Blvd. From downtown, take L St. (it becomes Minnesota Dr.) to Northern Lights Blvd. and turn right. The park is on your right after you cross Lakeshore Dr.

Eklutna Historical Park ⭑   The Native village of Eklutna has a fascinating old cemetery, still in use, in which each grave is enclosed by a highly decorated spirit house, the size of a large dollhouse. These little shelters excite the imagination in a way no ordinary marker would. The unique practice evolved in the melding of Athabascan and Russian Orthodox beliefs. There are two small Russian Orthodox churches on the site, including the **St. Nicholas Orthodox Church.** Built north of here of logs sometime before 1870, it is among the oldest buildings in the Southcentral region. Walk through by yourself or take an informative 30-minute tour for the same price. Wear mosquito repellent. If you come out this far, don't miss the Thunderbird Falls, described below under "Hiking."

About 25 miles out the Glenn Hwy. © **907/688-6026** or 907/696-2828. www.eklutna.com. Admission $6 adult, $3 ages 6–17. Summer daily 8am–6pm. Take the Glenn Hwy. to the Eklutna exit, then go left over the overpass.

SPECTATOR SPORTS

Most big events in Anchorage happen at the **Sullivan Arena,** at 16th Avenue and Gambell Street. The main ticket agency is California-based **Tickets.com** (© **800/478-7328**), which has counters at most Carrs grocery stores and operates the Alaska Center for the Performing Arts box office.

BASEBALL   Anchorage has two semipro baseball teams—the **Anchorage Glacier Pilots** (© **907/274-3627;** www.glacierpilots.com) and the **Anchorage Bucs** (© **907/561-2827;** www.anchoragebucs.com)—with college athletes playing short midsummer seasons in a six-team Alaska league. The quality may be uneven, but you may see diamonds in the rough: Among famed alumni are Mark McGwire, Rick Aguilera, Tom Seaver, Dave Winfield, Barry Bonds, Wally Joyner, and Randy Johnson. Check the *Anchorage Daily News* or websites for game times. Mulcahy Stadium is at 16th Avenue and A Street, a long walk or a short drive from downtown. Tickets are under $5. Dress warmly for evening games; a blanket is rarely out of order. A weekend day game is warmer, but then you won't get to see baseball played at night without lights.

BASKETBALL   The University of Alaska Anchorage men's basketball team (www.goseawolves.com) hosts a major Division I preseason tournament over

Thanksgiving weekend, the **Great Alaska Shootout,** and plays the regular season at the Sullivan Arena and at the University Sports Center, on campus on Providence Drive.

HOCKEY   The **Anchorage Aces** (© **907/258-2237;** www.anchorageaces.com) compete in the West Coast Hockey League against cities such as Phoenix, Tacoma, and San Diego. The **University of Alaska Anchorage** (www.goseawolves.com) fields an NCAA Division I hockey team, on hard times recently but sure to start winning in 2002.

5 Getting Outside

Anchorage is unique in Alaska (and anywhere else I know) for the number of places right near town to hike, bike, ski, and otherwise get into the wild. I've broken the options down by activities below. In town, the city's bike trails connect through greenbelts that span the noisy, asphalt urban core with soothing creekside woods. Kincaid Park and Far North Bicentennial Park are both on the trail system within the city, and encompass scores of miles of trails for Nordic skiing, mountain biking, and horseback riding. The Chugach Mountains, which form the backdrop to the town, offer tundra hiking, backpacking, mountain biking, and climbs that range from easy to technical. More trails and streams, only slightly farther afield, are covered in the "Out from Anchorage" sections later in this chapter.

Many cruises, tours, fishing charters, and sea-kayaking trips leave from nearby **Whittier,** easily managed as a day trip; see section 4 of chapter 7 for details.

INFORMATION   The **Alaska Public Lands Information Center** (© **907/271-2737;** www.nps.gov/aplic) offers guidance for all these areas. For information on the bike trails, Nordic skiing parks, and other city recreation, contact the **Municipal Division of Sports & Recreation** at © **907/343-4474** (www.muni.org/parks). The **Chugach State Park Headquarters** is in the Potter Section House on the Seward Highway at the south end of town (© **907/345-5014;** www.dnr.state.ak.us/parks/units/chugach/index.htm); downtown, get their *Ridgelines* newsprint guide through the public land information center. Chugach National Forest can be reached at © **907/271-2500** or www.fs.fed.us/r10/chugach.

The best trail guide to the entire region is Helen Nienhueser and John Wolfe Jr.'s *55 Ways to the Wilderness,* published by The Mountaineers (mountaineersbooks.org). It costs $12.95 and is available in any bookstore in the area. The best trail map is the Chugach State Park topographic trail map published in 2000 by Imus Geographics and sold at either of the sporting-goods stores mentioned below.

EQUIPMENT   You can rent most anything you need for outdoor activities. For bike rentals, see "Getting Around," in section 1 of this chapter. You can get advice and rent sea kayaks, skis, snowshoes, bear-proof containers, and mountaineering equipment at **Alaska Mountaineering and Hiking,** at 2633 Spenard Rd. (© **907/272-1811;** www.alaskan.com/amh). It's a small shop where the staff takes the time to help you plan a trip. A block away, at 1200 W. Northern Lights Blvd., **REI** has a large store (© **907/272-4565;** www.rei.com) that rents a wide range of gear, including canoes with car-top carriers, camping gear, and packs (but not bikes).

WALKING & BIKING

Anchorage has an award-winning network of paved **bike trails** spanning the city along wooded greenbelts. You rarely see a building and almost always cross roads and rail lines through tunnels and over bridges, so you're never in traffic. Here are two of the best.

TONY KNOWLES COASTAL TRAIL ★★★   Leading 10 miles from the western end of Second Avenue along the shore to **Kincaid Park,** the coastal trail is among my favorite things about Anchorage and a unique pathway to the natural environment from the heart of downtown. I've had moose stop me on the trail near the Kincaid Park end, while closer to downtown, I've ridden parallel to beluga whales swimming along the trail at high tide. The more popular entry is at **Elderberry Park,** at the western end of Fifth Avenue. **Westchester Lagoon** is 10 blocks south of Elderberry Park, making for a lovely stroll and an equally enjoyable destination for a picnic or to feed the ducks and geese.

LANIE FLEISCHER CHESTER CREEK TRAIL ★★   Starting at an intersection with the Coastal Trail at Westchester Lagoon, the trail runs about 4 miles east along the greenbelt to **Goose Lake,** where you can swim in a cool woodland pond at the end of a hot bike ride—still, improbably enough, in the middle of the city. South from the lake, a wooded trail leads partway through the university campus. The paved bike trails, including the Fleischer, stay well back in the trees, so you rarely see a building, and tunnels and bridges span all road and railroad crossings, so you're never in traffic.

HIKING & MOUNTAIN BIKING

KINCAID PARK ★★   Covered in more detail below, Kincaid Park is an idyllic summer setting for mountain biking and day hikes. Moose sightings are a daily occurrence on wide dirt trails that snake for about 30 miles through the birch and white spruce of the park's hilly 1,400 acres of boreal forest, often with views of the sea and mountains beyond. Within the park, wooded Little Campbell Lake is a picturesque but little-used swimming hole and a fun spot for family canoeing and fishing for stocked trout, salmon, and char; there is no lifeguard.

FAR NORTH BICENTENNIAL PARK ★   The 4,000-acre park, on the east side of town, is a unique patch of urban wilderness, a habitat for bears, moose, and spawning salmon. People use it for dog mushing and skiing in winter, and for exceptional mountain biking and day hiking in summer. The Alaska Botanical Garden, listed above, and the Hilltop Ski Area, below, are both within the park's boundaries. A good place to start a hike or ride through the woods is the **Campbell Creek Science Center** (© 907/267-1257), an educational facility operated by the Bureau of Land Management, where staff are often on hand to answer questions and where you can consult books and maps. To get there from downtown, take Gambell Street (it becomes New Seward Highway) south to Dowling Road, go east (toward the mountains), and turn right on Lake Otis Road and left on 68th Avenue, following it to the end.

FLATTOP MOUNTAIN & THE GLEN ALPS TRAILHEAD ★★★   There are many ways to reach the alpine tundra, intoxicating fresh air, and cinematic views of the Chugach Mountains behind Anchorage, but the easiest and best developed are at the Chugach State Park Glen Alps Trailhead. Even those who aren't up to hiking should go for the drive and a walk on a short, paved loop with incredible views and interpretive signs. If you are ready for a hike, you can start at the trailhead for trips of up to several days, following the network of trails or taking off across dry, alpine tundra by yourself, but usually within cellphone range. Camping is permitted anywhere off the trails.

Flattop Mountain is the most popular hike from the Glen Alps Trailhead, and a great family climb, if a bit crowded on weekends. It's a steep afternoon hike, easy for fit adults and doable by school-age children. There's a bit of a scramble at the top, easiest if you stick to the painted markers on the rocks. Dress warmly and don't go in the rain.

For a longer or less steep hike or a mountain-biking trip, follow the broad gravel trail that leads up the valley from the Glen Alps Trailhead to several other great routes. Trails lead all the way over the mountains to Indian or Bird Creek, on Turnagain Arm, up some of the mountains along the way or to round alpine lakes in high, rocky valleys. You're always above the tree line, so you don't need to follow a trail if you have a good map. This is wonderful backpacking country.

To get to the trailhead, take New Seward Highway to O'Malley Road, head east toward the mountains, then turn right on Hillside Drive and left onto Upper Huffman Road. Finally, turn right on the narrow, twisting Toilsome Hill Drive. Don't forget to bring cash for a self-service day-use fee of $5.

EAGLE RIVER VALLEY & CROW PASS ★★   The **Eagle River Nature Center,** at the end of Eagle River Road, 12 miles up Eagle River Valley from the Glenn Highway exit (✆ **907/694-2108;** www.ernc.org), is like a public wilderness lodge, with hands-on naturalist displays about the area and guided nature walks or talks daily in the summer and weekends year-round (call for times). Operated by a nonprofit concessionaire for Chugach State Park, it's open in summer Sunday through Thursday 10am to 5pm, Friday and Saturday 10am to 7pm; spring and fall 10am to 5pm except Monday; winter Friday through Sunday 10am to 5pm. There's a $5 parking fee.

The three-quarter-mile **Rodak Nature Trail,** with interpretive signs, leads to a viewing platform over a beaver pond. The **Albert Loop Trail** is a 3-mile route; a geology guide from the center matches with numbered posts on the way. Both have good bird and wildlife watching. The 25-mile **Crow Pass Trail,** a portion of the historic Iditarod Trail, continues up the valley into the mountains along the river, eventually surmounting the Chugach in alpine terrain, and passing near Raven Glacier before descending into Girdwood (see "Out from Anchorage: Turnagain Arm & Portage Glacier," later in this chapter). There are campsites with fire rings along the way, and a mile up the trail the center rents out a public-use cabin for $55 a night. A yurt on the Crow Pass Trail and another on the Albert Loop rent for the same price. Reserve well ahead for weekends. Availability is shown on the website.

THUNDERBIRD FALLS & EKLUTNA LAKE ★★   The hike to Thunderbird Falls is an easy, 1-mile forest walk with a good reward at the end; you can see the falls without the steep final descent to their foot. Take the Glenn Highway north to the Thunderbird Falls exit, 25 miles from Anchorage. Continuing 10 miles up the gravel Eklutna Lake Road, you come to a lovely state parks campground ($10 a night, $5 day-use fee) and the beautiful glacial lake for canoeing, hiking, and exceptional mountain biking. The Lakeside Trail leads 13.5 miles to Eklutna Glacier; you can camp on the way or stay at a state parks cabin at 3 miles (reservation required; see "State Parks Cabin Reservation Tricks" in section 1 of chapter 7), or in a communal hut at 12.5 miles ($10 per bunk). Rental bikes, kayaks, and other equipment, and guided kayak and boat tours, are offered by **Lifetime Adventures,** with a booth at the trailhead

(© **907/746-4644;** www.lifetimeadventures.net). For $70 you can kayak 8 miles to the other end of the lake and pick up a bike there to ride back. This glacial melt is also where Anchorage gets most of its city water. People bottle it and sell it as "glacier water."

ARCTIC VALLEY 🎿 The road to the Alpenglow Ski Area (see "Skiing," below) is a wonderful route into mountains of alpine tundra where you can romp on its soft carpet and hike or climb in any direction. Late summer berry picking is excellent. On top of the mountain to the left is an abandoned Cold War–era antimissile emplacement. The park charges a $3 day use fee. Take Glenn Highway to the Arctic Valley exit.

FISHING

There are hatchery salmon in many of Anchorage's streams, and stocked trout, salmon, or char in more than 25 lakes, so you need not leave town to catch a fish. The **Alaska Department of Fish and Game,** 333 Raspberry Rd., Anchorage, AK 99518-1599 (© **907/267-2218;** www.state.ak.us/adfg, click "Sportfish," then "Region 2"), publishes informative booklets on the web and on paper. There's also a recorded information line (© **907/267-2503**) with all the details on what's hot and lots of other advice. See chapter 2 for general guidance and license information, and information for planning a fishing vacation, and see chapter 7 for the most famous fishing opportunities on the Kenai Peninsula.

ROADSIDE FISHING Although the setting (under a highway bridge in an industrial area) might not be the wilderness experience you've dreamed about, the 40-pound king salmon you pull from **Ship Creek** may make up for it. From downtown, just walk down the hill to the railroad yard. A couple of shacks sell and rent gear in the summer. Fishing for kings is best in June and for silvers in August and September. Fish at or near high tide, especially at the end of the rising tide. You'll need rubber boots, preferably neoprene chest waders, for the muddy banks, but don't go too far out, as the mudflats are dangerous.

Bird Creek, 25 miles south of Anchorage on the Seward Highway (see "Out from Anchorage: Turnagain Arm & Portage Glacier"), carries a strong hatchery run of silver salmon, peaking in August. When silver fishing is hot, it gets crowded and parking is a problem. Pink salmon run from late June to early August. Other creeks along the Arm have similar but smaller runs.

FLY-IN FISHING 🎣🎣🎣 Serious anglers will use Anchorage as a base from which to fly to a remote lake or river with more fish and fewer people. Such a flight can be an unforgettable experience for those who are less than enthusiastic about fishing, too. The plane lifts off from Anchorage's Lake Hood floatplane base and within half an hour smoothly lands on a lake or river, often all alone. You climb out and watch as the plane lifts off and disappears, leaving behind the kind of silence unique to true wilderness. It's on these trips that avid anglers are made—or spoiled. I've heard people complain of how sore their arms got from pulling in too many salmon.

Several companies offer fly-in trips; two of the largest and best established are **Ketchum Air Service** (© **800/433-9114** or 907/243-5525; www.ketchumair. com) and **Rust's Flying Service** (© **800/544-2299** or 907/243-1595; www.fly rusts.com). They can take you out guided or on your own, just for the day or to stay for a while in a cabin or lodge. If you fly to a lake, they'll provide a boat. They can't make fish appear if none are running, but they will try to take you to the hot spots. You can bring your own gear, or they can provide it. Prices for an unguided day trip start around $250 per person, with a two-person minimum.

OTHER SUMMER ACTIVITIES

FLIGHTSEEING   Small planes are the blood cells of Alaska's circulatory system, and Anchorage its heart. There are several busy airports in Anchorage, and Lake Hood is the world's busiest floatplane base. More than two dozen operators want to take you on a flightseeing tour—check the visitor center for names—but the most comfortable and memorable is probably aboard the restored DC-3s operated by **Era Aviation** (© **800/843-1947** or 907/266-8351; www.eraaviation.com). The planes re-create 1940s air travel—you can pretend to be Ingrid Bergman or Spencer Tracy while gazing out the oversize windows at a glacier. The daily summer flights leave from hangars on Carl Brady Drive, off Raspberry Road, with itineraries determined by the weather: The plane has the speed and range to go where the best views are, including Mount McKinley, Prince William Sound, or Kenai Fjords National Park's Harding Ice Field. A 90-minute flight is $159 per person. The route is tailored to the weather and viewing opportunities. Era also offers helicopter flightseeing.

RAFTING   There are several white-water rivers within a 90-minute drive of Anchorage. **Nova Raft and Adventure Tours** (© **800/746-5753** or 907/745-5753; http://novalaska.com) has 25 years of experience offering multiday trips all over the state, and four different half-day floats in the Anchorage area. Rafting trips are available ranging from relatively easygoing Class II and III rapids on the Matanuska River to the Class IV and V white water of Six-Mile Creek, for which you may be required to prove your swimming ability before you can get in the boat. Self-paddling is an option on some trips. White-water rafting always entails risk, but Nova's schedule allows you to calibrate how wild you want to get. The half-day trips range in price from $65 to $125. Children 5 to 11 can go on the calmer Matanuska River float for $35. Other trips are suitable only for older children and adults. You'll need your own transportation to the river and may need to bring your own lunch.

SEA KAYAKING   Except at Eklutna Lake (see above), kayaking day trips from Anchorage go through Whittier, on Prince William Sound (see section 4 of chapter 7 for complete details).

WINTER ACTIVITIES

DOG MUSHING   In the last 20 years, dog mushing has become a recreational sport as well as the utilitarian transportation it once was in the Bush and the professional sport it has been for years. But keeping a dog team is a more than a hobby—it is a lifestyle revolving around the feeding, care, and exercise of at least a dozen dogs (the pros sometimes have 200). Some mushers offset the great expense by offering rides. In the Anchorage area, among the best are friendly and casual Angie and Tom Hamill, who keep two dozen dogs at their home in the Chugiak area, half an hour from downtown on the Glenn Highway. In winter only, they'll take you on as short a ride as 2 miles, riding in the sled basket while they drive, for $35. For $195, they'll teach you to mush in a 2½-hour session. They do expeditions, too, and own a bed-and-breakfast. The business is called **Birch Trails Adventures,** 22719 Robinson Rd., Chugiak (© and fax **907/688-5713**). For other options, see the sections on Girdwood and the Matanuska and Susitna valleys, later in this chapter.

ICE-SKATING   Westchester Lagoon, just 10 blocks from downtown (see "Walking & Biking," above), is a skating paradise in the winter. When the ice gets thick enough, usually by mid-December, the city clears a large rink and

"Anchorage." They have box offices at the Anchorage Center for Performing Arts and at Carrs grocery stores.

The arts season begins in the fall and ends in the spring, but traveling performers often come through in the summer as well. The **Anchorage Concert Association** (© 907/272-1471; www.anchorageconcerts.org) offers a fall-through-spring schedule of classical music, theater, dance, and other performing arts. **Whistling Swan Productions** (www.whistlingswan.net) promotes folk and acoustic alternative performers in intimate venues. The **Anchorage Festival of Music** (© 907/276-2465; www.festivalmusic.org) presents a classical music series in June. The **Anchorage Symphony** (© 907/274-8668; www.anchorage symphony.org) performs during the winter season. Anchorage also has lots of community theater, opera, and limited professional theater, including the experimental **Out North Contemporary Art House** (© 907/279-8099, www.outnorth.org), which produces local shows and imports avant-garde performers. Downtown, **Cyrano's Off Center Playhouse** (© 907/274-2599; www.cyranos.org), at Fourth Avenue and D Street, is a tiny theater with its own semiprofessional repertory company.

NIGHTCLUBS & BARS

For a fun, funny night out, nothing in town compares to **Mr. Whitekeys' Fly By Night Club,** on Spenard Road south of Northern Lights Boulevard (© 907/279-SPAM). The goateed proprietor, a consummate vulgarian, ridicules Anchorage in his crude, political, local-humor musical comedy shows, in which he costars with a fallen former Miss Anchorage. If you can laugh at dog poop, you'll love it. The summer show is at 8pm Tuesday to Saturday, with no smoking Tuesday to Thursday; live music follows Fridays and Saturdays. Tickets are $12 to $19, and reservations are necessary well in advance. They serve good food, too. (Believe me, I wrote this long before they started using a piece of my writing in one of their shows.)

Blues Central/Chef's Inn, 825 W. Northern Lights Blvd. (© 907/272-1341), is dedicated to showcasing the best blues performers available, virtually every night. Major names come through on a regular basis. Shows start at 9:30pm. They also serve excellent beef. The huge **Chilkoot Charlie's,** at Spenard Road and Fireweed Lane (© 907/272-1010; www.koots.com), has two stages for rock and one for swing. The place is huge, but can be claustrophobic when crowded, with low ceilings and a dark, roadhouse atmosphere. The **Long Branch Saloon,** 1737 E. Dimond Blvd. (© 907/349-4142), east of New Seward Highway, has live top-40 music every night and great burgers.

THE MOVIES

The most fun place to see a movie is the **Bear Tooth Theatrepub,** at 1230 W. 27th Ave. (© 907/276-4200; www.beartooththeatre.net), where you can watch art films and second-run movies while sipping craft brews and eating gourmet tacos, pizzas, and the like. There are several multiplexes in Anchorage playing all the current Hollywood output; check the *Anchorage Daily News* for listings. The closest larger theaters, the **Century 16** (© 907/929-FILM; www.centurytheatres.com) and the **Fireweed 7 Theater** (© 907/566-3328; www.regalcinemas.com), are a short cab ride away in midtown.

8 Out from Anchorage: Turnagain Arm & Portage Glacier

One of the world's great drives starts in Anchorage and leads roughly 50 miles south on the Seward Highway to Portage Glacier. It's the trip, not the

OTHER SUMMER ACTIVITIES

FLIGHTSEEING   Small planes are the blood cells of Alaska's circulatory system, and Anchorage its heart. There are several busy airports in Anchorage, and Lake Hood is the world's busiest floatplane base. More than two dozen operators want to take you on a flightseeing tour—check the visitor center for names—but the most comfortable and memorable is probably aboard the restored DC-3s operated by **Era Aviation** (✆ **800/843-1947** or 907/266-8351; www.eraaviation.com). The planes re-create 1940s air travel—you can pretend to be Ingrid Bergman or Spencer Tracy while gazing out the oversize windows at a glacier. The daily summer flights leave from hangars on Carl Brady Drive, off Raspberry Road, with itineraries determined by the weather: The plane has the speed and range to go where the best views are, including Mount McKinley, Prince William Sound, or Kenai Fjords National Park's Harding Ice Field. A 90-minute flight is $159 per person. The route is tailored to the weather and viewing opportunities. Era also offers helicopter flightseeing.

RAFTING   There are several white-water rivers within a 90-minute drive of Anchorage. **Nova Raft and Adventure Tours** (✆ **800/746-5753** or 907/ 745-5753; http://novalaska.com) has 25 years of experience offering multiday trips all over the state, and four different half-day floats in the Anchorage area. Rafting trips are available ranging from relatively easygoing Class II and III rapids on the Matanuska River to the Class IV and V white water of Six-Mile Creek, for which you may be required to prove your swimming ability before you can get in the boat. Self-paddling is an option on some trips. White-water rafting always entails risk, but Nova's schedule allows you to calibrate how wild you want to get. The half-day trips range in price from $65 to $125. Children 5 to 11 can go on the calmer Matanuska River float for $35. Other trips are suitable only for older children and adults. You'll need your own transportation to the river and may need to bring your own lunch.

SEA KAYAKING   Except at Eklutna Lake (see above), kayaking day trips from Anchorage go through Whittier, on Prince William Sound (see section 4 of chapter 7 for complete details).

WINTER ACTIVITIES

DOG MUSHING   In the last 20 years, dog mushing has become a recreational sport as well as the utilitarian transportation it once was in the Bush and the professional sport it has been for years. But keeping a dog team is a more than a hobby—it is a lifestyle revolving around the feeding, care, and exercise of at least a dozen dogs (the pros sometimes have 200). Some mushers offset the great expense by offering rides. In the Anchorage area, among the best are friendly and casual Angie and Tom Hamill, who keep two dozen dogs at their home in the Chugiak area, half an hour from downtown on the Glenn Highway. In winter only, they'll take you on as short a ride as 2 miles, riding in the sled basket while they drive, for $35. For $195, they'll teach you to mush in a 2½-hour session. They do expeditions, too, and own a bed-and-breakfast. The business is called **Birch Trails Adventures,** 22719 Robinson Rd., Chugiak (✆ and fax **907/688-5713**). For other options, see the sections on Girdwood and the Matanuska and Susitna valleys, later in this chapter.

ICE-SKATING   **Westchester Lagoon,** just 10 blocks from downtown (see "Walking & Biking," above), is a skating paradise in the winter. When the ice gets thick enough, usually by mid-December, the city clears a large rink and

long, wide paths on the pond, mopping the ice regularly for a smooth surface. In recent years, a 1-kilometer loop has wrapped around all the shorter paths. Skaters gather around burn barrels, well stocked with firewood, to socialize and warm their hands, and on weekends vendors often sell hot chocolate and coffee. Ice skates are for rent for $5 a day at **Champions Choice,** in the University Center Mall at Old Seward Highway and 36th Avenue (© **907/563-3503**).

SKIING   Kincaid Park is one of the best **cross-country skiing** areas in the country, with more than 50 kilometers of trails geared to every ability level, but mostly intermediate and expert. Besides the superb trails, it's a beautiful place to ski, through rolling hills of open birch and spruce, with views of the mountains and ocean. Trails are groomed for skating and classical techniques. Sixteen kilometers are lighted in winter (an important feature on short winter days). The **Kincaid Park Outdoor Center** (© **907/343-6397**) is open Monday to Friday from 1 to 9:45pm and Saturday and Sunday from 10am to 9:45pm. A gate closes at 10pm, so park outside it if you will be skiing later. Skiing often lasts through March. **Far North Bicentennial Park** also has some excellent trails— 32 kilometers total, 7 kilometers lighted—and a slightly longer season because of a hillside location. Start at Hilltop Ski Area. Many other parks and the bike trails have lengthy skiing routes, too, much of it lighted; ski right from downtown on the Tony Knowles Coastal Trail.

Anchorage has three **downhill ski areas.** The best, **Alyeska Resort,** is described in the Girdwood section, later. **Alpenglow at Arctic Valley** (© **907/ 428-1208**) is a good local ski area above the tree line, but it is in perennial financial trouble, so you should check before going (take the Glenn Highway to Arctic Valley Road). **Hilltop Ski Area,** in Bicentennial Park in town, is a great place to learn to ski, with one long beginner slope, at 7015 Abbott Rd. (© **907/ 346-1407;** www.hilltopskiarea.org).

6 Shopping

Some of the most interesting shops are mentioned earlier, in the walking tour of downtown, where most galleries and gift shops are located.

NATIVE ARTS & CRAFTS   Many stores in Anchorage carry Native Alaskan arts and crafts. Before making major purchases, know what you're buying (see "Native Art: Finding the Real Thing," in chapter 2). If you're going to the Bush, you'll find lower prices there but less selection.

Nowhere else will you find another business like the **Oomingmak Musk Ox Producers' Co-operative** (© **888/360-9665** outside Alaska or 907/272-9225; www.qiviut.com), located in the house with the musk ox on the side at Sixth Avenue and H Street. Owned by 250 Alaska Native women in villages across the state, the co-op sells only scarves and other items they knit of *qiviut* (*ki*-vee-ute), the light, warm, silky underhair of the musk ox, which is collected from shedding animals. Each village has its own knitting pattern. They're expensive—caps can cost over $100—but the quality is extraordinary. The website contains the women's fascinating correspondence.

The **Yankee Whaler,** in the lobby of the Hotel Captain Cook, at Fifth Avenue and I Street, is a small but well-regarded shop carrying Native arts. **The Rusty Harpoon,** at 411 W. Fourth Ave., also has authentic Native items, less expensive crafts, and reliable, longtime proprietors. Both buy only direct from Native artists they know. Farther afield, the **Alaska Fur Exchange,** at 4417 Old Seward Hwy., near Tudor Road, is a cross between an old-time wilderness trading post and a modern factory outlet. Rural residents bring in furs and crafts to sell and

trade, which are displayed in great profusion and clutter. If you're in the market for pelts, go no further.

Probably the best place for Native crafts in Anchorage is the **Hospital Auxiliary Craft Shop** in the Alaska Native Medical Center, off Tudor east of Bragaw (© **907/762-1122**), where everything is on consignment from those eligible to use the hospital. The work you find here is all authentic and entirely traditional. The shop is open Monday to Friday 10am to 2pm and some Saturdays. There's exceptional Native art on the walls of the hospital, too.

FURS & KUSPUKS   If you're in the market for fur, Anchorage has a wide selection and no sales tax. **David Green Master Furrier,** at 130 W. Fourth Ave. (www.davidgreenfurs.com), is an Anchorage institution. Others are nearby. **Laura Wright Alaskan Parkys,** at 343 W. Fifth Ave. (www.alaskan.com/parkys), makes and sells *kuspuks,* the brightly trimmed summer parkas really worn by Eskimos. Their winter-wear *parkys* often have fur trim, but that isn't a requirement for beauty and authenticity. Most of the coats are made to order by the friendly women in the shop.

GIFTS   There are lots of places to buy both mass-produced and inexpensive handmade crafts that aren't from the Bush. If you can be in town on a Saturday during the summer, be sure to visit the **Saturday Market** street fair, in the parking lot at Third Avenue and E Street, with food, music, and hundreds of miscellaneous crafts booths. You won't have any trouble finding gift shops on Fourth. Our favorite is the relatively classy **Cabin Fever,** at 650 W. Fourth. Other large, attractive shops include **Once in a Blue Moose,** at Fourth Avenue and F Street; **Grizzly's Gifts,** at Fourth and E; and **Trapper Jacks,** at Fourth and G. The **Kobuk Coffee Company,** at Fifth Avenue and E Street, next to the town square, occupies one of Anchorage's earliest commercial buildings; it's a cozy little candy, coffee, and collectibles shop. In midtown, on International Airport Road between the Old and New Seward highways, **Alaska Wild Berry Products** is a fun store to visit. There's a chocolate waterfall and a big window where you can watch the candy factory at work. The chocolate-covered berry jellies are simultaneously addictive and rich enough to make you dizzy if you eat more than a few.

FINE ART   Downtown has several galleries. Openings at all the galleries happen on the first Friday of each month, allowing for an evening of party hopping. The **Decker/Morris Gallery,** at Sixth Avenue and G Street, shows exciting and adventurous artists, even if they lack broad commercial appeal. **Artique,** 2 blocks north at 314 G St., is Anchorage's oldest gallery and has a much larger selection. Half of the gallery is given over to big oils and other gorgeous originals; the other half is chock-full of prints, less-expensive ceramics, and some mass-produced and/or corny stuff. At Fifth and G, **Aurora Fine Arts** carries more pottery, prints, and gifts.

7 Nightlife

THE PERFORMING ARTS

To find out what's happening, pick up a copy of Friday's edition of the *Anchorage Daily News* for the "8" section, which includes event listings and information on the club and arts scene. Their website, www.adn.com/weekend, allows you to check the calendar and listings from afar, or on days other than Friday.

Tickets.com (© **800/478-7328**), of Concord, California, is the main ticket agency. For a list of current events, go to their site and search under

"Anchorage." They have box offices at the Anchorage Center for Performing Arts and at Carrs grocery stores.

The arts season begins in the fall and ends in the spring, but traveling performers often come through in the summer as well. The **Anchorage Concert Association** (© 907/272-1471; www.anchorageconcerts.org) offers a fall-through-spring schedule of classical music, theater, dance, and other performing arts. **Whistling Swan Productions** (www.whistlingswan.net) promotes folk and acoustic alternative performers in intimate venues. The **Anchorage Festival of Music** (© 907/276-2465; www.festivalmusic.org) presents a classical music series in June. The **Anchorage Symphony** (© 907/274-8668; www.anchorage symphony.org) performs during the winter season. Anchorage also has lots of community theater, opera, and limited professional theater, including the experimental **Out North Contemporary Art House** (© 907/279-8099, www. outnorth.org), which produces local shows and imports avant-garde performers. Downtown, **Cyrano's Off Center Playhouse** (© 907/274-2599; www.cyranos. org), at Fourth Avenue and D Street, is a tiny theater with its own semiprofessional repertory company.

NIGHTCLUBS & BARS

For a fun, funny night out, nothing in town compares to **Mr. Whitekeys' Fly By Night Club,** on Spenard Road south of Northern Lights Boulevard (© 907/ 279-SPAM). The goateed proprietor, a consummate vulgarian, ridicules Anchorage in his crude, political, local-humor musical comedy shows, in which he costars with a fallen former Miss Anchorage. If you can laugh at dog poop, you'll love it. The summer show is at 8pm Tuesday to Saturday, with no smoking Tuesday to Thursday; live music follows Fridays and Saturdays. Tickets are $12 to $19, and reservations are necessary well in advance. They serve good food, too. (Believe me, I wrote this long before they started using a piece of my writing in one of their shows.)

Blues Central/Chef's Inn, 825 W. Northern Lights Blvd. (© 907/ 272-1341), is dedicated to showcasing the best blues performers available, virtually every night. Major names come through on a regular basis. Shows start at 9:30pm. They also serve excellent beef. The huge **Chilkoot Charlie's,** at Spenard Road and Fireweed Lane (© 907/272-1010; www.koots.com), has two stages for rock and one for swing. The place is huge, but can be claustrophobic when crowded, with low ceilings and a dark, roadhouse atmosphere. The **Long Branch Saloon,** 1737 E. Dimond Blvd. (© 907/349-4142), east of New Seward Highway, has live top-40 music every night and great burgers.

THE MOVIES

The most fun place to see a movie is the **Bear Tooth Theatrepub,** at 1230 W. 27th Ave. (© 907/276-4200; www.beartooththeatre.net), where you can watch art films and second-run movies while sipping craft brews and eating gourmet tacos, pizzas, and the like. There are several multiplexes in Anchorage playing all the current Hollywood output; check the *Anchorage Daily News* for listings. The closest larger theaters, the **Century 16** (© 907/929-FILM; www. centurytheatres.com) and the **Fireweed 7 Theater** (© 907/566-3328; www. regalcinemas.com), are a short cab ride away in midtown.

8 Out from Anchorage: Turnagain Arm & Portage Glacier

One of the world's great drives starts in Anchorage and leads roughly 50 miles south on the Seward Highway to Portage Glacier. It's the trip, not the

destination, that makes it worthwhile. The two-lane highway along Turnagain Arm, chipped from the foot of the rocky Chugach Mountains, provides a platform to see a magnificent, ever-changing, mostly untouched landscape full of wildlife. I've listed the sights in the style of a highway log, for there are interesting stops all the way along the road. It will take at least half a day, and there's plenty to do for an all-day excursion. Use your headlights for safety even in daylight and be patient if you get stuck behind a summertime line of cars—if you pass, you'll just come up behind another line ahead. Mileage markers count down from Anchorage.

Car rental is covered in "Getting Around," earlier. There are many bus tours that follow the route and visit Portage Glacier (see "Getting There: By Bus" under "Essentials," earlier). **Gray Line of Alaska** (© 800/544-2206 or 907/277-5581; www.graylineofalaska.com) offers a 7-hour trip that includes a stop in Girdwood and a boat ride on Portage Lake for $59 adults, $30 ages 2 through 11, twice daily in summer.

POTTER MARSH (Mile 117)   Heading south from Anchorage, the Seward Highway descends a bluff to cross a broad marsh formed by water impounded behind the tracks of the Alaska Railroad. The marsh has a boardwalk from which you can watch a huge variety of birds. Salad-green grasses grow from sparkling, pond-green water.

POTTER SECTION HOUSE (Mile 115)   Located at the south end of Potter Marsh, the section house was an early maintenance station for the Alaska Railroad. Today it contains offices of Chugach State Park, open during normal business hours, and, outside, a few old train cars and interpretive displays. Just across the road is the trailhead for the **Turnagain Arm Trail.** It's a mostly level path running down the arm well above the highway, with great views breaking now and then through the trees. You can continue 9 miles to Windy Corner, or break off where the trail meets the McHugh Creek picnic area and trailhead, about 4 miles out.

McHUGH CREEK (Mile 111)   Four miles south of Potter is an excellent state park picnic area and a challenging day hike with a 3,000-foot elevation gain to Rabbit Lake, which sits in a tundra mountain bowl, or to the top of 4,301-foot McHugh Peak. You don't have to climb all the way; there are spectacular views within an hour of the road.

BELUGA POINT (Mile 110)   The state highway department probably didn't need to put up scenic overlook signs on this pull-out, 1½ miles south of McHugh Creek—you would have figured it out on your own. The terrain is simply awesome, as the highway traces the edge of Turnagain Arm, below the towering cliffs of the Chugach Mountains. If the tide and salmon runs are right, you may see beluga whales, which chase the fish toward fresh water. Sometimes they overextend and strand themselves by the dozens in the receding tide, farther along, but they usually aren't harmed.

WINDY POINT (Mile 106)   Be on the lookout on the mountain side of the road for Dall sheep picking their way along the cliffs. It's a unique spot, for the sheep get much closer to people here than is usual in the wild; apparently, they know they're safe. Windy Point is the prime spot, but you also have a good chance of seeing sheep virtually anywhere along this stretch of road. If cars are stopped, that's probably why; get well off the road and pay attention to traffic, which still will be passing at high speeds.

Tidal Wave

Tides in Turnagain Arm rise and fall over a greater range than anywhere else in the world other than Nova Scotia's Bay of Fundy, with a difference between an extreme high and low of more than 41 feet. When the tide is rising, the water can grow deeper by as much as 7 feet an hour, or a foot of water every 8½ minutes. If your foot gets stuck in the mud, it takes less than an hour to drown (yes, that has really happened). Incredible as the normal rise of water is, what's even more breathtaking is when the tidal rush creates a 6-foot wall of water called a tide bore, a tidal wave that roars up Turnagain Arm twice a day.

You may also see windsurfers in the gray, silty waters of the Arm. They're crazy. The water is a mixture of glacial runoff and the near-freezing ocean. Besides, the movement of water that creates the huge tides causes riverlike currents, with standing waves like rapids.

INDIAN VALLEY (Mile 104)   Up the road by the Turnagain House restaurant is the **Indian Valley** trailhead, a gold rush era trail that ultimately leads 24 miles to the other side of the mountains. The path, while often muddy, rises less steeply than other trails along the Arm.

BIRD CREEK (Mile 100)   The **Bird Ridge Trail** comes first, at mile 102, a steep alpine climb rising 3,000 feet in a little over a mile. With the southern exposure, it's dry early in the year. The excellent state campground on the right, over the water, costs $10 a night. There is also a short trail, interpretive signs, an overlook, and a platform that makes fishing easier for people with disabilities. Pink salmon run late June to mid-August, silver salmon mid-July to August.

THE FLATS (Miles 96–90)   At Bird Point, where there is a large wayside, the highway descends from the mountainside to the mudflats. A fragment of bike trail parallels the highway for this 6 miles. At high tide, water comes right up to the road. At low tide, the whole Arm narrows to a thin, winding channel through the mud. Since the 1964 Good Friday earthquake, the Arm has not been navigable; before the earthquake, there was never much reason to navigate it. The first to try was Capt. James Cook, in 1778, as he was searching for the Northwest Passage on his final, fatal voyage of discovery (he was killed by Hawaiians later that year). He named this branch of Cook Inlet Turnagain Arm because the strength of the currents and shoals forced him to keep turning around.

TURNOFF TO GIRDWOOD (Mile 90)   This is the intersection with the road to Girdwood. The attractions of the town, covered below, are worth a visit, but the shopping center here at the intersection is not chief among them. Stop here for a simple meal, for a restroom break, or to fill your gas tank for the last time for many a mile.

OLD PORTAGE (Mile 80)   All along the flats at the head of Turnagain Arm are large marshes full of what looks like standing driftwood. These are trees killed by salt water that flowed in when the 1964 quake lowered the land as much as 10 feet. On the right, 9 miles beyond the turnoff for Girdwood, across from the former rail depot, a few ruins of the abandoned town of Portage are still visible, more than 35 years after the great earthquake. There is good bird-watching from the turnouts, but venturing out on Turnagain Arm's tidal mud carries the real risk of getting stuck in quicksandlike mud and drowning in the tide.

BIG GAME ALASKA WILDLIFE CENTER(Mile 79)   A 140-acre fenced compound on this glacial valley gives shelter to injured or orphaned deer, moose, eagles, owls, elk, bison, musk ox, bear, and caribou (© **907/783-2025;** www.biggamealaska.com). One moose is a movie star, but mostly the animals will spend their lives on display for visitors, who pick up a cassette tape and map and drive a short course looking at them in 3- to 5-acre enclosures. A large log gift shop is at the end of the tour. Admission is $5 for adults, $3 for military, seniors, and children 4 to 12, with a maximum of $20 per vehicle. In summer, it's open daily from 9:30am to 7:30pm; in winter, daily 10am to 5pm.

PORTAGE GLACIER (Take the 5.5-mile spur road at mile 78)   The named attraction at this, the most popular of all Alaska tourist attractions, has largely melted, receding out of sight of the visitor center. (The glacier you can see is Burns.) When the center was built in 1985, Portage Glacier was predicted to keep floating on its 800-foot-deep lake until the year 2020. Instead, it withdrew to the far edge of the lake in 1995. In 2001, the exhibits inside the **Begich–Boggs Visitor Center** were remodeled to focus on the Chugach National Forest as a whole, rather than just the glacier. The lakeside center is worth a stop.

Several short trails start near the center. Rangers lead nature walks on the one-quarter-mile, paved Moraine Trail up to six times a day. Another trail leads less than a mile to Byron Glacier, in case you're interested in getting up close to some ice. Always dress warmly, as cold winds are the rule in this funnel-like valley.

A **cruise boat** operated by **Gray Line of Alaska** (© **800/478-6388,** 907/277-5581 for reservations, or 907/783-2983 at the lake; www.graylineofalaska. com) traverses the lake to get right up to Portage Glacier on hour-long tours, ice conditions permitting. It costs $25 adults, $12.50 ages 2 to 12, and goes five times daily in summer, every 90 minutes starting at 10:30am. If this is your only chance to see a glacier in Alaska, it's probably a good choice, but if your itinerary includes any of the great glaciers in Prince William Sound, Kenai Fjords National Park, or the like, you won't be as impressed by Portage. You also can get a free view of the glacier by taking a left just before the visitor center and stopping at a pullout on the way to the Whittier Tunnel.

The best meals near Portage come from the **Tidewater Cafe** (© **907/783-2840;** eananook@aol.com), at the highway junction at mile 78.5. It's a

---

Gone But Not Forgotten

The **Begich-Boggs Visitor Center** at Portage Glacier is named for Hale Boggs, who was U.S. House majority leader, and Rep. Nick Begich, then Alaska's lone Congressmen, who disappeared together in a small plane during Begich's 1972 reelection bid. The most likely theory is that the small plane iced up in Portage Pass and then crashed into Prince William Sound near here. No trace was ever found, as with many other Alaskan planes that have simply flown off into oblivion. Begich was reelected anyway. His opponent, Republican Don Young, later won a special election and continues to serve as Alaska's lone congressman. Boggs's wife, Lindy, went on to serve out his term and eight more. Boggs's daughter, Cokie Roberts, is the famous broadcast journalist.

friendly diner with grand views of the valley; the menu includes homemade soup, pies, and cinnamon rolls as well as halibut, steaks, and good hot chili. There are no lodgings in Portage, but two **Forest Service campgrounds** are on the road to the visitor center, with 72 sites between them (more details are in the Chugach National Forest section in chapter 7). At the Williwaw Campground, there's also a place to watch red salmon spawning in mid-August, but no fishing.

9 Out from Anchorage: Girdwood & Mount Alyeska

Girdwood, 37 miles south of Anchorage, is proof that a charming little town can coexist with a major ski resort, as long as the resort goes undiscovered by the world's skiers. Girdwood still has a sleepy, offbeat character. Retired hippies, ski bums, a U.S. senator, and a few old-timers live in the houses and cabins among the big spruce trees in the valley below the Mount Alyeska lifts. They all expected a development explosion to follow the construction of an international resort here a few years ago, but it hasn't happened. That may not be good news for the Japanese investors in the resort, but it is for skiers and other visitors who discover this paradise. They find varied, uncrowded skiing through long winters, superb accommodations, and an authentically funky community.

The primary summer attractions are the hiking trails, the tram to the top of Mount Alyeska, and the Crow Creek Mine, described below. In winter, it's skiing. Mount Alyeska doesn't have the size of the famous resorts in the Rockies, but it's more than large and steep enough. Better still, it's uncrowded, half the mountain is above the tree line, and the snow lasts long. Olympian Tommy Moe trained here. Skiers used to tamer, busier slopes rave about the skiing here, with long, challenging downhills, no lift lines, and stunning views of the Chugach Mountains and glistening Turnagain Arm below.

ESSENTIALS

A **rental car** is the most practical route to Girdwood. If you will only ski, however, you may be able to take a shuttle; call the resort before you come, as these arrangements change frequently.

The **Girdwood Resort Association** maintains an extensive website at **www. girdwoodalaska.com**. For more information, check the Anchorage visitor information listed in section 1 of this chapter.

EXPLORING GIRDWOOD

Crow Creek Mine ⚓   This mine opened in 1898 and operated until 1940. The Toohey family has turned the paths and 14 small buildings into a charming tourist attraction where you can see the frontier lifestyle and watch rabbits and ducks wandering around. A bag of dirt, guaranteed to have some gold in it, is provided for gold panning, and you can dig and pan to get more if you have the patience for it, which few people do. Crow Creek Road, off the Alyeska Highway, is quite rough and muddy in the spring. Camping is $5 a night, with portable toilets.

Crow Creek Rd. (off the Alyeska Hwy.), Girdwood, AK 99587. © **907/278-8060.** $3 adults, free for children. Gold panning $5 adults, $4 children 11 and under. May 15–Sept 15 daily 9am–6pm.

Mt. Alyeska Tram ⚓ *Moments*   The tram isn't cheap, but I think it's worth it for anyone who otherwise might not make it to high alpine tundra during an Alaska trip. (In winter ride on your lift ticket, or in summer ride free with a meal at the acclaimed Seven Glaciers Restaurant at the top.) The tram takes

---

> **_Tips_ Ski Conditions**
>
> The weather is often different between the rain forest of Girdwood and dry Anchorage, so before heading down the road for a day of skiing you should check out the conditions. Snow conditions are at www. alyeskaresort.com/snow.html, or © **907/SKI-SNOW**. For visibility, check out the live cam at www.chairfive.com.

---

7 minutes in summer to get to the 2,300-foot level, where it stops at a station with an attractive but overpriced cafeteria. Whether or not you eat, the tram presents an opportunity for everyone, no matter how young, old, or infirm, to experience the pure light, limitless views, and crystalline quiet of an Alaskan mountaintop. Dress very warmly.

At The Alyeska Prince Hotel (see below). $16 adults ($12 Alaska residents), $15 ages 55 and older, $10 ages 8–17, $7 ages 7 and under. 7-min. summertime ride.

ACTIVITIES

For additional information about activities in this area, contact the **Alyeska Resort** (see "Accommodations," below).

SKIING   Mount Alyeska, at 3,939 feet, has 1,000 acres of skiing, beginning from a base elevation of only 250 feet and rising 2,500 feet. The normal season is early November to April, and it's an exceptional year when there isn't plenty of snow all winter. Skiing often lasts through Memorial Day weekend. The average snowfall is 560 inches, or 46 feet. Because it's near the water, the weather is temperate. Light is more of an issue, with the short days in midwinter.

There are 27 lighted trails covering 2,000 vertical feet on Friday and Saturday evenings mid-December to mid-March, but the best Alaska skiing is when the days get longer and warmer in the spring. There are nine lifts, including the tram. Two chairs serve beginners, with a vertical drop of around 300 feet. The other 89% of the mountain is geared to intermediate to expert skiers. It's a steep mountain, and the expert slopes are pretty extreme, but more than half is rated intermediate. Helicopter skiing goes right from the hotel as well.

An all-day lift ticket costs $45 for adults, $26 for ages 14 to 17, $19 for those ages 8 to 13 or over 60, and $7 ages 7 and under or over 70. Private and group instruction are available, and a basic rental package costs $22 a day for adults, $12 for age 13 and under or over 60.

There are groomed **cross-country trails** as well, and gear for rent, although the best Nordic skiing is in Anchorage.

A utilitarian **day lodge** with snack and rental counters is located at the front of the mountain, as is the **Sitzmark Bar,** a more comfortable place for a meal (burgers are around $8). The hotel is on the other side of the mountain, connected to the front by the tram to the top and beginner-level chair 7 (you can ski right from the door). It makes a quieter and more genteel starting point for day-trippers as well as guests, as it has its own rental counter and day lockers. There are several dining choices here and at the top of the tram (see "Accommodations," below).

A center operated by **Challenge Alaska** (© **907/783-2925** or 907/ 344-7399) allows skiers with disabilities to use the mountain, skiing down to the lift to start and back to the center at day's end.

SNOWMOBILING & DOG MUSHING   **Alaska Outdoor Adventures** (© **888/414-7669** or 907/783-7669; www.akadventures.com) offers snowmobile tours for raw beginners, with everything provided. Three-hour tours are $110 (an additional rider is about half off) and 5-hour tours to a glacier $175. This is a chance to get way back into the snowy mountains. They also offer hour-long dog sled rides; you ride in the sled, then get to drive the dogs yourself. It costs $60 adults, $45 children. The same firm does snowcat skiing.

HIKING   There are a couple of great trails starting in Girdwood. The Winner Creek Trail runs 5 miles through forest from behind the Westin Alyeska Prince Hotel to a roaring gorge where Winner Creek and Glacier Creek meet; it's muddy and snowy in the spring. The winter ski trail takes a separate route, through a series of meadows, to the same destination. The Crow Pass Trail rises into the mountains and passes all the way over to Eagle River, after a 26-mile hike that you can do in a couple of days. But you can make a long day hike of it to the pass and see the glaciers, wildflower meadows, and old mining equipment. The trailhead is up Crow Creek Road, off the Alyeska Highway.

ACCOMMODATIONS

Besides the resort hotel, there are plenty of condos and B&Bs in town. **Alyeska Accommodations,** on Olympic Circle (© **907/783-2000;** www.alyeska accommodations.com), offers condos, chalets, and houses. The **Girdwood Bed and Breakfast Association** (© **907/222-4858;** www.gbba.org) networks B&Bs in the area, inspected for quality.

Alyeska Prince Hotel ★★★   The Alyeska Resort's hotel is Alaska's best. The beauty of the building alone separates it from the competition. Studded with dormers and turrets, it impresses on first sight. Inside, sumptuous cherrywood and rich colors unite the welcoming common rooms and elegant guest rooms. Although not large, rooms have every convenience, and the maintenance and housekeeping are exceptional.

Five restaurants vie for attention, including the acclaimed Seven Glaciers, 2,300 feet above the lobby by tram on Mount Alyeska, which takes its name from its incredible view. The hotel's Japanese cuisine also has developed a reputation. The swimming pool is magnificent, with a cathedral ceiling and windows by the spa overlooking the mountain. As good as the property is, however, the location and activities alone make it worth visiting. To find such a place in a pristine mountain valley is a revelation. To spend a few days here skiing and swimming makes the rest of life seem too drab. One warning: On weekends, especially around holidays, families from Anchorage, like mine, descend on the hotel with noisy children. Couples would do well to come midweek.

1000 Arlberg Ave. (P.O. Box 249), Girdwood, AK 99587. © 800/880-3880 or 907/754-1111. Fax 907/754-2200. www.alyeskaresort.com. 307 units. Summer and Christmas $175–$435 double; $800–$1,600 suite. Winter $145–$280 double; $600–$1,100 suite. Extra adult $25; children stay free in parents' rm. AE, DC, MC, V. **Amenities:** 5 restaurants (steak and seafood, teppanyaki, sushi, café, cafeteria); 2 bars; pool; health club; spa; bike rental; children's programs; concierge; tour desk; shopping arcade; room service (7am–11pm); massage; baby-sitting. In room: TV w/pay movies, dataport, unstocked refrigerator, coffeemaker, hair dryer, iron, safe.

DINING

Chair 5 ★★ *Kids*   SEAFOOD/BURGERS/PIZZA   This is where Girdwood locals meet their friends and take their families for dinner, and it's also one of our favorites. One afternoon, Bob Dylan music accompanied a friendly game of pool while baseball played on the TV, and men with ponytails and beards sipped microbrews. Another evening, a guy in the entryway entertained the children with magic tricks and the waitress asked them to draw pictures to enter into a contest. The menu offered choices pleasing to each, including pizza, burgers, fresh fish, and entrees such as the rib-eye and mushroom fettuccine, a memorable meal for only $15.50. Every time we've gone, the food has been excellent and inexpensive, and the service friendly and quick.

Linblad St., town square. ℰ 907/783-2500. www.chairfive.com. All meals $6.50–$16.50; large pizza $15.50–$19.75. AE, MC, V. Daily 11am–midnight.

Double Musky Inn ⭐⭐ CAJUN   The ski-bum-casual atmosphere and rambling, cluttered dining room among the trees match the wonderful Cajun and New Orleans food in a way that couldn't have been contrived—it's at once too improbable and too authentic. Service is relaxed to a fault, and food takes a long time to arrive, but when it does it's flawless. The place isn't to everyone's taste, however; your senses can feel raw after the extreme noise, highly spiced food, and crowds, and parking can be difficult. Loud groups will enjoy it more than couples, and families don't really fit. They have a full bar.

Mile 3, Crow Creek Rd., Girdwood. ℰ 907/783-2822. www.doublemuskyinn.com. Main courses $18–$32. AE, DC, DISC, MC, V. Tues–Thurs 5–10pm, Fri–Sun 4:30–10pm. Closed Nov.

10 Out from Anchorage: The Matanuska & Susitna Valleys

For most visitors, the Mat-Su Valley, as the area is known, will be a place to pass through on the way to somewhere else—along the Glenn Highway to Valdez or the Alaska Highway, or up the Parks Highway to Denali National Park from Anchorage. But the area has some attractions of its own: the sweeping beauty of the Hatcher Pass area, the Matanuska and Knik glaciers, the Iditarod Sled Dog Race, and fishing in the rivers and dozens of lakes. This area isn't a destination for visitors with a limited schedule, but it is a worthy day trip from Anchorage or a refreshing stop between the state's major attractions.

The Matanuska Valley developed from the Great Depression until the 1970s as a farming area. The New Deal relocated colonists from other parts of the country to settle the prime growing land. But as transportation links improved both within the state and outside, farming in Alaska lost in competition with shipping goods in from Seattle. Farms became subdivisions, housing a population overflow from booming Anchorage, only an hour's drive south on the Glenn Highway. With its adamantly antigovernment philosophy preventing any community planning, Mat-Su's rush of development produced the worst kind of suburban sprawl. The area along the Parks Highway from its start at the Glenn Highway through Wasilla to Big Lake is plain ugly, the more profoundly so for the beauty it once contained.

The entire area is enormous. The county-level government, the Matanuska-Susitna Borough, covers an area about as large as West Virginia, vaguely defined by the drainages of the Matanuska and Susitna rivers. Most of the people live in the section near Anchorage, in and around the towns of Palmer and Wasilla. In 1996, the Big Lake area, west of Wasilla, was swept by the costliest forest fire in Alaska history, which destroyed more than 400 buildings and seared 35,000 acres of land. For the casual visitor, however, the fire's ravages are little evident.

The borough seat, **Palmer,** is a traditional small town built by the Depression-era colonists. One side of the quiet main street, Colony Way, is lined with little storefront businesses, hotels, and restaurants; the other is an open vista of the mountains. About 10 miles west, **Wasilla** was created mostly by a building boom of the 1970s and 1980s. The town exists primarily as a string of shopping centers along the Parks Highway, and you have to really look to find its center. The area is dotted with lakes surrounded by houses, where people water-ski and fish in the summer and snowmobile and run sled dogs in the winter. **Hatcher Pass** is in the Talkeetna Mountains on the north side of the Matanuska Valley. The Talkeetnas aren't as tall as other ranges, but they have the striking, rugged beauty of cracked rock. A historic mining site nestles in the pass, and it's a terrific place for summer hikes and winter recreation, including Nordic skiing and snowmobiling. **Talkeetna,** at the northern end of the Susitna Valley, is covered in chapter 8, on Denali National Park.

ESSENTIALS

GETTING THERE & GETTING AROUND   To get around the broadly spread valley you need a car and a map. The best map is by **Alaska Road and Recreation Maps,** widely available for $5.

VISITOR INFORMATION   The **Mat-Su Visitors Center,** Mile 35.5 Parks Hwy., HC 01 Box 6166J21, Palmer, AK 99645 (© 907/746-5000; www.alaska visit.com), is located on the right side of the Parks Highway just after the intersection with the Glenn Highway, as you enter the area from the south. It's open mid-May to mid-September daily from 8:30am to 6:30pm, closed in winter. The **Palmer Visitor Center,** in the center of town at 723 S. Valley Way, P.O. Box 45, Palmer, Alaska 99645 (© 907/745-2880; www.palmerchamber.org), has a small museum on the 1935 colony project that developed the valley. It's open mid-April to mid-September daily from 8am to 6pm, and in winter Monday to Friday 10am to 4pm.

 FAST FACTS: Wasilla & Palmer

Banks Several are on the Parks Highway in Wasilla and on Bailey Street or S. Colony Way in Palmer; they have **ATMs,** as do most shopping centers and grocery stores.

Hospitals The **Valley Hospital** is at 515 Dahlia Ave. in Palmer (© 907/746-8600). **West Valley Medical Campus** is at 950 E. Bogard Rd. in Wasilla (© 907/352-2800).

Internet Access Try **Mead's Coffee Shop,** 405 E. Herning Ave. (© 907/357-5633).

Police For nonemergency business, call the Palmer Police Department (© 907/745-4811), the Wasilla Police Department (© 907/373-9077), or, outside either town, the Alaska State Troopers (© 907/745-2131).

Post Office In Palmer at 500 S. Cobb St.; in Wasilla, on Main Street.

Taxes Palmer levies a 3% **sales tax;** Wasilla 2%. The Mat-Su Borough charges a 5% **bed tax** on top of the sales tax.

SPECIAL EVENTS   The **Iditarod Restart** (© 907/376-5155; www.iditarod. com), on the first Sunday in March, enlivens Wasilla at the end of a long winter. The Iditarod Trail Sled Dog Race starts officially in Anchorage the day before, but then the dogs are loaded in trucks and carried to Wasilla, where the trail becomes continuous to Nome. The restart is the real beginning of the race, and the area makes the most of it.

The **Alaska State Fair** (© 907/745-4827; www.akstatefair.org), held the 11 days leading to Labor Day, is the biggest event of the year for the valley, and one of the biggest for Anchorage; it's a typical fair, except for the huge vegetables. The good soil and long days in the valley grow cabbages the size of bean-bag chairs. A mere beach-ball-size cabbage would be laughed off the stage.

EXPLORING THE ROADS OF MAT-SU

A trip to Hatcher Pass combines one of the area's most beautiful drives, access to great hiking and Nordic skiing, and interesting old buildings to look at. If you're headed north to Denali National Park or Fairbanks, the rough, winding gravel road through Hatcher Pass to Willow makes a glorious alpine detour around the least attractive part of your drive. The road to the mine is scheduled for paving. Past the mine and skiing area, the road is open only in summer and is not suitable for large RVs. Just after the Parks Highway branches from the Glenn Highway, exit to the right on the Trunk Road and keep going north on Fishhook Road. From the Glenn Highway near Palmer, take Fishhook just north of town.

The **Independence Mine State Historical Park** ★★ (© 907/745-2827 or 907/745-3975; www.dnr.state.ak.us/parks/units/indmine.htm) takes in the remains of a hard-rock gold mine operation that closed down in 1943. Some buildings have been restored, including an assay office that's a museum and the manager's house that's a welcoming visitor center, while other structures sag and lean as picturesque ruins. It's undergoing a renovation, so many details about the park may change. At present, a $3 guided tour ($2 seniors, free under 10) leaves at 1:30pm and 3:30pm weekdays, plus 4:30pm weekends, or you can wander with the help of an excellent walking-tour map. The visitor center is open 11am to 7pm daily in the summer, but closes the week after Labor Day.

The high Talkeetna Mountains valley that the site occupies is idyllic for a summer ramble in the heather or for Nordic or Telemark skiing in winter. There are four hiking trails and two mountain-biking routes in the area—ask at the visitor center. One great hike is the 8-mile **Gold Mint Trail,** which starts across the road from the Motherlode Lodge on Fishhook Road and ends at the Mint Glacier, where you have to turn around to hike back.

The **Musk Ox Farm,** 2 miles north of Palmer on the Glenn Highway and left on Archie Road (© 907/745-4151), raises the beasts for research and breeding, and provides the underwool for Anchorage's Oomingmak cooperative (see "Shopping," earlier in this chapter). The farm offers tours 10am to 6pm daily in the summer season. It costs $8.50 for adults, $7 seniors and ages 13 to 18, and $5.50 ages 6 to 12.

The family-operated **Reindeer Farm,** in the Butte area (© 907/745-4000), raises reindeer as pets (as well as elk, moose, and deer) and puts them in harness each Christmas. The tour teaches all about reindeer and gives you an opportunity to feed them. Take the Old Glenn Highway to the intersection with Bodenburg Butte Road and Plumley Road, going toward the butte less than a mile. It's open 10am to 6pm daily in the summer. Admission is $5 for adults, $4 for seniors, and $3 for children 3 to 11. They offer horseback rides by appointment for $25 an hour. Across the road is a great short hike to the top of the butte.

The **Dorothy G. Page Museum,** at 323 Main St. in Wasilla (© 907/373-9071), preserves the early history of the area in a collection of pioneer buildings. Sometimes real valley pioneers are on hand to tell their stories. Several buildings are open for tours Tuesday to Saturday from 9am to 5pm in the summer, and the small museum is open Monday to Friday from 9am to 5pm in the winter as well. Admission is $3 for adults, $2.50 for seniors, and free for ages 12 and under.

The **Museum of Alaska Transportation and Industry** ⚸, off the Parks Highway at mile 47, west of Wasilla (© 907/376-1211; www.alaska. net/~rmorris/mati1.htm), is a paradise for gearheads and tinkerers. The volunteers have gathered every conceivable machine and conveyance—13 fire trucks and five locomotives, for example—and fixed up to running order as many as they can. An indoor museum displays their finished masterpieces, while the 15 acres outside are crammed with future projects—trains, aircraft, fishing boats, and mining equipment—all grist for memories and imagination. It's open summer 9am to 6pm daily, winter Tuesday through Saturday 9am to 5pm. Admission is $5 for adults, $4 for students and seniors, $12 for families, free under age 8.

GETTING OUTSIDE

The Alaska Public Lands Information Center, described in the Anchorage section, is the best place for advice on the outdoors. **Rafting** in the Mat-Su is described under "Getting Outside" in the Anchorage section, earlier in this chapter. The best **hikes, skiing,** and **snowmobiling** are at Hatcher Pass, described above.

DOG MUSHING   The Valley is a center of **sled-dog mushing,** both for racing and recreational dog driving. Raymie Reddington—son of Joe Reddington, father of the Iditarod race—offers trips up the Iditarod Trail, ranging from half an hour to several days, and will teach you to mush as well. The 30-minute ride is $35. Contact **Reddington Sled Dog Tours,** at mile 12.5, Knik–Goose Bay Road (© 907/376-6730). **Lucky Husky Mushing Adventures,** in Willow (© 907/495-6470; www.luckyhusky.com), offers summer and winter rides and lessons. They're located on the Parks Highway north of Willow. The summer rides include a kennel tour, and cost $24 per person. You bounce down the trail for about 5 minutes. Winter trips are, of course, longer and more authentic. For most of the ride you'll be in the basket, but they will also teach you to ride the runners, guiding the team with your voice. A 1-hour ride is $120; a half-day lesson with 2 hours on the sled costs $195.

FISHING   The Mat-Su area has many road-accessible salmon-fishing streams and stocked lakes, as well as plenty of campgrounds to get close to the fishing. Call the **Alaska Department of Fish and Game** (© 907/746-6300) for a recording with current fishing information, or check the web for most of what you need to know (www.state.ak.us/adfg, click "Sportfish," then "Region 2").

HIKING   For a challenging 7- to 10-hour climb, try 6,398-foot Pioneer Peak to the ridge below the top, with stupendous views. The trailhead is on Knik River Road, off Old Glenn Highway. See the description of Hatcher Pass, above for other choices.

HORSEBACK RIDING   This is farming country and one of the best places in the state for riding. Near Bodenburg Butte, **Flying G Ranch,** Palmer (© 907/745-7258), offers rides in beautiful country for $25 per person per hour, $15 for children under age 7. The reindeer farm, listed above, also offers rides.

ACCOMMODATIONS
ON THE GLENN HIGHWAY

If you're headed down the Glenn Highway, there are two good remote lodges near the **Matanuska Glacier,** 90 minutes from Palmer. In this remote area there is no TV and phones are in common rooms.

Majestic Valley Wilderness Lodge ⭐ This friendly lodge offers basic rooms with private bathrooms and serves excellent family-style meals to guests and others who reserve in advance. While most of the rooms are small and basic, they're set out of sight of the highway. A 30-kilometer network of exceptional cross-country skiing trails is groomed for diagonal or skate skiing—we enjoy going there for spring skiing weekends on the spectacular terrain. The lodge also offers guided skiing, snowmobiling, and hiking.

Mile 114.9, Glenn Hwy., HC03, Box 8514, Palmer, AK 99645. © **907/746-2930.** Fax 907/746-2931. www. majesticvalleylodge.com. 10 units, 2 cabins. $85 double; $105 cabin double. Extra adult $10; extra child ages 4–12 $5. AE, MC, V. **Amenities:** Restaurant; free-standing wood-fired sauna; activity desk.

Sheep Mountain Lodge ⭐ A historic roadside log lodge on a mountainside has become a center for cross-country skiing, with more than 15 kilometers of groomed trails. In the summer, hike and mountain bike over tundra mountains. Ten up-to-date log cabins with country decoration and sitting porches are arrayed on the hillside. They rent a sleeping bag bunkhouse, too. The cafe serves basic family style meals. A well-loved couple presides.

Mile 113.5, Glenn Hwy., HC 03, Box 8490, Palmer, AK 99645. © **877/645-5121** or 907/745-5121. Fax 907/745-5120. www.sheepmountain.net. 10 cabins. Summer $125 double, $15 each additional person. Winter $95 double, $10 each additional. Bunkhouse $60 for 6, $5 each additional. DISC, MC, V. **Amenities:** Restaurant; Jacuzzi; sauna.

AT HATCHER PASS

Hatcher Pass Lodge ⭐ *Finds* Nine lovely A-frame cabins with chemical toilets sit right in the treeless bowl of the 3,000-foot alpine pass, deeply buried in snow in winter and surrounded by heather in summer. Running water and showers are available in the fun, funky little restaurant. It's a great family place where, in the winter, you can ski out the front door on up to 20 kilometers of Nordic trails. Cabins lack phones, and there is no TV service.

P.O. Box 763, Palmer, AK 99645. © **907/745-5897.** Fax 907/745-1200. www.hatcherpasslodge.com. 9 cabins. $95–$115 cabin for 2. Extra person $15. AE, DC, DISC, MC, V. **Amenities:** Restaurant and bar; sauna; room service.

IN THE MID-VALLEY

Bed-and-breakfasts are a good choice in the valley. Besides those I've listed, some 30 others book through **Bed and Breakfast Association of Alaska, Mat-Su Chapter,** P.O. Box 873507, Wasilla, AK 99687 (© **800/401-7444** or 907/ 376-4461).

Agate Inn ⭐ *Value* The big, comfortable apartments and cottages come with full kitchens, while the attractive standard rooms have private bathrooms. Originally a home B&B, it's grown to take over two houses and an apartment building, and is still growing. They've even acquired a couple of reindeer for the guests' amusement and offer weeklong archaeological digs for college credit.

4725 Begich Circle, Wasilla, AK 99654. © **800/770-2290** or 907/373-2290. Fax 907/376-2294. www. agateinn.com. 9 units. $95 rm for 2; $125 apt for 2; $205 cottage. Rates include continental breakfast. AE, DISC, MC, V. **Amenities:** Coin-op laundry; fish cleaning and freezing. *In room:* TV, dataport and voice mail, microwave oven, fridge, coffeemaker, iron.

Best Western Lake Lucille Inn ★★ This well-run, attractive lakeside hotel right in Wasilla has the best standard hotel rooms in the valley. They're large and well appointed, and those facing the lake have balconies and a grand, peaceful view. Various kinds of boats can be rented for play on Lake Lucille, and flight-seeing trips take off right from the dock below the lawn. The **restaurant** is one of the best in the area, with a light, quiet dining room looking out on the water. It's open for three meals a day, with the beef and seafood dinner menu ranging from $15 to $38.

1300 W. Lucille Dr., Wasilla, AK 99654. ✆ 800/528-1234 for reservations, or 907/373-1776. Fax 907/376-6199. www.bestwestern.com/lakelucilleinn. 54 units. High season $139 double; $209 suite. Low season $89 double; $139–$159 suite. Extra person $10. AE, DC, DISC, MC, V. **Amenities:** Restaurant; bar; exercise room; Jacuzzi; sauna; room service during the day; coin-op laundry; small playground. *In room:* TV, dataport, coffeemaker, hair dryer, iron.

Colony Inn ★★ *(Finds)* This perfect country inn occupies a lovingly restored teacher's dormitory from the New Deal Colony Project, right in the middle of Palmer. The rooms feel fresh and new, yet at the same time wonderfully old-fashioned, with rockers and comforters but also Jacuzzi bathtubs and big TVs with VCRs. A large sitting room and a dining room downstairs are decorated with historic photographs that help tell the building's story. Excellent lunches and inexpensive dinners are served here during the summer at the **Inn Cafe** (✆ 907/746-6118). This is one of the best places to stay in Southcentral Alaska, and an incredible bargain.

325 E. Elmwood, Palmer, AK 99645. ✆ 907/745-3330. Fax 907/746-3330. 12 units. $85 double; $170 suite. Extra person $5. AE, DISC, MC, V. **Amenities:** Restaurant; free laundry use. *In room:* TV w/VCR, dataport.

DINING

Some of the best restaurants in the Valley are at the **Best Western Lake Lucille Inn,** the **Colony Inn,** and **Hatcher Pass Lodge,** described above.

In **Palmer,** don't miss **Vagabond Blues,** 642 S. Alaska (✆ 907/745-2233), a great little coffeehouse with hearty soups and breads, and folk, jazz, blues, and other performances on weekend nights. Sometimes nationally known acts show up in the very intimate setting.

In **Wasilla, Mead's Coffee Shop** (✆ 907/357-5633) is in the historic Tee-land's General Store, at 405 E. Herning Ave., by the Dorothy Page Museum (see above). They serve pastries, soups, salads, and vegetarian meals, roast their own coffee, and have entertainment on weekends, as well as Internet access. **The Windbreak Café** (✆ 907/376-4484), at 2201 E. Parks Hwy., uphill from Wal-Mart, is one of the area's most popular diners, with solid traditional food in an Alaska-theme dining room.

In **Big Lake, The Islander Lodge** (✆ 907/892-2892) sits on a tiny island in this large recreation lake north from Wasilla on the Parks Highway. In summer, guests call for a free 5-minute boat ride across; in winter, they drive on the ice; during breakup, the restaurant closes. The steak and seafood are fine, but it's the adventure that makes the experience. Call ahead for directions and to arrange for your boat. Plan to spend the whole evening.

7

The Kenai Peninsula & Prince William Sound

The Gulf of Alaska arcs at its northern edge, forming the rounded northern shore of the Pacific Ocean, a zone of great collisions. This is where the earth's tectonic plates collide, spewing forth froths of hot lava from dozens of volcanoes and fracturing and folding the earth with titanic earthquakes. Here the ocean's wildest weather hits mountains jutting miles high from the sea, growing immense prehistoric ice sheets and glaciers that carve the rock into long, deep, intricate fjords. The sea proffers prodigious biological wealth on these shores, including the salmon it unleashes into the rivers in furious swarms of life that climb over the mountains and into the Interior to spawn. Nature seems giant and superabundant in this magnificent arc of land and water.

Geography endowed this one stretch of coast with several of the world's great natural places. On the east, near Cordova, the **Copper River**'s immense, entirely unspoiled delta is the largest contiguous wetlands in the Western Hemisphere. On a day trip, you're immediately alone with flocks of rare, graceful waterfowl that congregate on shallow ponds surrounded by miles of waving grass. **Prince William Sound** is a vast protected sea of wooded, uninhabited islands and mammoth glaciers. On a summer day, I picnicked here with my family on the beach of a deserted bay next to a stream boiling with spawning salmon. A raft of hundreds of sea otters lolled on the sunny water before us while eagles circled low overhead. **Kenai Fjords National Park** takes in bays off the open ocean where the mountains soar a mile straight up from the water. Boats travel here among humpback, gray, and orca whales; spot otters, seals, and sea lions; and visit swarming colonies of puffins and other seabirds. The **Kenai River** harbors the world's biggest salmon, on the western side of the Kenai Peninsula; and on its southern tip, **Kachemak Bay** is like a miniature Prince William Sound. The bay has wildlife and glaciers and all that, but its shores also are dotted by tiny towns with lodges, art galleries on pilings, and some of Alaska's best restaurants.

The whole region is exceptionally accessible, by Alaska standards. The Kenai (*keen*-eye) Peninsula, in particular, is especially easy to get to without the expense and exhausting travel that can make much of the state difficult. Most of what you're looking for in Alaska lies along a few hundred miles of blacktop, within reach of a rental car and perhaps a tour boat ticket: glaciers, whales, legendary sportfishing, spectacular hiking trails, interesting little fishing towns, bears, moose, and high mountains.

People from Anchorage go to the peninsula for the weekend to fish, hike, dig clams, paddle kayaks, and so on, and certain places can get crowded. There's a special phrase for what happens when the red salmon are running in July on the Kenai and Russian rivers: *combat fishing*. At hot times in certain places, anglers stand elbow to elbow on a bank, each casting into his or her own 1-yard-wide slice of river, and still catch plenty of hefty salmon. The peninsula also exerts a powerful magnetic force on RVs, those road-whales that one finds at the head of strings of cars on the two-lane highways. During the summer, the fishing rivers, creeks, and beaches on the west side of the peninsula and the end of the Homer Spit can become sheet-metal cities of hundreds of Winnebagos and Itascas parked side by side. Often some local entrepreneur will be selling doughnuts or newspapers door-to-door.

Yet the decision is yours as to whether you spend time in the company of tourists. If the roadside fishing is hairy, hiking a little farther down the bank usually means you can be by yourself. In this chapter, I'll describe some towns of unspoiled charm, where you can kayak virtually from your room. Being alone is easy. You can paddle among otters in Resurrection Bay; tramp over the heather in Turnagain Pass; hike, bike, or ski one of the many maintained trails in Chugach National Forest. When you're ready to come back to the comforts of civilization, you'll find that some of the state's best restaurants and most interesting lodgings are here, too.

1 Exploring the Kenai Peninsula & Prince William Sound

THE TOWNS

Kenai, on Cook Inlet on the west side of the Kenai Peninsula, is the largest town in the region. Ten miles up the Kenai River, **Soldotna** is Kenai's twin, and together they form a unit with about a fourth of the Kenai Peninsula's population of 50,000. They're also the least interesting of the peninsula's communities. **Homer,** at the southern end of the peninsula, has wonderful art and character and lots of ways to get out on the water. **Seward,** on the east side, is smaller and quieter, but also charming and a gateway to Kenai Fjords National Park.

There are three major towns on Prince William Sound. **Valdez** is an oil town at the southern terminus of the trans-Alaska pipeline where tankers are loaded. **Cordova** is more attractive, a historic community on the eastern side of the Sound, with outdoor activities close at hand. **Whittier** is a grim former military outpost, but a convenient gateway to the protected fjords and glaciers of the western Sound.

GETTING THERE & GETTING AROUND

BY CAR Highways connect all the region's large towns, except Cordova. Like all of Alaska's main highways, they are paved two-lane roads. The Seward Highway runs south from Anchorage to the Kenai Peninsula. That route is described below. A new road completed in 2000, built in a railway tunnel, connects Whittier, on Prince William Sound, to the Seward Highway. The Glenn and Richardson highways reach from Anchorage to Valdez through Alaska's Interior. Stops along that route are described in chapters 6 and 9, and all the highways are summarized in chapter 9.

BY FERRY The ferry system connects Whittier with Valdez and Cordova. Valdez serves as the hub; ferries run straight between Cordova and Whittier only once a week. The ferry on these routes, the *Bartlett,* is one of the smallest in the fleet. There are no sleeping accommodations, but the boat is rarely very full and there is plenty of deck space and recliners for overnight runs. The restaurant has

The Kenai Peninsula & Prince William Sound

the best views you could hope for, and acceptable food (if short hours). The Chugach National Forest usually has rangers on board offering programs and interpretation in the observation lounge.

The ferry *Tustumena* connects Homer and Seward to Seldovia and Kodiak Island and the Aleutian Archipelago (covered in chapter 10), and also runs from Homer to Seldovia, with occasional trips to Seward, Whittier, and Prince William Sound villages as well. The schedule is not convenient for Seldovia, however, and it's much more practical to drive between Homer, Seward, and Whittier. Private passenger ferries serve the towns and remote sites around Kachemak Bay from Homer, described in sections 10, 11, and 12.

For details on the ferry system, see section 1 of chapter 5, call ℂ **800/ 642-0066,** or visit **www.state.ak.us/ferry**.

BY AIR Commuter airlines fan out from Anchorage to Kenai, Homer, Seward, Valdez, and Cordova; their names and phone numbers are given in the relevant sections of this chapter. You can also fly an Alaska Airlines jet to Cordova, with one flight from Anchorage every day, and another daily flight from Yakutat, Juneau, and Seattle. Scheduled and air-taxi services use these smaller towns as bases for the villages, carrying passengers, mail, and cargo, and flying to remote lodges and cabins for fishing or other outdoor activities. Valdez, Cordova, and Anchorage operators serve the Prince William Sound region. Kenai and Anchorage companies cover Cook Inlet and remote public lands such as Lake Clark National Park. Homer is the base for villages around Kachemak Bay and lower Cook Inlet bear viewing sites.

BY TRAIN The **Alaska Railroad** (ℂ **800/544-0552** or 907/265-2494; www.akrr.com) runs from Anchorage south to Seward and Whittier daily in the summer.

VISITOR INFORMATION

For information on the peninsula as a whole, contact the **Kenai Peninsula Tourism Marketing Council,** 150 N. Willow St., Kenai, AK 99611 (ℂ **907/ 283-3850;** www.KenaiPeninsula.org), which distributes a vacation planner (order at ℂ **800/535-3624**) and runs a website with information on businesses in the area; the staff will answer inquiries at the toll number during normal business hours. The **Kenai Peninsula Resource Network** (www.kenaipeninsula. com) is a commercial website with many links and useful information from all over the area.

See "Getting Outside," below, for outdoor information.

TRIP PLANNING & ITINERARIES

This is a busy area in mid-summer, and you will get the best places only by booking well ahead. Wilderness cabins book 6 months out, many lodges and better hotels for summer by late April. Mid-June to mid-August is the busiest, when finding any decent room can be difficult without reservations. Activities should be reserved a few weeks ahead; peak fishing times on the Kenai River earlier. Reservations are not necessary for camping. Leave plenty of time in your schedule around any boating or flightseeing excursions. Reputable tour and fishing operators simply won't go out in rough weather. If you have a backup day, you can spend the bad-weather day on shore and try again the next day. Check on weather-cancellation policies before you book any boat excursions.

I've arranged the sections below to match the ways you'll tour the region. First comes general information on the outdoors, next a road guide to the Kenai

Peninsula's Seward Highway, a section on Chugach National Forest, then the towns in the region in order of their distance from Anchorage. If you're considering taking a wildlife sightseeing cruise, compare the sections on Kenai Fjords National Park and the section on Whittier.

BY CAR   Driving is the easiest way to get around the region. One good itinerary of 10 days to 2 weeks would be to fly to Anchorage and spend a few days taking in the sights there (see chapter 6). Then rent a car to drive the Seward and Sterling highways, taking plenty of time to get down to Homer, perhaps with a couple of days to stop for fishing or hiking on the way in the Chugach National Forest, in Cooper Landing, or in the Kenai/Soldotna area. In Homer, plan several days, getting out on Kachemak Bay to Halibut Cove, Seldovia, or hiking and boating in Kachemak Bay State Park. Then drive back to Whittier and take the ferry through Prince William Sound to Valdez, seeing the glaciers and wildlife on the way. Spend a day in Valdez, then drive up the Richardson Highway, perhaps making a 2-day side trip to historic Kennecott in the spectacular Wrangell–St. Elias National Park (see chapter 9), then returning on the Glenn Highway to Anchorage or continuing up to Fairbanks, if there's time.

WITHOUT A CAR   A possible 10-day carless itinerary would be to fly to Anchorage, spend a few days sightseeing there, then take the Alaska Railroad to Seward, visiting Kenai Fjords National Park by boat, with a second day in Seward in case of bad weather or for a hike or fishing. Then return to Anchorage and fly to Cordova, taking the tour to Childs Glacier, visiting the quaint and welcoming town, and perhaps getting outdoors on a bike, a hike, a kayak, or a fishing excursion. Then take the ferry to Valdez, spend part of a day there, and board a tour boat to see Columbia Glacier and other glaciers in western Prince William Sound, either going all the way to Whittier and taking the train to Anchorage or returning to Valdez and flying back to Anchorage from there. If there's time left, use Anchorage as a base for further explorations.

GETTING OUTSIDE

The towns of the region are like beads strung along the laces of the highways; everything else is wilderness. You can find all the activities and isolation you seek here, yet the presence of the towns means that comfort is closer at hand than in other parts of Alaska.

Chugach National Forest takes in all of Prince William Sound and most of the eastern Kenai Peninsula. At 5.3 million acres, it's almost three times the size of Yellowstone National Park. Anywhere else but Alaska it would be a national park, and one of the largest and most spectacular, with some of the best sea kayaking, hiking, backpacking, wildlife watching, and scenery anywhere. General information, camping, and ideas on remote areas in the Chugach are covered below, in the Chugach National Forest section. Details about National Forest areas near towns are in the appropriate town sections.

Kenai Fjords National Park, taking in the outer edge and ice cap of the Kenai Peninsula's southern side, is incomparable in its remoteness, stark beauty, and abundance of marine wildlife. Access is though Seward. On the peninsula's western side, **Kenai National Wildlife Refuge** has Alaska's most accessible wilderness lake and river canoeing as well as extraordinary fishing, with access from roads near Soldotna. Each of those areas is covered in its own section, below.

Kachemak Bay State Park offers good sea-kayaking waters and wilderness hiking not connected to any road. The **Alaska Maritime National Wildlife**

Tips State Parks Cabin Reservation Tricks

Alaska's National Forest remote public cabins are getting famous (see the Chugach National Forest section, below), but Alaska's own state parks cabins remain our local secret. They are located in beautiful spots in several parts of the state, but most are in Southcentral Alaska—in this chapter, they're mentioned near Homer, Seward, and Valdez. Like the Forest Service cabins, it takes a hike, boat ride, or air taxi to get to the cabins, but once there you can experience the real Alaska all by yourself.

These cabins are popular, and getting reservations takes planning. Bookings open 6 months before the date of the stay, and the best dates can book up the morning they become available. If your reservation arrives early, they will hold it until the appropriate day and then hold a lottery if more than one applicant wants that date. You can reserve only in person, by mail, or by fax (you can ask questions by phone, but not apply). If you can't go in person, reserve by fax or the date you want could be booked in the 5 days it takes mail to get to Alaska. For fax reservations, you will need to use a Visa or MasterCard.

The reservations system doesn't make much sense and can be manipulated to your advantage. For example, you can reserve 7 days out from the first day that becomes available, giving you an exclusive shot at those days; cancel the earlier days if you don't want them (you can get a credit, not a refund). Also, the Fairbanks office opens at 9am, an hour earlier than Anchorage, so by sending your reservation there you beat out anyone using the Anchorage office (the Kenai and Mat-Su offices open at 8am, but accept only walk-in reservations).

The main information and reservations desk is the **Department of Natural Resources Public Information Center—Anchorage,** 550 W. Seventh Ave, Suite 1260, Anchorage, AK 99501-3557 (© **907/269-8400,** or 907/269-8411 TDD; fax 907/269-8901; www.dnr.state.ak.us/parks). In Fairbanks, it's 3700 Airport Way, Fairbanks, AK 99709 (© 907/451-2705, fax 907/451-2706). The website is the best source of information about the cabins, with a picture and description of each, a reservation form, and a real-time availability calendar. Cabins generally cost $50 a night.

Refuge protects the wildlife habitat of remote islands and seashores around the state. Both are covered in section 10 of this chapter, on Homer.

VISITOR INFORMATION The best and most central place to get outdoor information is the **Alaska Public Lands Information Center,** 605 W. Fourth Ave., Suite 105, Anchorage, AK 99501 (© **907/271-2737,** or 907/271-2738 TTY; www.nps.gov/aplic). Since most trips to the region start in Anchorage, the center makes a good first stop. You'll be able to get guidance from residents who have spent time in the places you'll be visiting, and there are exhibits on the wildlife and outdoor opportunities in the region—even maps showing where to find various species of fish. Land agencies present information on the whole state. Pick up books and maps here, too, and buy tickets for the ferries. Summer hours are daily 9am to 6pm, winter Monday to Friday 10am to 5:30pm.

Visitor centers particular to the Chugach National Forest, Kenai Fjords National Park, and Kenai National Wildlife Refuge are included in those sections below. Visitor centers for Kachemak Bay State Park and the Alaska Maritime National Wildlife Refuge are listed in section 10 of this chapter, on Homer.

2 The Seward Highway: A Road Guide

The Kenai Peninsula's main lifeline is the road down from Anchorage, a 127-mile drive to Seward on a good two-lane highway, most of it through public land without development or services. Highway 1, commonly known as the Seward Highway, is more than scenic—it's really a wonderful attraction in itself, designated a National Scenic Byway. There are excellent campgrounds and hiking trails all along the way in the Chugach National Forest, which I've covered in section 3 of this chapter.

The mileposts start in Seward. Here we count backward, since you'll likely start from Anchorage.

Mile 127–79   The highway begins at the south end of Anchorage, the only way out of town in that direction, and runs along Turnagain Arm 48 miles to the Portage Glacier. I've written about that spectacular portion of the drive in chapter 6 under section 8, "Out From Anchorage: Turnagain Arm & Portage Glacier."

Mile 79–75   Beyond the Portage Glacier turnoff, the road traverses the salt marshes to the south side of the Arm. These wetlands are good bird-watching grounds. The dead trees on the flats are left over from before the 1964 earthquake. The area was inundated in the quake, when the entire region—the Kenai Peninsula and Prince William Sound—sank 7 feet and moved several feet laterally. Besides being the second strongest earthquake ever recorded, the '64 quake moved more land than any other. People who were here tell of their surprise when the tide came far higher than they had ever seen it before in the days after the earthquake, until finally they realized that the land itself had sunk. Large parts of Homer, Hope, and Seldovia disappeared under the waves at high tide. Seward, Whittier, Valdez, and Kodiak were swept by destructive tsunami waves.

Mile 75–69   The highway steeply climbs through the spruce forest to the fresh, towering alpine terrain of the 1,000-foot-elevation **Turnagain Pass.** The vistas here are stupendous year-round.

Mile 69   If you find the meadow and tundra hard to resist for a walk, go ahead. Park at the pull-out with the toilets on the right side at the pass summit and amble off into the wildflowers (assuming the ground is dry when you're there). In the winter and spring, this is a backcountry skiing and snowmobiling paradise. Skiers go on the left side of the road and snowmobilers on the right. Always check with the Chugach National Forest (see section 3, below) for avalanche conditions first. An avalanche near here killed five riders in spring 1999.

Mile 69–57   The pass forms a divide, and now Granite Creek flows down toward the south. The road follows, falling back below the tree line of stunted spruce and then popping back up into sweeping views. Arcing to the northwest after the Granite Creek Campground, the highway follows another north-flowing river, Sixmile Creek.

Mile 57 and Hope Highway   The Hope Highway divides off to the north and west along Sixmile Creek while the Seward Highway continues south. Rafting

Why All the Dead Trees?

Whole mountainsides on the Kenai Peninsula and in Anchorage have turned brown. Thousands of dead trees topple in each windstorm. Homeowners all over the region have cleared treasured trees to reduce the fire danger from standing dead spruce.

The spruce bark beetle is to blame. Although a natural part of the forest ecology, the beetles' population exploded in the last 2 decades and swept across Southcentral Alaska, wiping out millions of acres of white spruce (the big Sitka spruces around Resurrection Bay and Prince William Sound aren't susceptible). The beetles bore under the outer bark layer to eat the trees' phloem, the soft inner bark that carries food manufactured in the needles down to the roots. The beetles reproduce in the tree, sending the next generation in flight in May and June in search of the next victim.

No one knows why spruce bark beetles have hit so hard now. Dry, stressed trees are more susceptible, because they lack thick-flowing sap that forces the beetles out of healthy trees. Perhaps the warmer weather blamed on global climate change is a factor. Or the blight may be caused by natural cycles. Whatever the cause, the landscape is changing for generations to come, as the forest begins its regenerative cycle. A natural succession of plants, shrubs, and deciduous trees will precede the eventual return of the white spruce. In the meantime, be careful with fire.

---

companies based in Anchorage use this wild stretch of water for some of their most challenging rides (see chapter 6).

A Side Trip to Hope   If you take a break, you'll find **Hope** at the end of the 17-mile Hope Highway. It's a charming gold rush era village with several hiking trails and the Porcupine Campground (the trails and campground are described in section 3, on Chugach National Forest). A few white frame buildings remain from the days when Hope was a gold-mining boomtown after a strike in 1895. Many of the newer buildings in the town center are quaint, too. Before the 1964 earthquake, the rest of the town used to stand where the creek gives way into a tidal meadow. Today, Hope's year-round population is 137. For information, contact the **Hope-Sunrise Community Library** (© **907/782-3121**), which is open daily in summer 11am to 4pm. The **Hope and Sunrise Historical and Mining Museum** is a one-room log cabin displaying historic objects and photographs. It's open noon to 5pm, Friday to Monday, Memorial Day to Labor Day.

If you need a room for the night in Hope, the best choice is the **Bear Creek Lodge** (© **907/782-3141**), with four pleasant cabins around a duck pond and two more on a creek for $85 double in summer. They share a bathhouse. The best place to eat in town is the **Discovery Café** (© **907/782-3274**), the community's hub and a place to get a generous burger and meet the beloved proprietor. The cafe burned to the ground in 1999 and was rebuilt almost entirely by volunteer labor, reopening in the summer of 2001.

Mile 57–46   The Seward Highway climbs steeply from the Hope Highway intersection, up the canyon of Canyon Creek, before leveling out above the tree line at about 1,400 feet elevation. Next come a series of alpine lakes in a narrow mountain valley.

Mile 46   The first business since the Portage Glacier, and the last for many miles, is on Summit Lake, the **Summit Lake Lodge,** at Mile 45.5 (© **907/ 244-2031**). It's a traditional log roadhouse that's been updated to house a comfortable and modern restaurant, open year-round from 8am to 10pm, and an hour earlier and later in the summer. The food is generally good, but service can suffer badly when weekend highway travelers overwhelm the staff. There's an ice-cream counter in the log gift shop by the lake. The six-room log motel has rooms for $80 double; they have private bathrooms, but lack TVs or phones. The canoeing photo in the color section at the front of this book was taken in this area; beware, however, of very cold water and sudden winds.

Mile 46–38   The highway continues through similar mountain terrain before descending into the trees again and branching at **Tern Lake.** There's a bird-watching platform with interpretive signs on the lake and, on the west end, a picnic area. This is a stirringly beautiful spot year-round, and a good place to get out and taste the fresh mountain air. To the right at the intersection, the Sterling Highway leads to Cooper Landing, Kenai, Soldotna, and Homer.

Mile 33–18   Trail Lake Fish Hatchery, on Upper Trail Lake, is on the first of a string of sparking mountain lakes that the road will follow for the next 15 miles.

Mile 30   The community of Moose Pass, with a population of 206, sits on the shore of Upper Trail Lake.

Mile 18–0   Down among the big spruces of the coastal forest, the highway comes to Seward.

3 Chugach National Forest: Do-It-Yourself Wilderness

I've lived near the Chugach National Forest all my life, but it wasn't until well into adulthood that I had seen all its parts and appreciated its vastness and variety. Still, I doubt I'll ever really know this seemingly infinite land.

Prince William Sound, just one of the National Forest's three parts, has 3,500 miles of shoreline among its folded islands and deeply penetrating fjords and passages. It would take a lifetime to really know all those cove beaches, climb all the island mountains, and explore to the head of every narrow bay under big rain forest trees. The **Copper River Delta** is another world entirely. Unlike the musty secrets of the Sound's obscure passages, the delta opens to the sky like a heavenly plain of wind and light, its waving green colors splashed by the airiest brushstrokes. It's another huge area: Just driving across the delta and back from Cordova takes most of a day. Finally, there's the western part of the national forest, on the **Kenai Peninsula.** This is largely an alpine realm. The mountains are steep, their timber quickly giving way to rock, tundra, and wildflowers up above. It's got remote, unclimbed peaks, but also many miles of family hiking trails, accessible fishing streams, and superb campgrounds. This is where you go in Alaska for multiday trail hikes.

The Chugach is managed primarily for recreation and conservation, although there is some logging, too. Visitors today may see large tracts of dead spruce and sometimes areas of cut timber, but these mostly are caused by a blight, the spruce bark beetle. The trees are cut in the forest and on private land to prevent fires in the standing deadwood. Logging in Prince William Sounds was slowed by the *Exxon Valdez* oil spill, when conservationists recognized the need to prevent further environmental damage to support recovery from the disaster. When Exxon was forced to pay $1 billion to a recovery fund, government trustees spent much of the money to buy back timber rights in the Sound and beyond to protect the trees. They bought 1,419 miles of coastline and almost as much land as is in all of Yosemite National Park. Still, that was only a sixth of the area the Chugach already encompassed.

ESSENTIALS

GETTING THERE & GETTING AROUND   There are many ways to the Chugach National Forest. For Prince William Sound, use Whittier, Valdez, or Cordova as gateways; for the Copper River Delta, go through Cordova. Trails and campgrounds on the Kenai Peninsula generally meet the Seward or Sterling highways, or spur roads from the highways. The individual town listings later in this chapter provide details on how to get there and into the national forest. Section 2, above, describes the Seward Highway.

VISITOR INFORMATION   The most central place for information on the national forest is the Alaska Public Lands Information Center in Anchorage, which is listed in full in section 1 of this chapter.

For general forest inquiries, you can also contact the **forest headquarters,** 3301 C St., Ste. 300, Anchorage, AK 99503 (© **907/271-2500;** www.fs.fed. us/r10/chugach).

The national forest also has three ranger district offices, where you can get up-to-date local information and personal advice: **Glacier Ranger District,** on Monarch Mine Road, near the Seward Highway off Alyeska Road, in Girdwood (© **907/783-3242);** **Seward Ranger District,** Fourth Avenue and Jefferson Street, in Seward (© **907/224-3374);** and **Cordova Ranger District,** Second and Browning streets, in Cordova (© **907/424-7661).** You can't reserve campground sites and remote cabins through these local offices—for that you must use the national system listed below under "Accommodations"—but you can call them with questions.

GETTING OUTSIDE
HIKING, MOUNTAIN BIKING & BACKPACKING
Alaska's best long trails lead through the mountain passes of Chugach National Forest, including historic gold rush trails and portions of the original Iditarod trail (the race doesn't use these southern portions). The Forest Service maintains **public cabins** on many of these trails, and in other remote spots reachable only with a boat or small plane. If the nights you need are available, you can use the cabins instead of a tent on a backpacking trip. Or make a cabin your destination and spend a few days there hiking or fishing.

I've covered trails near Cordova in section 14 of this chapter, and some shorter hikes are mentioned below with the campgrounds under "Accommodations." Also check for hikes outside the national forest in the town sections.

The best trail guide covering the peninsula is *55 Ways to the Wilderness* by Helen Nienhueser and John Wolfe Jr. (The Mountaineers, $13). *Kenai Pathways* (Alaska Natural History Association, $5) contains official guidance for 25 peninsula trails, which coordinate with numbers on the excellent **Trails Illustrated** plastic map (see "Fast Facts: Alaska," in chapter 2). Order from the publisher's website (www.AlaskaNHA.org) or buy at the Public Lands Information Center.

RESURRECTION PASS TRAIL   This gold rush trail begins 4 miles above the town of Hope (mentioned above in the preceding section on the Seward Highway) and runs over the top of the Kenai Peninsula to Cooper Landing (covered in section 7 of this chapter). It's a beautiful, remote, yet well-used trail for hiking, mountain biking, Nordic skiing, or snowshoeing; it rises through forest, crossing the alpine pass, and then descends again to a highway trailhead where you'll need to have transportation waiting. The 39-mile trail has eight public-use cabins, available for $35 to $45 a night. (See "Accommodations," below, for reservation information.) The cabins are well spaced to cover the trail in an easy 5 days, and those on lakes have boats for fishing. They are booked up well ahead winter and summer, but there are lots of good camping spots, too. The **Devil's Pass and Summit Lake trails** cut off from the Resurrection to the Seward Highway south of Summit Lake, shortening the route. The difficulty of doing the whole trail, by any of the entrances, is that you either need two cars or someone willing to drive you back to your starting point.

RUSSIAN LAKES TRAIL   This trail begins in Cooper Landing (covered in section 7 of this chapter), near the end of the Resurrection Pass Trail, and leads to three remote cabins and a series of lakes. There's excellent fishing and wildlife viewing (bears are common).

JOHNSON PASS TRAIL   The 23-mile trail climbs to a pair of lakes above the tree line at the 1,450-foot Johnson Creek Summit, tracing impressively narrow mountain valleys. The route, part of the Iditarod National Historic Trail, leads from near the Trail Lake Fish Hatchery, at mile 32 of the Seward Highway, to near the Granite Creek Campground, on the highway at mile 63. You need transportation at each end.

LOST LAKE TRAIL & PRIMROSE TRAIL   With their fields of alpine wildflowers and small lakes, these connected trails offer one of the most beautiful hikes in the area. Snow lasts until late in the season up top. The upper, northern trailhead is at the 10-site Primrose Campground, on vast Kenai Lake, 17 miles from Seward off the Seward Highway on Primrose Road. The trail rises through hemlock past a waterfall about 2 miles up (look for the spur to the right when you hear water), past an old mining cabin, and then through ever smaller trees and above the tree line. A Forest Service cabin is on a 2-mile spur about 11 miles along the 15.8-mile route. The south, Lost Lake trailhead is near Seward.

FISHING

The national forest contains some of the most famous, and crowded, fishing banks in Alaska, including the **Russian River,** near Cooper Landing, with its incredible run of red salmon in July and good fishing lasting into September. Easiest access is at the Russian River Campground, just west of the village. There are plenty of other roadside salmon streams and remote fishing rivers and lakes in the national forest where you can lose sight of other anglers. Some remote lakes have Forest Service cabins for rent on their shores, with rowboats. The Forest Service publishes information on these opportunities. See chapter 2 for other information sources.

SEA KAYAKING & BOATING

A variety of Prince William Sound tour boats are listed in the Whittier, Valdez, and Cordova sections of this chapter. Whittier is the best starting point, with the greatest number of choices.

All three communities also have operators offering sea-kayak rentals and guided outings of various lengths. The best sea kayaking is east of Whittier, an area of long fjords, calving glaciers, narrow passages, and Forest Service cabins, but to get out there you need a boat ride first—the waters right around Whittier aren't as interesting. The local sea-kayaking operators can help you arrange drop-off service. Cordova has more interesting waters right near town, so you can paddle right from the boat harbor. Those who haven't done much sea kayaking should only consider a guided trip; if you're a raw beginner, start with a day trip rather than an overnight.

For those who aren't up to paddling but don't want to ride a big tour boat, renting a skiff or chartering a small boat is a great alternative. Boat rental operators in the Valdez and Cordova harbors offer skiffs with fishing gear, and small-boat natural history tours go from Whittier. Exploring the Sound in a small boat is our family's favorite activity.

ACCOMMODATIONS
REMOTE CABINS
There is no more authentic Alaska accommodation than a pioneer cabin with a woodstove—a place to give you a better feel for the soul of a wild place. Chugach National Forest maintains more than 40 remote recreation cabins for rent to the public. This is simple shelter: Cabins don't have electricity or plumbing; you bring your own sleeping bags, cooking equipment, and other gear; and the cabin is only as clean as the last user left it. But no other room you can rent has a better location or greater privacy. Some cabins are along hiking and skiing trails, others on shores where boats and kayaks can pull up, and others on remote fishing lakes accessible only by floatplane. You can stay up to a week in most, with a summer limit of 3 days in the Resurrection Trail cabins.

The Forest Service prints a free listing of the cabins with short descriptions of each. The maps are rudimentary, so you will need a detailed map such as the Trails Illustrated plastic map mentioned in "Fast Facts: Alaska" in chapter 2, which shows cabin locations and names. Cabins rent for $35 or $45 a night, with most priced at $45 a night. Typically, the price of the cabin itself is not your major expense: You'll need a way to get there, either by plane, by boat, or by having a vehicle to drive to a trailhead and then hiking. If you're flying, contact flight services in the nearest town (listed in the sections below) to find out the cost *before* you book the cabin. Flight time is several hundred dollars an hour. You can rent the equipment you'll need at the businesses listed in the Anchorage section, but you should talk to a ranger first to get details about access and what to take.

The National Recreation Reservation Service (NRRS), operated by **Reserve America,** a company in upstate New York, handles the reservation system. Use them to book a cabin, but contact the ranger stations first to choose a cabin that is right for you and to find out what to expect. The easiest way to reserve a cabin is online at **www.reserveusa.com**, because you use its interactive maps and availability calendars to shop for open days at various cabins. To reserve by phone, call ✆ **877/444-6777,** 877/833-6777 TDD, or 518/885-3639 with toll from overseas. In the summer, the lines are open daily 8am to midnight eastern standard time; winter hours are daily 10am to 7pm. They take American Express, Discover, MasterCard, and Visa, or you can reserve on the phone and then pay by certified check. Campsites can be reserved starting 240 days ahead, cabins 180 days ahead.

CAMPGROUNDS
Forest Service campgrounds mostly have pit toilets and water from hand pumps, and roads usually are not paved. But some of these places are truly spectacular. I've listed them in order of distance from Anchorage, counting in reverse

direction on the Seward Highway mileposts. For information on campgrounds below mile 60, call the Seward Ranger District; for the others, call the Glacier Ranger District, in Girdwood (see "Visitor Information," above). Sites in a few of the following campgrounds, as noted, take reservations through the national system explained above.

Williwaw and Black Bear   These two campgrounds are next to each other near Portage Glacier, along a creek where you can watch spawning red salmon in mid-August (no fishing is allowed, though). Williwaw, one of the better-developed campgrounds in the national forest, with paved roads and pumped water, is intended primarily for RVs.

Mile 4, Portage Glacier Rd. (turn at mile 78.9 Seward Hwy.). Williwaw: 60 sites. $12 per night. Reservations accepted with additional fee. Black Bear: 12 sites. $12 per night.

Bertha Creek   This one's in the high country.

Mile 65.5, Seward Hwy. 12 sites. $10 per night.

Granite Creek   Near the Johnson Pass trailhead.

Mile 63, Seward Hwy. 19 sites. $10 per night.

Porcupine   This campground near the gold rush village of Hope is among the most beautiful in the Chugach National Forest. The sites are on a mountainside overlooking Turnagain Arm, five with sweeping ocean views. The thick trees make for privacy, but also mosquitoes. Bring repellent. Two good day hikes leave from the campground: The level 5-mile trail to **Gull Rock** makes a good family ramble, and with some effort you can scramble down to remote beaches along the way, where we've enjoyed a picnic. The **Hope Point Trail** is a stiff climb that rises 3,600 feet to expansive views. See "The Seward Highway: A Road Guide," earlier, for more on Hope.

At the end of the Hope Hwy. 24 sites. $10 per night.

Tenderfoot Creek   This pleasant campground lies across Summit Lake from the Seward Highway as it passes through a narrow mountain valley above the tree line. Campsites look out on the water from a peaceful, sunny hillside. The nearby Summit Lake Lodge, described in section 2 of this chapter on the Seward Highway, offers good meals, and is the only business for many a mile.

Mile 46, Seward Hwy. 27 sites.$10 per night.

Ptarmigan Creek and Trail River   Near the tiny towns of Moose Pass and Crown Point, the Ptarmigan Creek campground is at the trailhead for the trail to Ptarmigan lake, 4 miles away with only 500 feet elevation gain—a good place for a picnic or fishing for Dolly Varden char and rainbow trout. Trail River campground is a mile away and on the other side of the highway.

Mile 23, Seward Hwy. 16 and 63 sites, respectively. Reservations accepted, with additional fee. $10 per night.

Primrose   Another favorite, this lovely campground lies on the edge of Kenai Lake and at the base of the Primrose Trail to Lost Lake, one of the area's most beautiful (see "Getting Outside," above). This campground is the closest to Seward that has a sense of natural isolation.

Mile 17, Seward Hwy. 10 sites. $10 per night.

Russian River   This large, well-developed campground mainly serves fishermen pursuing red salmon on the river. When the fishing is good, the campground overflows and can be noisy. Overnight parking is $6. Reserve ahead.

Mile 52, Sterling Hwy., just west of Cooper Landing. Reservations accepted, with additional fee. 84 sites. 3 day limit. Flush toilets. $13 per night.

Cooper Creek   The campground is in Cooper Landing, with 10 sites right on the Kenai River.

Mile 50.7, Sterling Hwy. Reservations accepted. 26 sites. $10 per night.

Quartz Creek   This campground is on Kenai Lake, in Cooper Landing, with good lake and stream fishing.

Quartz Creek Rd., at mile 45 Sterling Hwy. 45 sites. Flush toilets, boat launch. $13 per night.

Crescent Creek   A couple of miles short of Cooper Landing, the campground is quieter and more secluded than the others, near the Crescent Lake trailhead. The 6.5-mile trail leads to the Crescent Lake Forest Service Cabin, where a boat is provided for grayling fishing.

Mile 3 Quartz Creek Rd., at mile 45 Sterling Hwy. $10 per night.

4 Whittier: Dock on the Sound

Whittier is Anchorage's portal to Prince William Sound. Although Anchorage itself is on Upper Cook Inlet, that muddy, fast-moving water is little used for recreational boating. Whittier, on the other hand, stands on the edge of a long fjord in the northwest corner of the Sound, whose clear waters are full of salmon, orcas, and otters, and bounded by rain forests and glaciers. In the past, getting to Whittier meant riding through a mountain by train. Now they're paved the railway tunnel, creating North America's longest highway tunnel and, in theory, putting Whittier only an hour away from the city. But only in theory, because the tunnel is also among the most inconvenient to use in North America. It has only one lane, and that lane must be shared by traffic and trains in both directions, and in between trips the tunnel often must be aired out. A wait is almost assured.

Whittier certainly has major advantages for visitors seeking to get out on the water. The water is calmer here than on excursions to Kenai Fjords National Park, so seasickness is rare, and the glaciers are even more numerous. One company's selling point is a "26-glacier cruise," all done in a day trip from Anchorage by rail and large tour boat (see below). Prince William Sound boats also see otters and sometimes whales; Kenai Fjords tours, on the other hand, more often see whales and see more birds. Sea kayakers also have great places to go from Whittier. Almost all of Prince William Sound is in Chugach National Forest, with its public-use cabins in lovely, remote spots on the shores (see the previous section).

There's little other reason to go to Whittier, unless you're on a quest to find the oddest towns in America. Most of the 182 townspeople live in a single 14-story concrete building with dark, narrow hallways. The grocery store is on the first floor and the medical clinic on the third. The rest of the people live in one other building. **The Begich Towers,** as the dominant structure is called, was built during the 1940s, when Whittier's strategic location on the Alaska Railroad and at the head of a deep Prince William Sound fjord made it a key port in the defense of Alaska. Today, with its barren gravel ground and ramshackle warehouses and boat sheds, the town maintains a stark military-industrial character. The pass above the town is a funnel for frequent whipping winds, it always seems to rain, and the glaciers above the town keep it cool even in summer. As one young town ambassador told me once when I was on a visit, "You're thinking, 'Thank God I

⌒ **Tips   Be Prepared**

An **ATM** is located at the liquor store near the boat harbor, but Whittier lacks a bank and other services, so bring what you need.

---

don't live here,' right?" The official boosters look more on the bright side: Having everyone live in one building saves on snow removal in a place that gets an average of 20 feet per winter. Kids don't even have to go outside to get to school—a tunnel leads from the tower to the school.

ESSENTIALS

GETTING THERE   By Car   Take the Seward Highway to the Portage Glacier Road, at mile 78.9 (48 miles from Anchorage). The road through the 2.8-mile long World War II rail tunnel to Whittier is only one lane and also accommodates trains, so you'll have to wait your turn. Get the schedule through the tunnel's website (www.dot.state.ak.us/whittiertunnel), its phone recording (© **877/611-2586** or 907/566-2244), or by tuning to 1610AM in Portage or 530AM in Whittier. Checking the schedule helps you avoid a wait of an hour or more if you miss the opening, but you can also wait if you arrive just on time, especially at peak weekend times, when there may be too many vehicles in line to get through during one open period. Here's a valuable tip: Choose the shortest line, not the line marked with the lowest number, as each line gets equal time for driving through. The tunnel closes altogether at night. Summer hours are daily 6am to 11pm; winter hours are shorter and changeable, so check ahead. The toll is $15 for cars; $40 for RVs, cars with trailers, or large vans. It is charged only going toward Whittier. Parking in Whittier is $5 a day. As I mentioned in the introduction, Whittier really isn't worth the trouble unless you are going out on the water.

By Train   If you plan to take a day trip on the Sound from a base in Anchorage—the way most people use Whittier—you can leave the car behind and take the train straight from the Anchorage depot. The large tour operators will book it for you when you buy your boat ticket. The **Alaska Railroad** (© **800/544-0552** or 907/265-2494; www.akrr.com) runs a daily train with self-propelled cars similar to those used on commuter lines timed to match the schedules of Prince William Sound tour boats. Unless you have planned an activity or tour on the water, however, you'll find the 6-hour stay in Whittier is too long to just hang around. The round-trip fare is $55, one-way $45, half price ages 2 to 11. The train ride is scenic and fun, but if there is more than one of you along, a rental car will save you money.

By Bus   Boat tour operators have buses that can save over the train. A regular summer bus daily except Monday meets the ferry in Whittier to and from Anchorage. **Grayline of Alaska**'s Alaskon Express (© **800/478-6388** or 907/277-5581; www.graylineofalaska.com) charges $25 one-way for adults, half price ages 2 to 11.

By Ferry   The **Alaska Marine Highway System** ferry *Bartlett* (© **800/642-0066**, or 800/764-3779 TDD; www.state.ak.us/ferry) makes a 7-hour run to Valdez several times a week, where you can drive north on the beautiful Richardson Highway, completing a circle back to Anchorage in 2 days or more. The fare is $76 for a car up to 15 feet long plus $64 for an adult passenger, with ages 2 to 11 roughly half price. The ferry also runs 7 hours once a week direct from Whittier to Cordova, or you can go by way of Valdez several times a week in roughly 15 hours. A Chugach National Forest ranger interprets the scenery in the observation lounge, and there is a serviceable little restaurant aboard. See section 1 of chapter 5 for more on the ferry system.

VISITOR INFORMATION   Contact the **Greater Whittier Chamber of Commerce,** P.O. Box 607, Whittier, AK 99693 (© **907/472-2461**); or you may have more luck calling the city clerk at © **907/472-2327.** There is no visitor center.

GETTING OUT ON THE SOUND

Whittier is the entrance to western Prince William Sound, at the end of one of many long, deep fjords where marine mammals and eagles are common. Glaciers at the heads of many of the fjords dump ice in the water for the tour boats that cruise from Whittier. Some small-ship overnight cruises start in Whittier, too; see chapter 4.

LARGE TOUR BOATS

Several companies with offices in Anchorage compete for your business for day-trip tours to the Sound's western glaciers. Besides having incredible scenery, the water is calm, making seasickness unlikely—for the queasy, this is a much better choice than Kenai Fjords National Park. Each operator times departures to coordinate with the daily Alaska Railroad train from Anchorage, described above, which means they have up to 6 hours for the trip. Some try to see as much as possible, while others take it slower to savor the scenery and wildlife sightings. Between the train and boat fare, expect to spend $175 per person for this day's outing, leaving Anchorage at 10am and returning at 9:30pm. You can save $10 to $15 a person and up to 3 hours by taking a bus the tour boat arranges instead of the train. If you have two or more people, you can save more by renting a car and driving. You will also have to buy some meals, although lunch is provided in the price on some boats.

Phillips' Cruises and Tours   The 26-glacier cruise travels the Sound on a fast three-deck catamaran, counting the glaciers as they go. The boat ride is 4½ hours, so if you use their bus you cut the total time from Anchorage to under 8½ hours.

519 W. Fourth Ave. Anchorage, AK 99501. © **800/544-0529** or 907/276-8023. www.26glaciers.com. $119 adults, $69 children under 12.

Major Marine Tours   This company operates a smaller, 149-passenger vessel at a slower pace than Phillips—they hit a mere 10 glaciers, but spend more time waiting for them to calve. They also put more emphasis on their food, which costs extra; the salmon or prime rib buffet is $12 for adults, $6 for children. Time on the water is 5 hours.

411 W. Fourth Ave., Anchorage, AK 99501. © **800/764-7300** or 907/274-7300. www.majormarine.com. $109 adults, $59 children ages 11 and under.

Prince William Sound Cruises and Tours   This Native-owned company offers a tour boat ride that crosses the sound from Whittier and Valdez, with sightseeing along the way, and a 6-hour glacier cruise from Whittier more like the other operators'. See section 13 of this chapter, on Valdez, for more on the company.

2525 C St., Ste. 3, Anchorage, AK 99503. © **800/992-1297** or 907/277-2131. www.princewilliamsound.com. Sightseeing cruise from Whittier $109 adults, $54 children under 12. Whittier to Valdez trip (one-way): $119 adults, $59 children.

SMALL BOAT TOURS

Instead of getting on a giant tour boat with a mob of people, you can go on a small boat with a local who you'll get to know as he shows off favorite places and lands on beaches to picnic and walk. If you see a whale or other point of interest, you stay as long or as short a time as you like. What you give up is the comfort of a large, tour-bus like vessel, and most small boats have a four-person minimum.

Sound Eco Adventures   Gerry Sanger is a retired wildlife biologist who spent years researching the waterfowl and ecology of Prince William Sound. Now he carries up to six passengers at a time on wildlife and glacier tours and does kayak drop-offs from his 29-foot aluminum boat, which has a large side door for wheelchairs and is perfect for landing on gravel beaches. He claims a 90% success rate on whale-watching trips, quite high for the Sound.

P.O. Box 707, Whittier, AK 99693. (© 888/471-2312 or 907/472-2312. www.SoundEcoAdventure.com. 10-hr. wildlife cruise $190 per person, 5½ hrs. $140, or charter the whole boat for $125/hr.

Honey Charters   This family runs small boats licensed for six to 10 passengers, specializing in personal tours, water transportation, and kayaker drop-offs. They operate with a minimum of 4 passengers; by paying the four-person minimum, you can have the boat to yourself. For larger groups, their new boat can carry 18 kayakers or 30 on a sightseeing cruise. They also book fishing charters.

On the Whittier waterfront (P.O. Box 708), Whittier, AK 99693. (© **888/477-2493** or 907/472-2493. www.honeycharters.com. 3-hr. cruise $99 per person, 6 hrs. $149 per person, 11 hrs. $199 person.

FISHING

More than a dozen charter fishing boats operate out of Whittier, the closest saltwater fishing to Anchorage, mostly targeting halibut but also getting salmon at certain times. The **Whittier Harbormaster** can give you a referral (© **907/472-2330**). **Bread N Butter Charters** (© **888/472-2396** or 907/472-2396; www.breadnbuttercharters.com) has been around for a while. They charge $185 per person for a day of fishing and have an office on the waterfront. Honey Charters, listed above under "Small Boat Tours," has a similar service.

SEA KAYAKING

Whittier is a popular starting point for kayak trips to beautiful and protected western Prince William Sound. Day trips for beginners paddle along the shore near Whittier, often visiting a bird rookery, or take a boat 5 miles from the harbor to Shotgun Cove and paddle back. Longer multiday trips go by boat to even more interesting waters where you can visit glaciated fjords and paddle narrow passages.

Several businesses compete in Whittier. **Alaska Sea-Kayakers** (© **877/472-2534** or 907/472-2534; www.alaskaseakayakers.com) offers 3- and 5-hour day trips, for $60 and $115, respectively, and paddles at Blackstone Glacier that begin with a charter boat ride, for $250. They also have an office in Whittier for kayak rentals. The **Prince William Sound Kayak Center** (© **877/472-2452** or 907/472-2452; www.pwskayakcenter.com) offers guided 3-hour trips starting at $55. They also take guests for day trips to Blackstone Bay, a place usually seen only on overnighters and escorted trips of 2 to 4 days. The 2-day trip is $140 per person, minimum two people. **Alaska Outdoor Adventures** (© **888/414-7669** or 907/783-7669; www.akadventures.com) is another good outfit. Experienced paddlers can plan their own trip, renting kayaks for out of Whittier for around $40 a day for a single, $60 double. Most people charter a boat to drop them off among the islands beyond the long, deep fjord in which Whittier is located. Honey Charters, listed above under "Small Boat Tours," offers a drop-off service. There are six Forest Service cabins in this idyllic area, which must be reserved 6 months ahead. Campsites are not easy to find on these rocky shores, which dropped in the 1964 earthquake, so do some research with the Forest Service or Alaska Public Lands Information Center in Anchorage before you go. For information and cabin reservations, see section 3, "Chugach National Forest: Do-It-Yourself Wilderness."

ACCOMMODATIONS & DINING

Most meals served in Whittier are for people grabbing a sandwich while waiting for a boat or otherwise passing through. The one standby that lasts year after year is the **Anchor Inn** (© **907/472-2354**), near the town's main building. It's a basic burger joint with a bar. The choice of inexpensive eateries in the shopping area at the east end of the boat harbor seems to change year to year, so I've given up listing them; you will certainly be able to find a sandwich or such.

June's Whittier Bed and Breakfast Condo Suites   These apartment units in the Begich Towers all have full kitchens and one, two, or three bedrooms. Some are nicely remodeled, with great views. The friendly hostess, June Miller, and her husband, Ken, also have a fishing charter and sightseeing business, Bread N Butter Charters, listed above.

P.O. Box 715, Whittier, AK 99693. © 888/472-2396 or 907/472-2396. Fax 907/472-2503. www. breadnbuttercharters.com. 7 units. $115–$220 double. Extra person over age 5 $15. AE, MC, V. **Amenities:** Coin-op laundry. *In room:* TV/VCR, kitchen.

5 Seward: Gateway to Resurrection Bay & Kenai Fjords

The main reason to go to Seward has always been Resurrection Bay and the access the port provides to Alaska. This agreeable little town started life as a place to fish and to get off the boat for Alaska, then continued as a place for Alaskans and visitors to get *on* boats and see the bay and Kenai Fjords National Park (described in section 6 of this chapter). With the growth of the cruise industry, Seward again is a place to get off the boat. Most cruises that cross the Gulf of Alaska start or end here, with their passengers taking a bus to or from the airport in Anchorage. That flow of people has brought a lot of tourist development to town, mostly of a quality that hasn't damaged the town's character.

Located by the broad fjord of Resurrection Bay, Seward is a mountainside grid of streets lined with old wood-frame houses and newer fishermen's residences. It's long been the sort of place where pedestrians casually wander across the road, hardly glancing for cars, for there likely won't be any, or, if there are, they'll be ready to stop. The growing tourism industry is bringing more traffic, but most of what's new has been good for the town. The largest addition, the Alaska SeaLife Center, is a research aquarium that's also open to the public. Combined with Seward's excellent ocean fishing, the national park, the wonderful hiking trails, and the unique and attractive town itself, the new center helps make Seward well worth a 2-day visit.

Seward's history is among the oldest in Alaska. The great Russian governor Alexander Baranof stopped here in 1793, named Resurrection Bay, and built a ship, which later sank, probably because Baranof's workers didn't have proper materials. Gold prospectors blazed trails from here to finds on Turnagain Arm starting in 1891, and in 1907 the army linked those trails with others all the way to Nome, finishing the Iditarod Trail. Today that route is discontinuous south

ACCOMMODATIONS ■
Best Western Hotel Seward **8**
Ballaine House
 Bed & Breakfast **5**
The Breeze Inn
 Restaurant and Motel **3**
Harborview Inn **4**
Hotel Edgewater **7**
Moby Dick Hostel **5**
Seward Windsong Lodge **1**

DINING ◆
Apollo Restaurant **6**
Ray's Waterfront **2**
Resurrection Roadhouse **1**

ATTRACTIONS ●
Alaska SeaLife Center **9**
Exit Glacier **1**
Seward Museum **5**

of Anchorage, but you can follow it through Seward and hike a portion of it through the Johnson Pass north of town (described above in section 3 of this chapter.

More relevant for current visitors and the local economy, the federal government took over a failed railroad-building effort in 1915, finishing the line to Fairbanks in 1923. Until the age of jet travel, most people coming to the main part of Alaska arrived by steamer in Seward and then traveled north by rail. The train ride to Anchorage, daily during the summer, is still supremely beautiful.

ESSENTIALS
GETTING THERE By Car See section 2 of this chapter, on the Seward Highway, for how to make the spectacular 127-mile drive down from Anchorage. All major car-rental agencies are represented in Anchorage.

By Bus The **Seward Bus Line** (© **907/224-3608** in Seward or 907/563-0800 in Anchorage; www.sewardbusline.com) makes one trip daily, year-round, starting in Seward and going to Anchorage and back; the fare is $35 one-way. They'll pick up and drop off passengers anywhere on route and, for an extra $5, take you to the airport.

The Park Connection (© **800/208-0200** or 907/245-0200; www. alaskacoach.com) connects Seward with Anchorage, Talkeetna, and Denali National Park with buses daily in each direction. The fare is $41 from Anchorage, $100 from Denali, half off under age 12.

By Train   The train ride between Anchorage and Seward is one of miraculous beauty. The **Alaska Railroad** (© **800/544-0552** or 907/265-2494; www. alaskarailroad.com) offers passenger service from Anchorage and back daily in summer. The route is even prettier than the highway, passing close by glaciers and following a ledge halfway up the narrow, vertical Placer River gorge, where it ducks into tunnels and pops out at bends in the river. The landscape looks just as it did when the first person beheld it. The railroad's young guides are well trained and provide an accurate and not overly verbose commentary. The fare is $55 one-way, $90 round-trip; children ages 2 to 11 half price. A rental car will almost always be cheaper, but the train ride is unforgettable. The railroad also offers packages that include a boat tour of Kenai Fjords National Park, but I advise against trying to get down from Anchorage, do the park, and return all in the same day—the 16-hour day is too much.

By Air   F.S. Air (© **907/248-9595** in Anchorage or 907/224-5920 in Seward) serves Seward from Anchorage twice a day for $69 one-way, $99 round-trip.

By Ferry   The ferry *Tustumena,* of the Alaska Marine Highway System (© **800/642-0066,** Seward terminal at 907/224-5485; www.state.ak.us/ferry), three times a month connects Seward with Valdez (11 hours to the east), with stops by reservation in the Prince William Sound Alaska Native village of Chenega Bay, and Kodiak (14 hours to the southwest). The adult passenger fare for Valdez is $58, Kodiak $54; ages 2 to 11 are about half price. Leaving from Homer cuts off more than 4 hours to Kodiak. Once a month in summer, the *Kennicott* travels from Juneau across the Gulf of Alaska to Valdez and then Seward. The $166 fare is a bargain, but it takes 50 hours. The terminal is at the cruise ship dock, on the outside of the small-boat harbor.

GETTING AROUND   You can easily cover downtown Seward on foot, although a little help is handy to get back and forth from the boat harbor. If it's not raining, a bike may be the best way. **Seward Mountain Bike Shop** (© **907/ 224-2448**), in a railcar near the depot at the harbor, rents high-performance mountain bikes and models good for just getting around town, plus accessory equipment. A cruiser is $12 half day, $19 full day. The **Chamber of Commerce Trolley** runs every half hour from 10am to 7pm daily in summer; it goes south along Third Avenue and north on Ballaine Street, stopping at the railroad depot, the cruise-ship dock, the Alaska SeaLife Center, and the harbor visitor center. The fare is $2 per trip, or $4 to ride all day. **Independent Taxi** (© **907/ 224-5678**) is one of the cab companies.

VISITOR INFORMATION   The **Seward Chamber of Commerce,** P.O. Box 749, Seward, AK 99664 (© **907/224-8051;** www.sewardak.org), has four visitor centers. The one on the right side of the Seward Highway as you enter town is open year-round (summer 8am–5pm Mon–Fri, 9am–5pm Sat, 9am–4pm Sun; winter closed weekends). Summer-only centers are at the Small Boat Harbor, downtown in an old Alaska Railroad car at the corner of Third Avenue and Jefferson Street, and in a kiosk on the cruise-ship dock. They can give business information and last-minute help finding a room.

In addition to these town information sources, the **Kenai Fjords National Park Visitor Center** is covered in section 6, later in this chapter. For contacts for the Chugach National Forest, see section 3.

SPECIAL EVENTS   The **Fourth of July** is the biggest day of the year in Seward, when the whole town explodes with visitors, primarily from Anchorage. Besides the parade and many small-town festivities, the main attraction is the

Mount Marathon Race, run every year since it started as a bar bet in 1915. The racers go from the middle of town straight up rocky Mount Marathon to its 3,022-foot peak, then tumble down again, arriving muddy and bloody at the finish line in town. Binoculars allow you to see the whole thing from town, including the pratfalls of the runners on their way down.

The **Silver Salmon Derby** starts the second Saturday of August, although the peak of silver season comes later. The chamber of commerce visitor centers can provide information.

 FAST FACTS: **Seward**

Bank **First National Bank of Anchorage** is at 303 Fourth Ave. **ATMs** can be found in the Eagle Quality Center grocery store at Seward Highway mile 2, and in the Alaska SeaLife Center, among other places.

Hospital **Providence Seward Medical Center** is at 417 First Ave. (*©* **907/ 224-5205**).

Internet Access Free at the **Seward Public Library,** Fifth and Adams.

Police For nonemergency situations, call the **Seward Police Department** (*©* **907/224-3338**) or, outside the city limits, the **Alaska State Troopers** (*©* **907/224-3346**).

Post Office At Fifth Avenue and Madison Street.

Taxes **Sales tax** is 5%. The **room tax** totals 9%.

GETTING OUTSIDE
Here I've described things to do out of Seward other than the national park, which includes the fjords and Exit Glacier. See section 6, "Kenai Fjords National Park," later in this chapter, for that information.

BOATING & SEA KAYAKING
Miller's Landing, at Lowell Point 3 miles south of town (*©* **907/224-5739;** www.millerslandingak.com) is a good place to know about if you intend to spend any time outdoors around Seward. The website is outstanding. They have a campground (described below), a boat launch with skiffs and sea kayaks for rent, sea-kayak lessons and tours, and fishing charters with experienced skippers. Skiffs rent for $65 for 4 hours; kayaks are $45 a day single, $55 double, $10 less after the first day; guided kayaking day trips are $47 to $179. Their kayak lessons are an unbelievable value: 4 hours of instruction, then a 3-hour guided paddle to salmon-choked (in season) Tonsina Creek, and then you keep the kayak until 10pm, all for $50. In the little bait shop and grocery store, a wood-stove burns and a coffee pot fuels ongoing discussions on fish and boats. The guys here will teach you how to fish for salmon and send you out on your own or on a guided charter. A water-taxi operation charges flat rates to get to remote beaches and public cabins around the bay or the national park, for sea kayakers or those who just want to get off on their own ($30 one-way to Caines Head, $250 round-trip to the park service cabin in Aialik Bay; children under 10 half price).

Sunny Cove Sea Kayaking (*©* **800/770-9119** for reservations, or 907/ 224-8810; www.sunnycove.com) offers day trips suitable for beginners as part of the Kenai Fjords Tours trips to its Fox Island, and day trips and multiday trips into the fjords themselves (see the Kenai Fjords National Park section later). On a budget, you also can take one of their tours right from Seward. They've earned a good reputation in more than 5 years of operation. They launch from Lowell Point, following the shore toward Caines Head State Recreation Area, where you can see sea otters, seabirds, intertidal creatures, and the salmon in Tonsina Creek. Three-hour paddles are $59; 8-hour trips are $125. A trip to Fox Island is more expensive but comes with a fjords boat tour, so it comes out roughly the same.

Book **sailing charters** on Resurrection Bay through the central agencies that are listed under "Fishing," below. The waters are beautiful, but it's a different experience than sailing in the Lower 48—if there's any wind, it's quite chilly.

FISHING
Seward is renowned for its saltwater silver salmon fishing. The silvers start showing up in the bay in mid-July and last through September. You can catch the fish from shore, from Lowell Point south of town, or even near the boat harbor, but your chances of success are far greater from a boat. I prefer small, six-passenger boats because you can get to know the skipper better and use that contact to learn more about fishing. If your party has the whole boat, you can control where it goes, perhaps adding whale-watching or sightseeing to the day. The going rate for a guided charter, with everything provided, is around $150 per person for salmon, or $170 for halibut (boats have to go farther for halibut). Andrew Mezirow, a marine biologist and diver for the SeaLife Center, can tell you about the bay while finding fish on his large, comfortable boat; his business is **Crackerjack Sportfishing Charters** (© **907/224-2606**; www.outdoorsdirectory. com/akpages/crackerjack). There are many others, mostly booked through central charter agencies, which make life simpler for visitors. **The Fish House,** located at the Small Boat Harbor, books charters, sells and rents ocean-fishing and spin-casting gear, and carries some fly-fishing supplies. For charters, reserve ahead at P.O. Box 1209, Seward, AK 99664 (© **800/257-7760** or 907/ 224-3674; www.thefishhouse.net). See "Boating & Sea Kayaking," above, for details on the much less expensive option of renting your own skiff and fishing without a guide.

HIKING
There are several excellent hiking trails near Seward. You can get a complete list and directions at the Kenai Fjords National Park Visitor Center (see the next section).

The **Mount Marathon Trail** is a tough hike to the top of a 3,000-foot mountain. The route of the famous Mount Marathon footrace is the more strenuous choice, basically going straight up from the end of Jefferson Street; the hikers' route starts at the corner of First Avenue and Monroe Street. Either trail rises steeply to the top of the rocky pinnacle and the incredible views there. Allow all day, unless you're a racer; in that case, expect to do it in under 45 minutes.

The **Caines Head State Recreation Area** (www.dnr.state.ak.us/parks/units/ caineshd.htm) has a 7-mile coastal trail south of town. Parts of the trail are accessible only at low tide, so it's best done either as an overnight or with someone picking you up or dropping you off in a boat at the far end—the Miller's Landing water taxi, mentioned under "Boating & Sea Kayaking," above, offers this service for $30 adults one-way, kids half price. The trail has some gorgeous views, rocky shores, and a good destination at the end (a promontory with the concrete remains of a World War II gun emplacement and bunker at Fort McGilvray). Three campsites are at Tonsina Point, 2 miles in, and a state park public-use cabin is 2 miles farther (see "Accommodations," below; and "State Parks Cabin Reservation Tricks," in section 1). At North Beach, 6½ miles from the trailhead, are two camping shelters, a ranger station, and trailheads to the fort, South Beach, and the 3-mile Alpine Trail. It's a beautiful and interesting hike. The trailhead is south of town on Lowell Point Road; pull off in the lot right after the sewage plant, then cross the road through the gate and follow the dirt road a bit until it becomes the actual trail. Stop at the Kenai Fjords National Park Visitor Center at the boat harbor for tide conditions and advice.

SLED DOG MUSHING

The dog-driving Seavey family, including the four boys (one is a Junior Iditarod champ), shows off their kennel off Exit Glacier Road in Seward and offers rides in summer and, for groups, in winter. A summertime ride on wheels isn't exactly the real thing, but you'll get a feeling for the dogs' amazing power and intelligence. The 75-minute tour costs $34 for adults, $15 for children 11 and under. Husky puppies are available for cuddling, too. They call their company **IdidaRide** (© **800/478-3139** or 907/224-8607; www.ididaride.com).

ATTRACTIONS IN TOWN

Besides the Alaska SeaLife Center (see below), most of Seward's attractions are of the modest, small-town variety. Explore downtown with the help of a **walking-tour map** provided by one of the visitor centers.

The **Iditarod Trailhead,** on the water just east of the SeaLife Center, is where pioneers entered Alaska. Walk along the paved path from there to the park, beach, and campground. The broken concrete and twisted metal you see on the beach here are the last ruins of the Seward waterfront, which was destroyed by a tsunami wave in the 1964 earthquake. The campground turns into an RV and tent city in the summer—at times a loud and rowdy one, unfortunately. Sometimes you can see sea otters swimming just offshore. During silver salmon season, in August and September, it's possible to catch them casting from shore here, although your chances are far better from a boat (see "Fishing," above).

The **Seward Museum,** at Third and Jefferson (© **907/224-3902**), is a charming grandma's attic of a place, with clippings, memorabilia, and curiosities recalling town history, painter Rockwell Kent, and the ways of the past. Admission is $3 for adults, 50¢ under age 18, and it's open during the summer, daily from 9am to 5pm.

The steep-roofed **St. Peter's Episcopal Church** is a delightful little chapel under the mountains at First Avenue and Adams Street. Go inside to see the mural in the front of the church, which shows what the Resurrection would have looked like if it had happened in front of Seward locals in the 1930s.

Alaska SeaLife Center ★★★   The center is a serious research institution and a superb aquarium of creatures from the nearby Alaska waters. You may have seen puffins diving into the water from a tour boat; here you can see what they look like flying *under* the water. Seabirds, harbor seals, and sea lions reside in three large exhibits that you can see from above or below. There are some smaller tanks with fish, crab, and other creatures, and a touch tank where you can handle starfish and other tide-pool animals. *Exxon Valdez* oil-spill settlement winnings from Exxon and federal grants built the center and an exhibit updates the status of spill-damaged populations of birds and marine mammals. The center is not as large as a big-city aquarium, however, and you're not likely to spend more than an hour or two here. Programs for kids and adults happen all day: To make the most of the admission price, call ahead so you can catch a program that interests you.

301 Railway Ave. (P.O. Box 1329), Seward, AK 99664. (© 800/224-2525 or 907/224-6300. www.alaskasealife. org. $12.50 adults, $10 children 7–12, free for children 6 and under. May–Aug daily 8am–8pm, Oct–Mar 10am–5pm, Sept and Apr 9am–6pm.

SHOPPING

Stop at the **Resurrect Art Coffee House Gallery,** at 320 Third Ave., in an old church. It's a coffeehouse and gathering place showing local fine art. The **Bardarson Studio,** 1317 Fourth Ave., at the boat harbor (www.bardarsonstudio. com), is a large gallery specializing in watercolor prints by Dot Bardarson and many other artists and has a wonderful, welcoming attitude. There's a children's cave under the stairs and a place to sit upstairs with videos and reading matter. Downtown, at 221 Fourth Ave., **Starbird Studio** (www.starbirdstudio.com) is another artist-owned gallery, in this case focusing on work by local artists. The **Resurrection Bay Galerie,** 500 Fourth Ave. (alaskafinearts.com), shows oils of wildlife and other Alaskan themes in a lovely old shingled house downtown—no prints, only originals.

ACCOMMODATIONS

Connections Seward (© 907/224-2323; www.alaskasview.com) is a hotel and B&B booking agency, and also books some tours and charters. The website has an impressive search function for B&B lodgings. You can get a list of B&Bs from the Chamber of Commerce Visitor Centers.

A friendly family runs the **Moby Dick Hostel,** at 423 Third Ave. (© 907/ 224-7072; www.mobydickhostel.com). They charge $16.50 for a bunk, $45 for private hostel rooms, and $60 for kitchenette rooms. They've been renovating and have made it a nice place.

Ballaine House Bed and Breakfast (Finds) This 1905 house near the center of downtown is a classic B&B, with its wooden floors, large living room, and tall, double-hung windows. It's on the National Historic Register and the town walking tour. Marilee Koszewski has decorated with antiques and handmade quilts and provides raincoats, binoculars, and other gear for outings, and will even do laundry. She also will give back the commission on boat bookings, normally amounting to a discount of up to 20%. Some of the rooms are small, they don't have phones or TVs, and all bathrooms are shared.

437 Third Ave. (P.O. Box 2051), Seward, AK 99664-2051. (© 907/224-2362. www.superpage.com/ballaine. 4 units, none with private bathroom. $77 double. Extra person $15. Rates include full breakfast. No credit cards. No smoking. No children under 10. **Amenities:** Tour booking; laundry service.

Best Western Hotel Seward (★) These rooms, while overpriced, are large, solid, and attractively decorated, and have good amenities. Many have big bay windows. The view rooms on the front go for a premium, although the view is largely blocked. A two-story log cabin on a cliff over the boat harbor also is part of the hotel (www.cliffcabin.com). With a large hot-tub spa on the magnificent deck, it's one of the most beautiful and luxurious accommodations in Alaska, renting for $339 a night.

221 Fifth Ave. (downtown), Seward, AK 99664. (© 800/222-2261 in Alaska only; 800/528-1234 national reservations; 907/224-2378. Fax 907/224-3112. www.bestwesternseward.com. 38 units. High season $192–$224 double. Low season $49–$99 double. Extra person $10. AE, DC, DISC, MC, V. In room: TV/VCR, fridge, coffeemaker.

The Breeze Inn ⭐ Located right at the busy boat harbor, this large, three-story, motel-style building offers good standard accommodations with the most convenient location in town for a fishing or Kenai Fjords boat trip. Rooms are frequently renovated. An annex building has excellent upscale rooms, some overlooking the harbor.

1306 Seward Hwy. (P.O. Box 2147), Seward, AK 99664-2147. © 888/224-5237 in Alaska only, or 907/224-5237. Fax 907/224-7024. www.sewardalaskamotel.com. 86 units. Summer $119–$160 double. Winter $49 double. Extra person $10. AE, DC, DISC, MC, V. **Amenities:** Restaurant (cafe); bar; courtesy van. *In room:* A/C, TV, fridge, coffeemaker, hair dryer, iron.

Harborview Inn ⭐⭐ The energetic and hospitable Jerry and Jolene King take great pride in their inn, which grew from their bed-and-breakfast operation. And for good reason, as theirs are among the most attractive rooms in town, with lots of light, Mission-style furniture, and Tlingit art based on Jolene's tribal crest. The rates are good by Seward standards, and the location, midway between the Small Boat Harbor and downtown, puts both within long walking distance. Two two-bedroom apartments on the beach along Ballaine Avenue rent for the same price as the motel rooms; they're a great bargain, and perfect for families. There's a nice one-bedroom apartment in the main section, too.

804 Third Ave. (P.O. Box 1305), Seward, AK 99664. © 888/324-3217 or 907/224-3217. Fax 907/224-3218. www.SewardHotel.com. 35 units, 3 apts. High season $129 double. Off-season $59 double. Extra person $10. AE, MC, V. *In room:* TV, dataport, coffeemaker, hair dryer.

Hotel Edgewater ⭐ Standing right across the street from the ocean and the SeaLife Center, this new hotel has excellent views from two sides and a three-story atrium inside. The rooms have fine furniture and the hotel has upscale amenities, but they've cut more corners than you would expect in a top-end place (lower-quality carpeting and wall coverings and a utilitarian elevator, for example), so it misses having an opulent feel. A few rooms that face the atrium instead of the bay rent for $99 double, a super value.

200 Fifth Ave. (Box 1570), Seward, AK 99664. © 888/793-6800 or 907/224-2700. Fax 907/224-2701. www.hoteledgewater.com. 76 units. High season $99–$245 double. Low season $65–$105 double. Extra person $10. Rate includes continental breakfast. AE, DISC, MC, V. **Amenities:** Exercise room; hot tub; sauna; concierge; tour desk; courtesy car; fish freezing. *In room:* TV/VCR, dataport, coffeemaker, hair dryer.

Seward Windsong Lodge ⭐ This hotel is the only one at Kenai Fjords National Park with a national park atmosphere: The 12-unit buildings with mock log siding and the large restaurant and lobby building sit among spruce trees on the broad, unspoiled valley of the Resurrection River. The rooms are crisp and new; all have two queen beds and rustic-style furniture. The Cook Inlet Region Native corporation, which owns this hotel, also owns Kenai Fjords Tours and other excellent properties; their **Alaska Heritage Tours** is listed in chapter 2 under "Escorted Tour or Do It Yourself?" The hotel restaurant, the **Resurrection Roadhouse,** is reviewed below, under "Dining."

½ mile, Exit Glacier Rd. (Mailing address: P.O. Box 93330, Anchorage, AK 99509-3330.) © 888/959-9590 or 907/265-4501 in Anchorage, or 907/224-7116 in Seward. www.sewardwindsong.com. 108 units. High season $179 double. Low season $129 double. Extra person over age 11 $10. AE, DISC, MC, V. Closed Oct–Apr. **Amenities:** Restaurant; tour desk; courtesy van. *In room:* TV/VCR, electric kettle.

CAMPING & CABINS

The Alaska State Division of Parks maintains two cabins for rent in the **Caines Head State Recreation Area,** south of town, and two in **Thumb Cove State Marine Park,** across the bay from Caines Head (see "State Parks Cabin

Reservation Tricks," in section 1 of this chapter). It's possible to hike to the Caines Head cabins (see "Hiking," above), but to get to Thumb Cove you need a boat. Water taxi service is offered for $50 round-trip by Miller's Landing (see "Boating & Sea Kayaking," earlier).

Cabins in Chugach National Forest and Kenai Fjords National Park are mentioned in those sections, as are the campgrounds in the national forest, but the national park's only campground is quite handy to Seward: near the **Exit Glacier,** at mile 8.5 of Exit Glacier Road. The campground is on willow-covered, gravely ground that plants haven't yet reclaimed from the retreating ice. Sites are far apart and almost completely private, but lack any amenities—no picnic tables, fire grates, or anything. Use the food lockers and central cooking to keep bears away. Snow lingers into early June. There is no fee for the 10 sites, and reservations are not taken. It's open for tents only and has pit toilets and hand-pump water.

The beachfront **Iditarod Trailhead Park** on Ballaine Avenue is acceptable for RV camping, but too crowded and exposed for tenters. Noise and drinking persist, despite a crackdown, and anyway the atmosphere is like a refugee camp on busy weekends. The fee is $6 for tents, $10 for RVs, and showers are $2. It's operated by the city parks and recreation department (© **907/224-4055**). A quieter but poorly developed town campground is **Forest Acres Park,** among the spruce trees at Hemlock and Sealion Boulevard, just off Seward Highway near the Army Recreation Center. Fees are the same.

More appealing is **Miller's Landing,** on Lowell Point Road south of town (© **907/224-5739;** www.millerslandingak.com). Sites are along the beach or among large spruce trees. Electric hookups are $25 a night, tent sites $20; rustic sleeping-bag cabins are $35 to $55; and cabins with kitchens and bathrooms run $65 to $100. There's lots to do here; see "Boating & Sea Kayaking," earlier.

DINING

There are various places at the harbor to grab a sandwich or other quick meal on the way out to sea; they change too frequently for me to include here. Downtown, the **Ranting Raven,** at 228 Fourth Ave. (© **907/224-2228**), is a great little coffee shop and gift shop serving pastries, sandwiches, and soup.

Apollo Restaurant ⭐ MEDITERRANEAN/SEAFOOD   This is a surprisingly good small-town restaurant. Seward families come back for a menu that includes anything they might want: Greek and southern Italian cuisine, seafood, pizza, and much more. But the cuisine is far more sophisticated and expertly turned out that you expect in such a place, especially the seafood dishes, and the service is fast and professional. The dining room, with many booths, takes the Greek theme as far as it will go—I especially enjoyed the miniature Doric columns.

229 Fourth Ave. © 907/224-3092. Main courses $10–$18. AE, MC, V. Daily 11am–11pm.

Ray's Waterfront ⭐⭐ STEAK/SEAFOOD   The lively, noisy dining room looks out from big windows across the small-boat harbor, with tables on terraces so everyone can see. The atmosphere is fun and the consistently good food is just right after a day on the water. While not perfect, it's more nuanced than the typical harborside place; the seafood chowder is great. Most important, they don't overcook the fresh local fish—and that's really all you can ask. Full liquor license.

At the small-boat harbor. © 907/224-5606. Main courses $16–$25; lunch $6–$15. AE, DC, DISC, MC, V. 15% gratuity added for parties of 6 or more. Daily 11am–11pm. Closed Oct to mid-Mar.

Resurrection Roadhouse ⭐ ALASKAN SPECIALTIES/PIZZA   This place has an annual shift in quality typical of seasonal restaurants, which explains why my Seward friends don't go much, but I've had wonderful food here. The menu includes fish, venison, and ribs smoked in-house. They also serve hand-thrown gourmet pizzas. The dining room lacks life, but the mountain view is great and there's plenty of space. The bar's collection of Alaska craft brews on tap is exhaustive. I temper my recommendation, however, as it may change by the time you read this.

⁷/₁₀ mile Exit Glacier Rd. ℂ 907/224-7116. Main courses $9–$24; lunch $9–$13. AE, DISC, MC, V. Daily 7am–2:30pm, 5–10pm. Closed mid-Oct to mid-Apr.

6 Kenai Fjords National Park

Kenai Fjords is all about remote rocks, mountains, and ice that meet the ocean, and the animals that live there. The park comprises 670,000 acres of the south coast and interior land mass of the Kenai Peninsula. The shore here is exposed to the Gulf of Alaska, whose wild, recurrent storms beat against the mountainous shore unbuffered by any landmass from the vast expanse of the Pacific to the south. Wildlife thrives, but humans have never made a mark.

The geological events that formed this landscape are vast and ongoing. The steep, coastal mountains amount to a dent in the earth's crust where the northward-moving Pacific tectonic plate is colliding and adding land to the southern edge of Alaska. As the Pacific plate pushes under Alaska, it slams islands onto the Alaska coast, then pulls them under into the molten layer down below. These mountains are shrinking measurably as the earth swallows them up. The 1964 earthquake dropped them by 6 to 8 feet. As your boat rides past the park's small, sharp, bedrock islands, now populated by seabirds and marine mammals, you are seeing the tips of ancient peaks that once stood far above the shore like today's coastal mountains.

The park's history has barely started. The fjords became a park only in 1980. In 1976, when the National Park Service explored more than 650 miles of coastline, including the park area, they didn't find a single human being. The same was true when geologists came in 1909. British explorer Capt. James Cook made the first maps of the fjords area in 1778, but the coast was too rugged and rocky for him to land. We don't know much about Native Americans who lived in the fjords. Scientists have found some areas where people lived, or at least had camps, but no one knows exactly who they were or what they were doing here. The earth, through earthquakes or glacial action, has erased most remains. Anthropologists call these people Unegkurmiut, and believe they were Alutiiq, Eskimos who lived on the Pacific coast, closely related to the Chugach people of Prince William Sound and the Koniag from Kodiak Island to the south. Those groups are still around; scientists are studying the Unegkurmiut and what happened to them from the little evidence they can find on the fjord's beaches.

The Natives probably never ventured inland over the impossibly rugged interior of the Kenai Peninsula, leaving its heart to be discovered in 1968, when the first mountain climbers crossed the Harding Ice Field, which covers most of the national park. **Exit Glacier** and all the glaciers of Kenai Fjords flow from this ice age leftover, which may be a mile thick. The ice field lies in a high bowl of mountains that jut straight out of the ocean to heights of 3,000 to 5,000 feet. When moisture-laden ocean clouds hit those mountains, they drop lots of rain and snow—up on the ice field 40 to 80 feet of snow falls each winter, with a water equivalent of 17 feet. Summer weather isn't warm enough to melt the snow at that elevation, so it packs down ever deeper until it turns into the hard, heavy ice of glaciers and flows downward to the sea.

The area's history finally got an ugly start in 1989, when the tanker *Exxon Valdez* crashed into a rock about 150 miles northeast of the park in Prince William Sound and spilled almost 11 million gallons of oil. Exxon did a poor job of catching the oil before it spread, and by the end of the summer the sticky, brownish-black muck had soiled beaches in the western Sound, across the fjords, and all the way to Kodiak Island and the Alaska Peninsula. More than 1,000 miles of shoreline were oiled to some degree, 30 miles in the park. Hundreds of sea otters and hundreds of thousands of seabirds were killed in the Sound and on the islands near the fjords. Nature scrubbed the oil off the rocks again, and you will see no evidence of it in the park today; but scientists say most of the affected species of birds and animals haven't come back completely. Nonetheless, you'll still see more wildlife on a boat ride here than anywhere else I know.

Exxon paid over $1 billion to the government in penalties for the oil spill, and that money has done a lot to help the area. Most of it was used to buy land in the spill area that otherwise would have been logged, including 35,000 acres of coastal land in the national park.

Most of the park is remote and difficult to reach. A large vessel, such as a tour boat operating out of Seward, is the only practical way for most people to see the marine portion of the park. That's not cheap or quick, and there are better destinations for people subject to seasickness. The inland portion is accessible only at Exit Glacier, near Seward.

ESSENTIALS

GETTING THERE Seward is the threshold to the park. Exit Glacier is 13 miles from the town by road; the Kenai Fjords National Park Visitor Center is at the Seward Small-Boat Harbor; and the tour boats that visit the park leave from Seward.

Many visitors try to see the park in a day, coming from Anchorage by train or road, touring the park by boat, then returning that evening. I do not recommend this. To really get to the park, you need to be on an all-day boat trip—most half-day trips barely leave Resurrection Bay and hardly see the park proper. More important, a lot of the visitors I saw riding the train back to Anchorage after a 16-hour marathon to Kenai Fjords were so tired they couldn't keep their eyes open for the extraordinary scenery passing by outside the train. A better plan is to spend a night in Seward and take in the full Kenai Fjords boat trip and Exit Glacier.

VISITOR INFORMATION At the **Kenai Fjords National Park Visitor Center,** Seward Small Boat Harbor (P.O. Box 1727), Seward, AK 99664 (© **907/224-3175;** www.nps.gov/kefj/), rangers answer questions and provide information on the all-important tour boats. They carry a good selection of books on Alaska natural history and occasionally show films. Call or drop by here for advice on Park Service cabins for rent in the fjords, guidance on a sea-kayaking expedition there, or information on places in the area to hike and trail conditions. They're open June to August daily from 8am to 7pm, and September to May Monday to Friday from 8am to 5pm.

ACCOMMODATIONS & CAMPING There are no hotels in the park; it's best to base yourself in Seward (see my recommendations earlier in this chapter). The **Exit Glacier Campground,** the only campground in the park, also is listed in section 5.

A free Park Service map shows the location of food lockers and hanging cables to keep your stuff away from bears in the kayaking waters of Aialik Bay and Northwestern Fjord. You can camp anywhere if you observe correct backcountry precautions. Send away for a packet of information from the park. They also rent out four **public-use cabins,** three in the fjords, reachable only by boat or floatplane. One is a mile from Exit Glacier, but is open only during the winter when the road is closed. It's accessible by ski, dogsled, or snow machine. Contact the park headquarters for a $35-a-day cabin permit, open for reservations starting January 2 each year.

SEEING THE PARK
SIGHTSEEING & WILDLIFE CRUISES

Kenai Fjords is essentially a marine park. On a boat tour, you'll see its mountains, glaciers, and wildlife. On any of the tours you're sure to see sea otters and sea lions, and you have a good chance of seeing humpback whales, orcas, mountain goats, and black bears. I saw all those on a recent trip to Aialik Bay. Gray whales come in the early spring and huge fin whales show sometimes, too. Birdwatchers will see bald eagles, puffins (both tufted and horned), marbled and Kittletz's murrelets, cormorants (red faced, pelagic, and double breasted), murres (common and thick billed), rhinoceros and parakeet auklets, and various other sea ducks, alcids, and gulls. The farther you go into the park, the more you'll see.

If you really want to see Kenai Fjords National Park and glaciers that drop ice into the water, the boat has to go at least into **Aialik Bay** to **Holgate Glacier. Northwestern Glacier** is even deeper in the park. Half-day Resurrection Bay cruises offer plenty of impressive scenery but do not get close to glaciers, have less of a chance of seeing whales, and see fewer puffins and other birds. The longest trips into the heart of the park proper encounter the greatest variety and number of birds and animals. If you're lucky with the weather, you can make it to the exposed **Chiswell Islands,** which have some of the greatest bird rookeries in Alaska, supporting more than 50,000 seabirds of 18 species. I've seen clouds of puffins swarm here. The day-long trips also allow more time to linger and really see the behavior of the wildlife. Whatever your choice, binoculars are a necessity; you may be able to rent them on board.

Prices are around $140 to go to Northwestern Glacier in Northwestern Fjord off Harris Bay, a 10-hour trip; $110 to go to Holgate Glacier in Holgate Arm off Aialik Bay, which takes 6 to 8 hours; and $60 to $70 for a 3- to 4-hour Resurrection Bay tour, which doesn't go to the national park at all. I have seen misleading publicity material from the tour operators, so ask exactly where the boat goes or get a map of the route. Children's prices are around half off.

Fares with each operator differ little, although you can sometimes get early season or web specials; instead shop for the destination, length of trip, food service, interpretation, and size or intimacy of the boat. Ask how much deck space there is outside so you can really see. What is the seating arrangement inside? How many passengers will be on board and how many crew members to answer questions? Is lunch provided, and what does it consist of? Another important point of comparison is if you have a ranger doing the commentary, or just the captain—some of these captains don't know when to shut up, and they can give inaccurate information.

Try to schedule loosely, so that if the weather is bad on the day you choose for your boat trip, you can wait and go the next day. If the weather's bad, you'll be uncomfortable, and the animals and birds won't be as evident, or the boat may not go out at all. If you pay up front to hold a reservation on a boat—

Tips It's Not Easy Being Green

An important factor in choosing your boat tour is your susceptibility to **seasickness.** To reach the heart of the park, vessels must venture into the unprotected waters of the North Pacific. Large, rolling waves are inevitable on the passage from Resurrection Bay to the fjords themselves, although once you're in the fjords, the water is calm. On a rough day, most boats will turn back for the comfort of the passengers and change the full-day trip into a Resurrection Bay cruise, refunding the difference in fare. Of course, they'd rather not do that, and the decision may not be made until the vessel is out there, often after many of the passengers are already vomiting over the side. If you get seasick easily, my advice is to stick to the Resurrection Bay cruise, or take a boat tour in protected Prince William Sound out of Whittier, where the water is smooth. In any event, ask about the tour company's policy on turning back and refunds, and take Dramamine *before* you leave the dock (once you're underway, it's probably too late to do any good).

probably a good idea in the busiest months—find out the company's refund policy.

Most operators offer packages with the Alaska Railroad and the SeaLife Center, which may save money, but make sure you have enough time to do everything you want to do in Seward. All have offices at the Small Boat Harbor in Seward. In addition to the large operators listed in full below, **Renown Charters and Tours** (© 907/272-1961; www.akol.com/renown) has smaller vessels, offering shorter, lower-priced cruises, and year-round operations. They can get you out on the bay for $49.

Kenai Fjords Tours　This is the dominant tour operator, with the most daily sailings and choices of destination. The main part of the operation uses 90- to 150-passenger vessels, some of which have forward-facing seats, like an airplane's. They're professionally staffed, but when the ships are crowded, the experience can be impersonal. The captain provides the commentary instead of a ranger. However, the same company also owns **Mariah Tours,** which operates 16-passenger vessels. Their trips are more spontaneous and go farther; the downside is that the smaller boats are less stable in the waves.

Most of the large Kenai Fjords vessels call on a lodge the company owns on **Fox Island,** in Resurrection Bay. It sits on the long cobble beach of **Sunny Cove,** where painter Rockwell Kent lived in seclusion with his son in 1918 and 1919 and produced the art that made him famous, as well as his classic book *Wilderness: A Journal of Quiet Adventure in Alaska* (Wesleyan University Press). It is an inspiring spot. The lodge itself stands on a narrow strip of land between the beach and a pond, which visitors overlook from large wooden decks. Boats stop for lunch of grilled salmon or a family style dinner, and some passengers spend the night. An overnight package on the island costs $220 per person, meals included. Half-day sea-kayaking paddles from the island are offered for day-trippers or overnight guests: $79 to $89 per person as an add-on for overnighters, or $149 to $169, including a Resurrection Bay tour boat ride for day-trippers.

At the Seward Small Boat Harbor and at 2525 C St., Ste. 405, Anchorage. © **800/478-8068,** 907/224-8068 in Seward, or 907/276-6249 in Anchorage. www.kenaifjords.com.

Major Marine Tours   This company pioneered first-class onboard dining and, at this writing, is the only cruise that brings along a park ranger to assure high-quality commentary, a decisive advantage in my judgment (after all, you're here for the park). Their boats are slower than some of the competitor's, so they don't make the long trip to Northwest Glacier; they either head into Aialik Bay to see Holgate Glacier or just tour Resurrection Bay around Seward. Instead of bringing sandwiches or stopping for a meal, they serve a fine-dining buffet of salmon and prime rib on board for $12 per person, $6 for children. The food is surprisingly good. While I like their table-seating arrangement to forward-facing seats, it can be an uncomfortable crush when the boat is crowded. Your seat is assigned, so there's no need to rush aboard or try to stake out your spot.

411 West Fourth Ave., Anchorage. (✆ **800/764-7300** or 907/274-7300, or 907/224-8030 in Seward. www. majormarine.com.

SEA KAYAKING

The fjords are calm yet rugged, intricate, and full of wildlife and soaring vistas. It's hard to imagine a better place for a sea-kayaking expedition. They also are extremely remote and very rainy, however, so a trip there is a poor choice for your very first outing. Experienced paddlers can rent kayaks and explore on their own, using the Park Service cabins for shelter (see below). I've listed the agencies that rent kayaks and offer guided trips and water taxis under "Boating & Sea Kayaking" in the Seward section, earlier in this chapter. One of them, **Sunny Cove Kayaking,** even has a kayaking day trip to Aialik Bay. They take guests out on a small charter boat for a wildlife tour, then you launch and paddle in front of the glacier. The price of $289 for the 1-day outing is not much more than you would pay for a separate boat tour and guided kayaking back in Resurrection Bay. For a visit where you get more of a feel for the place, spend a couple of days. Sunny Cove's 2-night trip costs $849.

EXIT GLACIER

When I visited Italy years ago, I got to the point where I thought I'd scream if I saw another painting of the Madonna. If your trip to Alaska is long, you may start to feel the same way about glaciers. But, although relatively small, Exit Glacier really is unique, and my family still enjoys visits there even as jaded life-long Alaskans. (And I've probably seen even more glaciers than Madonnas.)

You can walk close to Exit Glacier, see its brittle texture, and feel the cold, dense spires of ice looming over you. Cold air breathes down on you like air from an open freezer door. Approaching the glacier, you can see the pattern of vegetation reclaiming the land that the melting ice has uncovered, a process well explained by interpretive signs and a nature trail. At the same time, however, the area remains refreshingly primitive. The National Park Service's low-key presentation of the site makes it a casual, pleasant visit for a couple of hours (longer if you do a hike).

The easiest way to get to the glacier is to drive. The clearly marked 9-mile road splits from the Seward Highway 3.7 miles north of town. In winter, the road is closed to vehicles. If you don't have a car, van service is usually available; check with the visitor center to see who is currently offering service.

Following the road along the broad bed of the wandering Resurrection River, you'll see in reverse order the succession of vegetation, from mature Sitka spruce and cottonwood trees down to smaller alders and shrubs. It takes time for nature to replace the soil on sterile ground left behind by a receding glacier. As you get closer, watch for signs with dates starting a couple of centuries in the past; they mark the retreat of the glacier through time.

At the end of the road an entrance booth charges a **user fee of $5 per vehicle.** A simple **ranger station** and pit toilets are near the parking lot. **Ranger-led nature walks** start here on a sporadic schedule; check at the visitor center. The short **trail** to the glacier starts here. At the glacier, the trail splits: The steep route goes up along the side of the glacier, and the easy route runs on the flat gravel at its face.

One of the glacier's striking features is a high berm of gravel that fits around its leading edge like a necklace. This is a **moraine,** the glacier's refuse pile. The glacier gouges out the mountains with its immense, moving weight as new ice flows down from the ice field above and melts here. It carries along the rock and gravel torn from the mountain like a conveyor belt. This moraine is where the conveyor belt ends and the melting ice leaves the debris behind in a big pile. Probably without knowing it, you've seen hundreds of moraines all over North America, where the glaciers of the last ice age piled debris into hills, but this is the most obvious moraine I've ever seen, and it helps you understand how they work. Don't go beyond the warning signs; ice can fall off and crush you.

An all-day hike, 7 miles round-trip, climbs along the right side of the glacier to the **Harding Icefield**—the glacier gets its name for being an exit from that massive sheet. It's a challenging walk with a 3,000-foot elevation gain, but it's the easiest access I'm aware of to visit an ice field on foot. Because of snow, the trail doesn't open until late June or early July. The ice field itself is cold and dangerous, and there's an emergency shelter maintained by the Park Service. Don't trek out on the ice unless you know what you're doing. The Park Service sometimes guides hikes up the trail.

The **Resurrection River Trail,** in Chugach National Forest, begins from the road just short of the last bridge to the glacier. It's a pleasant day hike, with lots of wildflowers in the fall, or the start of a long hike deep into the mountains.

7 Cooper Landing: Road Meets River

The little roadside community of Cooper Landing, in a wooded mountain valley along Kenai Lake and the Kenai River, begins about 8 miles west of Tern Lake, where the Sterling Highway splits from the Seward Highway, and continues sporadically along the highway for about 7 miles. (The Sterling runs generally west until Soldotna, where it heads south again.) The frothing upper **Kenai River** is the community's lifeline, each summer bringing the salmon that in turn draw visitors, who fill hotels, restaurants, and the date books of fishing guides. The **Russian River** meets the Kenai at the western edge of the community, where the mad fishing frenzy of the July red salmon season occurs. A ferry takes anglers across the river from the highway. For information on how to fish the Kenai, see "Fishing," in section 8 of this chapter on Kenai/Soldotna; there's additional information in chapter 2.

If you're not an angler, there's not much here—a couple of operators do rafting trips, some trails start here, and some of the accommodations could provide a romantic mountain retreat. Cooper Landing is the starting or ending point for backpacking trips in the Chugach National Forest, described in section 3 of this chapter. Look there also for descriptions of several campgrounds for tents or RVs (there are also RV hookups at the Kenai Princess Lodge, reviewed below).

Cooper Landing has a post office, service stations, and small stores selling fishing gear and essentials, but it's not a real center of commerce. For banking or anything else not directly related to catching a salmon, you'll have to drive to Sterling, 30 miles away to the west, or Soldotna, 14 miles beyond that.

FISHING LODGES

The three lodges below can take care of everything, so you can set up your fishing and other activities with a single phone call. If all you need is a simple but comfortable, inexpensive room, try **The Hutch Bed and Breakfast,** Mile 48.5, Sterling Highway (© **907/595-1270;** www.arctic.net/~hutch).

Gwin's Lodge   This is the town's old original log roadhouse. Standing just a mile east of the Resurrection trailhead and the Russian River Campground, Gwin's is convenient and has loads of character. The owner, a dynamic former F-15 fighter pilot, keeps it open 24 hours a day all summer long to be the nerve center for the 24-hour fishing on the Russian River. It includes an extensive tackle shop, liquor store, and clothing shops, and they book fishing, rafting, and other activities. Most of the cabins are new. Among other choices, they include trailer-sized units with kitchenettes, mock log exteriors, and sleeping lofts with tiny dormers; a small house with a full kitchen and living room; and a real old log cabin. All have shower stalls, not tubs.

Over 50 years, the **restaurant** has welcomed many a tired angler or backpacker for a hearty meal, including me; after that, it's hard to be objective. Food in the seven-table dining room ranges from burgers to steaks and seafood. Servings are plentiful, satisfying, and generally quite good. Both the restaurant and bar are open around the clock in summer.

14865 (Mile 52) Sterling Hwy., Cooper Landing, AK 99572. © **907/595-1266.** http://ool.com/gwins/. 11 cabins. High season $99–$139 double. Low season $59–$69 double. DISC, MC, V. **Amenities:** Restaurant; bar; fishing rentals; activity desk. *In room:* Coffeemaker.

Kenai Princess Lodge ★★★   Built for Princess's cruise ship and package-tour business, this hotel also has rooms open for independent travelers. It's the most luxurious choice on the Kenai Peninsula. Each room feels like a remote cabin, with balconies overlooking the wooded valley, woodstoves stocked with firewood, and many unique details; yet they're luxurious hotel rooms at a resort with a gym, spa, and fine restaurant. The restaurant menu is varied and goes well beyond standard "steak and seafood." Even if you have no reason to stay in Cooper Landing, it could be a relaxing overnight stop or a place to get a meal a few steps up from highway fare. Anchorage couples use the hotel as a romantic getaway. They book guided fishing, horseback riding, tours, and other activities, and there are hiking trails nearby. An attractive 35-space RV park with full hookups is on-site, with access to the facilities. For summer, make reservations for rooms or RV sites well ahead.

Up Bean Creek Rd. above Cooper Landing (P.O. Box 676, Cooper Landing, AK 99572). © **800/426-0500** or 907/595-1425. Fax 907/595-1424. www.princessalaskalodges.com. 86 units. High season $229–$249 double. Low season $79–$119 double. RV sites $25. AE, DC, DISC, MC, V. **Amenities:** Restaurant; bar; exercise room; Jacuzzi; fishing rentals; concierge; tour desk; massage; coin-op laundry. *In room:* TV, dataport, coffeemaker.

Kenai River Sportfishing Lodge/Kenai Riverside Lodge ★★   The compound lies between the highway and the river, but down among the trees it feels like a remote lodge. I'd call the cabins faux rustic—I've never seen real bush cabins with smooth walls, wainscoting, and bright rag rugs, but these trim places still feel like the outdoorsy real thing, with no TVs or phones. The plumbing is in a central bathhouse. The location is the real advantage: White-water rafting rides and fishing floats leave right from the riverfront. The lodge also possesses

Floating the Kenai River

The Kenai is more famous for fishing than rafting, but the area is beautiful and the Kenai Canyon, below Cooper Landing and above Skilak Lake, has wild Class III water between vertical canyon walls. **Alaska Wildland Adventures,** at the Kenai Riverside Lodge (© **800/478-4100** or 907/595-1279), is the most established operator and has a great reputation. They offer a 7-hour float through the canyon for $110 adults, $69 children, and a placid 2½-hour float down the upper Kenai for $45 adults, $29 children. Their guided fishing is $200 for a full day. **Alaska Rivers Co.,** Mile 50, Cooper Landing (© **907/595-1226**), also has been around a while. They offer scenic rafting ($42, children half price), canyon floats ($85), and guided fishing ($135 all day).

a scarce resource in its coveted guide permits for the hot fishing river section that runs through the Kenai National Wildlife Refuge.

Everything comes with the one price: transportation from Anchorage, meals in a central lodge building, guided salmon fishing or fly-fishing for rainbow trout in drift or jet boats, and, on longer visits, halibut fishing (done from boats in salt water). You provide your own booze and fishing license and pay the tip. Many visitors use it as part of a "safari" package that takes them to various outdoor activities and sites; that's described in section 7 of chapter 2.

Alaska Wildland Adventures, Sterling Hwy. along the Kenai River, P.O. Box 389, Girdwood, AK 99587-0389. © **800/478-4100** or 907/783-2928. www.alaskasportfish.com. 16 cabins. 3-day, 4-night inclusive package $1,650. MC, V. **Amenities:** Restaurant (family style); sauna; river equipment included.

8 Kenai/Soldotna & Sterling: Giant Salmon

These quintessential western U.S. towns, dominated by shopping malls and fast-food franchises facing broad highways, have a single claim to fame, but it's a pretty good claim: The largest sport-caught king salmon in the world, almost 100 pounds, came from the Kenai River. The Kenai's kings run so large there's a different trophy class for the river—everywhere else in the state, the Alaska Department of Fish and Game will certify a 50-pounder as a trophy, but on the Kenai it has to be at least 75 pounds. That's because kings in the 60-pound class—with enough wild muscle to fight ferociously for hours—are just too common here. Anglers prepared to pay for a charter will be in their element on the river when the fish are running hot. Catching a big king is not easy or quick, however, and success rates vary greatly year-to-year and week-to-week.

Those not interested in fishing will find less than a day's sightseeing in these towns. Instead, use the towns as a base for the outdoors. Kenai has a strangely beautiful ocean beach and the Kenai River mouth, with its exceptional bird-watching. Outside town, you'll find a wealth of outdoor activities, primarily in the lake-dotted **Kenai National Wildlife Refuge,** which has its headquarters in Soldotna. The refuge is covered in the next section.

Kenai came into being with the arrival of the Russians at the mouth of the Kenai River more than 200 years ago, but it came into its own only with the discovery of oil on the peninsula in 1957. Today its economy relies on oil, commercial fishing, and, to a smaller extent, tourism. Soldotna, a smaller, newer, and less attractive town, is the borough seat and the primary destination for sportfishermen. Sterling is just a wide place in the road—incredibly wide, as a matter of fact (no one is quite able to explain why such a small town needs such a big road).

ESSENTIALS

GETTING THERE   From Anchorage, the drive on the Seward and Sterling highways to Soldotna is 147 miles. Allow 3 hours, without stops: In summer, traffic will slow you down; in winter, speeds are limited by ice and the fear of hitting moose.

The **Homer Stage Line** (© **907/235-7009** or 907/399-1847 on the van) connects Anchorage, Homer, Seward and points in between with van service, 6 days a week from Anchorage and 3 from Seward in the summer (less frequently in winter). The fare from Anchorage to Soldotna is $38 one-way, $65 round-trip. Tickets are for sale in Soldotna at the Goodnight Inn on the highway (© **907/262-4584**) or in Anchorage at the Seward Bus Line ticket office at 3339 Fairbanks St. (© **907/868-3914**).

Kenai receives very frequent flights from Anchorage from **Era Aviation** (© **800/866-8394** or www.eraaviation.com).

GETTING AROUND   The area is so spread out that walking most places really isn't possible, and there's no public transportation. Everyone here owns or rents a car; among the rental companies at the Kenai airport are **Hertz** (© **800/478-7980** or 907/283-7979; www.hertzcars.com) and **Payless** (© **800/PAY-LESS** or 907/283-6428; www.paylesscarrental.com). If you plan only to fish, however, you may not need one, instead getting rides from your guide, host, or a taxicab. There are several cab companies; try **Inlet Taxi Cab** (© **907/283-4711** in Kenai or 907/262-4770 in Soldotna).

VISITOR INFORMATION   The **Soldotna Visitor Information Center,** 44790 Sterling Hwy., Soldotna, AK 99669 (© **907/262-9814** or 907/262-1337; www.SoldotnaChamber.com), is located on the south side of town; drive through the commercial strip and turn right after the Kenai River Bridge. It's open daily in summer from 9am to 7pm; in winter, Monday to Friday 9am to 5pm and Saturday noon to 5pm. Besides the usual brochures, they maintain notebooks full of comparative information about lodgings, camping, and other services, and will help you find a room or charter. Anglers should stop in to see the world-record king salmon and a 20-pound rainbow trout.

In Kenai, don't miss the **Kenai Visitors and Cultural Center** at 11471 Kenai Spur Hwy., Kenai, AK 99611 (© **907/283-1991;** www.visitkenai.com). It's an attraction in itself. A fascinating museum does a good job of using artifacts to explain the cultures that passed through the Kenai: the Natives, the Russians who settled in 1791, and the later pioneers and oil workers. A natural history section will help you identify the birds and fish you see. Look for the "King of Snags," an immense conglomeration of lost fishing lures and sticks from the bottom of the river. In the summer, superb temporary art exhibitions are mounted, too (see below). To get there, follow the Spur Highway past Main Street and look for the large, well-landscaped building on your left. Museum admission is $3, free ages 12 and under in summer, free off-season. The center also offers free interpretive programs in summer; Monday on science, Wednesday art, and Friday history, at 3pm. They are open summer Monday to Friday 9am to 8pm, Saturday and Sunday 10am to 7pm; and winter Monday to Friday 8:30am to 5pm, Saturday 10am to 4pm.

SPECIAL EVENTS   May through July, the Kenai Visitors and Cultural Center (see above) will host **2002: Spirit of Alaska,** an invitational show of art in all media. Past art shows here have been extraordinarily good. Admission is $3 adults, children and students free. **The Kenai River Festival** (© 907/ 260-5449), over the second weekend of June, has food, music, crafts, and games.

In Soldotna, the **Tustumena 200 Sled Dog Race** (© 907/262-3270), held in late January, helps kick off the mushing season. **Progress Days** (© 907/ 262-9814), in late July, offers a parade, rodeo, car shows, and other festival events commemorating the completion of a gas pipeline in 1960—that's the area in a nutshell.

In Ninilchik, the **Kenai Peninsula State Fair** (© 907/567-3670), south at mile 136 on the Sterling Highway, is Friday to Sunday the third weekend in August, with a rodeo, crafts, games, agricultural exhibits, and other country attractions, plus a few kids' rides. Admission is $7 adults, $5 seniors, $4 children ages 6 to 12.

 FAST FACTS: **Kenai & Soldotna**

Banks Several are on the Kenai Spur Highway in the middle of town; in Soldotna, two banks are on the Sterling Highway commercial strip. In addition, ATMs are in grocery stores all over the area.

Hospital **Central Peninsula General** is in Soldotna at 250 Hospital Place (© 907/262-4404); from the Sterling Highway, take Binkley Street to Marydale Avenue.

Internet Access Connect to the web for free at the **Kenai public library,** 163 Main St. Loop (© 907/283-4378), or at the **Soldotna public library,** 235 Binkley St. (© 907/262-4227).

Police For nonemergencies in Kenai, call the Kenai Police Department (© 907/283-7879); in Soldotna, call the Soldotna Police Department (© 907/ 262-4455); outside city limits, call the Alaska State Troopers (© 907/ 262-4453).

Taxes 5% **sales tax** in Kenai and Soldotna, and 2% outside city limits.

FISHING

Fishing the Kenai River is the whole point of coming to the area for most visitors. Check at the visitor centers for information and regulation booklets. Or contact the **Alaska Department of Fish and Game,** 43961 Kalifornsky Beach Rd. Suite B, Soldotna, AK 99669 (© 907/262-9368 or 907/262-2737, for a recorded fishing report; www.state.ak.us/adfg). Serious anglers shouldn't miss that website; navigate through to the Region 2 Sportfish Division and download their treatises on Kenai River biology and fishing techniques or check current fish counts and escapement goals. Licenses are for sale on the site and in virtually any sporting-goods store. Also, read the "Salmon Primer" and "Fishing," in chapter 2.

There are more than two dozen public-access points over the 80 miles of the Kenai River. A **guide brochure** with a map is available from the state **Division of Parks,** P.O. Box 1247, Soldotna, AK 99669-1247 (© 907/262-5581; www.dnr.state.ak.us/parks); you also can pick up a copy at one of the visitor centers.

For anglers interested in less competition and more of a wilderness experience, Kenai is a gateway for vast wild lands accessible by air on the west side of Cook Inlet. There you can fish a stream packed with salmon without competition. Among others, **High Adventure Air** (© 907/262-5237; http://highadventureair.com) has day trips and packages with fly-in cabins. For a day trip, you'll pay $250 to $325 per person.

KINGS   King salmon, the monsters of the river, come in two runs. The early run, which sometimes has been limited to catch-and-release, comes from late May to the end of June, peaking in mid-June. These usually are the smaller fish and less plentiful, in the 20- to 40-pound range. The second run comes during the month of July and includes massive fish that range up to 90 pounds.

Regulations usually allow only the use of artificial lures with a single hook. Most people fish kings from a boat, floating with the current while the lure bounces along the bottom. Some also keep the boat stationary or back slowly down the river. Your chances from the bank are low; on average, with or without a boat, it takes 29 hours of fishing time to land a king (you'll likely get at least a dozen strikes for every fish that makes it into the boat). With a guide, the average time to land a fish is cut in half, but that still means that if you fish for only 1 day, chances are good that you'll get skunked. A boat of three anglers on a half-day guided charter has roughly a 50% chance of landing a king between them. You can increase your chances by fishing for several days, or when king and silver salmon are both in the river and both biting the same lures— a narrow window in late July.

A guided charter averages $125 to $150 for a 6-hour, half-day trip, $225 to $250 full-day. There are dozens of guides. Contact the visitor center in Kenai or Soldotna to get in touch with a guide; also, many hotels and lodges have their own. It's possible to rent a boat, but advisable only if you are experienced in boats and stay out of the hazardous, faster flowing parts of the river. The **Sports Den**, at 44176 Sterling Hwy. in Soldotna (© 907/262-7491; http://alaska sportsden.com), is one of the larger charter operators, with river and ocean trips, fly-in fishing, and hunting; they also rent condos, boats, and equipment for many kinds of outdoor activities. I've found them very friendly and helpful.

REDS   The area really goes crazy when the red, or sockeye salmon, join the kings in the river, mid-July to early August. You can fish reds from the bank or from a boat. Reds are plankton eaters and won't strike a lure. In the most popular fishing areas, near the confluence of the Russian and Moose rivers with the Kenai, regulations allow only the use of flies. Most people around here cast the flies with spinning gear, weighting the line 18 inches from the fly so it bounces along the bottom. Cast upstream from shore and allow the fly to drift down, keeping near the bank. The fish probably don't really attack the flies, but get caught when they instinctively move their mouths in an eating motion, which they do in quick-moving water.

SILVERS   Silvers come in two runs. The first, lighter run is late July to August, and the larger run arrives in September. They're easiest to catch anchored in a boat, but you can also do well from shore. Lures work well, as does bait of salmon eggs, but eggs aren't always allowed.

OTHER SPECIES   Trophy-size rainbow trout and Dolly Varden char also come out of the river. Anglers using light tackle may also get some enjoyment out of catching pink salmon, but most Alaskans turn up their nose at this 4-pound fish, which is plentiful in the Kenai during even-numbered years.

EXPLORING THE TOWNS

Kenai's historic sites, beach walking, and bird-watching can occupy you for most of a day. Start at the visitor and cultural center mentioned above and get a copy of the *Old Town Kenai Walking Map;* follow the numbered markers. Not many of the simple, weathered buildings remain from Kenai's life before oil, but those that do are interesting and lie only a few blocks down Main Street from the center, along the Cook Inlet bluff.

The **Holy Assumption Russian Orthodox Church** is the area's most significant building. The parish was founded in 1845 and the present church was built in 1895. It's a quaint, onion-domed church, brightly kept but with old icons. A donation is requested. Several nearby buildings are interesting for their interlocking log construction.

The bluff over the beach is nearby. When the salmon are running, you can occasionally see white beluga whales chasing them upstream from here, sometimes in great numbers. To get down to the sandy **beach** itself, go back up to the Kenai Spur Highway, turn to the west (left), then turn left on South Spruce Street. There you'll find a simple beach park and a place to begin a walk. It's easy to imagine the Russians' first arrival. On a calm day the beach sand, the mudflats, and the Inlet's gray, glacial water seem to meld together into one vast shimmering plain. Walking south, the beach wraps around and becomes the shore of the Kenai River. The water is far too cold for swimming.

The mouth of the river and the wetlands of its delta make for fine **bird-watching,** especially during spring and fall migrations. One of the best places to get to the tidal marshes is along Bridge Access Road, which branches from the Spur Highway. The state of Alaska has developed a viewing area near the bridge.

In Soldotna, there is one modest attraction, on Centennial Park Road, behind the visitor center. The free **Soldotna Historical Society Homesteader Museum** (© 907/262-3832) celebrates the town's brief history with a collection of cabins dating from as recently as the 1960s set among spruce trees to show what the area was like then. They house pioneer artifacts and old photographs. It's open summer only, Tuesday through Saturday 10am to 4pm.

A family looking for something to do while one parent is off fishing may enjoy the magnificent **North Peninsula Recreation Area Nikiski Pool** (© 907/776-8472), 10 miles north of Kenai on the Kenai Spur Road. The facility occupies a large dome and has a 136-foot water slide, mushroom fountains of water, and a raised hot tub from which parents can watch their children play in the pool below. Families travel from other towns just to swim here (including us). The water slide is open Tuesday to Sunday 1 to 5pm and 6 to 9pm in the summer (swimming without the slide opens those days at 7am); the winter hours are complicated, with the slide open only Friday through Sunday, so call for details. Pool admission is $3, or $6 to use the slide and pool. Weekends can be crowded.

ACCOMMODATIONS

Rates at all hotels are on seasonal schedules with three, four, or even more levels linked to the salmon runs. I've listed the highest and lowest.

Daniels Lake Lodge Bed and Breakfast ⭐ *(Finds* Located on peaceful and sparsely built Daniels Lake, this lovely, relaxing place has a boat and canoe you can rent for trout fishing right out the back door, among the resident ducks. The gregarious hosts share their Christian faith with guests, and, along with their dogs and rabbits, eagerly make friends. It's not a 1-night stopover, but a place to stay for a couple of days of relaxation, closer to the Nikiski Pool and the outlet of the Swanson River Canoe route of the Kenai National Wildlife Refuge than to any town.

21 miles north of Kenai (P.O. Box 1444), Kenai, AK 99611. ℂ **800/774-5578** or 907/776-5578. www. DanielsLakeLodge.com. 4 units, 2 cabins. High season $95–$130 double, $150–$250 cabin. Extra person $20. 2-night minimum in cabins. Low season $50–$80 any unit. Extra person $15. AE, DISC, MC, V. Deposits by check only. No smoking. **Amenities:** Jacuzzi; boat or canoe rental; babysitting; laundry machines. *In room:* TV, fridge, coffeemaker.

Great Alaska Adventure Lodge ⭐⭐
For anglers, it's the location that counts: a third of a mile of river frontage where the Moose and Kenai rivers converge, a hot fishing spot since time immemorial, as an ancient Native site attests. In the evening, they keep a guide and campfire on the beach so you can keep casting in the midnight sun. For guests interested in seeing wildlife and the glorious backcountry of the Kenai National Wildlife Refuge, there are cushy tent camps where you can use some muscle but sleep and eat in comfort. A bear camp across Cook Inlet takes day trips and overnights to watch three dozen resident brown bear up close, engaging in their natural behavior. The lodge itself, in Sterling, is nothing remarkable, but perfectly adequate.

Moose River, 33881 Sterling Hwy., Sterling, AK 99672 (in winter, P.O. Box 2670, Poulsbo, WA 98370). ℂ **800/ 544-2261** or 907/262-4515. Fax 907/262-8797 in summer, 360/697-7850 in winter. www.greatalaska.com. 22 cabins. Rates anywhere from $175–$249 for a day trip without lodging to $3,495 for a 7-day package. Rates include all meals, guide service, and travel from Anchorage. AE, MC, V. Closed mid-Oct to mid-May.

Harborside Cottages Bed and Breakfast ⭐
On a grassy compound at the top of the bluff over the mouth of the Kenai River in Old Town, these little white cottages make the most of a perfect site. The view and quiet can keep you occupied all day in a peaceful reverie. Inside, the cottages are as immaculate as if they were brand-new, each with its own light country decoration. The hostess stocks a self-serve breakfast the night before. There are no tubs, just shower stalls. Outside is a deck with a picnic table and gas barbecue.

13 Riverview Dr. (P.O. Box 942), Kenai, AK 99611. ℂ **907/283-6162.** www.harborsidecottages.com. 5 cottages. High season $150 double. Low season $125 double. Rates include continental breakfast. AE, DISC, MC, V. Closed winter. *In room:* TV, fridge, microwave oven, coffeemaker, iron.

Kenai River Lodge
Overlooking the river, next to the bridge in Soldotna, this roadside motel has the advantages of well-maintained standard rooms and a great location for anglers. The grassy front yard descends right to the water, with a barbecue where you can cook up your catch. They operate fishing charters from the hotel.

93 Riverside Dr., Soldotna, AK 99669. ℂ **888/966-4292** or 907/262-4292. Fax 907/262-7332. www.kenairiverlodge.com. 25 units. High season $120 double. Low season $60 double. Year-round $240 suite. Extra person $10. Fishing packages available. DISC, MC, V. **Amenities:** Car rental. *In room:* TV, fridge, coffeemaker.

Log Cabin Inn ⭐
Ted and Carol Titus built this huge log house specifically to be a B&B, but with its huge common room—with a fireplace and towering cathedral ceiling—it feels more like a luxurious wilderness lodge. Located off Kalifornsky Beach Road a little south of the bridge in Kenai, the house stands over an active beaver pond, with a deck and lots of windows to watch the beavers. The upstairs rooms, which cost $10 more, are well worth it—they're large and airy. A room on the main floor has French doors to a deck over the

pond. All the rooms are attractively decorated in a country style, although not all are so exceptional. Carol cooks a large breakfast at the time of your choosing.

9840 Eider Rd. P.O. Box 2886, Kenai, AK 99611. ✆ and fax **907/283-3653**. www.ptialaska.net/~tedtitus. 9 units, 3 cabins. $90–$100 double. Extra adult $25; extra child $10. Rates include full breakfast. AE, MC, V. **Amenities:** Hot tub.

CAMPING

Soldotna's appealing **Centennial Park Campground** lies atop a bluff along the Kenai River among thick spruce and birch trees. Turn right on Kalifornsky Beach Road just past the visitor center. Camping fees are $9 a night; day use is $5. There's a dump station, usable for a $10 fee. **Swiftwater Park** is a similar city-operated riverside campground near the Fred Meyer grocery store and Taco Bell as you enter town from the north.

RV parks are scattered about. **Beluga Lookout RV Park** (✆ **907/283-5999;** belugarv@ptialaska.net) is in Kenai's Old Town, at bluff's edge over the Inlet and the river's mouth, at 929 Mission Ave. Full hookups are $25 a night, with phone and cable TV at each site.

DINING

Franchise fast-food and burger-steak-seafood places dominate in Kenai and Soldotna. **Paradisos,** at Main Street and Kenai Spur Highway in Kenai (✆ **907/ 283-2222**), is a good multiethnic family restaurant. **Louie's,** at 47 Spur View Drive (✆ **907/283-3660**), serves good, solid food in a dining room much like the den of a maniacal sportsman—if the animal mounts come to life, you'll be crushed in a stampede.

Charlotte's Bakery, Café, Espresso ⊛ SANDWICHES   Rich-textured bread from the bakery anchors the sandwiches, and lettuce from a nearby garden completes the large, filling salads, but the motherly owner doesn't make a point of that—hers is not a trendy or gimmicky place. Locals fill the big wooden chairs in the bright dining room because the food is good, the service sweetly attentive, and the prices reasonable.

115 S. Willow, Kenai. ✆ **907/283-2777**. All items $5–$8. MC, V. Mon–Fri 7am–4pm, Sat 9am–3pm. Closed Sun.

Sal's Klondike Diner DINER   It certainly looks corny and touristy from the outside, but Sal's turns out to be a classic Western highway diner, with huge portions, fast service, and nothing fancy that doesn't have to be. Our meat loaf sandwich and halibut fish-and-chips, served on a plastic tablecloth, were just what we wanted for a quick lunch, and our coffee cups stayed full. The children's menu is good and cheap.

44619 Sterling Hwy., Soldotna. ✆ **907/262-2220**. Lunch $4.50–$9; dinner main courses $7–$10. AE, DISC, MC, V. Daily 24 hours.

9 Kenai National Wildlife Refuge

Floating through the Kenai National Wildlife Refuge in a canoe narrows the world into a circle of green water, spruce, and birch. You can paddle and hike for days without encountering more than a few other people, your only expense the cost of your canoe and the vehicle that carried you to the trailhead. Out there with my son, I once noticed that, other than his voice, the only sounds I had heard in 2 days were the gurgling of the water and the wind shushing in the birch leaves. You rely on yourself, but your greatest tests are not overly taxing.

Trail a line behind the canoe, and, when you catch a rainbow trout, land it and make a fire to cook it. Launch your body into the clear, frigid water to rinse off the sweat on a warm day. Float slowly, watching eagles circle the treetops and puffy clouds drifting like ships past your little world.

Most of the western half of the Kenai Peninsula lies within the 2 million acres of the refuge—it's almost as large as Yellowstone National Park—and much of that land is impossibly remote and truly dedicated to the wildlife. The Kenai River flows through part of the refuge, but the refuge is just a name to the anglers who pursue its salmon. (Information about fishing and rafting the river is above, in the Kenai/Soldotna and Cooper Landing sections.)

Canoeists will be more interested in the lowlands on the west side, west of the Sterling Highway and north of Kenai and Soldotna. The lakes there are as numerous as the speckles on a trout's back, or at least that's how they appear from the air. From the ground, the region is a maze of lakes connected by trails—more than 70 lakes you can reach on canoe routes stretching more than 150 miles. It's the easiest way to real Alaska wilderness I know.

ESSENTIALS

GETTING THERE   The refuge surrounds much of the land from Cooper Landing at the north to Homer at the south and Cook Inlet to the west. The Sterling Highway and roads that branch from it are the main ways to the lakes, trails, and rivers, and there is no practical way there without a vehicle.

VISITOR INFORMATION   Stop in at the **Kenai National Wildlife Refuge Visitor Center,** Ski Hill Road (P.O. Box 2139), Soldotna, AK 99669 (© **907/ 262-7021;** kenai.fws.gov), for guidance before plunging into the wilderness; they'll tell you about the land and the animals of the refuge. It's open in summer Monday to Friday 8am to 5pm, Saturday and Sunday 9am to 6pm; winter, Monday to Friday 8am to 4:30pm, Saturday and Sunday 10am to 5pm. The U.S. Fish and Wildlife Service, which manages the refuge, exhibits natural history displays here, and shows a film each hour in the afternoon in the summer. A mile-long nature trail has numbered stations. The staff offers advice and sells books and maps that you'll definitely need for a successful backcountry trip. The website contains detailed trip-planning information for the canoe routes. To find the center, turn left just south of the Kenai River Bridge, taking the dirt road uphill from the building-supply store.

CANOEING

From 1941 to 1980 the refuge was known as the Kenai National Moose Range. Its brushy wetlands are paradise for **moose,** rich in their favorite foods of willow and birch shoots and pond weeds. Moose like to dine while wading. Waterfowl and other birds, beavers, muskrats, and other aquatic animals are common on the lakes. People also must be partly aquatic to explore the lakes, paddling canoes across their surfaces, pushing through lily pad passages between lakes, and frequently hiking in rubber boots between lakes while carrying the canoe and camping gear.

There are two main canoe routes, both reached from Swanson River and Swan Lake roads, north of the Sterling Highway from the town of Sterling. The **Swan Lake Canoe Route** is a 60-mile network of 30 connected lakes. It meets Swan Lake Road twice, allowing a loop of several days, and in between adventurers can penetrate many lakes deep into the wilderness, visiting remote lakes they'll have all to themselves. It's also possible to canoe through to the Moose River and ride its current 17 miles over a long day back to the Sterling Highway.

Getting anywhere requires frequent portages of a quarter mile or so, and more ambitious routes have mile-long portages. You can skip all the portaging, however, by floating 2 days down the **Swanson River** to its mouth, at the Captain Cook State Recreation Area (see below), joining the river at a landing at mile 17.5 of Swanson River Road. The water is slow and easy all the way.

The most challenging of the routes is the **Swanson River Canoe Route,** which connects to the river's headwaters through a series of lakes and longer portages. The route covers 80 miles, including 40 lakes and the river float. Both routes have many dozens of remote campsites—just lakeside areas of cleared ground with fire rings—and most of the portages are well marked and maintained with wooden planking over the wet areas.

If you go, among your most important tools will be the book *The Kenai Canoe Trails,* by Daniel L. Quick, published by Northlite Publishing Company (33335 Skyline Dr., Soldotna, AK 99669-9752). This extraordinary guide contains superdetailed maps and directions, and advice on how to plan your trip and fish and camp on your way—I've never seen a trail guide like it. The author and publisher leads guided canoe trips on the routes; his company is **Northlite** (*©* **800/994-5997** or 907/262-5997; www.alaska.net/~northlit). For around $150 per person per day, you get his personal attention and everything you need but your own clothes. He offers day trips or paddles of up to a week. Quick shows his gorgeous photography of the area on his website, where you can also order the book.

Experienced canoeists don't need a guide, although, of course, you must be prepared before you go off on your own in this wilderness. I haven't provided detailed driving instructions because you'll need detailed maps to go at all. **Trails Illustrated** produces a good detailed map of the whole area, printed on plastic (see "Fast Facts: Alaska," in chapter 2 for details). A serviceable free map is distributed by the refuge visitor center. Coleman canoes and the gear to go with them, including car-top carriers, are for rent from the Sports Den in Soldotna for $35; rental information is listed under "Fishing," in section 8 (on Kenai/Soldotna) of this chapter. The refuge can provide you with a list of other rental agencies. But no one in the area I know of rents camping equipment or lightweight canoes, so a better plan might be to rent everything you need, including a canoe and camping gear, in Anchorage (see chapter 6).

There's much more to do in the refuge too, including several upland hiking trails. The refuge visitor center has a free guide map, and can give guidance on where to go.

CAMPING

For car camping away from all the fishing mayhem, the **Captain Cook State Recreation Area** is a lovely and underused 3,460-acre seaside area on Cook Inlet, 25 miles north of Kenai on the North Kenai Road, at the mouth of the Swanson River. There are lots of attractive sites among large birches, trails, beach walking, a canoe landing at the end of the Swanson River Canoe Route, and lake swimming. The camping fee is $10. **Daniels Lake Lodge,** listed above in section 8 (on Kenai/Soldotna) of this chapter, is nearby.

There are many campgrounds within the refuge, too, some of them lovely, quiet spots on the edge of uninhabited lakes, such as the small **Rainbow Lake** and **Dolly Varden Lake campgrounds,** on Swanson River Road near the start of the canoe routes. Get a complete listing from the visitor center. Generally, there is no camping fee.

10 Homer: Cosmic Hamlet by the Sea

Homer's leading mystic, the late Brother Asaiah Bates, always maintained that a confluence of metaphysical forces causes a focus of powerful creative energy on this little seaside town. It's hard to argue. Homer is full of creative people: artists, eccentrics, and those who simply contribute to a quirky community in a beautiful place. Indeed, Brother Asaiah may have been the quintessential Homerite, although perhaps an extreme example, with his gray ponytail, extraordinary openness and generosity, and flowery rhetoric about "the cosmic wheel of life." Homer is full of outspoken, unusual, and even odd individualists—people who make living in the town almost an act of belief. I can say this because I'm a former Homerite myself.

The geography of Homer—physical as well as metaphysical—has gathered certain people here the way currents gather driftwood on the town's pebble beaches. Homer is at the end of the road; the nation's paved highway system comes to an abrupt conclusion at the tip of the Homer Spit, almost 5 miles out in the middle of Kachemak Bay, and believers of one kind or another have washed up here for decades. There were the "barefooters," a communal group that eschewed shoes, even in the Alaska winter (Brother Asaiah came with them in the early 1950s). There are the Russian Old Believers, who organize their strictly traditional communities around their objection to Russian Orthodox church reforms made by Peter the Great. There are the former hippies who have become successful commercial fishermen after flocking here in the late 1960s to camp as "Spit rats" on the beach. And there are even the current migrants—artists and retired people, fundamentalist preachers and New Age healers, wealthy North Slope oil workers and land-poor settlers with no visible means of support—all people who live here simply because they choose to.

The choice is understandable. Homer lies on the north side of Kachemak Bay, a branch of lower Cook Inlet of extraordinary biological productivity. The **halibut fishing,** especially, is exceptional. The town has a breathtaking setting on the Spit and on a wildflower-covered bench high above the bay. The outdoors, especially on the water and across the bay, contains wonderful opportunities. And the **arts community** has developed into an attraction of its own. There are several exceptional galleries and the Pratt Museum, which has a national reputation.

You'll be disappointed, however, if you expect a charming little fishing town. Poor community planning has created a town that doesn't live up to its setting. Homer Spit in summer is a traffic-choked jumble of cheap tourist development and RVs. Homer began to take its modern form after two events: In the 1950s the Sterling Highway connected it to the rest of the world, and in 1964 the Good Friday earthquake sank the Spit, narrowing a much larger piece of land with a small forest into the tendril that now barely stands above the water. If not for constant reinforcement by the federal government, the Spit long since would have become an island, and Homer would hardly exist. As long as it survives, however, the town makes the most of that unique finger into the sea. Whether or not it is a cosmic focal point, it certainly is an exceptional launching point to one of the world's great marine recreation areas.

ESSENTIALS

GETTING THERE **By Car** At about 235 miles, Homer is roughly 4½ hours from Anchorage by car, if you don't stop at any of the interesting or beautiful places along the way. It's a scenic drive. If you take a rental car, drive it both ways, as the drop-off fees from Anchorage to Homer are high.

By Bus **Homer Stage Line** (© 907/235-7009 or 907/399-1847 on the van) runs to Anchorage and back six times a week during the height of summer, less frequently the rest of the year, and three times weekly to Seward. The Anchorage-Homer fare is $48 one-way, $85 round-trip. Tickets are for sale at **Quicky Mart,** 1242 Ocean Dr., in Homer (© **907/235-2252**). In Anchorage, buy tickets at **Seward Bus Line,** 3339 Fairbanks St. (© **907/868-3914**).

By Air **Era Aviation** (© **800/866-8394;** www.eraaviation.com) serves Homer from Anchorage several times a day. Small air-taxi operators use Homer as a hub for outlying villages and the outdoors.

By Ferry The **Alaska Marine Highway System** (© **800/642-0066;** www. state.ak.us/ferry) connects Homer to Seldovia, Kodiak, and points west along the Alaska Peninsula and Aleutian Archipelago, and to Seward and Valdez to the east, with the ferry *Tustumena.* The run to Kodiak takes 9½ hours and costs $53 for an adult walk-on passenger (children half off). It's a long trip, but a memorable one. A U.S. Fish and Wildlife Service naturalist rides the ferry to present programs and answer questions. The **Homer ferry terminal** is run by a contractor, and has its own toll-free number and website (© **800/382-9229** or 907/235-8449; www.akmhs.com), which may make it easier to get through to someone who can answer questions than through the state number above.

VISITOR INFORMATION The **Homer Chamber of Commerce Visitor Information Center,** 201 Sterling Hwy. (P.O. Box 541), Homer, AK 99603 (© **907/235-7740;** www.homeralaska.org), is on the right as you enter town. In summer, staff is on hand daily from 9am to 8pm to answer questions and to hand out brochures on local businesses—and you can buy tickets for the halibut derby. Winter hours are Monday through Friday 8am to 5pm. Get a copy of the *Homer Tourism and Recreation Guide,* published by the *Homer News,* at the center, or order it from the chamber's website. It includes a useful map.

On the right side of the highway as you arrive in town, the **Alaska Maritime National Wildlife Refuge Visitor Center,** 451 Sterling Hwy., Ste. 2, Homer, AK 99603 (© **907/235-6961;** www.r7.fws.gov/nwr/akmnwr), is the place to stop for outdoors information wherever you go in the area. It's open in summer daily 9am to 6pm, winter by appointment. The refuge itself consists of islands off Alaska from the Arctic to near British Columbia. The U.S. Fish and Wildlife Service manages these lands for the benefit of birds and marine mammals, and people rarely set foot on their shores, but rangers in Homer also offer bird and beach walks frequently in the summer, and show natural history films and give programs at the center. Call for times.

Call the **Kachemak Bay Bird Alert Information Line** (© **907/235-7337**) to find out about recent sightings and upcoming birder events, and to leave news of your own observations. It is operated by the wildlife refuge.

The **Kachemak Bay State Park District Office,** Mile 168.5 on the Sterling Hwy., 4 miles from town (P.O. Box 3248), Homer, AK 99603 (© **907/ 235-7024;** www.dnr.state.ak.us/parks), can help answer questions about planning a trip to the trails and beaches across Kachemak Bay from Homer and about booking remote cabin rentals. Depending on staffing, it should be open Monday through Friday 9am to 5pm.

GETTING AROUND The best way to get to and around Homer is by car. If you didn't bring one, you can rent a car at the airport from **Hertz**

ACCOMMODATIONS ■
Driftwood Inn **6**
Land's End **8**
Magic Canyon Ranch B&B **3**
Ocean Shores Motel **4**
Old Town B&B **5**
Seaside Farm **3**

DINING ◆
Boardwalk Fish and Chips **9**
Café Cups **1**
Duncan House Diner **2**
Fresh Sourdough Express
   Bakery and Cafe **7**
The Homestead Restaurant **3**

(✆ **800/654-3131** or 907/235-0734; www.hertz.com) or from **Polar Car Rental** (✆ **907/235-5998**), among others. There are two taxi companies in town, **CHUX Cab** (✆ **907/235-CHUX**) and **KacheCab** (✆ **907/235-1950**).

For strong riders, a bike is a good way around town. You do have to dodge traffic at times, and the Spit is 5 miles long. Some excellent mountain-biking routes are mentioned below. **Homer Saw and Cycle,** 1532 Ocean Dr. (✆ **907/ 235-8406;** homersaw@xyz.net), rents mountain bikes and trailers, starting at $15 half day; keeps track of trail conditions; and offers gear and repairs. They're open Monday to Friday 9am to 5:30pm, Saturday 11am to 5pm. It's wise to reserve bikes a day or two ahead, especially if an outing depends on getting one.

Homer Tours (✆ **907/235-6200;** www.ptialaska.net/~ericson) offers van and bus tours and shuttle service around town. A 1-hour driving tour is $20, and a 4-hour tour that makes stops, including the Pratt Museum, is $35, both with a two-passenger minimum. They also pick people up in Anchorage.

SPECIAL EVENTS **Homer's Winter Carnival,** in mid-February, is a big community event, a small-town celebration with a beer-making contest, parade, and snow-sculpture competition, among other highlights.

The **Kachemak Bay Shorebird Festival** (© **907/235-7740;** homeralaska. org/shorebird.htm), held in early May, includes guided bird-watching hikes and boat excursions, natural history workshops, art shows and performances, and other events. It's organized by Alaska Maritime National Wildlife Refuge and the Homer Chamber of Commerce to mark the return of the annual migration. **The Kachemak Bay Wooden Boat Festival,** which takes place at the same time as the Shorebird Festival, displays handmade boats from around the region and presents workshops and films.

Concert on the Lawn, put on usually the last Sunday in July by KBBI public radio (© **907/235-7721**), is a day-long outdoor music, craft, and food festival that brings together the whole town.

The **Jackpot Halibut Derby** (© **907/235-7740;** homerhalibutderby.com) lasting the whole summer long, has a top prize that has surpassed $31,000 for the biggest fish of the summer, and smaller monthly prizes and tagged fish prizes. Winning fish are usually 300 pounds or more. Of course, you must buy your $2 ticket before you fish.

 FAST FACTS: Homer

Bank **Wells Fargo,** with an ATM, is on the Sterling Highway near Heath Street.

Hospital **South Peninsula Hospital** is at the top of Bartlett Street, off Pioneer Avenue (© **907/235-8101**).

Internet Access **Eagle Eye Photo and Communications,** 601 E. Pioneer Ave. (© **907/235-8525;** www.eagleeyephoto.com), offers $5-an-hour Internet access and photo proccessing and business services.

Police For nonemergencies within the city limits, call the **Homer Police Department** (© **907/235-3150**); outside the city, phone the **Alaska State Troopers** (© **907/235-8239**). Both have offices located across Pioneer Avenue from the intersection with Heath Street.

Post Office Sterling Highway at Heath Street.

Taxes **Sales tax** in Homer is 5.5%. Outside the city, you pay 2%.

ATTRACTIONS

Homer's man-made attractions derive from its setting, from walks on the beaches and in the hilltop meadows, and from Kachemak Bay itself. The art this place has inspired is found in more than a dozen galleries and studios in town, not including those across the bay in Halibut Cove and Seldovia (see below). New shows open all over town on the first Friday of the month, when restaurants hold special evenings and the entire community comes out for an evening of gallery hopping.

A widely distributed brochure lists most of the galleries in town, with a map. Most of these places feature photography, inexpensive prints, pottery, and crafts as well as fine art, and some have other sidelines. Some of the smallest are also the best, where you get to see the mind of the gallery owner at work in his or her creation of a collection. Several good ones are on Pioneer Avenue, besides those I've described below.

Pratt Museum ★★★ The Homer Society of Natural History's museum is as good as any you'll find in a town of this size, and it has achieved a well-deserved national reputation. The Pratt displays art and explains local history, too, but it is strongest in natural history. Volunteers pioneered new technology that allows visitors to watch birds inside nesting burrows on Gull Island and bears feeding at the McNeil River State Game Sanctuary (the Gullcam and Bearcam), and you can zoom and pan the cameras live from controls in the museum. There is a saltwater aquarium housing local marine life, and if you're curious about all the fishing boats down in the harbor, you can find out about the different types of gear as well as the fish they catch. In the garden outside, you can learn to identify all the local wildflowers, and a forest trail teaches about the ecology there. There's much more to see, too.

3779 Bartlett St. (at Pioneer Ave.). ☏ **907/235-8635.** www.prattmuseum.org. Admission $6 adults, $5.50 seniors, $3 children ages 6–18, $20 family rate. High season daily 10am–6pm. Low season Tues–Sun noon–5pm. Closed Jan.

Bunnell Street Gallery ★★ This nonprofit gallery, located in a perfect space in an old hardware store near Bishop's Beach at the lower end of Main Street, is my favorite in Alaska. Unlike most other Alaska galleries, which double as tourist gift shops, Bunnell was made by and for artists, and the experience is noncommercial and often challenging. You may be tempted to become a member of the nonprofit corporation that runs it, for membership comes with a one-of-a-kind plate made by one of the artists. As with all Homer art, the themes of the work tend to be fishy, and the medium and style can be anything. A statewide juried art show is mounted every June. The gallery also puts on summer concerts, booking nationally known folk and classical performers into the most intimate of settings. Tickets are $10 to $12. Don't miss the **Two Sisters Bakery** and coffee shop next door.

106 W. Bunnell Ave. ☏ **907/235-2662.** www.xyz.net/~bunnell. Summer daily 10am–6pm. Winter, Mon–Sat 10am–6pm. Closed Jan.

Ptarmigan Arts Often staffed by the artists themselves, Ptarmigan Arts specializes in crafts, especially ceramics and fabrics, which are the most common media in Homer and are generally more affordable than fine art. Occasionally you can see a demonstration by one of the resident artists. There's always a tremendous array of work in various styles.

471 E. Pioneer Ave. ☏ **907/235-5345.** http://ptarmiganarts.com. High season, Mon–Sat 10am–7pm, Sun noon–5pm. Low season, Mon–Sat 11am–6pm, Sun noon–5pm.

Sea Lion Gallery Wildlife artist Gary Lyon and his family own and staff this small gallery among the T-shirt shops on one of the boardwalks on Homer Spit. It's pleasant but a little odd to see very valuable works by Lyon and others displayed in this intimate setting. Lyon's work captures Alaska wildlife in spectacular detail but also transforms his subjects with a distinctively dreamy vision. The rooms for rent upstairs are described under "Accommodations," later.

4241 Homer Spit Rd. (Central Charters Boardwalk). ☏ **907/235-3400.** sealion@xyz.net. Summer, Mon–Sat 11am–9pm, Sun noon–6pm. Closed in winter.

Norman Lowell Studio & Gallery ★ *Finds* Lowell built his own huge gallery on his homestead to show his life's work. The immense oils of Alaska landscapes, which are not for sale, hang in a building that counts as one of Alaska's larger art museums. Admission is free, and Lowell or his wife, Libby, often host guests who walk through. Their original homestead cabin also is a museum, showing pioneer life in Alaska as it was when they originally settled here. The studio/gallery sells Lowell's paintings, which range in price from $750 to $30,000; prints start at $100. They don't take credit cards.

Sterling Hwy. milepost 160.9 (near Anchor Point, about 12 miles out the Sterling Hwy. from Homer). © 907/235-7344. Mon–Sat 9am–7pm, Sun 1–5pm. Closed Oct–Apr.

GETTING OUTSIDE

The best **map of the Kachemak Bay area** is produced by Alaska Road and Recreation Maps, P.O. Box 102459, Anchorage, AK 99510. Available all over town, it costs around $5, depending on where you buy it.

ON THE HOMER SIDE OF KACHEMAK BAY

TIDE POOLING   Exploring Kachemak Bay's tide pools is the best way to really get to know the sea and meet the strange and wonderful animals that live in it, and it doesn't cost anything but the price of a pair of rubber boots. First, check a tide book, available for free in virtually any local store, or ask a local to check one for you. You need a low tide of –2 or lower, meaning that low water will be at least 2 feet below the normal low, some 25 feet below the high. Extralow tides expose more of the lower intertidal zone that contains the most interesting creatures. At a –5 tide, you could find octopus and other oddities. Also, the lower the tide, the more time you'll have to look. Keep track of the time: The tide will come in faster than you imagine, and you could get stranded and drown in the cold water.

The best place to go in town is reached from Bishop's Beach Park, near the lower end of Main Street. Walk west on the beach toward the opening of the bay to Cook Inlet. It's at least a half-hour brisk walk to the Coal Point area, where the sand and boulders end. This is where you'll find pools of water left behind by the receding tide, many full of life. Explore patiently and gently—look at the animals and touch them, but always put them back as they were and be careful not to crush them underfoot. Marine invertebrate identification keys and many other field guides are sold at the Wildlife Refuge Visitors Center, above under "Visitor Information," where rangers happily give advice. If you want to keep going, there's usually a sea otter raft offshore about 3 miles down the beach. Just continue walking, keeping your eyes on the water. As always with watching wildlife, binoculars will improve the experience.

HIKING   There are trails on the bench above Homer as well as across the bay at Kachemak Bay State Park (see below). The 6-mile **Homestead Trail** is an old wagon road used by Homer's early settlers. The largely informal trail is lovely

---

Tips Walk with an Expert

The **Wynn Nature Center,** operated by the nonprofit **Alaska Center for Coastal Studies** (© 907-235-6667; www.akcoastalstudies.org) is a chance to learn about the ecology of the area on an easy guided walk. The center encompasses 126 acres of spruce forest and wildflower meadow off Skyline Drive, with an 800-foot boardwalk accessible to people with disabilities. It is open daily 10am to 6pm mid-June through Labor Day, with guided walks every 2 hours. Fees are adults $5, seniors $4, under age 18 $3.

and peaceful, tunneling through alders, crossing fields of wildflowers, and passing old homestead cabins. From a hilltop meadow you can see all the way to the Inlet and the volcanoes beyond. A trailhead is at the reservoir on Skyline Drive—drive up West Hill Road from the Sterling Highway, turn right, and follow Skyline, turning left before the pond.

DRIVING OR MOUNTAIN BIKING   Several gravel roads around Homer make for exquisite drives or bike rides. Mountain bikers can use the Homestead Trail, above, too. Drive out **East End Road,** through lovely seaside pastures, a forest, and the village of Fritz Creek, then follow the bluff line through meadows toward the head of the bay. When the road gets too rough, explore onward on a mountain bike. **Skyline Drive** has extraordinary views of high canyons and Kachemak Bay; drive up East Hill Road just east of Homer. The two bike shops listed above, under "Getting Around," can give you many more ideas. The great mountain biking across the bay is described below.

HORSEBACK RIDING   Ranchers have worked around Kachemak Bay for decades. Drive east of town on East End Road and you can see pastures full of cattle overlooking views that anywhere else would be used for resort hotels. **Trails End Horse Adventures** (© **907/235-6393**), 11.2 miles out East End, offers half-day trail rides to the head of Kachemak Bay. They charge $20 for the first hour and $15 an hour thereafter and take all ages and raw beginners.

ON & ACROSS KACHEMAK BAY

Along the south side of the Kachemak Bay, glaciers, fjords, and little wooded islands are arrayed like a smorgasbord before Homer. A quick boat ride puts you there for sea kayaking, mountain biking on unconnected dirt roads, hiking in the mountains, or eating sushi in a top-flight restaurant on pilings. Or gallery hopping, or resting at a remote lodge, or studying at a nature center, or walking the streets of a forgotten fishing village. The far side of the bay has no road link to import the mundane, mass-produced world, but it does have people, and they make the landscape even richer and more enchanting than it would be alone. And underneath the water, there's a wealth of halibut and salmon.

There are two settlements across the bay, **Halibut Cove** and **Seldovia,** each with its own services and lodgings; they are described later in this chapter. Remote lodgings that aren't in any of the towns are described later under "Accommodations." Here I've covered the many places you can go for a day trip or longer away from town or lodge.

PLANNING AN OUTING

BOOKING AGENCIES   It's easy to set up a day on or across the water in Homer because almost everything can be set up through central agencies that represent many businesses.

The Bookie   This outfit represents more than 100 small, owner-operated businesses, including B&Bs and other things on land as well as fishing, kayak tours, watertaxis, and the like. Their website is useful and informative.

P.O. Box 195, Homer, AK 99603. © **888/335-1581** or 907/235-1581. www.alaskabookie.com.

Central Charters   This long-established booking agent represents businesses for some of the largest and most popular activities, including halibut fishing, boat tours to Seldovia and Halibut Cove, and the like. They have a ticket office on the right side of the Spit as you drive out.

4241 Homer Spit Rd., Homer, AK 99603. © **800/478-7847** or 907/235-7847. Fax 907/235-2895. www. centralcharter.com.

TRANSPORTATION ACROSS THE WATER Many water taxis operate from Homer to wilderness cabins and kayaking waters, the hiking and mountain biking roads accessible from the Jakolof Bay Dock, Seldovia, Halibut Cove, Kachemak Bay State Park, and other remote points. Rates vary little, around $50 to get to Kachemak Bay State Park, for example. All can be booked through the agencies mentioned above. Among the best is the **Jakolof Ferry Service** (© 907/ **235-2376** or 907/235-6384 summer only; www.jakolofferryservice.com), which operates two handsome wooden boats that carry up to 18 passengers, mostly seated outside, and can pull right up on the beach. It's a great way to get out. They also rent remote cabins across the bay for $60 to $75 a night. Another well-thought-of, long-time operator is **Mako's Water Taxi** (© **907/235-9055;** www.makoswatertaxi.com).

Besides these two destinations, see the sections on Halibut Cove and Seldovia later in this chapter.

JAKOLOF BAY A state-maintained dock opens an area of gentle shorelines, abandoned logging roads, and inexpensive cabins to visitors who seek the wilderness but can't afford to stay at a wilderness lodge. West of Kachemak Bay State Park and east of Seldovia, the lands have roads, but the roads aren't connected to anything and are used as much by mountain bikers as by anyone else. You can take the Jakolof Bay Ferry or another water taxi straight to the Jakolof dock. The ferry owners rent simple cabins, and the Across the Bay Tent and Breakfast, listed under "Wilderness Lodges" in the "Accommodations" section later, also has inexpensive lodgings.

There's plenty to do in the area. The waters of Jakolof, Little Jakolof, Kasitsna, and Little Tutka bays, and the tiny Herring Islands, are appealing and protected for sea kayaking. Supreme mountain biking trails lead along the shore and right across the peninsula through forest and meadows for berry picking. The Red Mountain and Rocky River roads are prime routes; check with one of the bike shops or the locals to find out about river crossings and other hazards. A maintained 10-mile road west leads to the charming village of Seldovia, described below.

KACHEMAK BAY STATE PARK The park comprises much of the land across the water that makes all those views from Homer so spectacular. For $100 round-trip, you can be dropped off there after breakfast, walk the beach, hike in those woods, climb the mountains, then meet your boat in time to be back in Homer for dinner and the first other people you've seen all day. This is heaven, as far as I'm concerned.

The park's main office is at the ranger station listed under "Visitor Information" earlier. Its center is the summer-only **ranger station** in Halibut Cove Lagoon, where there's a dock and mooring buoys for public use, three public rental cabins over the water, a campsite, and excellent king salmon fishing in mid-June.

The park has about 80 miles of trails, mostly linking at the ranger station; a free trail guide is available there, but just in case, get a map before you leave Homer. The trails generally start at tidewater among a lush, mossy forest of towering spruce and rise into the craggy mountains—up sharp peaks to a glacier, or, if you don't want to climb, over the hills to the next secluded beach. Bring mosquito repellent and review bear avoidance skills (see "Outdoors Health & Safety," in chapter 2). You can hike to a public rental cabin on secluded China Poot Lake less than 3 miles from the Halibut Cove dock.

The park's fifth cabin is on Tutka Bay, off the Halibut Cove trail network. You can also use these places as a base for self-guided sea kayaking. Cabin permits are

$50 a night and usually must be reserved 6 months in advance (see "State Parks Cabin Reservation Tricks," in section 1 of this chapter).

GULL ISLAND   The island is a rock across the bay from Homer Spit that is a busy bird colony in the summer. It's easy to get to, and boats can edge close as the water is deep all around. You can usually see tufted and horned puffins, black-legged kittiwakes, common murres, red-faced and pelagic cormorants, pigeon guillemots, and glaucus-winged gulls. Tour boats to Halibut Cove or Seldovia may often cruise by the island, and if you are taking a water taxi to Halibut Cove Lagoon, ask to take a look on your way.

ACTIVITIES

FISHING   Homer is known for **halibut,** those huge, flat bottom fish, and the harbor is full of charter boats that will take you out for the day for around $180 per person in the high season. Every day, a few people catch fish that are larger than they are, and halibut over 50 pounds are common. Getting out to where the fish are plentiful requires an early start and a long ride to unprotected waters. People who get seasick easily shouldn't go, as the boat wallows on the waves during fishing. (Take Dramamine *before* you set out; if you wait, it probably won't do any good.) Using gear and lines that look strong enough to pick up the boat, you jig the bait (chunks of herring or cod) up and down on the bottom. Halibut aren't wily or acrobatic, and fighting one can be like pulling up a sunken Buick.

Tips Getting Your Fish Home

A typical angler comes back from a halibut charter with around 50 pounds of fish that, when cleaned, will yield 30 pounds of filets. A hungry adult can eat half a pound of halibut at a sitting. Eat as much fresh as you can, as it will never be better, but be prepared for how you will deal with the rest of your bounty. The typical 30 pounds is worth around $250 in the grocery store (it's illegal to sell sport-caught fish). If it is properly and quickly frozen, it will retain much of its quality for several months; if not, you waste this superb food. If you're lucky enough to catch that much salmon, the problem is even more immediate, as salmon is more sensitive to proper handling. Most fishing towns have a sport processor who can vacuum-pack and flash-freeze your catch for under $1 a pound. If time is an issue, they'll often trade your catch for fish that is already processed. The best way to get it home is as checked baggage; the processor can provide sturdy fish boxes and cold packs. If you aren't leaving right away, processors will hold the fish, and many hotels have freezer facilities. If you have to ship it, use an overnight service (expensive) and make sure someone is there to put it in the freezer on the other end. Above all, keep the fish *hard frozen;* if it thaws, even only partially, refreezing will ruin it. Consider having some of your salmon smoked, making it a ready-to-eat delicacy that will last a long time and a very welcome homecoming gift. Halibut can be smoked, too, but because of its low fat content and delicate flavor it doesn't come out as well. In Homer, **Coal Point Trading Co.,** 4306 Homer Spit (✆ **907/235-3877;** www.welovefish.com), will process, pack, and ship your catch as ordered.

One good, large operator is **Silver Fox Charters** (© 800/478-8792 or 907/235-8792; silverfoxcharters.com). Their website has a handy primer on fishing Kachemak Bay. Others can be booked through Central Charters, listed above under "Planning an Outing," or you can find one on the **Homer Charter Association** website, which has a list and links to dozens of boats, at **homercharterassociation.com**.

Salmon feed in Kachemak Bay in winter and are fished with trolling gear year-round, not only when they're running in the streams. The town even has a Winter King Salmon Tournament in March (check with the chamber of commerce). But that's for the hardy and the lucky. Most people fish salmon in summer. Although not known for salmon, Homer does have some good spots. A small lagoon called the Fishing Hole on the Spit is stocked with terminal run king and silver salmon by the Alaska Department of Fish and Game. Silvers arrive early August through early October, and kings are in the lagoon starting in late May for most of the summer. These fish have nowhere to spawn, and some anglers scorn such "fish-in-a-barrel" fishing. At the end of the runs, snagging is permitted, which is something like mugging salmon and can be a lot of fun, if not something you'll brag about later at the Rod and Gun Club. For more natural salmon fishing, you can surf cast for silvers from the end of the Spit, head over to Halibut Cove Lagoon (see Kachemak Bay State Park, above) or Seldovia, or drive back up the Sterling Highway to the Anchor River, an excellent steelhead trout stream, and the other rivers that flow west into Cook Inlet. The **Alaska Department of Fish and Game** maintains a fishing hotline at © **907/235-6930.** They're located at 3298 Douglas Place (© **907/235-8191**).

NATURAL HISTORY TOURS   The nonprofit **Center for Alaska Coastal Studies** (© 907/235-6667; www.akcoastalstudies.org) is dedicated to educating the public about the shore. That means the group's emphasis isn't on making money, but on interpreting Kachemak Bay for visitors on half-day explorations of the Peterson Bay area. If the tides are right, they lead guests on a fascinating guided tide-pool walk (the good tide days are listed on their website); if not, you can take a woodland nature walk and visit an archaeological site. Their lodge has saltwater tanks containing creatures from the intertidal zone and microscopes to inspect your finds. It's very casual, often volunteer led, and truly Alaskan. They also offer sea kayaking and overnights. Reserve through **Mako's Water Taxi** (© 907/235-9055; www.makoswatertaxi.com). The price is $60 adults, $45 ages 6 to 12; add $15 for the minus-tide tours. Pack your own lunch, as none is provided, and bring footwear suitable for hiking and beach walks and warm clothing for the ride in Mako's open boat.

SEA KAYAKING   Silence fell as the boat pulled away from the beach, leaving us behind with the kayaks and our guide. For the rest of the day my son and I absorbed the water-reflected sunlight and glided past fancifully shaped rocks and resident sea otters around Yukon Island. We explored beaches, picnicked, raced, and discovered tiny bays too small for any other craft. At the end of the day, we had a new friend in our quietly cheerful guide, Allison O'Hara, and discovered that she'd imperceptibly taught us a lot about sea kayaking. O'Hara runs **True North Kayak Adventures** (© 907/235-0708; www.truenorthkayak.com) with Kevin Bell. Their 8-hour beginner day trips cost $125, including lunch and passage across the bay. Most kayaking day trips in Alaska towns barely get out of the small boat harbor. This trip doesn't feel so tame—it's more like a mini expedition. They also offer more challenging overnight and multiday trips to remote waters in the area, and a $199 package that includes the day tour, a night in the attractive Hesketh Island Cabins, and a second day of hiking. You can also book the cabins separately at **Porter's Alaskan Adventures** (© **907/776-3626;** www.portersak.com).

Various others offer Kachemak Bay kayak trips. Make a choice through the booking agencies listed above. The protected waters, tiny islands, and remote settlements are fascinating paddling no matter who you go with, or, for experienced paddlers, if you go on your own. Kayakers can take a water taxi across and explore at will, camping or staying in cabins over much of the bay. Check with Kachemak Bay State Park for guidance. True North Kayak rents to experienced paddlers for $60 a day double, $40 single, and also rents camping gear. Also see the Halibut Cove and Seldovia sections of this chapter (sections 11 and 12) for other rental and guided opportunities.

FLIGHTSEEING & BEAR VIEWING   There are several good air taxis in Homer, providing access to the very remote areas of the southern Kenai Peninsula and lower Cook Inlet that you can't easily reach by boat, but **Kachemak Bay Flying Service** (© **907/235-8924;** www.alaskaseaplanes.com) is really special. It offers spectacular scenic flights over the bay and glaciers starting at $120 per person. The personable Bill de Creeft, flying out of Homer since 1967, is experienced enough to qualify as a pioneer aviator, but the real old-timer is his favorite plane, a restored 1929 Travel Air S-6000-B, one of only six remaining examples of the executive aircraft, with mahogany trim and wicker seats. He'll also fly you into backcountry lakes. **Emerald Air Service** (© **907/235-6993;** www.emeraldairservice.com), operated by de Creeft alumni, offers saltwater landings, specializing in bear-viewing natural history trips to remote shores.

ACCOMMODATIONS

Homer has many good B&Bs. The Homer Chamber of Commerce (http://homeralaska.org) has links to a prodigious number of them.

In addition to the places I've listed in detail, **The Sea Lion Cove,** above the Sea Lion Gallery on Homer Spit (© **907/235-3400** in summer or 907/235-8767 in winter; www.AlaskaOne.com/sealion), has two comfortable rooms with kitchens and a deck right over the beach where you can hear the waves roll in at night. **Cranes' Crest Bed and Breakfast,** 59830 Sanford Dr. (© **907/235-2969;** www.akms.com/cranes), 5 miles out atop the beach behind the town, has nesting sandhill cranes that wander around like lawn ornaments, and sweeping, cinematic views you can sit and watch all day.

Besides the hotels listed in detail below, you'll find good rooms at the **Bay View Inn,** 2851 Sterling Hwy. (© **907/235-8485;** www.bayviewalaska.com), at the top of Baycrest Hill before you come into town on the Sterling Highway, with amazing views, attractive little rooms, peace, and reasonable prices. The **Best Western Bidarka Inn,** 575 Sterling Hwy. (© **866/685-5000** or 907/235-8148; www.ptialaska.net/~bidarka), on the right as you come into town, has standard motel rooms.

Driftwood Inn *Value*   The historic building a block from Bishop's Beach and across from the Bunnell Gallery resembles a lodge or B&B, with its large fireplace of rounded beach rock, the hot coffeepot and inexpensive self-serve breakfast in the lobby, and the owner's roving dog. The smallest rooms resemble Pullman compartments in size and configuration, but they are cute and clean and have some real style. And they're inexpensive. Nine bedrooms share two

Hermits on the Homestead

Late in October, the snow was holding back in the clouds like a strong emotion. The ground was frozen, the swamp grasses stiff, brittle, painted with frost. This was the one time of year when, with a stout four-wheel-drive truck, you could drive in to Ben's cabin. It stood on a small rise amid his hundreds of acres of swampy ground, the only spot where trees could get out of the dampness and grow. The heavy, lovingly peeled logs of the house lay horizontally amid big birch and white spruce trees. Ben had dragged these huge tree trunks from far afield, by himself, when he started his homestead nearly 40 years earlier, so he could keep living trees nearer to his house.

I'm not using his real name. Ben was a private guy. He generously invited us in, offered coffee from the percolator on top of the soapstone woodstove, but it was clear that he wasn't quite sure he remembered how to talk to people—where to look, for example—and he kept mumbling and looking at my feet or the sky. He showed us the huge rocks he'd dragged in to build a foundation, the cellar where he stored his food, the collection of moose racks. Food tended to walk by each fall—he never had to go far to get his moose. Everything about his home was exactly the way he wanted it, the product of immense effort to make it all with his own hands. I could see plainly how he'd spent his days all these years. But I could only imagine his nights all alone out here—the piles of *Reader's Digest* and *National Geographic* magazines, the insistent silence.

I finally asked Ben why he'd spent his whole adult life on this homestead, so far from other people. Why not move to town, where life is easier and there's someone to talk to? Well, he said, he did work construction in the summer for cash. But I knew that was an evasion. How, I asked, did he first end up out here, in the middle of nowhere, in a huge swamp? What made him want to be off by himself when he first came out here, so long ago? Pause—check the shoes, check the sky—well, he said, it seems there was a woman. She chose the other guy.

Alaska homesteaders are as varied as people in the city. They aren't all crazed war veterans any more than they're all victims of unrequited love, although those make the best stories. What they do have in common is a willingness to invest hard physical labor into the things the rest of us obtain effortlessly by turning a thermostat or a faucet handle.

Alaska's homesteaders came in waves. There were the prospectors from the gold rush who stayed. Then, after World War II, GIs with families looking for broad new opportunities came north and settled more land. The counterculture movement of the 1960s brought yet another group. Federal homesteading laws written to open the Great Plains to agriculture in the 19th century made getting land difficult and required Alaska homesteaders to do a lot of anachronistic, absurd work, such as clearing large tracts for farming that could never occur. The homesteaders had to survey the land, live on it, clear much of it, and then answer any challenges about their accomplishments at a hearing. If they passed the test, they received a patent to up to 160 acres.

The laws allowing homesteading on federal lands in Alaska were all repealed by 1986, but the state government still sometimes provides land to its citizens under laws that allow homesteading, lotteries, and sale of remote land. The parcels are very remote and smaller than the old federal homesteads, and the rules still don't make it easy—for a homestead, you have to live at least 25 months on the land in a 5-year period, for example. Many families try, with a Hollywood dream of living in the wilderness, only to give up when they learn firsthand of the hardship, privations, and cold. I know from experience that I want never again to live in a home where the heating is wood or the water is in jugs, and I've never done anything approaching building a homestead. Homesteading isn't like camping. Outdoor skills won't help unless you also know how to repair engines below zero, build houses without power tools, carry all your own water and firewood, and live poor, largely without an income or any of the things money can buy. You have to be willing to bathe rarely, be cold in winter, be eaten alive by mosquitoes in summer, and end up with land that isn't really worth anything.

Many successful homesteading experiences end with growing children. Kids don't care if they can take a bath, so long as the parents don't mind washing diapers by hand and being far from medical care. But when children get to a certain age, they need to go to school and be around other children. The families often expect to go back to the homestead someday, but, somehow, they rarely do. Areas that were thriving little communities of neighbors in the 1950s or 1960s now are deserted, perhaps with one hermit left—like my friend Ben.

My wife's parents homesteaded in the 1950s and '60s. Her father was a World War II veteran. Today the family still has some acreage, and a treasure trove of great stories—among them the tales of my late father-in-law's feats of strength and endurance, and my wife's memory of playing with dolls as a girl, then looking up to meet the eyes of a bear that had been watching her.

But my favorite is the story of Rose and her lover. They lived in the same area in Northern California where my wife Barbara's parents grew up. Everyone in town knew the story of the red-headed beauty who had an affair with an older man. Rose's parents refused to let her marry him and decreed that the couple couldn't see each other anymore. She entered a convent, and he disappeared, never to be seen in the town again. Many years later, after moving to Alaska, Barbara's parents were boating in Kachemak Bay when they got caught by bad weather on the opposite side of the bay from Homer. On their own in an open boat and looking for shelter, they found a cabin on a remote beach of an otherwise uninhabited island. They were taken in and befriended by the hermit who'd homesteaded there for years. After warming up with coffee, they got to talking about where they'd come from and how they'd ended up in Alaska. When it came time for their host to tell his story, it was about a beautiful young woman he'd loved, named Rose.

bathrooms. Larger rooms have more amenities, but not as much charm (most have only showers, no tubs). The walls are thin, so there's a no-noise policy during evening hours. There's also an appealing 22-site RV park.

135 W. Bunnell Ave., Homer, AK 99603. ℂ and fax **907/235-8019**. thedriftwoodinn.com. 20 units, 11 with private bathroom. High season $59–$124 double. Low season $60 double. RV sites $26–$29, full hookup. Extra person $10. DC, DISC, MC, V. No smoking. **Amenities:** Coin-op laundry; fish cleaning and freezing facility. *In room:* TV.

Land's End Resort ⭐⭐

Traditionally *the* place to stay in Homer, Land's End would be popular no matter what it was like inside because of its location at the tip of Homer Spit, the best spot in Homer and possibly the best spot for a hotel in all of Alaska. It's composed of a line of weathered buildings that straggle along the beach crest like driftwood logs, but the interior has been remodeled into comfortable rooms with occasionally fanciful decoration. There are about a dozen different classes of rooms, ranging from cute shiplike compartments to two-story affairs, and a complex rate schedule to match. The hotel is near the boat harbor, and you can fish right from the beach in front.

The **Chart Room restaurant** makes good use of its wonderful location, looking out over the beach and bay, with a casual, relaxing atmosphere. The deck outside has glass wind shields, making it a warm, satisfying place to sit over coffee on a sunny day. You can watch otters, eagles, and fishing boats while you eat. Excellent chefs have passed through from year to year, so it's hard to predict the quality of the cuisine. Locals discuss the current food at Land's End the way some towns talk about their baseball players. I've had simply prepared fresh seafood there that couldn't have been better.

4786 Homer Spit Rd., Homer, AK 99603. ℂ **800/478-0400** in Alaska only, or 907/235-0400. Fax 907/235-0420. www.lands-end-resort.com. 80 units. High season $119–$170 double. Low season $86–$120 double. Extra person $10. AE, DC, DISC, MC, V. **Amenities:** Restaurant; bar; moving-water lap pool; exercise room; outdoor Jacuzzi; sauna; massage. *In room:* TV, coffeemaker.

Magic Canyon Ranch Bed and Breakfast ⭐

At the top of a canyon road off East End Road, the Webb family shares its charming home, 74 unspoiled acres, a tree house, and sweeping views with guests, a cat, and a herd of retired llamas. The air is mountain clear and quiet between the high canyon walls—you start to relax as soon as you get out of the car. The Webbs serve sherry in the evening and a full breakfast in the morning. The four rooms, some nestled cozily under the eaves, are decorated in country and Victorian style, with some family antiques.

40015 Waterman Rd., Homer, AK 99603. ℂ and fax **907/235-6077**. magiccanyonranch.com. 4 units, 2 with private bathroom. High season $85–$100 double. Low season $55–$70 double. Extra adult $25; extra child $20. Rates include full breakfast. MC, V. **Amenities:** Meditation pond; sun deck; telescope; horseshoes; croquet. *In room:* Heirloom antiques and quilts.

Ocean Shores Motel ⭐

Buildings on a grassy compound overlook Kachemak Bay, with a path leading down to Bishop's Beach, yet the location is right off the Sterling Highway as you enter town, within walking distance of downtown Homer. Rooms are fresh and bright, most with private balconies, and many with kitchens. A few less expensive rooms aren't as up-to-date and lack the stunning views, but they still have cute touches. It's a family business, and they've decorated the place with photographs and art collected over five generations in Alaska. The hospitality matches.

451 Sterling Hwy. no. 1, Homer, AK 99603. ℂ **800/770-7775** or 907/235-7775. Fax 907/235-8639. http://oceanshoresalaska.com. 32 units. High season $99–$155 double. Low season $70–$75 double. Extra person $5. AE, DISC, MC, V. *In room:* TV, dataport, coffeemaker.

Old Town Bed and Breakfast *(Finds)*   Artist and lifelong Homer resident Asia Freeman and her husband, Kurt Marquardt, casually host a B&B that combines the artiness of the excellent Bunnell Street Gallery downstairs (see "Attractions," earlier) and the funky, historic feel of the old trading post/hardware store that the building used to house. The wood floors undulate with age and settling, and the tall, double-hung windows, looking out at Bishop's Beach, are slightly cock-eyed. Antiques and handmade quilts complete the charming ambience. They serve a full breakfast on weekends, and during the week you get a continental breakfast at the wonderful Two Sisters Bakery, downstairs. Not a good choice for people who have trouble with stairs.

106–D W. Bunnell, Homer, AK 99603. (C) **907/235-7558.** Fax 907/235-9427. www.xyz.net/~oldtown. 3 units, 1 with private bathroom. High season $70–$85 double. Low season 25% discount. Extra person $15. Rates include breakfast. MC, V. **Amenities:** Self-serve laundry.

Seaside Farm *(Finds)*   Take a step back in time—all the way to the 1960s. Mairis Kilcher's farm is populated by Morgan horses, cows, chickens, pigeons, and latter-day hippies, many of whom do chores in exchange for their room: 2½ hours of work equals a night in the hostel bunks, and 90 minutes earns a campsite in the pasture above the bay. Campers have use of an outdoor cooking and washing area, and autumn raspberry picking. Some of the primitive cabins sit in lovely, quiet places. The farm, its meadows dotted with cottonwood trees, slopes spectacularly to Kachemak Bay. Homer's pioneering Kilcher family spawned the singer Jewel (Kilcher), although you're not likely to see her around here anymore—she wrote a nasty autobiography trashing her family.

40904 Seaside Farm Rd. (5 miles from downtown off East End Rd.), Homer, AK 99603. (C) **907/235-7850.** www.xyz.net/~seaside. 4 units, 9 cabins, 12 hostel beds. $55 cabin for 2; $45 private rm with shared bathroom; $15 per person hostel bunk; $6 campsite. Extra person in rm or cabin $12. MC, V.

CAMPING

The most popular place to camp in Homer is out on the Spit, amid the sand and pebbles. Tenters camp on the beach, while RVs park on the beach or around the boat harbor. It can be windy and crowded, and toilet facilities are minimal; but waking up on a bright, pebbled beach makes up for much. The fee changes annually; at this writing, it's $6 for tents, $10 for RVs, payable at a booth on the right side of the Spit, across from the fishing hole. For information call Homer Public Works at (C) 907/235-3170. Tent campers will find a natural, pastoral setting at Seaside Farm, mentioned above.

If you want hookups for your RV, there are plenty of places to go off the Spit. See the Driftwood Inn, above. **Oceanview RV Park,** 455 Sterling Hwy. ((C) **907/235-3951**), has 100 spaces near the downtown area overlooking the water with a trail to the beach. Rates are $27 a night for full hookups, including cable TV and showers.

WILDERNESS LODGES

These four lodges all are based across Kachemak Bay from Homer, each in its own remote cove or bay, and each in its own market niche, from budget family lodgings to luxurious accommodations. It's wise to reserve rooms at any of these places months in advance (the preceding winter isn't too soon). More places to stay, some with wilderness-lodge qualities, are listed below under the Halibut Cove and Seldovia sections, later in this chapter. I've also listed remote cabin rentals in Halibut Cove below, and in Kachemak Bay State Park and rented by the Jakolof Bay Ferry and True North Kayak Adventures above.

Across the Bay Tent and Breakfast *Value*   Looking like a summer camp, large canvas tents on wooden platforms stand by themselves on a steep hillside among towering spruce trees. There's a central house for meals, an organic garden to produce the food, an outhouse with a stained-glass window, and a forest volleyball court for games. A long beachfront faces placid Kasitsna Bay—that's where water taxis drop off visitors and where guided sea-kayaking excursions depart ($95 per person). Up the stairs to the road, mountain bikes are for rent ($25 a day) to explore the area's network of abandoned logging roads or to pedal to Seldovia. The tents have beds, but you sleep in your own bag. For families, it's an easy and inexpensive way to the wilderness.

On Kasitsna Bay (P.O. Box 81), Seldovia, AK 99663 (winter P.O. Box 112054, Anchorage, AK 99511; © 907/ 345-2571). © **907/235-3633.** www.tentandbreakfastalaska.com. 6 tents. $58 per person with breakfast, $85 with all meals. Children 6–11 half price, children 5 and under free. MC, V. Closed mid-Sept to Memorial Day.

Kachemak Bay Wilderness Lodge 🌟🌟🌟   I can think of no more idyllic way to become acquainted with Alaska's marine wilderness than staying at this intimate, luxurious lodge, run for more than 25 years by hospitable and generous Mike and Diane McBride. I only wish it were affordable for more people, because it's a place of unforgettable experiences. The McBrides' meals are legendary, and their four cabins manage to seem rustic while having every comfort; it's easy to pretend you're the only guest. But their site, on China Poot Bay, is what's really special—it has excellent tide pooling, kayaking, a black-sand beach, and good hiking trails nearby. Experienced, environmentally conscious guide service is included for sea kayaking, hiking, and wildlife watching; outings by boat carry an extra charge.

China Poot Bay (P.O. Box 956), Homer, AK 99603. © **907/235-8910.** Fax 907/235-8911. www.xyz. net/~wildrnes/lodge.htm. 5 cabins. $2,500 per person for a 5-day stay. Rates include all meals and guide service. Mon–Fri package only. No credit cards; checks accepted. Closed Oct 15–May 1. **Amenities:** Hot tub and sauna; boating; kayaking and all guiding included; in-room massage.

Sadie Cove Wilderness Lodge 🌟   This place reminded me of *Swiss Family Robinson*. Its weathered buildings of rough-cut lumber—owner Keith Iverson hauled and milled them of driftwood—climb the steep shore of the Sadie Cove fjord amid the sound of clattering water from a creek that provides the electricity and fills the wood-fired hot tub, itself an old boat set into the ground. A fifth unit is a 45-foot ketch on the shore with an interior of teak, mahogany, and brass. Keith's wife, Randi, provides the softening touches and cooks the seafood dinners that complete the enchanting experience. Most activities, such as sea kayaking, fishing, and tours, are booked separately.

P.O. Box 2265, Homer, AK 99603. © **907/235-2350.** www.sadiecove.com. 5 units. $250 per person per night, including all meals. MC, V. **Amenities:** Hot tub; sauna; limited laundry service.

Tutka Bay Wilderness Lodge 🌟🌟🌟   John and Nelda Osgood's personalities are reflected in the amazing place they've built—open and enthusiastic, perfectionist and safety conscious, clean-cut but truly Alaskan. On pilings and on a narrow, grassy isthmus by the green water of the Tutka Bay fjord, they've put together what amounts to an upscale hotel in the wilderness, with cabins connected by long boardwalks, a deck large enough for a helicopter to land on, and a kitchen capable of producing gourmet meals. It's quite a feat—the water system alone is a wonder. There's plenty to do: guided tide-pool and forest walks, bird-watching, hiking, berry picking, and other activities around the lodge, and you can pay extra for guided fishing, kayaking, bear-viewing flights, fishing, and other outdoor experiences that go farther afield.

P.O. Box 960, Homer, AK 99603. (✆ **800/606-3909** or 907/235-3905. Fax 907/235-3909. www.
tutkabaylodge.com. 5 cabins. $325–$350 per person per night. Rates include all meals. 2-night minimum stay.
MC, V. Closed Oct–Apr. **Amenities:** Sauna. *In room:* TV/VCR, fridge, coffeemaker, hair dryer.

DINING

Besides those places listed here, don't miss the **Chart Room** at Land's End,
described under "Accommodations," above. For good fast food in an attractive
beachfront dining room, try **Boardwalk Fish and Chips** (✆ **907/235-7749**),
on the boardwalk across from the harbormaster's office on the Spit. The milk
shakes are great. **Two Sisters Bakery,** next to the Bunnell Gallery at the bottom
of Main Street (✆ **907/235-2280**), is a coffeehouse with terrific baked goodies
and a clientele of interesting folk.

Café Cups ★★★ CREATIVE/ECLECTIC   The facade of the yellow house
on Pioneer Avenue, with its elaborate bas-relief sculpture, is truthful advertising
for the arty restaurant and creative food to be found inside. Somehow, just
sitting in the small, hand-crafted dining room makes you feel sophisticated. The
menu specializes in surprises—fresh local seafood is prepared using combinations of international cooking styles in ways that no one may have thought of
before. The experiments seem to work, and now the restaurant is recognized as
one of the very best in the state. The service and hospitality are at once professional and warm. Beer and wine are available. The last time my wife and I dined
there, we emerged in the warm, sunny evening with an afterglow of complete
relaxation and sensual satisfaction.

162 W. Pioneer Ave. (✆ **907/235-8330**. Reservations recommended. Lunch $6–$10; dinner main courses
$16–$23. MC, V. High season Mon–Sat 11am–10pm. Low season Mon–Sat 11am–9pm.

Duncan House Diner DINER/STEAK/SEAFOOD   The locals nest on the
counter stools to sip coffee and tease the waitresses, who give as good as they get.
Most tables are in booths in the open dining room, which is decorated with
memorabilia such as old license plates, advertisements, clocks, and the like. The
hearty breakfasts and lunches are a cut above typical diner fare, and dinners
include steaks, halibut, fettuccine, and other items you'd expect to find only in
a fancier place. Breakfast is served all day, and people rave about the desserts,
which are baked in-house. The atmosphere can be smoky.

125 E. Pioneer Ave. (✆ **907/235-5344**. Lunch $4–$8.50; dinner main courses $10–$17. AE, DISC, MC, V.
Summer, Thurs–Sat 7am–9pm, Sun–Wed 7am–2pm. Winter, Thurs–Sat 7am–8pm, Sun–Wed 7am–2pm.

Fresh Sourdough Express Bakery and Cafe ★ BAKERY/CAFE   Ebullient
Donna and Kevin Maltz's organic eatery is quintessential Homer, starting with
its motto: "Food for people and the planet." But there's no New Age dogma
here. Sourdough Express is fun and tasty, even as it grinds its own grain and
recycles everything in sight. An inexpensive lunch menu includes a buffalo
burger, halibut hoagie, and reindeer grill, as well as various vegetarian choices.
The evening menu has grilled salmon and chicken, halibut cakes, and inexpensive choices. The staff will pack lunches for outings, too. Don't miss dessert from
the scratch bakery. The aptly named "Obscene Brownie," covered with espresso
and ice cream, left me in a happy daze for the rest of the afternoon.

1316 Ocean Dr. (✆ **907/235-7571**. www.freshsourdoughexpress.com. Breakfast $4–$8, lunch $5.50–$7.50;
dinner main courses $7.50–$18. DISC, MC, V. High season daily 7am–10pm. Low season daily 8am–3pm.
Closed Oct to mid-Apr.

The Homestead ★★ STEAK/SEAFOOD   The ambience is that of an old-
fashioned Alaska roadhouse, in a large log building decorated with local art and

lots of summer light. The food is wonderfully satisfying. After a day outdoors, it's a warm, exuberant place for dinner. Many menu items are charbroiled, but the cuisine is more thoughtful than you'd find in your typical steak-and-seafood place, including adventurous and creative concoctions along with the simple, perfectly broiled fish and meat. Service is cordial but sometimes slow. They have a full bar.

Mile 8.2, East End Rd. © 907/235-8723. Reservations recommended. Dinner main courses $17–$25. AE, MC, V. Summer daily 5–10pm. Apr–May Wed–Sat 5–9pm. Closed Oct–Mar.

HOMER NIGHTLIFE

The **Pier One Theatre** (© 907/235-7333; www.pieronetheatre.org) is a strong community theater group housed in a small, corrugated-metal building on the Spit, just short of the small-boat harbor on the left. Instead of the ubiquitous gold rush melodrama and Robert Service readings, Pier One often presents serious drama, musicals, and comedy—not just schlock. They also produce dance, classical music, and youth theater events during the summer. There's generally something playing Thursday to Sunday nights in the summer. Check the *Homer News* or the website for current listings. Tickets are available at the door or can be reserved by phone.

The landmark **Salty Dawg Saloon** is a small log cabin on the Spit with a lighthouse on top. It's the place to swap fish stories after a day on the water.

11 Halibut Cove: Venice on Kachemak Bay

A visit to the tight, roadless little community of Halibut Cove, across Kachemak Bay from Homer, encompasses all the best things about a visit to the bay: a boat ride, the chance of seeing otters or seals, a top-notch restaurant, several galleries and open studios with some of Alaska's best fishy fine art, and even cozy, welcoming accommodations. The settlement sits on either side of a narrow, peaceful channel between a small island and the mainland; the water in between is the road. Boardwalks connect the buildings, and stairs reach down to the water from houses perched on pilings over the shore. The post office is on a floating dock. The pace of life runs no faster than the tide.

It's also an essentially private community. Unless you have your own boat, an excursion boat owned by the community's restaurant is the only way to get there. Once there, you have to leave according to plan, as there's no business district and everything is privately owned. You're really a guest the whole time you're in Halibut Cove—the community is open for visitors, however they arrive, only between 1 and 9pm, unless you're staying at the Quiet Place Lodge or the cabins mentioned below. Not all nearby lodges have privileges to take their guests to Halibut Cove, so make sure you ask before booking.

GETTING THERE

The classic wooden boat *Danny J* (book through Central Charters at © 907/235-7847; www.centralcharter.com) leaves Homer daily in the summer at noon, brings back day-trippers, and takes over dinner guests at 5pm, then brings back the diners later in the evening. The noon trip includes bird-watching at Gull Island. Seating is mostly outdoors, and I wouldn't take the trip in the rain. You also take the *Danny J* if you're spending the night in Halibut Cove. The noon trip is $44 for adults, and the dinner trip is $22, but in the evening you're obliged to buy a meal at the restaurant, too. Kids 12 and under are $22 both times; seniors $36 at noon and $12 for dinner. When not everyone will fit on the *Danny J,* the steel *Storm Bird* goes, too. Reservations and fares are identical to those of the *Danny J.*

ATTRACTIONS

On an afternoon trip, you can bring lunch or eat at the Saltry, described below, and then explore the **boardwalk** that runs from the restaurant along Ismailof Island past the galleries, boat shops, and houses. There's also a barnyard where kids, who already will be in heaven, can look at rabbits, pigs, chickens, ponies, and other animals. Trails branch from the boardwalk across the island to broad views of the bay or to the quiet opposite end of the island. The time in Halibut Cove lasts 2½ hours, which some people find to be too little; bringing a sack lunch instead of eating at the Saltry will allow more time to walk.

Fine art is the major industry in this community. The census lists only 35 residents, but there are 17 artists and three galleries (I suspect the population is several times this in the summer). The summer-only **Halibut Cove's Experience Fine Art Gallery** (✆ **907/296-2215**) is first past the farm on the boardwalk, on pilings above the water. The airy room contains works by Halibut Cove artists only. Farther on, Diana Tillion, who, with her husband, Clem, pioneered the community, opens her **Cove Gallery** and studio to guests. Since the 1950s, she has worked almost exclusively in octopus ink, painstakingly extracted with a hypodermic needle. **Alex Combs,** a grand old Picasso-like figure among Alaska artists, takes visitors at his studio even though he often isn't there. The building is marked by a huge self-portrait and a sign reading, "Leave money, take pottery and paintings."

ACCOMMODATIONS

Besides the lodge listed below, inexpensive housekeeping cabins rent in Halibut Cove. **Halibut Cove Cabins** (✆ **907/296-2214** in summer or 808/322-4110 in winter) consists of two quaint cabins on a steep hill overlooking artist Sydney Bishop's private lagoon, at the opposite end of the island from the main part of town. **Cove House** (✆ **907/296-2255;** http://thecovehouse.com) is near Bishop's place, a two-bedroom house on the water, near the public dock.

The Quiet Place Lodge ★★ This family-run lodge sits perched on pilings that seem to climb up the side of the mainland across the water from the Saltry restaurant (see below). The five cabins looking out on the cove, linked by stairs and boardwalks, are cozy and attractively decorated, with local art, quilts, and flannel sheets. They share bathrooms in the main lodge, and there's also a large rec room with a library, refrigerator, microwave, and telephone for guests. The lodge also has a day spa for massage, facials, and the like. A full breakfast, sack lunch, and seafood dinners are included in the rate, as well as the use of classic wooden rowboats and sea kayaks to explore the Cove, and a water taxi to points around the cove.

P.O. Box 6474, Halibut Cove, AK 99603. ✆ **907/296-2212.** Fax 907/296-2241. www.quietplace.com. 5 cabins with shared bathrooms. $185 per person. Rates include all meals. MC, V. Closed Labor Day–Memorial Day. **Amenities:** Sauna; rowboat and sea kayak loan; courtesy boat.

DINING

Saltry ★★ *(Finds* SEAFOOD This restaurant operates in conjunction with the *Danny J.* It sits on pilings in an idyllic setting over the edge of the smooth, deep green of the cove's main watery avenue. You can sit back in the deck gazebo and sip microbrews and eat fresh baked bread, mussels, sushi, and locally grown salads, followed by fresh fish grilled over charcoal. For a basic lunch, however, there are few choices other than fish chowder and bread. Those who don't eat seafood have few choices. The high prices reflect an incredible location. Make reservations with Central Charters at the same time you reserve your *Danny J* tickets.

On the main channel, Halibut Cove. © 907/235-7847. Lunch $10–$18; dinner main courses $18–$20. MC, V. In season daily 1–9pm. Off-season, call ahead for hours.

12 Seldovia

One evening when my family and I were visiting this town of under 300 near the tip of the Kenai Peninsula, a group of children walked up to us in the empty main street and asked, in a friendly way, what we were doing there. That's how quiet Seldovia is. But early in this century, Seldovia was a metropolis, acting as a major hub for the Cook Inlet area with steamers coming and going with fish and cargo. Unconnected to the road system, the town's decline was steady until 1964, when the Good Friday earthquake destroyed most of what was left. The entire Kenai Peninsula sank, and high tides began covering the boardwalks that comprised most of the city. When the U.S. Army Corps of Engineers came to the rescue, they replaced the boardwalks with rock and gravel and erased much of the waterfront's charm.

A short section of the old boardwalk that remains runs along peaceful **Seldovia Slough,** where you can fish king salmon from shore in June and where a sea otter is in regular residence—you can get a close look at him, if you're patient. The other roads and trails around town make for pleasant walks and bike rides. Here you can wander in and out of the forest and along the beach, see what a real Alaska fishing town is like without seeing many other tourists, and maybe see wildlife—eagles, certainly, and maybe bears.

ESSENTIALS

GETTING THERE   The trip across Kachemak Bay to Seldovia is one of the best parts of going there. Go at least one way on the **Rainbow Tours** (© 907/235-7272; www.rainbowtours.net). Their tour leaves Homer at 9am and visits the Gull Island rookery and the islands of Eldred Passage on the way, with a good chance of seeing otters, puffins, and eagles. They leave the visitor in Seldovia all afternoon, with plenty of time for lunch, for a bike ride, and to see the town, while the boat continues on for whale-watching, returning to Homer at 6pm. Round-trip fares are $50 adults, $45 seniors, $30 children; one-way $30, $25, and $20.

Flying to Seldovia on one of Homer's air taxis costs little more and is a cheap way to do a flightseeing trip. **Homer Air** (© 907/235-8591; www.homerair. com) is one experienced operator.

The Alaska Marine Highway System ferry *Tustumena* (see section 10 of this chapter, on Homer) also visits Seldovia from Homer, but stays briefly. Passenger fare is $20 one-way.

VISITOR INFORMATION   Contact the **Seldovia Chamber of Commerce,** P.O. Box F, Seldovia, AK 99663-0150 (© 907/234-7612; www.xyz. net/~seldovia). The community also has an astonishingly good website at **www. seldovia.com**; it's worth a look as a window into the community even if you don't plan to visit.

FAST FACTS: Seldovia

Bank There is no bank or ATM, so get cash before leaving Homer.

Hospital The **Seldovia Medical Clinic** (✆ **907/234-7825**) at Main Street and Anderson Way is open Monday, Wednesday, and Friday 9am to 5pm.

Police For nonemergency help call ✆ **907/234-7640.**

Sales Tax 6¼% in summer, 4% in winter.

ATTRACTIONS & ACTIVITIES

The **Otterbahn Trail,** built by students at the Susan B. English School, leads through woods, wetlands, and beach cliffs to Outer Beach, where there's a picnic shelter. Allow a couple of hours. Unfortunately, there are few other hiking trails, but dirt roads around town lead to some fine **berry picking** grounds, where in late summer and fall you can quickly collect enough berries for a pie. Those roads also make for intriguing and secluded **mountain biking.** There are many miles to explore without encountering another soul. At this writing, bikes are for rent near the Boardwalk Hotel; if biking is a priority, call ahead or rent in Homer and bring the bike with you. With the lack of hiking trails, bikes really are needed to get into the woods.

The area is good for **sea kayaking.** Kayak'atak (✆ **907/234-7425;** www.alaska.net/~kayaks/), operating out of Herring Bay Mercantile, offers rentals and guided trips. The couple who do the tours, long-time Seldovia residents, take pride in showing off the wildlife and beauty of this little-used area. They charge $110 for a 5-hour tour, including lunch. They also rent kayaks and offer overnight trips.

King salmon spawn in Seldovia Slough, right in the middle of the town. The run peaks in mid-June, and you can fish right from shore. Seldovia also has an edge for halibut anglers, because you start out an hour closer to the **halibut** grounds than Homer. Find a charter through the visitor information sources listed above.

There are several **shops** worth visiting, all on the main street. A tiny, picturesque **Russian Orthodox church** stands on the hill above the town, built in 1891. Call the chamber of commerce to find out how to get in.

ACCOMMODATIONS

Dancing Eagles Cabin and Bed and Breakfast *Finds*   The boardwalk leads to this large house, cabin, and outbuildings, all nestled on rocks and pilings above the slough and connected by their own boardwalks. My muscles always seem to relax just standing on the central deck, among the weathered wood, rock and water. More than quaint, it's almost too good to be true, with the resident otter swimming by. Three rooms under the eaves upstairs are cute but small; two other rooms are larger, as is the cabin, which has a deck, a view of the boat harbor, and its own cooking facilities.

On the boardwalk (P.O. Box 264), Seldovia, AK 99663 (in winter, P.O. Box 240067, Anchorage, AK 99524). ✆ **907/234-7627** in summer or 907/278-0288 in winter. Fax 907/278-0289 in winter. www.dancingeagles. com. 5 units, none with private bathroom; 1 cabin. $110 double; $175 cabin for 2. Extra person in cabin $50. Rates include full breakfast except in cabin. No credit cards. Closed Oct–Apr.

Seldovia's Boardwalk Hotel ★ *Value*   It's quite unusual to find standard rooms as good as these in a town as small and remote as Seldovia. They're light, clean, and comfortable, with private bathrooms and phones; some are quite large. Although there's no real boardwalk attached, rooms on the front do have a sweeping view of the small boat harbor. Besides all that, the place is warm and friendly, just like the town. The hotel offers a $139 package from Homer, which includes a boat tour over and a flightseeing trip back—quite a deal. Other packages including sea kayaking also are well-priced.

243 Main St. (P.O. Box 72), Seldovia, AK 99663. ℂ **800/238-7862** or 907/234-7816. www.alaskaone. com/boardwalkhotel. 14 units. $89–$130 double, $20 each additional adult, $10 children under 12. DISC, MC, V. **Amenities:** Courtesy car; activities booking; bike rental.

DINING

The Buzz Coffeehouse Café CAFE   This espresso shop and community meeting place also serves meals: tasty quiche, calzone, baked goods, and vegetarian dishes.

231 Main St. ℂ **907/234-7479.** All meals $3.75–$7.75. MC, V. Daily 6am–6pm daily.

Mad Fish Restaurant 🐟🐟 SEAFOOD/ECLECTIC   A restaurant like this is unheard of in a town this small. Catherine Haralson is the chef while her husband, Jim, serves her creations, local seafood and beef prepared in ways that would put this in the first class of restaurants in Anchorage, a town that's larger by three orders of magnitude. The masterpiece is the grilled salmon with a lemon-honey wasabi that's gingery and complex but also mild enough to let the natural flavor of the fish shine through. The duck and chops are good, too; the blackberry halibut was a bit sweet for my taste, however. Reserve ahead; they have only seven tables and two seatings for dinner, and hours can suddenly change. The lunch menu is also varied and sophisticated, and even the burgers are done with a flourish.

At the south end of the harbor on Main St. ℂ **907/234-7676.** madfishalaska.com. Reservations recommended. Lunch $6.25–$13; dinner main courses $11.50–$28.50. MC, V. Daily 11:30am–3pm, 5–9pm. Closed mid-Sept to mid-May.

13 Valdez

Big events have shaped Valdez (val-*deez*). The deepwater port, at the head of a long, dramatic fjord, first developed with the 1898 Klondike Gold Rush and an ill-fated attempt to establish an alternative route to the gold fields from here. Later, the port and the Richardson Highway, which connected Valdez to the rest of the state, served a key role in supplying materials during World War II. On Good Friday, March 27, 1964, all of that was erased when North America's greatest recorded earthquake occurred under Miners Lake, west of town off a northern fjord of Prince William Sound, setting off an underwater landslide that caused a huge wave to sweep over the waterfront, killing 32 people. The town sank and was practically destroyed. The U.S. Army Corps of Engineers rebuilt a drab replacement in a new, safer location that slowly filled with nondescript modern buildings over the next 2 decades. A walking tour provides the locations of a few buildings that were moved.

The construction of the trans-Alaska pipeline, completed in 1977, brought a new economic boom to Valdez and enduring economic prosperity as tankers came to fill with the oil. Then, on March 24, 1989, on Good Friday 25 years after the earthquake, the tanker *Exxon Valdez*, on its way south, hit the clearly marked Bligh Reef, causing the largest and most environmentally costly oil spill ever in North America. The spill cleanup added another economic boom, but a decade later, most of the wildlife populations affected had yet to fully recover.

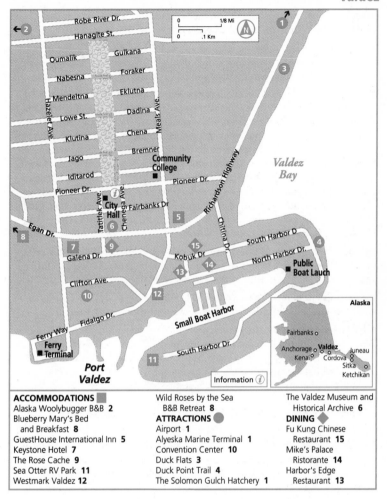

Information (i)

ACCOMMODATIONS ■
Alaska Woolybugger B&B **2**
Blueberry Mary's Bed
and Breakfast **8**
GuestHouse International Inn **5**
Keystone Hotel **7**
The Rose Cache **9**
Sea Otter RV Park **11**
Westmark Valdez **12**

Wild Roses by the Sea
B&B Retreat **8**
ATTRACTIONS ●
Airport **1**
Alyeska Marine Terminal **1**
Convention Center **10**
Duck Flats **3**
Duck Point Trail **4**
The Solomon Gulch Hatchery **1**

The Valdez Museum and
Historical Archive **6**
DINING ◆
Fu Kung Chinese
Restaurant **15**
Mike's Palace
Ristorante **14**
Harbor's Edge
Restaurant **13**

Today, Valdez is a middle American town, driven by industry but turning to the vast resources of Prince William Sound for outdoor recreation. In town you can tour two small museums and the fish hatchery, and take a hike or a river float. The town has made major strides in improving its appearance, especially on the waterfront, but it isn't the sort of historic or charming fishing village that justifies a trip all by itself. Instead, come for the setting—the wildlife, fishing, and sightseeing in the Sound, and the spectacular drive down the Richardson Highway.

Because Valdez lies at the end of a funnel of steep mountains that catches moisture off the ocean, the weather tends to be overcast and rainy in summer and extremely snowy in winter.

ESSENTIALS

GETTING THERE   By Car   The **Richardson Highway,** described in "Alaska's Highways a la Carte," in chapter 9, dramatically crosses Thompson Pass and descends into the narrow valley where Valdez lies. Try to do the trip in daylight, in clear weather, and stop at the Worthington Glacier. This is the only road to Valdez. The drive from Anchorage is 6 hours without stops.

By Bus   Gray Line's **Alaskon Express** (© **800/544-2206** or 907/835-4445; www.graylineofalaska.com/alaskon.cfm) runs to Anchorage 3 or 4 days a week in the summer, taking 10 hours for the trip; the fare is $71.

By Ferry   The **Alaska Marine Highway System** (© **800/642-0066** or 907/835-4436; www.state.ak.us/ferry) calls on Valdez daily in the summer with the *Bartlett*, a ferry connecting Valdez, Whittier, and Cordova. One time-tested way to see the Sound is to put your vehicle on the ferry in Whittier for the 7-hour run to Valdez, then drive north on the Richardson Highway. A forest ranger rides on board to present programs. The fare is $76 for a car up to 15 feet long and $64 for an adult passenger (children half price). The *Tustumena* comes from Seward roughly once a week. The *Kennicott* runs across the Gulf of Alaska between Valdez and Juneau once a month June through September. The 40-hour run costs $102 for adults, $49 to $170 for a cabin. See section 1 in chapter 5 for information about the system.

By Tour Boat   **Prince William Sound Cruises and Tours** (© **800/992-1297** or 907/835-4731; full listing below) offers summer cruises between Whittier and Valdez, including lunch, for $119 one-way ($59 ages 4 to 12).

By Air   **Era Aviation** (© **800/866-8394** or 907/835-2636; www.eraaviation. com) flies several times a day each way between Anchorage and Valdez.

GETTING AROUND   A bicycle is a good way to get around the central town area. **Beaver Sports,** 316 Galena St. (© **907/835-4727;** www.beaversports.net), rents mountain bikes for $6 an hour, $16 for 6 hours, and $20 per day. They also rent snowshoes and skies.

To get to the airport, taxis are available from **Valdez Yellow Cab** (© **907/835-2500**).

Valdez-U-Drive (© **907/835-4402**) and **Hertz** (© **800/654-3131** or 907/835-4378; www.hertz.com) are at the airport.

VISITOR INFORMATION   The Valdez Convention and Visitors Bureau maintains a **Visitor Information Center** at 200 Chenega Ave., a block off Egan Drive (P.O. Box 1603), Valdez, AK 99686 (© **800/770-5954,** 907/835-4636, or 907/835-2984 in winter; www.valdezalaska.org). Pick up the free town map and useful *Vacation Planner.* They're open in summer daily from 8am to 8pm, and normal business hours in the winter. A booking agency, **One Call Does It All,** at 210 N. Harbor Dr. (P.O. Box 2197), Valdez, AK 99686 (© **907/835-4988;** fax 907/835-5865; www.alaska.net/~onecall), reserves lodgings, fishing charters, activities, and tours in the area.

SPECIAL EVENTS   The **Valdez Ice Climbing Festival** (© **907/835-2984**) is held in late February or early March on the frozen waterfalls of Keystone Canyon. Three **summer fishing derbies** are organized by the Valdez Chamber of Commerce (© **907/835-2330**), with prizes that have totaled more than $75,000. The **Halibut Derby** runs all summer, the **Pink Salmon Derby** during most of July, and the **Silver Salmon Derby** is through August until early September. Buy a ticket at the boat-rental booth at the visitor center.

The Last Frontier Theater Conference (© **907/834-1612;** www.uaa.alaska. edu/pwscc) brings famous playwrights and directors to the community for seminars and performances in June. Arthur Miller, Edward Albee, and other famous writers have met the public here in fairly intimate settings.

FAST FACTS: Valdez

Banks Two **banks** are on Egan Drive, both with ATMs.

Hospital **Valdez Community** (📞 **907/835-2249**) is at 911 Meals Ave.

Internet Access Free at **Valdez Consortium Library** (📞 **907/835-4632**), but you may need to call ahead to reserve a time.

Police For nonemergencies phone the **Valdez Police Department** at 📞 **907/835-4560.**

Post Office On Galena Drive, 1 block back from Egan Drive.

Taxes Valdez has no sales tax but does charge a 6% **bed tax.**

GETTING OUTSIDE
SIGHTSEEING & WILDLIFE TOURS

For most visitors, a daylong ride on a tour boat into the Sound is likely to be the most memorable part of a visit to Valdez. After passing through the long fjord of Port Valdez, the boats enter an ice-choked bay in front of **Columbia Glacier.** Some also continue to an active glacier farther west, or continue all the way to Whittier.

Environmental activist Stan Stephens started and still runs the main tour boat company, now owned by the Chugach Alaska Native corporation. **Prince William Sound Cruises and Tours** (📞 **800/992-1297** or 907/835-4731; www.princewilliamsound.com) has its office at the west end of the small boat harbor. Stephens predicted and was working to prevent an accident like the *Exxon Valdez* grounding right up to the eve of the disaster, and he's still working for improved environmental safeguards for the oil companies. The company offers tours of various lengths to the glacier and other sites, often seeing seals, sea otters, and sea lions, and sometimes whales. Trips go to Whittier and Meares Glacier, but the primary destination is Columbia Glacier and the company's camp there, on Growler Island, where passengers get off and, on some trips, have a meal and can even spend the night and go boating. Prices range from $74 ($37 ages 4 to 12) for a 6-hour cruise to $119 to visit both glaciers and stop for lunch on the island ($59 kids). You can spend the night in a tent cabin on the island for as little as $200 double, meals included. See "Sea Kayaking & Sailing," below, for appealing options to add on a trip to Growler Island.

SEA KAYAKING & SAILING

Raven Charters, Slip C-25, Valdez Boat Harbor (📞 **907/835-5863;** www. alaska.net/~ravenchr), is run by a family living on its 50-foot boat who take clients sailing and exploring the Sound. The wind tends to be light and change-able, but a sailboat makes a comfortable base for discovering interesting, isolated places. All-inclusive prices start at $750 per night for up to four passengers, or $600 for a day charter, with discounts for longer trips.

Sea kayaking right around the town of Valdez is not as appealing as some other places you can choose, but experienced kayakers and outdoors people have unlimited possibilities in Prince William Sound. One idea is to take your kayak, perhaps rented in Valdez from **Anadyr Adventures** (📞 **800/TO-KAYAK** or 907/835-2814; www.alaska.net/~anadyr), on the ferry *Tustumena's* weekly trip from Valdez to Seward (see "Getting There," above), disembarking at the whistle stop in the village of Chenega Bay. This scheme allows you to inexpensively start out in deep wilderness. The ferry stops in Chenega only when a passenger has a reservation. Anadyr and **Pangaea Adventures** (© **800/660-9637** or 907/ 835-8442, www.alaskasummer.com) also offer expeditions in the Sound, including "mothership" trips which offer a soft bunk after each day's paddling.

FISHING & BOATING

The ocean waters around Valdez are rich in salmon and halibut. From shore, you can fish for salmon on Allison Point, along Dayville Road on the far side of the port from Valdez. Salmon here are returning to the Solomon Gulch Hatchery and are primarily pinks in June and July and silvers in August and September. The success rate is high when the fish are running—one wild year, fish literally jumped into boats—but it's not the most aesthetic fishing experience, right along a road with many other people. (See "Fishing," in chapter 2, for further advice.)

For more isolated fishing, use one of the **fishing charters** available in the boat harbor. Halibut charters cost around $150 per person, as they have to go a long way. Half-day salmon charters are around $80, and troll right in Port Valdez. Get a referral from the Valdez Chamber of Commerce or check the links on their website; you also can book through **One Call Does It All** (both are listed above under "Visitor Information"). **Popeye Charters** (© **907/835-2659;** www.alaska.net/~popeyes) is the best in town.

If you're up for running your own boat, they're for rent from **Valdez Harbor Boat and Tackle Rentals** (© **907/835-5002;** www.fishcentral.net/boatrentals. htm); a 16-foot boat costs $135 a day, plus fuel. You can get all the gear you need there. Or use the boat to explore the area, perhaps with a visit to Shoup Glacier, 20 minutes west. Renting a boat overnight, you can pull up on an uninhabited shore and set up camp.

Ketchum Air Service (© **800/433-9114** or 907/835-3789; www.ketchumair. com) offers fly-in fishing starting at $249 per person, and flightseeing trips.

HIKING & MOUNTAIN BIKING

The Valdez Trails Association and other agencies have been busy in recent years, and now Valdez has a broad selection of good day hikes and one superb overnight. The visitor center can advise you on choices beyond those I can list here.

The easiest is a pleasant forest and shore walk to **Dock Point,** starting at the east side of the boat harbor, at the end of North Harbor Drive. It's a peaceful, natural walk close to town, with boardwalks and overlooks and berries along the way in season.

> _Tips_ **Columbia Glacier Pros & Cons**
>
> The Columbia Glacier is immense—3 miles across at its face and 30 miles long—and it is retreating fast, dumping thousands of icebergs that float over miles of water in front. The smooth surface and weird white and blue shapes look like a vast Henry Moore sculpture garden that's been invaded by seals and other wildlife. The biggest drawback of visiting the Columbia is that you won't see it calve (when ice falls off the face) because boats can't get close enough through all the icebergs. For that you must go to glaciers in the western Sound, such as Meares. But those glaciers are closer to Whittier.

For a longer hike and perhaps an overnight, the new, state-maintained **Shoup Glacier Trail** runs 12 miles west from town along the shore of Port Valdez to the glacier. The going is generally flat, and there are many places to get down to the beach, with wild iris and many other flowers. Cool yourself in a waterfall. Camping is unrestricted, but be sure to bring mosquito repellent and review bear avoidance techniques (see "Outdoors Health & Safety," in chapter 2). If you plan to go all the way, reserve one of the three state parks cabins there, which costs $50 a night (see "State Parks Cabin Reservation Tricks," in section 1 of this chapter). The trail starts at the end of West Egan Drive.

The **Solomon Gulch Trail** starts across from the fish hatchery on Dayville Road (see below) and goes steeply up to Solomon Lake, where locals swim. Be prepared for bears.

Trails off **Mineral Creek Road,** above town off Hanagita Street, are great for walking, mountain biking, or berry picking, and in winter there is a fine cross-country skiing trail network.

The new **Valdez Goat Trail** runs from the spectacular Bridal Veil Falls at mile 13.8 of the Richardson Highway for a distance of 2½ miles on an abandoned roadbed, past some great views. The Trails Association hopes to connect this and other historic trail segments all the way through Thompson Pass 35 miles to Tsaina Lodge.

RAFTING

Keystone Raft and Kayak Adventures (© **800/328-8460** or 907/835-2606; www.alaskawhitewater.com) takes five trips a day 4½ miles down the amazing Keystone Canyon, a virtual corridor of rock with a floor of frothing water, past the crashing tumult of the 900-foot Bridal Veil Falls. It's a wild ride, and not without risk—serious mishaps do sometimes occur. They charge $35 per person. The company also has numerous longer trips, ranging from a day to 10 days, on many of the region's rivers.

FLIGHTSEEING

Besides several fixed-wing operators at the airport, **Era Helicopters** (© **800/843-1947** or 907/835-2595; www.eraaviation.com) offers a 1-hour, $199 trip that overflies Columbia Glacier and lands in front of Shoup Glacier; a landing on top of Valdez Glacier goes for $179.

ATTRACTIONS

The **Alaska Cultural Center,** at the airport (© **907/834-1690;** www.uaa. alaska.edu/pwscc), is called "The Whitney" by locals for its benefactors, Jesse and Maxine Whitney, who donated a large collection of Native Alaska arts and crafts and animal mounts. They're open May through mid-September Monday to Friday 9am to 6pm and charge $4 admission.

The Valdez Museum and Historical Archive 🐾★   The museum contains an exceptional history display that follows the story of the area from early white exploration through the oil spill. It's a little light on Alaska Native culture, but there are other museums for that. Each gallery is well designed and some are fun, like the restored bar room. There's also a saltwater aquarium and an area with transportation relics, including shiny fire engines dating from 1886.

The museum recently built a ¹⁄₂₀-scale model of how Valdez looked at its old site, before it was destroyed by the 1964 earthquake. Using photographs, records, and old timers' memories, they have tried to bring that lost city back to life in 400 miniature buildings. The **Historical Old Town Valdez Model** 🐾 is at the museum annex at 436 S. Hazelet Ave., which also has an interactive earthquake exhibit, including a shaking table, seismograph, and children's activities. It is open in the summer 9am to 4pm and admission is $1.50.

217 Egan Dr. (ℂ 907/835-2764. www.alaska.net/~vldzmuse. $3 adults, $2.50 over age 65, $2 ages 14–18, free for children under 14. Summer Mon–Sat 9am–6pm, Sun 8am–5pm. Winter Mon–Fri 11am–5pm.

The Solomon Gulch Hatchery ✦ When the pink salmon are returning from late June to early August, they swarm on the hatchery in a blizzard of fish. The hatchery releases more than 200 million pinks each year, as well as millions of chums and silvers (or coho). There is no stream for the salmon to return to, so they try to get back into the hatchery, crowding together in a solid sea of fighting muscle. Seals and birds come in to feed, and you can stand on shore and watch the spectacle. (Surefire fishing is allowed up the shore—see "Fishing," in section 14, below.) A self-guided walking tour leads around tanks and pools of fish, but it's the seasonal salmon run that makes it worth the trip.

On Dayville Rd. on the way to the tanker terminal. (ℂ **907/835-1329**. Free self-guided tours. Summer daily 9am–9pm.

Alyeska Pipeline Marine Terminal Bus Tour The 2-hour ride visits the terminal where tankers carrying much of the nation's oil supply are loaded. You can't enter any of the buildings. The highlights are a chance to see the big ships and a scenic overlook, the only point where you can get off the bus.

Operated by Valdez Tours, corner of Pioneer and Tatitlek sts. (ℂ **907/835-2686**. $17.50 adults, $8 children ages 6–11; free for children ages 5 and under. May–Sept.

ACCOMMODATIONS

Alaska Woollybugger B&B ✦ *Finds* Named for a fishing fly, this place takes its theme seriously, with bamboo rods on display, a fly tying center for guests' use, and even a hand-tied fly as a souvenir when you leave. It's also a sumptuously furnished and decorated B&B with many thoughtful touches, including thick robes and sheepskin slippers for the guests. Doug and Darla East gutted the striking white house in 1998 to create the B&B in the lower level. Dave is a master gardener whose award-winning flower garden is known for its bold colors. The common room has satellite TV and a full kitchen and dining area for guests' use. Breakfasts are rich and elaborate.

1130 Ptarmigan St. (P.O. Box 3563) Valdez, AK 99686. (ℂ **907/835-8505**. Fax 907/835-4596. www. alaska.net/~akwoolly. 2 units. High season $115 double, $20 each additional person. Low season $90 double, $15 each additional person. Rates include full breakfast. MC, V. **Amenities:** Well-equipped exercise room; free laundry machines.

Blueberry Mary's Bed and Breakfast ✦ *Value* A lucky few get to sleep under Mary Mehlberg's handmade quilts on her feather beds, gaze at the ocean views, bake in the sauna, and breakfast on her blueberry waffles made from wild berries that grow just outside the house. She only takes parties of two or less and sometimes closes for breaks. Those who do stay here get a terrific deal on immaculate, handcrafted rooms with private entrances and a prime location.

Blueberry Hill Rd., off West Egan Dr. (P.O. Box 1244), Valdez, AK 99686. (ℂ **907/835-5015**. www.alaska. net/~bmary. 2 units. $90 double, including tax. Rates include full breakfast. No credit cards. Closed Oct 1– May 1. **Amenities:** Sauna. *In room:* TV/VCR with free movies, fridge, microwave oven, coffeemaker, hair dryer, iron.

GuestHouse International Inn ✦✦ The best hotel in town, this is also the only hotel with standard rooms at the level you would find in a quality national chain. Gutted and rebuilt in 2000, the hotel has wide halls and spacious rooms decorated in burgundy, hunter green, and dark wood, with lots of amenities, large TVs, and mirrors. It's nothing exceptional if you're used to the hotels found around any big U.S. airport, except that it's in Valdez. A continental breakfast comes with the room.

100 Meals Ave., Valdez, AK 99686. ℂ **888/478-4445** or 907/835-4445. Fax 907/835-2437. www.guest housealaska.com. 78 units. High season $129–$149 double. Low season $74–$89 double. AE, DISC, DC, MC, V. **Amenities:** Exercise room; business center (computer, printer, copier, dataport); coin-op laundry. *In room:* TV/VCR, dataport, fridge, microwave oven, coffeemaker, hair dryer, iron.

Keystone Hotel 〈*Value*〉 This building, made of modular units, was built by Exxon to serve as its offices for the oil-spill cleanup operation but wasn't completed until late summer 1989, so the company occupied it for only about a month. It stood vacant for 5 years before a new owner remodeled it into a hotel, with small rooms that mostly have two twin beds or one double bed, though some have two doubles. Select a room when you check in, as they vary in decor; some have dark paneling, some are more modern.

401 W. Egan Dr. (P.O. Box 2148), Valdez, AK 99686. ℂ **888/835-0665** or 907/835-3851. Fax 907/835-5322. www.alaskan.com/keystonehotel. 104 units. $95 double. Extra person over age 12 $10. Rates include continental breakfast. AE, MC, V. Closed in winter. **Amenities:** Restaurant (outdoor salmon bake); coin-op laundry. *In room:* TV.

Wild Roses by the Sea B&B Retreat ★★ Light pours from bay windows that overlook the water and surrounding woods into large, elegantly appointed rooms with high ceilings, decorated with Asian and contemporary art, and finished in light colors, wood floors, and Berber style carpets. Best of all is the spacious and private "Ocean View Guesthouse," a downstairs suite with a kitchen, living room, and VCR. The hostess, Rose Fong, prepares elaborate breakfasts in the summer and feeds guests snacks and beverages all day.

620 Fiddlehead Lane (P.O. Box 3396), Valdez, AK 99686. ℂ **907/835-2930.** Fax 907/835-4966. www.bythe sea.alaska.net. 3 units. Summer $125–$145 double, including full breakfast. Winter $89 double, continental breakfast. Extra person $10. MC, V. *In room:* TV, dataport, hair dryer, iron.

CAMPING

Valdez is a popular RV destination. When the salmon are running, RVs can park, self-contained, at the **Allison Point** fishing area (ℂ **907/835-2282**) for $10 a night; water and portable toilets are available. The **Sea Otter RV Park,** P.O. Box 947, Valdez, AK 99686 (ℂ **800/831-2787** in Alaska only, or 907/ 835-2787), sits on the outside of the boat harbor breakwater, a mosquito-free spot with views and beachfront where you can fish for salmon or watch the harbor sea otters. They have a laundry and other facilities, and charge $25 for full hookups.

The town's **Valdez Glacier Campground** has 101 well-separated sites among alder and cottonwood trees near the airport, but the trees also make it a mosquito haven. They have pit toilets and well water. The fee is $10 a night.

The best campground in the area is the state's **Blueberry Lake Campground,** 24 miles out of town on the Richardson Highway, just below Thompson Pass. The campground is above the tree line, with mountaintop views and access to limitless alpine hiking. It can be windy and cold. The small lake is stocked with trout. Fifteen well-screened sites are $12 on a self-serve system. There are pit toilets.

DINING

Fu Kung Chinese Restaurant ★ CHINESE This long-established family restaurant in a Quonset hut near the harbor serves the best meals in town; in Valdez, that's not a huge claim to fame, but this place is good. The interior of the old metal building is clean and pleasant, with a fish tank, warm colors, and plenty of room. The food is plentiful and tasty, especially the gingery bean curd with vegetables, the hot and sour soup, and the kung pao chicken. The sushi is good, too. Service is fast and attentive. In winter, they often close earlier than the hours listed below.

207 Kobuk Dr. (1 block from the boat harbor). © **907/835-5255.** Lunch $6.75–$8.75; dinner main courses $11–$16,. MC, V. Daily 11am–11pm.

Harbor's Edge Restaurant ⭑ STEAK/SEAFOOD   This is the town's main place for a nice dinner out, with candles and linen tablecloths. Just across the street from the boat harbor, it has pleasant indoor and outdoor seating areas. The menu has typical waterfront beef and sea choices, plus a few more ambitious entrees and pasta. For lunch, it's a comfortable place with reasonable prices and choices that include wraps, soups, salads, and fish as well as the typical sandwiches and burgers.

107 N. Harbor Dr. © **907/835-5989.** Lunch $4–$10, dinner entrees $16–$39 (most $20–$30). AE, MC, V. Summer daily 6am–10pm. Winter 11am–9pm.

Mike's Palace Ristorante PIZZA/STEAK/SEAFOOD   This is a good family pizza restaurant, a place where Valdez residents come for a casual evening out. The calzone is good, the service skilled, and everything consistent. It's a warm, cheerful place, perfect after a day on the water—the boat harbor is right across the street. Mike's also has a place in history: Capt. Joseph Hazelwood was waiting for a take-out pizza here when he slipped next door to the Club Bar for his last drink before starting the fateful voyage of the *Exxon Valdez* that hit Bligh Reef. Mike also serves his national Greek cuisine and has a beer and wine license.

201 N. Harbor Dr. © **907/835-2365.** Lunch $5–$9; dinner main courses $9–$25. MC, V. Daily 11am–11pm.

The Rose Cache *Finds* ECLECTIC   A local pastor and his wife, Dan and Nancy Bower, have created an extravaganza of faux Victorian decoration so alluring that little girls celebrate their birthdays with tea parties here. Open regularly only for lunch, it has become so popular with the locals that reservations often are needed. The menu includes a lot of comfort food, but also exotic items the owners have picked up on their travels—they even do Ethiopian cuisine sometimes. Everything comes with a side salad, despite the reasonable prices. The desserts are famous.

321 Egan Dr. © **907/835-8383.** Lunch $6–$9. MC, V. Mon–Sat 11am–2pm. Closed Jan.

14 Cordova: Hidden Treasure

The first time I ever went to Cordova, my companion and I arrived at the Mudhole Smith Airport in a small plane and happened upon an old guy with a pickup truck who offered to let us ride in back with some boards the 10 miles to town. The highway led out onto a broad, wetland plain—the largest contiguous wetland in the Western Hemisphere, as it happens. Our guide's voice, studded with profanity, boomed through the back window as he told us proudly about the diversity of the wildlife to be found out there. Then, absolutely bursting with enthusiasm, he leaned on the horn and bellowed, "Look at them swans!" We looked; trumpeters paddling in the marsh looked back. He would have invited them along to the bar, too, if he'd known how.

Every time I've been to Cordova since, I've been taken under the wings of new friends. Although they usually don't express themselves the same way that first

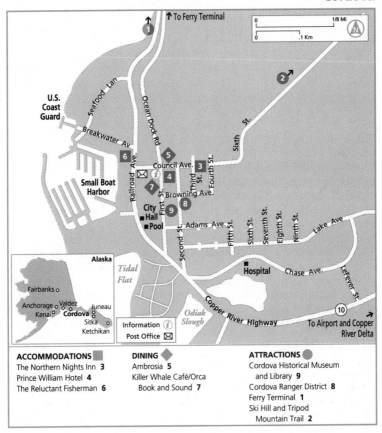

ACCOMMODATIONS ■
The Northern Nights Inn **3**
Prince William Hotel **4**
The Reluctant Fisherman **6**

DINING ◆
Ambrosia **5**
Killer Whale Café/Orca
Book and Sound **7**

ATTRACTIONS ●
Cordova Historical Museum
and Library **9**
Cordova Ranger District **8**
Ferry Terminal **1**
Ski Hill and Tripod
Mountain Trail **2**

gentleman did, they are just as enthusiastic to show off the amazing natural riches of their little kingdom. Tourists are still something of a novelty here, for Cordova isn't just off the beaten track—it's not on the track at all. There's no road to the rest of the world and the town is an afterthought on the ferry system. Boosters call their town "Alaska's Hidden Treasure." For once, they're right.

Our family has had some of our happiest times in Cordova, visiting the **Childs Glacier** and seeing the swans and geese on the delta; hiking into the mountains behind town; boating on the Sound to meet the sea otters, sea lions, eagles, and spawning salmon; hiking and canoeing at a remote lake cabin—and meeting no other people at all. In town, we made new friends whenever we turned around, and received hearty greetings from old friends from previous visits. Leaving on the ferry for Valdez, I've watched Cordova shrinking behind us with a wistful hope that it would never change.

So far, I've gotten my wish. You can feel a bit like an anthropologist discovering a tribe lost to time, for Cordova has the qualities small towns are supposed to have had but lost long ago in America (if they ever did have them). Walking down First Street, you pass an old-fashioned independent grocery store, the fishermen's union hall, and Steen's gift shop, run by the same family since 1909— no chains or franchises. People leave their keys in the car and their doors unlocked at night. When a friend of mine bought one of the quaint, moss-roofed hillside houses a few years ago, he didn't receive a key—the simple reason was that the front door didn't have a lock.

The commercial fishermen who power the economy have fought to protect Cordova from change. They pushed for the oil industry to improve its shipping practices years before the 1989 oil spill and then, after the disaster (which hurt Cordova worst of all), lobbied for the money won from Exxon to be spent on the Sound's environment. They have resisted building a road to Cordova, as well. Another faction in town, the merchants and tourism workers, want a road. The debate is hot, and several local elections between the two camps have been decided by a single vote.

This controversy has been going on for 50 or 60 years. The town's heyday was in 1911, when the Copper River and Northwestern Railroad opened, carrying copper ore down from the mine at Kennecott; it hit a low when the mine closed in 1938. Since then, boosters have been trying to get a road built on the old rail line, north along the Copper River to Chitina (that fascinating area is covered in chapter 9, under "Wrangell–St. Elias National Park and Kennecott"). The road builders have made it only about 50 miles out of town so far. From Cordova, the **Copper River Highway** provides access to the best bird-watching and, in my judgment, the most impressive glacier in Alaska, as well as trails and magnificent vistas and areas to see wildlife. In town, the small-boat harbor is a doorway to Prince William Sound.

ESSENTIALS

GETTING THERE   By Ferry   Cordova is served twice a week from Valdez, once from Whittier, by the ferry *Bartlett* of the **Alaska Marine Highway System** (© **800/642-0066** or 907/424-7333 local dock; www.state.ak.us/ferry). If you plan to make this trip, study the schedule carefully before planning the rest of your itinerary, as it can be a puzzle to do it both ways. The passenger fare for the 5½-hour run from Valdez is $33, while the 7-hour trip from Whittier is $64; children pay roughly half. It may pay to bring a car, depending on how much time you want to spend out the road, on the delta, and at the glacier. Taking a vehicle under 15 feet one way from Valdez to Cordova is $64. See section 1 of chapter 5 for information about the system.

By Air   Alaska Airlines (© **800/426-0333** or 907/424-7151; www.alaskaair.com) flies one jet daily each direction, from Anchorage to the west and Yakutat, Juneau, and Seattle to the southeast, with one or two more flights to Anchorage operated by **Era Aviation** (© **800/866-8394;** www.eraaviation.com).

The **Airport Shuttle** from the Reluctant Fisherman Hotel (© **907/424-3272**) meets all planes and charges $10 one-way. Taxis are usually available as well from **Wild Hare Cab** (© **907/424-3939**). At times a free van is available at the ferry dock, ask the purser.

GETTING AROUND   You can easily walk around downtown Cordova, but that's not where the most interesting sights are. To get out on the Copper River Highway, you'll need a car, bus, or, if you're vigorous, a bike.

Cars are for rent from the Reluctant Fisherman Hotel (listed later) for $75 a day, without mileage charges; the airport shuttle is free when you rent a car. **Cordova Auto Rentals** (© **907/424-5982;** www.ptialaska.net/~cars) charges comparable prices for cars, vans, and four-wheel-drive vehicles at the airport (they have canoes, too).

Rent bikes, kayaks, skiffs, canoes, and fishing and camping gear at **Cordova Coastal Outfitters,** at the boat harbor below the fishermen's memorial (© **800/ 357-5145** or 907/424-7424; www.cdvcoastal.com). They're described in full below.

To get to remote cabins and fly-in fishing, try **Fishing and Flying** (© **907/ 424-3324**), located at the airport, or **Cordova Air** (© **907/424-3289**), based on Eyak Lake.

VISITOR INFORMATION   A **Cordova Chamber of Commerce Visitor Center** (© **907/424-7260;** www.cordovachamber.com) is at 404 First St., north of Council Avenue (P.O. Box 99, Cordova, AK 99574). They're open Monday to Friday from 10am to 3pm; summer hours are longer, but vary. Besides the usual information, the center has a 60-minute recorded walking tour that you can listen to as it guides you around town.

The **Cordova Ranger District** of the Chugach National Forest, upstairs in the old white courthouse at Second Street and Browning (P.O. Box 280), Cordova, AK 99574 (© **907/424-7661;** www.fs.fed.us/r10/chugach), has displays and provides maps and guide information that's indispensable for planning outdoor activities. The staff will sit down and help you figure out what you want to do.

SPECIAL EVENTS   The **Cordova Ice Worm Festival** is a winter carnival the first full weekend in February; the big ice worm—or, to be precise, ice centipede—marches in a parade. **The Copper River Delta Shorebird Festival** (**907/424-7260;** www.ptialaska.net/~midtown) revolves around the coming of dizzying swarms of millions of shorebirds that use the delta and beaches near the town as a migratory stopover in early May. The whole community gets involved to host bird-watchers and put on a full schedule of educational and outdoor activities that lasts 5 days.

 FAST FACTS: Cordova

Banks There are two banks on First Street, with **ATMs.**

Hospital **Cordova Community Medical Center** is on Chase Street (© **907/424-8000**), off the Copper River Highway near the slough.

Internet Access Find it at the **Cordova Public Library** (© **907/424-6667**) and at **Laura's Liquor Shoppe** (© **907/424-3144**), both on First Street.

Police For nonemergency calls, call © **907/424-6100.**

Post Office At Railroad Avenue and Council.

Taxes Sales tax is 6%; rooms and car rentals carry an additional 6%.

ATTRACTIONS & HIKING NEAR TOWN

ATTRACTIONS   Cordova mostly is for outdoor activities (covered below), but save some time to wander around town, make discoveries, and meet people, possibly with the help of the **historic walking tour booklet** produced by the historic society, available from the chamber of commerce.

The **Cordova Historical Museum,** at 622 First St. (© **907/424-6665**), is a well-presented one-room display with some valuable artifacts reflecting

Cordova's eventful past. The three-seat kayak and other artifacts of Prince William Sound Native peoples are of particular interest. Cordova is the home of the last few Eyak, a Native people whose language now has only one speaker left. There's also a historic lighthouse lens, a Linotype machine, the interior of a fishing boat, and photographs of fishing and historic scenes. The museum is open summer Monday to Saturday 10am to 6pm, Sunday 2 to 4pm; winter Tuesday to Friday 1 to 5pm, Saturday 2 to 4pm. Recommended donation $1.

HIKING   Cordova has more good hiking trails per capita than any place I know. The Cordova Ranger Station can provide you with a free trail-guide booklet with lots of ideas and maps. There are three close to town (trails farther out are listed below, in the section on the Copper River Delta).

The **Tripod Mountain Trail** begins right from town and climbs 1,255 feet over less than a mile up the first mountain back from the shore, a half-day hike with views that present the Sound and Cordova like a map below you. The trail begins at the foot of the town ski lift, on Sixth Street—take Browning up the hill.

Partway up Tripod Mountain, near the middle drop off of the ski lift, a 1-mile trip links to the **Crater Lake Trail,** which eventually joins the **Power Creek Trail** on a loop of 12 miles. An easier start for that route is the Power Creek Road—take it along the north side of Eyak Lake to the end, 7 miles from town. The creek has spawning red salmon in July and attracts a lot of bears; watch, but don't get out of your car if you come upon one. The trail follows the creek through dramatic scenery 4.2 miles to the Power Creek Forest Service cabin, with a great view (reserve through the system described in section 3, Chugach National Forest, earlier).

THE COPPER RIVER DELTA

The delta and its star attraction, the **Childs Glacier,** make an unforgettable day trip by car or tour bus from Cordova, but if you have a couple of days, you can do more. The backwaters, sloughs, and ponds beg to be explored by canoe. Bird-watchers will especially enjoy such a paddle, or visits to the boardwalks and blinds set up by the Forest Service. You can raft the rivers. There are excellent hiking trails and mountain-biking routes branching from the road, and Forest Service cabins to stay in.

The delta seems to go on forever, a vast patchwork of marsh, pond, small hills of trees, and the huge, implacable gray river itself. The glacial silt it carries away—some two million tons a day—has built this 700,000-acre wetland. A well-maintained gravel road leads across it, all in Chugach National Forest, and the rangers have done a good job of providing ways and places to enjoy and learn about the area. The road itself is the old bed of the Copper River and Northwestern Railroad. It leads 48 miles to the **Million Dollar Bridge.** Built by Michael Heney, a magician of a 19th-century railroad builder who also constructed the White Pass and Yukon Route in Skagway, the 200-mile Copper River line was an engineering triumph that brought the mind-boggling wealth of the Kennecott Copper Mine to ships in Cordova (read more about the mine in the section on "Wrangell–St. Elias National Park and Kennecott," in chapter 9). The bridge over the Copper River went up in a race against time between two surging glaciers in 30-foot-deep, fast-flowing glacial water, in winter. The bridge stood 56 years, until the 1964 earthquake knocked down one end of one of the spans, augering it into the riverbed. But you can still drive across on a jerry-built ramp and go a few miles farther on unmaintained road.

GETTING THERE

BY CAR Driving gives you the most freedom. The road is gravel, but it's wide and level. Beyond the Million Dollar Bridge, however, it's a rough four-wheel-drive track at best, and if you get stuck you'll be there for a long time. Pick up the road guide from the Forest Service Cordova Ranger Station, and read the highlights below.

BY BIKE Mountain biking the highway is the adventurous way to travel, camping or staying in a Forest Service cabin on the way. The drawbacks are the distances, the delta's strong winds, and a lot of road dust. Of course, you don't have to ride all the way to see lots of birds and wildlife, and there are good mountain biking routes on the delta away from the road. The 3-mile **Saddlebag Glacier Trail,** at mile 25 of the Copper River Highway, leads to a stunning vista of a glacial lake surrounded by rocky peaks. Bikes are for rent from Cordova Coastal Outfitters (see "Out On the Sound," below) for $15 a day.

ALONG THE ROAD

Keep your eyes scanning the wetlands and mountains around you as you drive out the road. The **wildlife** you may see along the way includes black and brown bears, wolf, coyote, moose, and mountain goats. The entire world population of dusky Canada geese nests on the delta, and you're likely to see eagles and trumpeter swans without really looking. The ranger station provides a wildlife-viewing guide and several places to stop along the way designed for bird-watching. The first is a platform with interpretive signs as you leave town, as sort of an introduction to the delta; this stretch of the road is fine for bird-watching.

Don't miss the **Alaganik Slough Boardwalk.** Take the 3.2-mile spur road to the right 16.8 miles out the Copper River Highway; it's marked. The sky here is big and certain while the land is ambivalent—it doesn't know if it wants to be waving grass of green and gold or shallow, shimmering ponds and tendrils of water. The road leads out to a parking lot and small, free campground, the start of the 1,000-foot boardwalk. One part leads to a large blind where you can watch the ponds and brush for birds. The other takes you above a large pond that reflects the sun and the colors of the marsh. We were speechless when we stood there one evening at sunset, even in the complete absence of birds. Often in the summer you can see breeding trumpeter swans, ducks, and grebes, and in the spring and fall migrating waterfowl and shorebirds.

The highway ends with its best attraction, the **Childs Glacier.** This is the most amazing glacier I've ever seen, and no one seems to know about it outside Cordova. The wall of ice, 300 feet tall, comes right down to the quarter-mile-wide river, where flowing water cuts it off like a knife, eroding the base and bringing down huge chunks. As you sit on the opposite bank, the glacier on the opposite side is too large to see—it completely fills your field of vision, creating an eerie and hypnotic sense of scale. On a warm summer day, you can feel the glacier's thunder as the ice shifts, and see pieces fall off. A chunk the size of a car barely registers, but when an office building–size hunk falls, there's a roar and gray breakers radiate out across the river. Falling glacier pieces have made waves large enough to uproot trees here, not to mention hurling a few fish around—at the Forest Service viewing and picnic area across the river, salmon have been found high up in the trees and boulders in odd places. Several years ago, such a wave injured some visitors, and now the Forest Service warns that anyone who can't run fast should stay in the observation tower. A bit farther from shore there's a campground with pit toilets.

Don't miss seeing and at least walking on the **Million Dollar Bridge,** less than a mile from the glacier-viewing area.

ACTIVITIES

HIKING   The Forest Service maintains several trails on the delta. The **Alaganik Slough Boardwalk** and **Saddlebag Glacier Trail** are mentioned above.

The **Haystack Trail,** starting on the right just past the 19-mile marker on the highway, climbs through mossy rain forest from the delta's floor onto an odd little hill. The glaciers that once covered the delta spared this bedrock outcropping. The trail is steep in places but only 0.8 mile in length, and it leads to an overlook.

The **McKinley Lake Trail,** at mile 21.6 on the highway, leads 2.4 miles through rain forest vegetation to a lake bearing trout (although we got no bites), and a little further to the overgrown ruins of a gold mine. You can also get there by canoe (see below). There are two Forest Service cabins on the trail, the small McKinley Trail Cabin near the highway and the McKinley Lake Cabin, beautifully situated among big trees above the lake. Each costs $35 a night and can be reserved through the national system described in section 3 of this chapter, on the Chugach National Forest.

CANOEING   The delta's canoe routes are little used, leading to remote places where birds and aquatic animals rule. You can launch on Alaganik Slough at a picnic area right at mile 22 on the Copper River Highway, paddling placid waters into stunningly beautiful marsh lands. Taking the "Wrong Way" route that starts a couple of miles up the road, you can float several miles of more challenging water down to McKinley Lake, stay at the cabin, then float downstream again to the slough launch, back at the road. It's ideal overnight, or you could do it in a day, or, as we did, spend an extra day and night at the cabin. The couple who run **Cordova Coastal Outfitters** (see below, under "Out on the Sound") rents canoes for $30 a day and drops them off, and will help you decide what route to take. You can ride out on one of their bicycles and pick up the canoe already at the launch site. They rent camping gear, too.

RAFTING   The immense quantity of water draining the Wrangell–St. Elias Mountains through the Copper River Delta, and the Copper River Highway that provides river access, make this a perfect venue for rafting. **Alaska River Rafting** (© 800/776-1864 or 907/424-7238; www.alaskarafters.com) is well regarded by locals. Their diverse territory means they can offer quite a range of trips, from easy floating to white water, or even rafting right in front of the Childs Glaciers. Trips duration ranges from half-day to multi-day. A 3½-hour trip is $65 adults, $45 ages 6 to 12; all-day, with flightseeing, $250.

FISHING   The delta's lakes and streams harbor all five species of Pacific salmon, as well as Dolly Varden char and cutthroat trout. The Cordova Ranger Station can offer guidance and regulation booklets, or contact the Cordova office of the **Alaska Department of Fish and Game** (© 907/424-3212; www. state.ak.us/adfg). See "Fishing," in chapter 2 for general guidance.

OUT ON THE SOUND

The waters of Prince William Sound around Cordova, although lacking the tidewater glaciers found in the western Sound, are protected and rich in marine life. Sea otters are so common as to no longer receive a second glance from locals, congregating in rafts of many dozens or even hundreds. Sea lions can be found predictably, too, and orcas and humpback whales are not out of the ordinary. Bird watchers can expect harlequin ducks and many other marine birds.

Cordova Coastal Outfitters is a good place to start for any outdoor activities (© **800/357-5145** or 907/424-7424; www.cdvcoastal.com). Andy Craig and Seawan Gehlbach know the equipment, the skills, and the area, and they convey that knowledge with casual enthusiasm. Their booth is on the dock below the Alaska Commercial grocery store, on the south side of the boat harbor. They guide sea kayaking and rent kayaks and fully equipped motorized boats. If your group isn't up to kayaking, **renting a boat** might be the way to go—you won't believe the sense of freedom you feel clearing the harbor breakwater to explore Orca Inlet and the bays of Hawkins Island, on the far side. Boats rent for $115 to $135 a day, fishing gear included.

The **guided sea-kayaking trip** for beginners lasts 4 hours and costs $65, concentrating on wildlife sightings. A 4-hour trip for the same price paddles on Eyak Lake to see brown bears and great blue herons. They offer all-day and multiday trips, too. Single kayaks rent for $35 a day, doubles $50.

Dave Janka runs the classic wooden *Auklet* (© **907/424-3428;** www. auklet.com), a 58-foot former U.S. Fish and Wildlife Service patrol boat, to carry scientific researchers and natural history excursions into the Sound from Cordova, Valdez, and Whittier. You design your own trip with him, paying $180 per person per day, with a $450 minimum. The accommodations on board are nautical, not luxurious.

Several vessels are available for fishing charters or day trips to see whales and other wildlife. The chamber of commerce (see "Visitor Information," earlier) has links to other charter operators on its website, or call them for a referral.

ACCOMMODATIONS

The Northern Nights Inn ⭐ (*Value*)   These large rooms, many with views and all loaded with amenities, are an almost unreal value. All but one has a full kitchen, and breakfast supplies are provided. They're upstairs in Becky Chapek and Bill Myers's historic 1906 house, a couple of blocks above the main street. The family is charming and will make you feel like a local. Each room has been lovingly renovated, with antiques and quilts. One room is essentially an entire apartment.

500 Third St. (P.O. Box 1564), Cordova, AK 99547. © **907/424-5356.** Fax 907/424-3291. www.northern nights.com. 5 units. $60–$75 double. Extra adult $5. Children stay free in parents' rm. AE, DISC, MC, V. **Amenities:** Free bike loan; babysitting; free laundry machines; fish freezing. *In room:* TV/VCR, fridge, microwave, coffeemaker, hair dryer, iron.

Prince William Motel (*Value*)   A friendly and helpful family renovated this old building into a clean, comfortable, modern motel. The lower rooms look out onto an air shaft, but that may be an advantage if you're trying to get to sleep when it's still light out. Seven have kitchenettes, with a $20 premium. Not a good choice if you have trouble with stairs.

Second St. and Council (P.O. Box 908), Cordova, AK 99574. © **907/424-3201.** Fax 907/424-2260. 16 units. Summer $90–$110 double. Extra adult $10. Children 11 and under stay free in parents' rm. AE, MC, V. **Amenities:** Coin-op laundry; fish freezing; barbecue. *In room:* TV, fridge, coffee machine, microwave.

The Reluctant Fisherman ⭐⭐   Mayor Margy Johnson presides at Cordova's main hotel with limitless energy. She and her husband, Dick Borer, have created one of the best waterfront lodgings in Alaska, overlooking the small-boat harbor. The decor in the lobby, lounge, and restaurant capture the town's railroad and copper-mining history, with rich wood and pressed-copper ceilings, stained glass, and mementos of the couple's history here. The rooms are comfortable and modern, with local art. Those on the water side have good views, while an economy wing on the parking lot rents for only $75 a night. There's a gift shop and travel agency in the hotel; they also rent cars and operate the airport shuttle.

The **restaurant** 🔦 serves the town's best dinners. Main courses of fish, steaks, and pasta range from $15 to $27. Lunch is $4 to $10. A small deck overlooks the harbor for outdoor dining. Order the Copper River king or red salmon in season, broiled—the river produces exceptionally rich fish, a real delicacy that's made into delicious chili for lunch.

401 Railroad Ave. (P.O. Box 150), Cordova, AK 99574. © 800/770-3272 or 907/424-3272. Fax 907/424-7465. http://Cordovaak.com. 50 units. High season $75–$125 double. Low season $75–$95 double. Extra person $10. AE, DC, DISC, MC, V. **Amenities:** Restaurant; bar; car rental; coin-op laundry. *In room:* TV/VCR, dataport, coffeemaker.

DINING

Other than the restaurants listed here, try the **Reluctant Fisherman,** above. Also, the **Flying Dutchman Pub and Grill,** 531 First St. (© **907/424-3248**), serves good burgers, fish-and-chips, and soup at a counter overlooking the harbor. It's one of the least smoky bars in town. Some of Cordova's best lunches come from **Baja Taco** (© **907/424-5599**), a bus at the boat harbor with a covered dining area elevated on a small tower. The proprietor, who lives in Baja in the winter, specializes in salmon tacos and operates here May to September.

Ambrosia ITALIAN   This is a comfortable family restaurant with an extensive menu and pizza. It's the kind of place that stays in business in a small town: The food is reliable and the portions large, but nothing too challenging or unusual. Beer and wine license.

410 First St. © 907/424-7175. Main courses $5.75–$18.75. AE, MC, V. High season daily 11am–11pm. Low season daily 4–9pm.

Killer Whale Café CAFE   This cafe is worth a stop if only for the atmosphere. The dining area is in two lofts above a bookstore that is a nexus of local ecopeople. Oil-spill hero Kelly Weaverling owns Orca Book and Sound, and was the only member of the Green Party to hold elective office in the United States when he was Cordova's mayor a few years ago. (He later lost to Margy Johnson, of the Reluctant Fisherman, by one vote, but refused to ask for a recount.) Order soups, sandwiches, and the like at the counter. No liquor license.

In Orca Book and Sound, 507 First St. © 907/424-7733. All items $6–$9. No credit cards. Mon–Fri 7am–4pm, Sat 8am–3:30pm.

8

The Denali National Park Region

Denali (den-al-ee) stands alone among the nation's parks: It gives regular people easy access to real wilderness, with sweeping tundra vistas, abundant wildlife, and North America's tallest mountain. Other wilderness areas in Alaska may have equally inspiring scenery and even more animals, but Denali is unique because of its accessibility to visitors—and because that accessibility hasn't spoiled the natural experience, as it has at so many other parks.

It's a sad truth that even the largest national parks in the Lower 48 are too small to comprise complete ecosystems. The dream of leaving nature undisturbed is essentially lost in those places, and only through human intervention do the natural systems within the parks stay as close to their primeval state as they do (this is illustrated by the work of rangers at Yellowstone to drive bison back within park boundaries so they won't come to harm outside). Millions of cars driving through the parks further interfere with nature. At Rocky Mountain National Park, there's a crossing guard for bighorn sheep. Yosemite Valley and Grand Canyon Village can be choked with cars in summer, yet attempts to rid them have so far been thwarted.

On the other end of the spectrum, Alaska has many parks with immense, intact ecosystems that have remained unchanged, still existing as they did before the first white contact. More than two-thirds of America's national park acreage is in Alaska, taking in inconceivably huge swaths of land without roads, buildings, or landing strips. They're natural, all right, but almost no one goes there. Some of these parks receive a few hundred visitors a year—only the Alaska Natives of the surrounding region and the hardiest and wealthiest outdoors people. Just chartering a plane to get to some of these places can cost as much as most of us spend on our whole vacation. With as many people on the earth as we've got, wilderness survives only when it's rationed somehow. In most of Alaska, the rationing system is simply the expense and difficulty of getting to the wild.

At Denali, on the other hand, you can see the heart of the park for little more than it would cost you to visit Yellowstone. And when you get there, it's a pristine natural environment where truly wild animals live in a nearly complete ecosystem pretty much without human interference. A single National Park Service decision makes this possible: The only road through the park is closed to the public. This means that to get into the park, you must ride a bus over a dusty gravel road hour after hour, but it also means that the animals are still there to watch and their behavior remains essentially normal. From the window of the bus, you're likely to see grizzly bears doing what they would be doing even if you weren't there. It may be the only $20 safari in the world.

What's even more unique is that you can get off the bus pretty much whenever you want to and walk away from the road across the tundra, out of sight of the road, and be alone in this primeval wilderness. Unfortunately, many Denali visitors never take advantage of the opportunity, which normally would cost a lot of money or require a lot of muscle and outdoor skill. Being alone under God's big sky makes many people nervous. Most of us have never been entirely away from other people, much less apart from anything people have made. But that's the essence of Alaska—learning, deep down, how big creation is and how small you are, one more mammal on the tundra under the broad sky. At Denali, you can experience that wonder, and then, when you're ready to return to civilization, you can just walk to the road and catch the next bus—they come every half-hour.

The Denali experience spreads beyond the park. After all, the park boundary is an artificial line—the wildlife and the scenery of the Alaska Range don't observe its significance. To the east, the **Denali Highway** runs through the same extraordinary terrain, with opportunities for hiking over the tundra and canoeing on the lakes managed by the Bureau of Land Management. To the south, **Denali State Park** and the town of **Talkeetna** provide another vantage on Mount McKinley, with the advantage of salmon fishing in the rivers and

remote lake recreation. The construction of comfortable new lodges and a variety of good outdoor guides have helped make Talkeetna a popular alternative gateway to Denali. Even though it's 150 miles from the park entrance by car, Talkeetna is physically closer to the mountain than is the park headquarters.

Visitors often skip all the area's other attractions, however, and focus on **Mount McKinley,** which, at 20,320 feet, is the tallest mountain in North America. It is an impressive peak, but you don't need to go to the park to see it—in fact, most people who do go *don't* see it. Summer weather patterns usually sock in the mountain by midafternoon, at least as seen from the ground in the park.

Unfortunately, Denali has become a thing people feel they must do, and seeing Mount McKinley is a thing they must do when they visit Denali. Many package tours rush the park so quickly it becomes just a blur outside a window rather than an experience. If they miss the mountain, passengers may wonder why they traveled so far to stay at the ticky-tacky roadside development at the park's entrance and then ride on a bus over a bumpy road. A friend swears she overheard a tourist ask, as she boarded the train leaving Denali, "Why did they put the park way out here in the boondocks?"

The answer is there for you to find, at the bottom of the steps of the shuttle bus door.

1 Planning a Visit to the Park

ORIENTATION

The park is like a pivot in the center of Alaska, a huge slice of the Alaska Range—rock and ice robed in tundra and stunted black spruce. Denali National Park and Preserve encompasses 6 million acres, a roughly triangular polygon about 20% larger than Massachusetts. The only park entrance is 230 miles north of Anchorage and 120 miles south of Fairbanks on the paved George Parks Highway or the Alaska Railroad. Although **Mount McKinley** is visible from as far away as Anchorage, you can't see it at all from the park entrance (where you will find the railroad depot and all services accessible by private vehicle), since

Denali National Park

ACCOMMODATIONS & DINING ♦ ■

Camp Denali **2**
Denali Backcountry Lodge **3**
Denali Bluffs Hotel **27**
Denali Cabins **17**
Denali Crow's Nest Cabins **26**
Denali Mountain Morning Hostel **20**
Denali Princess Lodge and Summit Restaurant **25**
Denali River Cabins **16**
Grizzly Bear Cabins & Campground **18**
Kantishna Roadhouse **1**
McKinley Creekside Cabins & Cafe **19**
McKinley Resort Chalet **23**
McKinley RV and Campground **15**
Motel Nord Haven **13**
North Face Lodge **4**
The Overlook Bar & Grill **24**
The Perch **20**
Stampede Lodge **14**
White Moose Lodge **12**

ATTRACTIONS ●

Denali State Park **21**
Eielson Visitor Center **6**
Mt. Healy **22**
Polychrome Pass **8**
Riley Creek Campground **29**
Sable Pass **9**
Savage River Campground **11**
Teklanika Campground **10**
Toklat Ranger Station **7**
Visitor Center **28**
Wonder Lake Ranger Station and Campground **5**

it's on the far side of the park. A mile north of the park entrance on the Parks Highway, along a cliff-sided canyon of the Nenana River, hotels and restaurants have developed a seasonal town known locally as Glitter Gulch, or, for the benefit of the tourists, as the **Nenana Canyon Area.** Other services are at **Carlo Creek,** 13 miles south on the Parks, at another gathering of roadside development 7 miles south of the park entrance, and in the year-round town of **Healy,** 10 miles north of the park entrance. From the park entrance, a road accessible only by shuttle bus leads west 89 miles through the park, past a series of campgrounds and a visitor center, and ends at the **Kantishna district,** a patch of park-surrounded private land inholdings with wilderness lodges.

WHEN TO GO & HOW FAR AHEAD TO PLAN
Crowding is relative. Once you're out in the park, Denali is never crowded. A transportation bottleneck, the shuttle system, protects the park from overuse. What makes the July-to-mid-August busy season difficult is getting through that bottleneck from the crowded park entrance into the wilderness. At that time, travelers who just show up at the visitor center without any reservations often have to spend a day or two outside the park before they can get a seat on a shuttle bus, a campground site, or a backcountry permit.

The flow of visitors varies greatly from year to year. Some years, you need to make **reservations** by March for a July visit; other years, a few weeks of advance planning will do. To be on the safe side, get your shuttle tickets and campsites as soon as you know the dates of your visit. Lodgings also get tight in July, but are not as critical to the success of your visit. Reserve as far ahead as you can, but don't worry about getting stuck in a dive if you don't get your first choice of rooms or cabins, as there are few really bad places near the park.

The park is populated by people beginning in mid-May, when snow remains; the humans migrate south again in mid- to late September, when winter is closing in. In the off-season, fewer than 200 residents stay in the area and sled-dog-driving rangers patrol the backcountry. The visitor season gets into high gear in mid-June and starts to wind down in mid-August, providing a month of relative quiet and often reduced prices at the beginning of the season and another at the end. Reservations are easy to come by at those times.

Access within Denali doesn't begin until Memorial Day, so May is out, but fall is a wonderful time to go. The weather gets nippy at night, and there can be surprise snowfalls, but rain is less likely, and the trees and tundra turn wonderful colors. By early September, visitors are so few that the park no longer takes telephone reservations. By mid-September, private cars can drive on the park road for a few days—the Park Service holds a lottery in July to determine who will get that treat.

Another way to avoid the crowds is to book a stay in a **wilderness lodge.** Four lodges in Kantishna, listed in section 7 of this chapter, have the right to carry clients to their businesses over the park road in buses and vans, avoiding the bottleneck. Two more remote lodges outside the park's boundaries, on the Wood River and near Talkeetna, are listed, too.

SAMPLE ITINERARIES
The more you're willing to rough it, the closer you can get to the real Denali. There are no hotels inside the park.

THE HOTEL-STAY ITINERARY
Arrive by train at the park, checking into accommodations nearby—shuttles and courtesy vans will get you around. Attend a ranger talk, the *Cabin Nite* dinner-theater show, or go on a short **nature walk** around the park hotel in the evening.

Get to bed early, and the next morning take a shuttle bus before 7am into the park, riding to the **Eielson Visitor Center** to see the terrain and animals, and possibly to get a view of the mountain (arriving there in late morning). Now ride partway back toward the entrance before getting off the bus at a place of your choosing for a walk and to eat the bag lunch you've brought along with you (pack out all trash, of course), or take one of the **Park Service guided walks.** After enjoying the wilderness for a few hours, head back on the bus, finishing a long day back at the hotel. Next day try a rafting ride, a flightseeing trip, or another activity near the entrance to the park before reboarding the train.

THE FAMILY CAMPING ITINERARY
Arrive at the park entrance by car with your camping gear and food for a couple of nights. (You can rent the camping gear and car in Anchorage.) Camp that evening at the **Riley Creek Campground** near the visitor center and enjoy the evening ranger program or a nature walk, or go straight to a campsite farther within the park (either way, you'll need to reserve well ahead). Next day, catch a shuttle bus or camper bus to get deeper into the park for sightseeing and **hiking.** If you have another day after that within the park, you can do more hikes and have the cushion of a weather day. If you're staying 3 nights, you can drive your car to the **Teklanika Campground,** which offers good hiking on the Teklanika riverbed, and the advantage of having your home base well within the park. Finally, break camp early on the third or fourth day and return to the entrance. Add a rafting or horseback excursion at the park entrance before driving on, if you like, and possibly a night at a hotel to get washed up.

THE BACKCOUNTRY CAMPING ITINERARY
Arrive by train, bus, or car with your backpack, camping gear, and food for at least several days' hiking. Go immediately to the visitor center to orient yourself to the backcountry permit process, buy the information you need for your trek (see section 4 of this chapter), and choose the unit area that looks most promising. **Backcountry permits** cannot be reserved in advance; you can only apply for them in person for the next day, and they go fast. If you're lucky, permits will be left for the day after you arrive; more likely, you'll need to camp at the **Morino Backpacker's Campground,** 1.9 miles on the park road from the highway, and arrive at the visitor center by the 7am opening to get your permit for the following day. Now you've got another day to wait; if you've reserved a shuttle-bus seat, you can get a preview of the park and see some wildlife or, outside the park, go on a rafting trip. The next morning you can start your backcountry hike, taking the camper bus to your unit, then traveling for up to 2 weeks in a huge area of wilderness reserved almost exclusively for your use.

THE WILDERNESS LODGE ITINERARY
For those who can afford it, this may be the best way to see Denali. The lodge will fly you in—or, if it's in Kantishna, drive you through the park—and you'll immediately be away from the crowds in remote territory. The lodges all have activities and guides to get you out into the wilderness. If you're not staying in Kantishna, you may want to schedule a day to ride the shuttle bus into the park to see the mountain and wildlife anyway, with an evening in a hotel near the park or in Healy.

THE TALKEETNA OPTION
Drive only as far as Talkeetna, about 110 miles north of Anchorage, and board a flightseeing plane from there to the park, perhaps landing on a glacier on

The Denali Highway: The Drivable Denali

From Cantwell, 27 miles south of the Denali National Park entrance, the Denali Highway leads 133 miles east to another tiny village, Paxson, on the Richardson Highway. The little-known road is a lesson in how we're influenced by labels. It runs due east from the Denali National Park border, a natural extension of the park over the Alaska Range, with scenery that's equal to and in some ways more impressive than the park's. Yet without the national park name, the terrain along the Denali Highway is comparatively little used.

The Bureau of Land Management controls the land along the Denali Highway, and it's pretty much open for any recreational activity. The **Tangle Lakes** start a 3-day, 35-mile float trip (for experienced paddlers) to the Richardson Highway and host fine lake canoeing, where you can see an extraordinary variety of waterfowl, including trumpeter swans, sandhill cranes, and loons. Much of the highway passes through high, alpine terrain, with views that extend infinitely into the distance and good chances of seeing caribou, moose, and black and grizzly bear. At **Maclaren Pass,** at 4,086 feet, you stand in high Alaska Range terrain of tundra and rock, with views of Maclaren Glacier. The land invites you to walk at least a little way out across it.

Simply driving the road is an experience. If you're traveling to Denali National Park from Anchorage or Fairbanks, consider making a return trip via the Denali Highway and Richardson Highway. The road is gravel (plans are in the works to pave it, unfortunately), but you can cover its length in less than 4 hours. (Check with your car-rental agency to find out if you are allowed to drive on gravel highways; agencies that do

Mount McKinley. You'll stand a better chance of seeing the mountain than anyone else, since the weather tends to be better on the south side and you can fly above most clouds when they do come. You'll also save yourself hours of driving to the park and the bus ride into the park, and you'll have the pleasure of staying in a town with some character, unlike the park entrance area. But you'll miss the wildlife-viewing opportunities that can be had only on the ground in the park. (See section 10 of this chapter for more information.)

2 Park Essentials

VISITOR INFORMATION

Getting the information you need to plan your visit is especially important at Denali because of the need for advance reservations. Besides the centers here, you can stop by at an interagency **Alaska Public Lands Information Center;** there are locations in Anchorage, Fairbanks, and Tok, all listed in chapters 6 and 9.

The easiest places to make contact with the Park Service are via their handy website and in person at the information desk at the **Denali National Park Visitor Center,** Denali Park Rd., a half mile from the park entrance (P.O. Box 9), Denali National Park, AK 99755 (© **907/683-2294;** fax 907/683-9612;

allow it are listed under "Getting There" in both the Fairbanks section of chapter 9 and in Anchorage, chapter 6.) Small roadhouses are along the way. **Biking** the road is one of the best ways to see it. Trails and remote roads from the highway offer some exceptional mountain biking and hiking routes, especially in the Tangle Lakes National Register Archaeological District. There are **Bureau of Land Management campgrounds** along the highway at Brushkana Creek and Tangle Lakes, and you can camp anywhere you want outside a campground.

Be sure to get the BLM's *Denali Highway Points of Interest* road guide and *Trail Map and Guide to the Tangle Lakes National Register District*. They're available at the Alaska Public Lands Information Centers in Fairbanks, Anchorage, or Tok, or directly from the **Bureau of Land Management.** Their Glennallen District Office, P.O. Box 147, Glennallen, AK 99588 (© **907/822-3217;** www.glennallen.ak.blm.gov; open Mon–Fri 8am–4pm), manages the area, and rangers there can give you guidance on where to go.

Alaskan Bicycle Adventures (described in chapter 2; © **800/770-7242** or 907/243-2329; www.alaskabike.com) leads a variety of bike tours that include the Denali Highway, generally starting from Anchorage, looping up the Parks Highway and returning south on the Richardson and Glenn highways. They provide the bikes and all the gear, as well as the van and trailer carrying the gear to make the trip comfortable. **CampAlaska Tours** (also described in chapter 2; © **800/376-9438** or 907/376-9438; www.campalaska.com) covers this ground, too, with group camping excursions.

www.nps.gov/dena). Since there's no park entrance station, stop here for the park map, a copy of the *Alpenglow* park newspaper, and other handouts. A small bookstore offers a limited selection on the area, and films and programs take place in an auditorium. It's open June to mid-September, daily from 7am to 8pm; May and late September, daily 10am to 4pm. It's closed October to April.

The park's nonprofit publishing arm is the **Alaska Natural History Association,** Denali Branch. P.O. Box 230, Denali National Park, AK 99755 (© **907/683-1272** summer, 907/683-1258 off-season; www.alaskanha.org). They operate the shops in the park visitor centers, and you can use their website to order books and maps before coming.

At the **Eielson Visitor Center,** on Denali Park Road, more than 60 miles inside the park (accessible only on the shuttle bus), rangers answer questions about Mount McKinley, which on clear days presents a dramatic view from the center. There are displays on wildlife and geology, and a seismograph constantly measures earthquake activity. A ranger allocates open seats on inbound buses for passengers who want to return on a bus different than the one they rode into the park. Picnic tables outside make a good place to eat your sack lunch before you board the bus back. Closed October to mid-June.

Tips Train Choices

Alaska Railroad executives know that their fares are high for a simple ride to Denali. As one told me, "We're selling entertainment," and that's how you should judge your choices. So, to review the entertainment: All the cars are luxurious, and some are grand and highly memorable; the rail line follows a historic, unspoiled route through beautiful countryside; there's a good chance of seeing moose and caribou; the commentary by well-trained Alaska high school students is fresh and engaging; and the food is good—you can dine in a beautiful bistro car or in a truly extraordinary white-table-cloth dining car. There are disadvantages, too. The train is very expensive. You can rent a small car for a week for the same price as one round-trip on the train. It's slow, adding 3 hours to a trip from Anchorage to the park, and when it's late, it can be very late. And, once you arrive, you have to rely on shuttles and courtesy vans to get around outside the park.

After you decide to ride the train, you have to choose which train. The Alaska Railroad's locomotives also pull three sets of cars with full domes owned by cruise lines, two of which have seats for independent travelers (although 90 % or more are filled with their cruise-ship customers). **Princess Cruises and Tours** (© 800/835-8907; www.princess.com) has tall all-dome cars with table seating upstairs and dining rooms downstairs; there's plenty of head room and you can see a long way. Their special advantage is large balconies at the ends of the cars where you can ride outdoors. **Holland America Tours** (© 800/544-2206 or 907/277-5581; www.hollandamerica.com) has the same above and below arrangement, but the seating seemed more cramped and there was less head room; some passengers sit in sideways-situated couches. The decor, however, captures the mood of the golden age of rail, surpassing that of Princess. The Alaska Railroad cars are more traditional, with all seats facing forward, so you don't have to socialize with strangers if you don't want to and you have more freedom to get up and wander around and choose among the two dining options. The dome seats are limited, however, with a 20-minute limit. Seating on all three offerings is assigned; you can't walk from one to the other, but you can walk between cars in your own train section. Fares on the cruise-line operations run even higher than the railroad's fares, but they're mainly sold, and much more advantageously priced, as lodging packages in the company's Denali hotels.

Personally, I would choose the Alaska Railroad experience because I love trains, and their cars feel more authentic and somehow less controlled than the cruise-line offerings. All provide superb service, however, as a sort of Orient Express of the north that's as much about the ride as the destination.

Most important for planning your trip is the concessionaire, **ARAMARK/Denali Park Resorts,** 241 W. Ship Creek Ave., Anchorage, AK 99501 (© **800/622-7275** or 907/272-7275; fax 907/264-4684;

www.denalinationalpark.com). They handle the reservations system for the campgrounds and shuttle buses, as well as two hotels, bus tours, a rafting operation, and a dinner theater you can reserve. They have a shuttle desk in the main visitor center.

THE RESERVATIONS SYSTEM

Here's the system for reserving shuttle bus tickets and spots at the developed campgrounds. This section may look long, but paying attention to the details of the reservations system greatly improves your chances of a good visit to the park. (The backcountry permit system is covered in section 4 of this chapter.)

FOR ADVANCE RESERVATIONS

Sixty-five percent of shuttle-bus seats and all campground sites (except Morino, Sanctuary, and Igloo) are offered for booking by telephone, fax, or mail; the balance are held back for walk-ins.

Reservations by mail or fax open for the whole summer on December 1 of the preceding year. Reservations by phone open sometime in February. After that date, lines are answered daily 7am to 5pm Alaska time (remember, that's 4 hours earlier than Eastern Standard Time), but at times it's impossible to get through. By faxing, you bypass this problem and can get in before the phone lines open. Reservation forms to fax or mail are available on the park's website (**www.nps.gov/dena**) or the concessionaire's website (**www.denalinationalpark. com**). You will need to include the dates, times, and campgrounds you want, plus alternate dates; the names and ages of the people in your party; and entrance and reservation fees (see "Fees" below) along with a Visa, MasterCard, American Express, or Discover Card number, with expiration and signature. You don't have to figure out the total. You can also pay by check if you're reserving by mail. But don't use the mail unless you write several months ahead, as you could miss getting a reservation at all. Mail to Alaska takes about 5 days from the East Coast.

A **confirmation** should be sent out by mail or fax within 2 days of receipt. Take the confirmation to the "will call" desk at the visitor center when you arrive to exchange it for a camping permit and bus ticket. If you'll be arriving after the center closes at 8pm, you must call © **907/683-1266** in advance to avoid losing your site or shuttle seat.

FOR WALK-INS

Phone, mail, and fax orders shut down the day before the visit starts, but walk-in reservations begin 2 days out, offering the remaining 35% of the shuttle bus seats and any leftover car-camping sites, and all sites in two primitive backcountry campgrounds, Igloo and Sanctuary. If it's a busy time of year, desirable shuttle reservations are snapped up early in the day. That means you may not get a good reservation for the day of your arrival or even the day after, only the next day after that. That's why it's so critical to reserve in advance.

On the other hand, don't despair if you arrive without reservations, as the flow of visitors rises and falls unpredictably. It's perfectly possible that you'll walk into the visitor center and get a shuttle seat on the same day.

FEES

The **park entrance fee** is $10 per family or $5 per person, good for 7 days. There is no entrance station to collect the fee, but it is automatically added to your bill when you make shuttle or campground reservations. If you have a

National Parks Pass or a Golden Age or Golden Access pass, mention it when you call in order to get your discount.

Campground fees are $12 per night in the car campground, $6 in the primitive campground. In addition, a campground **reservation fee** of $4 is charged for the first night of any campground stay.

Another $6 fee is charged for canceling or changing a campsite or bus ticket, except for free children's tickets. You can cancel until 6pm for campground reservations, or 2 hours before departure for bus tickets.

Various bus fees are listed in the chart in section 3 of this chapter.

GETTING THERE
BY TRAIN
The **Alaska Railroad** (© **800/544-0552** or 907/265-2494; www.alaskarailroad.com) pioneered tourism to the park before the George Parks Highway was built in 1972. In summer, trains leave both Anchorage and Fairbanks daily at 8:15am, arriving at the park from Anchorage at 3:45pm and from Fairbanks at noon, crossing and going on to the opposite city for arrival at 8:15pm in each. The fare from Anchorage to Denali is $125 one-way for adults, half price for children. The full train runs only from mid-May to mid-September, with somewhat lower fares in the first and last few weeks of the season. During the winter, the Alaska Railroad runs a single passenger car from Anchorage to Fairbanks and back once a week—a truly spectacular, truly Alaskan experience.

BY CAR
Renting a car and driving from Anchorage is far cheaper than taking the train. The drive is about 4½ hours from Anchorage, 2½ from Fairbanks, on a good two-lane highway. Many of the views along the **Parks Highway** are equal to the views on the train, but large stretches, especially in the Matanuska and Susitna valleys, near Anchorage, have been spoiled by ugly roadside development (which you don't see on the train). A long but spectacular detour around the mess leads through **Hatcher Pass** on a mountainous gravel road open only in the summer. See section 10 of chapter 6, on the Matanuska & Susitna valleys. Farther north from Anchorage, the Parks Highway passes through Denali State Park. If the weather's clear, you can see Mount McKinley from the pull-outs there. The state park also contains several campgrounds and hiking trails and a veterans memorial.

BY BUS
Several van and bus services inexpensively connect Anchorage and Fairbanks to Denali. Most will carry bikes and other gear for an additional fee.

The **Parks Highway Express** (© **888/600-6001;** www.AlaskaShuttle.com) offers daily service between Anchorage and Fairbanks, with one bus each way, stopping at Denali and any other point on the way. In Anchorage, it leaves from the downtown Anchorage Youth Hostel, and in Fairbanks, from the visitor center. The one-way fare is $49 from Anchorage, $34 from Fairbanks.

The **Park Connection** (© **800/208-0200,** or 907/245-0200; www.alaskacoach.com) runs to Seward and Anchorage, with two buses daily in each direction. The fare is $59 to Anchorage, $100 to Seward. Children ride for half price.

BY AIR
Flightseeing trips to Denali from Anchorage are listed in section 5, "Getting Outside," under "Flightseeing." You also can charter to Denali from Anchorage or Fairbanks, although it's costly.

GETTING AROUND

If you take the train or bus, you'll find that most accommodations have arrangements to get you around, although this becomes less convenient as you get farther from the park entrance. Ask how it works when you book your room. The summer-only **Caribou Cab** (© **907/683-5000**) charges on a per-person basis ($6 from Healy to Denali, for example), with a $13 minimum. You can also rent a car in Healy from **Teresa's Alaska Car Rentals** (© **907/683-1377;** www.alaskaone.com/denalicar).

If you drive to the park, you'll still need to take the shuttle bus, described below, to get into its heart, except under certain circumstances. You can drive past mile 14 on the park road only if you have a 3-day camping permit at Teklanika Campground, 29 miles in; then your vehicle must remain parked at the campground for the entire 3 days. The rules loosen at the end of the season, when winners of a drawing can drive the road for a few days in late September (check with the Park Service for lottery details). After the permit driving is over, the road is open to anyone as far as mile 30 until the snow flies; then it's maintained only as far as the headquarters, 3 miles from the entrance.

Bicycles have free access to the park road. For that option, see section 5 of this chapter.

 FAST FACTS: **Denali National Park**

Banks A couple of **ATMs** are in Healy, 10 miles north of the park, including one at Wally's Service Station. Do your banking before leaving Anchorage or Fairbanks.

Emergencies © **911** will work inside the park, but be sure to tell the operator you are within Denali National Park.

Gear Rental **Denali Mountain Morning Hostel and Lodge** (© **907/683-7503**), listed in full under Accommodations, later, rents camping gear; a complete kit is $30 for the first day, $7 each additional day. Bikes are for rent; see section 5, later.

Hospital A **health clinic** (© **907/683-2211**) is located in Healy, 10 miles north of the park entrance; it's open 24 hours a day for emergencies, or normal office hours for nonemergencies.

Police The **Alaska State Troopers** (© **907/683-2232** or 907/768-2202) has a post in Healy, 10 miles north of the park, and in Cantwell, 28 miles south.

Post Office The post office is a mile within the park entrance.

Stores **McKinley Mercantile** (© **907/683-9246**) is at the Riley Creek Campground, near the park entrance. It's open daily from 7:30am to 8pm in the summer. Besides convenience groceries, they have firewood, some basic camping supplies, showers, and laundry machines. A larger convenience store and gas station, the **Park Mart** (© **907/683-2548**), is on the Parks Highway in the Nenana Canyon area, just north of the park entrance. Do major shopping before coming to the park.

Taxes The local **bed tax** is 7%. There is no sales tax.

The Alaska-Ohio Name Game, Round 4

We've long been taught that the Athabascans of Interior Alaska named the mountain *Denali,* "the high one," or "the great one." But at least one historian contends that the word *Denal'iy* actually referred to a mountain near Anchorage, now known as Pioneer Peak, and means "one that watches," and that the word for McKinley, "the high one," is actually *Doleika.* In any event, Alaska Natives made little use of the area, as it produced few fish or game, and white men came only in search of gold. In 1896, a prospector named the mountain after William McKinley of Ohio, who was elected president of the United States that year.

All well and good, except that most Alaskans prefer the name Denali and since 1975 have petitioned to change it officially back. Ohio won't allow it. Although congressmen from Alaska and Ohio compromised on the issue in 1980, changing the name of the national park to Denali and leaving the mountain named McKinley, Alaskans have kept pushing for Denali. But the U.S. Board on Geographical Names has refused to take up the issue. It seems that the board has a rule against considering an issue that is also before Congress, and Rep. Ralph Regula of Ohio repeatedly introduces a one-paragraph bill stating that the name should stay the same. His bill never goes anywhere, but just having it introduced has been enough to stop the name board. In 1999, Alaska representative Don Young brought the issue back to life with an opposing bill to change the mountain's name to Denali, saying that Regula should just name something in Ohio for McKinley. Young's bill also died quietly.

3 Denali by Shuttle Bus

Your visit to Denali will likely revolve around a ride on the shuttle bus into the park to see the wildlife and to stop for a walk in the wilderness. Some planning will make it a more successful trip.

CHOOSING YOUR DESTINATION

You can buy shuttle tickets to the Toklat (*toe*-klat) River, 53 miles into the park; the Eielson (*aisle*-son) Visitor Center at 66 miles; Wonder Lake at 85 miles; or Kantishna, at 89 miles (fares are listed in the "Denali Park Road Bus Facts" chart that accompanies this section). On any day trip, you have to go both ways, so you're in for a long drive. If you don't get off the bus along the way, the round-trip takes 6½ hours to Toklat, 8 hours to Eielson, 11 hours to Wonder Lake, and 12 hours to Kantishna.

In choosing your destination, you need to balance your stamina, your desire to save time for a day hike, and your desire to see wildlife. There are no firm rules about where wildlife shows up, but my own observations are that in the early morning, you can often see moose on the first part of the road; in mid-summer, brown (grizzly) bears seem to appear most in the higher country, beyond Toklat, which also is the best area for caribou; in the fall berry season, the grizzlies show up all along the drive.

The best views of Mount McKinley show up after mile 61, also beyond Toklat. The mountain is most likely to be visible in the morning, as clouds often pile up during the day. Going beyond Eielson to Wonder Lake provides more amazing views, including the land-covered Muldrow Glacier and many classic images of Mount McKinley. There's really no reason to go as far as Kantishna unless you are headed to a lodge there (see "Wilderness Lodges," in section 7 of this chapter). In general, I think **Eielson** is the best destination for most people, offering both the chance to see the mountain and some wildlife while leaving some time to get out and walk (I've included some ideas on where to hike later).

You won't be able to time your trip for **good weather,** as you need to book ahead. But don't despair if it rains—the sun may be out at the other end of the park. The best weather for wildlife sightings is cool, overcast skies without rain. One trick of the system that allows visitors to wait for sun is to stay at Teklanika Campground. If you drive to a campsite there, agreeing to stay for 3 days, you're eligible to buy a special shuttle ticket for $23 that is good for rides deeper into the park the entire time you're staying at the campground. Wherever you stay, you can buy a three-trip pass from the Park Service for the price of two.

Denali can be a challenge for families. Young children will go nuts on an 8-hour bus ride, and often can't pick out the wildlife—this isn't a zoo, and most animals blend in with their surroundings. Older children also have a hard time keeping their patience on these trips, as do many adults. The only solution is to get off the bus and turn your trip into a romp in the heather. When you've had a chance to revive, catch the next bus. Besides, just because you buy a ticket to Eielson doesn't mean that you have to go that far. Keep in mind, too, that if your child normally needs a car seat, you must bring it along on the bus, or borrow one from the Park Service.

ARAMARK also operates narrated bus tours, booked mostly as part of package tours. The **Natural History Tour** provides just a taste of the park, going 17 miles down the park road. The **Wildlife Tour** goes to Toklat when the mountain is hidden by clouds, and 8 miles farther, to Highway Pass, when it is visible. Food is provided, but you can't get off the bus along the way, and the route skips the beautiful grizzly and caribou habitat toward the Eielson Visitor Center. The **Kantishna Roadhouse** (listed in section 7 of this chapter) offers a 190-mile, 13-hour marathon with lunch and a dogsled and gold-panning program at the halfway mark, at the lodge. It's well done, with commentary, but you can't get off the bus along the way, and the return trip may be too rushed to stop for all wildlife sightings. The cost is $109.

GETTING READY

Reserve your shuttle ticket for as early as you can stand to get up in the morning. This strategy will give you more time for day hikes and enhance your chances of seeing the mountain and wildlife. Many animals are more active in the morning, especially on hot days. During peak season, the first bus leaves the visitor center

Bus Concerns & Complaints

ARAMARK, the Denali concessionaire, uses only school bus–type vehicles over the park road. We've received complaints from readers who allegedly were stuck on these buses while other visitors toured the park in luxury motor coaches, but this just isn't so: Only these tough, lightweight buses are allowed on the narrow, gravel park road. I've also heard from visitors complaining of white knuckles on the ride. It's true the buses act a bit like mountain goats on the heights of Polychrome Pass and near Eielson Visitor Center. The road climbs without guardrails, and if you're afraid of heights, it might not be to your liking.

at 5:15am and then roughly every 15 to 30 minutes in the morning. A few buses leave in the afternoon, mostly to pick up stragglers on the way back, returning late under the midnight sun.

By taking an early bus, you have more time to get off along the way for a hike, walking back to the road and getting the next bus that comes along with a spare seat. Time it right, and you could have more than 8 hours for hiking plus a tour of most of the park road before returning on a late bus. (To be on the safe side, don't push it to the very last bus.) The sun won't set until after 11pm May to July and it will be light all night. If you need to get back to the park entrance at a certain time, leave yourself plenty of time, because after getting off your westbound bus, you can't reserve seats going back the other way, and you may have to wait an hour for a bus with room to take you.

Before you leave for the visitor center to get on your shuttle bus, you'll need a packed lunch and plenty of water; you should wear sturdy walking shoes and layers of warm and lighter clothing with rain gear packed; you should have binoculars or a spotting scope at the ready; and you should have insect repellent. You may also want a copy of Kim Heacox's worthwhile booklet **"Denali Road Guide,"** available for $6 at the visitor center bookstore, published by the Alaska Natural History Association, listed earlier under "Visitor Information." It provides a milepost commentary you can follow as you ride. ANHA also publishes guides to Denali birds, mammals, geology, and trails. If you'll be doing any extensive day hiking, you may also want to bring a detailed topographic map printed on waterproof plastic (published by Trails Illustrated and sold for $9.95 from the visitor center or ANHA) as well as a compass; if you're just going to walk a short distance off the road, you won't need such preparations.

ON YOUR WAY

There are no reserved seats on the bus, but if you arrive early you can find a place on the left side, which has the best views on the way out. Most buses will see grizzly bears, caribou, Dall sheep, and moose, and occasionally wolves, but, as one driver said, the animals aren't union workers, and it's possible that you won't see any at all. Of course, you have to stay on the bus when animals are present.

The shuttle bus drivers generally offer commentary about the sights on the road, but they don't have to and haven't specifically been trained to teach about natural history. Some do a great job, some pass on inaccurate information, and some don't say much. The tour bus drivers are trained to give commentary.

A ROAD LOG

Here are some of the highlights along the road (check the visitor center or the Park Service information handouts to confirm times of the guided walks):

MILE 9   In clear weather, this is the closest spot to the park entrance with a view of Mount McKinley. This section also is a likely place to see moose, especially in the fall rutting season.

(*Tips*   **Shuttle-Bus Etiquette**

Shuttle-bus etiquette is to yell out when you see wildlife. The driver will stop, and everyone will rush to your side of the bus. After you've had a look, give someone else a chance to look out your window or to get a picture. Try to be quiet and don't stick anything out of the bus, as that can scare away the animals.

Denali Park Road Bus Facts

Bus	Purpose	Route	Frequency	Fare
ARA courtesy shuttle	Links hotels to park entrance	Hotels 1 mile north and 7 miles south and within park	Continuous loop	Free, even if not staying at an ARA hotel
Riley Creek Loop	Links facilities within park entrance area	Visitor center, Riley Creek Campground, rail depot	Continuous loop	Free
Savage River Shuttle	Public transport to hiking near the Savage River, which can also be reached by car	From visitor center to Savage River Day use area, about 14 miles into the park	Every 2 hours	$2 exact change, paid to driver
Camper shuttle	Access to campgrounds beyond the park entrance	From the visitor center to Wonder Lake Campground, 85 miles into the park	Several times a day	$18.50 adults, half-price ages 15–17, free 14 and younger
Backcountry shuttle (or just "the shuttle")	General access to the park and wildlife viewing; limited commentary, depending on the driver; no food service	From the visitor center as far as Kantishna, 89 miles away through the park	Every 30 minutes to Eielson Visitor Center, every Wonder Lake, hour to once daily to Kantishna	$17 to Toklat, $23 to Eielson, $30 to Wonder Lake, $33 to Kantishna; half-price ages 15–17, free 14 and younger
Tundra Wildlife Tour	7-hour guided bus tour with lunch provided; passengers may not get off en route	From the visitor center to the Toklat River or Highway Pass, 53 to 61 miles into the park	Twice daily	$71 adults, $38 ages 12 and younger (includes park entrance fee)
Natural History Tour	3-hour guided bus tour at the edge of the park	From the visitor center 17 miles into the park	Three times daily	$37 adults, $21 ages 12 and younger (includes park entrance fee)
Kantishna Roadhouse bus	All-day bus tour to a lodge in Kantishna and back (see section 7 of this chapter)	From the park entrance 95 miles to Kantishna	Once a day	$109, no discount for children, no children under 5

MILE 14   The end of the paved road at the Savage River Bridge. This is generally as far as private vehicles can go. A Park Service checkpoint stops anyone who doesn't have a proper permit. From the parking lot by the bridge, a simple climb over dry tundra leads to Primrose Ridge, also known as Mount Wright.

MILE 17   The portable toilets here are as far as the Natural History Tour bus goes.

MILE 29   An hour and 10 minutes into the drive, a large rest stop overlooks the Teklanika River, with flush toilets, the last plumbing until the Eielson Visitor Center. The Teklanika, like many other rivers on Alaska's glacier-carved terrain, is a braided river—a stream wandering in a massive gravel streambed that's much too big for it. The braided riverbeds, sometimes miles wide, were created by water from fast-melting glaciers at the end of the last ice age. Each is kept free of vegetation by its river, which constantly changes course as it spreads the rock and dust debris carried down from the glaciers. Flat plains in glacial terrain usually are laid down by this mechanism.

MILE 34   Craggy Igloo Mountain is a likely place to see Dall sheep. Without binoculars, they'll just look like white dots. Manageable climbs on Igloo, Cathedral, and Sable mountains take off along the road in the section from Igloo Creek to Sable Pass.

MILE 38–43   Sable Pass, a critical habitat area for bears, is closed to people. A half-eaten sign helps explain why. Bears show up here mostly in the fall. This is the start of the road's broad alpine vistas.

MILE 46   The top of 5-mile-wide Polychrome Pass, the most scenic point on the ride, and a toilet break, 2 hours and 25 minutes into the trip. Caribou look like specks when they pass in the great valley below you, known as the Plain of Murie after Adolph Murie, a biologist who pioneered study here and helped develop the Park Service's scientific ethic (the name does not always appear on maps, however). Note how the mountains of colored rock on either side of the plain match up—they once connected before glacial ice carved this valley. Huge rocks on its floor are glacial erratics, plucked from the bedrock by moving ice and left behind when it melted.

MILE 53   The Toklat River, another braided river, is a flat plain of gravel with easy walking. The glaciers that feed the river are 10 miles upstream; the river bottom is habitat for bears, caribou, and wolves, and a good place for picnics.

MILE 58   Highway Pass is the highest point on the road. In good weather, dramatic views of Mount McKinley start here. The alpine tundra from here to the Eielson Visitor Center is inviting for walking, but beware: Tundra is soft underfoot and can conceal holes and declivities that can twist an ankle.

MILE 64   Thorofare Pass, where the road becomes narrow and winding, is a good area to look for bears and caribou. Bus drivers know best where the animals are on any particular day; they exchange information among themselves.

MILE 66   The **Eielson Visitor Center,** the end of most bus trips, has flush toilets, a covered picnic area, and a small area of displays where rangers answer questions. Among the exhibits is one explaining why you probably can't see the mountain from this best of vantage points, just 33 miles from its summit (Mount McKinley creates its own weather and is visible only about a third of the time in the summer). There's also a seismograph on display, registering the frequent small earthquakes that accompany McKinley's prodigious growth—about an inch every 3 years. This region is a jumble of rocks pushed together by the expanding Pacific tectonic plate; the mountain, and the whole Alaska Range, are folding upward in that great collision. Starting in mid-June, a ranger-guided tundra walk occurs daily at 1:30pm, lasting no more than an hour; take a 9am or earlier bus to be there on time. If you leave the bus here for a hike, you can get a ride back later by signing up on the standby list kept by a ranger.

MILE 68.5 The incredibly rugged terrain to the north is the earth and vege-tation covering Muldrow Glacier. The ice extends to McKinley's peak and was the early and arduous route for climbers; these days, they fly to a base camp at 7,200-feet elevation on the Kahiltna Glacier, on the south side. McKinley's glaciers, falling 15,000 vertical feet and extending up to 45 miles in length, are among the world's greatest. The Ruth Glacier has carved the Great Gorge on the south side, which is almost 6,000 feet deep above the ice and another 4,000 below—almost twice the depth of the Grand Canyon. The park road comes within a mile of the Muldrow's face, then continues through wet, rolling terrain past beaver ponds, and finally descends into a small spruce patch near mile 82.

MILE 86 Wonder Lake campground is the closest road point to Mount McKinley, 27 miles away. Some buses continue another half-hour to Kantishna. The fact that McKinley looks so massive from this considerable distance, dom-inating the sky, is testament to its stupendous size. You'll likely never see a larger object on this planet. From its base (your elevation here is only 2,000 ft.) to its top is an elevation gain greater than any other mountain on earth. Other moun-tains are taller overall, but they stand on higher ground.

4 Denali on Foot: Day Hiking & Backpacking
DAY HIKING IN THE BACKCOUNTRY

One of the unique aspects of Denali is the lack of developed trails—you really can take off in any direction. I've covered some of the best hiking areas above, in "A Road Log," including Primrose Ridge, Teklanika River, Igloo and Sable mountains, and the Toklat River. The Park Service long resisted building any trails, but is giving in and recognizing some trails visitors have created, including those at Eielson Visitor Center and the new 2-mile path that leads from the Wonder Lake Campground to the McKinley River Bar, which extends far to the east and west. You can drive or take a $2 shuttle to the Savage River Day Use Area, at mile 15, which has a 1-mile loop trail and longer, informal routes for great alpine tundra hiking. No permit is needed for day hiking.

The broad, hard gravel flats of the **braided riverbeds,** such as the McKinley, Toklat, Teklanika, and Savage, are among the best routes for hiking in the park. **Stony Creek,** leading up a gorge to the north from the road at mile 60, is an excellent walk into the mountains. You can also hike on the tundra, of which there are two varieties: The **wet tundra** lies on top of permanently frozen ground called permafrost; it's mushy at best, like hiking on foam rubber laid over bowling balls. At worst, it's swamp. **Dry tundra** clothes the mountainsides, and generally makes for firmer footing and easier walking. The brush and stunted forest of the region are virtually impenetrable.

The major risks of hiking here relate to the weather and rivers. It can get cold and wet in midsummer, and if you're not prepared with warm, waterproof cloth-ing, you could suffer the spiraling chill of hypothermia. The rivers are danger-ous because of their fast flow and icy cold water. Experienced backcountry trekkers plan their routes to avoid crossing sizable rivers. See the notes on river crossings and hypothermia in the "Outdoors Health & Safety" section of

---

⌒ **Tips** **Ranger Programs in the Park**

Check the park newspaper, *The Alpenglow,* for ranger talks and slide shows that happen as often as several times a day in the frontcountry area and at the Riley Creek, Savage River, and Teklanika campgrounds.

---

chapter 2. Bears, which people worry most about, have never killed a Denali visitor. Tips on avoiding them are in chapter 2, and are widely distributed at the park.

For a first foray beyond the trails, consider joining one of the Park Service guided hikes. Two daily **Discovery Hikes** go somewhere near the Eielson Visitor Center and another route nearer the entrance end of the park. A ranger takes only 15 hikers, leading them into wilderness while teaching about the nature of the places they visit. Plan a 5- to 11-hour day, including the shuttle ride; actual hiking time is about 4 hours. The hikes generally are not too strenuous for families with school-age children, although it is wise to inquire how steep it will be if you have any doubts. They cost no more than the price of your shuttle ticket. You need to wear hiking shoes or boots and bring food, water, and rain gear. Reserve a place in advance, as hikes fill up in July and you'll need to know when and where to catch the special bus. Rangers also lead walks on the short Savage River Loop, 15 miles into the park. The **Eielson Stroll,** at 1:30pm daily starting in early June, is a short guided stroll from the Eielson Visitor Center, at mile 66 on the park road. Check in at the visitor center for late word on all the hikes before heading out on a long bus trip.

DAY HIKING IN THE PARK ENTRANCE AREA

There are six short trails at the park entrance, weaving through the boreal forest around small lakes, and one steep and spectacular hike to the **Mount Healy overlook,** a 5-mile round-trip. That trail breaks through the tree line to slopes of tundra and rock outcroppings, where you can see just how small the pocket of human infestation is at the park entrance area: The Alaska Range and its foothills extend far into the distance. If you were to continue on an all-day hike right to the top of Mount Healy, you could see all the way to McKinley on a clear day. The *Alpenglow* park newspaper contains a brief guide for these trails, and you can get a natural history guide, *The Nature of Denali,* by Sheri Forbes, at the visitor center.

BACKPACKING

Imagine backpacking over your own area of wilderness, without trails, limits, or the chance of seeing other people. There's no need to retrace your route to get back: Anywhere you meet the 89-mile Denali Park Road you can catch a bus back to the world of people. Any experienced backpacker should consider a backcountry trek at Denali.

Yes, it can be challenging. Hiking on the tundra, broken rock mountainsides, and braided rivers is tiring, and it's easy to fall or turn an ankle. You must be prepared for river crossings and cold weather, know how to find your way with a map and compass, and know how to avoid attracting bears. But if you've done a backpacking trip in a less challenging area, you surely can manage it here, so long as you prepare and don't underestimate the additional time you'll need in trail-less terrain. Nor do you need to trek far—you can camp just a few miles off the road and still be in a place that looks like no one has ever been there before.

You must be flexible about where you're going and be prepared for any kind of terrain, because you can't choose the **backcountry unit** you will explore until you arrive at the backcountry desk at the visitor center and find out what's available. This information, and a map of the units, is posted on a board behind the desk. Groups of four or more may have a hard time finding a place to hike, but there's almost always *somewhere* to go. You can reserve permits only 1 day in advance; you're unlikely to get one for the day you arrive, but you can reserve permits for continuation of your trip for up to 14 days at the same time. The first night of a trip is the hard one to get—for one thing, you can reserve only units that are contiguous to the park road for the first night—but after that, each night gets progressively easier. A couple of rangers are there to help you through the process. Buy the *Denali National Park and Preserve* topographical map, published by Trails Illustrated, available for $9.95 from the Alaska Natural History Association, listed earlier under "Visitor Information." Printed on plastic, the map includes the boundaries of the 43 backcountry units and much other valuable information. Also, you'll want a copy of *Backcountry Companion,* by Jon Nierenberg, which describes conditions and routes in each area and is published and sold by ANHA for $8.95. You'll find it at the visitor center, or you can glance at a well-thumbed copy kept at the backcountry desk.

The alpine units from the Toklat River to Eielson Visitor Center are most popular. That's where you get broad views and can cross heathery dry tundra, walking in any direction. But to go far, you'll also have to be ready to climb over some rugged, rocky terrain, and the tundra itself is deceptively difficult walking—it's soft and hides ankle-turning holes. The wooded units are the least popular, since bushwhacking through overgrown land is anything but fun. The best routes for making time here (and anywhere in the Alaska Bush) are along the braided river valleys and streambeds. You need to be ready for stream crossings.

Before venturing into the backcountry, everyone is required to watch an **orientation film** called the *Backcountry Simulator.* It's intended to teach you how not to attract bears, but it's intimidating enough to scare you out of the park—don't let it. The Park Service provides bear-resistant food containers in which you are required to carry all your food. Guns are not permitted in the park; carrying a pepper spray for self-defense from bears such as Counter Assault is allowed. You'll have to take the **camper bus** to get to your backcountry unit, at a cost of $18.50 for each adult.

Before you decide to go backpacking at Denali, however, you may want to broaden your thinking—if you're up to a cross-country hike without a trail, there are tens of millions of acres in Alaska available for backpacking that don't require a permit. Check with the Alaska Public Lands Information Center in Anchorage or Fairbanks for ideas about road-accessible alpine wilderness in Gates of the Arctic National Park, on the Denali Highway (see earlier); and in Wrangell–St. Elias National Park (in chapter 9). I've listed some great trail hikes in chapter 7, under Chugach National Forest, and in chapter 9, in the sections on Chena Hot Springs Road and the Steese Highway.

5 Activities Within the Park

MOUNTAIN BIKING

A bicycle provides special freedom in the park. Bicyclists can ride past the checkpoint where cars have to turn back, at mile 14 on the park road. Park campgrounds have bike stands, and you can take a bike on the shuttle or camper bus,

First to the Top

It's the biggest. That's why climbers risk their lives on Mount McKinley. You can see the mountain from Anchorage, more than 100 miles away. On a flight across Alaska, McKinley stands out grandly over waves of other mountains. It's more than a mile taller than the tallest peak in the other 49 states. It's a great white triangle, always covered in snow, tall but also massive and strong.

The first group to try to climb Mount McKinley came in 1903, led by Judge James Wickersham, who also helped explore Washington's Olympic Peninsula before it became a national park. His group made it less than halfway up, but on the trip they found gold in the Kantishna Hills, setting off a small gold rush that led to the first permanent human settlement in the park area. Wickersham later became the Alaska Territory's nonvoting delegate to Congress and introduced the bill that created the national park, but the government was never able to get back land in the Kantishna area from the gold miners. Today, that land is the site of four luxurious wilderness lodges, right in the middle of the park.

On September 27, 1906, renowned world explorer Dr. Frederick Cook announced to the world by telegraph that he had reached the summit of Mount McKinley after a lightning-fast climb, covering more than 85 miles and 19,000 vertical feet in 13 days with one other man, a blacksmith, at his side. On his return to New York, Cook was lionized as a conquering explorer and published a popular book of his summit diary and photographs.

In 1909, Cook again made history, announcing that he had beat Robert Peary to the North Pole. Both returned to civilization from their competing treks at about the same time. Again, Cook was the toast of the town. His story began to fall apart, however, when his Eskimo companions mentioned that he'd never been out of sight of land. After being paid by Peary to come forward, Cook's McKinley companion also recanted. A year later, Cook's famous summit photograph was re-created—on a peak 19 miles away and 15,000 feet lower than the real summit.

In 1910, disgusted with Cook, four prospectors from Fairbanks took a more Alaskan approach to the task. Without fanfare or special supplies—they carried doughnuts and hot chocolate on their incredible final ascent—they marched up the mountain carrying a large wooden

so you can get a lift when you need one, or ride one way. The longest stretch on the park road between campgrounds is 52 miles. On the downside, the buses kick up a lot of dust, and bikes may not go off-road. Pick up a copy of the bicycle rules from the backcountry desk before you start. **Denali Outdoor Center** (© **888/303-1925** or 907/683-1925; www.denalioutdoorcenter.com), located just north of the overlook in the Nenana Canyon area, rents front-suspension bikes for $40 for 24 hours, $25 for 6 hours, with discounts for longer rentals. The 2½ -hour guided rides are $65.

flagpole they could plant on top to prove they'd made it. But on arriving at the summit, they realized that they'd climbed the slightly shorter north peak. Weather closed in, so they set up the pole there and descended without attempting the south peak. Then, when they got back to Fairbanks, no one could see the pole, and they were accused of trying to pull off another hoax.

In 1913, Episcopal archdeacon Hudson Stuck organized the first successful climb to reach the *real* summit—and reported he saw the pole on the other peak. Harry Karstens led the climb (he would become the park's first superintendent in 1917), and the first person to stand at the summit was an Alaska Native, Walter Harper.

Although McKinley remains one of the world's most difficult climbs, about 10,000 people have made it to the top since Hudson Stuck's party. Since 1980 the number of climbers has boomed, making it crowded at the top (garbage disposal has even become a problem). In 1970, only 124 made the attempt; now more than 1,000 people try to climb the peak each year, with about half making it to the summit. The cold, fast-changing weather is what usually stops people. From late April into early July, climbers fly from the town of Talkeetna to a base camp at 7,200 feet elevation on the Kahiltna Glacier. From there, it takes about a month to get to the top, through temperatures as cold as –40°F.

Climbers lose fingers, toes, and other parts to frostbite every year, or suffer other, more severe injuries. During the season, the Park Service stations rescue rangers and an emergency medical clinic at the 14,200-foot level of the mountain, and keeps a high-altitude helicopter ready to go after climbers in trouble. They and the military spend about half a million dollars a year rescuing climbers, and sometimes much more. In 1998, a volunteer ranger lost his life trying to save a Canadian who had fallen; he was one of three people who died that year, bringing the total who have perished on McKinley to 91. None died in 1999, but in 2000, three volunteer rangers and their pilot died trying to fly into the Kahiltna Glacier base camp, and one climber was killed in an avalanche on nearby Mount Johnson. (No deaths were reported in 2001.) Most who died had fallen, but cold and altitude also took many and may have contributed to the falls. Monuments to those who never returned are in the cemetery near the airstrip in Talkeetna.

SLED DOG DEMONSTRATIONS

In the winter, rangers patrol the park by dogsled, as they have for decades. In the summer, to keep the dogs active and amuse the tourists, they run a sled on wheels around the kennel, and a ranger gives a talk, normally at 1, 2, and 4pm. Although it's no substitute for seeing dogs run on snow, you can get a sense of their speed and enthusiasm from the show. It was the highlight of my son's trip to Denali when he was 3 years old. There's a shortage of parking at the kennels, near the headquarters at mile 3.4 on the park road, so take a free bus from the visitor center a half-hour before each show. Times are listed in the *Alpenglow* park newspaper.

FISHING

Fishing is quite poor at Denali. There are grayling in some rivers, but the water is too cold and silty for most fish. Those who don't care if they catch anything, however, do enjoy fishing in this wonderful scenery. You don't need a fishing license within park boundaries, but you do have to throw back everything you catch. Bring your own gear, as it's unavailable in the park area.

CLIMBING MOUNT MCKINLEY

Because of its altitude and weather, Mount McKinley is among the world's most challenging climbs. Summer temperatures at the high camp average 20° to 40°F below zero. If you're looking here for advice, you're certainly not up to an **unguided climb.** A **guided climb** is a challenging and expensive endeavor requiring months of conditioning and about a month on the mountain. Get names of guides from the Park Service's **Talkeetna Ranger Station,** P.O. Box 588, Talkeetna, AK 99676 (© **907/733-2231**). The climbing season lasts from late April or early May until the snow gets too soft, in late June or early July. Climbers fly from Talkeetna to a 7,200-foot base camp on Kahiltna Glacier. About 1,000 climbers attempt the mountain annually in about 300 parties; about half typically make it to the top each year, and usually a few die trying.

6 Attractions & Activities Outside the Park

FLIGHTSEEING

Getting a good, close look at Mount McKinley itself is best accomplished by air. Frequently you can see McKinley from above the clouds even when you can't see it from the ground. Best of all, some Talkeetna operators that fly mountaineers also land visitors on the mountain, a unique and unforgettable experience (see section 10 of this chapter; also see chapter 6, on Anchorage, for an air excursion from there). Regardless of how close you approach the mountain, however, a flight does show how incredibly rugged is the Alaska Range.

Small planes and helicopters fly from the park airstrip, private heliports and airstrips along the Parks Highway, and the Healy airstrip. **Denali Air** (© **907/ 683-2261;** www.denaliair.com) has an office in the Nenana Canyon area, and flight operations at mile 229.5 of the Parks Highway. An hour-long flight going within a mile of the mountain costs $190 for adults, half price for children ages 12 and under. **Era Helicopters** (© **800/843-1947** or 907/683-2574; www. eraaviation.com) has hour-long flights for $215, including van pickup from the hotels. Their helihikes land for a 4-hour hike on a mountain ridgeline, the difficulty tailored to the customers' ability; it costs $295. A 75-minute glacier-landing flight costs $299.

RAFTING

Rafting on the Nenana River, bordering the park along the Parks Highway, is fun and popular. Several commercial guides float two stretches of the river: an upper portion, where the water is smoother and the guides explain passing scenery; and the lower portion, where the river roars through the rock-walled Nenana Canyon, and rafts take on huge splashes of silty, glacial water through Class III and IV rapids. Guides take children as young as 5 on the slow trip (although I wouldn't let my kid go at that age); the youngest accepted for the fast portion is age 12. White-water rafting carries risks you shouldn't discount just because a lot of people do it, as a fatal accident on the supposedly easy tour confirmed in 1999. Each session takes 2 to 2½ hours, including safety briefings, suiting up, and riding to and from the put-in and take-out points. Prices vary from $53 to $65 for adults, with discounted rates for children (from $10 less to half off).

Denali Outdoor Center (© **888/303-1925** or 907/683-1925; www. denalioutdoorcenter.com) is a professional operation, offering rafting trips and instruction in river techniques. There are four firms in competition, however, so you may be able to save by shopping around. When reserving, be sure to ask what kind of gear is provided: Dry suits will keep you comfortable, while you're likely to get drenched if all they give you is rain gear or Mustang flotation suits. If you're camping, plan a shower afterward—the silt in the river water will stick to your skin and hair.

HORSEBACK RIDING

There is no riding in the park itself, but you have several opportunities in similar terrain outside its boundaries. Various companies offer rides, although the lineup of firms seem to change every year. One- to two-hour rides cost from $65 to $85. Among the operators are **Denali Saddle Safaris** (© **907/683-1200;** www.denalisaddlesafaris.com), which also offers pack trips and extended journeys, and **Tumbling B Ranch** (© **907/683-6000;** www.tumblingbranch.com).

7 Accommodations

PARK SERVICE CAMPGROUNDS

I've explained how to make camping reservations in section 2 of this chapter, under "The Reservations System." Note that reservation fees are added to camping fees.

Only Riley Creek Campground is open after September (water is off in winter). The rest reopen when the snow is gone, in May for all but Wonder Lake, which opens in June.

CAR-ACCESSIBLE CAMPGROUNDS

In addition to these, see **Teklanika River campground** under "Bus-Accessible Campgrounds," below; you can drive to it as long as your stay is 3 days long.

Morino Backpacker Campground   This campground is simply an area of trees near the entrance where you can self-register, put up a tent, and use a portable toilet. There's no parking, and only two people are allowed per site.

1 mile from park entrance, near railroad depot. $6 per night; tents only.

Keeping Clean at Denali

None of the campgrounds at Denali have showers. The larger camp-grounds have the typical cold-water bathrooms found in the national parks. Better bathrooms are at the hotels and visitor center. You can grab a shower and wash clothes at **McKinley Mercantile,** at the Riley Creek Campground. You pay by the shower: There is no time limit or coin machine to feed. You also can take showers, even if you're not a guest, at **McKinley RV and Campground** (listed below) for $2.50. It has a token-operated laundry, too.

Riley Creek ⭐   This large campground right across the road from the visitor center is best for those who want to be in the middle of things. It's near the store, showers, a bus stop for the free front-country shuttle, and a pay phone. Sites are wooded with small birch and spruce, and they're adequately separated, but this isn't exactly wilderness camping. Reservations are relatively easy to get. The park's only sewage dump station is here.

Near the visitor center. $12 per site. 100 sites; RVs or tents. Campfires allowed; flush toilets, dump station.

Savage River ⭐⭐   On the *taiga*—the thin spruce forest and tundra—this is a wonderful campground with unforgettable views. Campers can wander from their sites on some of the park's best hikes. This is the only campground you can readily drive to that's away from the activity at the park entrance. There is no telephone.

On Denali Park Rd., 13 miles from entrance. $12 per site. 33 sites; RVs or tents. Campfires allowed; flush toilets.

BUS-ACCESSIBLE CAMPGROUNDS

To use these campgrounds, you'll need a camper ticket on the shuttle bus, which costs $18.50 for adults, half price ages 15 to 17, free 14 and under. There are no businesses and no phones beyond the park entrance area; you must bring in everything you need.

Igloo Creek and Sanctuary River ⭐   These two primitive campgrounds, each with seven tent sites, offer a backcountry experience, away from cars. There's a $6 camping fee and no campfires are allowed, only stoves. You can't reserve sites in advance; you can only reserve in person at the visitor center when you arrive. Both campgrounds have only chemical toilets.

On Denali Park Rd., 23 miles and 34 miles from park entrance, respectively.

Teklanika River ⭐⭐   This is the only car campground that's beyond the checkpoint on the Park Road. You can drive in only if you don't move your vehicle for 3 days; otherwise, take the camper bus. Sites are among the small trees of the boreal forest. One big advantage of staying here is that you begin the morning much closer to the heart of the park, cutting the time you have to spend on the bus, and one bus ticket lasts your whole 3-day stay. Using this base for 3 days, you can really explore different areas of the park in varying kinds of weather.

On Denali Park Rd., 29 miles from entrance; access by camper bus, or drive in with a minimum 3-night stay. $12 per site. 53 sites; RVs or tents. Campfires allowed; flush toilets.

Wonder Lake ⭐⭐⭐   It takes almost 6 hours to get here on the bus, but this campground by placid Wonder Lake, at the foot of Mount McKinley, puts you in the most beautiful and coveted area of the park. Set among a patch of spruce trees on the mountain side of the lake, the sites can be tough to get.

On Denali Park Rd., 85 miles from entrance. $12 per site. 28 sites; tents only. No campfires, stove only; flush toilets.

COMMERCIAL CAMPGROUNDS

There are two commercial campgrounds in the area. **Denali Grizzly Bear Cabins and Campground** (📞 **907/683-2696;** www.AlaskaOne.com/dengrzly) is about 7 miles south of the park entrance, and has some exposed sites and others on a hillside among small trees. Small cabins and tent cabins dot the property as well. There is a coin-operated shower. Tent sites are $17.50 for up to four people, with electrical and water hookups $6 more.

A campground with birch trees and attractive sites is 10 miles north of the park, in Healy. **McKinley RV and Campground,** at mile 248.5 on the Parks Highway (© **800/478-2562** or 907/683-2379; www.mtaonline.net/~rvcampak), has a deli and espresso bar, a gas station, token-operated laundry, hot showers, and a small playground. Basic tent sites are $16.25, full hookups $27.

HOTELS

Patterns of land ownership and the uncontrolled development around Denali have led to a hodgepodge of roadside hotels, cabins, lodges, campgrounds, and restaurants in pockets arrayed along more than 20 miles of the Parks Highway. There are rooms of good quality in each of the pockets, but the going rates vary widely.

The most expensive rooms, and the first booked, are in the immediate area of the park entrance. Next are the hotels south of the park. Both these areas are entirely seasonal. The best deals are in **Healy,** 10 miles north of the park, where you can find a room for $50 less than a comparable room near the park entrance. Of course, if you don't have a car, it's most convenient to stay in or near the park.

The other choices are to stay in **Talkeetna,** the back door to the park (described in section 10 of this chapter), or at a wilderness lodge in the **Kantishna** area or outside the park.

Despite their high prices, rooms can be hard to find in the high season, and it's wise to book well ahead. If you don't mind gambling, however, you can often get great last-minute deals from hotels that have had large cancellations from their package-tour clients.

NEAR THE PARK

This area, known formally as Nenana Canyon or more commonly as "Glitter Gulch," extends about a mile north of the park entrance on the Parks Highway. Two huge hotels that primarily serve package-tour passengers dominate the area, the **Denali Princess Lodge,** Mile 238.5, Parks Hwy. (© **800/426-0050;** fax 206/336-6100; www.princessalaskalodges.com), and the **McKinley Resorts Chalets,** Mile 239.1, Parks Hwy. (book through Denali Park Resorts, under "Visitor Information," earlier). If they have a cancellation, you may be able to get attractive rooms at one of these places at the last minute for a fraction of their astronomical rack rates. The McKinley Resorts Chalets also is a good place to book activities.

Since most readers of this book are independent travelers, I've concentrated instead on smaller lodgings that cater to individual bookings. In addition to those I've listed, you'll find good standard rooms at **Denali River View Inn,** Mile 238.4, Parks Hwy. (© **907/683-2663;** www.alaskan.com/denaliriverview), for $139 double; and at **Denali Sourdough Cabins,** Mile 238.5, Parks Hwy. (© **907/683-2773;** www.denalisourdoughcabins.com), which has comfortable little cabins in the woods below the highway for similar prices.

All of the hotels in this area are open only during the tourist season, roughly May 15 to September 15.

Denali Bluffs Hotel ✦ A series of 12 buildings on a steep mountainside looks down on the Nenana Canyon area from above the highway. The light, tastefully decorated rooms have two double beds and good amenities, and those on the upper floor have vaulted ceilings and balconies with great views. The courtesy van will take you anywhere in the area. The Mountain Café serves simple, American meals for breakfast and lunch.

Mile 238.4, Parks Hwy. (P.O. Box 72460, Fairbanks, AK 99707). ✆ **907/683-7000.** Fax 907/683-7500. http://denalibluffs.com. 112 units. High season $185 double. Low season $132 double. Extra person $10. AE, DISC, MC, V. **Amenities:** Restaurant (American); tour desk; courtesy van; coin-op laundry. *In room:* Satellite TV, fridge, coffeemaker.

Denali Crow's Nest Log Cabins ⭐   Perched in five tiers on the side of a mountain above the Nenana Canyon area, looking down on Horseshoe Lake and the other, larger hotels, the cabins are roomy and comfortable, especially those on the 100 and 200 level. A log cabin and the warmth of the Crofoot family create more of a true Alaskan feeling than the modern, standard rooms that have filled the canyon. You spend a lot of time climbing stairs, however; and despite the great views and the price, the cabins are simple, not luxurious; the rooms have shower enclosures, not tubs. All rooms are nonsmoking. The restaurant, **The Overlook,** is recommended separately under "Dining," later in this chapter.

Mile 238.5, Parks Hwy. (P.O. Box 70), Denali National Park, AK 99755. ✆ **888/917-8130** or 907/683-2723. Fax 907/683-2323. www.denalicrowsnest.com. 39 cabins. High season $154 cabin for 2. Low season $79 cabin for 2. Extra person $10. MC, V. **Amenities:** Restaurant; bar; outdoor hot tub; tour desk; courtesy van.

IN HEALY

Healy is 10 miles north of the park entrance, but a world away. It's a year-round community with an economy based primarily on a large coal mine and only secondarily on the park. It sits in a large, windy valley with a few patches of stunted trees and big, open spaces of tundra. There are many hotels and B&Bs with rooms that cost from $20 to $90 less than those near the park. They say the water tastes better, too. On the downside, you need a car to stay in Healy.

Besides my two favorites below, the **Stampede Lodge,** Mile 248.8, Parks Hwy., Healy (✆ **800/478-2370** or 907/683-2242; www.AlaskaOne.com/stampede), has small but attractively decorated rooms in a renovated 1946 railroad building; they go for $89 double in summer. A reasonably priced restaurant inside serves three meals a day beginning in May.

Motel Nord Haven ⭐ *(Value)*   This fresh little gray hotel with a red roof has large, immaculate rooms, each with one or two queen-size beds. They're equal to the best standard rooms in the Denali Park area and a lot less expensive. Bill and Patsy Nordmark offer free newspapers, coffee, tea, hot chocolate, extra phone lines for the Internet, and a sitting room with a collection of Alaska books. The rooms, decorated with Alaska art and oak trim, all have interior entrances and have been smoke-free since their construction. Up to four people can stay in the rooms with two beds for the price of a double. They have three kitchenette units. A continental breakfast is served for $5 and a sack lunch will be packed for $8.

Mile 249.5, Parks Hwy. (P.O. Box 458), Healy, AK 99743. ✆ **800/683-4501** or 907/683-4500. Fax 907/683-4503. www.motelnordhaven.com. 28 units. High season $112–$131 double. Low season $70 double. AE, MC, V. *In room:* TV, dataport, hair dryer.

White Moose Lodge *(Value)*   This old, low-slung building among stunted black spruce contains an unlikely find—comfortable, cheerfully decorated rooms with flower boxes, and a small greenhouse. The breakfast served in the small lobby consists of coffee, tea, orange juice, and pastries.

Mile 248, Parks Hwy. (P.O. Box 68), Healy, AK 99743. ✆ **800/481-1232** or 907/683-1231. Fax 907/683-1232. www.whitemooselodge.com. 12 units. High season $90 double. Low season $70 double. Extra adult $10, extra child $5. Rates include continental breakfast. AE, DC, DISC, MC, V. Closed Oct to mid-May. *In room:* TV, 2 double beds, private bath.

SOUTH OF THE PARK

Lodgings south of the park are in widely separated pockets of private land concentrated 7 and 14 miles south of the park. (Anything south of that is in Talkeetna, covered in section 10 of this chapter.) I've listed just a few of the best in detail below, but you may also want to try these others: **McKinley Creekside Cabins,** 13 miles south at Mile 224, Parks Hwy. (© **888/5DENALI** or 907/683-2277; www.mckinleycabins.com), which has cabins with private or shared bathrooms starting at $99 double; or **Denali Cabins,** Mile 229, Parks Hwy. (© **888/560-8489** or 907/683-2643; 907/783-8448 in winter; www.alaskan.com/denalicabins).

Denali Mountain Morning Hostel and Lodge _Value_   This new place is operated by energetic outdoors people who offer a cozy place to stay in an octagonal log building and rental of the equipment you'll need for an adventure in the park. Accommodations include hostel bunks, private rooms, or a separate private cabin, all advantageously priced. All use the shared bathhouse. They are located near McKinley Creekside Café and the Perch.

Mile 224, Parks Hwy. (P.O. Box 208), Denali National Park, AK 99755. © 907/683-7503 or 866/D-HOSTEL, within Alaska only. www.hostelalaska.com. Bunk $22 adult, $17 child. Private rm $65 double; cabin $80 double; $10 each additional adult, $5 child 5–13, free under 5. DISC, MC, V.

Denali River Cabins _★★_   These cedar cabins arrayed on a maze of boardwalks above the Nenana River are fresh and well appointed. Unlike most accommodations outside Denali, they have an outdoorsy, national park feel, lent in part by the riverside location. They have shower stalls, not tubs, and lack closets. Those cabins on the river, with decks over the water, are $20 more. The sauna has a picture window on the river, and there's a Jacuzzi and a comfortable lobby. It's owned by the same Native corporation that owns the Kantishna Roadhouse, listed under "Wilderness Lodges," below. Don't confuse this place with Denali Cabins.

Mile 231, Parks Hwy. (P.O. Box 210), Denali National Park, 99755. (Winter mailing address: P.O. Box 81670, Fairbanks, AK 99708). © 800/230-7275 or 907/683-2500. Fax 907/683-2502. (Winter © 907/459-2121; fax 907/459-2160.) www.denalirivercabins.com. 54 cabins. High season $139–$159 cabin for 2. Low season $99–$119 cabin for 2. Extra adult $10, children under 11 free. AE, DISC, MC, V. **Amenities:** Restaurant (American); bar; Jacuzzi; sauna; tour desk; courtesy car; coin-op laundry. _In room:_ No TV or telephone.

The Perch _★_ _Value_   In the trees along rushing Carlo Creek, 13 miles south of the park entrance, cabins range from large, modern units with private bathrooms to adorable if spartan A-frames with lofts that share a bathhouse. There's a sense of privacy and of being out in the woods along the wooden and gravel walkways. It's an exceptional value, open year-round. You will need a car to stay here. The **restaurant and bar,** set atop a steep hill, are described below under "Dining."

Mile 224, Parks Hwy. (P.O. Box 53) Denali National Park, AK 99755. © 888/322-2523, or phone/fax 907/683-2523. www.denaliperchresort.com. 20 cabins, 14 with private bathroom. $65–$95 cabin for 2. Extra person $10. AE, DISC, MC, V. **Amenities:** Restaurant/bar.

WILDERNESS LODGES

For those who can afford it, a lodge allows you to experience real wilderness in complete comfort. Here I've listed the three lodges in the Kantishna district, an old gold-mining inholding near McKinley, and one fly-in lodge east of the park. You get to Kantishna on a private bus or van over the 89-mile park road, guided by your host. Once there, you can explore the park using a special pass for shuttle rides starting in Kantishna, which costs $16.50, available from your lodge, space available. All are open only in summer. A year-round wilderness lodge reached from Talkeetna is covered in section 10, below.

Camp Denali/North Face Lodge ★★★ At this pioneering ecotourism establishment, you can wake to the white monolith of Mount McKinley filling your window. The naturalist guides here have the right to use the park road free of the shuttle system for hikes, biking, lake canoeing, bird-watching, photography sessions, and other outdoor learning activities. During some sessions, nationally reputed academics and other experts lead the program. All arrivals and departures are on fixed session dates and start with a picnic on the park road on the way out of camp. Each of the Camp Denali cabins has its own outhouse, and all share a central bathhouse and wonderful lodge common rooms—it would be my first choice for anyone who can get by without his or her own flush toilet. North Face Lodge has smallish traditional rooms with private bathrooms. A conservation ethic pervades the operation, from the homegrown vegetables to the proprietors' efforts to preserve the natural values of private land in the park.

Kantishna District (P.O. Box 67), Denali National Park, AK 99755. © **907/683-2290**. www.campdenali.com. 17 cabins, none with private bathroom (Camp Denali); 15 units with bathroom (North Face Lodge). $345 per person per night, double occupancy. Rates include all meals. Minimum stay 3 nights. No credit cards. No smoking in buildings or vehicles. **Amenities:** Restaurant (meals included in rate); canoes, mountain bikes, and fishing gear included.

Denali Backcountry Lodge ★★ Thirty comfortable, modern cedar cabins sit in rows on a deck next to babbling Moose Creek and a two-story lodge building. Guests can sit in a screened porch away from the mosquitoes and watch the day go by, or join a choice of guided hikes, natural history programs, or other activities around the lodge. Each cabin has its own bathroom, with a shower stall. To go out into the park, you're on your own, either on a lodge mountain bike or the shuttle, although the ride in from the entrance in a 15-passenger van is treated as a safari. It's run by Alaska Wildland Adventures, which offers a variety of well-regarded ecotourism packages all over the state, including some that include a stay at the lodge and the Denali Wilderness Lodge, listed below.

Kantishna District, Denali National Park (mailing address: P.O. Box 810, Girdwood, AK 99587). © **800/841-0692** or 907/783-1342. Fax 907/783-1308. www.denalilodge.com. 30 cabins. $330 per person per night, double occupancy. Rates include all meals. 3-night minimum recommended. MC, V. **Amenities:** Restaurant (meals included in rate); mountain bikes and activities included.

Denali Wilderness Lodge ★★ The extraordinary log buildings were built by the late big-game guide Lynn Castle along the Wood River, but they don't kill the animals anymore: Now they're more valuable to look at alive, and the lodge has become an ecoestablishment, flying guests in for horseback riding, hiking, talks by naturalists, and other activities. This is the best place for riders, with a sizable stable and a daily ride included in the price. While not luxurious, the cabins are quite comfortable and have private bathrooms. The location is distant from Mount McKinley, in a remote valley 30 miles east of the park entrance.

Wood River (P.O. Box 50), Denali Park, AK 99755. © **800/541-9779** year-round or 907/683-1287 summer only. www.DenaliWildernessLodge.com. (In winter: P.O. Box 120, Trout Lake, WA 98650.) 22 units. $330 per person per night, double occupancy. Rates include all meals. Plane fare from Denali $80 one-way. MC, V. **Amenities:** Restaurant (meals included in rate); bar; horseback riding included.

Kantishna Roadhouse ★★ This well-kept property of many buildings along Moose Creek in the old Kantishna Mining District trades on both the mining history and outdoor opportunities of the area. Some rooms are large and luxurious, while others are in smaller single cabins with lofts. The log central lodge has an attractive lobby with people coming and going—it's got more of a hotel feel and might be more attractive to an older, less active set or to families than the other lodges in the Kantishna District. It's also somewhat less expensive, has a bar, and accommodates 2-night stays. Guided hikes, wagon rides, biking, and gold panning are included in the rate.

A sled dog demonstration (http://denaliwildlifetour.com) coincides with the arrival of a day trip the lodge offers called the Kantishna Wilderness Trails (the same bus brings lodge guests). That ride is the only choice in the park for a nar-rated day tour that covers the entire park road. At 13 hours, it's a marathon, and not suitable for children. The fare, including lunch at the lodge, is $109.

Kantishna District, Denali National Park (mailing address: P.O. Box 81670, Fairbanks, AK 99708). ℭ **800/942-7420** or 907/683-1475. Fax 907/683-1449. (Winter: ℭ 907/459-2120; fax 907/459-2160.) www.kantishnaroadhouse.com. 27 units. $310 per person per night, double occupancy. Rates include all meals. 2-night minimum. AE, DISC, MC, V. **Amenities:** Restaurant (meals included in rate); bar; sauna; mountain bikes; activities included in rate.

8 Dining

Since Denali is entirely seasonal, it lacks the range of inexpensive family restau-rants that develop in year-round communities. For that, head north to Healy, where the **Stampede Lodge** has reasonably priced burgers, sandwiches, and steaks, or south, to the two places described below near Carlo Creek.

Nearer the park, most meals are overpriced by 25% to 50%, a cost of the short season and captive audience. The large hotels in the canyon each have fine dining and casual restaurants; I've described the best in detail below, at the Denali Princess Lodge. The **Chalet Center Cafe** at the McKinley Resorts Chalets serves casual meals in a large, light room (a ham sandwich is $9). You can't miss the tacky highway frontage of the **McKinley Denali Salmon Bake** in the Nenana Canyon area. Although casual to the point of indifference, it can be a fun place to eat in a picnic setting, and the food is adequate and relatively inex-pensive. We can't recommend Lynx Creek Pizza, despite its convenience and popularity; the prices are too high and the quality too low.

McKinley Creekside Café ℜ 🄺🄸🄳🅂 This is a cozy and friendly spot in the Carlo Creek area, south of the park, where you can dine on salmon or halibut (the latter with a Parmesan, artichoke, and spinach sauce) for around $20, or order a main-course salad or burger for around $8. The food is consistently good, including breakfast, and craft brews and wine are served. It's a good choice for families, as parents can see the playground from their tables. They also pack substantial sack lunches for the shuttle bus ride.

Mile 224, Parks Hwy. ℭ **907/683-2277.** www.mckinleycabins.com. Lunch $6–$10, dinner $8–$21. DISC, MC, V. Summer daily 6am–9:30pm.

The Overlook Bar and Grill ℜ BURGERS/STEAK/SEAFOOD This fun, noisy place has the feel of a classic bar and grill, with a vaulted ceiling of rough-cut lumber and a spectacular view of the Nenana Canyon. There are two dining rooms, one with the bar, and another, behind a glass partition, which is quieter and has tablecloths. A huge variety of craft beers is available, with several on tap. At times I've gotten superb fare here, but at other times it has been merely acceptable and not worth the prices, which are high.

Mile 238.5, Parks Hwy., up the hill above the Denali Canyon area. ℭ **907/683-2641.** Lunch main courses $9–$15; dinner main courses $16–$30. MC, V. 11am–11pm daily. Closed mid-Sept to mid-May.

The Perch STEAK/SEAFOOD   The odd, knoblike hill the restaurant stands on provides reason for the name (the attractive cabins described above sit below the restaurant). It's a friendly, family-run place serving a straightforward steak and seafood menu—they don't try anything fancy. The home-baked bread is noteworthy. The dining room is light, with well-spaced tables, and makes up for a somewhat stark quality with big picture windows on three sides. At this writing they were planning a deli on the highway.

Mile 224, Parks Hwy., 13 miles south of the park. © 888/322-2523 or 907/683-2523. www.denaliperchresort. com. Dinner main courses $14–$40. Summer daily 6am–10pm. Winter hours vary. AE, DISC, MC, V.

The Summit Restaurant ★★ STEAK/SEAFOOD   We've decided this is the best place to eat at Denali. First, there's the dining room, perched on the edge of the Nenana Canyon, where you can watch screaming rafters floating by during your meal. Then there's the food and service, which are up to Princess Tours' excellent standards—steak and salmon, the usual choices for Alaska tourists—but done well.

In the Denali Princess Lodge, Mile 238.5, Parks Hwy. © 907/683-8812. Reservations recommended. Breakfast $7–$10, dinner main courses $17–$28. Summer daily 5am–10:30am, 5:30–10pm. AE, DC, DISC, MC, V.

9 Denali Nightlife

The main evening event is the concessionaire's **Cabin Nite Dinner Theater,** at the McKinley Resorts Chalets (© **800/276-7234** or 907/683-8200), a professionally produced musical revue about a gold rush era woman who ran a roadhouse in Kantishna. You can buy the $44 tickets (half price for kids under age 11) virtually anywhere in the area. The actors, singing throughout the evening, stay in character to serve big platters of food to diners sitting at long tables, doing a good job of building a rowdy, happy atmosphere for adults and kids.

Princess Cruises and Tours puts on its own evening show, **The Music of Denali,** at the Denali Princess Lodge. (The local rap says: better food, show not as good.) The performance lasts an hour; with dinner, it lasts 2 hours. Tickets are for sale at the hotel's tour desk (© **800/426-0500** or 907/683-2282) for $37 (half price ages 6 to 12 and younger), or $14 for the show without the meal.

10 Talkeetna: Back Door to Denali

Talkeetna, a historic and funky little town with a sense of humor but not much happening, slept soundly from its decline around World War I until just a few years ago. Now there are paved streets (both of them), a fancy National Park Service building, a new railroad depot, and two large luxury lodges. It seems that while Talkeetna slumbered in a time capsule, an explosion of visitors was happening at Denali National Park. Now, not entirely voluntarily, Talkeetna finds itself enveloped in that boom.

As a threshold to the park, Talkeetna has significant pros and cons that you should take into account. On the positive side, it's closer to Anchorage; the development is much more interesting and authentic than that at the park entrance; there's lots to do outdoors; and great views of the mountain are less frequently obscured by clouds. On the negative side, a big minus: You can't get into the park from here. That means you miss the dramatic scenery, easy backcountry access, and unique wildlife viewing on the park road.

The town dates from the gold rush, and has many charming log and clapboard buildings. With 15 sites of historic note, the entire downtown area has been listed on the National Register of Historic Places. You can spend several hours looking at two small museums and meeting people in the 2-block main street, then go out on the Talkeetna or Susitna rivers for rafting, a jet-boat ride, or fishing, or take a flightseeing trip to the national park.

ESSENTIALS

GETTING THERE   Talkeetna lies on a 13-mile spur road that branches from the Parks Highway 99 miles north of Anchorage and 138 miles south of the park entrance.

The **Alaska Railroad** (© **800/544-0552** or 907/265-2494; www. alaskarailroad.com) serves Talkeetna daily on its runs to Denali National Park during the summer, and weekly in the winter. (See section 2 of this chapter for additional details.) The summer fare from Anchorage to Talkeetna is $75 one-way for adults, half price for children.

The **Talkeetna Shuttle Service** (© **907/733-1725** office, or 907/373-8548 cellular) runs back and forth to and from Anchorage for $50 one-way, $90 round-trip. The **Parks Highway Express** (© **888/600-6001;** www. AlaskaShuttle.com), listed earlier in section 2, also serves Talkeetna.

VISITOR INFORMATION   Built to serve people aiming to climb Mount McKinley, the **Denali National Park Talkeetna Ranger Station,** downtown Talkeetna (P.O. Box 588), Talkeetna, AK 99676 (© **907/733-2231;** www. nps.gov/dena), makes a fascinating stop for anyone curious about mountaineering. Inside the handsome structure, you'll find a large sitting room with a river rock fireplace, climbing books, and pictures of the mountain—it's like an old-fashioned explorers' club. Records open for inspection cover the history of McKinley climbs. Rangers are on hand to answer questions, too. It's open May through August daily 8am to 6pm; winter, Monday to Friday 8am to 4:30pm.

The **Denali/Talkeetna Visitor Center,** located in a tiny cabin at the intersection of the Parks Highway and Talkeetna Spur Road (P.O. Box 688), Talkeetna, AK 99676 (© **800/660-2688** or 907/733-2688; www.alaskan. com/talkeetnadenali), is a commercial center belonging to a local flight service and providing brochures, information, and advice while earning commissions from bookings. It's the handiest commercial information stop in the region. The center is open daily 8am to 8pm in summer, and they respond to inquiries year-round with free trip-planning help.

 FAST FACTS: **Talkeetna**

Bank There is none, but the coin-operated laundry and store at the Three Rivers gas station on Main Street has an **ATM.**

Hospital Go to **Sunshine Community Health Center,** mile 4.4 on the Talkeetna Spur Road (© **907/733-2273**).

Police The **Alaska State Troopers** (© **907/733-3513**), is at mile 97.8 on the Parks Highway, just south of the intersection with the Talkeetna Spur Road.

Post Office In the town center, near the intersection of Talkeetna Spur Road and Main Street.

Taxes There is no **sales tax. Bed tax** in the area is 5%.

GETTING AROUND   You can walk everywhere in Talkeetna, but there are good **mountain biking** routes, too. **CGS Bicycles,** on Main Street (© 907/733-1279), is a full-service bike shop, renting mountain bikes for $16 for an 8-hour day.

SPECIAL EVENTS   The **Talkeetna Moose Dropping Festival,** held over the second weekend in July, is the big event of the year, a community fair finishing its third decade as a fundraiser for the Talkeetna Historical Society (© 907/733-2487; www.moosedrop.com—note that the site is dead in the off-season). The main event doesn't involve dropping moose, as an aggrieved animal lover once complained, but dropping moose droppings. There's also a parade and many other events.

ATTRACTIONS & ACTIVITIES IN TOWN

Talkeetna is famous for its laid-back atmosphere and outdoors, not for "attractions," but there are several places to stop in to get the sense of the place. One is the ranger station mentioned earlier in section 5, "Climbing Mount McKinley." If you come in May or June, you're sure to meet many international mountain climbers; you'll have no difficulty picking them out.

The **Fairview Inn** is a historic bar with the rough edges still in place. Along Main Street are shops where artists and craftspeople often can be found at work.

The **Talkeetna Historical Society Museum,** in three buildings on the Village Airstrip a half block south of Main Street (© 907/733-2487), is well worth a stop. The first building contains artifacts and displays on local mining history, including engaging photographs and biographies of individual characters. The second is an attempt to re-create the old railroad depot. The third holds climbing displays and a huge scale model of Mount McKinley and the nearby mountains (don't miss it if you will fly over the mountain). The museum also is a handy information stop. It is open daily in summer, 10:30am to 5:30pm, winter weekends only. Admission is $2.50, free for children 12 and under.

I've found the most affecting site in town to be the **mountain climbers' memorial** at the town cemetery, near the airstrip on the east side of the railroad tracks. Besides a granite memorial of plaques for lost mountaineers, there is a small garden of monuments to many individual climbers, some in Japanese. The bodies of 34 climbers who died on the mountain have never been recovered.

GETTING OUTSIDE
FLIGHTSEEING

The only way you'll get into the park from Talkeetna is by flying with one of the glacier pilots who support McKinley climbs, which typically begin with a flight from here to the 7,200-foot level of the Kahiltna Glacier. There is no more dramatic or memorable experience available to the typical tourist in Alaska. These immense mountains grow ever larger as you fly toward them until, like a tiny insect, you fly among their miles-tall folds, watching the climbers toiling on the ice below you. I was simply speechless.

Several operators with long experience offer the flights. The least expensive excursions cost around $100 (if the plane is full) and approach McKinley's south face. Rates often depend on how many are going, so if you can put together a group of four or five, or the operator can add you to a group, you can save as much as half. If at all possible—and if the weather is good—buy an extended tour that circles the mountain and flies over its glaciers, for $120 to $200 with a full plane. Best of all, in May and June you can arrange a landing on the mountain itself, just as the climbers do (the snow is too soft starting in July). The Don Sheldon Amphitheater on the Ruth Glacier is a stunning spot high on McKinley; only after you stand there do you realize the incredible scale of what you have seen from above. These landings are usually treated as add-ons to the tours mentioned above, for an additional price of around $40 per person.

Try any of these three renowned glacier pilot operations, all operating out of the Talkeetna airport: **Talkeetna Air Taxi** (© 800/533-2219 or 907/733-2218; www.talkeetnaair.com); **K2 Aviation** (© 800/764-2291 or 907/733-2291; www.flyk2.com); and **Doug Geeting Aviation** (© 800/770-2366 or 907/733-2366; www.alaskaairtours.com).

FISHING & JET BOAT TOURS

Talkeetna is at the confluence of the wild Talkeetna and Susitna rivers. **Mahay's Riverboat Service** (© 800/736-2210 or 907/733-2223; www.mahaysriverboat.com) is a large guide service, with 2-hour tours on a unique 51-foot jet boat for $45 per person, operating several times a day from a dock near the public boat launch on the Talkeetna River. Owner Steve Mahay is legendary, the only person ever to shoot Devil's Canyon in a jet boat. He offers fishing charters as well.

RAFTING

Talkeetna River Guides, on Main Street (© 800/353-2677 or 907/733-2677; www.talkeetnariverguides.com), offers a 2-hour wildlife river-rafting tour, without white water, over 9 miles of the Talkeetna three times a day for $55 adults, $22 children under 12. They also offer longer trips and guided fishing.

ACCOMMODATIONS & DINING
ON THE ROAD SYSTEM

There are good restaurants at each of the lodgings listed here. One other place stands out, **Café Michele,** in a quaint little house at the corner of Talkeetna Spur Road and Second Street (© 907/733-5300). It's a classy little bistro, serving sandwiches on homemade focaccia bread for lunch, and dinner entrees under $20. It's easy to find a burger or sandwich on the Main Street.

Mt. McKinley Princess Lodge ★★ The Princess Cruise Line built the main lodge building to take advantage of a striking view of the mountain, only 42 miles away as the crow flies. The property isn't really near anything—100 miles south of the park entrance and about 45 road miles from Talkeetna—but, like a resort, they offer everything you need on-site and a full set of activities, including a short network of trails. The design and decoration are an inspired modernization of the classic national park style.

Mile 133.1, Parks Hwy., Denali State Park, AK 99755 © 800/426-0500 or 907/733-2900. Fax 907/733-2922. www.princessalaskalodges.com. 238 units. Summer $189 double; $289 suite. Spring and fall $99 double; $199 suite. AE, DISC, DC, MC, V. Closed mid-Sept to mid-May. **Amenities:** 2 restaurants (steak and seafood, café); bar; exercise room; tour desk; coin-op laundry. *In room:* TV, hair dryer.

Swiss-Alaska Inn *Finds* This place is more the essence of Talkeetna than the flashy newer places. It's a friendly family business with a small restaurant serving good, familiar American meals, plus a few German dishes. There are large, attractive rooms with oak furniture and Jacuzzis in the newer of the two buildings. The rooms in the old building are nice too, but quite small.

F St., near the boat launch (P.O. Box 565), Talkeetna, AK 99676. © 907/733-2424. Fax 907/733-2425. www.swissalaska.com. 20 units. $100 double. Extra person $10. AE, DISC, MC, V. **Amenities:** Restaurant; bar; courtesy car (to railroad station).

Talkeetna Alaskan Lodge ★★ Built of big timbers and river rock, this sumptuous hotel was opened in 1999 by Cook Inlet Region, a Native corporation. It stands just 2 miles from the town but feels like it's out in the wilderness. The view from on top of a high river bluff is a broad-canvas masterpiece of the Alaska Range, with McKinley towering in the center. Unlike other large hotels in the area, this place is open year-round and employs mainly local people; its philosophy shows in the Alaska art and style of the place—it's not faked. Rooms and hallways are thoughtfully crafted with regional birch trim and understated stylish touches. Those in the main building are somewhat larger and have either king- or two queen-size beds.

Mile 12.5, Talkeetna Spur Rd. (P.O. Box 93330, Anchorage, AK 99509-3330). ✆ **888/959-9590** or 907/265-4501. Fax 907/263-5559. www.talkeetnalodge.com. 200 units. Summer $179 double. Winter $99 double. Extra person $12. AE, DISC, MC, V. **Amenities:** 2 restaurants (International, café); bar; Jacuzzi; tour desk; courtesy van; fish freezing. *In room:* TV, dataport, coffeemaker, hair dryer.

A WILDERNESS LODGE

Caribou Lodge This lodge sits on an alpine lake amid the tundra of the Talkeetna Mountains with Mount McKinley looming out back. The location, far from any road, offers an opportunity to live for a few days in terrain much like Denali's, with only a few other people in many a mile, while you're hosted by a family who've made a life in this remote wilderness. They'll guide you hiking, canoeing on the lake, and watching the wildlife of the area. In the winter, come for cross-country skiing, snowshoeing, and dog mushing when the endlessly rolling hills are buried in snow—all included in the price (snowmobiling is extra). The accommodations are simple, with shared bathrooms. Access is by air only—a floatplane is $125 from Talkeetna; a ski plane $150.

20 miles east of Talkeetna (P.O. Box 706) Talkeetna, AK 99676. ✆ and fax **907/733-2163**. www.caribou lodgealaska.com. 3 cabins. Summer $235 per person per day. Winter $210 per person per day. Rates include all meals and guiding and are based on double occupancy. No credit cards. **Amenities:** Restaurant (family style, included in rate); guided activities included in rate; sauna.

9

The Alaskan Interior

A warm summer evening in a campground; a slight breeze rustling the leaves of ghostly paper birches, barely keeping the mosquitoes at bay; the sounds of children playing; a perpetual sunset rolling slowly along the northern horizon—this is Interior Alaska. You know it's time to gather up the kids, separate them according to who belongs to whom, and put them to bed; it's 11 o'clock, for heaven's sake. But it's too difficult to feel that matters, or to alter the pace of a sun-baked day that never ends, meandering on like the broad, silty rivers and empty two-lane highways. Down by the boat landing, some college kids are getting ready to start on a float in the morning. An old, white-bearded prospector wanders out of the bar and, offering his flask to the strangers, tries out a joke while swatting the bugs. "There's not a single mosquito in Alaska," he declares. Waits for the loud, jocular objections. Then adds, "They're all married with big, big families." Easy laughter; then they talk about outboard motors, road work, why so many rabbits live along a certain stretch of highway. Eventually, you have to go to bed and leave the world to its pointless turning as the sun rotates back around to the east. You know it'll all be there tomorrow, just the same—the same slow-flowing rivers, the same long highways, the same vast space that can never be filled.

Interior Alaska is so large—it basically includes everything that's not on the coasts or in the Arctic—you can spend a week of hard driving and not explore it all. Or you can spend all summer floating the rivers and still have years of floating left to do before you see all the riverbanks. It's something like what the great mass of America's Midwest once must have been, perhaps a century and a half ago, when the great flatlands had been explored but not completely civilized and Huckleberry Finn could float downriver into a wilderness of adventures. As it happens, I have a friend who grew up on a homestead in the Interior and ran away from home at age 15 in that exact same fashion, floating hundreds of miles on a handmade raft, past the little river villages, cargo barges, and fishermen. During an Interior summer, nature combines its immensity with a rare sense of gentleness, patiently awaiting the next thunderstorm.

Winter is another matter. Without the regulating influence of the ocean—the same reason summers are hot—winter temperatures can often drop to –30°F or –40°F, and during exceptional cold snaps, much lower. Now the earth is wobbling over in the other direction, away from the sun. The long, black nights sometimes make Fairbanks, the region's dominant city, feel more like an outpost on a barren planet, far off in outer space. That's when the northern lights come, spewing swirls of color across the entire dome of the sky and crackling with electricity. Neighbors get on the phone to wake each other and, rising from bed to put on their warmest parkas and insulated boots, stand in the street, gazing straight up. Visitors lucky enough to come at such times may be watching from a steaming hot-spring tub. During the short days, they can bundle up and watch sled-dog racing or race across the wilderness themselves on snowmobiles.

Fairbanks stands second in Alaska in population, with over 80,000 in the greater area, but the Interior otherwise is without any settlements large enough to be called cities. Instead, it's defined by roads, both paved and gravel, which are strands of civilization through sparsely settled, often swampy land. Before the roads, development occurred only on the rivers, which still serve as thoroughfares for the **Athabascan villages** of the region. In the summer, villagers travel by boat. In the winter, the frozen rivers become highways for snowmobiles and sled-dog teams. White homesteaders and gold miners live back in the woods, too. Gold rush history is written on the land in piles of old gravel tailings and abandoned equipment, as well as in the prettier tourist attractions and historic sites. Gold mining goes on today, in small one-man operations and huge industrial works employing hundreds.

1 Exploring the Interior

Having your own car in the Interior, more than anywhere else in Alaska, provides you with the freedom to find the out-of-the-way places that give the region its character. Bus service connects Fairbanks with the ferry terminus at Haines or Skagway, and trains and buses run between Fairbanks and Anchorage. But that approach will show you only the larger, tourist-oriented destinations.

If you have the time and money, you may enjoy driving one of the remote gravel highways, or just poking along on the paved highways between the larger towns, ready to stop and investigate the roadhouses and meet the people who live out in the middle of nowhere. You'll find them mostly friendly and, often, downright odd—*colorful,* to use the polite term. As I drove an abandoned highway recently, I saw a hand-lettered sign advertising coffee. It wasn't your typical espresso stand, just a log cabin dozens of miles from the next nearest building. A squinting high plains drifter stepped out, wearing a cowboy hat on his head and a huge revolver on his hip, and asked, "Yeah?" The coffee came from a percolator warming on the woodstove, and the proprietor and I struck up a good conversation in his dark little dwelling. He was living the life of the old-time frontier. Another favorite roadside sign, sighted on the Alaska Highway, in spray paint on plywood: SALE—EEL SKINS—ANVILS—BAIT. I've always wished I'd stopped in to window-shop and meet the person who came up with that business plan.

Of course, not every mile of back road is scenic, nor are all the stops interesting. Driving a car through Alaska takes a long time, including many hours spent in dull, brushy forest, and calls for a high tolerance for greasy hamburgers. Paved highway sections can develop frost heaves in this often-frozen land—backbreaking dips and humps caused by the freeze and thaw of the road base and ground underneath. The gravel roads generate clouds of dust and quickly fatigue drivers, and windshield and headlights often succumb to their flying rocks.

LIKELY ITINERARIES

You can shorten your driving time by flying or taking the train to Fairbanks, then renting a car for an exploration. Renting a car one way is a good way to go, too, if you can stand the drop-off fee.

One itinerary is to rent a car in Fairbanks, explore eastward to Dawson City along the Alaska Highway and unpaved Taylor and Top-of-the-World highways,

Rollin' on the River

Floating any of the thousands of miles of the Interior's rivers opens great swaths of wilderness. Beginners will want to take a guided trip before venturing on their own. (See the lists of operators in chapter 2.) To plan your own trip, get Karen Jettmar's *The Alaska River Guide* (Alaska Northwest Books, $17), which includes details for floats on more than 100 river trips across the state. Also, check with the **Alaska Public Lands Information Center** in Fairbanks, Tok, or Anchorage for guidance on setting up your trip. Among the most accessible and historic rivers in the region are the Chena, Chatanika, Yukon, and Fortymile (see the sections on Chena Hot Springs Road, the Steese Highway, Dawson City, and Eagle in this chapter, respectively).

---

then drive south through the Yukon Territory to drop the car in Skagway. There you can board the ferry south to fly out from Juneau, Sitka, or Ketchikan. I'd allow a good 10 days for such a plan, and expect a drop-off fee of around $300. If you prefer to return the car to the starting point in Fairbanks, take it on the ferry from Skagway to Haines, then follow the Alaska Highway back.

Another idea, staying on pavement, is to make a loop through Anchorage. From Fairbanks, take the Richardson Highway to Kennecott, in Wrangell–St. Elias National Park (take the van in to avoid driving the dirt road), then continue to Valdez, take a ferry to Whittier, and drive back north on the Seward Highway to Anchorage, continuing on the Parks Highway to Denali National Park and back to Fairbanks. That will take 10 days to 2 weeks, depending on how long you stay in each place. For a shorter loop, cross through the Alaska Range on the unpaved Denali Highway, which links the Richardson and Parks highways at their midpoint, or leave the Richardson Highway at Glennallen and take the Glenn Highway to Anchorage.

Or simply base yourself in Fairbanks and take a few days to experience the Steese or Dalton highways or Chena Hot Springs Road, perhaps with hot springs soaking, hiking, or canoeing on the way.

An especially fun way to go is with an **RV.** They're everywhere on these highways, so services are well developed even in many remote areas. An RV offers much of the freedom of camping, but sidesteps a lot of the problems of tent camping in a cool climate so far from home. Perhaps most important, it allows spontaneity. You don't have to stick so closely to an itinerary tied to hard-to-get hotel reservations. But RVs are expensive: Just the rental can cost as much as staying in hotels, renting a car, and eating out for your meals. High-season rates are around $200 a day, plus the large amount of fuel you use and sometimes mileage charges of over 30¢ a mile beyond certain minimums. Campgrounds with full utility hookups cost $20 to $30 a night, or you can go self-contained at public campgrounds that cost half as much, dumping your tanks later. Also, an RV can easily get damaged on remote gravel roads.

The Milepost (Morris Communications, $25), a highway guide to Alaska and northwestern Canada, has long been considered the indispensable handbook for Alaska drivers, and it's fun to follow the mile-by-mile road logs. If you want campground information, *Traveler's Guide to Alaskan Camping,* by Mike and Teri Church (Rolling Home Press, $20), has far greater depth and objectivity.

Alaska's Highways a la Carte

You won't need a detailed highway map of Alaska, because Alaska doesn't have detailed highways. A single triangle of paved two-lane highways connects Tok, Fairbanks, and Anchorage. From this triangle, a few routes reach to discrete destinations, and gravel roads penetrate the periphery of the Bush. Beyond a few miles of freeway around Fairbanks and Anchorage, highways are narrow strips of asphalt or gravel through the wilderness.

MAIN HIGHWAYS

Alaska Highway (Route 2 from the border to Delta Junction)   Running nearly 1,400 miles from Dawson Creek, British Columbia, to Delta Junction, Alaska, a couple of hours east of Fairbanks on the Richardson Highway, this World War II road is paved, but that doesn't mean it's always smooth. Like other northern highways, it's subject to bone-jarring frost heaves and spring potholes. Two tiny towns lie on the Alaska portion of the road, Delta Junction and Tok. The prettiest part is on the Canadian side, in the Kluane Lake area. Driving the highway all the way to Alaska is a real adventure, covered later in this chapter.

Denali Highway (Route 8)   I simply couldn't believe my eyes when I first drove this 133-mile gravel road connecting the midpoints of the Parks and Richardson highways. The stunning alpine vistas high in the Alaska Range rival those within Denali National Park but are open to all drivers, with a rich network of trails and mountain lakes and a good chance to see caribou, bear, moose, and waterfowl. It's popular with mountain bikers, canoeists, anglers, and hunters. See chapter 8.

Glenn Highway (Route 1 from Anchorage to Tok)   This is the road you'd take if you were coming from the Alaska Highway on your way to Southcentral Alaska, including Prince William Sound, Anchorage, and the Kenai Peninsula. It connects Tok to Anchorage, 330 miles southwest. (The section between Glennallen and Tok is sometimes called the "Tok Cut-Off.") The northern section, from Tok to Glennallen, borders Wrangell–St. Elias National Park, with broad tundra and taiga broken by high, craggy peaks. That area is covered later, in this chapter. Glennallen to Anchorage is even more spectacular, as the road passes through high alpine terrain and then close by the Matanuska Glacier, where it winds through a deep canyon valley carved by the glacier's river. A pair of lodges on that part of the road are covered in chapter 6.

Parks Highway (Route 3)   The George Parks Highway is a straight line from Anchorage to Fairbanks, 358 miles north, providing access to Denali National Park. There are some vistas of Mount McKinley from south of the park, but the Parks Highway is mostly just a transportation route, less scenic than the Richardson or Glenn highways. From the northern (Fairbanks) end, the highway passes Nenana, then Denali and Talkeetna (chapter 8), and finally the towns of the Matanuska and Susitna Valleys (chapter 6).

Richardson Highway (Route 4 from Valdez to Delta Junction, Route 2 from Delta Junction to Fairbanks)   The state's first highway, leading 364 miles from tidewater in Valdez to Fairbanks, lost much of its traffic to the Parks Highway, which saves more than 90 miles between Anchorage and Fairbanks, and to the Glenn Highway, which saves about 120 miles from Glennallen to Tok. But it's still the most beautiful paved drive in the Interior. From the south, the road begins with a magnificent climb through Keystone Canyon and steep Thompson Pass, just out of Valdez (see chapter 7), then passes the huge, distant peaks of southern Wrangell–St. Elias National Park. North of Glennallen, the road climbs into the Alaska Range as it snakes along the shores of long alpine lakes. The road descends again to the forested area around Delta Junction and meets the Alaska Highway before arriving in Fairbanks.

Seward Highway (Route 1 from Anchorage to Tern Lake, Route 9 from Tern Lake to Seward)   The highway leaves Anchorage on the 127-mile drive to Seward following the rocky edge of mountain peaks above a surging ocean fjord. Abundant wildlife and unfolding views often slow cars. Later, the road climbs through high mountain passes above the tree line, tracing sparkling alpine lakes. Alaska's best trail hikes are here. The section from Anchorage 50 miles south to Portage Glacier is covered in chapter 6; the remainder, to Seward, in chapter 7.

Sterling Highway (Route 1 from Tern Lake to Homer)   Leading 142 miles from the Seward Highway to the tip of the Kenai Peninsula, the highway has some scenic spots but is mostly a way to get to the Kenai River, the Kenai National Wildlife Refuge, Kachemak Bay, and the towns of Cooper Landing, Soldotna, Kenai, and Homer.

RURAL ROADS
Each of these mostly gravel roads is covered in detail later in this chapter.

Chena Hot Springs Road   A more civilized road into the outdoors, this paved 57-mile highway east of Fairbanks meets hiking and river routes on the way to Chena Hot Springs.

Dalton Highway (Route 11)   Built to haul equipment to the Prudhoe Bay oil fields, about 500 miles north of Fairbanks, the Dalton punctures the heart of the wilderness, crossing the Brooks Range and the North Slope.

Edgerton Highway & McCarthy Road (Route 10)   Running east from the Richardson Highway south of Glennallen, the Edgerton leads to the tiny town of Chitina, where the McCarthy Road, a muddy one-lane track, penetrates Wrangell–St. Elias National Park to the historic sites at McCarthy and Kennecott. The journey of 93 miles takes half a day.

Steese Highway (Route 6)   This gravel road climbs the rounded tundra mountains 162 miles east of Fairbanks to the Native village of Circle, on the Yukon River. It's a route to the real Alaska.

Taylor Highway (Route 5)   At times rough, narrow, and a little scary, this dirt road leads 161 miles from a junction on the Alaska Highway east of Tok to the fascinating Yukon River village of Eagle, an island in time.

Top of the World Highway (Yukon Route 9)   Connecting to the Taylor Highway and crossing the Canadian border to Dawson City, a distance of 79 miles, the road rides mountaintop to mountaintop, above the tree line nearly the entire way.

2 Fairbanks: Alaska Heartland

If the story of the founding of Fairbanks had happened anywhere else, it wouldn't be told so proudly, for the city's father was a swindler, and its undignified birth contained an element of chance not usually admitted in polite society. As the popular story goes (and the historians' version is fairly close), it seems that in 1901, E. T. Barnette decided to get rich by starting a gold-mining boomtown like the others that had sprouted from Dawson City to Nome as the stampeders of 1898 sloshed back and forth across the territory from one gold find to the next. He booked passage on a riverboat going up the Tanana with his supplies to build the town, having made an understanding with the captain that, should the vessel get stuck, he would lighten the load by getting off with the materials on the nearest bank. Unfortunately, the captain got lost. Thinking he was heading up a slough on the Tanana, he got sidetracked into the relatively small Chena River. That was where the boat got stuck and where Barnette got left, and that was where he founded Fairbanks.

Fortunately for Barnette, an Italian prospector named Felix Pedro had been looking for gold in the hills around the new trading post, and made a strike on the Tanana. On that news, Barnette dispatched his Chinese cook off to Dawson City to spread the word. The cook's story showed up in a newspaper that winter, and a stampede of hundreds of miners ensued, heading toward Fairbanks in weather as cold as –50°F. Barnette's town was a success, but the cook nearly got lynched when the stampeders found out how far he'd exaggerated the truth. Much more gold was found later, however, and half the population of Dawson City came down river to Fairbanks. Barnette had made it big.

The town's future was assured thanks to a political deal. Barnette did a favor for the territory's judge, James Wickersham, by naming the settlement for Wickersham's ally in Congress, Sen. Charles Fairbanks of Indiana, who later became vice president. Wickersham then moved the federal courthouse to Fairbanks from Eagle—he loaded his records on his dogsled and mushed here, establishing the camp as the hub of the region. Wickersham's story is interesting, too. He was a notable explorer, Alaska's first real statesman as a nonvoting delegate to Congress, and father of the Alaska Railroad. Houses he lived in are preserved at Alaskaland in Fairbanks and in Juneau just up the hill from the capitol building. Barnette didn't do as well in history's eyes: He was run out of the town he founded for bank fraud.

Fairbanks is Alaska's second-largest city now, with a population of about 30,000 in the city limits and 82,000 in the greater metropolitan area, but it has never learned to put on airs. It sprawls, broad and flat, along big highways and the Chena. It's a friendly, easygoing town, but one where people still take gold and their independence seriously. They're still prospecting and mining for gold around here, fighting off environmental regulation, and maintaining a traditional Alaskan attitude that it's us against the world. Fairbanks is the birthplace of strange political movements, including the secessionist Alaskan Independence Party. It's an adamant, loopy, affable place; it doesn't seem to mind being a little bizarre or residing far from the center of things. And that makes it an intensely Alaska city, for those are the qualities Alaskans most cherish in their myth of themselves.

Fairbanks can strike a visitor a couple of ways, depending on what you expect and what you like. Fairbanks can come across as a provincial outpost, a touristy cross between Kansas and Siberia. Driving one of the franchise-choked

Greater Fairbanks

Alaska

Fairbanks ○
Anchorage ○ Valdez Juneau ○
Kenai ○ ○ Cordova Sitka ○
Ketchikan ○

To Fox, Chena Hot
Springs Road, and
Prudhoe Bay

Wedgewood Rd.
Margaret Ave.
Blanch Ave.

College Rd.
Old Steese Hwy.

Hall St.
Dunkel St.
Noble St.
Lacy St.
Griffin Park
Slater Dr.
Minnie St.
Illinois St.
1st Ave.

See Downtown
Fairbanks Map

Richardson Hwy.

To North
Pole and
Delta Jct.

Cushman St.

Jesse St.

Alaska Railroad
Depot
Barnette St.
2nd Ave.
8th Ave.
Wein Park

17th Ave.
Turner St.

23rd Ave.
27th Ave.
Mitchell Expwy.

Fairbanks
Memorial
Hospital
19th Ave.

16th Ave.
Lathrop St.
Cowles St. East
Davis Rd.

Hez Rey
Recreation
Complex

ⓘ Information
✉ Post Office

Wedgewood Rd.

Johansen Expwy.
Alaska Railroad
Chena River

Noyes Slough

Cowles St.

Phillips-Field Rd.
Growden
Memorial
Park
1st Ave.

Wilbur

Peger Rd.

Airport Way

College Rd.

Farmer's Loop Rd.

UNIVERSITY
OF ALASKA
FAIRBANKS

University Ave.

Geist Rd.
Pierce
Park
Birch Lane

Fairbanks St.

Sportsman
Way

Chena River
State
Recreation
Site

Chena Ridge Rd.

George Parks Hwy.

Airport Way
Old Airport Way

Fairbanks
International
Airport

BROADMOOR
ACRES
Discovery Dr.
Dale Rd.

Chena Pump Rd

Chena River

To Esther, Denali Park
and Anchorage

1/2 Mi
N
0   1/2 Km
0   .5 Km

ACCOMMODATIONS & DINING ■

The Bakery **19**
Fairbanks Exploration Inn **17**
Fairbanks Princess Riverside Lodge **12**
Forget-Me-Not Lodge
& The Aurora Express B&B **5**
Golden North Motel **11**
Minnie Street B & B **18**
Pike's Landing and Pike's Waterfront Lodge **13**
The Pump House Restaurant **6**
River's Edge Resort Cottages **9**
River's Edge RV Park and Campground **10**

Sam's Sourdough Cafe **4**
Wedgewood Resort **16**

ATTRACTIONS ●

Alaskaland **14**
Creamer's Field **15**
Georgeson Botanical Garden **3**
Large Animal Research Station **1**
Riverboat *Discovery* **7**
7 Bridges Boats & Bikes **8**
University of Alaska Museum **2**

commercial strips, you can wonder why you went out of your way to come here, and the deserted downtown area can be downright depressing. Or you can relax and take Fairbanks on its own terms, as a fun, unpretentious town that never lost its sense of being on the frontier.

My children love it here. There's plenty for families to do in Fairbanks, much of it at least a little corny and requiring drives to widespread sites at the university, on the Chena River, in the gold mining area north of town, and at a big town park called Alaskaland. (You *must* have wheels in Fairbanks.) There are good opportunities for hiking and mountain biking, and great opportunities for canoeing and slow river float trips.

ESSENTIALS

GETTING THERE **By Car or RV** Fairbanks is a transportation hub. The Richardson Highway heads east 98 miles to Delta Junction, the end point of the Alaska Highway, then south to Glennallen and Valdez. The Parks Highway heads due south from Fairbanks to Denali National Park, 120 miles away, and Anchorage, 358 miles south.

By Bus Gray Line's **Alaskon Express** (© 800/478-6388 or 907/451-6835; www.graylinealaska.com/alaskon.cfm) offers service from Skagway, up the Alaska Highway to the Westmark Fairbanks (the fare is $216), with stops along the way. The **Parks Highway Express** (© 888/600-6001; www.AlaskaShuttle. com) offers daily service in summer to and from Denali National Park and Anchorage (one-way fares are $34 and $69 respectively), and less frequent service to and from Valdez and even Dawson City and other remote spots.

By Train The **Alaska Railroad** (© 800/544-0552; www.alaskarailroad.com) links Fairbanks with Denali National Park and Anchorage, with tour commentary provided along the way. The high-season one-way fare is $50 to Denali and $175 to Anchorage (about twice the cost of flying).

By Air **Fairbanks International Airport** has direct jet service from Anchorage on several airlines, with **Alaska Airlines** (© 800/252-7522; www.alaska air.com) having the most flights. Round-trip fares are generally under $200. The airport is a hub for various small carriers to Alaska's Interior and Arctic communities. A cab downtown from the airport is $16 to $18 with **Yellow Cab** (© 907/455-5555).

VISITOR INFORMATION The **Fairbanks Log Cabin Visitor Information Center** is in a large log building at 550 First Ave., on the Chena River at the center of town, at Cushman Street, Fairbanks, AK 99701 (© 800/327-5774 or 907/456-5774; fax 907/452-2867; www.explorefairbanks.com). The staff provides a road map and detailed walking and driving tour maps, and will help you find a room with their daily vacancy listing. The center is open summer daily 8am to 8pm, winter Monday to Friday 10am to 5pm. When you stop by, take a look at nearby Golden Heart Plaza for a shot of civic pride.

The **Alaska Public Lands Information Center,** 250 Cushman St. (at Third Ave.), Suite 1A, Fairbanks, AK 99701 (© 907/456-0527; TTY 907/456-0532; fax 907/456-0514; www.nps.gov/aplic), is an indispensable stop for anyone planning to spend time in the outdoors, and an interesting one even if you're not. The staff is remarkably knowledgeable and can tell you about trips and activities based on first-hand experience. Besides providing maps and other details, the center houses a small museum about the state's regions and the gear needed to explore them. Daily free films and naturalist programs show in a small auditorium. Open daily 9am to 6pm in summer, winter Tuesday through Saturday 10am to 6pm.

GETTING AROUND   Fairbanks is designed around the car, and that's the practical way to get around. Without one, sticking downtown, you will leave with a low opinion of the place. The city is too spread out to use taxis much.

If you flew in and need to rent a car, you'll find many agencies. **Avis** (© **800/ 331-1212** or 907/474-0900; www.avis.com) is located at the airport. **National Car Rental,** downtown at 1246 Noble St. (© **800/227-7368** or 907/451-7368), rents SUVs and will allow some vehicles to go on gravel roads such as the Dalton and Steese highways, an important consideration in this region. Several local firms rent RVs in Fairbanks, including **Diamond Willow RV Rentals,** 350 Old Steese Hwy. N. (© **888/724-7373** or 907/457-2814).

The Fairbanks North Star Borough's **MACS bus system** links the university, downtown, the nearby North Pole community, shopping areas, and some hotels. Service is every 30 minutes, at best, worse Saturday and nonexistent Sunday. Pick up timetables at the visitor center. All buses connect at the transit park downtown, at Fifth Avenue and Cushman Street. The fare is $1.50.

Fairbanks' car-oriented layout does not lend itself to using bikes as the primary means of transportation. But bikes are for rent from **Beaver Sports,** 3480 College Rd. (© **907/479-2494;** www.beaversports.net). Downtown you can rent bikes by the hour at the **Fairbanks Hotel,** 517 Third Ave. (© **888/329-4685** or 907/456-6411).

 FAST FACTS: **Fairbanks**

Banks Fairbanks has numerous banks with **ATMs** in the downtown area and along the commercial strips. **Key Bank** is at 100 Cushman.

Business Services **Kinko's Copy Center** is at 418 Third St. (© **907/ 456-7348**).

Hospital **Fairbanks Memorial** is at 1650 Cowles St. (© **907/452-8181**).

Internet Access **Café Latte** is at 519 Sixth Ave. (© **907/455-4898**).

Police For nonemergency police business, call the **Alaska State Troopers** (© **907/451-5100**) or, within city limits, the **Fairbanks Police Department** (© **907/459-6500**).

Post Office At 315 Barnette St.

Taxes Fairbanks has no sales tax. North Pole charges 3%. **Bed tax is 8%.**

SPECIAL EVENTS   A recording of current local happenings can be reached at © **907/456-INFO,** maintained by the Fairbanks Convention and Visitors Bureau, which also posts an event calendar at **www.explorefairbanks.com**.

The **Yukon Quest International Sled Dog Race** (© **907/452-7954;** www.yukonquest.org) starts February 9, 2002, in Fairbanks (Fairbanks has the start in even-numbered years; Whitehorse, Yukon Territory, hosts the start in odd-numbered years). Mushers say this rugged 1,000-mile race is even tougher than the Iditarod.

The **Nenana Ice Classic** (© **907/832-5446;** www.ptialaska.net/~tripod) is a sweepstakes held annually since 1917 based on who can guess closest to the exact minute when the ice will go out on the Tanana River. The classic starts with Tripod Days, the first weekend in March, when they set up the so-call four-legged tripod; when it moves 100 feet it trips a clock, determining the winner.

The Tripod Days celebration includes dance performances, dog mushing, and other activities. The **World Ice Art Championships** (© 907/451-8250; www.icealaska.com), March 6 through 17, 2002, brings carvers from all over the world to sculpt immense, clear chunks cut from a Fairbanks pond. Among ice carvers, Fairbanks' ice is famous for its clarity and the great size of the chunks. Some spectacular ice sculptures stand as tall as a two-story building. Check the website for pictures of past winners. The **North American Sled Dog Championships** (© 907/488-1357) is the oldest running, taking place over a weekend in mid-March. Sprint mushers from all over the world compete with teams of as many as 24 dogs, streaking away from the starting line on Second Avenue.

Lots of events happen around the **summer solstice,** usually June 21. A street fair happens downtown (© 907/452-8671), there's a big 10K race open to walkers and people in funny costumes (© 907/452-7211), and the **Midnight Sun Baseball Game**, hosted by the semipro Fairbanks Goldpanners (© 907/451-0095), begins at 10:30pm, and there are no artificial lights. Also in June, the **Fairbanks Summer Music Festival** (© 907/488-0556; www.alaskafolkmusic.org/faifolkfest) fills an Alaskaland lawn with music, food, and art booths for a full day and evening.

Golden Days, over 2 weeks in late July, includes crafts fairs and a parade (© 907/452-1105). **The Fairbanks Summer Arts Festival,** held on the University of Alaska Fairbanks campus over 2 weeks in late July and early August (© 907/474-8869; www.fsaf.org), brings artists of international reputation for workshops and performances in music, dance, theater, opera, and the visual arts.

The **Tanana Valley State Fair** (© 907/452-3750; www.tananavalleyfair.org), in early August, shows off the area's agricultural production, arts and crafts, and entertainment, and includes rides, a carnival, and a rodeo. Mid-August to mid-September, Friends of Creamers Field (© 907/452-5162) hosts an annual **Sandhill Crane Festival,** with nature walks, lectures, and other activities, mostly at Creamers Field (see "Special Places," later).

The **Athabascan Fiddling Festival** (© 907/452-1825), held in early November, draws together musicians and dancers from the Interior region for performances and workshops. The **Top of the World Classic,** in mid-November, brings NCAA Division I basketball teams to the University of Alaska—Fairbanks for a weekend tournament (© 907/474-6830).

ATTRACTIONS & ACTIVITIES
STROLLING AROUND DOWNTOWN

If you want to explore downtown for an hour or two, pick up the walking tour map available at the visitor center. Among the highlights is the **Golden Heart Park,** a waterfront plaza with a fountain and a bronze of a Native family, where community events often occur.

The town's most interesting building is the Roman Catholic **Church of the Immaculate Conception** ✛, across the river on Cushman Street. The white clapboard structure, built in 1904, has ornate gold rush decoration inside, rare for its authenticity, including a pressed-tin ceiling and stained-glass windows—an appealing if incongruous mix of gold rush and sacred decor.

At First Avenue near Kellum Street, east from the visitor center, **St. Matthew's Episcopal Church** is a cute old log church with a working rope-pull bell. It was founded by missionary and dog-sled explorer Hudson Stuck in 1904, an early advocate for Alaska's Natives. The original church burned; the present structure dates from 1948.

Seeing the Aurora Borealis

One fall evening I left the house of friends in Fairbanks to the sight of a swirling green glow that filled the dark sky. I knocked on the door and brought them out to see, only to have my friends laugh in my face. They informed me, with mock contempt for my Anchorage home, that in Fairbanks they don't even bother to bend their necks back for northern lights as dim as these. It's true—a bright aurora borealis is routine in Fairbanks. Some of the world's top experts on the phenomenon work here, at the University of Alaska's Geophysical Institute (their aurora predictions, in season, and extensive background on the aurora are posted at **www.gi.alaska.edu**; click on "Research"). Hours-long displays can be incredibly spectacular and even moving.

Unfortunately, few visitors ever see these wild strands of bright colors whipping across the sky, because when most visitors come, the sky is never dark. Alaskans rarely see the stars from late May through early August, and to see the aurora well you need an especially dark night sky. To improve your chances, plan your trip in the fall or winter. An early September trip offers brilliant fall foliage, dark night skies, and the remnants of summer weather. In midwinter, the sky is dark all night and most of the day. Many hotels near Fairbanks cater to travelers coming to see the aurora in winter, as well as visitors who come for such winter sports as dog mushing and snowmobiling. See chapter 2 for tips on planning a winter trip.

At Second Avenue and Lacey Street, the **Fairbanks Ice Museum** ★ (© 907/451-8222) aims to show summer visitors what winter is like, with a freezer you can enter to feel the cold and view 60,000 pounds of ice sculptures. A striking high-tech slide show plays hourly, explaining the annual World Ice Art Championships (see "Special Events," above), and freezers contain impressive ice tableaux. Admission is $8 for adults, $4 ages 6 to 12. It's open 10am to 6pm daily June to mid-September.

At 410 Cushman St., the former city hall contains the volunteer-operated **Fairbanks Community Museum** (© 907/452-8671), which shares quarters with the Yukon Quest International Sled Dog Race (see "Events," above) and displays dog-mushing material, a miner's cabin, and old Fairbanks photographs. Hours are Tuesday to Saturday 10am to 6pm.

ALASKALAND ★★

Built for the Alaska purchase centennial in 1967, **Alaskaland** is the boiled-down essence of Fairbanks on grounds at the intersection of Airport Way and Peger Road (© 907/459-1087; co.fairbanks.ak.us/Parks&Rec/Alaskaland). It's called a theme park, but don't expect Disneyland or anything like it. Instead, Alaskaland is a city park with a theme. It's relaxing and low-key, entrancing for young children and interesting for adults if you can give in to the charm of the place. Admission to the park is free and the tours and activities are generally inexpensive. The park is open year-round, but the attractions operate only Memorial Day to Labor Day, daily from 11am to 9pm. Pick up a map and schedule when you arrive; here I've listed the highlights, but there is more to see. Depending on the pace you like to keep and the age level of your group, you can spend anything from a couple of hours to most of a day here.

The **SS *Nenana*** ★★ (© 907/456-8848) is the park's centerpiece. Commissioned by the federally owned Alaska Railroad in 1933, the large stern-wheeler plied the Yukon and Tanana rivers until 1952. In 1967 the *Nenana* came to Alaskaland but was unmaintained and had nearly collapsed from rot when it was saved by a community restoration effort, completed in 1992. There are five decks of sumptuous mahogany, brass, and white-painted promenades. The wheelhouse and engine room remain well preserved, too. A guided tour is $5 for adults, $3 children. You can see the ground-floor cargo deck anytime without paying, and it contains an engaging set of dioramas showing all the riverside towns and villages where the boat called, modeled as they looked in its heyday.

Much of Fairbanks's history has been moved to Alaskaland. A village of log cabins contains shops and restaurants, each marked with its original location and place in town history. **Judge Wickersham's house,** built around 1904, is kept as a museum, decorated appropriately to the period of the town's founding. The house is less than grand—it may remind you of your grandmother's—but it's worth a stop to strike up a conversation with the historical society volunteers who keep it open. **Pres. Warren Harding's railcar,** from which he stepped to drive the golden spike on the Alaska Railroad, sits near the park entrance. The **Pioneer Air Museum** (© 907/451-0037) is housed in a geodesic dome toward the back of the park. Besides the aircraft there are displays and artifacts of the crashes of Alaska's aviation pioneers. Admission is $2 adults, $1 children.

If you have children, you certainly won't escape Alaskaland without a ride on the **Crooked Creek and Whiskey Island Railroad** that circles the park twice, with a tour guide pointing out the sights; rides cost $2 for adults, $1 for children, free for senior citizens and children under age 4. Kids also will enjoy the large **playground,** with equipment for toddlers and older children, where lots of local families come to play, and the 36-hole miniature golf course. The only carnival ride is a nice old **merry-go-round,** which costs $1.

Tour groups generally come to Alaskaland in the evening mid-May to mid-September for the **Alaska Salmon Bake,** at the mining display (© 907/ 452-7274), and the **Golden Heart Revue,** at the Palace Theater (© 907/ 456-5960; www.akvisit.com). Costs for the halibut, ribs, steak, or brown-sugar salmon are under $25. Beer and wine are available. The revue, nightly at 8:15pm, mid-May to mid-September, covers the amusing story of the founding of Fairbanks with comedy and song in a nightclub setting; admission is $14 for adults.

UNIVERSITY OF ALASKA—FAIRBANKS

The state university's main campus contains several interesting attractions and makes a point of serving tourists. The campus is on the west side of town; look for University Avenue. A widely distributed brochure lists tours, hours, and fees. A free 2-hour **walking tour,** led by students, meets at the museum Monday through Friday at 10am, June to August except July 4. Call ahead (© 907/ 474-7581) to confirm the time and any weather cancellations. (See www.uaf. edu/univrel/Tour/index.html for information on all university tours and maps.)

University of Alaska Museum ★★★   This rich, interdisciplinary museum explains the nature and culture of each of the state's regions. It's Alaska's best natural history museum and its most scholarly, with information presented at advanced as well as elementary levels. Some of the objects have a real wow factor, such as Blue Babe, the petrified Steppe Bison, and a 5,400-pound copper nugget. Despite the museum's small size, a curious person can spend most of a day here. The only major weakness is that it tries to do too much in too small a space and seems cluttered. A display on emission spectrums is side by side with a stuffed lynx, a woven root basket, and a broad-view aurora camera. They're currently raising money for an expansion.

In the summer, catch the shows in the auditorium. UAF scientists lead the world in the study of the **northern lights,** and their aurora show depicts and explains the phenomenon daily at 10am and 3pm; admission is $4 adults, $3 youth (7–17), $2 children. A show on Alaska Native culture is at 11am and 2pm and costs $6.50 for adults, $4 youth, $2 children.

907 Yukon Dr. (P.O. Box 756960), Fairbanks, AK 99775-6960. ✆ 907/474-7505. www.uaf.alaska.edu/museum. June–Aug daily 9am–7pm; May and Sept daily 9am–5pm; Oct–Apr, Mon–Fri 9am–5pm, Sat–Sun noon–5pm. Admission $5 adults, $4.50 ages 60 and older, $3 ages 7–17, ages 6 and under free.

Georgeson Botanical Garden ✦   I really enjoy the mix of science and contemplation I find at this relaxed working garden. Plots are laid out to compare seeds and cultivation techniques, usually well posted with explanatory information on the experiment; but at the same time the flowers and vegetables are spectacular, and there are peaceful memorials and places to picnic. You don't need a tour to enjoy the garden. Nearby, the barn of the university's experimental farm is open for visitors to wander through and view the cows, pigs, and reindeer.

W. Tanana Dr. ✆ 907/474-1744. www.lter.uaf.edu/salrm/gbg. Admission $1. Open daylight hours; store open May 15 to Labor Day daily 10am–6pm; free guided tours Fri at 2pm.

Large Animal Research Station   The university studies captive musk ox and caribou here, on a property more commonly known as the musk ox farm. Hour-long tours are given five times a week in the summer, but just walking along the fence in the cool morning or evening hours with binoculars, you can see the animals behaving naturally in the large pastures.

Yankovich Rd. (drive north from campus, turn left on Ballaine Rd., left again on Yankovich). ✆ 907/474-7207. Tours June–Aug Tues, Thurs, and Sat 11am and 1:30pm; Sept Sat 1:30pm. Admission $5 adults, seniors $4, students $2, ages 6 and under free.

COMMERCIAL TOURIST ATTRACTIONS AROUND FAIRBANKS

Three major for-profit attractions around Fairbanks pack in visitors by the hundreds of thousands, most of them on group tours. These places are educational and fun, as I've described below, but I think they all charge excessive prices; whether they're worth your money depends on how much you've got and your level of interest.

The Riverboat *Discovery* ★★   The *Discovery* belongs to the pioneering Binkley family, which has been in the riverboat business since the Klondike gold rush and whose family has run this attraction for 50 years. The *Discovery* is a real stern-wheeler, a 156-foot steel vessel carrying 700 passengers on as many as three trips a day. There's nothing intimate or spontaneous about the 3½-hour ride, which mostly carries package-tour passengers off fleets of buses, but the Binkleys still provide a fun, educational experience that doesn't feel cheap or phony. After loading at a landing with shops off Dale Road, near the airport, the boat cruises down the Chena and up the Tanana past demonstrations on shore—among others, a bush plane taking off and landing, fish cutting at a Native fish camp, and a musher's dog yard (in recent years, it was five-time Iditarod champion Susan Butcher's yard, and she'd often show off the dogs herself). Finally, the vessel pulls up at the bank for a tour of a mock Athabascan village.

1975 Discovery Dr., Fairbanks, AK 99709. © 866/479-6673 or 907/479-6673. www.riverboatdiscovery.com. Sailings mid-May to mid-Sept daily at 8:45am and 2pm. Admission $39.95 adults, $29.95 ages 3–12.

The El Dorado Gold Mine ⭐ A train such as you would find at an amusement park carries visitors though an impressively staged educational tour, much like the Riverboat *Discovery* tour operated by the same family, but the gold miners who act as hosts are the real attraction here. Visitors gather around a sluice to hear the amusing and authentic Dexter and Lynette (a.k.a. Yukon Yonda) Clark and watch a swoosh of water and gold-bearing gravel rush by. You pan the resulting pay dirt, and everyone goes home with enough gold dust to fill a plastic locket—typically $5 to $35 worth. Drive out to the mine after making reservations, or take a free shuttle.

Off the Elliott Hwy., 9 miles north of town. © 907/479-7613. www.eldoradogoldmine.com. Tours daily; call for times. Admission $27.95 adults, $19.95 ages 3–12.

Gold Dredge Number 8 ⭐⭐ This is the area's best gold-mining historic site, because it's real. The centerpiece is a 1928 gold dredge, similar to machines in Dawson City and Nome, that stands five decks tall on a barge floating in a pond it created. When it operated, huge scoops would dig from one end, the mechanism inside would digest the gold from the gravel, and then it would dump the spoils out the back—in this way, the pond and the dredge it supports crept 21 miles across the frozen ground north of Fairbanks. Many sterile areas you see in this area were created by these earth-eaters, for nothing grows on their tailings for decades after. The tour company that bought the historic site added to the dredge with museums housed in relocated gold camp buildings, showing the drab life lived by the miners A 90-minute tour starts with a film, then a half-hour on the dredge, and finally a chance to pan for gold yourself, with success assured. A large cafeteria is mostly for package-tour bus passengers.

1755 Old Steese Hwy., Fairbanks, AK 99712. © 907/457-6058. Mid-May to mid-Sept daily 9am–6pm; tours hourly 9:30am–3:30pm. Admission $17 adults, $13 children ages 4–12; add $4 for gold panning; add another $8.50 for a cafeteria lunch. To get there, go north on the Steese Expressway from town, turn left on Goldstream Rd., and again on the Old Steese Hwy.

SHOPPING

Fairbanks has a few good shops downtown. **New Horizons Gallery,** at 519 First St. (© **907/456-2063**), occupies a large space with a combination of large oils by Alaska's best serious artists, inexpensive prints, and gifts. The **Arctic Travelers Gift Shop,** at 201 Cushman St. (© **907/456-7080**), specializes in Native crafts, carrying both valuable art and affordable but authentically Alaska gifts. The staff is friendly and knowledgeable.

Near the airport, at 4630 Old Airport Rd., the **Great Alaskan Bowl Company** (© **907/474-9663;** www.woodbowl.com) makes and sells bowls of native birch—salad bowls, of course, but also for many other purposes. They can carve up to eight nested bowls from one piece of wood. Through a glass wall looking into the shop, you can see workers cutting the bowls from raw logs.

GETTING OUTSIDE

In this section, I've described the outdoor opportunities local to Fairbanks, but some other choices are barely farther afield: Check out sections 3 and 4 of this chapter, on Chena Hot Springs Road and the Steese Highway.

The **Alaska Public Lands Information Center,** 250 Cushman St. (at Third Ave.), Suite 1A (© **907/456-0527;** www.nps.gov/aplic), is a great resource. The staff will advise you on outings, outfitters, and where to find rental equipment.

SPECIAL PLACES

CREAMER'S FIELD   At 1300 College Rd., right in Fairbanks, this migratory waterfowl refuge is a 1,800-acre former dairy farm that was saved from development in 1966 by a community fund drive. The pastures are a prime stopover point for Canada geese, pintails, and golden plovers in the spring and fall. Sandhill cranes, shovelers, and mallards show up all summer. The **Friends of Creamer's Field** (© 907/452-7307; www.creamersfield.org) operates a small visitor center with bird and history displays, open June through August Tuesday through Friday from 10am to 5pm and on Saturday from 10am to 4pm, and offers guided nature walks in summer Saturday and Wednesday at 9am and Tuesday and Thursday at 7pm. You don't need a guide, however; I especially enjoyed the boreal forest nature walk, interpreted by an excellent booklet you can pick up at the visitor center or from a stand at the trailhead when the visitor center is closed.

CHENA LAKES RECREATION AREA   This is a wonderful and unique place for a family camping trip. A birch-rimmed lake created for a flood-control project has been developed by the local government to provide lots of recreational possibilities: flat walking and bike trails; a swimming beach; fishing; a place to rent canoes and paddleboats; a self-guided 2½-mile nature trail; a playground; big lawns; and the terrific campground, with 80 camping sites, from pull-throughs for RVs to tent sites on a little island you can reach only by boat. In the winter, it's a popular area for cross-country skiing, ice fishing, and dog mushing. Camping costs $10; day use is $3. Drive 17 miles east of Fairbanks on the Richardson Highway and turn left on Laurance Road as you leave North Pole. For information, contact Fairbanks North Star Borough Chena Lakes Recreation Area (© 907/488-1655). Follow the same directions (drive along the dam past the recreation area) to the **Moose Creek Dam Salmon Watch,** a picnic and viewing area built by the U.S. Army Corps of Engineers atop the flood control project to watch spawning salmon in crystal-clear water late June through July. Use of the area is free, so tell the recreation area gatehouse you are going there.

ACTIVITIES

CANOEING   The Chena River is slow and meandering as it flows through Fairbanks, and you have your pick of restaurants on the bank. Farther up river, the canoeing passes wilder shores, and near its headwaters becomes more challenging (covered in the "Chena Hot Springs Road" section, later). For beginners, try the wilderness section from the Chena Lakes Recreation Area downstream (see above). It's 12 to 16 hours from there all the way into town, or you can take out at one of the roads that crosses the river along the way. The **U.S. Army Corp of Engineers** (© 907/488-2748) produces a float map with put-in and take-out points and float times, available at the Alaska Public Lands Information Center (see "Visitor Information," earlier). The Public Lands Center can provide guidance for all the trips, and a list of companies that rent equipment. **7 Bridges Boats and Bikes** rents canoes and kayaks for $30 per day, $100 per week, and provides the valuable service of dropping you off at the river and picking you up at your destination for $1.50 per mile out of town, with a $15 minimum. They're at the 7 Gables Inn, 4312 Birch Lane (© 907/479-0751; www.7gablesinn.com/7bbb).

BIKING & HIKING   **7 Bridges Boats and Bikes** (see contact info immediately above) rents street and mountain bikes for $20 a day. Another rental agency is under "Getting Around," earlier. Traffic goes fast in Fairbanks, and the separated bike trails are few, but strong cyclists can get by. Mountain biking and hiking are good on the remote dirt roads and trails out of town, especially off the Steese Highway and Chena Hot Spring Road, described later. Inquire at the Alaska Public Lands Information Center for more ideas (see "Visitor Information," earlier).

FISHING   Salmon fishing isn't as good here as nearer the coast, where the fish are brighter, and the season is brief. Most fishing is in the streams and stocked lakes for pike, grayling, and various kinds of trout. You can fish right in the Chena as it flows through town, although getting out of town and hiking away from a road yields better results. Fly-in fishing will further increase your chances, but the expense of around $300 a day is easier to justify from Anchorage, where you can target salmon as well as freshwater fish. The Alaska Public Lands Information Center (earlier) offers guidance, or contact the **Alaska Department of Fish and Game,** at Creamer's Field, 1300 College Rd., Fairbanks, AK 99701 (© **907/459-7207;** sport fish information recording 907/459-7385; www.state. ak.us/adfg).

WINTER RECREATION   Fairbanks has real Jack London winters, with long darkness and temperatures that commonly linger well below zero, but that doesn't stop people from getting outdoors for Nordic skiing, snowmobiling, and sled-dog mushing. You can count on snow and have excellent chances of seeing the Northern Lights. Many local dog mushers offer rides; get a referral from the visitor center. There are several cross-country-ski trail networks, including 50 miles of groomed trails at the University of Alaska and hilly, well-maintained trails at the **Birch Hill Recreation Area,** off Farmers Loop Road just east of the Steese Highway. Both have lighted loops.

ACCOMMODATIONS

Going the bed-and-breakfast route is a good choice in Fairbanks, where good budget motel rooms are few. At the B&Bs I've listed below, you can save money over a hotel and get just as good a private room while staying in a unique place with interesting people. The **Fairbanks Association of Bed and Breakfasts,** P.O. Box 73334, Fairbanks, AK 99707-3334, lists many more on its website at **www.ptialaska.net/~fabb.** You also can get B&B information at the Fairbanks Log Cabin Visitor Information Center (see "Visitor Information," at the beginning of this section).

VERY EXPENSIVE

Fairbanks Princess Riverside Lodge ★★   This well-thought-out gray clapboard structure in a wooded area on the banks of the Chena, near the airport, was built to serve Princess cruise-line passengers. The rooms, while not large, are trim and stylish, and many look out on the river. The convenient location, amenities, and efficient service make it a good choice for business travelers. The lobby is attractive, and a bar and restaurant have a large deck overlooking the river.

4477 Pikes Landing Rd., Fairbanks, AK 99709. © **800/426-0500** or 907/455-4477. Fax 907/455-4476. www. princessalaskalodges.com. 325 units. High season $199–$209 double. Low season $129–$139 double. Year-round $199–$349 suite. Extra person $10. AE, DC, DISC, MC, V. **Amenities:** Restaurant; cafe; bar; exercise room; steam room; tour desk; courtesy van; business center; laundry service. *In room:* A/C, TV, dataport, hair dryer.

Other Upscale Hotels in Fairbanks

There are many more expensive hotels than we can list. I've described in full those with the most character, but these others are in the same league, each

ACCOMMODATIONS ■

All Seasons Inn **4**
Bridgewater Hotel **5**
Fairbanks Hotel **10**
Westmark Fairbanks **15**

DINING ◆

Gambardella's Italian Cafe **6**
Souvlaki **14**
Thai House **9**

ATTRACTIONS ●

Alaska Public Lands Information Center **7**
Early Fairbanks homes **3**
Fairbanks Community Museum **8**
Fairbanks Ice Museum **13**
Golden Heart Park **12**
Church of the Immaculate Conception **1**
Fairbanks Log Cabin
    Visitor Information Center **11**
St. Matthew's Episcopal Church **2**

charging $170 to $190 a night. **Pike's Waterfront Lodge,** near the airport at 1850 Hoselton Rd. (© **877/456-4500** or 907/456-4500; www.pikeslodge.com), is like a big, luxurious wilderness lodge on the river, with many amenities. Downtown, at 575 First St., **Marriott SpringHill Suites of Fairbanks** (© **888/ 236-2427** or 907/451-6552; www.springhillsuites.com) charges $179 for up to six guests in suites that are like little homes. West of downtown, **Comfort Inn Chena River,** 1908 Chena Landings Loop (© **800/228-5150** or 907/479-8080; www.comfortinn.com), has attractive rooms and a small pool on a lovely wooded site near the river.

EXPENSIVE

Fairbanks Exploration Inn ★★ *(Finds* Executives of the Fairbanks Exploration Co. lived in these bungalows—the inn takes its name from that early gold mining operation—then left them vacant for 20 years to be rescued, lovingly restored, and made into Alaska's best historic accommodation, near the rail depot. Light streams in through screen porches and big, double-hung windows onto wood floors. There are white walls framed with varnished moldings and hung with contemporary fine art, as well as crisp period furnishings and working fireplaces. The service is professional. Port and sherry in the evening and a full breakfast in the morning are included in the price of the room. It's not flawless, though. Besides the high prices, the rooms can be too cool, most rooms have only showers (no tubs), many lack closets, all have only one bed (you can get a rollaway in a suite), and TVs are in common rooms only.

505 Illinois St., Fairbanks, AK 99701. © **888/452-1920** (outside Alaska) or 907/451-1920. Fax 907/ 455-7317. www.feinn.com. 16 units, 14 with private bathroom. Summer $149 double; $209 suite. Winter $85 double; $100 suite. Extra person in suite $25. Rates include full breakfast. AE, MC, V. **Amenities:** Tour desk.

River's Edge Resort Cottages ★★★ An afternoon on a sunny riverbank exemplifies the best of Interior Alaska; this place is built around that knowledge. Trim little cottages stand in a grassy compound along the gentle Chena River, where guests can fish for grayling. Inside, each light, airy cottage is an excellent standard hotel room, with high ceilings and two queen beds. Outside, they're like a little village, where guests can sit on the patio, watch the river go by, and socialize. The owners got the idea for the place from their RV park next door, when they noticed how their guests enjoyed visiting together in the open with their own private units to retreat to. It's perfect for families, as the outdoor areas are safe for playing and noise inside won't bother the neighbors. A large restaurant sits at river's edge, with dining on a deck or inside at round, oak tables. Dinner entrees range up to $30—steak, seafood, and down-home cooking; a burger is $8. A breakfast buffet is served in the summer for $8.95.

4200 Boat St., Fairbanks, AK 99709. Take Sportsman Way off Airport Way to Boat St. © **800/770-3343** or 907/474-0286. Fax 907/474-3665. www.riversedge.net. 86 cottages, 8 suites. High season $173 double. Low season $89 double. Extra person age 12 and over $10. AE, DISC, MC, V. **Amenities:** Restaurant; bar; tour desk; couresy van; laundry service. *In room:* TV, dataport, coffeemaker, hair dryer.

A Taste of Alaska Lodge ★ Situated atop a grassy slope on 280 acres, facing Mount McKinley, the hand-crafted log main building feels like a wilderness lodge but is less than half an hour from Fairbanks. They maintain a team of huskies for dogsled rides. Rooms are decorated with handmade quilts, brass beds, and other reproductions; and each has a door straight onto the grounds, where moose are often seen wandering. The cabins are large and especially luxurious.

551 Eberhardt Rd. (turn right 5.3 miles out Chena Hot Springs Rd.), Fairbanks, AK 99712. © **907/488-7855.** Fax 907/488-3772. www.tasteofalaska.com. 8 units, 2 cabins. $150 double; cabin $175–$200. Extra person $25. Rates include full breakfast. AE, MC, V. No smoking. **Amenities:** Hot tub. *In room:* TV.

Wedgewood Resort ★★ Off College Road near the Creamer's Field Refuge, this huge, well-kept hotel sprawls across a grassy, 23-acre complex in eight large buildings. Seven of them are converted three-story apartment buildings, newly remodeled, without elevators but with large living rooms, separate dining areas, fully equipped kitchens, air conditioners, TVs, balconies, and phones with voicemail in both the living room and bedroom. The main difference from home is that someone else cleans up after you. Another 157 standard hotel units are large and thoughtfully designed but mostly house package tour groups in summer and are closed in winter. I would choose an apartment, but if you don't have your own car, you'll be hiking back and forth to the buildings and up the stairs a lot, so travelers with mobility issues might prefer the more centrally located though smaller regular rooms. A scheduled courtesy van runs to the airport and train depot and various tourist sites in the summer.

212 Wedgewood Dr., Fairbanks, AK 99701. © **800/528-4916** or 907/452-1442. Fax 907/451-6376. www. fountainheadhotels.com. 157 units, 294 apts. High season $182 double; $160 apt for 2. Low season $80 apt for 2, regular double rms not offered. Extra person in apt $10. AE, DC, DISC, MC, V. **Amenities:** 2 restaurants (summer only, indoor and outdoor cafes); bar; tour desk; courtesy van; coin-op laundry; same day dry cleaning; evening lectures; historic exhibits. *In room:* A/C, TV, dataport, coffeemaker, hair dryer, iron.

Westmark Fairbanks ★ Taking up a full block downtown, the Westmark Fairbanks (not to be confused with the seasonal and somewhat less expensive Westmark Inn on South Cushman Street) fulfills the role of the city's grand, central hotel. A recent remodeling helps it hold that image, with an impressive lobby on Tenth Street, but the rooms, in a series of buildings surrounding a central courtyard, remain uneven in quality. Some are large and fresh, with new furniture, while others are worn, dated, and grossly overpriced. Make a choice when you check in. Facilities include a gift shop.

813 Noble St., Fairbanks, AK 99701-4977. ℂ **800/544-0970** (reservations), or 907/456-7722. Fax 907/451-7478. www.westmarkhotels.com. 244 units. High season $179–$199 double. Low season $99–$129 double. Extra person $15. AE, DC, DISC, MC, V. **Amenities:** Restaurant (cafe); bar; tour desk; courtesy van; coin-op laundry and laundry service. *In room:* A/C, TV with pay movies.

MODERATE

All Seasons Inn ★★   This charming and comfortable country inn stands on a pleasant residential street a couple of blocks from the downtown core. Each cozy room has its own inspired decorative details in bold colors, and the housekeeping has always been perfect on our many visits. For socializing with the personable hostess or other guests, a series of large, elegant common rooms connect downstairs, where you'll find a bar with hot drinks and a sun porch with books and games. Complimentary newspapers come with the full breakfast.

763 Seventh Ave., Fairbanks, AK 99701. ℂ **888/451-6649** or 907/451-6649. Fax 907/474-8448. www.allseasonsinn.com. 8 units. High season $135 double. Low season $75 double. Extra person $25. Rates include full breakfast. DC, DISC, MC, V. No smoking. **Amenities:** Coin-op laundry. *In room:* TV, dataport, hair dryer, iron.

Forget-Me-Not Lodge and the Aurora Express Bed and Breakfast ★★
Finds   Susan Wilson's late grandmother appeared to her in a dream and told her there would be a train on a bank below her house, on the family's 15 acres high in the hills south of Fairbanks. So Wilson went out and got a train—a still-growing collection that includes a pair of 1956 Pullman sleepers, a dining car, a locomotive, a caboose, and a World War II hospital car—and her husband, Mike, brought it all up the mountain to install below the house, right in the spot indicated. Some cars are close to their original form, and Susan says older guests sometimes weep over the memories they bring back. Others were elaborately remodeled into small rooms on themes related to Fairbanks history. A full breakfast is served in the dining car, which also houses the common area, TV, and phone. One 85-foot-long car is meant for families, with railroad-theme decor, puzzles, and toy trains. Then there's the incredible caboose, dedicated to Grandma. They're located 6.5 miles out of town, so you will need your own car if you stay here.

1540 Chena Ridge Rd. (P.O. Box 80128), Fairbanks, AK 99708. ℂ **800/221-0073** or 907/474-0949. Fax 907/474-8173. www.aurora-express.com. 7 units. $115–$150 double. Extra person $25. Rates include full breakfast. MC, V. Closed Oct–Apr. No smoking.

Minnie Street Bed & Breakfast Inn ★   Just across the river from the downtown center, near the rail depot, two buildings around a garden courtyard contain clean, brightly decorated rooms with many amenities, custom-designed carpeting, handmade quilts, and stylish furniture. A full breakfast is served in a dining room with a high vaulted ceiling. The one- and two-bedroom suites have kitchens, and one has a Jacuzzi and guest computer.

345 Minnie St., Fairbanks, AK 99701. ℂ **888/456-1849** or 907/456-1802. Fax 907/451-1751. www.minniestreetbandb.com. 10 units, 6 with private bathroom. High season $100–$130 double; $145–$195 suite. Low season $65–$75 double; $100 suite. Extra person $25. Rates include full breakfast. AE, DISC, MC, V. **Amenities:** Car rental; business center; in-room massage; coin-op laundry. *In room:* TV, CD player, hair dryer, robes.

INEXPENSIVE

Cloudberry Lookout Bed and Breakfast ★ *Finds*   Back amid the spruces on the edge of town, near its own small pond, a house with a 60-foot wooden tower in its center rises like a vision. Sean McGuire and Suzi Lozo took 7 years to build this masterpiece of log carpentry, with huge, airy common rooms that radiate from a central spiral staircase that ascends to a high perch for viewing the aurora and countryside. Rooms vary greatly in size, but all are comfortable and decorated with family antiques. The couple serves a large breakfast and can tell you about their work in the local environmental community. Since the house is on wetland it has finicky marine toilets, and the stairs make it unsuitable for children or people with disabilities.

Off Goldhill Rd. (P.O. Box 84511), Fairbanks, AK 99708. ℂ 907/479-7334. www.mosquitonet.com/~cloudbry. 5 units, 4 with private bathroom. $85–$105 double. Extra person $25. Rates include full breakfast. AE, DISC, MC, V. Closed Dec–Feb.

Fairbanks Hotel *Value*   Four women transformed a notorious flophouse into a trim Art Deco–style historic hotel, in the core of downtown. The proprietors aim for the feel of a small European hotel. Although quite small, the rooms are light and attractively decorated, including brass beds and other period touches. The neighborhood remains gritty, however, and the building has quirks, so it's wise to choose your room when checking in. Only the bottom floor of three is nonsmoking. In the winter, they rent arctic parkas, boots, hats, and mittens for only $5 a day.

517 Third Ave., Fairbanks, AK 99701. ℂ 888/329-4685 or 907/456-6411. Fax 907/456-1792. www.alaska. net/~fbxhotl. 35 units, 11 with private bathroom. High season $85–$109 double. Low season $40–$59 double. AE, DISC, MC, V. **Amenities:** Bike rental; courtesy van. *In room:* TV.

Golden North Motel *Value*   The Baer family, owners since 1971, keep the rooms in this two-story motel in good shape, making it a good bargain favored by Alaskans who've come to town from the Bush to shop or just visit by car. They're always remodeling something, and where carpets and furniture are worn they're quite clean. The standard rooms are small, but the reasonably priced suites are a good choice for families. The building is a nondescript brown rectangle, but bright flower boxes lighten the outdoor walkways and the location is near the airport. The motel provides a free continental breakfast and coffee in the office.

4888 Old Airport Rd., Fairbanks, AK 99709. ℂ 800/447-1910 or 907/479-6201. Fax 907/479-5766. www. goldennorthmotel.com. 62 units. $69 double; $99 suite. Rates include continental breakfast. AE, DC, DISC, MC, V. **Amenities:** Courtesy van. *In room:* TV.

CAMPING & HOSTEL

There are several hostels in Fairbanks. Among the best is the homey **Billie's Backpackers Hostel,** off College Road near the University, at 2895 Mack Blvd. (ℂ 907/479-2034; www.Alaskahostel.com).

Tent camping is a good way to go in Fairbanks, with its mild summers and ample public lands. Right in town, the **Chena River State Recreation Site** (not to be confused with the recreation "area" of the same name described in the next section of this chapter), is located where University Avenue crosses the river. Riverside sites are surrounded by birch. The self-service fee is $15, $10 for walk-in camping. Getting a bit out of town, there are superb public campgrounds at Chena Lakes Recreation Area (see "Special Places," earlier) and along Chena Hot Springs Road (covered in section 3 of this chapter).

Fairbanks has plenty of RV parks, some with full service and then some. Pick up a list at the visitor center. Among the best is **River's Edge RV Park and Campground,** at a wooded riverside bend of the Chena at 4140 Boat St., off Airport Way and Sportsman Way (© **800/770-3343** or 907/474-0286; www. riversedge.net), with lots of services, including free shuttles and organized tours. Full hookups are $27 and tent camping $16. The same people operate the cottage resort and restaurant next door.

DINING
DOWNTOWN

Gambardella's Italian Cafe ★★ ITALIAN   Gambardella's style and food are a level above those almost anywhere else in town. My halibut was fresh and deftly seasoned on light, rich pasta, with mixed vegetables that were all done perfectly, even mushrooms and carrots side by side. The lasagna is famous. Dining rooms are narrow and long, with high ceilings and well-scuffed wooden floors, and bend around a corner—pleasingly noisy but intimate at the same time. On a sunny day, eat on the patio among the hanging flowers. The service is quick and professional, the prices reasonable, and the desserts, baked in-house, not to be missed. They serve beer and wine.

706 Second Ave. © **907/456-3417.** www.gambardellas.com. Main courses $9.50–$17; lunch $6–$10. 15% gratuity added for parties of 5 or more, or for split checks. AE, MC, V. Mon–Sat 11am–10pm, Sun 4–10pm, closing an hour earlier off-season.

Souvlaki GREEK   Drop in here for a quick, inexpensive lunch or dinner. Besides the tasty Greek dishes, they serve sandwiches, salads, and some Mexican food from a brief menu. Servings are light. Families will do well, occupying one of the small, single-party rooms off the main dining room. The desserts, baked in-house, are memorable. Souvlaki also operates a take-out place at Alaskaland in the summer.

310 First Ave. © **907/452-5393.** Main courses $3.75–$6.25. MC, V. Summer, Mon–Fri 10am–9pm, Sat 10am–6pm. Winter, Mon–Sat 10am–6pm.

Thai House ★★ THAI   In a small, brightly lit storefront in the downtown area, this is a simple, family-run restaurant with authentic Thai cuisine. Every time we've dined here the food came quickly and was deftly seasoned and cooked to a turn. You tend to check the bill because it seems too small. Such gems may be common in cities with large ethnic communities, but in Fairbanks, this place stands out.

526 Fifth Ave. © **907/452-6123.** Lunch items $6.75–$8; dinner main courses $9–$12. MC, V. Mon–Sat 11am–4pm and 5–10pm.

WITHIN DRIVING DISTANCE

Besides the restaurants listed here, there's the salmon bake at Alaskaland, described earlier, and the Ester Gold Camp, below. Also, in town, near the university at 3702 Cameron St. off University Road, **Sam's Sourdough Cafe** (© **907/479-0523**) is a masterpiece in the art of the greasy spoon, with quick, friendly service, creative burgers, great milk shakes, and breakfast all day. They're open 6am to 10pm, and it's a bit smoky.

The Bakery ★ (Finds) DINER   There are an infinite number of old-fashioned coffee shops in and around Fairbanks—the kind of place where a truck driver or gold miner can find a hearty, down-home meal, a motherly waitress, and a bottomless cup of coffee. This is the best of the lot, which is really saying something. The sourdough pancakes are memorable, the menu is long and inexpensive, portions are huge (sometimes they require two plates), the service is fast and friendly, and the quality of the baked goods testified to by the number of police cars always in the parking lot. The Formica tables are worn down from years of wiping. They have no liquor license.

69 College Rd. © **907/456-8600.** Lunch items $5–$8; dinner main courses $7–$17. MC, V. Mon–Sat 6am–9pm, Sun 7am–4pm.

Pike's Landing ☀ STEAK/SEAFOOD   The large dining room overlooking the Chena River near the airport serves consistently good steak and seafood and some more ambitious fare. It's all well prepared, with huge servings and occasional flashes of creativity in the more sophisticated fish dishes. Sunday brunch is big and delicious. For an inexpensive meal, the bar serves basic food on the deck over the river from 2:30pm to closing time. It's a pleasant choice on a sunny day, less so in cool or rainy weather, when it remains in operation behind plastic.

4438 Airport Way. © **907/479-6500.** Main courses $22–$39; lunch items $7.50–$10.75. AE, DC, DISC, MC, V. Daily 11:30am–2:30pm and 5–11pm.

The Pump House Restaurant and Saloon ☀ STEAK/SEAFOOD   The historic, rambling, corrugated tin building on the Chena River is elaborately decorated and landscaped with authentic gold rush relics. Sitting on the deck, you can watch the riverboat paddle by or a group in canoes stop for appetizers and drinks from the full bar. It's a jolly place, good for groups. The dinner menu includes steak and seafood, and the food is good. They serve a big Sunday brunch.

1.3 Mile, Chena Pump Rd. © **907/479-8452.** www.pumphouse.com. Main courses $17–$29. AE, DISC, MC, V. Summer Mon–Sat 11:30am–2pm and 5–10pm, Sun 10am–2pm and 5–10pm; winter Mon–Sat 5–9pm, Sun 10am–2pm and 5–9pm.

Two Rivers Lodge/Tuscan Gardens ☀☀ STEAK/SEAFOOD/ NORTHERN ITALIAN   Inside the log lodge building, chef Tony Marsico turns out food a cut above what you would expect, although the menu, like those of almost all fine-dining establishments in the area, is primarily steak and seafood. From the appetizer list order a light meal of the creamy, complex king crab bisque in a bowl of sourdough bread topped with a layer of cheese. Service is friendly but not necessarily quick—it's a place to settle in for an evening of dining. Outside, on a deck over the duck pond, a whole separate operation serves meals from a brick Tuscan oven in the open air, operating only in fine weather. Start there for appetizers, or eat a whole inexpensive Tuscan meal under the evening sun. There are full bars at both spots. The drive from Fairbanks is about 25 minutes.

4968 Chena Hot Springs Rd. © **907/488-6815.** Main courses $12–$28. AE, DC, DISC, MC, V. Mon–Fri 5–10pm, Sat–Sun 3–10pm.

NIGHTLIFE

Fairbanks has a lot of tourist-oriented evening activities, as well as entertainment also attended by locals. Call the 24-hour event recording of what's playing currently (© **907/456-INFO**) or get a copy of the *Fairbanks Daily News-Miner.* The best of the summer arts scene is at the **Fairbanks Summer Arts Festival** (© **907/474-8869;** see "Special Events," at the beginning of this section). There also are **movie theaters**—a large multiplex is located on Airport Way. The evening show at the **Palace Theater** is discussed earlier under "Alaskaland."

The **Ester Gold Camp** (© 800/676-6925 or 907/479-2500; www.akvisit. com) is an 11-building historic site, an old mining town that's been turned into an evening tourist attraction. The main event is a gold rush theme show at the Malamute Saloon, with singing and Robert Service poetry, nightly at 9pm; admission is $14. A "photosymphony" slide show about the aurora takes place every summer evening at 6:45 and 7:45 and costs $8. There's also a restaurant that serves a buffet and has mess-hall seating; prices approach $30 a plate, although it's less for kids or if you abstain from crab. The gift shop is open in the evening, and there are simple, inexpensive rooms in the old gold mine bunkhouse. A free bus is available from major hotels in Fairbanks.

The **Howling Dog Saloon,** north of town in Fox (© 907/457-8780), claims to be the "farthest north rock 'n' roll club in the world." That's questionable, but the bar with the dancing dog on the roof does have a reputation for a rowdy good time. The music is classic rock and blues; a selection of 17 craft brews is on tap at $4 each, while regular American beer is $2.75; and there's no cover charge. Outside there are volleyball nets, horseshoe pits, and the like. The saloon usually closes for a few months in midwinter.

3 Chena Hot Springs Road

The 57-mile paved road east from Fairbanks is an avenue to an enjoyable day trip or a destination for up to a week's outdoor activities and hot-spring swimming. Of all the roads radiating from Fairbanks, this short highway will be most rewarding to outdoors people, as well as provide some of the best remote lodgings accessible on the Interior road system.

The road travels through the Chena River State Recreation Area, with spectacular hikes and float trips and well-maintained riverside campgrounds, and leads to the Chena Hot Springs, where there's a year-round resort perfect for soaking in hot mineral springs and for use as a base for summer or winter wilderness day trips. The resort is open to people who want to rent one of the comfortable rooms or to campers and day-trippers, and it's equally as popular in the winter as in the summer (the slow seasons are spring and fall).

The paved road leads through a forest of birch, spruce, and cottonwood, first passing an area of scattered roadside development and then following the Chena River through the state recreation area. It's a pleasant drive, around 1¼ hours each way from Fairbanks, but not particularly scenic. On a sunny summer weekend, the people of Fairbanks migrate to the riverside and the hiking trails; on a sunny winter weekend, they take to the hills on snowmobiles, cross-country skis, or dogsleds.

A pair of prospectors, the Swan brothers, discovered the hot springs in 1905, having heard that a U.S. Geological Survey crew had seen steam in a valley on the upper Chena. Thomas Swan suffered from rheumatism; incredibly, he and his brother poled up the Chena River from Fairbanks, found the hot springs, built a cabin and rock-floored pool, and spent the summer soaking. He was cured! More visitors followed, drawn by stories that whole groups of cripples were able to dance all night after soaking in the pools—by 1915 a resort was in operation, drawing worn-out miners and gold rush stampeders and many others as well. The resort has been in constant use ever since.

ESSENTIALS

GETTING THERE   The Chena Hot Springs Road meets the Steese Expressway about 10 miles north of downtown Fairbanks. (Details on renting a car in

Fairbanks can be found at the beginning of section 2 of this chapter.) The resort offers rides from Fairbanks for $30 per person round-trip with a minimum of two passengers; one-way fares are not available.

VISITOR INFORMATION   For outdoors information, check the Fairbanks **Alaska Public Lands Information Center,** 250 Cushman St. (at Third Ave.), Suite 1A, Fairbanks, AK 99701 (© **907/456-0527;** TTY 907/456-0532; fax 907/456-0514; www.nps.gov/aplic).

The **Alaska Division of Parks,** at 3700 Airport Way, Fairbanks, AK 99709 (© **907/451-2695;** www.dnr.state.ak.us/parks/units/chena/index.htm), manages the area and produces trail, river, and road guides, which are available at trailhead kiosks or from the public lands center, on the website, or in their Trailmaker newspaper, which you can also order from the web. Contact them, also, with questions about the public cabins in the area (see "State Parks Cabin Reservations Tricks," in section 1 of chapter 7, for how to reserve).

The **Chena Hot Springs Resort** owns and operates the springs; they're discussed below. Also on the road are the **Two Rivers Lodge,** a fine-dining establishment and bar, and **A Taste of Alaska Lodge,** a bed-and-breakfast. They are listed in "Dining" and "Accommodations" respectively in section 2 of this chapter.

THE CHENA RIVER STATE RECREATION AREA

The recreation area takes in 254,000 acres along the river valley and over the rolling mountains of heather around it. Some of Interior Alaska's best hiking and floating are found here. As everywhere in the Interior, the mosquitoes are brutal.

ACTIVITIES

HIKING & BACKPACKING   The best trail hikes in the Fairbanks area are in the Chena Hot Springs State Recreation Area. Backcountry camping requires no permit, and many of the trails go above the tree line, so it's a good area for backpackers to get into the wilderness.

The **Angel Rocks Trail** is a sometimes steep 3½-mile loop to an immense granite outcropping, an impressive destination with good views of the valley below. The trail mostly stays below the tree line. The trailhead is well marked, at mile 48.9 of the road.

The 15-mile loop of the **Granite Tors Trail,** starting at mile 39 of the road, is a challenging day hike, rising through forest to rolling alpine terrain, but the towering tors more than reward the effort. Like surrealist experiments in perspective, these monolithic granite sentinels stand at random spots on the broad Plain of Monuments, at first confounding the eye's attempts to gauge their distance and size. Like the Angel Rocks, they were created when upwelling rock solidified in cracks in the surrounding earth, which then eroded away. Water is scarce, so bring along plenty. This is an excellent overnight hike, with the driest ground for camping right around the tors, and there is also a public shelter halfway along.

For a longer backpacking trip, the **Chena Dome Trail** makes a 30-mile loop, beginning at mile 50.5 and ending at mile 49. The 3 miles nearest the road at either end pass through forest, but the remaining 23 miles are above the tree line, marked with cairns, with expansive views, summiting 4,421-foot Chena Dome after the 10-mile mark. The trail can be quite wet and muddy in parts and steep and rocky elsewhere. A public shelter is on the trail.

RIVER FLOATING   The Chena is a lovely river, growing from a clear, frothy creek near the end of the road to a lazy Class I river as it flows off toward Fairbanks, several days downstream. Where you choose to start depends on your experience. Easier water is downstream from Rosehip Campground (mile 27), with the slowest of all nearer Fairbanks, but the upper portion is more popular if you are up for something a bit more challenging. The road crosses the river several times, and the state park system has developed other access points, so it's possible to plan a float that exactly matches your time and abilities. Use the state park river guide to choose your route.

Canoe Alaska (© 907/883-2628) offers instruction and guided trips; an introductory clinic is $165. 7 Bridges Boats and Bikes, 4312 Birch Lane, Fairbanks (© 907/479-0751; www.7gablesinn.com/7bbb), rents canoes for $30 per day, and will drop you off and pick you up for $1.50 per mile out of town.

FISHING   Several of the ponds are stocked with trout, which you can keep; signs along the road mark access points. You can catch-and-release arctic grayling in the Chena, depending on the current regulations and bait restrictions. Check with the **Alaska Department of Fish and Game,** 1300 College Rd., Fairbanks, AK 99701 (© 907/459-7228; www.state.ak.us/adfg).

CAMPING & CABINS

Three beautiful campgrounds with water and pit toilets lie along the road by the Chena River, managed by the Alaska Division of Parks (see "Visitor Information," above). Although they can't be reserved ahead, the campgrounds are unlikely to be full. The **Rosehip Campground,** at mile 27, has 37 sites, well separated by spruce and birch, with six suitable for RVs. Some sites are right on the river, and some are reserved for more private tent camping, in the woods. The **Granite Tors Campground** is across from the trailhead at mile 39; it has 24 sites, seven suitable for RVs. Some sites have river frontage, and, as at Rosehip, float trips start here. Sites at each of those campgrounds are $10 a night. The **Red Squirrel Campground,** at mile 42.8, has 12 sites and a pleasant picnic area on the grassy edge of a small, placid pond, where swimming is permitted. Camping is $5 per vehicle.

There are several public-use cabins in the recreation area, two of them easily accessible to summer visitors and not hard to book a month or two ahead. (See "State Parks Cabin Reservation Tricks," in section 1 of chapter 7 for how to get one.) These are primitive cabins; you must bring your own sleeping bags, lights, and cooking gear. The **North Fork Cabin** is at mile 47.7 of the road, and the **Chena River Cabin** faces the river at mile 32.2. You can get to either by car or canoe, and they cost $35 a night. Other public cabins in the area primarily serve winter users and are difficult to reach when the ground thaws.

THE HOT SPRINGS

Our family has enjoyed wonderful days here swimming and exploring, but this is not a sophisticated resort. It's a place to romp in the pool, hike through the woods, and enjoy the sound of the wind in the trees. The hot springs heat the buildings and, mixed with cold water, supply an indoor pool, a series of indoor and outdoor hot tubs and spas, and a rock-lined outdoor hot pond (100 to 104 degrees), with evaporative cooling by a fountain and waterfall. Kids are limited to the indoor swimming pool, which is kept cool enough to swim, allowing adults to escape the noise outside. The locker rooms are undersized, so guests will want to change in their rooms. Having various hot tubs and spas allows you to soak at your chosen temperature, inside or outside. The swimming facility is open daily 7am to midnight. Swim passes come with your room if you're staying at the resort; for campers or day-trippers, a day pass is $10 adults, $7 ages 6 to 13, free children 5 and under; a 10-punch pass is $60 for all ages.

ACCOMMODATIONS

The resort has an RV parking area without hookups, and two primitive campgrounds. A tent campground with outhouses wraps itself around the bends in a creek. All sites are $20 per night. Campers can use a dump station free.

The Chena Hot Springs Resort ★★   The resort, set on 440 acres of land in a bowl of mountains, invites a slow pace, with plenty of time spent soaking or walking. Families love it, while couples may prefer to go during school days when the pool is quieter. In the winter, the aurora viewing is exceptional here, away from city lights, and you can enjoy Nordic skiing, snow-cat and snow-machine tours, skating, sled-dog rides, and more. In the summer, you can go horseback riding, rafting, hiking, gold panning, flightseeing, or mountain biking. There's also a large new activity building. A 6-mile alpine ridge trail links to the Angel Rocks trail described above.

The rooms range from the crude, original cabins built by the prospectors who discovered the area to large new hotel rooms with televisions, phones, and coffeemakers. The larger cabins—not the prospectors' originals—are crude but adequate for a family or group looking for inexpensive lodgings and not particular about indoor plumbing. The lodge building contains the restaurant and bar, with a brief but sufficiently varied menu with prices only slightly above those in town.

Mile 56.5, Chena Hot Springs Rd. (P.O. Box 73440), Fairbanks, AK 99707. © **800/478-4681** or 907/452-7867. Fax 907/456-3122. www.chenahotsprings.com. 80 units, 11 cabins. $125–$170 double; $190–$200 suite. Extra person $20. AE, DC, DISC, MC, V. **Amenities:** Restaurant; bar; indoor and outdoor pools; hot tubs and Jacuzzis; bike rental; tour desk; massage; coin-op laundry. *In room* (excluding cabins): TV, coffeemaker, hair dryer.

4 The Steese Highway

The Steese Highway leads from Fairbanks 162 miles northeast to Circle, a village on the Yukon River about 50 miles south of the Arctic Circle (they were mistaken about the town's exact location when they named it—oh well). The historic gold rush route parallels the Davidson Ditch, a huge aqueduct and pipe that carried water to the mining operations near Fairbanks. Small-time miners and prospectors still scratch the hills. They bring their gold into the bar in Central, where they can get a shower and where the current metal price is posted on the wall. **Arctic Circle Hot Springs** is out here, too, with a big, hot outdoor pool.

There are a couple of good hikes from the road, and it provides many access points to **river floats.** The clear, Class I water of the Chatanika River is perfect for day trips or relaxed expeditions of a week or more, if you know how to handle river hazards such as sweepers and snags that show up on any Alaska stream. And the road meets two National Wild and Scenic Rivers: Beaver Creek, for trips of a week or more over easy Class I water, and Birch Creek, for more experienced paddlers. Get *The Alaska River Guide,* mentioned at the beginning of this chapter in a sidebar called "Rollin' on the River," for detailed guidance, and check with the Alaska Public Lands Information Center, below.

The Steese is paved only for the first 40 miles, and you can drive only so fast on these rural gravel roads without bouncing into a ditch. Besides the bumps, you must go slowly and pull to the side to avoid rocks thrown up by vehicles going the other direction. Consequently, you'll spend much of your day in the car—driving both ways in one day would be absurd. On the other hand, the overnight accommodations to be had on the highway are below many people's standards, and if you're not interested in a hike, float trip, or hot springs soak, there isn't that much to do. Arctic Circle Hot Springs is the main attraction—more on that below. Above all, take mosquito repellent.

ESSENTIALS

GETTING THERE   The Steese turns to gravel 40 miles out of Fairbanks. Most car rental agencies won't allow their vehicles to drive gravel roads, but **National Car Rental,** at 1246 Noble St. in downtown Fairbanks (℃ **800/ 227-7368** or 907/451-7368), is an exception.

VISITOR INFORMATION   For information on the outdoors, check with the **Alaska Public Lands Information Center,** 250 Cushman St. (at Third Ave.), Suite 1A, Fairbanks, AK 99701 (℃ **907/456-0527;** TTY 907/456-0532; fax 907/456-0514; www.nps.gov/aplic).

The federal **Bureau of Land Management (BLM),** 1150 University Ave., Fairbanks, AK 99709 (℃ **907/474-2200;** aurora.ak.blm.gov), manages most of the land and campgrounds. Their website contains detailed information about campgrounds, trails, and rivers (click on "Site Map" and scroll down to "Recreation").

Check for business information with the **Fairbanks Convention and Visitors Bureau,** at 550 First Ave. (at Cushman St.), Fairbanks, AK 99701 (℃ **800/ 327-5774** or 907/456-5774; www.explorefairbanks.com).

A HIGHWAY LOG

11 MILES   The Steese and Elliot highways split, the Steese heading east into hilly, wooded land. The big piles of gravel and the machinery you may see in the trees are the many-years-old remains of the environmentally destructive form of mining practiced in this region, which requires the excavation and sorting of large amounts of gravel.

28 MILES   Chatanika, an old gold-mining settlement, has a couple of roadhouses where you can stop for a burger, a beer, and, if necessary, a room or place to park your RV. **Chatanika Lodge,** 5760 Old Steese Hwy. N (℃ **907/ 389-2164**), is a thriving and authentic roadhouse with a large bar in which to immerse yourself in local ways amid every kind of animal trophy, a collection of signed dollar bills, and 28,000 Christmas lights (we didn't count them, but the proprietor seemed honest). The place serves good, simple food and rents clean rooms with TVs for $60 a night double. It's a popular snowmobiling hangout and the scene of an **Outhouse Race** during Chatanika Days, the second weekend in March. Snowmobiles rent next door at **Snow RV** (℃ **907/389-7669**) for $55 for 2 hours, and you can hire a guide for $65 for that time.

Beyond Chatanika, there's little more in the way of any kinds of services from here to Central.

30 MILES   The University of Alaska's **Poker Flat Research Range** (℃ **907/ 474-7558**) is marked by a small rocket by the road. This is where the Geophysical Institute launches rockets to study the aurora and other high-altitude phenomena. Tours are scheduled every other Thursday in the summer at 1:30pm. Call to confirm before making the drive.

39 MILES The inviting state parks' **Upper Chatanika River Campground** sits on the river below a bridge on the highway, with 35 sites, pit toilets, and a hand pump for water. Camping is $10. There are grayling in the river, and it's a good spot to start or end a Chatanika float trip. State Parks produces a brochure covering the 12-hour float to the Elliot Highway, available from the Alaska Public Lands Information Center. The road is paved for another 5 miles, slowly rising along the Chatanika with some good views.

42.5 MILES A pull-out here at the McKay Creek Trailhead offers access to the **White Mountains National Recreation Area,** a one-million-acre area managed by the BLM with some summer hiking trails, lots of rafting opportunities, and more than 200 miles of winter trails with cabins.

57 MILES The 1928 **Davidson Ditch** water pipeline is along here—it's not much to look at, just a big rusted pipe. It siphoned water 80 miles to mining operations nearer Fairbanks. The U.S. Creek Road intersects to the left, or north, branching after 6 miles into the Nome Creek Road, which runs east and west along the creek to two campgrounds, trails, and river recreation within the BLM's White Mountains National Recreation Area. It's a well-maintained gravel way over scenic hills. The 19-site **Ophir Creek Campground** is 12 miles west of the T (18 miles from the Steese Highway), a put-in for a weeks-long float of Beaver Creek. The self-service camping fee is $6. At the other end of the road, 4 miles east of the T (10 miles from the Steese), is the **Mount Prindle Campground,** with 13 treeless sites and a $6 fee. The high country beckons here by way of the 16-mile Quartz Creek Trail, open to all-terrain vehicles and hikers.

60 MILES The 12-site BLM campground at **Cripple Creek** has a half-mile nature trail and put-in for Chatanika River floats. This is the last public campground on the highway. The fee is $6.

86 MILES The drive becomes really spectacular from here to just short of Central, as it climbs over rounded, windblown, tundra-clothed mountaintops at **Twelvemile Summit.** There's a parking lot for interpretive signs and the lower end of the BLM's 27-mile **Pinnell Mountain Trail,** a challenging 3-day hike over this amazing terrain. (The upper trailhead is at Eagle Summit.) There are two emergency shelters on the way for protection from the ferocious weather that can sweep the mountains. Get the free BLM trail guide from one of the agencies listed above. Over the next 20 miles, the scars you see in the land are from gold mining.

94 MILES The **Upper Birch Creek** wayside is the put-in point for a challenging 126-mile wild river float trip, taking out at mile 140. For a more doable trip, put in at mile 140 and float an easy 16 miles of Birch Creek through scenic country to a bridge at mile 147.

107 MILES **Eagle Summit,** at 3,624 feet, is the highest place on the highway, and the best place to be on June 21 each year (the summer solstice). Although it's still a degree of latitude below the Arctic Circle, the sun never sets here on the longest day because of the elevation and atmospheric refraction. People come out from Fairbanks and make a celebration of it. The midnight sun is visible for about 3 days before and after the solstice, too, assuming the sky is clear. The BLM has installed a toilet and a viewing deck on a 750-foot loop trail at the trailhead to the Pinnell Mountain Trail. Wildflowers are good here in mid-June.

CENTRAL

After descending from the mountains and entering a forest of spruce that continues to the Yukon, the road at mile 128 suddenly reaches a stretch of pavement and is surrounded by the spectral white trunks of paper birches—like a breath of fresh air after hours bouncing over gravel. You're in the friendly little gold-mining town of Central. We were made to feel like we were the first tourists ever to come this far. From Central you can turn right for the 8-mile drive to Arctic Circle Hot Springs, or continue straight on the Steese for a featureless 34-mile drive to Circle.

The big annual event is the all-day **miners picnic** the first Saturday in August, an old-time community event. Admission is $8 or less. The town's main attraction is the **Central Museum** (℗ **907/520-1893**), which concentrates on the gold mining that has sustained the area since 1893. It's surprisingly good for a town of this size. Admission is $1 for adults, 50¢ for children; it's open Memorial Day to Labor Day, daily from noon to 5pm.

There are two restaurants, both with rural diner food. The **Central Motor Inn** (℗ **907/520-5228**) serves food daily from 7am to 11pm all year (the bar is virtually always open). Its six rooms, with TVs and private bathrooms, rent for $60 as a double. A shower is $3, and there's a coin-op laundry and a gas pump. The other establishment, **Crabb's Corner** (℗ **907/520-5599**), at the corner of Circle Hot Springs Road and the Steese, has basic food in the bar as well as a tiny grocery, a liquor store, a gas station, and cheap rooms. Their pleasant campground among the birches costs $7 a night. Both places accept at least MasterCard and Visa.

Don't miss taking the 8-mile side trip to **Arctic Circle Hot Springs,** mile 8, Circle Hot Springs Rd. (℗ **907/520-5113**). The main draw is the large outdoor pool, fed directly by the hot springs. (A daily pool pass is $5; families of four or more pay $16.) In wintertime, Fairbanksans like to come out here for snow-mobiling and to swim outdoors in subzero weather, toasty warm in the water while their hair freezes. The hotel offers massage and can arrange flightseeing and dogsledding, but it's not a center of resort activities as much as a place to taste, for a day or two, a slice of Alaska's rural past. The patched authenticity of the big, frame lodge is undeniable, confirmed by the blend of lacy antiques and simply old stuff dating from the 1940s through the '60s. The main house has 24 rooms with shared bathrooms; there are 12 cabins, some with water and some without; and there are five hostel cubbyholes in the eaves of the lodge. Everything is unique, but the hospitable management will try to suit your taste. Rates in the main building range from $74 to $125; cabins are $85 to $110; and hostelers pay $20. They accept MasterCard and Visa, and it's wise to reserve ahead for holiday periods. The camping area is suitable only for self-contained RVs. The comfortable dining room is typically open 8am to 9pm, year-round, and was serving excellent home-style meals from a short menu when we last visited.

5 The Dalton Highway

Although it was built to service the trans-Alaska pipeline, one of humankind's largest private construction projects, the glory of the 414-mile Dalton Highway is the wilderness it passes through. Running straight through Interior Alaska to the Arctic coast, the Dalton crosses all kinds of scenic terrain, including forested rounded hills, the rugged peaks of the Brooks Range, and the treeless plains of the North Slope. This is still some of the most remote and untouched land on the globe. To the west of the highway, Gates of the Arctic National Park protects 8.4 million acres of the Brooks Range, part of protected wilderness that spans from the Canadian border to the Chukchi Sea. Beyond the thin ribbon of the gravel highway, only a few thousand human beings a year venture into that vastness.

Wildlife shows up all along the road, from grizzly bears to sport fish to songbirds. The road passes through Alaska's history of mineral extraction, too—there's the gold rush era town of Wiseman and the current oil industry complex at Prudhoe Bay. Also, the Dalton provides Fairbanks's closest access to the Yukon River. But surely the reason most people drive all the way on the Dalton is because of where it goes, and not what's there. It goes to the very end of the earth, as far north as you can drive. It's quite a rough trip to nowhere, but a dramatic one if you have the time and endurance.

The Dalton is known to most Alaskans as the Haul Road—it was built to haul supplies to the Prudhoe Bay oil field and the northern half of the 800-mile pipeline. It remains a wilderness route, with little in the way of human habitation along the way. Coldfoot is the northernmost truck stop in the United States. Wiseman is 15 miles up the road from Coldfoot, where the 2000 census counted 21 people.

That's it for another 240 miles of gravel, until you reach the modern industrial complex at Prudhoe Bay, where you must join a shuttle or tour to see the Arctic Ocean or the oil field.

DALTON HIGHWAY ESSENTIALS

PRACTICAL TIPS   You can drive the highway yourself, staying in the few motels along the way or in a tent or motor home. **National Car Rental,** in downtown Fairbanks at 1246 Noble St. (© **800/227-7368** or 907/451-7368), will allow renters to take some of its vehicles on the Dalton, though most other firms do not. The highway starts north of Fairbanks at mile 73 of the Elliot Highway—take the Steese Highway north from town until it becomes the Elliot. The total road distance from Fairbanks to the Arctic Ocean is 497 miles. Road conditions are notorious on the gravel-and-dirt Dalton, but now much of it is kept in good condition. Speeds of 50 miles per hour are possible on some of the road, while doing 35 will keep you in one piece on rougher spots. The drive takes 12 hours each way, without stops. It's dusty, shoulders are soft, and flat tires are common. For **road conditions,** call the state hotline (© **907/456-7623**).

Driving the Dalton Highway gets you into some remote territory, and you must take **precautions.** Services are always many hours drive apart. Drive with your headlights on at all times. Bring at least one full-sized spare tire and extra gasoline. Insect repellent is an absolute necessity. Truck traffic is dominant. Slow down or even stop to allow trucks to pass you either way, and be careful on bridges, as some are not wide enough for two vehicles to pass safely. Also, pull off for views or pictures—don't just stop in the middle of the road, as some people do.

For those who want to let someone else do the driving, bus packages are listed in section 9 of chapter 10, on Prudhoe Bay.

VISITOR INFORMATION   The best source of information on the Dalton Highway is Fairbanks's **Alaska Public Lands Information Center,** at 250 Cushman St. (at Third Ave.), Suite 1A, Fairbanks, AK 99701 (© **907/456-0527;** TTY 907/456-0532; fax 907/456-0514; www.nps.gov/aplic). Rangers there drive the road annually to keep their advice up to date.

Much of the road runs through land managed by the **Bureau of Land Management,** 1150 University Ave., Fairbanks, AK 99709 (© **907/474-2200;** http://aurora.ak.blm.gov/arcticinfo). They publish extensive information for driving and recreation on the highway on their web page and in the *Dalton Highway Road Guide,* which includes an indispensable map.

For information about businesses along the highway, try the **Fairbanks Convention and Visitors Bureau,** at 550 First Ave. (at Cushman St.), Fairbanks, AK 99701 (© **800/327-5774** or 907/456-5774; fax 907/452-2867; www. explorefairbanks.com).

Along the highway, there are two visitor information stops, both open summer only. A cabin **contact station** at the Yukon crossing is staffed by BLM volunteers and open daily in summer 9am to 6pm. It has no phone. A larger, **interagency center** is in Coldfoot (© **907/678-5209**), open 10am to 6pm daily.

ON THE ROAD

The bridge over the Yukon River at mile 56 is the only crossing in Alaska, and many people drive the Dalton just to get to the **Arctic Circle** at mile 115, where you'll find a colorful sign for pictures as well as a crude camping area. A number of places along the highway have incredible views, including Finger Mountain at mile 98; Gobbler's Knob at mile 132, which offers the first view of the Brooks Range; and 4,739-foot Atigun Pass at mile 245, where the road crosses the Brooks Range, winding through impossibly rugged country. The pass is the highest point on the Alaska road system, and you may find summer snow. All along the highway are opportunities to see birds and animals, including rabbits, foxes, wolves, moose, Dall sheep, bears, and caribou. Sit still if you want to see the skittish caribou, as they may wander closer to an unmoving vehicle.

The road parallels the 4-foot-wide **trans-Alaska pipeline.** The line, completed in 1977, serves America's largest and second-largest oil fields, Prudhoe Bay and Kuparuk, carrying the hot crude 900 miles from the Arctic Ocean to docks in Valdez, where tankers pick it up for shipment primarily to the West Coast. The public road ends before reaching the Prudhoe Bay complex and the Arctic Ocean. The only way through the gate is with a tour operator. See section 9 of chapter 10, on Prudhoe Bay, for details.

HIGHWAY SERVICES: FOOD, FUEL & LODGINGS

Among the three places offering services along the 414 miles of the Dalton, you won't find anything luxurious, or even similar to budget chains.

Yukon Ventures Alaska, at mile 56, just past the Yukon River Bridge (© **907/655-9001**), has a motel, a restaurant, a gift shop, fuel, and tire repair. The motel is a former pipeline construction camp and the food includes salmon, halibut, and Italian dishes.

The truck stop in Coldfoot, run by **Sukakpak Inc.,** at mile 175 (© **907/ 678-5201**), offers a variety of services, including lodging, a 24-hour restaurant, fuel, minor repairs, towing, RV hookup, laundry, a post office, and a gift shop. As at Yukon Ventures, the inn is made of surplus construction worker housing— not fancy, but with private bathrooms. The park service has a small campground 5 miles north.

After Coldfoot, the next service area is at **Deadhorse,** at the end of the road 240 miles north, with rooms, fuel, restaurants, a post office, vehicle maintenance, a general store, and an airport. See the Prudhoe Bay section in chapter 10.

GETTING OUT OF THE CAR
ACTIVITIES

HIKING   The road has no established hiking trails, but most of the area is open to self-reliant hikers who know how to pick their own route. The country opens up in the alpine **Brooks Range,** north of the Chandalar Shelf at mile 237. At upper elevations, you can avoid the vast swamps of the wet tundra, but you still will run into tussocks and stream crossings. Forests and brush make cross-country traveling more difficult south of the shelf. A popular destination is the **Gates of the Arctic National Park and Preserve,** to the west of the road, but consider going east. The country is more open, and major rivers lie between the road and the park. Topographical maps and advice on hiking the Brooks Range are available at the sources listed under "Visitor Information," above. Remember, this is remote wilderness; do your research, be prepared, and tell someone where you're going and when you'll be back.

FISHING   The Dalton is not a top fishing area, but there are fish in streams and lakes along the highway. Many of the streams have grayling, but you'll want to hike farther than a quarter mile from the road to increase your chances. A good bet is the **Jim River area** between miles 135 and 144, where the river follows the road and fishing pressure is more spread out. Many of the lakes along the road have grayling, and the deeper ones have lake trout and Arctic char. For detailed information, contact the Alaska Public Lands Information Center, or the **Alaska Department of Fish and Game,** 1300 College Rd., Fairbanks, AK 99701 (© **907/459-7228;** www.state.ak.us/adfg).

CAMPING

The Bureau of Land Management has several camping sites along the road, mostly just gravel pads left over from construction days. They are at:

- **Mile 60:** Artesian well, outhouses, and dump station.
- **Mile 98** (Finger Mountain): Nice views, outhouse, and wheelchair-accessible trail with interpretive signs.
- **Mile 115** (Arctic Circle): Outhouses and picnic tables, an interpretive display, and undeveloped campground without water.
- **Mile 150** (Grayling Lake): Pull-out with outhouse.
- **Mile 175** (Coldfoot): A private campground with hookups is part of the truck stop described above.
- **Mile 180** (Marion Creek): A developed BLM campground with 27 campsites, 11 of them for large RVs (no hookups). The campground has a well and outhouses; the self-service fee is $8.
- **Mile 235** (Arctic tree line): No improvements.
- **Mile 275** (Galbraith Lake): Undeveloped campground with outhouses about 5 miles off-road; state-operated landing strip.

6 The Alaska Highway

Detailed coverage of the entire 2,400-mile drive to Alaska is beyond our scope, but chapter 2's "Getting There" section provides the planning basics. Here I've covered the Alaska portion of the road, the 200 miles of the Alaska Highway that runs from the border with Canada to the terminus, in Delta Junction. This is mostly boring driving, hours of stunted black spruce and brush, either living or burned out. It's a relief when you hit the first major town, **Tok** (rhymes with Coke), 100 miles along. But don't get your hopes up. This is the only place where I've ever walked into a visitor center and asked what there is to do in town, only to have the host hold up her fingers in the shape of a goose egg and say, "Nothing." Another 100 miles (I hope you brought plenty of cassette tapes, because no radio station reaches out here) and you've made it to **Delta Junction.** There's a little more to do here, but it's still not a destination. Another 100 miles and you're in Fairbanks.

The main sources of information for the drive are based in Tok, the first town you hit after you cross the border. It acts as a threshold for the entire state. To plan the journey ahead, contact them, and see "Exploring the Interior," at the beginning of this chapter. One useful website, with many links, specializes in advice for Alaska Highway travelers: **www.alcanseek.com.**

I've arranged this section in order from the border with Canada heading west.

CROSSING THE BORDER

Remember to set your watch back an hour when crossing the border east to west—it's an hour later in Yukon Territory. Also, if you make significant purchases or rent rooms in Canada, you may be able to get a refund on the 7% goods and services tax (GST). See section 7 of this chapter, on Dawson City, for details.

CUSTOMS   Crossing the U.S./Canadian border either way is usually as simple as exchanging a few pleasantries with a smiling guard, but occasionally it can get more complicated. Visas are unnecessary going either way, but U.S. and Canadian citizens should carry **proof of citizenship** and **proof of residence.** A driver's license is usually enough, but a passport, voter's card, or birth certificate could be required. **Children** with their parents may need a birth certificate; children or teens under 18 unaccompanied by parents may need a letter from a parent or guardian, and children with a single parent should carry a letter from the other parent. There are no duties on products made in the United States or Canada; for items that you buy that originated in other countries, or alcohol or smoking supplies, see chapter 3. Products you buy in Alaska made of **ivory, fur, or other wildlife** will probably require special permits to be taken out of the United States, and it's easiest to have the store where you bought the item take care of it (see chapter 3 for details). Going into Canada, **firearms** other than hunting rifles or shotguns generally are not allowed, and you need to fill out a form and pay a $50 fee for guns that are allowed; contact the Canadian Firearms Center (© 800/731-4000; www.cfc.gc.ca) before you go to avoid problems. **Dogs and cats** require rabies certificates. If in doubt, call before you go, as the border is a long way from anywhere: **Canadian Customs** in Whitehorse (© 867/667-3943) or **U.S. Customs** in Anchorage (© 907/271-2675).

FROM THE BORDER TO TOK

The first 60 miles after entering the United States the road borders the Tetlin National Wildlife Refuge, whose broad wetlands are a summer home to duck and lesser sandhill cranes, as well as 114 other nesting species. Caribou show up all along the road in the winter. A **visitor center,** 7 miles past the border, at mile 1,229 (© 907/774-2245, headquarters 907/883-5312), overlooks rolling hills and lakes. It is open Memorial Day to Labor Day daily 8am to 5pm. The refuge also has two small campgrounds over the next 27 miles: Deadman, at mile 1,249, with 16 sites; and Lake View, at mile 1,256, with 8.

TOK

Originally called Tokyo Camp, a construction station on the highway, the name was shortened to Tok when it became unpopular after Pearl Harbor. Since then,

Tok's role in the world hasn't expanded much beyond being a stop on the road. With its location at the intersection of the Alaska Highway and the Glenn Highway to Glennallen—the short way to Anchorage and Prince William Sound—the town has built an economy of gas stations, gift stores, cafes, and hotels to serve highway travelers.

ESSENTIALS

GETTING THERE   You're surely passing through Tok with your own set of wheels. If you get stuck for some reason, one bus service or another can get you to Fairbanks, Anchorage, Whitehorse, or even Dawson City. **Parks Highway Express** (© **888/600-6001;** www.AlaskaShuttle.com) offers the most service. The most established is Gray Line's **Alaskon Express** (© **800/478-6388** or 907/883-2291; www.graylinealaska.com/alaskon.cfm).

VISITOR INFORMATION   Local boosters and public land agencies have combined to operate a large, informative visitor center to introduce highway travelers to Alaska. The government's part, the **Alaska Public Lands Information Center,** P.O. Box 359, Tok, AK 99780 (© **907/883-5667;** www.nps.gov/aplic), is open daily from 8am to 7pm in summer and from 8am to 4:30pm in winter. Besides answering questions, rangers offer talks and nature walks in the summer. The commercial portion, the **Main Street Visitor Center,** operated by the Tok Chamber of Commerce, P.O. Box 389, Tok, AK 99780 (© **907/883-5775;** www.TokAlaskaInfo.com), provides information on Tok and anywhere else you may be bound on the highway. They're open May 1 to September 15 daily 8am to 7pm.

 FAST FACTS: **Tok**

Bank   Tok has no bank, but ATMs are in the Three Bears store and at the Texaco station across the road from Fast Eddy's restaurant.

Hospital   **Tok Clinic** is on the Tok Cut-Off across from the fire station (© **907/883-5855**).

Police   Contact the **Alaska State Troopers** (© **907/883-5111**), near the intersection of the Alaska Highway and Glenn Highway.

Post Office   At the highway junction next to the Westmark Hotel.

Taxes   There are none in the region.

ACCOMMODATIONS

The motels are numerous and competitive in Tok. There also are many B&Bs; check at the visitor center.

The **Tok International Youth Hostel** (© **907/883-3745;** stout@aptalaska. net) occupies a MASH tent a mile off Mile 1322 Alaska Highway, 8 miles west of town, on Pringle Drive. Guests use an outhouse and need mosquito repellent. There are a shower and limited cooking facilities. Beds are $10 apiece; reservations are not necessary. It's closed September 15 to May 15.

Be sure to get the 25¢ state highway and campground map from the public lands center, which includes all the public campgrounds in Alaska. Three attractive state park campgrounds lie near Tok on the three highway links that radiate from the town. Each has a $10 self-service fee. There are lots of competitive RV parks in Tok, too. One that has wooded sites suitable for tent camping as well is the **Sourdough Campground,** 1½ miles south of town on the Glenn Highway (*©* **800/789-5543** Alaska and Yukon only, or 907/883-5543). They charge $24 for full hookups, $16 dry.

Snowshoe Motel & Fine Arts and Gifts *Value*   The 10 newer no-smoking rooms near the front are a real bargain. Each is divided into two sections by the bathroom, providing two separate bedrooms—great for families. The house-keeping seemed exceptionally good when I visited, and the outside walkways were decorated with flowers. The gift shop carries some authentic Native art as well as highway kitsch.

Across the highway from the information center (P.O. Box 559), Tok, AK 99789. *©* **800/478-4511,** in Alaska, Yukon, and part of B.C., or 907/883-4511. Fax 907/883-4512. snowshoe@aptalaska.net. 24 units. High season $72 double. Low season $52 double. Rates include continental breakfast in summer. Extra person $5. MC, V. *In room:* TV.

Westmark Tok   The central hotel in town is closed in the winter, as its clientele is primarily the package tour bus trade. It's made up of several buildings connected by boardwalks. The older rooms are narrow, without enough room at the foot of the bed for the TV, but they're comfortable and up-to-date. The new section has larger, higher-priced rooms. There's a "factory outlet" gift store in the lobby that sells remainders from Westmark's other shops for lower prices. A greenhouse grows huge vegetables. The restaurant serves three meals a day, with dinners in the $14-to-$20 range.

Intersection of Alaska and Glenn hwys. (P.O. Box 130), Tok, AK 99780-0130. *©* **800/544-0970** (reservations) or 907/883-5174. Fax 907/883-5178. www.westmarkhotels.com. 92 units. $109–$129 double. AE, DC, DISC, MC, V. Closed Sept 16–May 15. **Amenities:** Restaurant (cafe); bar. *In room:* TV.

Young's Motel   Good standard motel rooms occupy three one-story structures on the parking lot behind Fast Eddy's restaurant, where you check in. Eighteen newer, smoke-free rooms are the pick of the litter, but all are acceptable.

Behind Fast Eddy's Restaurant on the Alaska Hwy. (P.O. Box 482), Tok, AK 99780. *©* **907/883-4411.** Fax 907/883-5023. edyoung@aptalaska.net. 43 units. High season $76 double. Low season $55 double. Extra person $5. AE, DISC, MC, V. **Amenities:** Restaurant (described below); bar. *In room:* TV, dataport.

DINING

The only noteworthy restaurant in town is **Fast Eddy's** (*©* **907/883-4411**), on the right as you enter town from the east. Begun as a typical roadside cafe, it has developed into a place where a wine list and fine-dining entrees don't seem out of place. Yet the proprietor knows that most highway travelers just want a simple, relaxing meal, and the varied menu offers anything they might have in mind. I relish the salad bar and light dishes that offer a break from the usually carnivorous greasy-spoon choices found elsewhere along the highway. The dining room is decorated in dark wood and brass. They're open in summer 6am to midnight, in winter 7am to 11pm.

DELTA JUNCTION

This intersection with the Richardson Highway, which runs from Valdez to Fairbanks, is the official end of the Alaska Highway. It's an earnest little roadside town set in a broad plain between the Delta and Tanana Rivers. People make their living from farming and tourism, and at a trans-Alaska pipeline pump station south of town. Fort Greely, the recently closed Army base south of town, may become a nerve center for the national missile defense system, if that is ever built. For visitors, there are two historic roadhouse museums and several good campgrounds, but not enough to hold most for more than a few hours.

ESSENTIALS

VISITOR INFORMATION A helpful **visitor center** run by the Delta Chamber of Commerce, P.O. Box 987, Delta Junction, AK 99737 (*C* **877/ 895-5068** or 907/895-5068; 907/895-5069 summer only; www.deltajunction alaska.com), stands at the intersection of the Alaska and Richardson highways, in the middle of town; it's open May to mid-September.

 FAST FACTS: **Delta Junction**

Bank **Wells Fargo** is on the Richardson Highway at the center of town, with an ATM.

Hospital The **Family Medical Center** is at Mile 267.2 Richardson Highway, 2 miles north of the visitor center (*C* **907/895-4879** or 907/895-5100).

Police The **Alaska State Troopers'** emergency number is *C* **907/895-4800.** For nonemergencies, call *C* **907/895-4344.**

Post Office On the Richardson, 2 blocks north of the visitor center.

Taxes None of any kind.

ATTRACTIONS & ACTIVITIES

Before construction of the first road to Fairbanks in 1917 (today's Richardson Highway), travelers to the Interior followed a trail on basically the same route by horse in summer and dogsled in winter, stopping at roadhouses that provided food and shelter a day apart on the 2-week trip. Two well-preserved examples of the roadhouse system survive near Delta Junction.

In 1996, the Army saved the 1905 **Sullivan Roadhouse,** which had stood abandoned since 1922 on what became an Army bombing range. Today the log building stands next to the town visitor center and is open in summer 9am to 5:30pm Monday through Saturday as a free museum. Many of the Sullivan's original belongings have been set back in their original places, giving a strong feel for frontier life, but the heart of the restoration is the authentic hospitality of the local volunteers who show off the place with great pride.

The next stop on the trail was 16 miles toward Fairbanks. **Rika's Roadhouse and Landing,** 10 miles northwest of Delta on the Richardson Highway (*C* **907/895-4201;** http://rikas.com), still makes a pleasant stop on your drive. This roadhouse lasted later than the Sullivans' because drivers had to board a ferry here to cross the Tanana River until the 1940s, and the shore was the end of the line for Tanana stern-wheelers. The 1906 log building has been altered too much to feel real, but the grassy compound completes a vivid scene of Alaska pioneer life with surviving outbuildings, a gorgeous vegetable garden, and a pen of domestic fowl. A concessionaire manages the site for the Big Delta State Historical Park, with a restaurant serving soups, salads, and sandwiches daily 9am to 5pm; the grounds and museum are open 8am to 8pm, May 15 to September 15. An impressive suspension bridge carries the trans-Alaska pipeline over the Tanana River, and boaters use the shoreline, at the confluence of the Tanana and Delta rivers, as a landing.

ACCOMMODATIONS

The cute, funny, and hospitable **Kelly's Country Inn,** at the intersection of Richardson and Alaska highways (📞 **907/895-4667;** www.kellysalaskacountry inn.com), has rooms for $89 (double) right in the middle of town. You'll find basic rooms for $70 (double) at **Alaska 7 Motel,** 3548 Richardson Hwy. (📞 **907/895-4848;** www.alaskan.com/ak7motel). Check at the visitor center for a referral to one of the many B&Bs.

CAMPING

Alaska State Parks maintains five campgrounds on the rivers and lakes in and around Delta Junction and a couple of public cabins. Right on the highway near town, the **Delta State Recreation Area campground** lies among large spruce and birch trees, the sites well separated, some with walk-in privacy. It is the most attractive campground on the highway. The **Quartz Lake State Recreation Area,** 11 miles northwest of town on the Richardson Highway and down a 3-mile turnoff, has an 80-site campground on the shallow fishing lake. The camping fee at each is $10. For information, contact the **Department of Natural Resources Public Information Center,** 3700 Airport Way, Fairbanks, AK 99709 (📞 **907/451-2705;** www.dnr.state.ak.us/parks).

To park an RV, or if you're tent camping and need a shower, **Smith's Green Acres RV Park and Campground,** 1½ miles north on the Richardson Highway from the visitor center (📞 **800/895-4369** or 907/895-4369; www.akpub.com/ akbbrv/smith.html), has grassy sites and tent sites among the trees, cabins, a small playground, and laundry.

DINING

Buffalo Center Diner DINER   The locals eat here, for good reason. The dining room is light and clean and the menu covers everything you would hope for in a simple family restaurant—plus a seasonal list of buffalo dinners in honor of the Delta herd. Service is friendly and quick, and the waitress called me "Hon."

1680 Richardson Hwy. 📞 907/895-5089. Main courses $6.25–$25. MC, V. Summer Sun–Thurs 6am–9pm, Fri–Sat 6am–10pm. Winter Sun–Thurs 6am–8pm, Fri–Sat 6am–9pm.

7 Dawson City: Gold Rush Destination

A gold rush scatters the seeds of civilization promiscuously. It is an irrational force of history, driven by hysterical greed for a metal that could show up almost anywhere, and its unpredictable results have the dramatic allure of madness, leaving cities behind on the landscape as if at random. Dawson City's presence at the confluence of the Yukon and Klondike rivers is just such a historic accident. Certainly, no other chain of events could have built it here, in such a remote place, nor filled it with such an extraordinary cast of characters. Today, no other town I know of preserves so well the true look and setting of a gold rush city. Being so far from the rest of the world, Dawson City never had the chance to change.

Approaching by road accentuates the town's weird isolation, especially coming from the west over the Top of the World Highway. Hour after hour you bounce over the gravel, surrounded by the silhouettes of rounded mountains that stand all around in countless, receding layers, all quiet, all empty. Other than the border post and a nearby lodge, there are no signs of humankind. Vehicles pass rarely. Then, turn a corner, and there it is: a grid of city streets.

Dawson City, once the second largest city on the west coast of North America, is still way out in the middle of nowhere 100 years later.

In town, people stroll the wide, straight streets, gazing at well-kept old buildings. Inside a museumlike visitor center, guides dressed in period costumes provide tourists with directions and sell them tickets to shows. Looking back at the hill across the river, at the wilderness so close at hand, it's suddenly easy to understand the incongruity and shock of the gold rush. A little more than 100 years ago, the world suddenly went mad, rushed to this riverbank beyond the edge of civilization, and created an instant city. It arrived as suddenly as it arrives in your windshield on the highway.

Dawson City was the destination for some 100,000 stampeders hoping to strike it rich on the Klondike River in 1898, about 30,000 of whom actually made it here. Mining for gold and other minerals continues today, but the town's main focus is on the visitors who come to see a well-preserved gold rush boomtown. Parks Canada does a good job of keeping up the buildings that make up part of the **Klondike National Historic Sites** and providing activities that bring history alive; you can easily spend 2 full days here, if you're interested in the period the town celebrates. Dawson City sometimes feels like one big museum, and it doesn't suffer from the commercialism that pervades Skagway, the other major gold rush town in the region.

Since winter temperatures can drop to –40°F, Dawson gets mighty quiet in the off-season. Before the second week of May or after the second week of September, you're unlikely to find any attractions open, and few other businesses. The town wakes a little for winter dog mushing and snowmobiling events, but a visit then wouldn't include the historic aspect more people go for.

ESSENTIALS

GETTING THERE   Most visitors drive to Dawson City by making a long detour from the Alaska Highway into Canada. The paved **Klondike Highway,** also known as **Yukon Highway 2,** splits from the Alaska Highway a few miles west of Whitehorse, heading 327 miles north over scenic, fairly smooth road to Dawson City. For guidance on that part of the trip, get *Canada's Yukon Official Vacation Guide* from **Tourism Yukon,** P.O. Box 2703, Whitehorse, Yukon, Canada Y1A 2C6 (© **867/667-5340;** fax 867/667-3546; www.touryukon.com). The gravel **Top of the World Highway** heads west from Dawson City, crossing the border before connecting with the rough **Taylor Highway,** which leads north to Eagle and south to rejoin the **Alaska Highway,** 175 miles after Dawson City. The 502 miles for the detour compare to 375 miles if you stay on the pavement of the Alaska Highway. You do miss the spectacular vistas on Kluane Lake, but maybe you can see that on the way back. The border is open May 15 to September 15, 8am to 8pm Alaska time. See section 6 of this chapter, on the Alaska Highway, for a note on Customs.

Air North (© **867/993-5110**) flies round-trip between Fairbanks and Dawson City on Tuesdays, Thursdays, and Sundays, with fares starting at around US$200. **Gold City Tours** (© **867/993-5175**) offers an airport limousine, $10 one-way.

VISITOR INFORMATION   Parks Canada's **Dawson City Visitor Reception Centre,** King and Front streets (P.O. Box 390), Dawson City, YT, Canada Y0B 1G0 (© **867/993-5566;** http://parkscan.harbour.com/khs), is a mix of information center, museum, and theater of historic films, and is an indispensable stop.

Dawson City Area

ACCOMMODATIONS & DINING ■ ◆

Aurora Inn **15**
Bombay Peggy's Inn and Lounge **13**
The Bunkhouse **12**
Dawson City River Hostel **2**
Eldorado Hotel **11**
5th Ave. Bed & Breakfast **16**
Goldrush Campground RV Park **7**
Klondike Kate's Restaurant **6**
Ruby's Hideaway **10**
Triple J Hotel **9**
Westmark Inn Dawson **14**
Yukon River Campground **1**

ATTRACTIONS ●

Bear Creek Historic Mining Camp **3**
Commissioner's Residence **18**

Dawson City Museum **19**
Diamond Tooth Gertie's **8**
Gold Dredge # 4 **4**
Jack London Cabin **21**
Palace Grand Theatre **5**
Robert Service Cabin **20**
St. Paul's Anglican Church **17**

The hosts are knowledgeable and provide free maps and guides, as well as sell tickets to all the Klondike National Historic Sites tours, events, and shows. They're open daily in summer from 8am to 8pm. If you plan to do all or most of the town and gold field attractions, the six-tour pass sold here for Can$20 is a good deal.

The **Klondike Visitors Association,** housed in the same building as the Parks Canada center, above (P.O. Box 389P, Dawson City, YT, Canada Y0B 1G0; © **867/993-5575;** fax 867/993-6415; www.DawsonCity.com), offers information on local businesses, accommodations, and community events. The **Klondike Centennial Society** maintains the only year-round visitor center, at Third and King streets (© 867/993-1996); they're celebrating the gold rush centennial (now 4 years old) through 2002.

GETTING AROUND   You probably got to Dawson City in a car or RV. If not, cars are for rent from **Budget** (© **800/527-0700** or 867/993-5644; www. budget.com). Dropping off in Whitehorse adds around $250.

Bikes are a fun way to get to the outlying sights for strong riders and are available for rent at the **Dawson City River Hostel,** listed later in this chapter.

The free **George Black Ferry** crosses the Yukon 24 hours a day May to September, except for servicing early Wednesday mornings. The landing is at the north end of Front Street. On the other side is the Top of the World Highway, a provincial campground, and the hostel.

FAST FACTS: Dawson

Bank The **Canadian Imperial Bank of Commerce** at Second Avenue and Queen Street has an ATM.

Hospital For an **ambulance**, call ✆ **867/993-4444**. A **nursing station** is located at Sixth and Mission streets (✆ **867/993-4444**).

Police In an emergency, call the **Royal Canadian Mounted Police,** on Front Street near Turner (✆ **867/993-5555**).

Post Office On Fifth Avenue near Princess Street. A historic post office, with limited services, is at Third Avenue and King Street.

Time Zone Dawson City is on Pacific time, 1 hour later than Alaska. The time changes at the border.

Taxes The 7% goods and services tax (GST) applies to almost everything. See "Money Matters," below, for how to get some back.

SPECIAL EVENTS The **Yukon Quest International Sled Dog Race** passes through Dawson City each year on its way between Fairbanks and Whitehorse. It's held, naturally, in the deep cold of February.

The **Commissioner's Grande Ball,** in early June, is the social event of the year in Dawson City. **The Yukon Gold Panning Championships** and **Canada Day Celebrations** are on July 1. **The Dawson City Music Festival,** a miniature Woodstock (but better behaved), occurs in late July.

GOLD RUSH ATTRACTIONS

Start your visit at the Parks Canada **Dawson City Visitor Reception Centre,** at King and Front streets (see "Visitor Information," above), where you can get advice and maps and buy tickets to attractions. Parks Canada leads a daily **town walking tour** from here for $5. The guides are well trained and can open historic buildings you won't get to look inside otherwise. Without joining the tour, you can rent a 90-minute cassette tape version with headphones. Or you use one of the maps they distribute to make up your own walking tour; there are interesting buildings almost anywhere you wander. Here are some of the highlights.

On Front Street, just south of the visitor center, the newly restored steamer *Keno* sits on timbers. Next door, the **Canadian Bank of Commerce** is receiving a foundation-up restoration. At Third Avenue and Princess Street, **Bigg's Blacksmith Shop** is next to a gold rush era building that is slowly sinking into the permafrost. At Front and Church streets, 2 blocks south, **St. Paul's Anglican Church** is a charming, creaky 1902 structure on the riverfront. Next door, the **Commissioner's Residence,** an impressive mansion with a wraparound porch, standing amid beautifully planted grounds, has been restored with mostly original furnishings. A tour goes through daily at 4pm for $5. In back of the house, you'll find a log building that was part of the 1897 **Fort Herchmer,** and later a jail.

The **Dawson City Museum** ⚐, on Fifth Avenue between Church and Turner streets (✆ 867/993-5291), is the best-presented gold rush museum I've seen. The fascinating, tin-roofed neoclassical building housed the Territorial Government from 1901 until it moved to Whitehorse, and upstairs one of the galleries still doubles as an impressive courtroom. The galleries downstairs display gold rush artifacts in a way that makes them seem immediate and alive. The clutter

---

Tips Money Matters

Except as noted, *all the prices in this section are listed in Canadian dollars.* At this writing, a U.S. dollar would buy about C$1.55. Current rates are listed in the newspapers, or click on "Exchange Rates" at http://finance.yahoo.com. It's wise to exchange your currency at a bank or using an ATM, or to use credit cards, rather than exchanging money at a point of sale. Most Alaska businesses will accept Canadian small change at face value, but not dollar coins or bills.

Non-Canadians can get a refund on the 7% **goods and services tax (GST)** they pay on goods and accommodations, but not food, services, rentals, transportation, fuel, and the like, so long as the pre-tax expenditure on eligible items totals more than $200. You can get up to $500 back at a duty-free shop or any amount by applying to **Visitor Rebate Program,** Canada Customs and Revenue Agency, 275 Pople Rd., Ste. 104, Summerside, PE, C1N 6C6 Canada (© **800/668-4748** in Canada; 902/432-5608 outside Canada; www.ccra-adrc.gc.ca/visitors). Be sure to keep your receipts and present them and your goods as you leave Canada to get a Proof of Export. Pick up a booklet containing all the rules and an application from the visitor center.

---

common to this kind of museum is confined to the "visible storage" gallery upstairs, where a rich collection is housed inside glass-fronted cabinets. A cafe serves soup, muffins, coffee, and tea, and there's a gift shop. Admission is $5; the museum is open Victoria Day to Labour Day, daily from 10am to 6pm. Next door is a free display of 19th-century locomotives from the short-lived Klondike Mines Railway, which ran 32 miles up Bonanza Creek.

The **Jack London Cabin,** at Eighth Avenue and Firth Street along the foot of the bluff, is a replica with some logs from the original cabin where London probably spent his winter in the Klondike. (The rest of the logs are in a replica in Oakland, California, where London also lived.) A small museum with a guide is at the site. London found a gold mine of material for his classic adventure stories, but little actual gold, when he stampeded north.

Poet **Robert Service** spent more time at his cabin, at Eighth Avenue and Hansen Street, just down the road. Service wrote his ballads about the North while working as a bank clerk in Dawson City, reciting them for free drinks in the bars. Today you can hear them in tourist shows all over Alaska and the Yukon.

After the initial gold rush, the Rothschilds and Guggenheims financed large-scale industrial gold mining here. The remains of that impressive technical effort are preserved outside of town. **Gold Dredge No. 4,** 8 miles down Bonanza Creek Road south of town, is maintained by Parks Canada to show how these incredible earth-eating machines worked their way across the landscape, sifting gold out of the gravel; similar dredges are in Fairbanks and Nome. Hour-long tours, which circle the outside of the machine but don't go inside, take place hourly June to mid-September from 9am to 5pm and cost $5. Another 7 miles up the road, the site of the original Klondike strike is marked. Parks Canada also manages the **Bear Creek Historic Mining Camp,** 7 miles up the Klondike Highway. The camp was headquarters for the company that owned the gold diggings. It's been kept as if the workers just left, including warehouses and workshops full of odd and interesting mechanical relics. The highlight is the gold room, where the gold was melted into bricks. At the end, you can watch a documentary film about the mining made before the operation shut down in 1966. The tour takes place twice daily, at 1:30 and 3pm, and costs $5.

ON THE RIVER

Dawson City is the largest town on the Yukon River after Whitehorse, and the most developed access point near Alaska. The Yukon, flowing 5 to 10 miles per hour, is a slow-paced westward-flowing highway. Here you can join its journey, either on a tour boat or on your own, floating with the current in a canoe.

Gray Line Yukon, with an office at Front and King streets (© 867/993-5599; www.graylineofalaska.com), operates the *Yukon Queen II*, a large, high-speed catamaran that runs daily from late May to early September 104 miles down-river to Eagle. The boat leaves at 9am for a 4-hour narrated ride to Eagle with breakfast; once there, you can eat at the cafe and visit the museum. It returns at 3pm, going upstream in 5 hours and serving dinner before arriving back in Dawson City. Most passengers are on Holland America Tours packages, but you can book a seat if space is available. It's US$87 one-way, $144 round-trip. The office is across Front Street from the Visitor Reception Centre.

One popular trip is to float 3 or 4 days in a canoe or raft to Eagle (you can come back on the *Yukon Queen II,* paying $50 to carry your canoe on board). There are other, more remote floats in the area, or you can keep floating down the Yukon to Circle, or even farther. A company offering gear for one-way floats to Eagle is listed below, in section 8 of this chapter, on Eagle; their Dawson City office is at the hostel mentioned below. The **Dawson Trading Post** (© 867/993-5316; www.dawsontradingpost.yk.ca) rents canoes and camping gear, and operates a shuttle that can drop you off on the more remote Stewart River for $175. Canoes rent for $150 a week.

ACCOMMODATIONS

In addition to the hotels and inn listed below, there are several good B&Bs in Dawson City, including the **5th Avenue Bed and Breakfast,** on Fifth Avenue next door to the museum (© 867/993-5941; 5thave@dawson.net). It has seven fresh, basic rooms. Three have their own bathrooms, and there are two kitchens for guests to use. **Triple J Hotel** has inexpensive rooms and cabins right in town at Fifth Avenue and Queen Street (© 867/993-5323; www.triplejhotel.com).

Dieter Reinmuth operates the **Dawson City River Hostel** (© 867/993-6823; www.yukonhostels.com), across the Yukon from Dawson City on the free ferry mid-May through September. Bunks in cabins, private rooms, and camping are available. A bunk is $16.50 for nonmembers, a private room $34 double. He also rents bicycles and canoes for $20 a day.

The wooded provincial **Yukon River Campground,** just down the road, has 98 sites, many on the riverside; the fee is $8. The **Goldrush Campground RV Park,** at Fifth Avenue and York Street (© 867/993-5247), is a conveniently located lot right downtown.

Aurora Inn ⭐ This pleasant little inn behind a false front on a boardwalk street has the added advantage of proprietors, Romy and René Jansen, who value an uncluttered atmosphere and immaculate housekeeping. On each visit, every-thing has been perfectly kept. Rooms have their own tiled bathrooms with shower stalls and are decorated with quilts and stripped-log furniture. To watch TV you must visit the comfortable front room. They serve a continental break-fast for $9.

Fifth and Harper sts. (P.O. Box 1748), Dawson City, Yukon Y0B 1G0. ℂ **867/993-6860.** Fax 867/993-5689. www.wildandwooly.yk.net. 18 units. High season $119 double; $180 suite. Low season $80 double; $140 suite. MC, V. **Amenities:** Jacuzzi; concierge; courtesy van; tour desk; business center; laundry service. *In room:* Dataport, hair dryer.

Bombay Peggy's Inn and Lounge ★★   This small inn occupies an impressive gold rush building—at various times it was a mining company office, a boardinghouse, and a brothel. Now it is one of the best lodgings in the region. Spaces with high ceilings and hardwood floors are decorated in a heavy Victorian theme fitting for the time period the inn recalls, carried all the way through to the antique bathtubs. Free sherry is served in the afternoon. Atypically for Dawson City, the inn is open year-round.

First and Princess sts. (P.O. Box 411), Dawson City, YT, Y0B 1G0. ℂ **867/993-6969.** Fax 867/993-6199. www. klondikeweb.com/bombay. 9 units, 6 with private bathroom. High season $89 shared bathroom, $159 private bathroom, $179 suite. Low season $79 shared bathroom, $119 private bathroom, $139 suite. $10 each additional person. MC, V. No smoking, no children. **Amenities:** Bar; courtesy van. *In room:* TV/VCR, hair dryer.

The Bunkhouse *Value*   This is a unique place—it looks like a riverboat from the outside, and is fresh and trim, but it's intended for budget travelers. The rooms, all no-smoking and each with its own exterior entry, have varnished wooden floors and attractive fabrics. The beds are really bunks—no bedsprings. Those that share bathrooms are quite small; the bathrooms are clean, but the showers for men and women are in the same room, shielded only by stalls with doors. The rooms with private bathrooms have telephones and TVs.

Front and Princess sts. (Bag 4040), Dawson City, YT, Canada Y0B 1G0. ℂ **867/993-6164.** Fax 867/993-6051. 31 units, 5 with private bathroom. $59 double without bathroom, $89–$95 double with bathroom. Extra person $5. MC, V. Closed in winter.

Westmark Inn Dawson ✿   The modern, well-run Westmark is the best hotel in town. I especially liked the newer Jack London and Robert Service wings, where wide, well-lit hallways lead to large rooms with crisp gold rush–theme decorative touches. The older rooms are good, too, but are smaller and have older decor. Ask for the "highway rate." A patio in the grassy courtyard is the site of a daily barbecue. **Belinda's Restaurant,** with light-wood decor and well-spaced tables, is open daily from 6am to 9pm.

Fifth Ave. and Harper St. (P.O. Box 420), Dawson City, YT, Canada Y0B 1G0. ℂ **800/544-0970** (reservations) or 867/993-5542. Fax 867/993-5623. www.westmarkhotels.com. 131 units. $129–$169 double. AE, DC, MC, V. Closed Sept 15 to May 15. **Amenities:** Restaurant (cafe); bar; coin-op laundry. *In room:* TV.

DINING & NIGHTLIFE

I've described the restaurant at the Westmark Inn Dawson, above. Bombay Peggy's Inn and Lounge also serves good finger food. The restaurant at the **Triple J Hotel,** at Fifth Avenue and Queen Street (ℂ **867/993-5323**), has a broad and varied menu and nice outdoor dining area. **Klondike Kate's Restaurant,** in a historic building at Third Avenue and King Street (ℂ **867/993-6527**), offers decent food for low prices, and has a fully licensed bar. The patio is pleasant.

For fine dining, the best (and really the only) choice is **Ruby's Hideaway,** at Second and Queen streets (ℂ **867/993-5721**), which specializes in Cajun and French cuisine, but also serves steak and seafood. It's an intimate, handcrafted experience—each table is set differently—with lace, stained glass, and antiques. Lunch is $8 to $10, dinner $18 to $33.

Some of Dawson City's most famous and fun activities are in the evening. **Diamond Tooth Gertie's,** at Fourth Avenue and Queen Street (ℂ **867/993-5575**), operated by the Klondike Visitors Association, is a gambling hall and bar, with tame cancan dancing and cabaret singing floor shows. It's a fun place to go with a group. The shows, each different, play three times nightly. It's open Tuesday to Sunday from 7pm to 2am, and admission is $6 for all evening, with only those at least 19 years old admitted.

The *Gaslight Follies* is a 2-hour vaudeville show nightly at 8pm in the **Palace Grand Theatre,** a historic building at Second Avenue and King Street that has been renovated by Parks Canada. Tickets ($15 to $17 for adults, $7.50 for children) are on sale at the box office from 3pm. Parks Canada also leads tours through the theater at 10:30am daily; it costs $5 at the Visitors Reception Centre.

8 A Detour to Eagle via the Top of the World & Taylor Highways

Sometime before World War I, the tiny town of Eagle got lost in an eddy in the stream of history, where it still awaits discovery by the outside world. The town was founded in 1898 as a subtle fraud, when a group of prospectors staked out the land then cleverly created a buzz in Dawson City, just upriver across the border, of a gold discovery. The federal government followed the rush, and in 1900, Judge James Wickersham chose Eagle for a new courthouse to try to bring law to the wild country. But when gold really was found in Fairbanks, the attention of prospectors and of Wickersham moved on, leaving Eagle slowly to decline to a ghost town of only nine residents by 1953.

But that's where the really exceptional part of the story begins. The few remaining people recognized the value of the history that had been left behind—Wickersham's papers were still in his desk where he'd left them—and formed the historical society that today is the main activity for the town's 150 residents. Visitors can tour the courthouse, customs house, and five museums, and use Eagle for the start or end of a history-drenched Yukon River float. You'll also see the places John McPhee wrote about in his classic *Coming into the Country.*

The reason Eagle is still so interesting is that it's still isolated, 173 dusty miles from Tok or 144 from Dawson City. It's a major side trip from the route between the two cities, which are 187 road miles apart, adding at least a day to your trip.

The **Taylor Highway** runs 160 miles north from the Alaska Highway just east of Tok to Eagle, 4 or 5 hours over a rough gravel road that's open only in summer. This is the Fortymile Country, around the past and current gold mining of the Fortymile River drainage. It's a remote country, mostly managed by the **Bureau of Land Management,** Tok Field Office, P.O. Box 309, Tok, AK 99780 (© **907/883-5121;** wwwndo.ak.blm.gov/fortymile/FMwelcome.html). There are no services or signs of human development on the way except at the town of **Chicken,** barely a wide spot in the road 66 miles north, with gas, a couple of shops, a bar, and a cafe, but no phone. The drive does have impressive views in spots, and at mile 96, the Taylor meets the Top of the World Highway, described below. That's the road more traveled. If you instead choose to go on to Eagle, you turn to the north for the last 66 miles of rough, winding road through lovely canyons and forest. That distance doesn't sound great, but at best it takes the better part of 2 hours, one-way, on this crude dirt road. There are two **campgrounds** along the Taylor, at mile 49 and mile 82, maintained by the BLM office mentioned above. The fee for each is $8. The BLM also is responsible for the **Fortymile National Wild and Scenic River,** a system with several floats of various lengths and levels of difficulty. The BLM or the public land information center in Tok can provide a river guide brochure and advice, or get

The Alaska River Guide, mentioned at the beginning of this chapter in a sidebar called "Rollin' on the River."

The **Top of the World Highway** connects mile 96 of the Taylor with Dawson City, 79 miles east. If you're starting this drive in Dawson City, you might take the Top of the World to connect with the Taylor, which continues on to Eagle. The Canadian part of the gravel highway is better maintained and stunningly beautiful on a clear day. You drive over the tops of mountains, treeless alpine vistas spreading far to the horizon. Just west of the border, 13 miles from the junction, there's a small roadhouse at a place called Boundary, the only habitation on the way. Open when the border is open, it has no phone. The border is open May 15 to September 15 8am to 8pm Alaska time. (Don't forget that it's an hour later in Yukon.) The road closes entirely in winter. See section 6, "The Alaska Highway," earlier, for information on Customs.

Don't plan on making 60 miles an hour on any of these unpaved roads. In the Canadian section, most of the road is fairly broad and smooth, but speeds over 45 or so contribute to losing control or losing a headlight or windshield to a rock from a passing vehicle. On the U.S. side, the road is poorly maintained in places, and you sometimes have to go quite slowly. Part of the Taylor Highway itself was mined for gold a few years ago.

Eagle has the historic sites and the Yukon River. The **Eagle Historical Society and Museum** (© **907/547-2325**) offers town walking tours Memorial Day to Labor Day, daily at 9am; the 3-hour tour costs $5. Or for the admission plus $10 more for a group, they'll do the tour anytime you like, winter or summer. The guides are local people, brimming with pride and knowledge about the area. Find them at the courthouse at Second and Berry streets. Even if you don't take the tour, a great little museum downstairs is open around the middle of the day. The tour takes you through various historic buildings loaded with the original materials left behind after the gold rush, including five buildings in the army's 1899 Fort Egbert, where Gen. Billy Mitchell had his first major assignment, in 1901 (before he was a general), to build a telegraph line to Valdez. You'll also notice the monument to Norwegian explorer Roald Amundsen, who stopped off in Eagle in 1905 during his journey through the Northwest Passage—400 miles away by dogsled—to use the telegraph.

The office of the **Yukon–Charley Rivers National Preserve** is across the airstrip on the west side of town. The preserve starts a few miles downstream on the Yukon and extends almost to Circle. The **National Park Service field office,** P.O. Box 167, Eagle, AK 99738 (© **907/547-2233;** www.nps.gov/yuch), is a good place to get information on floating the river and to register your journey. It's open Memorial Day through September, daily from 8am to 5pm, and normal business hours year-round. The staff can also provide lots of information on the area's natural history and historic sites.

You can start or finish a **river float** in Eagle. From Dawson City to Eagle is 108 miles and takes 3 or 4 days, and from Eagle to Circle is 158 miles and 5 to 7 days. Mike Seger's **Eagle Canoe Rentals,** based in Eagle (© **907/547-2203** in Eagle or 867/993-6823 in Dawson City; paddleak@aptalaska.net), allows you to drop off the canoe at the end of your float, and also rents rafts. The Dawson City office is located at the Dawson City River Hostel on the west side of the river next to the free ferry landing. The price, including return of the canoe, is $110 for up to 4 days Dawson to Eagle, $165 up to 5 days Eagle to Circle, and additional days are $20. You can take the *Yukon Queen* tour boat back upriver (see section 7 of this chapter, on Dawson City).

The **Eagle Trading Company** (© 907/547-2220) is the main business in town, with a grocery store, gas station, public showers, restaurant, and motel. Their **Riverside Cafe** offers inexpensive food in a dining room overlooking the river. The nine **motel rooms** also are good, with TVs and phones, tubs with showers, two queen beds in each, and a rate of only $70 double. An attractive **BLM campground** with well-wooded sites is located in the woods above Fort Egbert. It costs $8 per night. Contact the BLM for information.

9 Wrangell–St. Elias National Park & Kennecott

Looking at a relief map of Alaska, you'd think the portion drained by the Copper River was so overweighted with mountains that it might topple the whole state into the Pacific. The Alaska Range, in the center of the state, has the tallest mountain, but this Gulf of Alaska region, straddling the Alaska-Yukon border, has more mass—the second- and fourth-tallest mountains in North America (Logan and St. Elias), plus 9 of the tallest 16 peaks in the United States. Four mountain ranges intersect, creating a mad jumble of terrain covering tens of millions of acres, a trackless chaos of unnamed, unconquered peaks. The Copper River and its raging tributaries slice through it all, swallowing the gray melt of innumerable glaciers that flow from the largest ice field in North America. Everything here is the largest, most rugged, most remote; words quickly fall short of the measure. But where words fail, commerce gives a little help: These mountains are so numerous and remote that one guide service makes a business of taking visitors to mountains and valleys that no one has ever explored before.

Ironically for such a wild land, the area's main attraction for visitors is its history. The richest copper deposit in the world was found here in 1900 by a group of prospectors who mistook a green mountaintop for a patch of green grass where they could feed their horses. It was a mountain of almost pure copper, with metallic nuggets the size of desks (one is at the University of Alaska Museum in Fairbanks). The deposit produced trainloads of 70% copper ore so rich it required no processing before shipping, lots more copper that did need minimal processing, and much more lower-grade ore still left underground. The Alaska Syndicate, an investment group that included J. P. Morgan and Daniel Guggenheim, built the Kennecott Copper Corporation from this wealth (its name was a misspelling of the Kennicott River and Glacier, where the copper was found). To get the copper out, they paid for an incredible 196-mile rail line up from Cordova (see chapter 7), and created a self-contained company town deep in the wilderness, called **Kennecott.** When the high-grade ore was gone, in 1938, they pulled the plug, leaving a ghost town of extraordinary beauty that still contains machinery and even documents they left behind.

Wrangell–St. Elias National Park and Preserve now owns Kennecott and more than 13 million acres across this region of Alaska. It's the largest national park in the United States by a long shot, six times the size of Yellowstone and about 25% larger than the entire country of Switzerland. The protected land continues across the border in Canada, in **Kluane National Park,** which is similarly massive. Most of that land is impossibly remote, but Wrangell–St. Elias has two rough gravel roads that allow access to see the mountains from a car. The main route is the abandoned roadbed of the Copper River and Northwestern Railroad leading to Kennecott and the historic sites there. It's an arduous but rewarding journey by car, requiring at least 2 days to do it right. Air taxis, river guides, and remote lodges offer other ways into the park's untouched wilderness, mostly starting from **McCarthy,** a historic village near Kennecott. There are a few trails near Kennecott, but only for day hikes. Rare in the world, this is a country where experienced outdoors people can get away from any trace of humans for weeks on end.

THE KENNECOTT & MCCARTHY AREA

This historic copper area is the only part of the park most visitors see, as it's the most accessible and has the most services, interesting sites, and paths to explore. It's still not easy to get to, however—that's why it's still so appealing—and there's little point in going without adequate time. You can hit the highlights at Kennecott and McCarthy in one long, full day, but just getting there takes time. My family and I spent 3 nights on our last visit and could have stayed longer.

The main event is the ghost town at **Kennecott,** whose red buildings gaze from a mountainside across the Kennicott Glacier in the valley below. Now owned by the Park Service, the buildings made up an isolated company town until 1938, when it abruptly shut down. Tourists coming here as late as the 1960s saw it as if frozen in time, with breakfast dishes still on the tables from the day the last train left. Most of that was looted and destroyed in the 1970s, but when I toured the company store recently, old documents still remained, and the powerhouse and 14-story mill buildings still had their heavy iron and wood equipment. Besides the buildings, there are excellent hiking trails, including one that traverses the glacier. The town now has only a few year-round residents, but in summer there's a lodge, a couple of bed-and-breakfasts, guide services, and a Park Service meeting hall.

Five miles down the road, Kennecott's twin town of **McCarthy** served the miners as a place to drink, gamble, and hire prostitutes on their rare days off— the company didn't allow any frivolity in Kennecott or in the bunkhouses high up on the mountain. McCarthy retains the relaxed atmosphere of its past, with businesses and residents living in false-front buildings not much changed from Wild West days. More of a year-round community, McCarthy has restaurants, lodging, flight services, and other businesses.

Yet even this most populous part of the park is isolated and sparsely inhabited, with few services. Only 42 people live in the greater area year-round. You will find no banking services, general stores, gas stations, clinics, police, or anything else you're used to relying on. Phones came to McCarthy and Kennecott only within the last few years; there still are few, and none along the McCarthy Road. Bring what you need.

ESSENTIALS

GETTING THERE   By Car   The **Edgerton Highway** starts 17 miles south of Copper Center on the Richardson Highway, then runs east for 33 miles to the tiny, dried-up former railroad town of **Chitina** (*chit*-na), the last reliable stop for groceries, gas, and other necessities until you return here. Do fill your tank; prudence also demands a full-sized spare tire. Heading east, into the park, the **McCarthy Road** continues along the roadbed of the Copper River and Northwestern Railroad. It's 60 miles of narrow dirt road, rutted and prone to mud holes in wet weather, but the drive is a fun adventure. The road passes through tunnels of alders and crosses rivers on some of the original wooden railroad trestles; one wood-decked bridge spans a canyon more than 200 feet deep. There are virtually no services and no more than two or three buildings on the entire 3-hour drive. There's a good chance you won't encounter another vehicle. The road ends at a crude campground, a parking lot, and collection of temporary businesses on the banks of the Kennicott River. Here you must leave your vehicle; parking costs $5 a day (© **907/554-4401**). From there, walk across a footbridge or two. Late in the summer the Kennicott Glacier releases a flood from a glacier-dammed lake, but at other times the second channel is a dry wash and the second bridge isn't needed. Handcarts are available to move your luggage across, and on the other side you can catch a van. The place you are staying will send one, or you can buy a ticket on a **van** operated by **Wrangell Mountain Air** (© **907/554-4411**) for $5 per person, one-way. A free public telephone and an information kiosk are near the bridge; use the phone to call the van or your lodgings.

By Bus   The **Backcountry Connection** (© **866/582-5292** or 907/822-5292; bakcntry@alaska.net) runs a van from Glennallen and Chitina to the footbridge daily in summer except Monday, leaving at 7am and 8:30am, respectively, arriving at the bridge at 11:45am; it returns at 4pm, getting back to Chitina at 7pm and Glennallen at 8:30pm. The fare is $80 round-trip from Chitina, $99 from Glennallen, and $10 more if you return on a different day. I think a 4-hour stay would be too brief.

By Air   The simplest way to Kennecott and McCarthy is to fly there on one of the air taxis, then get around on one of the vans that shuttles back and forth over 5 miles of dirt road. **Wrangell Mountain Air** (© **800/478-1160** or 907/554-4411; www.wrangellmountainair.com) offers twice-daily service from Chitina for $140 round-trip. You can charter from anywhere. A five-passenger plane is $795 from Anchorage, $495 from Valdez, one-way. Another reputable operator is **McCarthy Air** (© **888/989-9891** or 907/554-4440; McCarthyAir. com). Both operators also offer charters to remote park valleys and glaciers for backcountry trips, covered below under "Getting Outside: Hiking & Backpacking." It's also possible to fly a small, prop mail plane from Anchorage to Gulkana and then Gulkana to McCarthy for a total of about $230 one-way. **Security Aviation** (© **907/248-2677**) flies to Gulkana, and Ellis Air Taxi (© **907/822-3368**; www.ellisair.com) flies from there to McCarthy.

VISITOR INFORMATION   The park visitor center is just north of Copper Center, a mile off the Richardson Highway on the old Richardson Highway (© **907/822-5234**; www.nps.gov/wrst). A new center, right on the highway, should be completed sometime in 2002. Stop in to buy maps and publications or to get advice from a ranger on outdoor treks. The office is open Memorial Day to Labor Day, daily from 8am to 6pm; in winter, Monday to Friday from 8am to 4:30pm. You can write for information at P.O. Box 439, Copper Center, AK 99573.

The **Chitina Ranger Station** (© **907/823-2205**) is along the most popular way to the park, in Chitina, 33 miles down the paved Edgerton Highway, which starts about 17 miles south of Copper Center on the Richardson Highway. The center is arranged like a reading room, with lots of material to consult, historic photographs on display, and rangers who help visitors figure out backcountry trips. There's a picnic table out front. Like almost all visitor services in the area, it is closed in winter. Summer hours are 10am to 6pm daily.

The Park Service is just starting to develop **visitor services in Kennecott** itself. Usually you'll find a ranger there during the day and often giving a talk in the evening in the hall across the road from the lodge. A visitor center is planned.

The **Kennicott-McCarthy Chamber of Commerce**, P.O. Box MXY, McCarthy, AK 99588, lacks a phone or office, but you can find lots of information about the area on the web at **www.mccarthy-kennicott.com**, including the charming bimonthly newspaper, a link to the chamber, and an online visitor guide.

GETTING AROUND   A great way to get around on your own is by bicycle. You can rent bikes for $20 a day at the **Glacier View Campground,** a half-mile short of the footbridge on the McCarthy Road (© **907/554-4490**).

ATTRACTIONS & ACTIVITIES IN THE TOWNS

CHITINA   Chitina lost its reason to exist in 1938, when the last train ran on the Copper River line, but it lives on with 123 residents supporting themselves largely with salmon in the river, produce from their gardens, berries from the forests, and the few tourists who stop. There's a general store and a couple of gas stations (the last gas for many a mile), a wayside at the site of the old depot, a pond where you can often see trumpeter swans, the ranger station, and, down by the river, lazily rotating fish wheels built by Alaska Natives to pluck fish from the river. The Copper River is too turbid for angling, but clear water tributaries and stocked lakes in the area have fish. You can also explore about 20 miles south on the old Copper River rail line and even through the tunnels; check with a local or the ranger station for advice and current conditions before trying it. The best stop in town is **Spirit Mountain Artworks** (© **907/823-2222;** Spirit-Mountain@mindspring.com), where an old building has been lovingly restored into a historic landmark to house fine art and crafts.

MCCARTHY   McCarthy feels authentic as soon as you walk down the dirt main street between the false fronts. On a summer evening young backpackers and locals stand in the road—there is no traffic, since there are almost no vehicles—meeting and talking, carrying their glasses of beer from the lodge over to the ice cream shop, laughing loudly, walking around the dogs that are having their own party. Along the street, there are flight service offices to arrange a trip out, a couple of restaurants, and a lodge. Then, a street beyond, unbroken wilderness for hundreds and perhaps thousands of miles. The people here know it's unique, and everyone hopes it doesn't change. No one wants a big flood of tour-bus visitors—that's why they fought the state government when it wanted to build a road bridge over the Kennicott; they prefer to have the McCarthy Road rough instead of smooth. The foot-bridge should keep too many casual visitors at bay. Those who do make it are treated like one of the community.

KENNECOTT   This has got to be one of the world's greatest ghost towns, with some 40 buildings, mostly in good enough condition to be reused today—indeed, until the current Park Service restoration project began, the community still played basketball in one structure. Some historic buildings have become lodgings, and the Park Service plans to eventually move into the store. Locals still pick rhubarb and chives from the company garden. History has the same kind of immediacy here that you get from holding an old diary in your hand, quite different from the sanitized history-through-glass that you're used to at more accessible sites.

The Park Service bought most of the buildings a few years ago and has closed everything up while they are stabilized and made safer. When we walked through, on the eve of the takeover, items remained out on the ground or on store shelves that would be in museums in many places. If Kennecott were an ordinary industrial site, that would be interesting enough, but this place was something well out of the ordinary: an outpost beyond the edge of the world where men built a self-contained city almost a century ago. The hardship of the miners' lives and the ease of the managerial families' lives also present a fascinating contrast.

You can take in some of it by wandering around with a walking tour booklet (available at a Park Service kiosk in the ghost town) and reading signs, but it would be a mistake to miss going inside, and to do that you need to join a **guided tour.** One good company offering these is **St. Elias Alpine Guides** (© **888/993-5427** or 907/544-4445; full listing below under "Hiking and Backpacking"); they charge $25 per person. Their tour lasts much of the afternoon and goes into real depth on the geology and history, as well as climbs to the perilous 14th floor of the mill building.

GETTING OUTSIDE

HIKING & BACKPACKING   There are a few trails radiating from Kennecott, for which crude maps are available from the rangers and others around town, or buy the **Trails Illustrated** topographic map, printed on plastic, also for sale at the ranger stations (see "Fast Facts: Alaska," in chapter 2). An impressive walk continues through the ghost town up the valley, paralleling the Kennicott Glacier and then its tributary, the Root Glacier. You can either climb along the Root's edge to a towering ice fall, or traverse the glacial ice on a trail branch. It's wise to join a group if you want to walk on the glacier, as it can be dangerous. St. Elias Alpine Guides, listed below, accepts walk-ins for daily glacier day hikes and other hikes and tours. A half day on the glacier goes for $50 a person, while all-day hikes are $80 and ice-climbing lessons $100. Another fascinating hike you can do on your own leads straight up the mountain behind the Kennecott buildings to the old mines and bunkhouses, 3,000 feet higher on the alpine tundra.

Beyond the trails, the park is endless miles of trackless wilderness—one of earth's last few places that really deserves that name. Fit hikers without the backcountry experience to mount their own expedition should join one of the guides who work in the area. **St. Elias Alpine Guides** (© **888/933-5427** or 907/ 554-4445; winter 907/345-9048; www.steliasguides.com) offers day hikes, rafting, backpacking trips, and alpine ascents, but specializes in guiding extended trips to unexplored territory. Bob Jacobs, president of the company, stopped guiding on Mount McKinley years ago because of the crowds. He claims never to have seen another party in more than 20 years of guiding expeditions in Wrangell–St. Elias, and has led more than 45 parties of customers up previously unclimbed peaks. By definition, you can't get farther from civilization. A 2-week trek and climb, including 4 days of mountaineering instruction, is a big commitment and costs $3,000 and up, but then, first ascents are a finite resource. The St. Elias catalog will make anyone who loves backpacking drool. Trips begin at $775 for a 4-day Donoho Peak trek. They are all-inclusive, but not without hardship and risk—nothing can take away from the severity of this wild country.

Hiking on your own in a wilderness largely without trails is a whole new kind of experience for veteran backpackers and outdoors people who are used to more crowded parts of the planet. You feel like an explorer rather than a follower. At times, there's a fairy-tale sense of the world unfolding around you, as fresh as creation. If you're not prepared to select your own route—a task only for those already experienced in trackless, backcountry traveling—there are various established ways through the park you can follow with a topographic map. You can get a trip synopsis from the visitor center or ranger station, or download from their website (www.nps.gov/wrst). Rangers can help you choose a route to suit your party, although none are easy. Some routes start from the roads, but a better way to go is to charter a flight into a remote valley from one of the two **air services** in McCarthy. The planes land on gravel strips, river bars, glaciers, and any other flat places the pilots know about. These companies make a business of flying out backpackers, and so have established rates for different landing sites and can help with determining a route that's right for you, as well as provide a list of supplies. You can do it for $70 to $300 per person, with at least two passengers. Or fly in to a lake or river for fishing and exploring from a base camp, eliminating some of the worry about how much you pack. Two operators are listed above, under "Getting There."

Note: I wouldn't want to scare off anyone who would really be able to manage one of these trips, but people do get in trouble in the Alaska wilderness every year, and some of them don't come back. Before you head out into the backcountry, you must know how to take care of yourself where help is unavailable, including how to handle river crossings, bear avoidance, preventing hypothermia, basic first aid, and other issues. Unless you have plenty of backpacking experience in less remote areas, I wouldn't recommend starting here.

MOUNTAIN BIKING   Anywhere else, the 60-mile road that leads to this area would be considered a mountain-biking trail. You also can make good use of bikes between McCarthy, Kennecott, and the footbridge. An old **wagon road** parallels the main road that connects the two towns, 4.5 miles each way; the road itself is a one-lane dirt track. Advanced cyclists can also ride the trails around Kennecott described above under "Hiking & Backpacking."

RAFTING   Many great, wild rivers drain these huge mountains, which are still being carved by enormous glaciers. The **Kennicott River,** starting at the glacier of the same name, boils in Class III rapids for some 40 minutes starting right from the footbridge at the end of the McCarthy Road. As the area lacks roads, however, most trips must include a plane ride at least one way, and that makes white-water rafting day trips here more expensive than outings near Anchorage or Valdez. At times, hour-long, drive-back floats have been available on a walk-in basis at the footbridge, but most trips punch deeper into the backcountry. The Kennicott River meets the Nizina, passing through a deep, dramatic canyon; then the Nizina River flows into the Chitina River, which meets the Copper River near the town of Chitina, 60 miles from the starting point. The Copper River flows to the ocean. A float from the footbridge through the Nizina Canyon takes all day, with lunch and bush plane flightseeing back, which could include a glacier fly-over. St. Elias Alpine Guides (see "Hiking & Backpacking," above) charges $245. Other trips continue 3 or 4 days to Chitina, for $575 to $850 per person; or 10 to 13 days, 180 miles all the way to the Copper River Delta and the sea (see "Cordova" in chapter 7), for $2,500 to $2,900 per person. This is Alaska on its largest and most grandiose scale, accessible only from the banks of these great rivers.

ACCOMMODATIONS

There's no standard hotel room in the Kennecott-McCarthy area, but there are several attractive places to stay, all thick with the history the towns represent. Besides the three recommended below, I was impressed with houses for rent behind the Kennecott ghost town. The two I saw were **Kennicott Cottage** (© **907/242-1392** in Kennicott or 907/345-7961 in Anchorage; www.alaska. net/~kenncott/kcc.htm), and, right next door, 17 **Silkstocking Row** (© **612/ 722-3678;** www.alaska.net/~lei). You can rent one room, a two-bedroom suite, or the whole three-bedroom house, with breakfast fixings provided. Although they lack electricity, they have running water and showers, propane light, heat, and refrigeration. The only drawback of the attractively restored houses is a lack of flush toilets.

A family that lives here year-round hosts guests in a house next door to their own, a historic, unspoiled residence in the woods behind the ghost town, once the home of the family of a Kennecott Copper manager. Their warmth is infectious, giving guests a chance to make friends of people living a real pioneer lifestyle. The rental unit even has indoor plumbing. You can rent one room for two with shared bath, or take both units for four and have the house to yourself. Cook your own meals in the full kitchen.

Silk Stocking Row, Kennicott. (McCarthy no. 4, P.O. Box MXY, Glennallen, AK 99588). 🕿 **907/554-4469.** Fax 907/554-4469. 2 units. $175 for 2, $250 for 4. Extra adult $25, child 4–12 $15. Rates include continental breakfast. MC, V.

Kennicott Glacier Lodge ★★ This is the area's largest and most comfortable accommodation, a first-class place that takes the edges off the isolation. The lodge accurately re-creates an old Kennecott building, with the same red-and-white color scheme, right amid the historic structures of the ghost town. You can't get any closer to what you want to see. Guests can sip drinks on a long front porch overlooking the glacier, or relax on a lawn with the same view. The rooms are not large, and bathrooms are down the hall—although all were quite clean each time we visited.

Filling dinners are served family style, at long tables, with a fixed menu for a fixed price (a turkey dinner was $22.50, for example). Breakfast and lunch are a la carte. There's nowhere else to eat right in Kennecott, so plan to spend about $40 per person on food, or simply book the package that includes meals, for $265 per person for two. A brief tour of the ghost town is included.

P.O. Box 103940, Anchorage, AK 99510. 🕿 **800/582-5128** or 907/258-2350. In season only, 907/554-4477. Fax 907/248-7975. www.KennicottLodge.com. 25 units, none with private bathroom. $179 double. AE, DISC, MC, V. Closed mid-Sept to mid-May. **Amenities:** Restaurant; tour desk; courtesy van; bicycle rental.

McCarthy Lodge The lodge is the center of the relaxed village of McCarthy, 5 miles from the historically more buttoned-up Kennecott. The small rooms are in a false-front building that you might see in an old Western movie, except that it's real and unrestored, with a shared bathroom. The decor is lace and rough-cut lumber.

The lodge is an authentic Bush roadhouse, serving dinner family style. Reserve for the single 7pm seating. Dinners range from $16 to $22.

P.O. Box MXY, McCarthy, AK 99588. 🕿 **907/554-4402.** Fax 907/554-4404. 18 units, none with private bathroom. $130 double. MC, V. Rates include continental breakfast. Closed Oct–Memorial Day. **Amenities:** Restaurant; bar; courtesy van.

Camping & Hostelling

There is no campground on the Kennecott-McCarthy side of the Kennicott River footbridge. The Park Service allows camping anywhere in the park without a permit, but there are few appropriate spots on public land (remember, much of the land along the roads is private).

A couple of primitive private campgrounds, and a hostel, are at the end of the McCarthy Road. **Glacier View Campground** (🕿 **907/554-4490,** 907/243-6677 off-season) charges $10 a night for camping and $5 for showers, rents bikes, and serves barbecue. **Kennicott River Lodge and Hostel** (🕿 **907/554-4441** summer, 907/479-6822 winter; www.ptialaska.net/~grosswlr/) is just up the road, with bunks for $25 per person and cabins for $85 double plus $15 for each additional person. Showers and bedding cost extra, as they have to haul their water. There is a common kitchen.

There are three campgrounds on the way to the footbridge. The most attractive is the State Parks' **Liberty Falls Campground,** at mile 23 on the Edgerton Highway, which is set among big trees at the foot of a crashing waterfall. Many of the sites are walk-ins, with wooden tent platforms and lots of privacy. The self-service camping fee is $10 per vehicle; the day use fee is $1. There are pit toilets, and no running water. At mile 11 on the McCarthy Road, the 30-site **Silver Lake Campground** (no telephone) sits in a lovely, peaceful spot along the shore of a lake with rainbow trout. Skiffs with outboards and canoes are for rent. The sites are most attractive for RVs, and there is an outhouse. The camping fee is $10.

DINING

The main restaurants in the Kennecott area are at the Kennicott Glacier Lodge and McCarthy Lodge, described above. Both require reservations for dinner, but you can walk in for breakfast or lunch at Kennicott Glacier Lodge. I also enjoyed pizza and beer in a screened porch at **Taylor-Made Pizza** in McCarthy (© **907/ 554-4455**). It's open 10am to 10pm daily in the summer. There's usually a food stand at the footbridge, too.

10 Glennallen & the Copper River Country

The people of the Copper River Country, as this cold, arid region along the great river is known, live on homesteads and tiny settlements, and in a couple of towns near the regional hub of **Glennallen,** at the intersection of the Glenn and Richardson highways. Other than one planned luxury hotel, this sparsely settled land is for rugged outdoor activities. The volunteer-run **Copper River Visitor Center** is in a log cabin right at the intersection of the highways (P.O. Box 469, Glennallen, AK 99588; © **907/822-5555;** www.traveltoalaska.com); in summer it's open daily from 8am to 7pm. Glennallen has a bank with an ATM, a post office, a medical center, and government offices.

At this writing, the best standard accommodations in the area are at the **New Caribou Hotel,** at mile 187 of the Glenn Highway (© **800/478-3302** or 907/ 822-3302; www.alaskan.com/caribouhotel). The rooms are the equal of a good chain. A double is $137 in the summer. Unfortunately, the hotel books up many months ahead with bus tours. Their **Caribou Restaurant** is inexpensive and good for comfort food—meat loaf, pork chops, steak, and salmon. The other place where my family likes to eat while passing through Glennallen is the **Great Alaskan Freeze** (© **907/822-3923**), a clean burger joint and local hangout with wallpaper and fine art on the walls. Besides big burgers, they also serve Mexican dishes and good milkshakes.

Fourteen miles south of Glennallen, **Copper Center** is a tiny Athabascan community on the old Richardson Highway. A historic roadhouse, the **Copper Center Lodge** (© **888/822-3245** or 907/822-3245; www.alaska.net/~ccl/) is worthy of a stop for dinner or even overnight. Rooms in the big old log building rent for $89 a night with a shared bathroom, $99 with a private bathroom. The restaurant here has a good reputation all over the region for hearty, satisfying meals. It's open 7am to 9pm, and the staff brags especially of its sourdough pancakes, made with starter more than 100 years old. (Gold rush prospectors carried sourdough starter, a mixture of live yeast and flour, always growing more so they never ran out. Alaskans sometimes track their pedigree by the lineage of their sourdough starter.) The history of the lodge dates from the bizarre gold rush origins of Copper Center and Valdez, when about 4,000 stampeders to the Klondike tried a virtually impossible all-American route from Valdez over the glaciers of the Wrangell–St. Elias region. Few made it, and hundreds who died are buried in Copper Center. The original lodge was built of the stuff they left behind. The existing building dates from 1932.

Copper Center has one great country-road attraction, a huge model train diorama of the Copper River and Northwestern Railroad and Kennecott Mine (see the previous section), which Ron Simpson built in his bar, **The Copper Rail Depot** (© 907/822-3522). It's on the loop road off the Old Richardson Highway, near the Copper Center Lodge; look for the martini glass sign.

Big changes are in store for Copper Center with the construction of the **Copper River Princess Wilderness Lodge** by Princess Cruises (© 800/426-0442; www.princessalaskalodges.com), 4 miles north of the National Park Visitor Center. Their other Alaska lodges are first rate; this one is planned to open in 2002, but few details were available at this writing.

Other than Wrangell–St. Elias National Park, most of the public land in the Copper River Country is managed by the **Bureau of Land Management Glennallen District,** with a log cabin office in town on the north side of the Glenn Highway, P.O. Box 147, Glennallen, AK 99588 (© 907/822-3217; www.glennallen.ak.blm.gov), open Monday to Friday 8am to 4pm. Information also is available from the public land information centers in Anchorage, Fairbanks, and Tok. This huge area, about the size of a midsize eastern U.S. state, is more accessible than the park, an advantage for outdoor recreation, but it's still a rough, remote land with few high-quality visitor facilities. There are several large alpine lakes, two National Wild Rivers, many hiking trails, and five campgrounds (including the State Parks campground just north of Glennallen), all reached on the Richardson, Glenn, and Denali highways. Guides are available for **rafting** and **fishing** in the rivers. Check at the visitor center or BLM office for referrals. The salmon are not as desirable this far inland as they are near the coast, as they've begun to turn red, soften, and lose oil content with their spawning changes.

10

The Bush

The Bush is most of Alaska. On a map of the state, the portion with roads and cities is a smallish corner. Yet most visitors—and, indeed, most Alaskans—never make it beyond that relatively populated corner. Recently a lifelong Anchorage resident was elected to the legislature and appointed chair of its rural issues committee, only to admit he had never been to the Bush. It's common for children to grow to adulthood in Anchorage, Fairbanks, or Southeast Alaska without traveling to the Arctic, the Aleutians, or the vast wetlands of western Alaska. It happens for the same reason most tourists don't go to Bush Alaska—getting there is expensive, and there's not much in the way of human activity once you arrive. Bush Alaska is one of the planet's last barely inhabited areas. But that's a reason to go, not a reason to stay away. You can meet indigenous people who still interact with the environment in their traditional way, and see virgin places that remain to be explored by self-reliant outdoors people.

Although there are few people in the Bush, the hospitality of those you do meet is special and warming. In Bush Alaska, where the population is overwhelmingly Alaska Native, it's not uncommon to be befriended by total strangers simply because you've taken the trouble to come to their community and are, therefore, an honored guest. Even in the larger towns, people smile as you pass in the street. If you have a questioning look on your face,

they'll stop to help. Living in a small place where people know each other and have to work together against the elements makes for a tight, friendly community.

Alaska's Native culture is based more on cooperative than competitive impulses. Respect and consensus carry greater weight than in individualistic white society. Cooperation requires slowing down, listening, not taking the lead. People from our fast-paced culture can leave a village after a visit wondering why no one spoke to them, not realizing that they never shut up long enough to give anyone a chance. The cultural differences here are real, unlike the shadows of past differences we celebrate in most regions of the homogenous United States. Long pauses in conversation are normal, looking down while addressing a person demonstrates respect, punctuality is highly relative, child care is a community function, and when gifts are offered, people really mean it—turning down even a cup of coffee is gauche. (For more on the culture of Alaska's Native peoples, see the appendix.)

The Native people of the Bush also have terrible problems trying to live in two worlds. There's too much alcohol and too many drugs in the Bush, too much TV, but not enough of an economic base to provide for safe drinking water or plumbing in many villages. Even in some of the relatively prosperous village hubs described in this chapter, visitors will glimpse a kind of rural poverty they may not have seen before—where prices are extremely high and where steady jobs are scarce and interfere with traditional hunting and food gathering. But if you ask why they stay, you're missing something. In a world where so few indigenous cultures survive, people here are working to retain traditions that give their lives meaning while also adopting what they need from modernity. It's a work in progress, but there's no question they're slowly succeeding. They control their own land, they're building an economic base, and Native ways are being passed on to younger generations.

The Natives' physical environment is extreme in every respect—the weather, the land, even the geography. There's a special feeling in walking along the Arctic Ocean, the virtual edge of the earth, on a beach that lies between flat, wet tundra and an ocean that's usually ice. The quantity and accessibility of wildlife are extreme, too, as are the solitude and uniqueness of what you can do. Unfortunately, the prices also are extreme. Getting to a Bush hub from Anchorage costs more than getting to Anchorage from Seattle, and a flight to the Aleutians costs up to four times as much. And once you're at the hub, you're not done. Getting into the outdoors can cost as much again. Many travelers can't afford to make a Bush sojourn, instead satisfying their curiosity about the state's unpopulated areas on Alaska's rural highways. Most who can afford the trip usually make the most of their time and money with brief prearranged tours or trips directly to wilderness lodges. Only a few explorers head for the Bush unguided, although there are some good places to go that way—Nome, Kodiak, and Unalaska among them.

Covering the Bush is also a challenge for the writer of a book like this one. There are more than 200 Alaska villages, many lodges, camps, and guides, and a vast, undefined territory to describe. All that information would fill a larger book than this one, but would be of little use to the great majority of readers. I've taken the approach, instead, of providing sections on those few Bush hubs that are most accessible and popular with visitors, that have modern facilities, and that can be used as gateways to much more of the state for those who want to step out beyond the fringe of civilization.

If you find yourself in a town such as **Nome, Kotzebue, Barrow,** or **Kodiak,** all hubs for outlying Native villages, there's a simple and relatively inexpensive way to get out and see how village people live: Mail and scheduled passenger planes, typically small, single-engine craft, make daily rounds of the villages from each hub. Without the difficulty, expense, and dubious interest of going for a longer trip to a village, you can fly out on one of these planes for a quick day trip, walk around and meet people, then fly back to the hub city on the next flight to come through. *One warning:* Don't make such an excursion in lowering weather, as you could get stranded at a remote village. A journalist friend of mine was weathered in for more than 2 weeks on one occasion. You'll find the air-taxi operators—true Bush pilots—friendly, informal, and most willing to oblige you in working out your Bush adventure. To find out where to go, just walk into the office and tell them what you're interested in seeing and how much time and money you want to spend. It's also an inexpensive way to go flightseeing.

1 Exploring the Bush

Alaska's Bush is better defined by what it's like than by where it is. The most common and convenient conception says the Bush is everything beyond the road system. On a map, everything north and west of Fairbanks obviously meets that definition, but many Bush villages lie elsewhere in the Interior, in South-central, and in Southeast Alaska. In fact, there are some Bush villages you can drive to. No simple definition works. You know a Bush community by how it feels. It's a place where the wilderness is closer than civilization, where people still live off the land and age-old traditions survive, and where you have to make a particular effort to get in or out.

THE REGIONS

THE ARCTIC   The Arctic Circle is the official boundary of the Arctic. The line, at 66° 33' north latitude, is the southern limit of true midnight sun—south of it, at sea level, the sun rises and sets, at least a little, every day of the year. But in Alaska, people think of the Arctic as beginning at the **Brooks Range,** which is a bit north of the circle, including **Barrow** and **Prudhoe Bay.** The northwest Alaska region, which includes **Kotzebue** and, slightly south of the Arctic Circle, **Nome,** also is Arctic in climate, culture, and topography. The biggest geographic feature in Alaska's Arctic is the broad **North Slope,** the plain of tundra that stretches from the northern side of the Brooks Range to the Arctic Ocean. It's a swampy desert, with little rain or snowfall, frozen solid all but a couple of months a year.

WESTERN ALASKA   This is the land of the massive, wet **Yukon-Kuskokwim Delta** and the fish-rich waters of Bristol Bay. The Y-K Delta, as it's known, was never really exploited by white explorers, and the Yup'ik people who live there have maintained some of the most culturally traditional villages. In some, Yup'ik is still the dominant language. **Bethel** is the main hub city of the delta but holds little attraction for visitors. **Bristol Bay** is known for massive salmon runs, and avid anglers may be interested in its wilderness lodges, using **Dillingham** as a hub.

SOUTHWEST ALASKA   Stretching from the Aleutians—really a region of their own—to the Alaska Peninsula, Kodiak Island, and the southern part of the mountainous west side of Cook Inlet, this is a maritime region, like Southeast, but far more remote. The hub of the wet, windy **Aleutians** is **Unalaska** and its port of **Dutch Harbor. Katmai National Park** and the adjoining wild lands are the main attraction of the Alaska Peninsula, although there also are fishing lodges on the salmon-rich rivers and on the lakes to the north, including areas in **Lake Clark National Park** and **Iliamna Lake.** The lakes and west side of **Cook Inlet** are accessed primarily by Kenai, Homer, and Anchorage flight services for fishermen and hunters. **Kodiak** is hardly a Bush community, but fits better in this chapter than anywhere else, and the town is a hub for villages on Kodiak Island.

GETTING AROUND

With a few exceptions for strongly motivated travelers, who can take the ferry to Kodiak and Unalaska or drive to Prudhoe Bay, getting to each town in this chapter will require flying. **Alaska Airlines (***©* **800/252-7522; www.alaskaair. com)** offers the only jet service to Bush hubs. Other, smaller operators serve these towns as well, mostly with prop aircraft. Throughout the chapter, I've listed the plane fare to various communities from Anchorage, based on flying coach and getting a significant discount for advance purchase, weekend stayover, and some restrictions. Full Y-class fares cost more. With the way airfares fluctuate, it would be unwise to use these numbers as anything more than rough guides. To get the current best fare, use a travel agent or the Internet.

Kodiak, which barely fits in a chapter on the Bush, is the most accessible of the communities in this chapter, but it still requires either a 10-hour ferry ride from Homer or a $250 round-trip plane ticket from Anchorage. This charming, historic town is similar to towns in Southeast Alaska or Prince William Sound; but it is also a hub for Native villages on the island. **Unalaska/Dutch Harbor,** in the Aleutian Islands, is an interesting place to go way off the beaten path while staying in complete comfort. A visit requires an $800 round-trip plane ticket. **Kotzebue** and **Barrow** are the most purely Native of the communities in the chapter. **Nome** has the advantages of Arctic surroundings easily accessible on gravel roads, but is more of a gold rush town than a Native village. **Prudhoe Bay,** at the end of the Dalton Highway, is an industrial complex without a real town associated with it. Fares range from $400 to $700 for these communities. Buying an **Alaska Airlines package tour** saves a lot of money to Nome, Kotzebue, or Barrow, and gives you something to do when you arrive.

2 Kodiak: Wild Island

The habitat that makes Kodiak Island a perfect place for bears also makes it perfect for people. Runs of salmon clog unpopulated bays and innumerable, unfished rivers; the rounded green mountains seem to beg for someone to cross them; the gravel beaches and protected rocky inlets are free of people, but full of promise. But, in this respect, bears are smarter than people. Brown bears own the island, growing to prodigious size and abundant numbers, but Kodiak is as yet undiscovered by human visitors. That's a part of the wonder of the place. I'll never forget flying over the luxuriant verdure of Kodiak's mountains and the narrow string of glassy Raspberry Strait on a rare sunny day, seeing no sign of human presence in the most beautiful landscape I had ever beheld.

The narrow streets of the town of Kodiak are a discovery, too. Twisting over the hills in little discernible order, they were the original stomping grounds of **Lord Alexander Baranof,** the first Russian ruler of Alaska, who arrived here in 1790. Kodiak has the oldest Russian building in North America. It was nearly lost in the 1964 Good Friday earthquake, which destroyed most of the town, explaining the general lack of old buildings. The quake brought a 30-foot wave that washed to the building's doorstep. A marker near the police station on Mill Bay Road shows the wave's incredible high-water point. Before the Russians, the **Koniag** people lived off the incomparable riches of the island. They're still here, recovering their past in a fascinating little research museum.

The town looks to the sea. Along with the Coast Guard base, fishing makes Kodiak prosperous, creating a friendly, energetic, unpolished community. Kodiak is separate from the rest of Alaska, living its own commercial fishing life without often thinking of what's going on in Anchorage or anywhere else. It's off the beaten path because it doesn't really need anything the path provides.

For the visitor, Kodiak is an undiscovered gem. A few days just scratches the surface of the charming, vibrant town and the easily accessible wild places around it, yet, even in midsummer, you will see few if any other tourists.

There are seven **Native villages** on the island. A flight to one of them and back on a clear day is a wonderful, low-cost way to see remote areas of the island and to get a taste of how Alaska Natives live. **Ranches** on the road system around town offer riding and lodging. You can fly out to see the famous bears on a day trip, or stay at one of several **wilderness lodges** for wildlife watching, fishing, sea kayaking, and hunting, and even participating in a Native-led archaeological dig.

ESSENTIALS

GETTING THERE   It's a 1-hour flight from Anchorage to Kodiak on **Alaska Airlines** (℃ 800/252-7522; www.alaskaair.com). **ERA Aviation** (℃ 800/ 866-8394; www.eraaviation.com) also serves the route. A round-trip ticket from Anchorage costs $250 and up, depending on the deal you get. A **cab,** from **Ace Mecca** (℃ 907/486-3211) or **A and B Taxi** (℃ 907/486-4343), runs around $15 from the airport.

The ferry *Tustumena,* of the **Alaska Marine Highway System** (℃ 800/ 642-0066 or 907/486-3800; www.state.ak.us/ferry), serves Kodiak from Homer and Seward. If you have the time for the 10-hour run from Homer—the closest port with a road—this boat ride is truly memorable. The vessel leaves land behind and threads through the strange and exposed Barren Islands. The ocean can be quite rough, and when it is, lots of passengers get seasick; take Dramamine *before* boarding. A cabin is a good idea for an overnight run. The U.S. Fish and Wildlife Service staffs the trips with a naturalist. The adult passenger fare is $53, children half price. The Kodiak terminal is in the same building as the visitor center.

VISITOR INFORMATION   The **Kodiak Island Convention and Visitors Bureau,** 100 Marine Way, Kodiak, AK 99615 (℃ 907/486-4782; fax 907/486-6545; www.kodiak.org), occupies a small building on the ferry dock. The staff and website are helpful. Hours vary according to the ferry schedule, but essentially follow this pattern: summer Monday 8am to 8:30pm, Tuesday to Friday 8am to 5pm, Saturday 10am to 4pm, Sunday 1 to 8:30pm; winter Monday to Friday 8am to 5pm, closed for lunch.

The **Kodiak National Wildlife Refuge Visitors Center,** Buskin River Road, near the airport 4 miles south of town (℃ 907/487-2600; www.r7.fws.gov), is headquarters for a refuge that covers most of the island and is home of the famous Kodiak brown bear. There are remote public-use cabins all over the refuge, reachable by chartered plane. Permits are $30, available 3 months in advance. The center has exhibits and is a good place to stop for outdoors information. They're open mid-June to August daily 8am to 4:30pm; the balance of the year Monday to Friday only.

ORIENTATION   The Kodiak Archipelago contains Kodiak, Shuyak, and Afognak islands, and many other, smaller islands. Kodiak is the nation's second-largest island (after Hawaii's Big Island). The city of Kodiak is on a narrow point on the northeast side of Kodiak Island, surrounded by tiny islands. There are seven Native villages on other parts of the island. The airport and Coast Guard base are several miles southwest of town on **Rezanof Drive,** which runs through town and comes out on the other side. The center of Kodiak is a hopeless tangle of steep, narrow streets—you need the excellent map given away by the visitor center, but it's all walkable. The ferry dock is on **Marine Way,** and most of the in-town sights are right nearby. Several gravel roads, totaling 100 miles, make wonderful exploring from Kodiak to deserted shorelines, gorgeous views, pastures, recreation areas, and salmon streams. The visitors guide contains a mile-by-mile guide to each drive.

GETTING AROUND   Several companies rent cars, including **Budget** (② **800/527-0700** or 907/487-2220; www.budget.com), which has offices at the airport or downtown.

If it's not raining, a bike is a great way to get around Kodiak, and strong riders will enjoy touring the roads out of town. Bikes are for rent at **Fifty-Eight Degrees North,** a full-service bike shop at 1231 Mill Bay Rd. (② **907/ 486-6249**). Front-suspension mountain bikes rent for $30 for 24 hours.

 FAST FACTS: Kodiak

Banks Several downtown have ATMs, including **Key Bank** on the mall at the waterfront.

Hospital **Providence Kodiak Island Medical Center** is at 1915 E. Rezanof Dr. (② **907/486-3281**).

Internet Access **Office Express** is at 202 Center St. (② **907/486-8780**).

Police Contact the **Kodiak Police Department** at ② **907/486-8000.**

Post Office Near Lower Mill Bay Road and Hemlock Street.

Taxes **Sales tax** is 6% within city limits. The **room tax** inside the Kodiak city limits totals 11%, while outside the city it's 5%.

SPECIAL EVENTS   **Russian Orthodox Christmas,** coming about 2 weeks after the Roman Catholic and Protestant celebration, includes the **Starring Ceremony,** in which a choir follows a star in the evening to sing at the homes of church members. The late-March **Pillar Mountain Golf Classic** (② **907/ 486-4782**) is played on a one-hole par-70 course that climbs 1,400 feet from tee to flag; dogs, chain saws, two-way radios, and tracking devices are prohibited, and cursing the officials carries a $25 fine. Hand saws and hatchets are allowed. The 5-day **Kodiak Crab Festival** (② **907/486-5557;** www.kodiak. org/crabfest.html), on Memorial Day weekend, is a big event, including many fun events and the solemn blessing of the fleet and memorial service for lost fishermen. The **Bear Country Music Festival** over 2 days in mid-July includes many styles of popular and folk music (② **907/486-6117**). In early September, the **Kodiak State Fair and Rodeo** (② **907/485-4959**) has all kinds of small-town contests. The **Harbor Stars** (② **907/486-8085**), in mid-December, is a fleet parade of vessels decorated for Christmas. The visitor bureau maintains a complete community calendar online at **www.kodiak.org/calendar. html**.

ATTRACTIONS & ACTIVITIES

A **walking tour** in the local visitors guide will show you what's available in town (a version is on the web at **www.kodiak.org/walk.html**). The highlights include the **Fishermen's Memorial,** near the harbormaster's office at the head of the St. Paul Harbor, where a soberingly long list of Kodiak fishermen who have lost their lives at sea is posted on plaques. The warship set in concrete on Mission Way is the *Kodiak Star,* the last World War II Liberty Ship built. It came here as a fish processor after the 1964 earthquake destroyed the canneries, and is still in use. At Kashevarof and Mission, the **Holy Resurrection Russian Orthodox Church** was founded in 1794, although the present building dates only to 1945, when it was rebuilt after a fire.

Half-hour **Native dance performances** take place June to August at the Kodiak Tribal Council Barabara, at 713 E. Rezanof Dr. (℃ **907/486-4449**). Admission is $15 adults, kids half price.

Alutiiq Museum ⋆   This exceptional Native-funded and -governed museum seeks to document and restore the Koniag Alutiiq people's culture, which the Russians virtually wiped out in the 18th century. Besides teaching about Alutiiq culture in a single gallery, the museum manages its own archaeological digs (see "Getting Outside," below) and repatriates Native remains and artifacts, which researchers removed by the thousands in the 1930s. The archaeological repository now includes 100,000 objects.

215 Mission Rd. ℃ 907/486-7004. www.alutiiqmuseum.com. Admission $2 adults, free for kids under age 12. Summer, Mon–Fri 9am–5pm, Sat 10am–5pm. Winter, Tues–Fri 9am–5pm, Sat 10:30am–4:30pm.

The Baranov Museum ⋆   The museum occupies the oldest Russian building of only four left standing in North America; it was built in 1808 by Alexander Baranof as a magazine and strong house for valuable sea otter pelts. It stands in a grassy park overlooking the water across from the ferry dock. Inside is a little museum rich with Russian and early Native artifacts. The guides know a lot of history and show 30 educational albums on various topics. The gift store is exceptional, selling antique Russian items and authentic Native crafts.

101 Marine Way. ℃ 907/486-5920. www.ptialaska.net/~baranov. Admission $2; free for children 12 and under. Summer, Mon–Sat 10am–4pm, Sun noon–4pm. Winter, Mon–Wed and Fri–Sat 10am–3pm. Closed Feb.

GETTING OUTSIDE
TWO RECREATION AREAS
A couple of miles north of town on Rezanof Drive, the **Fort Abercrombie State Historical Park** encompasses World War II ruins set on coastal cliffs amid huge trees. Paths lead to the beaches and good tide-pool walking, a swimming lake, and lots of other discoveries. The gun emplacements, bunkers, and other concrete buildings defended against the Japanese, who had seized islands in the outer Aleutians and were expected to come this way. A group of local World War II buffs, led by Joe Stevens, known as Crusty Old Joe, have built a museum of war artifacts from the Alaska fighting in one of the bunkers (see "The Aleutians: The Quiet After War," later), as well as other military operations in Alaska. Hours change annually, but will be posted at www.kadiak.org, or they'll open it any time by appointment (℃ **907/486-4700**). The website is truly exhaustive. A wonderful 13-site campground sits atop the cliffs among the trees and ruins. Camping is $10. The **Division of State Parks,** Kodiak District Office, 1400 Abercrombie Dr., Kodiak, AK 99615 (℃ **907/486-6339;** fax 907/486-3320; www.ptialaska.net/~kodsp/), maintains an office here where you can pick up a walking-tour brochure or, during the summer, join the Saturday-night interpretive program or a guided tide-pool walk, scheduled to coincide with the tides. Or investigate the tide pools on your own, picking up an identification guide at a bookstore or the Fish and Wildlife Service visitor center.

The **Buskin River State Recreation Site,** 4 miles south of town off Rezanof Drive near the Fish and Wildlife Service visitor center, has 15 sites, a hiking trail, and access to fishing. Camping is $10.

ACTIVITIES

ARCHAEOLOGY Dig Afognak, 215 Mission Rd., Suite 212 (© **800/ 770-6014** or 907/486-6014; www.afognak.com/dig), operated by the Afognak Native Corporation, offers visitors a chance to help in scientific excavations of Koniag sites on Afognak Island, an effort by the Native group to reassemble their cultural heritage. Visitors are instructed in the natural history of the beautiful area as well as archaeology, but they're also expected to work, digging and working in a remote lab. Each weeklong session has a different educational emphasis, with scientists or elders on hand to enrich the learning. Accommodations are in heated tents, and you have to bring your own sleeping bag. Dinner often is seafood caught in nets at the beach. A 7-day session is $1,650, including transportation from Kodiak.

BROWN BEAR VIEWING To see Kodiak's famous bears, you need to get out on a plane or boat. The easiest way is a Kodiak-based floatplane; expect to pay at least $400 per person, with a two- or three-person minimum (prices can fluctuate depending on the size of your party, the type of plane, how far you have to fly, and so on). Landing on the water, you may watch from the safety of the plane's floats, or put on rubber boots to get closer. Bears congregate only when salmon are running, so the timing of your visit is critical. If seeing bears on Kodiak is an important element of your trip, call ahead to the **Kodiak National Wildlife Refuge** (© **907/487-2600;** see "Visitor Information," above) to make sure you come at the right time, since salmon runs and the hot bear-viewing spots can vary from year to year. When the salmon aren't running, Kodiak flight services fly over to the east coast of the Alaska Peninsula to watch bears digging clams from the tidal flats; it's fascinating behavior and a spectacular flight, but flying that far is expensive. If bear viewing is the whole reason you're going to Kodiak, it makes more sense to time your visit for the salmon run, or to try to see bears from a base in Homer (see chapter 7) or King Salmon (see section 3 of this chapter, on Katmai National Park) instead. Several small flight services offer bear viewing, including (I have no preference): **Highline Air** (© **907/486-5155;** www.ptialaska.net/~highline), **Sea Hawk Air** (© **800/ 770-4295** or 907/486-8282; www.seahawkair.com), or **Kodiak Air Service** (© **907/486-4446**).

FISHING The roads leading from Kodiak offer access to terrific salmon and trout fishing. The visitor center provides a list of where to fish and the names and addresses of guides for remote fishing. The **Alaska Department of Fish and Game** is at 211 Mission Rd., Kodiak, AK 99615 (© **907/486-1880;** www. state.ak.us/adfg). To fish the remote areas, you'll need to charter a plane, going for a day or staying at a remote public-use cabin or wilderness lodge. Several boats are available for ocean salmon and halibut fishing. Check with the visitor center.

HIKING & BIRD-WATCHING There aren't a lot of trails on Kodiak, but there are some good day hikes. Pick up a copy of the *Kodiak Hiking Guide* at the visitor center for a variety of mountain climbs and day hikes from the road system. They'll also have the field-trip program of the **Kodiak Audubon Society,** which includes guided hikes and bird-watching trips.

HORSEBACK RIDING The lush green hills that cover much of the island are idyllic grounds for riding. The **Kodiak Cattle Co.** (© **907/486-3705**) is one of several outfits offering rides. They often see deer, eagles, and bears on their day trips, which start at $45 per person with a two-person minimum.

SEA KAYAKING The Kodiak Archipelago, with its many folded, rocky shorelines and abundant marine life, is a perfect place for sea kayaking. Kayaks were invented here and on the Aleutian Islands to the west. Several operators offer kayaking services and tours in and around Kodiak, and on the shore of Katmai National Park. **Mythos Expeditions** (© **907/486-5536;** www.mythos-expeditions.com) offers introductory paddles from the boat harbor—surprisingly complex and attractive waters for kayaking—starting at $40 per person. Their real specialty, however, is taking kayakers along the Katmai coast for multi-day bear viewing trips; guests paddle by day and sleep and eat aboard a converted commercial fishing boat. They also go to **Shuyak Island State Park,** 54 miles north of Kodiak. The park is a honeycomb of islands and narrow passages in virgin Sitka spruce coastal forest. The Division of State Parks (see addresses under "Two Recreation Areas," above) distributes a free kayaking guide with route descriptions and maintains four public-use cabins, which rent for $65 a night. These cabins can be quite hard to get. See "State Parks Cabin Reservation Tricks," in section 1 of chapter 7, and read up on the special rules for Shuyak Island on the website mentioned there. Mythos Expeditions rents kayaks for use in the park.

ACCOMMODATIONS

Besides the hotels listed below, you'll find good standard rooms for under $80 a night at **Shelikof Lodge,** 211 Thorsheim Ave. (© **907/486-4141;** www.ptialaska.net/~kyle), and the **Russian Heritage Inn,** 119 Yukon (© **907/486-5657;** www.ak-biz.com/russianheritage). I've listed places in town, but there also are more than two dozen wilderness lodges on and around Kodiak Island. You can get a list from the visitor center, and their website contains links to most of them.

Best Western Kodiak Inn 🎯 This is the best hotel in downtown Kodiak, with attractive, up-to-date rooms perched on the hill overlooking the boat harbor, right in the center of things. Rooms in the wooden building vary in size and view, but all are acceptable standard rooms with good amenities.

The **Chart Room** restaurant, specializing in seafood and with a great view of the water, is a good choice for a nice dinner out, with entrees in the $15 to $25 range.

236 W. Rezanof Dr., Kodiak, AK 99615. © **888/563-4254** or 907/486-5712. Fax 907/486-3430. www.ptialaska.net/~kodiakin. 81 units. High season $149 double. Low season $99 double. Extra person over age 12 $15. AE, DC, DISC, MC, V. **Amenities:** Restaurant (seafood); bar; outdoor Jacuzzi; courtesy van; tour desk. *In room:* TV, fridge, microwave oven, coffeemaker.

Buskin River Inn 🎯 This quiet, well-kept hotel with standard rooms is near the airport, not the downtown sights; you will need a rental car if you stay here. Rooms on one side look out on the river, the other side on the parking lot. It's near the wildlife refuge visitor center, a hiking trail, and the nine-hole golf course at the Coast Guard base. The Buskin makes a specialty of booking activities and offering package discounts for outdoor explorations of the island. The **Eagle's Nest Restaurant** has reliable food from a complete beef and seafood menu, and a pleasant setting.

1395 Airport Way, Kodiak, AK 99615. © **800/544-2202** or 907/487-2700. www.kodiakadventure.com. 50 units. High season $145 double. Low season $125 double. Extra person over age 12 $15. AE, DC, DISC, MC, V. **Amenities:** Restaurant; courtesy van; tour desk; coin-op laundry. *In room:* TV, voicemail, fridge, coffeemaker, hair dryer.

Kodiak Bed and Breakfast Hospitable, active Mary Monroe runs this comfortable, homey place with a big, friendly golden retriever, Buffy. There is a porch where you can eat breakfast on sunny mornings, overlooking the harbor (fish is often on the morning menu). The location is convenient, right downtown, and the entry for the bedrooms and shared sitting room downstairs doesn't require you to walk through Monroe's own living quarters.

308 Cope St., Kodiak, AK 99615. ℂ 907/486-5367. Fax 907/486-6567. www.ptialaska.net/~monroe. 2 units, both with shared bathroom. $95 double. Rates include breakfast. MC, V. **Amenities:** Fish freezing. *In room:* Phone, TV in common room.

Wintels Bed and Breakfast A long walk from downtown (you'll need a car if you stay here), this house stands with the ocean on one side and a lake on the other, so all rooms have water views. The owners, a family of longtime residents, can tell you a lot about Alaska and show off their mounted sea ducks and furs. The rooms are attractive and the breakfasts large.

1723 Mission Rd. (P.O. Box 2812), Kodiak, AK 99615. ℂ and fax **907/486-6935**. www.wintels.com. 3 units, 1 with private bathroom. $80–$100 double. Extra person $35. Rates include breakfast. AE, MC, V. **Amenities:** Sauna; Jacuzzi; laundry service. *In room:* Hair dryer.

DINING

Besides the hotel restaurants listed above at the Best Western Kodiak Inn and Buskin River Inn, Kodiak has a selection of family restaurants.

Downtown, **El Chicano,** at 103 Center St. (ℂ **907/486-6116**), is a good Mexican family restaurant, with friendly service and reasonable prices. **Beryl's** is a nice little sandwich and breakfast shop on a pedestrian way at 202 Center St. (ℂ **907/486-3323**). It started out as a candy and ice-cream place but now serves meals all day until 6pm. **Harborside Coffee and Goods,** at 216 Shelikof St. (ℂ **907/486-5862**), on the south side of the boat harbor, is a comfortable coffeehouse with soup and bagels, popular with commercial fishermen and young people. **Henry's Great Alaskan Restaurant,** at 512 Marine Way (ℂ **907/ 486-8844**), on the waterfront mall, is a popular but very smoky bar and grill.

A mile from downtown, **Mongolian Barbecue,** 1247 Mill Bay Rd. (ℂ **907/ 486-2900**), is the best family restaurant in town. Diners choose their thinly sliced meat and vegetables raw and watch the chef toss them on the grill. An all-you-can-eat dinner is $13, half-price for kids. It's fun and the food is great.

3 Katmai National Park

Most of the land of the Alaska Peninsula, pointing out to the Aleutian Archipelago, is in one federally protected status or another, centering on Katmai National Park. The park, pronounced "*cat*-my," lies just west of Kodiak Island, across the storm-infested Shelikof Strait. Bear and salmon are the main attractions. **Brooks Camp,** with a campground and lodge within Katmai, is probably the most comfortable place for foolproof bear viewing in Alaska. Here, in July and September only, you can sit back on a deck and watch 900-pound brown bears walk by, going about their business of devouring the spawning salmon that contribute to their awesome size. (A brown bear is the genetic twin of the grizzly, but generally larger due to its coastal diet of salmon.) Staying the night will require you to reserve a place in the 16-space campground the previous winter (see "Reservations & Fees," below) or stay in the pricey lodge, where rooms book up over a year ahead for the bear season. You can go for a day trip with less planning, if you can afford round-trip airfare of around $500 from Anchorage (see "Reservations & Fees," below).

Katmai was set aside in 1918, 6 years after the area exploded into world consciousness with the most destructive volcanic eruption to shake the earth in 3,400 years. When Katmai's Novarupta blew, it released ten times more energy than Mount St. Helens' eruption of 1980 and displaced twice as much matter as 1883's Krakatoa. In Kodiak, the sky was black for 3 days, and 2 feet of ash crushed houses and choked rivers. People could clearly hear the blast in Juneau; acid rain melted fabric in Vancouver, British Columbia; and the skies darkened over most of the northern hemisphere. At ground zero, all life was wiped out in a 40-square-mile area and buried as deep as 700 feet. But so remote was the area, then still unnamed, that not a single human being was killed. The **Valley of Ten Thousand Smokes,** the vast wasteland created by the blast, belched steam for decades after. Today Novarupta is dormant and the steam is gone, but the area is still a barren moonscape, making a fascinating day tour or hiking trip.

ESSENTIALS

GETTING THERE   The most common way to get to Katmai is to fly from Anchorage to the village of **King Salmon,** which lies just west of the park, and then continue by air taxi to **Brooks Camp. Alaska Airlines** (© 800/252-7522; www.alaskaair.com) flies to King Salmon, charging around $350 round-trip. A floatplane from there to Brooks Camp is about $140, round-trip. Various air taxis make that jump, including **Katmai Air,** operated by park concessionaire Katmailand (© 800/544-0551 or 907/243-5448; www.bear-viewing.com). This company also offers round-trip airfare packages that may save you money.

As an alternative to Brooks Camp, more and more visitors are exploring the supremely rugged wilderness on the east side of the park from the beaches along **Shelikof Strait.** Air-taxi operators make drops-offs and do bear-viewing day trips from Homer or Kodiak (see section 2 of this chapter, above, on Kodiak, or see the Homer section in chapter 7), and boats out of Kodiak go across for extended cruising and kayak expeditions. In this park, with more than 2,000 brown bears resident (the world's largest protected population), it's easy for pilots to find them digging clams on the tidal marshes, then land on floats for a good, close look.

RESERVATIONS & FEES   To go to the bear-viewing area at Brooks Camp, you must pay the use fee of $10 per person, per day. In addition, once you're there you have to sign up for an hour on the bear viewing platforms (see below). Camping costs $5 per person per night. There are only 16 sites, and they are in very high demand during the bear season in July. The crowds are less in September, but the bears are not quite as numerous. All sites become available for the entire summer on January 15. There are no limits on day-use permits, so everyone gets in. To reserve, call the **Park Service national reservation system,** which is operated by Biospherics (© 800/365-2267 or 301/722-1257; http://reservations.nps.gov). You can reserve online (note, there is no "www" on the URL). If you're using the phone system, enter **KAT#** at the prompt. If reserving a campsite, make sure also to get a day-use permit. Lodge guests get their permit automatically.

VISITOR INFORMATION   Besides the **Katmai National Park Headquarters,** P.O. Box 7, King Salmon, AK 99613 (© 907/246-3305; www.nps.gov/katm), there's also a **visitor center** at the airport in King Salmon (© 907/246-4250), staffed jointly by the National Park Service, U.S. Fish and Wildlife

Service, and local governments. It is open May through mid-October daily 8am to 5pm, winter Monday through Saturday 8am to 5pm. At Brooks Camp, the park service has a center where all visitors are required to attend a 20-minute orientation called "The Brooks Camp School of Bear Etiquette," designed to train visitors (not bears) and keep them out of trouble. In Anchorage, you can get information at the **Alaska Public Lands Information Center,** at Fourth Avenue and F Street (© **907/271-2737;** see the complete listing in section 1 of chapter 6).

GETTING AROUND   Once you've made it to Brooks Camp, a **bus** carries visitors to the Valley of Ten Thousand Smokes, 23 miles by gravel road from the camp. The park concessionaire, **Katmailand,** charges $72 per person, round-trip, for the all-day excursion, plus $7 more for lunch. One-way transfers for hikers are $42.

 FAST FACTS: Katmai

Bank **Wells Fargo,** with an ATM, is on King Salmon Highway.

Hospital The **Camai Clinic,** in Naknek (© **907/246-6155**), is open during normal business hours; calls to the number go to emergency dispatchers after hours.

Police In **King Salmon,** call © **907/246-4222;** elsewhere, call **Alaska State Troopers** at © **907/246-3346** or 907/246-3464. There are no phones or cellular service out in the park.

EXPLORING KATMAI

Katmai's famous bear viewing occurs at **Brooks Camp** when the bears congregate near the Brooks River to catch salmon during July and September, and maybe the last week of June or the first week of August. This is when you're assured of seeing bears from the elevated platforms near the Brooks River falls, half a mile from Brooks Camp, even on a day trip. Forty to sixty bears feed here. Rangers escort visitors to the platforms to keep them separate from the bears, but you do get quite close to them. The Park Service recommends that people with mobility problems avoid this trail when bears are present, which pretty much means you shouldn't go to Brooks Camp if you have trouble getting around. Due to the popularity of the experience, there is a 1-hour limit on the platforms. After your turn is up, you can sign up on a waiting list to get another chance. Outside of the short salmon runs, there are better places to see bear, so don't spend the money to come here. Bears feed all summer on clams on Katmai's east shore. See "Getting There," above.

The Brooks Camp area has a small park service campground, visitor center, and lodge, located where the Brooks River flows into Naknek Lake. Unfortunately, when the area was first developed for fishing in the 1950s, the camp was placed in the middle of a bear corridor and on top of a valuable archaeological site. The park service plans to move facilities and people to the south side of the Brooks River and to impose limits on how many visitors can come, but that's still years away. The most comfortable way to stay in the camp is at the **Brooks Lodge,** operated by Katmailand (see contact info under "Getting There," above). The lodge has 16 units, with private bathrooms with shower stalls. To save money, book the lodge rooms as packages with air travel. The least expensive, 1-night visit is $693 per person, double occupancy, meals not included; 3 nights is $1,123. A double room without airfare is $412. The place books up 18 months ahead; reservations open January of the year before the visit and are full within a couple of weeks. Three buffet-style meals are served daily for guests and visitors who aren't staying in the lodge. Breakfast is $12, lunch $14, and dinner $22. For food, they take plastic at the lodge: American Express, Master-Card, and Visa. Also at Brooks Camp, there's a small store, the park service visitor center, and the 16-site campground. See "Reservations & Fees," above, for info on campground reservations, which should be made 6 months in advance. The rangers require special precautions to keep bears away from campers.

The rivers and lakes of Katmai lure human anglers as well as ursine ones. Katmailand operates two lodges within the park other than Brooks Lodge for remote fishing, the **Kulik** and **Grosvenor lodges.** Check their website at www.katmailand.com for fishing details. The park service also has a list of dozens of fishing, hiking, and air guides. There is no central clearinghouse for remote fishing, but you can find and book a good place through an agency such as **Sport Fishing Alaska,** 9310 Shorecrest Dr., Anchorage, AK 99515 (© **907/ 344-8674;** www.alaskatripplanners.com), listed in full under "Planning an Outdoor Vacation" in chapter 2.

Backcountry hiking in Katmai means crossing a wilderness without trails, and only experienced backpackers should plan extended trips. The park service asks hikers to obtain a voluntary permit for backcountry travel, thereby clueing them in to your plans in case you need to be rescued. Anyone can walk for the day without such precautions in the desolate **Valley of Ten Thousand Smokes.** This 40-square-mile plain remains a moonscape 90 years after the titanic volcanic blast that buried it, little changed except that the famous plumes of smoke are gone and rivers have sliced through the debris in places to create narrow, white-walled canyons. Although it looks like a desert and is subject to dust storms, rain is common and temperatures rarely go higher than 65°F. Katmailand operates a tour bus from Brooks Camp, mentioned above under "Getting Around." The visitors on those tours usually stick to a short trail on the valley's rim. Longer hikes into the valley bring you into contact with more of the bizarre landforms created by the eruption.

4 Dutch Harbor/Unalaska: Aleutian Boomtown

After a lifetime of hearing how desolate the Aleutians (uh-*loo*-shens) were, I felt like I was leaving the edge of the earth the first time I traveled to Unalaska (oon-ah-*las*-ka). Shortly after I arrived, a storm started slinging huge raindrops horizontally through the air so hard that they stung as they splattered on my face. People went on about their business as if nothing special was happening—stormy weather constantly batters these rocks that pop up from the empty North Pacific. My expectations seemed justified.

But the next day, the storm cleared like a curtain opening on a rich operatic scene—simultaneously opening the curtain of my dark expectations. Unalaska may lack trees, but it's not a barren rock. The island is covered with heather and wildflowers. Rounded mountains that invite wandering exploration rise from the ocean like the backs of huge beasts. For sightseeing, it has only a half a day's attractions, but for outdoor exploring, bird-watching, and halibut fishing, few places come close.

With the protected port of Dutch Harbor so far out in a ferocious ocean habitat rich in crab and bottom fish, Unalaska has grown in 3 decades from a tiny, forgotten Native village to the nation's largest fishing port. The pattern of growth followed the form of the early gold rushes. There was a wild, lawless time in the 1970s when crab fishermen got rich quick and partied like Old West cowboys. Then the overfished crab stocks crashed, only to be replaced, starting in the mid-1980s, by an even bigger boom, when waters within 200 miles of the U.S. shore were rid of foreign vessels and American bottom fishing took off. Big factory ships began unloading here, and huge fish plants were built on ground chipped from the rock. Today that expansion has reached a more steady state, and more women and families are coming to town—another part of the gold rush pattern. But domestication isn't done yet. Most of the population lives in bunk houses and flies back to Seattle, Mexico, and the Philippines when the processing plants close for the season. Unalaska may be the best current example of the American cultural phenomenon of the frontier boomtown.

Ironically, Unalaska is Alaska's oldest town as well as its newest city. The value of a good port out in the middle of the ocean was recognized from the beginning by the Aleuts. In 1759, the Russians began trading here, and fought a war with the Aleuts from 1763 to 1766, the outcome of which was slavery for the Aleut hunters and the massacre of their people. The Russians built a permanent settlement here in 1792, their first in Alaska. Unalaska also was a key refueling stop for steamers carrying gold rush stampeders to Nome a century ago, which brought an epidemic that killed a third of the indigenous population. In 1940, Dutch Harbor—the seaport on Amaknak Island associated with the town and island of Unalaska—was taken over by the U.S. Navy to defend against Japanese attack. That attack came: In June 1942, Japanese planes bombed Unalaska, killing 43. The Aleut people were removed from the islands for the duration of the war and interned in inadequate housing in Southeast Alaska, where many died of disease. The military pulled out in 1947, but the remains of their defenses are interesting to explore, part of a unique unit of the national park system. Thanks to a 1971 act of Congress settling Native claims, the Aleut-owned Ounalashka Corporation owns much of the island. But the National Park Service protects and interprets the World War II historic sites on Native-owned land.

ESSENTIALS

GETTING THERE Several operators fly to Dutch Harbor from Anchorage, including **Alaska Airlines** (© 800/252-7522; www.alaskaair.com). You're likely to pay $800 round-trip. An air/hotel package makes sense and saves money—see the Grand Aleutian Hotel, described under "Accommodations," below.

The **Alaska Marine Highway System** ferry *Tustumena* (© **800/642-0066;** www.state.ak.us/ferry) runs once a month from Homer, leaving Tuesday and arriving in Unalaska on Saturday after stopping in Kodiak and the villages along the way. The passenger fare is $266, and an outside cabin, with facilities, is $361 more. I'm told this open sea adventure is beautiful. Of course, unless you want to spend only 5 hours on a Saturday morning in Unalaska and then make the long return trip, you'll need to fly back.

VISITOR INFORMATION The **Unalaska/Port of Dutch Harbor Convention and Visitors Bureau,** P.O. Box 545, Unalaska, AK 99685 (© **877/ 581-2612** or 907/581-2612; http://arctic.net/~updhcvb), is at Fifth Street and Broadway, in the old part of town.

A new $1 million visitor center for the **Aleutian WWII National Historic Area** (© 907/581-1276; www.nps.gov/aleu) in a war-era building at the airport should be completed by 2002. The historic area encompasses Native-owned lands with World War II ruins on the island. The website is interesting (click on "In Depth").

GETTING AROUND   The main historic part of the town is a tiny street grid on a narrow peninsula facing Iliuliuk Bay. The **Bridge to the Other Side** (that's the official name) leads to Amaknak Island, the site of the airport, the Grand Aleutian Hotel, and the fishing industrial area of Dutch Harbor. Traveling down the road in the other direction leads a little way up into the mountains, a starting point for walks.

Van taxis are the main way of getting around town for the hordes of fishermen. One company is **Blue Checker Taxi** (© 907/581-2186).

You can rent a car, truck, or forklift from **North Port Rentals** (© 907/581-3880) or a couple of other companies. Small cars rent for $40 a day.

In good weather, bikes are a good way to cover the town, which has only a few miles of road. **Aleutian Adventure Sports** (© 888/581-4489 or 907/581-4489; www.aleutianadventure.com) rents bikes for $30 a day, as well as sea kayaks, and offers guided tours and outdoor activities.

FAST FACTS: Dutch Harbor/Unalaska

Bank **Key Bank** is near the Alaska Commercial Store.

Hospital **Iliuliuk Family and Health Services** (© 907/581-1202) offers clinic services.

Internet Access Free at the **public library** (© 907/581-5060).

Police **Unalaska** Department of Public Safety (© 907/581-1233) is just above the bridge on the Unalaska side.

Taxes **Sales tax** is 3%; **room tax** is 8%.

ATTRACTIONS & ACTIVITIES

Unalaska's most significant historic site is the **Holy Ascension Cathedral.** Completed in 1896 on the site of churches that had stood since 1808, the white church with green onion-shaped domes contains 697 icons, artifacts, and artworks—a significant collection that has been continuously in use by the Aleut congregation. The congregation was founded by Fr. Ivan Veniaminov, who translated the Gospel into Aleut and has been canonized as St. Innocent. A $1.3 million restoration completed in 1996 has left the church looking bright and trim on the edge of sparkling Iliuliuk Bay.

The new, professionally curated **Museum of the Aleutians,** next door to the Ounalashka Corporation on Margaret Bay in Dutch Harbor (© 907/581-5150; www.aleutians.org), contains some of the Aleuts' best artifacts anywhere, including some from North America's oldest coastal sites on Umnak and Unalaska islands. Exhibits also cover the town's history, with World War II artifacts and other items left behind by the successive waves of occupiers. Every summer the museum mounts archaeological digs on the island, inviting visitors to join in the work, earn college credit while digging, work to clean the artifacts

The Aleutians: The Quiet After War

Once thousands of men died for the rocky islands of the Aleutians, a bizarre and bitter tale with few parallels in American history. What began as a military diversion became a ferocious fight for honor with little strategic meaning. When the fighting was done, it turned out that no one even wanted the land enough to stay. The islands remain uninhabited, littered with military ruins. Sixty years later, with the construction of a new National Park Service visitor center in Unalaska, the battle for the Aleutians is only beginning to enter national consciousness.

The Japanese attacked the islands of **Kiska** and **Attu** at the start of the Pacific war to divert the main core of the American navy away from what became the Battle of Midway. But the Americans had intercepted and decoded Japanese transmissions, and weren't fooled. Meanwhile, the Japanese had sent 24 ships, including two aircraft carriers, on a fool's errand to bomb the new American naval base at Dutch Harbor/ Unalaska and occupy islands in the western Aleutians. Those ships could have tipped the balance at Midway, among the most important battles of the war. Instead, the Japanese met stiff antiaircraft fire in 2 days of bombing at Dutch Harbor; although 43 Americans were killed, the defensive function of the base was not greatly impaired.

The Japanese then took Kiska and Attu, meeting no resistance from 10 Americans staffing a weather station or from a small Aleut village whose few inhabitants were all—even the children—sent to a prison camp in Japan to mine clay for the duration of the war. About half the prisoners survived to return to Alaska.

The Americans had their own plan to remove the Aleuts, but the idea of depopulating all the islands had been turned down. Now, with the Japanese attack, it was swiftly put into effect. All the Aleuts were rounded up and put on ships. As they pulled away from their ancestral islands, they could see the glow of huge fires destroying their villages— the U.S. military had torched the villages to deny the modest assets of the islands to the Japanese, should they advance farther. With little thought given to their living conditions, the Aleuts were interned in abandoned summer camps and similarly inadequate facilities in Southeast Alaska. Shunned by the local communities and without the basic necessities of life, 10% died due to poor sanitation. The U.S. Fish and Wildlife Service took Aleut hunters to hunt furs as virtual slaves, much as the Russians had done 200 years before.

The Japanese and American military fared not much better on their new real estate. Although the Aleutians quickly became irrelevant to the rest of the war, significant resources were committed to a largely futile air and sea battle in the fog and endless storms. Flying at all was difficult and extremely dangerous, and finding the enemy in the fog over vast distances close to impossible. The Americans couldn't spare a land invasion force at first, and had to rely on bombing Kiska and Attu to punish the Japanese and try to deter a further advance up the chain. To that end, they built a large base at Adak, among others, so shorter-range fighter escorts could accompany the bombers. Construction in the spongy tundra was difficult in any case, made more so by the length of supply lines.

The Japanese high command never had any intention of advancing up the chain, but also saw no reason to abandon their new Kiska air base when it was causing the Americans to exert such effort—even if it had no strategic value to either side. The Japanese concentrated on fortifying Kiska, which became a honeycomb of underground bunkers and heavy antiaircraft guns and withstood constant bombing raids by the Americans.

Finally, on May 11, 1943, almost a year after the Japanese took the islands, Americans landed on Attu, and a brutal 18-day battle for the rugged island began. The Japanese were massively outnumbered but heavily dug in. Finally, with only 800 soldiers left from an original force of 2,600, the Japanese mounted a banzai attack. Only 28 were taken prisoner—the rest were killed in battle or committed suicide. The Americans lost 549 killed, 1,148 wounded, and 2,132 injured by severe cold, disease, accident, mental breakdown, or other causes. In the end, it was the second most costly island battle in the Pacific, after Iwo Jima.

The battle for Kiska was less dramatic. The Japanese withdrew under cover of fog. After a massive bombardment of the empty island and the rallying of heavy reinforcements, the Americans landed to find that no one was there. Still, 105 American soldiers died in the landing in accidents and fire from their own forces.

After the Aleutian battle was over, American forces in Alaska declined drastically, but never went away altogether. Before the war, the absurd little Fort William Seward, in Haines, had been the totality of Alaska's defenses, with a couple of hundred men armed with Springfield rifles and no reliable means of transportation. Afterward there were large bases in several areas of the state. Military spending became the biggest economic boom the territory had ever seen, connecting it by a new road to the Lower 48 and bringing precious year-round jobs. A new wave of postwar settlers, many former GIs looking for a new opportunity, brought a population boom. Alaska's prime strategic location in defense against the Soviet Union brought ever-greater increases in military spending in Alaska. To this day, the military is one of the largest sectors of the Alaska economy.

The end of the war was more bitter for the Aleuts. Returning to villages they had departed hastily 3 years before, they found homes and subsistence gear ruined and even historic Russian Orthodox churches and icons severely damaged. Many who had survived internment never returned. Some villages never revived; bureaucrats managing the evacuation wiped them off the map as a cost-saving measure.

Awareness of this injustice began to resurface in the 1980s, and in 1988 Congress and President Reagan formally apologized to the Aleuts and paid compensation of $12,000 to each survivor, then about half the 900 who were evacuated. That act also helped fund restoration of the five historic churches, including the beautiful church in Unalaska, and construction of one replacement. That work was recently completed.

Today, the Aleuts own their islands. It's fitting that the National Park Service's Aleutian World War II National Historic Area is their guest, on their land, and the new visitor center belongs to a Native corporation. Stop in here to learn about the lives sacrificed here, and wonder why.

in the museum, and hear evening lectures. Admission is $2. It's open summer Monday through Saturday 10am to 5pm, Sunday noon to 5pm; in winter Wednesday to Saturday 11am to 4pm, Sunday noon to 4pm.

There are several **World War II military ruins** around town, including some that are still in use, such as the submarine dry dock that today fixes fishing boats. You can walk to other sites outside town, including the U.S. Army Fort Schwatka, on Mount Ballyhoo, about an hour's hike from the airport. The fort once had over 100 buildings. Many remain, including the best-preserved gun mounts and lookouts of all the nation's coastal defenses from the war. Besides, it's a spectacular site where you can see the ships returning. You will need to buy a hiking permit from the Ounalashka Corp. (see "Hiking," below). Also stop by the new Park Service visitor center at the airport.

The activity at the port is interesting to see, too, if only for the size of the vessels and harvest and the incredible investment in buildings and equipment.

GETTING OUTSIDE

BIRD-WATCHING Flip through the crisp, unused pages of your bird book to find out what you may see in the Aleutians. Several rare bird species nest in the area, and Asian birds occasionally drop in as accidentals. The whiskered auklet and red-legged kittiwake are among the birds commonly found around Unalaska that you probably haven't seen. You'll have greatest success taking a boat to a seabird colony. The Grand Aleutian Hotel (below, under "Accommodations") offers packages; it's also possible to combine halibut fishing and bird-watching on your own chartered boat (see "Fishing," below). You're also likely to encounter sea lions and other marine mammals.

FISHING You can fly out for salmon fishing from black-sand beaches, but Unalaska has become more famous for huge **halibut.** In 1995, a local sport fisherman caught a 395-pound halibut from an 18-foot skiff within a half mile of town; to kill the behemoth he had to beach it and beat it over the head with a rock. The next year, Fairbanks angler Jack Tragis landed the world's record halibut here, which weighed 459 pounds. If you're having trouble imagining a fish that big, drop by City Hall, where a replica hangs stuffed in the lobby. If you plan to fish, buy a $7 derby ticket from the visitor center; if you break the world record, you could win $100,000. (The world record was broken twice here recently.) John Lucking's **Far West Outfitters** (© 907/581-1647) brought in the 459-pounder. Charters are around $165 per person for a 4- to 6-hour trip, with a two-person minimum. Also check on packages with the place where you are staying, which can save money.

HIKING The island's green heather and rounded mountains of wildflowers are inviting for a walk. You can walk pretty much in any direction, looking at the abandoned World War II defenses; making a goal of a beach or one of the small peaks around the town; or, for the ambitious, even heading to the top of an active volcano, Mount Makushin. There are no bears and not many bugs, but there's great berry picking and beachcombing. The weather can be a threat, however, and fox holes can trip you up. As always in remote outdoor areas, you must be suitably dressed and leave word of where you're going and when you'll be back.

Hikers have to pay a fee to the **Ounalashka Corp.,** at 400 Salmon Way near the Grand Aleutian Hotel (© 907/581-1276), the Native village corporation that owns much of the island. Hiking is $6 per person per day, camping $11.

They're open Monday to Friday from 8am to 5pm; if you arrive when they are closed, you can get a permit from OC Security (the guys driving around town in the white pickup trucks with "SECURITY" written on the side in blue). For extended hikes, also go to the Department of Public Safety (see "Fast Facts: Dutch Harbor/Unalaska," above) for a travel-planning guide and to report your route on a travel plan that will assist with a search if you don't come back (not necessary if you're just going for a short ramble in the hills around town).

SEA KAYAKING   The Aleuts invented the kayak to hunt and travel. **Aleutian Adventure Sports** (see "Getting Around," above) rents kayaks and offers daily beginners' harbor tours (3½ hours, $50) as well as longer day trips and multiday expeditions. They also lead treks and volcano climbs, and rent mountain bikes.

ACCOMMODATIONS

If you're traveling alone, budget rooms in a clean, hostel-like place are available at **The Bunkhouse** (© 907/581-6247). They charge $55 per bed per night.

Carl's Bayview Inn   The building, in town on Iliuliuk Bay, looks a bit like a Dutch Harbor warehouse from the outside, but the eight kitchenette units and six suites inside are comfortable and attractive, with many amenities, pastel colors, and sweeping views. The double rooms, although clean, showed more signs of wear. Few rooms are reserved for nonsmokers.

606 Bayview (P.O. Box 730), Unalaska, AK 99685. © 800/581-1230 or 907/581-1230. Fax 907/581-1880. bayview@arctic.net. 30 units. $90 double, $125 double with kitchenette; $150 suite. Extra person $20. AE, DISC, MC, V. **Amenities:** Restaurant (pizza); bar; courtesy van; coin-op laundry; fish freezing. *In room:* TV.

Grand Aleutian Hotel ★★★   It's almost unreal to arrive at this big, luxurious hotel in a hard-driving Alaska Bush community. The Grand Aleutian is among the best hotels in Alaska, to say nothing of the Bush. For the same room in Anchorage, you'd pay considerably more, yet here you are minutes away from some of the best halibut fishing and bird-watching anywhere. The rooms are well designed and comfortable, many with good water views; the lobby is grand, with a huge stone fireplace; and there's a piano bar. As you walk outside into a driving gale, it's like teleporting from a big city hotel back to an exposed rock out in the North Pacific.

The **Chart Room** restaurant, on the second floor, allows bird-watchers to see waterfowl in the bay while dining on steak, seafood, or pasta. The menu, although brief, is Unalaska's most sophisticated. Dinner entrees range from $18 to $28. The **Margaret Bay Cafe,** downstairs, also has a good view, with grilled sandwiches and some lighter fare. A hamburger is $8.

The Japanese-owned UniSea fish-processing company (which built the hotel) has developed a full scope of sportfishing and birding packages to entice visitors, and booking one of those packages, including airfare, should save money. A 2-night package, which includes a boat visit to the Baby Islands bird colony to see the whiskered auklet, tufted and horned puffin, albatross, and other creatures, starts at about $1,300 per person, double occupancy. Longer packages with more birding trips are available, as well as fishing packages at about the same price.

498 Salmon Way (P.O. Box 921169), Dutch Harbor, AK 99692. © 800/891-1194 or 907/581-3844. Fax 907/581-7150. www.grandaleutian.com. 112 units. $175 double; $230 suite. Extra person $20. Packages available. AE, DC, DISC, MC, V. **Amenities:** 2 restaurants (see above); 2 bars; activities desk; courtesy van; limited room service; laundry service; fish freezing. *In room:* TV, hair dryer.

DINING

Two of the town's best restaurants are at the **Grand Aleutian Hotel,** described above. Here's the other contender.

Tino's Steak House AMERICAN   They pack in the commercial fishermen and other locals by serving huge portions of authentic Mexican food fast, as well as steaks, a few seafood items, and lots of sandwiches and burgers. I'm told you save money but get virtually the same meal by ordering from the lunch menu—the dinner prices are on the Unalaska scale, with most over $20.

11 N. Second St. at Broadway. © 907/581-4288. Lunch items $7–$14; dinner main courses $15–$40. AE, DISC, MC, V. Daily 8am–11pm.

5 The Pribilof Islands: Birder's Paradise

The Pribilof Islands of St. Paul and St. George sit out in the middle of the Bering Sea, due north of Unalaska, teeming with marine mammals and seabirds. Some 600,000 fur seals meet at the breeding rookeries in the summer, and 2 million birds of more than 200 species use the rocks. Bird-watchers visit St. Paul for one of the most exotic and productive birding and wildlife-viewing opportunities in Alaska. It's best during the spring migration, from mid-May to mid-June, when great numbers of birds show up, including rare Asian accidental species; the fall migration comes in late July and August. You can count on making rare sightings any time during the summer. Indeed, the National Audubon Society's *Field Guide to North American Birds* calls this "perhaps the most spectacular seabird colony in the world."

The islands are extremely remote, however, and the accommodations simple; if you're not interested in birding or spending a lot of time watching wildlife, it's probably too much money and trouble. There is only one hotel, the **King Eider,** which has basic rooms and shared bathrooms. There is no restaurant on the island, so guests are issued food vouchers for the mess hall at the Trident Seafoods fish-processing plant, near the hotel. Three meals a day come from a buffet there, and cost $10 to $17; you settle up at the end of your stay depending on how many vouchers you've used. There is also a grocery store across from the hotel.

Visitors generally come on tours, which are sold as a package with airfare and guiding by Aleuts and expert birders. With the guides' help and radio communication, your chances of seeing exotic species are much enhanced. The tours are offered by **Tanadguix Corp.,** 1500 W. 33rd Ave., Anchorage, AK 99503 (© 877/424-5637; www.alaskabirding.com). Check the website for birding news and species details. Packages from Anchorage start at $1,096 for a 2-night visit. Travelers can choose to ride on a bus as a group or hike on their own. Permanent blinds are in place for watching birds and seals. The weather is always cool and damp.

6 Nome: Arctic Frontier Town

The accidents of history deposited the streets and buildings of this lusty little town on the shore of Norton Sound, just south of the Arctic Circle in Northwest Alaska, and gave it qualities that make Nome an exceptionally attractive place for a visitor to go. For once, the local boosters' motto—in this case, "There's no place like Nome"—is entirely accurate, and that's because Nome, although itself nothing special to look at, combines a sense of history, a hospitable and somewhat silly attitude, and an exceptional location on the water in front of a tundra wilderness that's crossed by 250 miles of road. Those roads are the truly unique thing, for Nome is the only place in Arctic Alaska where a visitor can drive or bike deep into the open country, coming across musk oxen, reindeer, rarely seen birds, Native villages, undeveloped hot springs, and even an abandoned 1881 elevated train from New York City. Elsewhere, you're obliged to fly from rural hubs to get so far into the Bush, a more expensive and ambitious undertaking for casual explorers.

The accidents of history have been rather frequent in Nome. History has been downright sloppy. Start with the name. It's essentially a clerical error, caused by a British naval officer who, in 1850, was presumably in a creative dry spell when he wrote "? Name" on a diagram rather than name the cape he was sailing past. A mapmaker interpreted that as "Cape Nome." Or so goes one widely accepted explanation. The original gold rush of 1898 was caused by prospectors in the usual way, but a much larger 1899 population explosion happened after one of the '98 stampeders, left behind by an injury in a camp on the beach, panned the sand outside the tent—and found that it was full of gold dust. By 1900, a fourth of Alaska's white population was in Nome, sifting the sand. Small-time operators and tourists are still at it. A huge floating gold dredge of the kind that makes for major historic sites in Fairbanks and Dawson City sits idle on the edge of town. In Nome, it stopped operation only in recent years. There are two other, smaller dredges in town, too. Historic structures are few, however, as fires and storms have destroyed the town several times since the gold rush.

Nome has a particular, broad sense of humor. It shows up in the *Nome Nugget* newspaper and in silly traditions like the Labor Day bathtub race, the pack-ice golf tournament, and the Memorial Day polar bear swim. The population is half white and half Native, and the town is run largely by the white group. Some see Nome as a tolerant mixing place of different peoples, while the town strikes others as a bit colonial. Booze is outlawed in Kotzebue, the Native-dominated city to the north; but in Nome there is still a sloppy, gold rush style saloon scene. That sort of thing is prettier as historic kitsch than when it shows up in the form of a staggering Front Street drunk.

But you can ignore that, instead taking advantage of the great bargains to be had on Inupiat arts and crafts. And, most important, you can use one of the pleasant little inns or bed-and-breakfasts as a base to get into the countryside that beckons you down one of the gravel roads. Nome is popular with birdwatchers, who find the roads especially useful.

ESSENTIALS

GETTING THERE   Flying is the only way to get to Nome. **Alaska Airlines** (© **800/252-7522** or 907/443-2288; www.alaskaair.com) flies 90 minutes by jet either direct from Anchorage or with a brief hop from Kotzebue. Prices range from $350 to $600. Many visitors come on a package sold by **Alaska Airlines Vacations** (© **800/468-2248**), which first visits Kotzebue, starting at $496 per person, double occupancy; it is described in section 7 of this chapter, on Kotzebue.

All taxis operate according to a standard price schedule you can get from the visitor center. A ride to town from the airport is $5. Call **Nome Cab** (© **907/443-3030**) or **Checker Cab** (© **907/443-5521**).

VISITOR INFORMATION   The **Nome Convention and Visitors Bureau,** Front and Hunter streets (P.O. Box 240), Nome, AK 99762 (© **907/443-6624;** www.nomealaska.org), is exceptionally well run, providing maps and detailed information for diverse interests, and screening videos for those interested. The office is open mid-May to mid-September daily 9am to 7pm, mid-September to mid-May daily 9am to 6:30pm.

The **Bering Land Bridge National Preserve Headquarters,** Front Street (P.O. Box 220), Nome, AK 99762 (© **907/443-2522;** www.nps.gov/bela), is a good source of outdoors information from the rangers who staff a desk and are responsible for a rarely visited 2.3-million-acre national park unit, which covers much of the Seward Peninsula north of the Nome road system.

Also check the *Nome Nugget* website, at **www.nomenugget.com,** a real window into the community.

GETTING AROUND   The town is a street grid along the ocean. **Front Street** follows the sea wall, **First Avenue** is a block back, and so on. A harbor is at the north end of town, and the gold-bearing beach is to the south. You can mostly walk to see this area. Three roads branch out from Nome. I've described them below, under "On the Road." To get out on the roads, you need to take a tour or rent a car, or bring a bike with you.

Several local car-rental agencies operate in town; the visitor center maintains a list, with rates. **Stampede Rent-A-Car,** 527 Front St. (© **800/354-4606** or 907/443-3838), charges $75 a day for an SUV, $115 for a van. The same people operate the Aurora Inn (see "Accommodations," below).

FAST FACTS: Nome

Bank   **Wells Fargo,** with an ATM, is at 250 Front St.

Hospital   **Norton Sound Regional** is at Fifth Avenue and Bering Street (© **907/443-3311**).

Internet Access   **Nome Public Library** is at 200 Front St. (© **907/443-5133**).

Police   At Bering Street and Fourth Avenue (© **907/443-5262**).

Post Office   At Front Street and Federal Way.

Taxes   The **sales tax** is 4%; tax on **rooms** totals 8%.

SPECIAL EVENTS   The **Tesoro Iron Dog Snowmachine Race** (© **907/ 563-4414;** www.irondog.org), in mid-February, is the world's longest, at over 2,000 miles, running from Wasilla to Nome over the Iditarod Trail, and then ending up in Fairbanks.

The biggest event of the year is the **Iditarod Trail Sled Dog Race** (© **907/ 376-5155;** www.iditarod.com), a marathon of more than 1,000 miles that ends in Nome in mid-March. The sled dog racers and world media descend on the town for a few days of madness, with lots of community events planned. The activities last for the whole month; contact the Nome visitor center for a calendar. Among the most exciting vacations you could plan would be to volunteer to help put on the Iditarod; call the race headquarters at the number above well in advance to get the information you need. One of the March Iditarod events, showcasing Nome's well-developed sense of humor, is the **Bering Sea Ice Golf Classic** (© **907/443-5162**)—six holes are set up on the sea ice. The pressure ridges constitute a bad lie.

Various similar silly events take place all year, including the **Polar Bear Swim,** which occurs in the Bering Sea on Memorial Day, ice permitting, and the Labor

Day **Bathtub Race.** The **Midnight Sun Festival** (© 907/443-5535) celebrates the summer solstice, around June 21, when Nome gets more than 22 hours of direct sunlight, with a parade, softball tournament, bank holdup, raft race, and similar events. Winners of the raft race get possession for a year of the fur-lined honey bucket (known some places as a chamber pot).

ATTRACTIONS & ACTIVITIES IN TOWN

Most of Nome's original buildings were wiped out by fires or by storms off Norton Sound that tore across the beach and washed away major portions of the business district. A seawall, completed in 1951, now protects the town. An interesting **Historical Walking Tour,** produced by the Alaska Historical Commission and the Lion's Club, is available from the visitor center; it covers 20 sites, including a turn-of-the-20th-century church and saloon, and a bust of Roald Amundsen, who landed near Nome, in Teller, after crossing the North Pole from Norway in a dirigible in 1926. Below the library, at Front Street and Lanes Way, the small **Carrie M. McLain Memorial Museum** (© 907/443-2566) contains an exhibit on the town's gold rush. The museum is free and open summer daily noon to 8pm, winter Tuesday to Saturday from noon to 6pm.

In good weather, a pleasant walk is to be had southeast of town, along the **beach.** Small-time miners may be camped there, but the gold-bearing sand extends for miles more of solitary walking. You can buy a gold pan in town and try your luck, but the sand has been sifted for nearly 100 years, so don't expect to gather any significant amount of gold. The **Swanberg Dredge** you can see from here operated until the 1950s; a large dredge north of town worked into the mid-1990s. The 38 gold dredges that once operated on the Seward Peninsula crept across the tundra, creating their own ponds to float in as they went. The **cemetery,** with white wooden crosses on top of a little hill just out of town, also is worth a look.

Several companies offer **organized tours. Nome Discovery Tours** (© 907/443-2814; Discover@dwarf.nome.net) has the asset of talented professional actor Richard Beneville as the van driver and tour guide. He'll pick you up and drive you anywhere in the area, sharing his quirky enthusiasm and extensive knowledge of the surroundings. The highlight is the wildlife and scenery on the roads out of town, and he also visits an ivory carver and working gold mine. Half days are $45 per person, full days $85. **Nome Tour and Marketing,** at the Nugget Inn, at Front and Bering streets (© 907/443-2651), is a more traditional tour, with a dogsled demonstration and gold panning. It is timed to meet flights bringing in visitors on packages, running in the summer only, and costs $52 per person. Bike tours are listed below under "On the Road."

If you're in the market for walrus ivory carvings and other **Inupiat arts and crafts,** you'll find low prices and an extraordinary selection in Nome. Jim West has a legendary collection for sale, assembled in the bar room of the historic **Board of Trade Saloon** that is attached to a shop on Front Street. The **Arctic Trading Post** is more of a traditional gift shop and also has a good ivory collection. **Sitnasuak Heritage Gallery** and **Maruskiya's** are both also on Front Street. **Chukotka-Alaska,** at 185 West First Ave., is an importer of art and other goods from the Russian Far East, and is really worth a look. Alaska Native art you find in Nome is likely to be authentic, but still ask; see "Native Art: Finding the Real Thing" in chapter 2. International visitors should see chapter 3 to find out about the special permit you need to carry ivory out of the United States.

ON THE ROAD

The modest attractions downtown would hardly justify a trip to Nome, but the city's surroundings do. The roads provide unique access to a large stretch of the Seward Peninsula. Unlike other Arctic Bush areas, where you need to have someone take you where you want to go, in Nome all you have to do is rent a car and go. There are few cars in Nome (they have to be flown in or shipped by barge), so you won't see many other vehicles on a huge expanse of spectacular territory, with wildlife-viewing opportunities as good as anywhere in the state.

Most of the land is managed by the **Bureau of Land Management (BLM),** P.O. Box 925, Nome, AK 99762 (© **907/443-2177;** aurora.ak.blm.gov). The **Alaska Department of Transportation** (© **907/443-3444**) can provide current information on road conditions. You have a good chance of seeing moose, reindeer, owls, foxes, bears, and musk ox anywhere you drive, but check in with the visitor center or the **Alaska Department of Fish and Game,** at Front and Steadman streets, to find out the best locales to see animals. They can also give you guidance on fishing along the roads and a "Nome Roadside Fishing Guide," or download it from www.state.ak.us/adfg (click on "sportfish," then "region 3," then "northwest"). Check "Getting Around," above, for how to get out on the roads.

ROAD HIGHLIGHTS   None of the three roads radiating from Nome have services of any kind—just small Native villages, a few dwellings, and some reindeer herders—so you must be prepared and bring what you need with you, including insect repellent and a good spare tire. The visitor center provides a good road guide. Here are some highlights:

The **Nome-Council road** heads 72 miles to the east, about half of that on the shoreline. It turns inland at the ghost town of Solomon, an old mining town with an abandoned railroad train known as the Last Train to Nowhere. The engines were originally used on the New York City elevated lines in 1881, then were shipped to Alaska in 1903 to serve the miners along this line to Nome. This is a great scenic spot for bird-watching, and fishing is good in the Solomon River, all along the road. Council, near the end of the road, has a couple of dozen families in the summer. A 3-foot-deep river separates the road from the village.

The **Nome-Taylor road,** also known as the Kougarok Road, runs north of town into the Kigluaik Mountains, 85 miles from Nome, eventually petering out and becoming impassable. About 40 miles out, you reach lovely Salmon Lake, with a lakeshore campground with picnic tables, grills, and outhouses. A few miles farther, a road to the left leads to the 125° Pilgrim Hot Springs, near a Catholic church. Access is limited to when the caretaker is on hand, so check with the visitor center before going.

The **Nome-Teller road** leads 73 miles to the village of Teller, which has 266 residents, a gift shop, and a store. It's an opportunity to see an authentic Arctic Native village.

MOUNTAIN BIKING   The roads of Nome are one of the world's great, undiscovered mountain biking destinations—where else can you bike past musk oxen and reindeer? Keith Conger's **Bering C Bikes** (© **907/443-4994**) offers guided bike day trips and van-supported multiday camping expeditions. Keith, a biologist (and high school volleyball coach), leads the tours and teaches about the ecology of the land they pedal through. He also sells and fixes bikes, but, unfortunately, no one in town rents bikes. For bike enthusiasts, it may be worth renting one in Anchorage or bringing yours from home.

BIRD-WATCHING   Bird-watchers will make many discoveries out on the Nome roads, using new pages of their bird books. A bird list is available at the visitor center, and they can tell you where to look—each of the three roads has a different habitat. The best times to visit for birding are right around Memorial Day, and from July to mid-August. Lana and Richard Harris are Nome's leading birders of long standing, and the only local members of the American Birding Association. Lana can most easily be reached at the visitor center, where she now works, but the couple also maintains a **birders' hotline** on their home phone recorder (℃ **907/443-5528**); please don't call before 6am or after 10pm, Alaska time. There's a chance to see Siberian birds, and you can count on bluethroats, yellow wagtails, wheatears, Arctic warblers, and Aleutian and Arctic terns. Nome is the only place to see a bristle-thighed curlew without chartering a plane. You don't need a guide, although guided trips are available (check with the visitor center). As Lana put it, "If you haven't found a yellow wagtail, you haven't left the bar yet."

IN THE AIR

Nome is a hub for Bush plane operators. Flightseeing charters are available, or you can fly on one of the mail-run routes out to the villages and spend a couple of hours touring for as little as $90; check how long the plane will stay in the village, as you may want to fly back on a different run to get more time. The visitor center or the flight services will help you figure it out. Among the operators are **Olson Air** (℃ **800/478-5600** in Alaska only, or 907/443-2229; drdonny@nook.net) or **Cape Smythe Air** (℃ **800/478-5125** in Alaska only, or 907/443-2414; www.capesmythe.com). Don't go in bad weather—you'll see little and may get stuck in a tiny village. You can also fly 150 miles over the International Dateline and see Russia from the air and the narrow water that divides our two nations. **Bering Air** (℃ **800/443-5465** in Alaska only, or 907/443-5620; www.beringair.com) specializes in these trips, which cost $150 for a 2-hour flight.

ACCOMMODATIONS

There are several good B&Bs and motel rooms besides those listed in full below. The **Nanuaq Manor** (℃ **907/443-5296**), **Nugget Inn** (℃ **877/443-2323** or 907/443-2323), and **Ponderosa Inn** (℃ **907/443-5737**) all have decent rooms, in decreasing order of cost. **Ocean View Bed and Breakfast** (℃ **907/443-2133**) is nice. Staying at a B&B makes sense, as your host can introduce you to the community in a less contrived way than a formal tour company. I do not recommend the Polaris Inn; I would cancel a trip to Nome before staying there.

Aurora Inn and Executive Suites ⟨★⟩   Choose, at the same price, among these two comfortable buildings with different styles of accommodations under the same ownership. The Aurora Inn offers the best traditional hotel rooms in town in a brand-new mock country inn on the town's main street. The Executive Suites comprise a dozen apartmentlike units, ranging from rooms with kitchenettes to two-bedroom apartments with full kitchens and living areas. That building, too, is only a couple of years old. Uniquely in town, they have lots of no-smoking rooms. Don't put too much faith in the rates listed here; instead, call and see what kind of deal you can work out.

Inn is located at 527 Front St.; Executive Suites is located at 226 W. D St. (P.O. Box 1008), Nome, AK 99762. ℃ 800/354-4606 or 907/443-3838. Fax 907/443-6380. 35 units. www.aurorainnome.com. Summer $120 double; $175 suite. Extra person over age 15 $10. AE, MC, V. **Amenities:** Sauna; car rental; coin-op laundry. *In room:* TV, dataport, hair dryer.

June's Bed and Breakfast *Finds* June Engstrom hosts this traditional little B&B, proudly declaring, "I really am a gold digger's daughter." Her sourdough pancake starter came over the Chilkoot Trail in 1898, and she gives it and the recipe away to guests (the starter is the yeast concoction that prospectors cultivated on the trail). The rooms are cozy, not commodious, but June's gregarious hospitality makes it special. Each has one of her handmade quilts.

231 E. Fourth Ave. (P.O. Box 489), Nome, AK 99762. © 800/494-6994 or 907/443-5984; Oct–May 206/547-7826. 3 units, none with private bathroom. $80 double. Rates include full breakfast. No credit cards. Closed Oct–May. **Amenities:** Courtesy car; free laundry use. *In room:* No telephone.

Sweet Dreams B&B Again, it's the host who makes this place special, in this case Nome Mayor Leo Rasmussen, a personable and funny man and a deep well of Nome history and local knowledge. The two-story house has a rustic, old-fashioned feel, with lots of Alaskan memorabilia and a sun room on top.

77 W. Fourth St. (P.O. Box 2), Nome, AK 99762. © 907/443-2919. leaknome@noak.net. 3 units, none with private bathroom. $95 double. Rates include full breakfast. MC, V.

DINING

There's not a selection of places where you'd go out of your way to dine, but you can find an adequate family meal at various establishments in Nome, all along Front Street.

Several restaurants are operated by immigrant families, who offer their national cuisine along with standard American-style fare. There sometimes is a language barrier with the servers. **Nachos,** at 503 Front St. in the Old Federal Building (© **907/443-5503**), has OK American-style Mexican food, barbecue, and good Chinese. The $11 lunch buffet is popular. **Milano's Pizzeria** (© **907/ 443-2924**), in the same building, serves Italian and Japanese meals; its pizza gets highly recommended by the locals. **Twin Dragons,** on Front Street near Steadman Street (© **907/443-5552**), has made it for years with Chinese food alone, which is consistently good; it's probably the best you can reliably get in Nome. All of these take Visa and MasterCard.

The other flavor of restaurant in Nome, and the most popular locally, is the classic American greasy spoon. The ethnic restaurants mentioned above all have a way to escape the smoke; these burger habitats tend to be smoky throughout. The **Polar Cub Restaurant,** at 225 Front St. (© **907/443-5191**), has an extensive dinner menu and prices that are reasonable for the Alaska Bush. **Fat Freddy's Restaurant,** in the Nugget Inn (© **907/443-5899**), serves more expensive fare in the evening, such as steaks and fried fish, in addition to the usual sandwiches; their prices are higher than those in the Polar Cub.

The **Fort Davis Roadhouse,** on the beach about 2 miles east of town on the Nome-Council Road (© **907/443-2660**), is the only fine-dining experience in town, with open views of the tundra and water. The roast beef and buffet are the best choices. It's open Monday through Friday 6pm to 10pm, Saturday and Sunday 6pm till midnight.

7 Kotzebue: Big Village

Although its 3,082 residents make Kotzebue (*kotz*-eh-biew) a good-size town, with a bank, a hospital, and a couple of grocery stores, I've heard it called a village instead. A "village," in Alaskan parlance, is a remote Native settlement in the Bush, generally with fewer than a few hundred residents, where people live relatively close to the traditional lifestyle of their indigenous ancestors. Kotzebue is a support hub for the villages of the Northwest Arctic, with jet service and a booming cash economy, but it's populated and run by the Inupiat—fish-drying racks and old dogsleds are scattered along the streets, and Native culture is thriving. It does feel like a village.

For visitors, this characteristic makes Kotzebue unique because you can see real Eskimo culture without leaving the comforts of jet travel and standard hotel rooms behind. Or, if you don't mind giving up some of those comforts, you can get even closer to the Inupiat way of life. For adventurous outdoors people, Kotzebue offers access to huge areas of remote public land through which you can float on a raft or canoe. **Kobuk Valley National Park,** with its bizarre sand dunes, **Noatak National Preserve,** and **Cape Krusenstern National Monument** are among the largest national park units in the country, and among the least visited.

It's important to realize from the outset, however, that outside of an organized bus tour, there's absolutely nothing to do in Kotzebue. As I was told, "You have to shoot something or burn a lot of gas to have any fun around here." Kotzebue is not set up for independent travelers except those of the most intrepid ilk, and they will most likely use the town as a way to get into the remote public lands. Nome offers more for the independent traveler interested in something in between an organized tour and a wilderness expedition.

The dominant business in town is the **NANA Corporation,** a regional Native corporation representing the roughly 7,000 Inupiat who live in this Northwest Arctic region the size of Indiana. NANA, which stands for Northwest Arctic Native Association, is a successful example of how the 1971 Alaska Native Claims Settlement Act gave the indigenous people control over their own destiny. With huge land and resource holdings and the cash to develop them, NANA is making money for its Inupiat shareholders and providing them with jobs in institutional catering and oil drilling, and at the Red Dog zinc mine near Kotzebue, the world's most productive. More relevant for visitors, NANA also owns the main hotel and tourist businesses in Kotzebue.

ESSENTIALS

GETTING THERE The only way to Kotzebue is by air. **Alaska Airlines** (© **800/252-7522;** www.alaskaair.com) has several daily jets from Anchorage and Fairbanks in the summer. You'll pay in the range of $350 to $600 round-trip from Anchorage. They also fly from Kotzebue to Nome. The cheapest and really the only sensible way for most tourists to go to Kotzebue is to take a package offered by **Tour Arctic** and **Alaska Airlines Vacations,** described under "Attractions & Activities," below.

VISITOR INFORMATION There is no town visitor center. The National Park Service staffs the **Iñiaigvik Education and Information Center** at Second Avenue and Lake Street (P.O. Box 1029), Kotzebue, AK 99752 (© **907/ 442-3760;** www.nps.gov/noaa), providing information and displays on the immense area of protected land in the region and offering classes in topics such as basket weaving and medicinal plants. Employees will answer questions about the town as well. It's open in summer daily from 8am to 6pm, by appointment in winter.

The local headquarters of the Park Service, Fish and Wildlife Service, and Bureau of Land Management are open during normal business hours all year. The **Park Service headquarters** is behind the post office on Shore Avenue (© 907/442-8300), and the other agencies are at 120 Second Ave.

GETTING AROUND Kotzebue is 26 miles north of the Arctic Circle on the Chukchi Sea. About a mile by 2 miles in size, it sits on a low spit of land extending into the shallow Kotzebue Sound. You can walk pretty much everywhere you need to go or take a cab if you have luggage. The main hotel is a 15-minute walk from the airport, and taxis are available from **Polar Cab** (✆ **907/442-2233**). If you're on the Tour Arctic package, buses will pick you up at the plane and deliver you and your luggage to the hotel. The gravel streets are on a warped grid radiating from **Shore Avenue,** also known as **Front Street,** which runs along the water. Roads extend only a few miles out of town.

 FAST FACTS: Kotzebue

Alcohol Legality The sale of **alcohol** is illegal in Kotzebue, but possession for personal use is permitted.

Bank **Wells Fargo,** with an ATM, is at the corner of Lagoon Street and Second Avenue.

Hospital The **Maniilaq Medical Center,** with a 24-hour emergency room, is at Fifth Avenue and Ted Stevens Way (✆ **907/442-3321**).

Police For nonemergency calls, contact the **Kotzebue Police Department** at ✆ **907/442-3351** or the **Alaska State Troopers** at ✆ **907/442-3222**.

Post Office Shore Avenue and Tundra Way.

Taxes **Sales tax** is 6%; the **tax on rooms** totals 12%.

SPECIAL EVENTS The **Fourth of July** is something special in Kotzebue. Besides the Independence Day celebration, it's the earliest you can count on all the snow being gone.

ATTRACTIONS & ACTIVITIES

There is only one activity in town, and it's part of an organized tour. **Tour Arctic** (✆ **907/442-3747**) hosts around 10,000 visitors annually in its cultural and natural-history program, the centerpiece of which is the seasonal **NANA Museum of the Arctic,** across from the airport. For most people, the packages, also sold through **Alaska Airlines Vacations** (✆ **800/468-2248**), are the only sensible way to go to Kotzebue. You'll learn about the Arctic and Native culture, but the tour is scripted and there are no spectacular sights on the way. Owned and operated by the Inupiat, the company employs real Eskimo guides who offer commentary for about 5 hours while keeping customers comfortable, mostly in buses and indoors. A show at the museum includes children dancing, a blanket toss, and a high-tech slide show about the struggle to save Inupiat culture. The tour also includes a talk and demonstration in a tent about the clothing and survival techniques of the Eskimos. There's also a brief opportunity to walk on the tundra. Independent travelers in town for outdoor activities can attend the hour-long museum program only for $35, the culture camp for $20, or the whole tour for $90; museum shows are timed to match the arrival of flights, at 4 and 6:30pm. The price is high, but it's the only thing to do in town.

Day-trip packages are $366 from Anchorage, less than a full-fare ticket. The same tour with an overnight stay and a day in Nome is $496 per person, double occupancy. You can choose to spend the night in Kotzebue at NANA's

Nullagvik Hotel or in Nome at the Nugget Inn; choose Kotzebue for the lodgings, Nome for the variety of things to do in your off-tour hours. Any of those visits will feel brief, with little time for anything but the structured tours. A 2-night trip, one each in Nome and Kotzebue, is $547 per person, double, and adds more free time. Adding an excursion to the village of Kiana and a lengthy flightseeing trip over the Northwest Arctic region, including the Kobuk Sand Dunes, requires another night and an additional $350 per person, double.

GETTING OUTSIDE

A FISH CAMP   Some rugged and curious travelers may want something a bit less pampered and scripted than the Tour Arctic program. **Arctic Circle Educational Adventures** (© **907/442-6013** in summer, 907/276-0976 in winter; http://fishcamp.org) offers a chance to stay at a camp similar to the fish camps where Native people spend the summer gathering food for the winter—and to participate in set-net fishing, fish cutting, food gathering, and other traditional subsistence activities as well as hiking, town tours, and bird-watching. The camp on the beach 5 miles south of town is crude, and only for people who don't mind using an outhouse or sleeping in a plywood cabin. Elderhostel groups sometimes come for a week. Rates are $150 to $250 a day for the tour activities plus $95 per person per day for lodgings and meals. The season is late June to mid-August.

FLIGHTSEEING   You can get an idea of what Native villages look like and see the **Kobuk Valley National Park,** including the Great Kobuk Sand Dunes, a desertlike area of shifting 100-foot dunes, from the air by buying a round-trip seat on one of the scheduled bush planes that serve the area. **Cape Smythe Air** (© **907/442-3020;** http://capesmythe.com) charges $189 for its loop that includes Shungnak and Kobuk and overflies the dunes (make sure to tell the pilot what you want to see). For $118, you can fly a shorter, northern loop to Noatak and Kivalina, over the **Cape Krusenstern National Monument.**

FLOAT TRIPS   There are several remote rivers near Kotzebue with easy self-guided floating for experienced outdoors people. This is a rare chance to get deep into the Arctic on your own. The great Noatak River originates in the Brooks Range and flows 450 miles through America's largest undisturbed wilderness, in the impressive scenery of the Noatak National Preserve. The Selawik, Squirrel, and Kobuk rivers all have long sections of easy water. **Alaska Discovery,** and **Equinox Wilderness Expeditions,** listed in chapter 2 under section 6, "Planning an Outdoor Vacation," have float trips in the area, although not necessarily every year. Expect to pay $3,000 per person, including air travel.

⸢ *Tips* **Which Arctic Tour to Choose**

Visitors can encounter Alaska Native culture on guided tours in Kotzebue, with an optional add-on to Nome, or in Barrow. Nome is best visited as an independent traveler, but the tours make more sense in the other two communities. The tours are similar, involving a ride in a small bus and indoor presentations of Inupiat dance, culture, and crafts. Kotzebue's tour was more informative and seemed better thought-out when I took it, but Barrow has the better sights: the nation's northernmost point, the brand-new Inupiat Heritage Center, and the chance, at least, of seeing a whale landed on the beach.

Most river running in the region is self-guided. Get details from *The Alaska River Guide,* by Karen Jettmar, director of Equinox (Alaska Northwest Books). Obviously you should be experienced in the outdoors and in river floating before heading out for a multiday trip in the Arctic. And plan ahead, arranging details well in advance with the Park Service and your pilot. Most visitors bring all their gear from Anchorage, but Buck Maxson of **Arctic Air Guides** (© 907/442-3030) rents rafts and canoes for $35 a day. An experienced bush pilot, he can fly you wherever you want to go, charging $320 an hour. You can minimize your costs by putting in or taking out at villages along the river and using scheduled air services (see "Flightseeing," above).

ACCOMMODATIONS & DINING

Dining options in Kotzebue are limited. Besides the hotel restaurant listed below, you'll find good breakfasts and great burgers at the **Bayside Inn,** right next door (© 907/442-3600). I cannot recommend their rooms, however. There is also **Mario's Pizza and Deli,** at 606 Bison St. (© 907/442-2666), a Japanese-Chinese-pizza-burger take-out place that serves sushi.

To save some money and meet friendly local people, stay at **Lagoon Bed and Breakfast,** 227 Lagoon St. (© 907/442-3723; mar81wsw@otz.net).

Nullagvik Hotel ⚐   The NANA-owned hotel is thoughtfully designed and comfortably furnished. The clean, up-to-date rooms have all the features of a good chain hotel. Their windows angle out from the building so that all get at least some ocean view. It can be startling to see Eskimo women wearing summer parkas called *kuspuks* cleaning in the halls; they certainly do a thorough job. By booking with an Alaska Airlines Vacations package, you save considerable money on stays here.

The **restaurant** is clean and nicely decorated, with a good view and flowers on the table. Certainly it is the best in town. Reindeer steak and Arctic salmon are on the menu for the tourists. Locals are more likely to come in for the popular Sunday breakfast, or order the less expensive sandwiches and beef for lunch. It is closed October through mid-May.

Shore Ave. and Tundra Way (P.O. Box 336), Kotzebue, AK 99752. © 907/442-3331. Fax 907/442-3340. 73 units. High season $149 double. Low season $121 double. AE, DC, DISC, MC, V. **Amenities:** Restaurant. *In room:* TV, telephone.

8 Barrow: Way North

The main reason visitors go to Barrow is its latitude. The Inupiat town is the northernmost settlement on the North American continent, above the 71st parallel. Here half-liquid land comes to an arbitrary point at the north tip of Alaska. The tundra around Barrow is dotted with lakes divided by tendrils of swampy tundra no more substantial than the edges of fine lace. On this haven for migratory waterfowl, the flat, wet land and the ocean seem to merge. Indeed, for all but a few months, it's all a flat, frozen plain of ocean and land. For 65 days in the winter, the sun never rises. In the summer, it doesn't set, and the ice recedes from the shore only for the months of the brief summer. Such extreme geography is a magnet—people want to stand in such a place, perhaps dip a toe in the Arctic Ocean.

And then what do you do next? If you're on a package trip, you can see an Eskimo blanket toss and dancing, look at whale bones and maybe buy Native crafts, and see some other manifestations of traditional Inupiat life amid a modern, oil-enriched town. An **Inupiat Heritage Center,** completed in 1999, exhibits and teaches about the culture. But there's no need to spend the night if your only interest is sightseeing. You can do it in a day and be back in Fairbanks or Anchorage in the evening.

The town of 4,581 is culturally unique. It's ancient, and still a center of whaling from open boats, with a summer festival celebrating a successful hunt and distribution of the meat to the community. But Barrow also is the seat of the North Slope Borough, a county government encompassing a larger area than the state of Nebraska, in which lies North America's largest oil field. The borough has everything money can buy for a local government, yet the people of the villages still must contend with crushing ice, snooping polar bears, and utter isolation.

ESSENTIALS

GETTING THERE   **Alaska Airlines** ($\mathcal{C}$ **800/252-7522;** www.alaskaair.com) flies to Barrow daily from Anchorage and Fairbanks, and offers 1-day and overnight tour packages, described in "Attractions & Activities," below. The packages are a good deal, competitive with round-trip tickets alone from Anchorage, which range from $450 to $700. Book them through **Alaska Airlines Vacations** ($\mathcal{C}$ **800/468-2248**).

VISITOR INFORMATION   A chamber of commerce **visitor center,** at Momegana and Ahkovak streets, near the airport, operates in the summer only 10am to 2pm, with a guide to talk to but little else. The town lacks a central tourism authority, but you can write ahead for information from the City Barrow, Office of the Mayor, P.O. Box 629, Barrow, AK 99723 ($\mathcal{C}$ **907/852-5211;** fax 907/852-5871; barrowmayor@nuvuk.com).

GETTING AROUND   Facing the Chukchi Sea, Barrow has two sections, lying on each side of Isatkoak Lagoon. **Browerville,** to the east, has the Inupiat Heritage Center and the Alaska Commercial store, with a food court and many services. **Barrow,** containing most businesses, is to the west. The northern tip of Alaska, **Point Barrow,** is north of the town on a spit. The road leads 6 miles in that direction to a point tour companies advertise as the "farthest north point navigable by bus," but the absolute end is farther out, beyond the road. **All-terrain vehicles** are for rent in town, if you're going to be compulsive about it. Gas Field Road is the only other route out of town, leading 10 miles out onto the tundra.

Taxis are handy, charging a flat $5 anywhere in town ($3 for seniors), plus $1 for each additional passenger. **Barrow Taxi** ($\mathcal{C}$ **907/852-2222**) is one cab service.

Barrow has an extraordinary bus system. The exact location of the buses is broadcast on TV channel 57 so riders can step right out the door without waiting; this saves them from standing in –40° weather in the company of polar bears. The fare is 50¢.

Jim Vordestrasse, the mayor ($\mathcal{C}$ **907/852-5211**), rents bicycles for $20 a day and offers tours by appointment for $20 an hour, proudly showing off the town while riding a bike trail that goes all over.

SPECIAL EVENTS   The return of the sun after 2 months below the horizon is met by traditional celebrations on **January 21.** The **Piuraagiaqt,** a spring festival, takes place in mid-April. If the traditional bowhead whaling season is a success, the **Nalukataq festival** in late June celebrates the event. The length of the celebration depends on the number of whales landed. If you're very lucky, as I once was, you'll be there when a whale is landed, pulled up on the town beach, and butchered by the community.

FAST FACTS: Barrow

Alcohol Legality The sale of alcohol is illegal in Barrow, and importation for personal use controlled. If it's an issue, call ahead.

Bank At Agvik and Kiogak streets, with an ATM.

Hospital Find one on Agvik Street (℃ **907/852-4611**).

Police Contact the borough **Department of Public Safety** (℃ **907/ 852-6111**).

Taxes There is no sales or bed tax in Barrow.

ATTRACTIONS & ACTIVITIES

The new **Inupiat Heritage Center** (℃ **907/852-4584**) is the town's main attraction. Completed in 1999, it is part museum, part gathering center, and part venue for living culture. Inside is a workshop for craftspeople and a performance space for storytellers and dancers. In the museum area, displays of Inupiat artifacts change regularly; for at least part of 2002, it will house an exhibit of dolls and figurines from ancient times to the present. If you have time, you can even join classes on myths and legends, ivory carving, the Inupiaq language, or many other topics. The center is open May 15 to September 15 Monday to Friday 8:30am to 3pm to the public, and is open for the Tundra Tours cultural show 3 to 5pm (see below). Admission is $5 adults, $2 ages 6 to 17, free 5 or younger or over age 55.

The main tourism business in town, Native-owned **Tundra Tours** (℃ **800/ 882-8478** or 907/852-3900; www.AlaskaOne.com/topworld), along with the Top of the World Hotel, is owned by the Arctic Slope Regional Corp., a Native corporation covering the region. Their tour (the same one sold through Alaska Airlines Vacations) presents the town to visitors who arrive with little idea of what to expect. The 6-hour summer tour, in a small bus, drives around the town to show off the modest sights, including the school, an Eskimo boat, the cemetery, a stop for a dip of toes in the Arctic Ocean at the farthest north point, and so on. It's interesting to drive one of the short roads out of town to find snowy owls and Arctic fox. The owls stand still out on the flat tundra like bowling pins. The tour visits the new Inupiat Heritage Center for a blanket toss and cultural presentation, with a drumming and dance performance, and a valuable chance to buy gifts from local craftspeople.

The day-trip tour is $399 from Anchorage, or $450 per person, double occupancy, to spend 1 night in Barrow at the Top of the World Hotel, giving you a chance to walk around a bit on your own; both prices include air fare and are less than buying a plane ticket alone. Book the tour through Alaska Airlines Vacations or with Tundra Tours at the numbers listed above. If you buy the tour separately, it's $65. They also offer a more expensive winter tour for seeing the Aurora.

ACCOMMODATIONS

If you spend the night on the package tour, you'll stay at the **Top of the World Hotel** (℃ **907/852-3900**; www.AlaskaOne.com/topworld), which has standard hotel rooms, some overlooking the water. Here are choices for independent travelers.

> **Fun Fact Bush Softball**
>
> Barrow is mad for the game. You can hear the play-by-play on the radio, but to attend you will need a car: that's how the spectators watch on the chilly Arctic evenings, honking for good plays. And remember: If a ball disappears completely from view in a puddle, runners can advance no more than two bases.
>
> On the rocky, mountainous Aleutian island of Unalaska, their problem was too small a field, so home runs carried heavy penalties. Hit three in a season and you were permanently expelled from the league. But that's all past: They recently built a new, larger field, at a cost of nearly $3 million, including the cost of bringing nine shipping-van containers of sod out from Palmer.

Barrow Airport Inn   These relatively economical rooms in a family-operated establishment are clean and come with a continental breakfast and many homey amenities. Nine have full kitchens for the same price.

1815 Momegana St. (P.O. Box 933), Barrow, AK 99723. ✆ **907/852-2525**. Fax 907/852-2528. 16 units. $115 double. Rates include continental breakfast. MC, V. **Amenities:** Travel agency. *In room:* TV, fridge, microwave oven, coffeemaker.

King Eider Inn ⭐   The best rooms in town are found in this new building near the airport. With the large stone fireplace in the lobby and large seating area, it feels like a lodge. The rooms are fresh and attractive; eight have kitchenettes, stocked with microwave popcorn. Bathrooms have showers only, not tubs.

1752 Ahkovak St. (P.O. Box 1283), Barrow, AK 99723. ✆ **907/852-4700**. Fax 907/852-2025. www. kingeider.net. 19 units. Summer $185 double. Winter $160 double. Extra person $30. AE, MC, V. **Amenities:** Sauna; car rental; courtesy van. *In room:* TV, telephone.

DINING

There are several decent restaurants in Barrow. Generally, they stay open very late, have TVs always on, offer free delivery, and don't offer decaffeinated coffee—I have no idea why.

Adjoining the Top of the World Hotel, **Pepe's North of the Border,** at 1204 Agvik St. (✆ **907/852-8200**), is the most famous place in town, serving large portions of familiar American-style Mexican food, steak, and seafood. The tours come here for lunch, and host Fran Tate hands out souvenirs. Summer hours are Monday through Saturday 6am to 10pm, Sunday 8am to 10pm; winter is the same except 9am to 9pm Sunday.

Arctic Pizza, at 125 Apayauk St. (✆ **907/852-4222**), has two dining rooms, a family place downstairs, and a no-kids-allowed room upstairs, with a gorgeous view of the Arctic Ocean. It is open Sunday through Thursday 11:30am to 11pm, Friday and Saturday 11:30am to midnight.

You'll find a menu with something for everyone in a fine-dining atmosphere at **Northern Lights Restaurant,** at 5122 Herman St. (✆ **907/852-3300**), open daily 11am to midnight. **Teriyaki House,** 1906 Takpuk St. (✆ **907/852-2276**), serves good Japanese, Chinese, and Korean food in a well-worn dining room. Open Monday through Friday 11:30am to midnight, they don't take credit cards.

9 Prudhoe Bay: Arctic Industry

The Prudhoe (*prew*-dough) Bay complex is no ordinary oil field: It's a historic and strategic site of great importance and a major technological achievement. It was built the way you'd have to build an oil field on the moon, with massively complex machinery able to operate in winters that are always dark and very, very cold. But in some ways, it might be simpler to build on the moon—here, the industry has to coexist with a critical habitat for migrating caribou and waterfowl, on wet, fragile tundra that permanently shows any mark made by vehicles. It works, and that's quite an achievement. Workers are forbidden even to set foot on the tundra, and as you look from the edge of one of the gravel pads the heathery ground looks as undisturbed as a calm sea.

To see Prudhoe Bay, you have to sign up for a tour. Everything is behind security checkpoints. The tour visits the Arctic Ocean and gives you a chance to see the tundra and touch the pipeline, but it doesn't go inside any of the buildings where the heavy-duty, high-tech equipment handles the oil and readies it for passage down the line. From the outside, these buildings and the oil wells don't look like much—just metal-sided industrial buildings. The grim town of **Deadhorse,** which serves the oil facility, is really more of an industrial yard, barely deserving to be called a town; it certainly isn't anything you'd travel to see. Frankly, I can't recommend taking the time and expense required for a Prudhoe Tour. If you're curious about the Arctic, a trip to Barrow, Kotzebue, or Nome makes more sense. (The oil companies' VIP tours, which do go inside, are fascinating, but you have to be a VIP.)

If you still want to go, fly up from Fairbanks or Anchorage for the day and take the tour from Deadhorse. There's no need to spend the night if you fly, as the tour takes less than 3 hours and there's nothing else to do and nowhere else to go. Or, if you drive up on the Dalton Highway, you can engage a tour in Deadhorse, or just get a lift to the water, through the oil complex. See chapter 9, on the Interior, for information on driving the Dalton. **Alaska Airlines** (© **800/252-7522;** www.alaskaair.com) serves Prudhoe Bay. A round-trip ticket costs around $600 from Anchorage.

Once at Prudhoe, the **Arctic Caribou Inn,** P.O. Box 340112, Prudhoe Bay, AK 99734 (© **907/659-2368** in summer or 907/659-2840 in winter), provides visitor services, including a hotel and cafeteria, plus tours and a shuttle service to the Arctic Ocean. Rooms start at $120 double. The restaurant has a buffet for breakfast ($10.50) and dinner ($18), and menu service for lunch. The hotel is near the airport in Deadhorse and serves as the starting point for the tours. The oil complex tour costs $50. It includes a video and lasts 2½ hours. It doesn't go inside any of the buildings, but it does stop at the shore of the Arctic Ocean. The 1½-hour round-trip just to touch the ocean costs $25.

Gray Line of Alaska (© **800/544-2206,** or 907/277-5581 in Anchorage; www.graylineofalaska.com) operates summer trips from Fairbanks that fly one way and drive the other over the Dalton Highway in buses. The 3-day, 2-night trip starts at $649, and can be added to a longer tour or a cruise.

Appendix: Alaska in Depth

An old photo album opens, emitting a scent of dust and dried glue. Inside, pale images speak wanly of shrunken mountains and glaciers, a huge blue sky, water and trees, a moose standing way off in the background. No family photographer can resist the urge to capture Alaska's vastness in the little box of a camera, and none, it seems, has ever managed it. Then, turning the page, there it is—not in another picture of the landscape, but reflected in a small face at the bottom of the frame: my own face, as a child. For anyone who hasn't experienced that moment, the expression is merely enigmatic—slightly dazed, happy but abstracted. But if you've been to Alaska, that photograph captures something familiar: It's an image of discovery. I've seen it on the fresh, pale faces in photographs stamped with the dates of my family's first explorations of Alaska 35 years ago. And then, researching this book, I got to see it once again, on my own young son's face. And I knew that, like me, he had discovered something important.

So what, exactly, am I talking about? Like anything worth experiencing, it's not simple to explain.

Tour guides try to get it across with statistics. Not much hope of that, although some of the numbers do give you a general idea of scale. Once you've driven across the continental United States and know how big that is, seeing a map of Alaska placed on top of the area you crossed, just about spanning it, provides some notion of size. Alaskans always like to threaten that we'll split in half and make Texas the third-largest state. Alaska has 627,000 residents. If you placed them an equal distance apart, each would be almost a mile from any other. Of course, that couldn't happen. No one has ever been to some parts of Alaska.

But none of that expresses what really matters. It's not just a matter of how big Alaska is or how few people it contains. It's not an intellectual conception at all. None of that crosses your mind when you see a chunk of ice the size of a building fall from a glacier and send up a huge splash and wave surging outward, or when you feel a wave lift your sea kayak from the fall of a breaching humpback whale. Or when you hike for a couple of days to stand on top of a mountain, and from there see more mountaintops, layered off as far as the horizon, in unnamed, seemingly infinite multiplicity. A realization of what Alaska means also can come in a simple little moment. It can come at the end of a long day driving an Interior Alaska highway, as your car climbs into yet another mountain range, the sun still hanging high in what should be night, storm systems arranged before you across the landscape, when you realize that you haven't seen another car in an hour. Or standing on an Arctic Ocean beach, it could happen when you look around at the sea of empty tundra behind you, the sea of green water before you, and your own place on what seems to be the edge of the world. Or you might simply be sitting on the sun-warmed rocks of a beach in Southeast or Southcentral Alaska when you discover that you're occupying only one of many worlds—a world of intermediate size, lying in magnitude between the tiny tide-pool universes of life all around you and the larger world seen by an eagle gliding through the air high above.

What's the soul alchemy of such a moment? I suppose it's different for each person, but for me it has something to do with realizing my actual size in the world, how I fit in, what it means to be just another medium-sized mammal, no longer armed with the illusions supplied by civilization. On returning to the city from the wilderness, there's a re-entry process, like walking from a vivid movie to the mundane, gray street outside—it's the movie that seems more real. For a while, it's hard to take human institutions seriously after you've been deep into Alaska.

Some people never do step back across that boundary. They live their lives out in the wilderness, away from people. Others compromise, living in Alaskan cities and walking out into the mountains when they can, the rest of the time just maintaining a prickly notion of their own independence. But anyone can make the same discovery with the courage to come to Alaska and the time to let the place sink in. You don't have to be an outdoors enthusiast or a young person. You only have to be open to wonder and able to slow down long enough to see it. Then, in a quiet moment when you least expect it, things may suddenly seem very clear and all that you left behind oddly irrelevant.

How you find your way back to where you started is your affair.

1 Natural History: Rough Drafts & Erasures

THE SURGING ICE

In 1986, Hubbard Glacier, north of Yakutat, suddenly decided to surge forward, cutting off Russell Fjord from the rest of the Pacific Ocean. A group of warm-hearted but ill-advised wildlife lovers set out to save the marine mammals that had been trapped behind the glacier. Catching a dolphin from an inflatable boat isn't that easy—they didn't accomplish much, but they provided a lot of entertainment for the locals. Then the water burst through the dam of ice and the lake became a fjord again, releasing the animals anyway.

Bering Glacier can't decide which way to go. Surging and retreating on a 20-year cycle, it recently reversed course after bulldozing a wetland migratory bird stopover, and speedily contracted back up toward the mountains. Yanert Glacier surged 100 yards a day in 2000 after moving 100 yards a year since 1942. In 1937, surging Black Rapids glacier almost ate the Richardson Highway. Mount McKinley's glaciers take off regularly. In Prince William Sound, Meares Glacier has plowed through old-growth forest. On the other hand, some glaciers are so stable they gather a layer of dirt where trees and brush grow to maturity. When Malspina Glacier retreated, the trees on its back toppled. And on a larger scale, all the land of Glacier Bay—mountains, forests, sea floor—is rising 1½ inches a year as it rebounds from the weight of melted glaciers that 100 years ago were a mile thick and 65 miles longer.

Yet these new and erased lands are just small corrections around the margins compared to all the earth has done in setting down, wiping out, and rewriting the natural history of Alaska. In the last Ice Age, 15,000 years ago, much of what is Alaska today was one huge glacier. Looking up at the tops of granite mountains in Southeast Alaska, especially in the Lynn Canal, you can see a sort of high-water mark—the highest point the glaciers came in the Ice Age. Even looking from the deck of a boat, thousands of feet below, you can see where mountain shoulders, rounded by the passage of ice, are much smoother than the sharp, craggy peaks just above, which stuck out of that incredible sheet of ice.

Some 7-year-old children worry about the bogeyman or being caught in a house fire. When I was that age, living with my family in Juneau, I learned how

Gastineau Channel was formed and then went to see Mendenhall Glacier. I was told how it was really a river of ice, advancing and retreating, and with this knowledge I developed a deeper fear: ice. I was afraid that while I slept, another Ice Age would come and grind away the city of Juneau.

It's possible that a glacier *could* get Juneau—the city fronts on the huge Juneau Ice Field—but there would be at least a few centuries' warning before it hit. Glaciers are essentially just snow that doesn't get a chance to melt. It accumulates at higher altitudes until it gets deep enough to compress into ice and starts oozing down the sides of the mountain. When the ice reaches the ocean, or before, the melt and calving of icebergs at the leading edge reaches a point of equilibrium with the snow that's still being added at the top. The glacier stops advancing, becoming a true river of ice, moving a snowflake from the top of the mountain to the bottom in a few hundred years. When conditions change—more snow or colder long-term weather, for example—the glacier gets bigger; that's called advancing, and the opposite is retreating. Sometimes, something strange will happen under the glacier and it will surge. Bering Glacier started to float on a cushion of water, and Yanert Glacier slid on a cushion of mud. But most of the time, the advance or retreat is measured in inches or feet a year.

It took some time to figure out how glaciers work, and the living glaciers of Alaska, like living fossils from the last Ice Age, helped show the way. In the 1830s, scientists in Switzerland found huge rocks (now called glacial erratics) that appeared to have moved miles from where they had once been a part of similar bedrock. They developed the theory that ancient glaciers shaping the Alps must have moved the rocks. **John Muir,** the famous writer and naturalist, maintained in the 1870s that the granite mountains of Yosemite National Park had been rounded and polished by the passing of glaciers that melted long ago (he was only partly right). He traveled to Alaska to prove it. Here, glaciers were still carving the land—they had never finished melting at the end of the last glacial period—and Muir could see shapes like those at Yosemite in the act of being created. Glacier Bay, which Muir "discovered" when guided there by his Alaska Native friends, was a glacial work in progress, as it still is today.

When you visit, you can see for yourself how the heavy blue ice and white snow are streaked with black rock and dust that were obviously gouged from mountains and left in hills at the face and along the flanks of the glaciers, in debris piles called moraines. At Exit Glacier in Kenai Fjords National Park, you can stand on a moraine that wraps the leading edge of the glacier like a scarf and feel the cold streaming off spires of clicking ice—like standing in front of a freezer with the door open. Find another hill like that, no matter where it is, and you can be pretty sure a glacier once came that way. Likewise, you can see today's glaciers scooping out valleys in the mountains. Fjords and valleys all over Alaska surely were made by the glaciers of the 50 ice ages that have covered North America in the last 2.5 million years.

We still don't know exactly why these glacial periods come and go. The best theory to date holds that the wobbles and imperfections in the earth's spin and orbit around the sun alter energy flow into the climate enough to bring on the ice. Indeed, ancient ice samples suggest that the last 10,000 years, in which mankind developed agriculture and civilization, have been an extremely rare period of benign and stable climatic conditions. That stability could be ending. The earth is warming, probably aided by human release of carbon dioxide into the atmosphere, and the effects are being felt more strongly in the Arctic than anywhere else on earth. Forests are moving north, wetlands are drying, sea ice is withdrawing, and permanently frozen ground is warming. But no one knows how glaciers will change. If global warming brings more precipitation, they may grow.

Today, Alaska's 100,000 glaciers cover about 5% of its landmass, mostly on the southern coast. There are no glaciers in the Arctic—the climate is too dry to produce enough snow. The northernmost large glaciers are in the Alaska Range, such as those carving great chasms in the side of Mount McKinley. The mountain's height creates its own weather, wringing moisture out of the atmosphere and feeding its glaciers. The Kahiltna Glacier flows 45 miles from the mountain, losing 15,000 feet downhill over its course. The Ruth Glacier has dug a canyon twice as deep as the Grand Canyon, half filled with mile-deep ice.

THE TREMBLING EARTH

Despite my early glacier phobia, I never had a similar fear of earthquakes. Living in Anchorage, I'd been through enough of them that, as early as I can remember, I generally didn't bother to get out of bed when they hit. Alaska has an average of 13 earthquakes a day, or 11 percent of all the earthquakes in the world, including three of the six largest ever recorded. Of course, Alaska is large; in Anchorage, we feel only a few earthquakes a year.

It's all part of living in a place that isn't quite done yet. Any part of Alaska could have an earthquake, but the Pacific Rim from Southcentral Alaska to the Aleutians is the shakiest. This is where Alaska is still under construction. The very rocks that make up the state are something of an ad hoc conglomeration, still in the process of being assembled. The floor of the Pacific Ocean is moving north, and as it moves, it carries islands and mountains with it. When they hit the Alaska plate, these pieces of land, called **terranes,** dock like ships arriving, but slowly—an island moving an inch a year takes a long time to travel thousands of miles. Geologists studying rocks near Mount McKinley have found a terrane that used to be tropical islands. In Kenai Fjords National Park, fossils have turned up that are otherwise found only in Afghanistan and China. The slowly moving crust of the earth brought them here on a terrane that makes up a large part of the south coast of Alaska.

The earth's crust is paper thin compared to the globe's forces, and, like paper, it is folding where the two edges meet. Alaska's coast is bending down; and farther inshore, where McKinley stands, it is bowing up. The steep little rock islands you see flocking with birds at Kenai Fjords National Park are old mountaintops; the monolith of McKinley is a brand new one.

Here's how it works. Near the center of the Pacific, underwater volcanoes and cracks that constantly ooze molten new rock are adding to the tectonic plate that forms the ocean floor. As it grows from the middle, the existing sea floor spreads at a rate of perhaps an inch a year. At the other side of the Pacific plate, where it bumps up against Alaska, there's not enough room for more crust, so it's forced, bending and cracking, downward into the planet's great, molten recycling mill of magma. Landmasses that are along for the ride smash into the continent that's already there. When one hits—the so-called Yakutat block is still in the process of docking—a mountain range gets shoved up. Earthquakes and volcanoes are a byproduct.

Living in such an unsettled land is a matter of more than abstract interest. The Mount Spurr volcano, which erupted most recently in 1992, turned day to night in Anchorage, dropping a blanket of ash all over the region. A Boeing 747 full of passengers flew into the plume and lost power in all its engines, falling in darkness for several minutes before pilots were able to restart the clogged jets. After that incident, the airport was closed until aviation authorities could find a way to keep volcanic plumes and planes apart. More than 80 volcanoes have been active in Alaska in the last 200 years. Earthquakes between 7 and 8 on the Richter scale—larger than the 1994 Los Angeles quake—occur once a year on average, and huge quakes over 8 averaged every 13 years over the last century. The worst of the quakes, on March 27, 1964, was the strongest ever to hit North America. It ranked 9.2 on the Richter scale, lowering an entire region of the state some 10 feet and moving it even farther laterally. No other earthquake has ever moved so much land.

The earthquake destroyed much of Anchorage and several smaller towns, and killed about 131 people, mostly in sea waves created by underwater landslides. In Valdez, the waterfront was swept clean of people. In the Prince William Sound village of Chenega, built on a hill along the water, people started running for higher ground when the wave came. About half made it. But the earthquake could have been much worse. It occurred in the early evening, on Good Friday, when most public buildings were empty. An elementary school in Anchorage that broke in half and fell into a hole had no one inside at the time.

But even that huge earthquake wasn't an unusual occurrence, at least in the earth's terms. Geologists believe the same Alaska coast sank 6 feet in an earthquake in the year 1090.

THE FROZEN TUNDRA

The Interior and Arctic parts of the state are less susceptible to earthquakes and, since they receive little precipitation, they don't have glaciers, either. But there's still a sense of living on a land that's not quite sure of itself, since most of northern Alaska is solid only by virtue of being frozen. When it thaws, it turns to mush. The phenomenon is caused by **permafrost,** a layer of earth a little below the surface that never thaws—or at least, you'd better hope it doesn't. Buildings erected on permafrost without some mechanism for dispersing their own heat— pilings, a gravel pad, or even refrigerator coils—thaw the ground below and sink into a self-made quicksand. You occasionally run across such structures. There's one in Dawson City, Yukon Territory, still left from the gold rush, that leans at an alarming angle with thresholds and lower tiers of siding disappearing into the ground.

Building sewer and water systems in such conditions is a challenge still unmet in much of Alaska's Bush, where village toilets are often "honey buckets" and the septic systems are sewage lagoons on the edge of town where the buckets are dumped. Disease caused by the unsanitary conditions sweeps the villages as if rural Alaska were a Third World country. Large state and federal appropriations are resolving the problem one village at a time, but still many years of work are left.

Permafrost makes the land do other strange things. On a steep slope, the thawed earth on top of the ice can begin to slowly slide downhill like a blanket over a pile of pillows, setting the trees at crazy angles. These groves of black spruce—the only conifer that grows on this kind of ground—are called drunken forests, and you can see them in Denali National Park and elsewhere in the Interior. Permafrost also can create weird ground with shaky tussocks the size of basketballs that sit a foot or two apart on a wet, muddy flat. From a distance it looks smooth, but walking on real basketballs would be easier.

The Arctic and much of the Interior are a swampy desert. Annual precipitation in Barrow is the same as in Las Vegas. Most of the time, the tundra is frozen in white; snow blows around, but not much falls. It melts in the summer, but it can't sink into the ground, which remains frozen. Liquid water on top of the permafrost layer creates huge, shallow ponds. Alaska is a land of 10 million lakes, with three million larger than 20 acres. Birds arrive to feed and paddle around those circles and polygons of deep green and sky blue. Flying over the Arctic in a small plane is disorienting, for no pattern maintains in the flat green tundra, and irregularly shaped patches of water stretch as far as the eye can see. Pilots find their way by following landmarks like tractor tracks etched into the tundra. Although few and far between, the tracks remain clearly delineated for decades after they're made, appearing as narrow, parallel ponds reaching from one horizon to the other.

The permafrost also preserves much older things. The meat of prehistoric mastodons, still intact, has been unearthed from the frozen ground. On the Arctic Coast, the sea eroded ground near Barrow that contained ancient ancestors of the Eskimos who still inhabit the same neighborhood. In 1982, they found a family that apparently was crushed by sea ice up to 500 years ago. Two of the bodies were well preserved, sitting in the home they had occupied and wearing the clothes they had worn the day of the disaster, perhaps around the time Columbus was sailing to America.

Sea ice is the frozen ocean that extends from northern Alaska to the other side of the world. For a few months of summer it pulls away from the shore. Then, in September, when the ocean water falls below 29°F, ice forms along the beach and expands from the North Pole's permanent ice pack until the two sides meet. The clash of huge ice floes creates towering pressure ridges, small mountains of steep ice that are difficult to cross.

At its extreme, in March, the ice extends solidly all the way south to the Pribilof Islands, when it becomes possible to drive a dog team across the Bering Sea to Siberia. The National Weather Service keeps track of the ice pack and issues maps and predictions you can find on the Internet (www.alaska.net/~nwsar). Crab boats like to tempt its south-moving edge in the fall and shippers look for the right moment in the summer to venture north with barges of fuel and other supplies for the coast of the Arctic Ocean—they barely have time to get there and back before the ice closes in again in the fall.

The Arctic and Interior are relatively barren biologically compared with the southern coastal areas of the state. Polar bears wander the Arctic ice pack, but they, like the Eskimos, feed more on marine mammals than on anything found on the shore. A 1,200-pound adult polar bear can make a meal of a walrus, and they're expert at hunting seal. In the summer, herds of caribou counted in the tens of thousands come north to their Arctic calving grounds, but they migrate south when the cold, dark winter falls unremittingly on the region.

Higher, Higher

The Eskimo blanket toss—the game of placing a person in the center of a walrus-skin blanket and bouncing him or her high in the air—traditionally was used to get hunters high enough to see over the pressure ridges so they could spot game.

In Barrow, the sun doesn't rise for more than 65 days in the winter. In February, the average daily high temperature is –12°F, and the average low is –24°F. The Inupiat people learned to survive in this climate for millennia, but life was short and terribly hard. Today they've made some sensible allowances while holding onto many cultural traditions. For example, the school in Barrow has wide, light hallways and a large indoor playground.

THE RAIN FOREST

By comparison, southern coastal Alaska is warm and biologically rich. Temperate rain forest ranges up the coast from Southeast Alaska into Prince William Sound, with bears, deer, moose, wolves, and even big cats living among the massive western hemlock, Sitka spruce, and cedar. This old-growth forest, too wet to burn in forest fires, is the last vestige of the virgin, primeval woods that seemed so limitless to the first white settlers who arrived on the east coast of the continent in the 17th century. The trees grow on and on, sometimes rising more than 200 feet high, with diameters of 10 feet, and falling only after hundreds of years. When they fall, the trees rot on the damp moss of the forest floor and return to soil to feed more trees, which grow in rows upon their nursery trunks.

Here at least, Alaska *does* seem permanent. That sense helps explain why cutting the rain forest is so controversial. Just one of these trees contains thousands of dollars' worth of wood, a prize that drives logging as voraciously as the federal government, which owns most of the coastal forest, may choose to allow. Already the vast Southeast lands owned by Alaska Native corporations have been stripped of their old trees.

The rivers of the great coastal forests bring home runs of big **salmon,** clogging in spawning season like a busy sidewalk at rush hour. The fish spawn only once, returning by a precisely tuned sense of smell to the streams where they were hatched as many as 7 years before. When the fertilized eggs have been left in the stream gravel, the fish conveniently die on the beach, making a smorgasbord for bears and other forest animals. The huge **Kodiak brown bear,** topping 1,000 pounds, owes everything to the millions of salmon that return to the island each summer. By comparison, the grizzly bears of the Interior—the same species as browns, but living on grass, berries, and an occasional ground squirrel—are mere midgets, their weight counted in the hundreds of pounds. Forest-dwelling black bears grow to only a few hundred pounds.

TAIGA & FIRE

Rain forest covers only a small fraction of Alaska. In fact, only a third of Alaska is forested at all, and most of this is the boreal forest that covers the central part of the state, behind the rain-shadow of coastal mountains that intercept moist clouds off the oceans. Ranging from the Kenai Peninsula, south of Anchorage, to the Brooks Range, where the Arctic begins, this is a **taiga**—a moist, subarctic forest of smaller, slower-growing, hardier trees that leave plenty of open sky between their branches. In well-drained areas, on hillsides and southern land less susceptible to permafrost, the boreal forest is a lovely, broadly spaced combination of straight, proud white spruce and pale, spectral paper birch. Along the rivers, cottonwoods grow, with deep-grained bark and branches that spread in an oaklike matrix—if they could speak, it would be as wise old men. Where it's wet and swampy, over more and more land as you go north, all that will grow are low, brushy willow and the glum black spruce, which struggles to become a gnarled stick a mere 3 inches thick in 100 years, if it doesn't burn first. As the elevation grows, the spruce shrink, turning into weirdly bent, ancient shrubs just before the tree line and the open alpine tundra.

Forest fires tear through as much as a million acres of Alaska's boreal forest each summer. In most cases, forest managers do no more than note the occurrence on a map. There's little commercially valuable timber in these thin stands, and, anyway, it isn't possible to halt the process of nature's self-immolation over the broad expanse of Alaska. The boreal forest regenerates through fire—it was made to burn. The wildlife that lives in and eats it needs new growth from the burns as well as the shelter of older trees. When the forest is healthiest and most productive, the dark green of the spruce is broken by streaks and patches of light-green brush in an ever-changing succession.

This is the land of the **moose.** They're as big as large horses, with long, bulbous noses and huge eyes that seem to know, somehow, just how ugly they are. Their flanks look like a worn-out shag carpet draped over a sawhorse. But moose are survivors. They thrive in land that no one else wants. In the summer, they wade out into the swampy tundra ponds to eat green muck. In the winter, they like nothing better than an old burn, where summer lightning has peeled back the forest and allowed a tangle of willows to grow—a moose's all-time favorite food. Eaten by wolves, hunted and run over by man, stranded in the snows of a hard winter, the moose always come back. In the summer, the moose disperse and are not easily seen in thick vegetation. In the winter, they gather where walking is easy, along roads and in lowlands where people also like to live. Encounters happen often in the city, until, as a resident, you begin to take the moose for granted. Then, skiing on a Nordic trail one day, you round a corner and come face to face with an animal that stands 2 feet over you. You can smell the beast's foul scent and see his stress, the ears pulled back on the head and the whites of the eyes showing, and you know that this wild creature, fighting to live until summer, can easily kill you.

THE LIGHT & THE DARKNESS

There's no escaping the stress of winter in Alaska—not for moose or people— nor any shield from the exhilaration of the summer. In summer it never really gets dark at night. In Fairbanks in June, the sun sets in the north around midnight, but it doesn't go down far enough for real darkness to settle, instead rising again 2 hours later. It's always light enough to keep hiking or fishing, and, in clear weather, always light enough to read by. You may not see the stars from early May until sometime in August (the climate chart in chapter 2 gives seasonal daylight for various towns). Visitors have trouble getting used to it: Falling asleep in broad daylight is hard. Alaskans deal with it by staying up late and being active outdoors. In the winter, on the other hand, you forget what the sun looks like. Kids go to school in the dark and come home in the dark. The sun rises in the middle of the morning and sets after lunch. At high noon in December, the sun hangs just above the southern horizon with a weak, orange light, a constant sunset. Animals and people go into hibernation.

As you go north, the change in the length of the days gets larger. In Ketchikan, the longest day of the year, the summer solstice is 17 hours, 28 minutes; in Fairbanks, 21 hours, 48 minutes; and in Barrow, the longest day is more than 2 months. In contrast, in Seattle the longest day is 16 hours, and in Los Angeles 14 hours, 26 minutes. On the equator, days are always the same length, 12 hours. At the North and South poles, the sun is up half the year and down the other half.

2 Politics & History: Living a Frontier Myth

The occupations of prospector, trapper, and homesteader—rugged individualists relying only on themselves in a limitless land—would dominate Alaska's economy if the state's image of itself were accurate. Alaskans talk a lot about the Alaskan spirit of independence, yearn for freedom from government, and declare that people from "Outside" just don't understand us when they insist on locking up Alaska's lands in parks and wilderness status. The bumper sticker says, simply, "We don't give a damn how they do it Outside." A state full of self-reliant frontiersmen can't be tied down and deterred from their manifest destiny by a bunch of Washington bureaucrats. At the extreme, there has even been a movement to declare independence as a separate nation so Alaskans can extend the frontier, extracting its natural resources unfettered by bunny-hugging easterners.

But just because you wear a cowboy hat doesn't mean you know how to ride a horse. In Las Vegas you find a lot more hats than horsemen, and Alaska is full of self-reliant pioneers who spend rush hour in traffic jams and worry more about urban drug dealing and air pollution than where to catch their next meal or dig the mother lode. As for self-reliance and independence from government, Alaska has the highest per capita state spending of any state in the nation, with no state income or sales taxes and an annual payment of about $2,000 a year to every man, woman, and child just for living here. The state government provides such socialistic benefits as retirement homes and automatic income for the aged; it owns various businesses, including a dairy, a railroad, and a subsidized mortgage lender; it has built schools in the smallest communities, operates a state ferry system and a radio and television

Dateline

- **Approximately 15,000 years ago** First human explorers arrive in Alaska from Asia.

- **1741** Vitus Bering, on a mission originally chartered by Peter the Great, finds Alaska; ship's surgeon and naturalist Georg Steller goes ashore for a few hours on Kayak Island, the first white to set foot in Alaska.

- **1743** Russian fur traders enter the Aleutian Islands; Aleuts are enslaved to hunt sea otter and massacred; when they try to revolt, Aleut cultural traditions are eliminated, and over the coming decades they are relocated as far south as California for their hunting skills.

- **1772** Unalaska, in the Aleutian Islands, becomes a permanent Russian settlement.

- **1776–79** British Capt. James Cook makes voyages of exploration to Alaska, seeking the Northwest Passage from the Pacific to the Atlantic, and draws charts of the coast.

- **1784** Russians build a settlement at Kodiak.

- **1799** Russians establish a fort near present-day Sitka, which will later become their capital; Tlingits attack and destroy the fort, but are later driven off in a counterattack; the Russian-America Company receives a 20-year exclusive franchise to govern and exploit Alaska.

- **1821** Russian naval officers are placed in control of the Russian-America Company, which begins to decline in profitability.

- **1824** Boundaries roughly matching Alaska's current borders are set by treaty between Russia, Britain, and the United States.

- **1839** The British Hudson's Bay Company, surpassing Russia in trade, begins leasing parts of Southeast Alaska and subsequently extends trading outposts into the Interior.

- **1843** First overtures are made by American officials interested in buying Alaska from the Russians, so U.S.

continues

network, and owns nearly a third of the landmass of Alaska. And although the oil money that funds state government has been in decline in recent years, forcing the legislature to dig into savings to balance its books, the independent, self-reliant citizens have successfully resisted having to pay any taxes.

That conflict between perception and reality grows out of the story of a century of development of Alaska. The state is a great storehouse of minerals, oil, timber, and fish. A lot of wealth has been extracted, and many people have gotten rich. But it has always been because the federal government let them do it. Every acre of Alaska belonged to the U.S. government from the day Secretary of State William Seward bought Alaska from Russia in 1867. Since then, the frontier has never been broader than Uncle Sam made it.

Yet the whole conception of ownership didn't fit Alaska well from the first. Did the Russians really own what they sold? Alaska Natives didn't think so. They'd been living on this land for more than 100 centuries, and at the time of the purchase, most had never seen a white face. How could Russia hold title to land that no Russian had so much as explored? As Americans flooded into Alaska to search for gold at the turn of the century, this conflict became obvious. Alaska Natives, never conquered by war or treaty, began their legal and political fight to recover their land early in the century—a fight they would eventually win.

The concept of ownership has changed in other ways, too. When the United States bought Alaska and, for the next 100 years afterward, the vast majority of the state was public domain—like the Old West of frontier lore—federal land and its surface and hard-rock resources were there for the taking. They belonged to everyone, but only until someone showed

instead of British power could expand there.

- **1867** In need of money and fearful that Russia couldn't hold onto Alaska anyway, Czar Alexander II sells Alaska to the United States; Secretary of State William Seward negotiates the deal for a price of $7.2 million, roughly 2¢ an acre; the American flag is raised in Sitka, and the U.S. military assumes government of Alaska.

- **1870** The Alaska Commercial Company receives a monopoly on harvesting seals in the Pribilof Islands and soon expands across the territory (the company remains a presence in the Alaska Bush today).

- **1879** Naturalist and writer John Muir explores Southeast Alaska by canoe, discovering Glacier Bay with Native guides.

- **1880** Joe Juneau and Richard Harris, guided by local Natives, find gold on Gastineau Channel and found city of Juneau; gold strikes begin to come every few years across the state.

- **1884** Military rule ends in Alaska, but residents still have no right to elect a legislature, governor, or congressional representative, or to make laws.

- **1885** Protestant missionaries meet to divide up the territory, parceling out each region to a different religion; they begin to fan out across Alaska to convert Native peoples, largely suppressing their traditional ways.

- **1898** After prospectors arrive in Seattle with a ton of gold, the Klondike gold rush begins; gold rushes in Nome and Fairbanks follow within a few years; Americans begin to populate Alaska.

- **1906** Alaska's first (nonvoting) delegate in Congress takes office; the capital moves from Sitka to Juneau.

- **1908** The Iditarod Trail, a sled dog mail route, is completed, linking trails continuously from Seward to Nome.

- **1913** The first territorial legislature convenes, although it has few powers; the first automobile drives the Richardson Highway route, from Valdez to Fairbanks.

- **1914** Federal construction of the Alaska Railroad begins; the first tents

continues

up to lay private claim. Today, amid deep conflicts about whether areas should remain natural or be exploited for natural resources, federal control stands out far more clearly than it did during the gold rush, when the land's wealth was free to anyone with strength enough to take it. Alaskans who want to keep receiving the good things that government brings today equate the frontier spirit of the past with their own financial well-being, whether that means working at a mining claim or at a desk in a glass office tower. But other Americans feel they own Alaska, too, and they don't necessarily believe in giving it away anymore. They may want the frontier to stay alive in another sense—unconquered and still wild.

White colonization of the territory came in boom-and-bust waves of migrants arriving with the goal of making a quick buck and then clearing out—without worrying about the people who already lived there. Although the gold rush pioneers are celebrated today, the **Klondike rush of 1898** that opened up and populated the territory was motivated by greed and was a mass importer of crime, inhumanity, and, for the Native people, terrible epidemics of new diseases that killed off whole villages. Like the Russians 150 years before, who had made slaves of the Natives, the new white population behaved as if the indigenous people were less than human. Until Franklin Roosevelt became president, federal policy was to suppress Alaska Native cultures; missionaries forbade Native peoples from telling the old stories or even speaking in their own languages. Segregation ended only after World War II. Meanwhile, the salmon that fed the people of the territory were overfished by a powerful, outside-owned canning industry with friends in Washington, D.C. Their abuses destroyed salmon runs. Formerly rich Native villages

go up in the river bottom that will be Anchorage, along the rail line.

- 1917 Mount McKinley National Park is established.
- 1920 The first flights connect Alaska to the rest of the United States; aviation quickly becomes the most important means of transportation in the territory.
- 1923 Pres. Warren Harding drives the final spike on the Alaskan Railroad at Nenana, then dies on the way home, purportedly from eating bad Alaska seafood.
- 1925 Leonhard Seppala and other dog mushers relay diphtheria serum on the Iditarod Trail to fight an epidemic in Nome; Seppala and his lead dog, Balto, become national heroes.
- 1934 Federal policy of forced assimilation of Native cultures is officially discarded and New Deal efforts to preserve Native cultures begin.
- 1935 New Deal "colonists," broke farmers from all over the United States, settle in the Matanuska Valley north of Anchorage.
- 1940 A military buildup begins in Alaska; bases built in Anchorage accelerate city's growth into a major population center.
- 1942 Japanese invade Aleutians, taking Attu and Kiska islands and bombing Dutch Harbor/Unalaska (a U.S. counterattack the next year drives out the Japanese); Alaska Highway links Alaska to the rest of the country overland for the first time, but is open to civilians only after the war.
- 1949 Massive cold war military buildup feeds fast economic growth.
- 1957 Oil is found on Kenai Peninsula's Swanson River.
- 1959 Alaska becomes a state.
- 1964 The largest earthquake ever to strike North America shakes Southcentral Alaska, killing 131 people, primarily in tsunami waves.
- 1968 Oil is found at Prudhoe Bay, on Alaska's North Slope.
- 1970 Environmental lawsuits tie up work to build the Alaska pipeline, which is needed to link the North Slope oil field to markets.

continues

faced famine when their primary food source was taken away.

It was only with **World War II,** and the Japanese invasion of the Aleutian Islands, that Alaska developed an industry not based on exploitation of natural resources: the military industry. The war brought the construction of the territory's first road to the outside world, the Alaska Highway. After the war, military activity dropped off, but only briefly. By the late 1940s, Alaska was on the front line on the Cold War. Huge Air Force and Army bases were built and remote radar stations installed to detect and repel Soviet bombers and missiles. To this day, the federal government remains a key industry whose removal would deal the economy a grievous blow.

The fight for **Alaska statehood** also began after the war. Alaskans argued that they needed local, independent control of natural resources, pointing to the example of overfishing in the federally managed salmon industry. Opponents said that Alaska would never be able to support itself, would always require large subsidies from the federal government, and therefore should not be a state. But the advocates pointed out that Alaska's lack of self-sufficiency came about because its citizens did not control the resources—Alaska was a colony, with decisions and profits taken away by the mother country. If Alaskans could control their own land, they could use the resources to fund government. The discovery of oil on the Swanson River on the Kenai Peninsula in 1957 helped win that argument. Here was real money that could fund a state government. In 1959, Alaska finally became the 49th state. Along with the

1971 Congress acknowledges and pays the federal government's debt to Alaska's indigenous people with the Alaska Native Claims Settlement Act, which transfers 44 million acres of land and almost $1 billion to new Native-owned corporations.

1973 The first Iditarod Trail Sled Dog Race runs more than 1,000 miles from Anchorage to Nome.

1974 Congress clears away legal barriers to construction of the trans-Alaska pipeline; Vice Pres. Spiro Agnew casts the deciding vote in the U.S. Senate.

1977 The trans-Alaska pipeline is completed and begins providing up to 25% of the U.S. domestic supply of oil.

1980 Congress sets aside almost a third of Alaska in new parks and other land-conservation units; awash in new oil wealth, the state legislature abolishes all taxes paid by individuals to state government.

1982 Alaskans receive their first Alaska Permanent Fund dividends, interest paid on an oil-wealth savings account.

1985 Declining oil prices send the Alaska economy into a tailspin; tens of thousands leave the state and most of the banks collapse.

1989 The tanker *Exxon Valdez* hits Bligh Reef in Prince William Sound, spilling 11 million gallons of North Slope crude in the worst oil spill ever in North America.

1994 A federal jury in Anchorage awards $5 billion to 10,000 fishermen, Natives, and others hurt by the Exxon oil spill; Exxon appeals continue today.

1996 Wildfire rips through the Big Lake area, north of Anchorage, destroying 400 buildings.

1999 Alaskans vote 87% against a plan to use Permanent Fund earnings to cover a state budget shortfall.

rights of entering the union, Alaska received a dowry, an endowment of land to develop and pay for all future government. The Statehood Act gave the new state the right to select 103 million acres from a total landmass of 365 million acres. Indeed, that land does pay for state government in Alaska, in the form of oil royalties and taxes—but, to this day, the federal government still spends a lot more in Alaska than it receives.

Oil revenues supported the new state as it began to extend services to the vast, undeveloped expanse of Alaska. Anchorage boomed in the 1960s in a period of buoyant optimism. Leaders believed that the age-old problems of the wide-open frontier—poverty, lack of basic services, impenetrable remoteness—would succumb to the new government and new money, while the land still remained wide open. Then the pace of change redoubled in 1968 with the discovery of the largest oil field in North America at **Prudhoe Bay** on land that had been a wise state selection in the federal land-grant entitlement. The state government received as much money in a single oil lease sale auction as it had spent in total for the previous 6 years. This was going to be the boom of all booms.

The oil bonanza on the North Slope would change Alaska more than any other event since the gold rush. Once, opening the frontier meant letting a few prospectors scratch the dirt in search of a poke of gold. But getting this immense pool of oil to market from one of the most remote spots on the globe would require allowing the world's largest companies to build across Alaska a pipeline that, when completed, could credibly claim to be the largest privately financed construction project in world history. With the stakes suddenly so much higher, it came time to figure out exactly who owned which parts of Alaska. The land couldn't just be public domain any longer.

That division wouldn't be easy. Much of the state had never even been mapped, much less surveyed, and there were some large outstanding claims that had to be settled. Alaska Natives, who had lost land, culture, and health in 2 centuries of white invasion, finally saw their luck start to turn. It wouldn't be possible to resolve the land issues surrounding the pipeline until their claims to land and compensation were answered. Native leaders cannily used that leverage to assure that they got what they wanted.

In the early 1970s, America had a new awareness of the way its first people had been treated in the settlement of the West. When white frontiers expanded, Native traditional homelands were stolen. In Alaska, with the powerful lure of all that oil providing the impetus, Native people were able to insist on a fairer resolution. In 1971, with the support of white Alaskans, the oil companies, and Pres. Richard Nixon, who threatened to veto any settlement that Natives did not support, Congress passed the **Alaska Native Claims Settlement Act,** called ANCSA. The act transferred 44 million acres of land and $962.5 million to corporations whose shareholders were all the Native people of Alaska. The new Native corporations would be able to exploit their own land for their shareholders' profit. In later legislation, Natives also won guaranteed subsistence hunting and fishing rights on federal land. Some Natives complained that they'd received only an eighth of the land they had owned before white contact, but it was still by far the richest settlement any of the world's indigenous people had received at that time. Today, the Native corporations are Alaska's largest and most powerful homegrown businesses.

It was a political deal on a grand scale. It's unlikely that Natives would have gotten their land at all but for the desire of whites to get at the oil and their need for Native support. Nor could the pipeline have overcome environmental challenges without the Natives' dropping their objections. Even with Native support in place, legislation authorizing the pipeline passed the U.S. Senate by only one vote, cast by Vice President Spiro Agnew.

But there were other side effects of the deal that white Alaskans didn't like so well. The state still hadn't received a large portion of its land entitlement, and now the Native corporations also had a right to select the land they wanted.

There still remained the question of who would get what, and of the wild lands that Congress, influenced by a strong new environmental movement, wanted to maintain as national parks and wilderness and not give away. That issue wasn't settled until 1980, when the **Alaska National Interest Lands Conservation Act** passed, setting aside an additional 106 million acres for conservation, an area larger than California. Alaska's frontier-minded population screamed bloody murder over "the lock-up of Alaska," but the act was only the last, tangible step in a process started by the coming of big oil and the need its arrival created to draw lines on the map, tying up the frontier.

When construction of the $9 billion pipeline finally got underway in 1974, a huge influx of new people chasing the high-paying jobs put any previous gold rush to shame. The newcomers were from a different part of the country than previously, too. Alaska had been a predominately Democratic state, but oil workers from Texas, Oklahoma, and other Bible Belt states helped shift the balance of Alaska's politics, and now it's solidly Republican. In its frontier days, Alaska had a strong Libertarian streak, but now it became more influenced by fundamentalist Christian conservatism. A hippie-infested legislature of the early 1970s legalized marijuana for home use. Conservatives at the time, who thought the government shouldn't butt into its citizens' private lives, went along with them. After the pipeline, times changed, and Alaska developed tough antidrug laws.

Growth also brought urban problems. As the pipeline construction boom waned in 1977, a boomtown atmosphere of gambling and street prostitution went with it, but other big-city problems remained. No longer could residents of Anchorage and Fairbanks go to bed without locking their doors. Both cities were declared "nonattainment" areas by the Environmental Protection Agency because of air pollution near the ground in cold winter weather, when people leave their cars running during the day to keep them from freezing.

But the pipeline seemed to provide limitless wealth to solve these problems. For fear that too much money would be wasted, the voters altered the state constitution to bank a large portion of the new riches. The new Permanent Fund would be off limits to the politicians in Juneau, with half the annual earnings paid out to citizens as dividends. The fund now contains more than $26 billion in savings and has become one of the largest sectors of the economy simply by virtue of paying out more than $1 billion a year in dividends to everyone who lives at least a year in the state. All major state taxes on individuals were canceled, and people got used to receiving everything free from the government.

Then, in 1985, oil prices dropped, deflating the overextended economy. Housing prices crashed and thousands of people simply walked away from their mortgages. All but a few of the banks in the state went broke. Condominiums that had sold for $100,000 went for $20,000 or less a year later. It was the bust that always goes with the boom, but it still came as a shock to many. The spending associated with the *Exxon Valdez* **oil spill** in 1989 restarted the economy and it continued on an even keel for a decade after, but the wealth of the earlier oil years never returned.

Meanwhile, the oil from Prudhoe Bay started running out. Oil revenues, an irreplaceable 85% of the state budget, started an irrevocable downward trend in the early 1990s. The oil companies downsized. Without another boom on the horizon, the question became how to avoid, or at least soften, the next bust. At this writing, that question remains unanswered. In 1999, the governor and legislature asked the voters to approve reducing their Permanent Fund dividends to cover a $1 billion budget gap. Conservatives said the state should just cut the budget; liberals said reducing the dividend would amount to a head tax, hitting hardest the poor people who rely on the money for necessities. The plan failed, with 87% voting no. The legislature, with a temporary budgetary reprieve provided by higher oil prices, backed away from doing anything. With the political system in deadlock, the disadvantages of individualism seemed apparent. Some asked if Alaskans had lost their capacity for collective sacrifice. More asked when the next big project would get the good times rolling again, such as a natural gas pipeline from the North Slope to middle America or oil development in the Arctic National Wildlife Refuge (ANWR).

Culture moves slower than politics, and Alaskans still see themselves as gold rush prospectors or wildcat oil drillers, adventuring in an open land and striking it rich by their own devices. Even as the economy blends ever more smoothly into the American corporate landscape, Alaskans' myth of themselves remains strong. Today, the state's future is as little in its own hands as it has ever been. Whether anyone gets to explore for oil in ANWR will be decided in Congress and distant corporate boardrooms, not here. Ultimately, an economy based on exploiting natural resources is anything but independent.

3 The People: Three Ways to Win an Argument in Alaska

NUMBER ONE: WAIT FOR SPRING

A small town in Alaska in March. Each time it snows, you have to throw shovels of it higher over your head to dig out. The air in the house is stale and the view out the window is black, white, and gray. Everyone's going nuts with winter. It's time for a good political ruckus.

No one can predict exactly what will set it off—it could just be an ill-considered letter to the editor in the local newspaper, or it could be something juicier, like a controversial development proposal. At some point, when the cabin fever gets bad enough, it almost doesn't matter what sparks the inferno. Alaskans can generate outrage about almost anything, with a ritual of charges and countercharges, conspiracy theories, and impassioned public testimony.

But all that outrage dries up as soon as the salmon started running. Then most of the city council meetings would be canceled and those that weren't would be brief and sparsely attended. If anything really important came up, the council would be smart enough to postpone it till fall. In the summer, Alaskans have more important things to attend to than government.

The sun shines deep into the night so you can catch fish and tourists, not sit inside. It's the season when the money is made. The streets are full of new people, like a bird rookery refreshed by migrants. Everyone stays awake late pounding nails, playing softball, and fly-casting for reds. Office workers in Anchorage depart straight from work for a 3-hour drive down to the Kenai Peninsula, fish through the night, catch a quick nap in the car in the wee hours, and make it to work on time the next morning, with fish stories to share. Sleep is expendable—you don't seem to need it that much when the sky is light all night.

In the Native villages of the Bush, everyone has gone to fish camp. Families load everything in an aluminum riverboat and leave town, headed upriver. On the banks and beaches, they set up wall tents and spruce-log fish-drying racks, maybe a basketball hoop and campfire, too. Extended families work as a unit. Men gather in the salmon, and the women gut them with a few lightning strokes of a knife and hang them to dry on the racks. Children run around in a countryside paradise, watched by whatever adults are handiest.

Suddenly, August comes. For the first time in months, you can see the stars. It comes as a shock the first time you have to use your car headlights. The mood gets even more frantic. There's never enough time in the summer to do everything that needs to get done. Construction crews can count the days now till snow and cold will shut them down. Anything that's not done now won't be done until next May. Labor Day approaches as fast as 5pm on a busy business day.

As September turns to October, the last tourists are gone, and T-shirt shops are closed for the season. The commercial fishing boats are tied up back in the harbor, and the fishermen prepare for vacation. Cannery workers are already back at college. For the first time in months, people can slow down long enough to look at each other and remember where they left off in the spring. It's time to catch up on sleep, make big decisions. The hills of birch turn bright yellow, the tundra goes brick red, and the sky turns gray—there's the smell of wood smoke in the air—and then, one day, it starts to snow.

It's not the velvet darkness of midwinter that gets you. December is bearable, even if the sun rises after the kids get to school, barely cruises along the horizon, and sinks before they start for home. Nowhere is Christmas more real than in Alaska, where carolers sing with cheeks tingling from the cold. January isn't so hard. You're still excited about the skiing. The phone rings in the middle of the night—it's a friend telling you to put on your boots and go outside to see the northern lights. February is a bit harder to take, but most towns have a winter carnival to divert your attention from the cold.

March is when bizarre things start to happen. People are just holding on for the end of winter, and you never know what will set them off. That's when you hunker down and lay low, watch what you say, bite your tongue when your spouse lets hang a comment you'd like to jump on like a coho hitting fresh bait. Hold on—just until the icicles start to melt, the mud shows around the snowbanks, and the cycle starts fresh.

NUMBER TWO: BE HERE FIRST

There's a simple and effective way to win an argument in Alaska—state how long you've lived here. If it's longer than your adversary, he'll find it difficult to put up a fight. This is why, when speaking in public, people will often begin their remarks by stating how many years they've been in Alaska. It's a badge of authenticity and status in a place with a young, transient population that's grown fast. No one cares where you came from, or who you were back there, and there's no such thing as class in Alaska—anyone who tries to act superior will quickly find that no one else notices. But if you haven't made it through a few winters, you probably don't know what you're talking about.

It's also traditional—although, sadly, a fading tradition—to treat strangers as friends until they prove otherwise. The smaller the town you visit, the more strongly you'll find that hospitality still alive. Visitors find it pleasantly disorienting to arrive in a small town and have everyone in the street greet them with a smile. These traditions of hospitality run deepest in Alaska's **Native people.** (Alaskans use the word *Native* to mean all the indigenous peoples of Alaska.) But instead of beginning a conversation by stating how long they've lived here, Natives—who've always been here—try to find a relation with a new person by talking about where their families are from.

Theories differ about how North America was originally populated. The traditional notion is that the first people walked across a land bridge from Asia through the dry Bering Sea around 15,000 years ago, when glacial ice sequestered enough of the earth's water to lower sea level. The bridge, up to 1,000 miles wide, included the entire west coast of Alaska at its largest size, and lasted longest in the area between Nome and Kotzebue.

But new archaeology and geology throw doubt on the theory, suggesting a migration story that's much more complex. People who know the Arctic know the land bridge simply wasn't necessary for migration: In the winter you can walk between Siberia and Alaska even today, and the seafaring skills of Alaska's Aleuts and Eskimos would have enabled them to travel back and forth to Asia at any time. Siberian and Alaskan Natives share language, stories, and kin. Perhaps the connection across the north was continuous and followed many routes after northern people learned to sew skin boats and clothing about 15,000 years ago. Certainly, the idea they walked seems increasingly questionable. Geologists now believe the route south was an impassable sheet of ice during the last glacial period; if migrants did use it, they could only have done so by making a tricky sea journey connecting coastal pockets that remained green.

However and whenever the first people arrived, they quickly spread through the Americas, creating cultures of incredible complexity and diversity. Most scientists believe migrants through Alaska were the ancestors of all the indigenous people of the hemisphere, from the Inca to the Algonquin. Those who stayed in Alaska became the Eskimos, who include the Inupiat of the Arctic, the Yup'ik of the Southwest, and the Alutiiq of the Gulf of Alaska coastline. They also became Indians: the Athabascans of the Interior and the Tlingit, Haida, and Tsimshian of Southeast Alaska and British Columbia. And seafaring Pacific people landed in the Aleutian Chain, becoming the Aleuts, who are neither Eskimo nor Indian.

The Native groups of Alaska have a lot in common culturally, but before the white invasion, they had well-defined boundaries and didn't mix much. They didn't farm, and the only animal they domesticated was the dog—dog teams and boats were the primary means of transportation and commerce. But they generally were not nomadic, and no one in Alaska lived in igloos. Where there was no wood, houses were built of whale bone and sod; where wood was plentiful, large and intricately carved houses sheltered entire villages. Typically, a family-connected tribal group would have a winter village and a summer fish camp for gathering and laying up food. Elders guided the community in important decisions. A gifted shaman led the people in religious matters, relating to the spirits of ancestors, animals, trees, and even the ice that populated their world. Stories passed on through generations explained the universe.

Those oral traditions kept Native cultures alive. Twenty distinct **Native languages** were spoken. Some elders still speak only their Native language today, and only one language, Eyak, is essentially extinct. The languages break into four major families: Eskimo-Aleut, Athabascan-Eyak-Tlingit, Haida, and Tsimshian (the last two are primarily Canadian). The Eskimo-Aleut language group includes languages spoken by coastal people from the Arctic Ocean to the Gulf of Alaska, including Inupiaq, in the Arctic; Yup'ik, in the Yukon-Kuskokwim and Bristol Bay region; Aleut, in the Aleutian Islands; and Alutiiq, on the Alaska Peninsula, Kodiak, and Prince William Sound. There are 12 Athabascan and Eyak languages in Alaska, and more Outside, including Apache and Navajo. In Southeast Alaska, Tlingit was spoken across most of the Panhandle. Haida was spoken on southern Prince of Wales Island and southward into what's now British Columbia, where Tsimshian also was spoken.

An Alaska Glossary

If Alaska feels like a different country from the rest of the United States, one reason may be the odd local usage that makes English slightly different here—different enough, in fact, that the Associated Press publishes a separate style-book dictionary just for Alaska. Here are some Alaskan words you may run into:

breakup   When God set up the seasons in Alaska, He forgot one: spring. While the rest of the United States enjoys new flowers and baseball, Alaskans are looking at melting snowbanks and mud. Then, in May, summer miraculously arrives. Breakup officially occurs when the ice goes out in the Interior's rivers, but it stands for the time period of winter's demise and summer's initiation.

bunny boots   If you see people wearing huge, bulbous white rubber boots in Alaska's winter, it's not necessarily because they have enormous feet. Those are bunny boots, superinsulated footwear originally designed for Arctic air force operations—and they're the warmest things in the world.

cheechako   A newcomer or greenhorn. Not used much anymore, because almost everyone is one.

dry or damp   Many towns and villages have invoked a state law that allows them to outlaw alcohol completely (to go dry) or to outlaw sale but not possession (to go damp).

Lower 48   The contiguous United States.

Native   When capitalized, the word refers to Alaska's indigenous people. "American Indian" isn't used much in Alaska, "Alaska Native" being the preferred term.

Native corporation   In 1971, Congress settled land claims with Alaska's Natives by turning over land and money; corporations were set up, with the Natives then alive as shareholders, to receive the property. Most of the corporations still thrive.

The first arrival of whites was often violent and destructive, spanning a 100-year period that started in the 1740s with the coming of the Russian fur traders, who enslaved the Aleuts, and continued to the 1840s, when New England whalers and other mariners first met the Inupiat of the Arctic. There were pitched battles, but disease and nonviolent destruction of oral traditions were more influential. Christian missionaries, with the support of government assimilation policy, drove the old stories and even Native languages underground. Lela Kiana Oman, who has published traditional Inupiat stories to preserve them, told me of her memories of her father secretly telling the ancient tales at night to his children. She was forbidden to speak Inupiaq in school and did not see her first traditional Native dance until age 18.

Oman's work is part of today's Native cultural renaissance. It's not a moment too soon. In some villages, children know more about Beverly Hills, which they see on television, than about their own culture. Some don't share a language with their own grandparents. But schools in many areas have begun requiring Native language classes, or even teach using language immersion techniques. For

oosik   The huge penile bone of a walrus. Knowing this word could save you from being the butt of any of a number of practical jokes people like to play on cheechakos.

Outside   Anywhere that isn't Alaska. This is a widely used term in print, and is capitalized, like any other proper noun.

PFD   No, not personal floatation device; it stands for Permanent Fund Dividend. When Alaska's oil riches started flowing in the late 1970s, the voters set up a savings account called the Permanent Fund. Half the interest is paid annually to every man, woman, and child in the state. With more than $26 billion in investments, the fund now yields more than $1,700 in dividends to each Alaskan annually.

pioneer   A white settler of Alaska who has been here longer than most other people can remember—25 or 30 years usually does it.

salmon   There are five species of Pacific salmon, each with two names. The king or Chinook is the largest, growing up to 90 pounds in some areas; the silver or coho is next in size, a feisty sport fish; the red or sockeye has rich red flesh; the pink or humpy and the chum or dog are smallish and not as tasty, mostly ending up in cans and dog lots.

Southeast   Most people don't bother to say "Southeast Alaska." The region may be to the northwest of everyone else in the country, but it's southeast of most Alaskans, and that's all we care about.

tsunami   Earthquake-caused sea waves are often called tidal waves, but that's a misnomer. The destructive waves of the 1964 Alaska earthquake were tsunamis caused by underwater upheavals like landslides.

village   A small, Alaska Native settlement in the Bush, usually tightly bound by family and cultural tradition.

the Aleut, whose cultural traditions were almost completely wiped out, the process of renewal involves a certain amount of invention. On the other hand, some traditional villages remain, especially deep in the country of the Yukon-Kuskokwim Delta, where Yup'ik is still the dominant language and most of the food comes from traditional subsistence hunting and gathering, altered only by the use of modern materials and guns.

Alaska Natives also are fighting destruction fueled by alcohol and other substance-abuse problems. Rates of suicide, accidents, and domestic violence are high in the Bush. Statistically, virtually every Alaska Native in prison is there because of alcohol. A sobriety movement is attacking the problem one person at a time. One of its goals is to use traditional Native culture to fill a void of rural despair where alcohol flows in. Politically, a "local option" law provides communities the choice of partial or total alcohol prohibition; it has been successfully used in many towns but remains controversial in others, where repeated local option elections sometimes divide Native and white residents, with whites more often voting against prohibition.

There are social and political tensions between Natives and whites on many levels and over many issues. The lives of the Alaskan city and village share less in common than do most different nations. Although village Natives come to the city to shop, get health care, or attend meetings, urban Alaskans have no reason to go to the villages, and most never have made the trip. The most contentious rural-urban issue concerns allocation of fish and game. Some urban outdoorsmen feel they should have the same rights to hunt and fish as the Natives do, and the state Supreme Court has interpreted Alaska's constitution to say they're correct. Rural Natives have federal law on their side, however, and Alaska faced the prospect of a federal takeover of fish and game management in the majority of the state that is federally owned unless the Alaska constitution was amended to provide a rural preference for fish and game. Over a decade of political stalemate, a legislative minority was able to block any constitutional amendment, and in 2000 the feds finally stepped in. Many Natives were glad to see it finally happen, as humiliating as the move was for independent-minded Alaskans. Natives feel subsistence hunting and fishing are an integral part of their cultural heritage, far more important than sport, and should take priority. Darker conflicts exist, too, and it's impossible to discount the charges of racism that Native Alaskans raise.

Alaska Natives have essentially become a minority in their own land. In 1880, Alaska contained 33,000 Natives and 430 whites. By 1900, with the gold rush, the numbers were roughly equal. Since then, whites have generally outnumbered Natives in ever greater numbers. Today there are about 98,000 Alaska Natives—27,000 of whom live in the cities of Anchorage and Fairbanks—out of a total state population of 627,000 people of all races. Consequently, Alaska Natives must learn to walk in two worlds. The North Slope's Inupiat, who hunt the bowhead whale from open boats as their forefathers did, must also know how to negotiate for their take in international diplomatic meetings. And they have to use the levers of government to protect the whale's environment from potential damage by the oil industry. The Alaska Native Claims Settlement Act created a new class, the corporate Native, responsible for representing rural needs but also obliged to function as an executive for large, far-reaching business concerns.

Non-Natives traveling to the Bush also walk in two worlds, but they may not even know it. In a Native village, a newly met friend will ask you in for a cup of coffee; it can be rude not to accept. Looking a person in the eye in conversation also can be rude—that's how Native elders look at younger people who owe them respect. If a Native person looks down, speaks slowly, and seems to mumble, that's not disrespect, but the reverse. Fast-talking non-Natives have to make a conscious effort to slow down and leave pauses in conversation, because Natives usually don't jump in or interrupt—they listen, consider, and then respond. Of course, most Native people won't take offense at your bad manners. They're used to spanning cultures. When I was in a village recently, I looked in confusion at a clock that didn't seem right. "That's Indian time," my Athabascan companion said. Then, pointing to a clock that was working, "White man time is over there."

Urban visitors who miss cultural nuances rarely overlook the apparent poverty of many villages. Out on a remote landscape of windswept tundra, swampy in summer and frozen in winter, they may secretly wonder why Natives endure the hardships of rural Alaskan life when even the most remote villager can see on television how easy it is in Southern California. Save your pity. As Yup'ik social observer Harold Napoleon has said, "We're poor, all right, but we've got more than most people. Our most important asset is our land and our culture, and we want to protect it come hell or high water."

NUMBER THREE: BE A REAL ALASKAN

Alaska's history books are full of the stories of economic booms, the people who came, what kind of wealth they were after, and how they populated and developed the land. In a largely empty place, you can make it into history just by showing up. But every wave is followed by a trough, the bust that comes after the boom when those who came just for the money go back where they came from. Those are the times when the real Alaskans—those who live here for the love of the place, not only the money—are divided from the rest. The real Alaskans stay; the others leave. It's the perfect way to settle an argument.

Other people have other definitions of what it takes to be a real Alaskan. One definition, which I once read on a placemat in a diner in Soldotna, holds that to be a real Alaskan, you have to know how to fix a Caterpillar tractor. Similar definitions require various feats in the outdoors—hunting, fishing, or shooting—and even acts in the barroom or the bedroom. They all assume that a real Alaskan is a big, tough, white, male, bulldozer-driving type of guy. But those can be the first to leave when the economy goes down the tubes.

The first group to leave were the Russians sent by the czar and the Russian-America Company. On October 18, 1867, their flag came down over Castle Hill in Sitka in a solemn ceremony, got stuck, and had to be untangled by a soldier sent up the pole. The territory was virtually empty of Russians before the check was even signed, as Congress didn't much like the idea of the purchase and took a while to pay. The gold rush stampeders were the next to leave. The population of Nome went from 12,500 to 852 after the stampede was over. The oil years have seen the same phenomenon, as people who can't find work in the bust years pack up and leave.

But each time the boom has gone bust, enough have stayed so that Alaska ended up with more people than it had before. Over the long term, the population has kept growing dramatically. And each set of migrants has been similar: young, transplanted from the West, but from other parts of the United States, too. Most people who have come to Alaska have been white—minority populations are smaller than in the nation as a whole—but there are strong minority communities in Anchorage. In Kodiak, the canneries are run by a tight Filipino community started by just a few pioneer immigrants.

Still, Alaskans have always been well paid. Until recently, the popular explanation always held that prices are higher because of shipping costs, so salaries needed to match. That's still true in rural Alaska and for some purchases in the large cities. But generally, fierce competition in the retail trade has driven prices down. Today the cost of living in Anchorage, Fairbanks, and Juneau compares to the cost in most parts of the country, and Wal-Mart has even moved into such remote towns as Ketchikan and Kodiak. Wages have gone down a little, but the federal government still pays a premium to its Alaskan employees, and oil workers, fishermen, and other skilled workers make a very good living.

The non-Native part of Alaska, 100 years old with the anniversary of the gold rush in 1998, hasn't had time to develop a culture of its own, much less an Alaskan accent. It's a melting pot of the melting pot, with a population made up of odds and ends from all over the United States. Everyone arrives with a clean slate and a chance to reinvent himself or herself, but on occasion, that ability to start from scratch has created some embarrassing discoveries, when the past does become relevant. There have been a series of political scandals uncovered by reporters who checked the resumes of well-known politicians, only to find out they had concocted their previous lives out of thin air. One leading legislative candidate's husband found out about his wife's real background from such a news story.

If an Alaskan culture hasn't had time to develop, Alaska does have traditions, or at least accepted ways of thinking, among them tolerance and equality, hospitality, independence—and a propensity for violence. In the late 1980s in Homer, a gunfight over a horse left a man lying dead on a dirt road. In the newspaper the next week, the editorial called for people not to settle their differences with guns. A couple of letters to the editor shot back, on the theme, "Don't you tell *us* how to settle our differences." Guns are necessary tools in Alaska. They're also a religion. I have friends who actually exchanged handguns instead of rings when they got married.

The tradition of tolerance of newcomers has made Alaska a destination for oddballs, religious cults, hippies, and people who just can't make it in the mainstream. Perhaps the most interesting of the religious groups that formed its own community is the Old Believers, who in recent decades have built villages of brightly painted, gingerbreadlike houses around Kachemak Bay, near Homer. Their resistance to convention dates from Peter the Great's reforms to Russian Orthodoxy in the 18th century, which they reject. In Alaska they've found a place where they can live without interference—in fact, they've thrived as fishermen and boat builders. You see them around town, in their 18th-century Russian peasant dress. Until recently, even the girls' high-school basketball team wore long dresses, with their numbers stitched to the bodice.

Nikolaevsk was the first of the Russian Old Believer villages. In the public school there, they don't teach about dinosaurs or men landing on the moon—that's considered heresy. Yet other Old Believers rebelled, convinced that Nikolaevsk was making too many compromises and was bound to lose the next generation to decadent American ways. They broke off and formed another village, farther up the bay, unreachable except by all-terrain vehicle, and adhered to stricter rules. They, in turn, suffered another schism and another village was formed, farther up the bay, virtually inaccessible and with even stricter rules. The process continues. The fight against assimilation may be hopeless, as children will ultimately do as they please, but it's the Old Believers' own struggle. No one in Homer pushes them to change. No one pays any attention at all, except to buy their fish and their top-quality boats.

After several decades, it looks as if the Old Believers are here to stay. Whether they speak English or not, I'd say they're real Alaskans.

Index

FROMMER'S® COMPLETE TRAVEL GUIDES

Alaska
Amsterdam
Argentina & Chile
Arizona
Atlanta
Australia
Austria
Bahamas
Barcelona, Madrid & Seville
Beijing
Belgium, Holland & Luxembourg
Bermuda
Boston
British Columbia & the Canadian
  Rockies
Budapest & the Best of Hungary
California
Canada
Cancún, Cozumel & the Yucatán
Cape Cod, Nantucket &
  Martha's Vineyard
Caribbean
Caribbean Cruises & Ports of Call
Caribbean Ports of Call
Carolinas & Georgia
Chicago
China
Colorado
Costa Rica
Denmark
Denver, Boulder & Colorado Springs
England
Europe
European Cruises & Ports of Call
Florida
France

Germany
Great Britain
Greece
Greek Islands
Hawaii
Hong Kong
Honolulu, Waikiki & Oahu
Ireland
Israel
Italy
Jamaica
Japan
Las Vegas
London
Los Angeles
Maryland & Delaware
Maui
Mexico
Montana & Wyoming
Montréal & Québec City
Munich & the Bavarian Alps
Nashville & Memphis
Nepal
New England
New Mexico
New Orleans
New York City
New Zealand
Nova Scotia, New Brunswick &
  Prince Edward Island
Oregon
Paris
Philadelphia & the Amish Country
Portugal
Prague & the Best of the Czech
  Republic

Provence & the Riviera
Puerto Rico
Rome
San Antonio & Austin
San Diego
San Francisco
Santa Fe, Taos & Albuquerque
Scandinavia
Scotland
Seattle & Portland
Shanghai
Singapore & Malaysia
South Africa
South America
Southeast Asia
South Florida
South Pacific
Spain
Sweden
Switzerland
Texas
Thailand
Tokyo
Toronto
Tuscany & Umbria
USA
Utah
Vancouver & Victoria
Vermont, New Hampshire
  & Maine
Vienna & the Danube Valley
Virgin Islands
Virginia
Walt Disney World & Orlando
Washington, D.C.
Washington State

FROMMER'S® DOLLAR-A-DAY GUIDES

Australia from $50 a Day
California from $70 a Day
Caribbean from $70 a Day
England from $70 a Day
Europe from $70 a Day

Florida from $70 a Day
Hawaii from $80 a Day
Ireland from $60 a Day
Italy from $70 a Day
London from $85 a Day

New York from $90 a Day
Paris from $80 a Day
San Francisco from $70 a Day
Washington, D.C., from $70
  a Day

FROMMER'S® PORTABLE GUIDES

Acapulco, Ixtapa & Zihuatanejo
Alaska Cruises & Ports of Call
Amsterdam
Aruba
Australia's Great Barrier Reef
Bahamas
Baja & Los Cabos
Berlin
Big Island of Hawaii
Boston
California Wine Country
Cancún
Charleston & Savannah
Chicago
Disneyland

Dublin
Florence
Frankfurt
Hong Kong
Houston
Las Vegas
London
Los Angeles
Maine Coast
Maui
Miami
New Orleans
New York City
Paris

Phoenix & Scottsdale
Portland
Puerto Rico
Puerto Vallarta, Manzanillo &
  Guadalajara
San Diego
San Francisco
Seattle
Sydney
Tampa & St. Petersburg
Vancouver
Venice
Virgin Islands
Washington, D.C.

FROMMER'S® NATIONAL PARK GUIDES

Family Vacations in the National
  Parks
Grand Canyon

National Parks of the American
  West
Rocky Mountain
Yellowstone & Grand Teton

Yosemite & Sequoia/
  Kings Canyon
Zion & Bryce Canyon

FROMMER'S® MEMORABLE WALKS

Chicago
London

New York
Paris

San Francisco

FROMMER'S® GREAT OUTDOOR GUIDES

Arizona & New Mexico
New England

Northern California
Southern New England

Vermont & New Hampshire

SUZY GERSHMAN'S BORN TO SHOP GUIDES

Born to Shop: France
Born to Shop: Hong Kong,
  Shanghai & Beijing

Born to Shop: Italy
Born to Shop: London

Born to Shop: New York
Born to Shop: Paris

FROMMER'S® IRREVERENT GUIDES

Amsterdam
Boston
Chicago
Las Vegas
London

Los Angeles
Manhattan
New Orleans
Paris
Rome

San Francisco
Seattle & Portland
Vancouver
Walt Disney World
Washington, D.C.

FROMMER'S® BEST-LOVED DRIVING TOURS

Britain
California
Florida
France

Germany
Ireland
Italy

New England
Scotland
Spain

HANGING OUT™ GUIDES

Hanging Out in England
Hanging Out in Europe

Hanging Out in France
Hanging Out in Ireland

Hanging Out in Italy
Hanging Out in Spain

THE UNOFFICIAL GUIDES®

Bed & Breakfasts and Country
  Inns in:
    California
    New England
    Northwest
    Rockies
    Southeast
Beyond Disney
Branson, Missouri
California with Kids
Chicago
Cruises
Disneyland

Florida with Kids
Golf Vacations in the
  Eastern U.S.
The Great Smokey &
  Blue Ridge Mountains
Inside Disney
Hawaii
Las Vegas
London
Mid-Atlantic with Kids
Mini Las Vegas
Mini-Mickey
New England & New York
  with Kids

New Orleans
New York City
Paris
San Francisco
Skiing in the West
Southeast with Kids
Walt Disney World
Walt Disney World for
  Grown-ups
Walt Disney World for Kids
Washington, D.C.
World's Best Diving Vacations

SPECIAL-INTEREST TITLES

Frommer's Adventure Guide to Australia & New
  Zealand
Frommer's Adventure Guide to Central America
Frommer's Adventure Guide to India & Pakistan
Frommer's Adventure Guide to South America
Frommer's Adventure Guide to Southeast Asia
Frommer's Adventure Guide to Southern Africa
Frommer's Britain's Best Bed & Breakfasts and
  Country Inns
Frommer's France's Best Bed & Breakfasts and
  Country Inns
Frommer's Italy's Best Bed & Breakfasts and Country
  Inns
Frommer's Caribbean Hideaways

Frommer's Exploring America by RV
Frommer's Gay & Lesbian Europe
Frommer's The Moon
Frommer's New York City with Kids
Frommer's Road Atlas Britain
Frommer's Road Atlas Europe
Frommer's Washington, D.C., with Kids
Frommer's What the Airlines Never Tell You
Israel Past & Present
The New York Times' Guide to Unforgettable
  Weekends
Places Rated Almanac
Retirement Places Rated

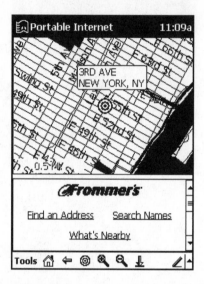